This book belongs to:

BY STEALTH AND DECEPTION

TRANSFORMATION

and its Parallel to the

EUROPEAN UNION

Best Wishes!

Orlean Koehle

Orlean Koehle

" For God, Family, and Country "

There are also plans for a new currency, just as the EU now has one currency.

Underneath is a picture showing the flags of the United States and the European Union side by side, signifying that the USA is also involved in a second merger—a "Transatlantic Partnership," a "Transatlantic Policy Network," and a "Transatlantic Common Market" between the USA and the European Union. Mexico and Canada have also formed their own partnerships with the EU, as has the Caribbean and other countries in South America.

The block letters of the USA being chipped away is a symbol of all that is incrementally disappearing in our nation as these various mergers take place: our U.S. Constitution is being replaced by international laws; limited representative government is being replaced by broad, sweeping regional government. Our U.S. sovereignty, borders, Judeo-Christian heritage, language, culture, traditions, education, economy, free enterprise system, health system, individual rights and liberties are being chipped away to be replaced with what President Obama calls a "transformed" America. Some of us don't want a transformed America. We liked America how it used to be. Its original design by our founding fathers was what made this nation great. It stood as the "shining light on a hill," the beacon of hope and liberty for people across the globe. We do not want America transformed, we want it restored!

Stealth and deception are the techniques being used to form the American transformation, mergers, partnerships, and the "chipping away of the USA." It is all being done "in a very quiet way," as stated by Utah Senator Bob Bennett, who served as the first Chairman of the Transatlantic Policy Network (TPN), and is now serving as its Honorary President. The mergers and partnerships are being done under the table with no congressional oversight, no vote by Congress or by the people. Americans have been kept in the dark.

Stealth and deception were also the techniques used for years creating the EU, until it was too late. People awoke one morning and found out that they had been lied to. What they had thought was just an innocent free trade agreement among neighboring nations was now a large political union, which has primacy over their own national governments and constitutions. Europeans have lost independence, sovereignty, autonomy, liberty, and prosperity. In the case of Germany, the euro devalued the German mark by 2/3; other countries are also finding out that their economy has greatly suffered from this union. Europeans are discovering that they are part of a vast "*coup d'etat.*" As two British authors describe it—"the most spectacular *coup d'etat* in all history."

The purpose of this book is to wake up not only USA Americans, but Canadians, Mexicans, Central and South Americans, Europeans, Africans, Asians, Australians, New Zealanders, citizens of the South Pacific Islands, actually people of every nation to the fact that deceptive planning behind the scenes for integration, merger, economic and political unions are already underway for your nations and continents as well. You will not be left out. There is a planned "*coup*" for you, too. If you are proud of your nation and believe in its sovereignty, independence, autonomy and liberty, please become informed, share this information with others, and take a stand against these mergers and transformations before it is too late.

BY STEALTH AND DECEPTION

TRANSFORMATION

and its Parallel to the

EUROPEAN UNION

Orlean Koehle

1st Printing March 2008
2nd Printing May 2008
3rd Printing with New Cover June 2008
4th Printing September 2008
5th Printing in Copybook Format and by New Publisher, Xlibris, 2010

ISBN: Hardcover   978-1-4415-0099-1
               Softcover   978-1-4415-0098-4

Printed in the United States of America

1st Printings were by
Small Helm Press Associate
Santa Rosa, CA
707-539-8393

James 3: 4—"Behold also the ships, which though they be so great, and are driven of fierce winds, yet are they turned about with a very small helm . . ."

"Just as a very small helm can turn about a great ship, it only takes one person, armed with truth and courage and willing to speak out, who can sometimes change the course of history." Orlean Koehle

To order additional copies of this book, contact:
Xlibris Corporation
1-888-795-4274
www.Xlibris.com
Orders@Xlibris.com
54953

Acknowledgments

This book is dedicated to all patriotic Americans who have been willing to take a stand and fight for their country, freedom and independence, including my own ancestors who fought in America's War for Independence—the Revolutionary War, and my father, H. Julian Miller, a World War I veteran.

To my pioneer parents, grandparents, and great grandparents who were willing to sacrifice and endure many hardships to help settle the western states and to secure a plot of ground on which to raise their children and grandchildren, to help them realize the American dream of freedom and liberty that comes with the right of property ownership.

To all courageous Americans who love their country, their freedoms, their traditions, and would like to preserve them; to those who speak out and write articles, letters, speak on radio and television to let others know of the threat that is going on now to America and to our way of life.

To my mother, Lelah Wright Miller, whose natural Dutch curiosity I must have inherited. She taught me a love for reading, writing, researching, questioning and to not give up until I found the answers.

To my husband W. Kurt Koehle, who has helped with research and with his expertise on his native country of Germany and the European Union.

And to our six children and grandchildren and to their children, for whom I want to preserve the precious blessings of liberty and the Judeo-Christian heritage upon which our nation was founded.

Special Thanks

*I would especially like to acknowledge Phyllis Schlafly and Dr. Jerome Corsi for their invaluable research, the many articles they have written and Dr. Corsi's book, **The Late Great USA**, exposing the movement to form a North American Union to the light of day. I would like to thank them both for a special week of training that I and other Eagle Forum state presidents and leaders had under their tutelage on this subject back in Washington D.C. in November of 2006. That week is what opened my eyes to the great danger our nation and our Constitution are now facing and is what motivated me to start doing my own research of how this all came to be. I would like to thank them for their continuous up-to-date coverage and their willingness and courage to speak out on these issues.*

I would like to thank editors of The New American, who have been writing for many years about the various free trade agreements, such as: NAFTA, CAFTA, The FTAA, which have led up to the Security and Prosperity Partnership (SPP), the movement to form a North American Union (NAU, a Transatlantic Partnership, and "deeper integration," with the European Union. I would like to thank them also for their past outstanding summer youth camps, "Freedom Generation," where I served as a counselor and speaker and from which I learned invaluable truths about our inspired Constitution, form of government, founding fathers, our Godly heritage, what "Americanism" is all about and what are the biggest threats trying to destroy it. Much of that information I have included in this book.

Special thanks to Attorney Brad Dacus and the Pacific Justice Institute for all that they are doing to defend "Americanism" and our Judeo-Christian heritage, values, and beliefs.

I would like to thank the many radio and television hosts who have the courage to speak out on issues that are deemed "nonpolitically correct," such as: Dr. Stan Monteith of Radio Liberty for his excellent radio programs, books, and tapes; former talk show host John Spring; Lou Dobbs formerly of CNN; Lee Rodgers, the former morning talk show host for KSFO; Brian Sussman, who has taken his place; Barbara Simpson, who is on weekends on KSFO of San Francisco; Sharon Hughes of Changing World Views, KDIA Radio; national radio and TV personalities: Glenn Beck, Rush Limbaugh, Sean Hannity, Mark Levin, Roger Hedgecock, and Michael Savage.

Special thanks to former Congressmen Tom Tancredo, Duncan Hunter, and Congressman Ron Paul for their courage to speak out against the NAU, the SPP, and the NAFTA Super Highway, even though such talk is not politically correct. Thanks to State Senators Sam Rohrer of Pennsylvania and Randy Brogdon of Oklahoma for their efforts in their own states to stop the Real ID Act, that would have changed state drivers' licenses into national and international ID cards. Senator Brogdon also passed legislation in Oklahoma to stop the Trans Texas Corridor (TTC) from coming into his state. (The TTC would be the first leg of the long NAFTA Super Highway crossing the USA into Canada). Thanks to Congresswoman Michele Bachmann of Minnesota for her strong stand against the plunge to socialism and the transformation of the USA where President Obama is leading us.

Thank you also to the following writers, authors, and speakers for their great information: Patrick Wood of August Review; Cliff Kincaid of Accuracy in Media; writers for Judicial Watch; Howard Phillips of Stop the NAU; Donna Hearne of the Constitution Coalition; Kitty Werthman of Eagle Forum in South Dakota; Edward Spalton of Campaign for an Independent Britain, Connie Fogal of the Canadian Action Party; authors Charlotte Iserbyt and Dr. John Coleman. Thanks to researchers Bernadine Smith, Debbie Niwa, Vicky Davis and Ferne Abbot.

Thanks to Michael Shaw, Michael Coffman, Tom DeWeese, and Henry Lamb of Freedom 21; Fred Grant, Margaret and Dan Byfield of American Stewards of Liberty; and Terri Hall, founder of Texans United for Reform and Freedom (TURF). They have all helped me to better understand the environmental movement, sustainable development, and the property rights battles we are facing across the nation. Loss of personal property rights is part of the plan and deeply intertwined with losing our national sovereignty.

Thanks to Scott Hartley at ARC Copy (Advanced Reproduction Center) of Santa Rosa, California, for the cover design and first printings, and thanks to my editors: Dick and Mary Wolbert, Ysabel Johnson, Carol Pascoe, Jennifer Delaney, Marian King, George Bruner, Marge Sorbi and Frank Henry.

My appreciation to the publishers, Xlibris Corporation, for their patience in waiting for the updated version for the paper back and hard back printings of 2010. Many changes and additions have been included because of the "transforming" of America under the Obama administration and because of the discovery of additional mergers that are happening across the globe, also "in very quiet ways"—by stealth and deception.

CONTENTS

Preface

I have a great love and passion for independence and freedom. Perhaps this was inherited from my pioneer ancestors who came to this country seeking religious liberty, or maybe it came from farther back from my colonial forefathers who fought in the Revolutionary War—what I prefer calling "The War for Independence" against Great Britain.

I also learned from the example of my parents and my ancestors that freedom is not free. As citizens of this great nation, we are to assume our responsibility in protecting the freedoms upon which it was founded. My father ran for Congress in Utah, served as Mayor of our small farming community of Roberts, Idaho, and in his free time was constantly reading and learning to better stay informed and to do his part as a citizen of his state and nation. Fortunately, I inherited many of his political books.

My mother also served in various positions in Republican women and Daughters of the American Revolution. Our evening meals and family discussions usually were centered on politics. My uncle Earl Wright was an Idaho state Senator. Our visits with him and other relatives also included discussions of politics. I assumed this is how every American grew up, but I have since discovered that is not the case.

For many people, politics has become a taboo subject, not to be discussed in polite society. I have been kicked under the table for bringing up the topic. It is as if we are no longer supposed to have a healthy discussion, especially if there are people who disagree. I'm sorry, but it will take more than a few kicks under the table to keep me silent.

Just as our founding fathers had to fight a long and bloody war for their independence, Americans who love their freedom have had to keep that battle going. Today it is not a battle with guns. It is a battle of words, ideas and principles. Some call it a "culture war," where the culture upon which this nation was founded is under attack and is being destroyed. What is that culture? It is our Judeo/Christian foundation of religious freedom, high moral standards and ethics, love and charity, the belief that basic rights come from God, not man and not government.

As the Declaration of Independence states, our founding fathers believed that our basic rights of life, liberty, property—all that it takes to "pursue your own happiness"—were inalienable, not ever to be taken away, that the sole purpose of government was to protect and "secure" those rights. They did not come from government; therefore, government has no authority to assume control over them. However, that is vastly different now, as the reader will find out from reading this book. Government has usurped so much authority over the American people and our basic rights that America is almost becoming a police state.

I consider liberty a very precious gift bestowed by a loving Father in Heaven on his children—all of his children, not just those living in the United States. I believe the Constitution was inspired of God to be a beacon of light, hope and liberty, not only for this nation, but for all people everywhere. For more than 200 years, America was considered the "shining city on the hill, the beacon of light to the world," that attracted people to her shores from every country who were seeking that light, hope, and liberty and wanting to live "the American dream." However, that is vastly different now.

What has happened to America to cause our rights and liberty to be so fleeting? As the title of this book points out, it has happened by stealth and deception by some very evil and cunning people, who have been exercising control behind the scenes over government for hundreds of years. These people are pursuing a different agenda and are either professing atheists or believe in and worship a different God. Instead of wanting life, liberty, and happiness for mankind, they want just the opposite—death, enslavement, misery and poverty. But for themselves, they want immense power, control, great wealth, and to rule and reign over the rest of mankind in a vast world government. The plan, however, is to first break up nations and boundaries by putting them into large regional governments such as a European Union.

The European Union is a role model and learning tool for the rest of all the nations. Do we really want to follow it and form similar unions? Has it been good for the people of the nations involved or just the opposite?

Chapter 1 begins with my husband's personal experiences growing up in war-torn Germany and how stealth and deception were used to convince the German people that it was because of evil nations that wars were started, thus the necessity of forming a union. The reader will also learn of the "Sixteen Ds of Deception" that were used in Europe and are being used now in America to form these mergers. Is this all a conspiracy theory or conspiracy facts?

Chapters 2-10 show how the European Union was formed by stealth and deception, how America is being led down the same trail towards regional and world government through the United Nations and through the many secretive groups who founded it and continue to support its aims and purposes.

Chapter 11-12 tell of CFR member Robert Pastor, known as the "Father of the North American Union," and his stealth campaign to push a North American merger upon all three countries. His plan called for a national ID card, which is written about in the Chapter 12, "Big Brother is Watching You," which tells just how far the USA has come to becoming a police state.

Chapter 13-14 tell of the planned financial crisis, the groups and people most responsible for it, and about President Obama, who is very much a part of the plan bringing us on a fast track towards socialism, communism, regionalism and world government.

Chapters 15-17 tell of the plans for a world religion, a theocracy, with Christianity out, paganism and Islam in; of the NAFTA superhighway and its part in the merger plan; and Chapter 17 gives a timeline of the last 100 years—events leading towards a totally transformed USA and North American merger.

Chapter 18 gives us hope, telling what others have done and what we can do to make a difference. It also tells what we can do to be prepared for a rough road ahead.

Chapter 19 gives almost a hundred quotes about the "new world order," world government, world economy, world religion and world socialism/communism by people warning us against them and those supporting them.

It is my hope that this book will help people better understand what is going on around them and take action to try to stop it before America is too far down the slippery slope to total transformation and loss of freedoms, and there is no turning back. I also hope that the reader will realize how important personal preparation is for some very difficult times ahead. Here is an additional quote that tells us how important the actions of just one person can be.

"I am one. I cannot do everything, but I can do something. And because I cannot do everything, I will not refuse to do the something that I CAN do. What I can do, I should do. And what I should do, by the grace of God, I will do." **Edward Everett Hale.**

Chapter One

Koehle Family Story During World War II;
Deceptive Preparations for the EU in Germany;
Sixteen Ds Strategy for a Stealth Plan;
Conspiracy Theories or Conspiracy Facts?

Koehle Family's Personal Experience with the Tragedies of War: In the twilight years of the life of my German mother-in-law, Johanna Koehle, who has since passed away, I tape-recorded and later transcribed her life story. She told me of her terrifying experiences during World War II. She and her two-year old son, Kurt, who later became my husband, were living in an apartment building in Mannheim, Germany. Her husband, Kurt Sr. was away fighting in the war in Northern Germany.

Late at night, Johanna heard the high pitched, shrilling warning sounds of an approaching air raid. She rushed to pick up her sleeping son with one arm, grabbed a suitcase with the other and fled down into the neighborhood bomb shelter. She and her frightened, whimpering little son sat crowded together with other German people in the dark, damp, cold shelter through the night, listening to the deafening sounds, feeling the earth shaking and rumbling from the dropping bombs.

The next morning when the bombing was over, they ascended from the shelter to a horrifying sight—devastation, destruction, debris everywhere and fires still burning. Their apartment building was totally destroyed, left in a pile of cinderblocks and debris with just crumbled walls remaining. Fires were still burning inside of it. The only thing that was left of the Koehle Family possessions was a laundry basket that had been blown off the balcony.

Johanna's husband, after receiving word of the bombing of Mannheim, was given leave for the weekend to move his homeless family to his parents' residence in Hilzingen, a small town in Southern Germany.

The shock and trauma of the bombing and losing their home had a profound effect on Johanna and a new baby whom she was expecting, Gerhard. He was, consequently, born with a severe heart condition. Even though he was operated on, and the doctor thought all was well, he died on his 8th birthday.

The death of little Gerhard was extremely hard on the whole family, but especially on his older brother. They were very close. The family considered this death just one more of the terrible tragedies of war-torn Germany.

So horrific were some of the war-related experiences that most of Kurt's early childhood is a total blank in his memory. He does remember, however, that there was very little food. He recalls having to go with his mother to glean some of the farmer's fields to try to get what little vegetables they could find to feed the family.

Lessons Taught in German Schools in Preparation for a European Union: Kurt and other children growing up in Germany were taught repeatedly how terrible war was, so terrible that some sort of an agreement with other European countries would be a good thing, if it could help prevent war. Kurt remembers hearing the big word, *Wirtschaftsgemeinschaft*, translated "Economic Community," and how good that would be for Germany and all of the countries of Europe that would belong to it. Never does he remember being taught, however, that the ultimate goal was an economic and political union for all of Europe. That was never mentioned.

When Kurt was 23, he came to the United States to finish his college education at Brigham Young University in Provo, Utah. He was doing graduate work in political science the year that we met. I was finishing my senior year. A month after our marriage, we left for Boston where he attended Fletcher, a graduate school in international relations, started by Tufts and Harvard University. He received two masters' degrees, one in international law and the other in diplomacy.

Shortly after graduation, he accepted a job offer that took us back to Germany where he began working in international affairs and taught political science at a German *"gymnasium"* (similar to a high school and junior college combined) in Lingen in Northern Germany.

Because of what Kurt had been taught in his master's programs, and from his own experience growing up in Germany, he also taught his students that the European Common Market, a "free-trade agreement" with other European countries, would be a good thing for Germany. However, again, he had no idea that such an agreement would lead to a political union. No one was told that a union was the ultimate goal.

In 1976, we returned to the United States. Kurt received two more degrees: an MBA and a PhD in Education Administration from the University of Nebraska in Lincoln. On his 40th birthday, he received one of his most prized possessions, his American citizenship. At the time of the writing of this book, he has been working for 27 years as an administrator at Sonoma State University in Northern California, close to Santa Rosa, where our home is located.

Kurt and I still have much contact with Germany and used to go there at least once a year to visit his parents, who have both since passed away. His father died the summer of 2009, at the age of 95. We have seen the many changes that have taken place since Germany became part of the European Union. We also used to hear from Kurt's father on how bad things have become since the EU has come into existence. Kurt's father had been very active in politics. He was on the city council and served as Vice Mayor of his town of Hilzingen for 25 years. He also served one term of what would be equivalent in the USA of a state senator.

The European Union Has not Been Good for Europe: The economy is much worse. There is high unemployment. The Euro has caused prices to be much higher. The EU parliament is very socialistic with unelected "commissioners" making most of the major decisions. The German people have little say in what is going on. With the open border policy, Germany is being flooded with foreigners, mainly Muslims, who are not the least bit interested in assimilating into German culture, but they are changing the culture to fit what Muslims believe. They are the ones producing most of the children and are being given money by the government to help take care of their children.

This book will also reveal what many British people are saying about the devastating effect membership in the EU is having on their nation.

Membership in the EU has not helped the economy of Greece, which is in a state of financial collapse. Other EU nations which are in dire economic conditions are Spain, Portugal, Italy, Ireland and many Eastern countries who were once part of the Soviet Union.

By Stealth and Deception: These are the descriptive words chosen for the title of the book, because they are the techniques that have been used in establishing the European Union and are being used for establishing economic and political trans-nationalist unions for North, Central and South American and other continents of the world. Such unions first start with innocent sounding "free trade agreements" such as: the European Common Market, NAFTA (North American Free Trade Agreement), CAFTA (Central America Free Trade Agreement), and the attempt to establish the FTAA (Free Trade Area of the Americas), which was stopped by many American people finally waking up to what was happening and harassing their Congressmen to vote against it. (However, the reader will discover that the FTAA is progressing anyway under a stealth agreement between Latin American countries and the European Union.)

The plan for the American continent is similar to what has happened in Europe. Powerful "trans-globalists" seek to form economic and political unions out of the various trade agreements and to bring them all together in one big American union of all of the Americas. That union would be combined with a transatlantic common market with the European Union and eventually form a large economic and political union between the two continental unions. The EU is already doing the same with other unions being formed, such as the African Union, Asian Union, South Pacific Union, etc.

Why is all this happening? The goal, as you will find out, is to incrementally chip away and destroy national sovereignty, pretending it is for the best good of the countries. The nations are promised "security and prosperity," when just the opposite is happening to every country that enters into these agreements.

A Transformed Socialist State Necessary Before Unions Can be Formed: The countries that have entered into unions throughout the world are pretty much on the same socialist page, so to speak, politically, economically, and with their social welfare programs, so it was much easier for them to form unions.

In the USA, under President Bush, that was not quite the case. We were coming closer, but we did not have the same socialism going on politically, economically, or with our social welfare programs. So the move towards forming a full-fledged North American Union had to be put on hold for awhile.

With the financial crisis in the fall of 2008, President Bush did give us a big socialist push with his passage of the TARP legislation. He started the nationalization of our mortgage companies, insurance companies, banks and auto industry. And he began the propaganda campaign that the "free enterprise" system was just not working any more in the USA.

However, under Obama's administration, socialism is now essentially the form of government the USA has been "transformed" into. Not only have our banks, mortgage companies, insurance companies, and auto industry been taken over by the federal government, but the health industry, one-sixth of our economy, has now become nationalized.

The USA is much closer to its two neighbors, Canada and Mexico, as a fellow socialist state. A North American merger could be much more a possibility, perhaps right on track. The goal was to have it all take place in the year 2010.

The Sixteen-Ds Strategy for Implementing a Stealth Plan: There are many different strategies being used in the stealth campaign to transform America, move us closer to socialism, destroy our sovereignty and to prepare us for a merger into regional government. I discovered most of them start with D, so I lumped them into a list of sixteen and give a description explaining how they are being used: 1) Deceive, 2) Deny, 3) Distract and Divert, 4) Deride and Discredit, 5) Degrade, 6) Dumb-Down, 7) Use Disinformation, 8) Use Duplicity, 9) Use Delusion 10) Divide and Conquer, 11) Dialectic Manipulation to Create a Crisis; 12) Delphi Technique to Form Consensus; 13) Depression, 14) Despair/Desperation, 15) Devolution and 16) Deluge.

1) **Deceive**: People in Europe were deceived, just as the American people are being deceived. The vast majority of Europeans did not have a clue that such a thing as a European Union was being planned. Most Americans have never heard of a Security or Prosperity Partnership or have any idea that regional government was being planned—a North American Community or Union—for the USA, Mexico, and Canada. Nor have they heard of a Transatlantic Partnership between the U.S. and the European Union. What has transpired up until now is by stealth. The powers behind the scenes use deception to not let the citizens know anything about their plans until it is too late.

    They also use the deception of changing names. If the people begin to catch on to one term and are upset about it, then often it will just disappear for awhile. The people think they have won, but low and behold, the same thing comes back, but with a new sugar-coated, nice sounding name. For example, because many people were beginning to catch on and protest about the Security and Prosperity Partnership, the forerunner to a North American Union, the name is no longer used. As of April, 2008, it is being called "North American Leaders Summit." Instead of using the name North American Union, it is called North American Community, or it might be called a Union of North America (UNA) or Union of North American Nations (similar to what was formed in May of 2008 for South America (UNASUR)—Union of South American Nations.) Or the popular term now is "trans-nationalism," and those who like the idea are called "transies." The latest deception is to no longer mention anything about a movement towards any merger of the USA, Canada, and Mexico, as if it never existed. Nor is very little attention paid to the Transatlantic Partnership with the EU.

2) **Deny:** If the citizens suspect something is going on, the powers behind this movement (the executive branches of all three nations) use denial and assure us that no such plan is in the works. They pretended that the SPP (Security and Prosperity Partnership) was just an innocent expansion of NAFTA, the North American Free Trade Agreement, which all three countries had entered into. In Europe, the same thing happened. Heads of state denied that a European Union was ever being planned. They also said it was just an expansion of their

free trade agreement, the European Common Market. The common citizen, and the majority of parliament members, did not know a union was being formed until it was a done deal and too late to get out of it.

3) **Distract and Divert:** The next tactic is to keep the attention of the nation and the media constantly distracted on something else. The terrible tragedy of 9/11, the pursuing War in Iraq and Afghanistan, the continuous "War on Terror" were long-lasting diversions during the Bush administration.

Another diversion was the 2008 election with its many presidential candidates and endless debates (but never a question asked about the SPP, or the NAFTA Superhighway, or the movement to form a NAU. I think once Ron Paul was asked a question about the NAFTA highway by someone on the internet, but his answer received much ridicule.)

Other good diversions are, of course, fear tactics over environmental scares (such as global warming and the latest gulf oil spill.) The many Americans who pay no attention to the news are easily diverted by video games, sports, television, movies, and especially the many scandals of movie stars and politicians.

One of the biggest distraction is, of course, the financial crisis that is affecting not only our nation but the whole world. This diversion will hold the attention of the media for a long time, while the movement to integration will continue right on track, by stealth and deception, with the citizens of the USA., Canada, Mexico, the Caribbean, and South America remaining in the dark as long as possible.

As if all these distractions were not enough, in the later part of April, 2009, came the swine flu scare that began to be called an epidemic. Some people had predicted that it might take a mutual health scare (such as a swine flu or avian flu epidemic) to force the USA, Mexico and Canada to work more closely together to stop whatever epidemic it is. A health emergency would be a good excuse to use to cause the three countries to form some kind of a union. (Laws have already been passed in each of the three countries regarding their working together for such an emergency.)

Beginning in the summer of 2009 and continuing on through 2010, came the endless debates, discussions, protest rallies and many town hall meetings regarding Obama Care, the health plan to bring socialized medicine to the United States. Many versions and varieties of lengthy bills were presented, most of them 1000-2000 pages long, which, of course, no Congressman had time to read before voting on them. This took up much media attention and distracted the American people for a long time.

Once the bill was finally passed and signed into law by Obama, March 23, 2010, the attention on health care did not end. There are many threatened law suits about its unconstitutionality that will go on for a long time and take up more media attention. Who knows what has been going on behind the scenes while all the attention has been on health care?

4) **Deride and Discredit:** For many years in Europe, the heads-of-state and the media ridiculed the people who suggested that a union was being formed. Here in America, the same thing happened. Ordinary citizens and conservative media, who would dare to suggest that the SPP was laying the framework for a North American Union, were ridiculed and discredited by the Executive branches of all three countries. Citizens, who are concerned and have written about an economic and political union being formed between the U.S. and the EU, are also discredited.

The media and even some elected officials tried to discredit people such as Dr. Jerome Corsi and Phyllis Schlafly for writing and speaking about the movement towards a North American Union. Congressman Ron Paul and former Congressmen Tom Tancredo and Duncan Hunter were discredited and ridiculed because they were the only 2008 Presidential candidates who spoke out freely against the movement towards an NAU and the NAFTA superhighway.

There is another way in which the method of "deriding and demonizing" is being used by the insiders. It is a precedural trick that they use to get support for a controversial bill that conservatives normally would never support. Insiders pretend to deride, discredit and demonize someone or some entity who really is secretly on their side and promoting the same legislation, because they have much to gain from it.

It is also using the Hegelian Dialectic that you will read about in #11, creating a common "enemy" for the people to rally against, when really the enemy is on the same side as the insiders and working with them.

This will be illustrated in Chapter Thirteen in how the Federal Reserve (the Fed) came into existence. They waged a war against the powerful bankers and "demonized" them to create a common enemy, when most of the insiders behind the "Fed" were the actual powerful bankers themselves and had the most to gain from its creation.

It was also the same technique used by Obama to get his health care bill passed. He pretended that the powerful health insurance companies were the enemy and derided and demonized them. They, however, were secretly supporting him, for they will greatly benefit by his bill when everyone in America will be forced to have health insurance or be fined.

5) **Degrade and Devalue America:** Many of our children, growing up in our public schools and attending American universities today, seldom hear any good things about their country that make them proud to be Americans. They, instead, hear all the bad things, revised history that degrade and devalue our American history, the free-enterprise system, our form of government, our Constitution and Bill of Rights.

   Why is this going on? Americans will be more willing to give up our form of government for a new socialist/communist system, for a merger with other countries, for even a global government, all for "hope and change," if we have been so programmed to believe that we don't have anything special anyway, and we are ashamed of it.

6) **Dumb-down:** A second book that will follow this one, *The Incremental Chipping Away of the Once Great USA*, shows in the chapters on education, that much of what is now being taught in our public schools and universities under "civics and history" has been greatly dumbed down. Even the ability to read has been so dumbed down through programs such as "whole language," that many adults who have graduated from American public schools are only able to read on a 3rd or 4th grade level. Such people certainly don't want to read difficult or complex words that are found in American history books or to even read the U.S. Constitution, which has equally big, complicated words. Since reading is hard for them, many people would much prefer watching movies, sports, playing video games, etc.

7) **Disinformation:** Much of what is taught is actual "disinformation" that is portraying American history, our founding fathers, our Constitution, Bill of Rights, and our Judeo/Christian heritage in a bad light. One can understand why children are graduating from our public schools and universities with very little pride or patriotism in our country. Much of what comes over the media is the same. One cannot expect the American people to understand or to make wise decisions about what is going on in their nation when they are so deliberately misinformed.

   As this book was going to print in the spring of 2010, there was another form of "disinformation" campaign brewing by the media against anyone who belongs to: "Tea Party Groups;" "Patriotic Groups;" "The 9/12 Project Groups" and other grass-root conservative organizations. They were being labeled by the Democrat Party leaders and the liberal media as "hateful, bigoted, racist, right-wing, fascist, neo-Nazi, and dangerous."

   In fact, the Department of Homeland Security tried to make it appear that these people are the new "terrorists" and sent out a memo to the police warning them of such.

Why was this attack going on? Because these various groups have been so effective. They have woken up the silent majority; they are growing in number— millions of Americans are now part of some such patriotic group, and they have taken a strong stand against the socialization and transformation of America under Obama's administration. Their activism prevented Obama's health care bill from being passed for over a year. Thus, Obama, his handlers and the controlled media are trying to discredit them and to silence them through spreading "disinformation" about them. (More is written about all of the activities of these groups in Chapter 18, letting us know that there is still hope.)

8) **Duplicity:** In Webster's dictionary, duplicity means double-minded. In other words, it is describing someone who is not honest and speaks with "a forked-tongue" or out of both sides of his mouth. It can also be used to describe some politicians, whose principles or statements depend on "which way the wind is blowing"—right or left. They will say one thing when speaking to conservatives and something entirely different to liberals. Their "principles" depend on what is popular at the time.

Duplicity could also be used to describe the technique being used to get many bills passed. Obama's health care bill had many **duplicate** versions, each having something a little different. A person thinks he has downloaded the bill and studies it carefully and speaks or writes against it, and the opposition can say, "but what you have said is not in the bill." It is because they have a different version.

Duplicity is also used when a bill fails. Often it is just given a new name and attached to the end of some other important, necessary bill that is sure to pass, because the funding is needed for a very necessary cause, such as funding for the current war effort. The Defense Authorization Bill of 2009 had the controversial Hate Crimes Bill snuck into it at the last minute and got it passed that way.

9) **Use Delusion:** Many Americans, for the longest time, were being deluded by the media and politicians to think "all was well." "Sure we have a few problems to worry about but not enough for me to actually get involved and do something about them. All I need to do to be a good American is to vote now and again. That's all."

The one good thing about the financial crisis and the outrageous bills passed by Bush (TARP) and Obama (the Stimulus Bill) and the nationalization of our banks, mortgage companies, auto industry and the health care industry, it is causing people to wake up and come out of their apathy and delusion thinking that all is okay in America. Millions of

Americans have now become involved in the political process, attending rallies, town-hall meetings, writing letters to the editor, and writing and calling their elected representatives. Many have joined groups to become better informed as to what is really going on.

10) **Divide and Conquer**: The powerful elitists behind the European Union, the SPP, the NAU, and the Transatlantic Partnerships use division to further their goals. "Divide and conquer" has always been a good technique by would-be tyrants. Just as with the European Union, before it was formed, a huge amount of foreigners were being allowed into the major countries of Europe, weakening their internal culture, language, long-standing traditions and Judeo-Christian beliefs. The division in our nation is also coming from the invasion of millions of illegal aliens, as well as the millions coming with H-1 work visas, who do not share our same heritage, culture, Judeo-Christian beliefs, traditions, love of country, love for our form of government, or for our Constitution and the freedoms it has brought us.

　　The division is also coming from confusion, lack of true information, and understanding of what is really going on, which causes people to support issues that they would not support if they were told the truth about them.

11) **Dialectic Manipulation to Create a Crisis:** This is a term that became popular with a German philosopher George Frederick Hegel. It was known as the "Hegelian Dialectic." To simplify: Hegel believed there is a three-stage pattern of events that happens naturally which helps society progress: A thesis—the status quo of how things are presently; an antithesis—opposition to the thesis that seeks to change it; and the synthesis—the solution when the thesis and antithesis work together to solve their differences and society supposedly improves.

　　Karl Marx got a hold of this philosophy and decided rulers could manipulate it, speed it up and always make the synthesis come out the way that they would want it to. The thesis has now become a crisis that leaders create but blame it on something or someone else, of course. The antithesis is the opposition that the leaders say has caused the crisis.

　　Often the opposition is actually a group of paid thugs whom sinister leaders hire to do the damage to cause the crisis. An example is Hitler, who paid his men to set fire to the Reichstag building (the seat of government) in Germany and then blamed it on the communists and Jews. He used this crisis to have himself declared supreme *Fuhrer* to fight the terrible "terrorists," the unrest, and poor conditions that existed in Germany after World War I.

　　The synthesis is the solution to the crisis that is formed by the leaders getting the opposition to work with them, to have a consensus of thought. Or in the case of Hitler, he used the crisis to get rid of the opposition—people a leader does not like. He caused that communists, revolutionaries, Jews, Gypsies, and Christians, anyone who would dare speak out against him were gathered up and put in concentration camps.

Marx' version of the dialectic always results in bigger government, less freedom and more controls on the people, and amazingly, it is always followed by another crisis which brings the same results.

12) **Delphi Technique:** This is the technique that is being used to help bring about the dialectic—how the heads of governments get leaders and citizens to go along willingly with their pre-conceived plans. Carefully trained, skilled "facilitators" manipulate those participating in the planning meetings into going along with the pre-conceived plans by making the participants think they were their own ideas. Everyone is brought to "consensus" and willing to implement the plan.

13) **Depression:** This word can have two different meanings, both of which apply—depression dealing with economy and depression dealing with the effect a financial crisis is having on the emotional state of our citizens. You will read more about all this in the chapter about the financial crisis.

14) **Despair/ Desperation:** When people lose their jobs; their homes go into foreclosure; their way of life and standard of living are greatly diminished; when they see what is happening to our nation, our expanding big government, our diminished freedoms, then, of course, they are filled with despair. They lose all hope or desire to try again. People full of despair are often desperate and gullible and more easily led by any new leader using fear tactics and promising "hope and change."

This is what happened to Germany after World War I. The people were in a state of great despair, surrounded by the ruins of war. The country was in a terribly depressed financial condition. They had enormous war debts to pay off; to do so, the government mass produced the German mark, causing hyper-inflation and the mark became worthless. It took a wheelbarrow of marks to buy a single loaf of bread. The German people were starving and desperate and willing to follow any "savior" or "charlatan" who came along and promised them a better life. They were even willing to accept a new form of government with a supreme dictator running things instead of a parliament. Adolph Hitler filled that role perfectly. He was elected and rose to become the supreme *"Fuhrer."*

Some people believe it was under such a state of despair that people voted for Obama, falling for his mantra of "hope and change." Now with his Stimulus Plan of $787 billion and a budget of almost over $3 trillion (all which we have to borrow because America is broke), people are expecting enormous "hyperinflation" of the American dollar to soon kick in, making the dollar become almost worthless. That will also bring a state of greater despair and desperation, and people will be willing to fall again for any plan "of hope and change"—maybe even a plan to give up our sovereignty, form a union with Canada and Mexico, or with the European Union, accept a new currency to save our economy—anything that is offered that people might think will help their desperate situation.

15. **Devolution:** The EU is breaking up the 27 countries that belong to it into regions, ignoring the long-standing, traditional provinces and locally elected government officials and "devolving" (transferring) powers to the EU-selected officials of the newly formed regions. It is only through these EU-selected officials that the regions will receive any authorized funding coming from the EU, thus local government and locally-elected officials are slowly become powerless, meaningless and will be faded out.

   It is interesting to read the definition of "devolution" given in the *World Book Dictionary* of 1985, (p. 574). It comes from the Latin word, "*devolvere,*" which means to "roll down." Along with the definition of "transferring of rights, duties, responsibility, authority to another," a fifth definition is given under the title Biology—"reversed evolution, degeneration, regression, extinction." That is exactly what is happening to local, representative government in the EU countries. It is what is planned for all nations of the world, as they are transformed into unions. Local, representative, self government "of the people, by the people, and for the people" is degenerating, regressing and will soon become extinct.

16. **Deluge:** Webster's Dictionary describes deluge as "a great flood, a heavy rainfall, or an overwhelming rush of anything."

   One of the tactics of those seeking to transform our nation is to so "deluge" us with an overwhelming rush of restricting legislation, either in our states, or in Congress, or locally with our own city councils or our county boards of supervisors, that we just can't fight them all. The intent of this deluge is to so wear us down and to tire us out that we will eventually just throw in the towel and give up.

   It is as if we are fighting a giant octopus with so many evil tentacles, and as you fight one restricting tentacle bill going through Congress, or your state legislation, there are seven others that are equally bad that are trying to choke the life out of you.

   So few bills and laws that are passed are actually beneficial for the people. Most of them are just the opposite. There are bills that: devalue life—such as those that allow for abortion and euthanasia; devalue our traditional morals and marriage—such as those that take away any teaching of abstinence in our schools, or promote same sex marriage; bills that devalue property rights—such as restrictions on the use of your own land and your own water. Thanks to the signing into law of Obama Care, we no longer have the right to decide for ourselves our own health care. There are so many more examples of laws that are taking away "our pursuit of happiness" and our rights and liberties, all the while raising taxes, or fees and fines, so the government can pay for all of the above.

Transformations of Countries and Union-Forming Around the Globe: The thought occurred to me if transformations, trans-nationalism, and union-forming are going on in Europe and America, what about the rest of the world? Is this a trend happening everywhere? I did a word search for "African Union" and amazing websites and information popped up. I continued and did the same for "South America Union," "Asian Union," "South Pacific Union;" again, much information was found. I even found information about a union of both North and South America combined, called "Americas-Union," with a charter, a sort of constitution, already written. Several articles mentioned union currencies (similar to the euro) being planned for these various "integrations."

Who are the People Behind the Transformation of Nations and What are Their Motives? Behind the movement to transform nations and governments and form various unions around the globe are some very powerful men and women who actually call themselves "transies" and are very proud of it. They want to transform the world. Their eventual goal is to link all the regional governments or unions together in one big world government.

These people are not concerned about improving the countries or the quality of life of the people inside those unions; though, as already mentioned, that is what they are pretending and promising with nice sounding names like "Security and Prosperity Partnership" or "Transatlantic Common Market." They are only interested in their own agendas, which are all about power, control, and greed. They like power. They like control, and they like money, lots of it. They truly believe that their elite status, their "blood line," their wealth, their intellect makes them far superior to the rest of mankind; they are to be the ones in charge to make the decisions for all the rest of us.

Conspiracy Theories or Conspiracy Facts: When people first hear of strange, unbelievable things going on in politics that do not make any sense, such as a movement to form a North American Union, or the transformation of the USA into a socialist state, they usually have one of three reactions:

1) They deny or scoff at what they are hearing. They say, "The government would never let that happen;"

2) They discredit the messenger who is bringing the message, saying such things as, "You don't know what you are talking about. You must be a conspiracy nut;" or "You must be racist to speak out against Obama like that;"

3) If they finally have to accept what they are hearing as fact, then they say it is just happening "by chance, by accident," no matter how strange or incomprehensible it all is.

Seldom do people think that there could be a conspiracy involved. Conspiracy does not exist in the vocabulary of most Americans, except for speaking of the Mafia and organized crime.

It is very hard for most people to be jarred out of their comfort zone to accept such an idea. They would rather deny it.

Someone told me that he compares the denial by most Americans of a governmental conspiracy to children who are in a dysfunctional family with abusive parents. As bad as the situation is, the children want to go on believing that their parents still love them and want the best for them.

Most Americans are like that with their "nanny-state" government. As bad as the president and his administration are (no matter if they are democrat or republican), just like little children, nanny-state Americans, would like to go on believing that the President loves them and only wants the best for them, and they trust him to do what is right for them, no matter how many times he violates that trust.

But what if the president has an entirely different agenda and mind-set for our nation? What if he is not really the one who is making the decisions at all, but is like a puppet on a string— having to do and say what his "handlers" order him to do and say? What if something similar is going on in other lands with other rulers?

The definition of a conspiracy is 1) "a secret planning to do something unlawful or wrong" or 2) "a secret combination of persons for an evil or unlawful purpose." (*World Book Dictionary*, 1985, p. 444.)

According to these definitions, we could have people in government involved in "conspiracies" every day. President Bush was meeting with the Prime Minister of Canada and the President of Mexico over several years in secret meetings, setting up the Security and Prosperity Partnership and planning for a North American Union and the NAFTA Superhighway system. There is nothing in the Constitution that authorized such, so such acts were illegal.

President Obama has met often with his many czars and other members of Congress in meetings trying to push through one socialist scheme after another. The Speaker of the House and the Head of the Senate are doing the same as they try to pass their socialist bills. Such socialist legislation is not authorized by the Constitution, so would you say their acts are illegal as well?

Very few of the bills that go through Congress and are signed into law are actually authorized by our U.S. Constitution. Many of our Congressmen seem to have little regard for the Constitution and think of it as antiquated or not relevant and they, for the most part, ignore it.

So, officially, does that make the majority of bills that are being passed and have no authorization by the Constitution— illegal? Does that make the people involved in doing these illegal actions part of a conspiracy? There would certainly be many Congressmen and state legislators then who should be labeled "coconspirators."

These would just be small conspiracies. But what if there was and has been for a long time a conspiracy of great magnitude, well organized and powerful, that is in control of the world's banks and finances, the political policies and parties of all nations, the major media, the environmental movement and the intelligence community?

It is hard for most people—even those suffering the most from the socialization that is going on in our nation today and our serious financial crisis— to accept that the great hardships that they and others are experiencing could have been deliberately orchestrated, all part of a bigger plan, a conspiracy, to bring down our nation's economy and put us into enormous debt.

It doesn't make sense. Why would anyone want to do any of the above to a nation or to its people? Usually when something does not make sense, the best answer is— "follow the money trail." We have to remember that powerful bankers and lenders make lots of money when a nation is in debt from the interest owed on that debt. In the case of the USA and our debt, it involves trillions of dollars.

If people still have a hard time thinking that there might be a conspiracy involved, and that governments could do this to their own people, I ask them to do their own research. Read Chapters Three and Four about how the EU was formed and check out the references and footnotes.

The EU is the example we are following. It was done by stealth and deception— by conspiracy— by the executives of the governments involved, with no parliamentary vote. Very few, if any, elected representatives knew what was going on, until it was a done deal.

Before the transformation of nations into a giant European union could take place, however, they all had to be somewhat on the same "socialist," "statist" page. Socialism and central control, including a powerful central bank, had to have taken over their governments, so the people had little say and little control in what was going on. The same is going on in the USA today, as we become closer to a socialist state with more powerful top-down central control.

As the reader will find out, the transformation of the USA and union building has been the goal of top government leaders for many years. However, they are not going to tell us about it (not until it is a done deal). They are doing it by stealth. They don't want any congressional oversight or a vote of the people to stop them. They may try to deceive us with a new fancy name for their union, or they just might put it on hold and go more deeply underground with it, waiting for the USA to become more socialistic, and the opportune time (or crisis) to bring forth their plans again.

If people still believe that what is happening in our nation and the world today is just occurring by chance or by accident, I give them the following quote by Franklin Delanor Roosevelt, Obama's idol. FDR said, "In politics, nothing happens by accident. If it happens, you can bet it was planned that way." (Gary Allen, *None Dare Call It Conspiracy*, Concord Press, Seal Beach, CA., 1972. p. 8.)

When people tell me that they do not believe in "conspiracy theories," I tell them, "I agree. I do not believe in conspiracy theories either. I only believe in conspiracy facts." This book is full of such facts. They are becoming easier to find as the conspirators become bolder and more brazen in their words and actions, so sure of themselves now. They believe there is no turning back from America's head-on course to world government.

The concluding chapter is full of quotes, many straight from the "insider's mouths"—all promoting a "New World Order," regional and world government, based on a centrally-planned and controlled society similar to socialism and communism, a one-world economy, one-world environmental controls, one-world religion, with no free press, no free enterprise system, no 2nd Amendment rights. Many of these quotes are coming from the original sources, from the actual members of the elite, who are now so confident and bold that they are admitting the truth about their real agenda and motives. The following are five examples:

David Rockefeller, one of the most powerful ringleaders, published a book about his life called *Memoirs*, wherein he reveals his family's agenda of a "one world political and economic structure" and he is very proud of it: (emphasis added).

*Some even believe we are part of a secret cabal working against the best interest of the United States, characterizing my family and me as 'internationalists' and of conspiring with others around the world to build a more integrated global political and economic structure—**one world, if you will**. If that's the charge, **I stand guilty, and I am proud of it.** (*David Rockefeller, Memoirs, Random House Inc. New York, 2002, p. 405)

Richard Gardner, a good friend of the Rockefeller Family and fellow member of the elitist group for the USA, the Council on Foreign Relations, wrote an article in their monthly publication called *Foreign Affairs,* in which he states how national sovereignty will have to be eroded away, "piece by piece" before world government can be established.

*. . . In short, the **house of world order** will have to be built from the bottom up rather than from the top down. It will look like a great booming, buzzing confusion, to use William James famous description of reality, but an end run around national sovereignty, eroding it piece by piece, will accomplish much more than the old-fashioned frontal assault.* (Richard Gardner, "The Hard Road to World Order," *Foreign Affairs,* April, 1974, pp. 558-559.)

Joseph Stalin, former communist dictator of the Soviet Union, responsible for the death of millions of his own people, wrote a book, *Marxism and the National Question,"* published in 1942, in which he gives the plan for how to best erode national sovereignty, break up nations first into regional governments:

Populations will more readily abandon their national loyalties to a vague regional loyalty than they will for a world authority. Divide the world into regional groups as a transitional stage to total world government. Later the regional groups can be brought all the way into single world dictatorship. (Joseph Stalin, *Marxism and the National Question,"* 1942.)

Brooke Chisholm, a Canadian doctor and former Director of the UN World Health Organization, who was awarded "Humanist of the Year" for 1959. He made the following statement, which helps us to better understand the anti-Americanism, anti-family, anti-religious indoctrination that is going on in our schools and media:

To Achieve World Government it is necessary to remove from the minds
of men their individualism, their loyalty to family traditions and national
identification.

Dr. Carroll Quigley, professor at Georgetown University, teacher and mentor for
Bill Clinton. When Clinton was asked to whom he would give the most credit
for his becoming President of the United States, he cited Quigley. The following
quote is taken from a 1300-page book that Quigley wrote called *Tragedy and*
Hope, published in 1966. The message that Quigley gives in his book is that it
is a tragedy that the truth about the movement to a one-world government is
being kept secret, for he believes that it is the hope for the world that it should
be revealed and established. However, as soon as Quigley's book was published,
the Macmillan Company stopped printing it. The powerful elite did not feel
the world was ready yet for the revelation of who they were and what they were
about. ((The entire quote is found in Chapter Nineteen. Quigley's book can
now be purchased at RadioLiberty.com.):

> *There does exist and has existed for a generation, an*
> *international. . . network which operates, to some extent, in the way the*
> *radical right believes the Communists act. In fact, this network, which we*
> *may identify as the Round Table Groups, has no aversion to cooperating*
> *with the Communists, or any other groups and frequently does.*
>
> *I know of the operation of the network because I have studied it*
> *for twenty years and was permitted for two years, in the early 1960s, to*
> *examine its papers and secret records. I have no aversion to it or to most*
> *of its aims and have, for most of my life been close to it and to many of*
> *its instruments. . . in general my chief difference of opinion is that it*
> *wishes to remain unknown, and I believe its role in history is significant*
> *to be known. . .*
>
> *The powers of financial capitalism has another far reaching aim,*
> *nothing less than to create a world system of financial control in private*
> *hands able to dominate the political system of each country and the*
> *economy of the world as a whole.*

The Incremental Chipping away of the Foundations of National Sovereignty:
The elitists have learned throughout history that one-world government building
is not done very well top down by force. It is best done by deception, by slowly
chipping away at the foundations of national sovereignty, by first forming trade
and economical unions between countries that later morph into political unions

and regional governments. People are naturally suspicious when they hear that there might be a movement towards world government. But they will be more accepting and not as aware of what is going on if the movement happens just a little bit at a time, and especially if it is cloaked under the disguise of nice-sounding words such as a "free trade agreement," or "common market," or "security and prosperity partnership," or as Richard Gardner said, under a bunch of "booming and buzzing confusion" so most people won't have a clue as to what is going on. This book will reveal much of that booming and buzzing confusion. It appears that the more confusing it is, the more success the elitists have in getting it implemented.

A One-World Government Vision: Yes, there are such people as David Rockefeller, Richard Gardner, Joseph Stalin, Brooke Chisholm and Carroll Quigley, who all have a very different one-world vision for our nation and the world. As you will become aware throughout this book, these people are becoming bolder, more arrogant, believing there is now no stopping them. These people are extremely powerful, wealthy, and in high positions of prominence, either in government, finances, corporations, academia, entertainment, or in the media. But if Americans and citizens of other nations can just be awakened to the seriousness of the situation we find ourselves in and become united in stopping them, we can thwart their agenda. The next to the last chapter gives some of the successes that have already happened and hope that these can continue, but we must become aware, united and activated. Knowledge is power, but only if it is put to use.

Protecting American sovereignty, our God-given freedoms and rights, our Judeo-Christian heritage, and our inspired U.S. Constitution are to me the most important issues that are at stake right now in the battle to preserve our nation and our future. I would like to be able to pass on to my children and grandchildren the freedoms, rights, American traditions and way of life that I hold so dear. That is why I have written this book.

A second book, later to be published, *the Incremental Chipping Away of the Once Great USA*, explains for those of us who like to have all the answers, just how, over the years, the foundation of our nation has been chipped away, making such a present-day transformation of America possible.

The inspiration for the second book came from a quote by a famous historian, Will Durant. He states in his first Volume of *Civilizations of the World*, that for any civilization to exist and to continue there must be four elements present: a form of government, a system of economy, morals based on religion, and education, to pass on to the next generation what the civilization values and feels is important. I examine each of these elements, how they were when they were first established in our nation, and what has happened to them since. Here is a brief idea of what *the Incremental Chipping Away of the Once Great USA*, says about the following:

1. Our Form of Government: Our representative-Republic, based on an amazingly well-written, divinely inspired Constitution, has been slowly changed to a democracy and now an oligarchy, with an elite few making all the decisions for the rest of us, and the Constitution is essentially ignored.

2. Our Free-Enterprise System and Economy: These have been changed to a central banking system under the Federal Reserve, and, with the bailout and takeover of our banks and financial institutions that started with President Bush and was continued "with gusto" by President Obama, we are becoming a nationalized, socialist economic system.

3. The Moral and Judeo-Christian Religious Foundation of Our Nation: These have been so chipped away that they are hardly recognizable. As a teacher, I had one student in the 7th grade ask me what morals are? Can you believe that—in the seventh grade! Very few young people seem to be taught morals at home; very few attend any church; and there is very little moral instruction going on at school, other than tolerance. Tolerance is the only virtue that many teachers teach. It essentially means "anything goes," and no one should pass judgment on anyone else. The exception is, of course, if you are a conservative or a Christian or both, and if you should dare to express any of your beliefs in class, then it is "open season" on you. The teacher and students can pass judgment on you and call you every name in the book: "intolerant, hateful, homophobe, discriminatory, bigoted, racist," and they receive no punishment, because they are the politically correct "tolerant" ones.

Thus, conservative and Christian students soon learn, that if you have strong moral principles, especially if you are opposed to abortion, to same-sex marriage, to free love, if you profess a belief in God, in creation and not evolution, in abstinence, absolute truths, in right and wrong, and if you want to survive in the public schools and universities, then you must just keep your beliefs to yourself—don't ever write about them or mention them in class. Your teachers and fellow students, however, can talk about their secular/humanist/atheist beliefs, their belief in evolution, in abortion, in same-sex marriage, and their disdain for any conservative president or any conservative elected official, and they are perfectly acceptable. But you are not allowed to express a different view or that will be called "hate speech."

Our Judeo-Christian foundation as a nation is also no longer taught or greatly played down. And, as you probably remember hearing on the news about Obama's statement on his trip to Turkey, he told the audience he was speaking to that "America is no longer a Christian nation."[1] If the president of our nation already believes that, how much quicker will any last semblance of Christianity be washed away.

4. Our Education System has been Greatly Dumbed Down: Many of our children no longer know or care to know what the history of this great nation is, and so many don't even want to stay in school and graduate. On an ABC radio news broadcast, October 23, 2008, I heard the following education statistics: 1 out of 4 teenagers in our nation today is dropping out of school, and those that stay in are not receiving the equivalent of the education their parents received. That is pretty sad news. In the Los Angeles School District it is even worse; it is 1 out of 3 who are dropping out.

The Incremental Chipping Away of the Once Great USA also tells of the birth and promotion of the environmental movement, the attack on property rights, more on United Nations invasive treaties, and illegal immigration and what it is doing to our nation. The book concludes with many pages of inspirational freedom quotes by famous Americans to help give us hope and encouragement to go on with the battle to stand up for our freedoms and try to preserve them for the next generation.

Chapter Two

Government by Stealth and Deception,
The War on the Middle Class,
The Parallel of the Formation of the European Union
with the Foundation for a North American Merger

To Most Americans, Sovereignty and Nationhood are Regarded as Precious.:
Most American citizens, even those who are somewhat disgruntled with what is going on in our nation today, still are proud of being Americans and would like to keep our Stars and Stripes flag and keep the United States as we know it for our children and grandchildren. We know that our founding fathers and even our own fathers and grandfathers have fought to win and keep the independence and freedoms our nation has enjoyed for more than 230 years. We know our founding fathers worked hard to write a courageous Declaration of Independence and magnificent and inspired U.S. Constitution with its attached Bill of Rights that have protected and preserved our freedoms. We would like to keep our independence, keep our Constitution and our freedoms and pass them on to the next generations for years to come, forever, if it were possible.

Most Americans, if they were asked if they wanted to give up our independence, give up our U.S. Constitution and Bill of Rights, our American sovereignty, our borders, and become part of a North American Union with Mexico and Canada, or form a partnership with the European Union, or become a transformed, socialist nation, they would look you square in the face and say, "Those are the silliest things I have ever heard of, of course not! What has gotten into you to come up with such crazy ideas?"

Most Americans know very little or nothing about either the movement towards a North American Union or integration with the EU. It was all being done by stealth, without any congressional oversight in our country, and without any or very little parliamentary oversight in Mexico or Canada. The executive branches of all three countries, with all their cabinet heads involved, and with assigned "working groups," were the ones who were scheming and planning and working hard to bring this integration about, without any pesky objections from other branches of government or a vote of the people. One would think such an important decision as forming a North American Union would be worthy of a vote of the people, but that was not the case. Very few people in Mexico and Canada were being told about this either. Those who found out were equally upset.

Most Americans are catching on to the amazing socialist "transformation" that is taking place in our nation because of President Obama's administration. Many, who voted for him, have now been hit in the pocket books, with either greatly reduced incomes, or total loss of incomes because of loss of jobs, and loss of homes. Many, who still have jobs, are facing higher taxes. These people are realizing that Obama's "hope and change" mantra is not what they thought it would be. People are catching on to what the USA transformation really entails, and they are not at all happy about it. Many changes, however, are also being done under the carpet. Obama is not the "transparent" president he promised he would be.

Government by Stealth, Government for the Elite, Government against the People: As you will see from reading the facts in this book, we no longer seem to have a government that is open and honest with the American people. It is government by stealth. Our representative government "of the people, by the people, and for the people" is fading fast. It is becoming government "of the elite, by the elite, and for the elite," and it seems to be more and more against the people, especially against those who would disagree with the ruling class.

Why Integration, Why Form Economic and Political Partnerships with Other Nations, Why Regional Governments? As you read in the preface, people are naturally suspicious when they hear that there might be a movement towards world government. So the elitists believe they can do it incrementally, first by bringing people into regions, where they have more in common with neighbor nations.

Here is another quote that supports regionalization by a more modern globalist, Zbigniew Brzezinski. He has been the advisor to many U.S. presidents, including Obama, and a member of several influential globalists organizations such as the CFR and the Trilateral Commission (of which you will be reading in later chapters). Brzezinski stated, *"We cannot leap into world government in one quick step. The precondition for genuine globalization is progressive regionalization."*[2]

The Attack on the Middle Class: One of the tactics that the elite are using to bring about their agenda is to destroy the middle class, not only in America, but in all nations that still have a middle class. Why is that? As you will read from the following quotes, the middle class in America has been her foundation, the strength of the country, the fabric of society, the ones who still believe in the American dream, individual rights, and in binding the elite down by the chains of the U.S. Constitution. The middle class are the ones who do the most complaining, letter writing, speaking out when they see their hopes, dreams, and rights being trampled on. They are the vast majority who make up the Tea Party movement in America.

The Middle Class are America's Hard Working Foundation Who Believe in Traditional Values, Individual Rights and Responsibilities: In his book, *The War on the Middle Class,* by former television and radio journalist Lou Dobbs, he tells why the elites are out to destroy it:

> For more than two hundred years, the American middle class has been the core of a work ethic, a tradition of values, and a belief that every citizen is an important part of a greater good. This heritage has made the United States a unique nation with shared goals and ideals. Our middle class is America's foundation, and it is in its hearts and minds that the ideal of America is held strongest and brightest.
>
> Individual rights and responsibilities are the core of America . . . But today we live in a postmodern society in which we've allowed interdependence to overpower individualism. The essential respect for the importance of the rights of the individual is eroding in America.[3]

The Middle Class Believe in God-Given Liberty and in Binding the Elite by the Chains of the U.S. Constitution: Taylor Caldwell, the famous author of many best selling novels such as *Captain and the Kings, the Story of an American Dynasty,* learned firsthand that there was truly a conspiracy to destroy the middle class of America. In an article published in the *New American*, she states:

> The elite hated the middle class which challenged them in the name of God-given liberty. And little wonder that this hatred grew deeper as the middle class became stronger and imposed restrictions through which all the people, including the most humble, had the right to rule their own lives and keep the greater part of what they earned for themselves . . . The middle class laughed and said, "We will bind you with the chains of our Constitution, which you must obey also, lest we depose you, for

*we are now powerful and we are human beings and we wish to be free
from your old despotism."*[4]

How Are the Elite Waging War on the Middle Class? One of the ways they are
doing this is by outsourcing and eliminating the manufacturing base of our nation
and over three million jobs, bringing our economy down to a third-world level.
Read the following quotes from people who are losing their jobs across our nation
taken from William Norman Grigg's book, *America's Engineered Decline:*

> *What does it do when you take away all these jobs from people who
> support families, who raise families? . . . Manufacturing has been the
> strength of this country. If we can't make anything here anymore, what
> does that do? The fabric of this society is falling apart.* (Statement by
> Jim Greathouse, age 55, 30-year employee of a Hoover vacuum
> factory in Canton, Ohio, after losing his job in June, 2003, because
> the company was closed down.)

> *We're basically liquidating our whole middle class, polarizing people on
> the two extremes, haves and have-nots . . . We'll be a third-world country."*
> (Roger Chastain, former president of the Mount Vernon Mills of
> Greenville, South Carolina, a textile mills that is now closed.)

> *It makes me wonder if there is some merit to the 'conspiracy theory'—the
> idea that all of this is part of a deliberate scheme to wipe out the middle
> class. The middle class is always a pain in the neck where government's
> concerned. It's where you find most of the people who complain about
> taxes, regulations, and other policies. If you wipe them out, you just have
> the ultra-rich and the poor—a perfect arrangement for a dictatorship.*
> (Jerry Skoff, former owner of Badger Tech Metals in Menomonee,
> Wisconsin.)[5]

Elitists, who seek to transform America, would like to do away with the
middle class. We are a pain in the neck to them. They would like a society of
either rich or poor with the problem of the pesky middle class eliminated. The
very rich, for the most part, have been bought off or are part of the governing
elite, and the poor are so busy working to eke out the bare minimum of existence
that they have no free time or money to bother about keeping a check on
government, or the poor are on the welfare dole and would not dare to speak
out against the hand that feeds them. The elitists are then free to do whatever

they want to do: take more rights and property away, raise more taxes and use that money any way they would like, and put the people into greater bondage, kind of like the good old "feudal system" of yesteryears.

Government Without a Pesky U.S. Constitution, of Unelected Commissioners, Patterned After the European Union: The U.S. Constitution has also been a big pain in the neck to the elitists. It has restricted their globalist plans and held them at bay for over 200 years. They have chipped away at it, a little at a time. Now they have chosen, for the most part, to simply ignore it.

If all goes according to plan, the U.S. Constitution will be totally done away with as we "harmonize" our laws with those of Canada and Mexico in forming a North American Union or as we harmonize U.S. laws with those of the European Union. Either way, the form of government that would be established for us would be a parliament. You cannot "harmonize" our government with parliamentary systems and expect to keep our form of government or our U.S. Constitution. We would end up with a system similar to that of the European Union, a government of unelected Commissioners who are running the parliament, but who are not voted in by the people. They are, thus, no longer accountable to the people and are free to do whatever they want to do, without any fear of not being reelected, easily tempted to heap more power unto themselves and form tyrannical regimes.

In the EU, each country sends ministers to the parliament, but the unelected EU Commissioners and their assistants essentially run the show and tell the ministers what they are voting on and how to vote. Then back home in each nation, their parliament merely rubber stamps what the EU is telling them. They have essentially lost their own autonomy.

Britain Held Hostage:—Lindsay Jenkins is author of two books exposing the origins of the European Federation and the emergence of the European Union, *Britain Held Hostage and the Last Days of Britain.* She states:

> *"Today, over 80 percent of everything that goes through the House of Commons and the House of Rules, merely rubberstamps Brussels [the seat of government for the EU], and there is an awfully lot of it. We recently 'celebrated,' if that is the right word, our 40,000th directive coming from Brussels and having attacked central government. Now Brussels is attacking our local government structure. So we have lost, just to recap in the following areas: We have lost 100% (or near enough) of our control*

of the environment, the British scenery and countryside, and everything
that comprises environment—including health and safety regulations. We
have lost 100% control of our fishing; 100% or our farming; and we
have lost 100% control of our trade policy, and that loss is of particular
significance . . ."[6]

Why is the Loss of their Trade Policy so Significant? Free trade was the main
excuse given to sell the idea of forming some kind of a free-trade agreement to
the European nations, first as an organization to better help in the production
and trade of steel and coal, called the ECSC, European Coal and Steel Company.
(Notice the parallel to NAFTA, our free-trade agreement, laying the framework
for a stronger union between the USA, Canada, and Mexico.) Slowly the ECSC
evolved into the European Common Market, sold to the member nations as a
better way to enhance trade and to compete with the United States and other
big trading countries.[7]

The Great Deception: According to two British authors, Christopher Booker,
a columnist for the *Sunday Telegraph,* and Dr. Richard North, a former research
director at the European Parliament, who wrote a book about the EU called *The
Great Deception*, the decades-long stealth campaign that gave birth to the EU
was a "slow-motion *coup d'etat*, the most spectacular *coup d'etat* in history." All
mention of political union was suppressed, and if anyone even mentioned that
they were concerned about such a union developing, they were scoffed at and
ridiculed. Sounds familiar to what is going on with the SPP and the movement
to form an NAU today, doesn't it? The following is a brief summary of the
book, *The Great Deception*, by a British on-line company from which you can
order the book:

> *The Great Deception* shows how the most ambitious political project
> of our time has for more than 50 years been based on a colossal
> confidence trick—the systematic concealment from the peoples
> of Europe of what the aim of this project has always been since its
> inception in the late 1940s. As it reveals for the first time the true story
> behind the long-term plan to build a politically united Europe, the
> authors show how all previous attempts to reconstruct the history of
> this project—whether written by Europhiles or Eurosceptics—have
> got it wrong, at almost every step along the way. With all the suspense
> of a detective story, drawing on thousands of books, papers and official

documents, many of which have only become publicly available in the past few years, the book traces how a handful of determined visionaries set out more than half a century ago to weld the countries of Europe into a single political state."[8]

The Common Market: It was sold as "no more than a deal to promote trade and prosperity." Is it not interesting that those who created the SPP for the North American countries chose that same nice sounding word—"prosperity"—The Security and Prosperity Partnership? As we see with Europe, the Common Market and the EU have not brought prosperity or security, but just the opposite. Member nations have lost their sovereignty, autonomy and so many of their freedoms in the process. Their currencies have been devalued; many are forced to live in public housing; and their nations are not more secure as the borders have been opened wide, bringing in many unsavory characters and more crime, drugs, and people with vastly different cultures and religions who do not want to assimilate in their new country.

The nation of Greece, in the beginning of 2010, became bankrupt, affecting other nations since their economies are all linked together with the euro as their common currency. This is one more example of how the EU and the euro has been bad for the nations of Europe who belong.

To form a vast trade organization involving many countries, it would be necessary to have a government structure set up to oversee that organization. Incrementally, that structure became stronger and evolved into a political union, the EU, what the original goal was all along. The 27 nations that belong to it now have lost control over making their own policies, including their own free trade, what the European Union was supposed to be all about in the first place. There is no "free" trade. There is nothing free when government has taken over. There are always many strings attached.

The Primacy of the EU Constitution: The EU Constitution was produced in 2004 and sent to all member nations to ratify. It boldly stated, "This Constitution . . . shall have primacy over the law of Member States." It also expressed, repeatedly, conformity with the Charter of the United Nations. President Vaclav Klaus of the Czech Republic said the following about what full ratification of the Constitution would mean, *"There will be no more sovereign states in Europe and only one will remain."* Spanish Foreign Minister Miguel Angel Moratinos said, *"We are witnessing the last remnants of national politics."*

The Poster to Promote the EU: For many years a poster of the Tower of Babel started appearing in public places all over Europe to get the Europeans used to the concept of forming some kind of a more united community of nations working together, that rebuilding the Tower of Babel would be a good thing. The picture on the poster was based on a famous painting of the Tower of Babel done back in 1563 by the Flemish artist, Pieter Bruegel.

God Established Nations: What the European Union leaves out in the promotion of their poster is that it is God who destroyed the Tower of Babel and separated people up into nations with different languages. Why? Because God believes in nations. Nations provide a check and a balance of power just as the fifty states in our nation help provide a check and balance to an all-powerful U.S. federal government. The Bible actually mentions the word "nations" 44 times. In Psalms 86:9, it states that God made the nations. Several verses mention

The Poster to Promote the European Union Using the Same Design as the Painting by the Flemish Artist Pieter Bruegle "The Building of the Tower of Babel,"—1563, (shown on page 31). The writing on the poster says, "Europe—Many Tongues—One Voice."

that nations are blessed when they worship the Lord such as "Psalm 33:12 "Blessed is the nation whose God is the Lord" and Proverb 14:34 "Righteousness exalteth a nation." (King James Version of the Bible)

Who Is it Who Seeks to Destroy Nations? The prophet Isaiah gives us the answer in Isaiah 14:12: "Lucifer . . . didst weaken the nations." Lucifer does not want nations because they limit his power and the power of his followers.

It is also interesting to see the shape of the stars on the poster that was used to promote the European Union. They are in the shape of an inverted pentagram, an occult symbol, supposedly showing the head of a goat with horns, on top, the ears below and a goatee at the bottom. In the occult, the goat is also a symbol for Satan, who some depict as also having horns and a goatee. The inverted pentagrams are an affront to God, as is the movement to destroy individual nations that God wants for the world.

"Europe, Many Tongues One Voice.": The slogan shown on the poster was trying to convince the people of Europe that they needed to be more united—to speak with one voice so they could be a powerful unit to wield greater influence in the global marketplace, especially in competing with the United States. (As you will see in Chapter 5, which tells of the formation of other unions, "to better compete with the USA" is always the big excuse given for why these unions of nations are necessary.)

There are many tongues in those 27 nations that now belong to the EU. The sad thing is they are speaking more and more in one voice, something most of the people in the various countries do not want. They still want their own voice to be heard. They are proud of their individual countries and their nationhood. But that is all different now. but most of the people of the various countries do not really want it that way. Individual voices, even those of their own parliaments are being ignored and not listened too. The "one voice" is a very powerful "socialist" voice that is becoming a dictator for the member nations.

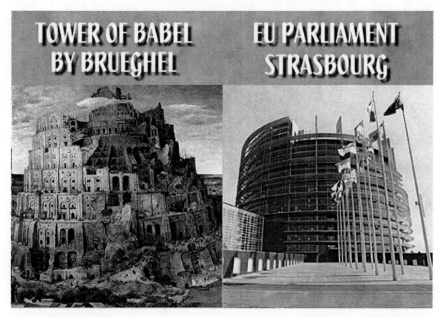

"The Building of the Tower of   EU Parliament Building in Strasbourg,
Babel,"1563,   France
by Flemish artist Pieter Bruegle

Notice how the EU parliament building in Strasbourg, France, has been specifically designed to resemble the unfinished Tower of Babel. Again it shows how strongly the European Union is intent on bringing back the old tower, symbolizing the dissolving of nation states and forming an all-powerful super union in their stead.[10]

In the next chapter you will read of the "politically correct" history of the European Union, painting a very rosy picture of the union and a very negative one of "nationalism," which is blamed for all wars and all the evils of the world.

Chapter Three

The Politically Correct History of the European Union, "The Evils of Nationalism"

To find the politically correct version of the EU and how wonderful it is, google "History of the EU." It is quite amazing what comes up. It is hard to find a website that does not give a favorable impression of how necessary and wonderful the European Union is (until one digs deeper). The writers are not hiding the fact at all that the original intent was a political union from the very beginning. But, as has been mentioned, at the time of forming the EU and getting member nations to sign on to it, the designers kept any mention of a union hidden. It was promoted as a "community of nations," united only to help in trade and commerce, just as in the case of NAFTA, and the SPP, and the partnership going on between the USA, Mexico, and Canada now.

The websites continue to try to convince the reader that the European Union is a good thing by painting an evil picture of "nationalism," which to them was the cause of both World War I and II. In the introduction, the writers say, "Europe's capacity to react to war depended on its ability to overcome the aggressive nationalism that had dragged our continent to the catastrophe and to adopt the ideal of a united and peaceful Europe as a common project."

As you have already read and will read in later chapters, proponents of a North American Union also believe that nationalism and sovereignty are evil and must be done away with, "piece by piece."

1914-1919—World War I: Many nations of Europe were involved, and the "evils of nationalism" were blamed as the reason for the War.

1923—A United States of Europe: After World War I, an Austrian Count, Richard Coudenhave-Kalergi, gave a talk to some political leaders in Vienna. He suggested that the only hope for the stopping of future wars and conflicts and "the mutual hate that poisons the atmosphere is . . . by means of the union of Europe's nations." He even called it a "United States of Europe." He said, "The biggest obstacle to the accomplishment of the United States of Europe is the 1,000 year old rivalry between the two most populated nations of Pan-Europe, Germany and France."

1929—European Federal Union: A second name for the union was suggested by the French Prime Minister, Aristide Briand, September 5, 1929, before the newly formed League of Nations. In his speech, he proposed a "European Federal Union," based on solidarity and the pursuit of economic prosperity and political and social cooperation."

1931—The "Monster" of Nationalism: A book called *The United States of Europe* was published by another Frenchman, Edoard Herriot, but his hopes of a united Europe had to be delayed. The United States of America would not go along with the League of Nations. The Great Depression hit in the 1930s, which not only affected America, but had repercussions around the world. Hitler rose to power in 1933. Soon everyone was at war again. This is how the article on this part of the EU's history ended:

> Adolf Hitler's rise to the post of German chancellery in 1933 involved the definitive end of the European harmony and the **rebirth of the monster of nationalism** in its worst form. Europe and, with her, the world were heading for a new catastrophe.[11]

1939-45—"Nationalist Rivalry Caused World War II": Again, all war is blamed on nationalism and the rivalry between nations. Nothing is mentioned about the designs of evil dictators and leaders, and their agenda for world dominance, power and control. Nor is anything mentioned about who was funding the wars— wealthy international bankers, who loaned money to both sides to keep the wars going. That way, it did not matter who won or lost, the bankers always came out as winners.

1945-1957—The End of the II World War, the Shuman Declaration of 1950, and the Treaty of Rome in 1957: This section again blames war on nationalism. There is nothing about the famous statement by Lord Acton, "power corrupts and absolute power corrupts absolutely," which had happened to Hitler and those supporting him and funding him.

The article states, "Europe had to witness a second catastrophe, World War II (1939-1945), so that it fully becomes aware of the suicidal absurdity that **nationalist rivalry** had led the continent to. The necessity of some type of European integration in a new way to reorder the European political map became evident."

Why Europeans Were Willing to Form Some Kind of a Union: According to the politically correct websites promoting the EU, Europeans wanted a union because of the following three reasons:

1) They realized their own weakness in comparison with the USA and the Soviet Union, which had been demonstrated in the war to have a "superior economic, political and military might."

2) They wanted to avoid, by all means possible, any further confrontation among European States. They did not want any further battles on European soil. They must, therefore, find an "accommodation" between France and Germany, a compromise that would be endorsed by the USA. "The European integration will pave the way to guarantee peace."

3) They now had a desire "to create a freer, fairer and more prosperous continent in which the international relationships were developed in a framework of concord."[12] (Don't these statements sound a little bit like pure propaganda? I wonder which "Europeans" were being quoted? Could it have been just a few of the elitists who were the ones behind such a union and probably the ones who wrote this article? Just as in America, the vast majority of the common ordinary citizen did not know anything about "some kind of a union" being planned.)

1943—Jean Monnet, Regarded as the Father of the European Union: Monnet had been working many years behind the scenes forging an alliance between the French and the British against Germany. As a member of the National Liberation Committee of the free French government in Algiers, Monnet addressed the committee and made the following statement:

> There will be no peace in Europe if the States rebuild themselves on the basis of national sovereignty, with its implication of prestige politics and economic protection . . . The countries of Europe are not strong enough to be able to guarantee prosperity and social development for their peoples. The states of Europe must therefore form a federation or a European entity that would make them into a common economic unit.[13]

Monnet was most instrumental in forging this "federation," mainly by emphasizing economic unity and hardly mentioning any political unity.

1944—The Benelux Customs Union was Formed: It was a small union among three countries: Belgium, the Netherlands and Luxembourg. In 1948, it introduced a common external tariff.

1946—Winston Churchill Proclaims His Belief in a United States of Europe: Even the leaders who one would think would be the most patriotic of their own nation and nationhood, after World War II, seemed to think some European integration was necessary. One of those was Winston Churchill, British Prime Minister from 1940-45 and 1951-55. This is what is said of him and his statements on a different website. Notice again, the attack on "nationalism:" (I have put in bold the words to be emphasized.)

> Following the experience of the Second World War, he [Churchill] was convinced that only a united Europe could guarantee peace. His aim was to eliminate the European **ills of nationalism** and war-mongering once and for all. He formulated his conclusions drawn from the lessons of history in his famous 'Speech to the academic youth' held at the University of Zurich in 1946: 'There is a remedy which . . . would in a few years make all Europe . . . free and . . . happy. It is to re-create the European family, or as much of it as we can, and to provide it with a structure under which it can dwell in peace, in safety and in freedom. **We must build a kind of United States of Europe.**'[14]

1948—Marshall Plan "Free Trade" Necessary to Receive U.S. Aid: The article mentions that for the European countries that were recovering from the devastations of war to receive economic aid from the United States, there had to be some kind of a free trade agreement in place. Why? Because the American government felt a lack of free trade was one of the things that had helped cause the "Nazi and Fascist autarchy." (Autarchy means an independence of imports from other countries which leads to autocracy, where government has absolute power over its citizens.) The U.S. government officials stated a free trade agreement would help curb the expansion of the Soviet Union and impede the spread of Communism. For these reasons, the Marshall Plan was [supposedly] launched.

1948—Organization for European Economic Cooperation (OEEC): There had to be an organization to implement the Marshall Plan, thus was launched the OEEC to administer and organize the delivery of the massive economic aid of the Marshall Plan. This was one of the first institutions that involved a great part of Western European countries. "OEEC helped to liberalize the trade among the member States, introduced ideas in favor of monetary agreements and enhanced economic cooperation."

1949—NATO, North Atlantic Treaty Organization: NATO was organized following an American initiative. Most of Western European democratic states belonged, along with the USA and Canada. It was "supposedly" formed as a great Western military alliance to guard against the Soviet Union. (The reader will find out much more about NATO in Chapter Ten, about who really formed it and what its real purpose is.)

1949—The Council of Europe was Formed: (Notice how the writers try to negate that any true political union was intended and they assure that no surrender of sovereignty will ever take place.)

> The Council tried to incite political cooperation among European countries. However, its statutes did not claim as an objective neither the union, nor the federation of States, and no sort of surrender of sovereignty is expected from the member States. Their main function has been to reinforce the democratic system and the human rights in the member States.[15]

May 9, 1950—Schuman Declaration Given by Robert Schuman, Minister from France: He suggested that France, Germany and other nations wishing to join them pool their coal and steel resources.

> Europe will not be made all at once, or according to a single plan. It will be built through concrete achievements which first create a de facto solidarity. The coming together of the nations of Europe requires the elimination of the age-old opposition of France and Germany. Any action taken must in the first place concern these two countries. With this in view, the French Government proposes that action be taken immediately on one limited but decisive point. It proposes that Franco-German production of coal and steel as a whole be placed under a common High Authority, within the framework

of an organization open to the participation of the other countries of Europe. The pooling of coal and steel production should immediately provide for the setting up of common foundations for economic development as a first step in the federation of Europe.

1951—A European Defense Community (EDC) Proposed by the French Government: It proposed a strong military and political integration, but it was aborted in 1954, when the French Legislative Assembly vetoed its application. It was substituted by the Western European Union (WEU). Since NATO and WEU overlap, it has had a minor role in European defense.[16]

April 18, 1951—The Treaty of Paris was Signed Forming the European Coal and Steel Community, (ECSC): The treaty was based on the Schuman plan and signed by six countries. The French minister in charge was Jean Monnet. Since coal and steel were needed to build weapons of war, and since they would then be under common management, no one country could make the weapons to turn against the others, as in the past. The six countries who signed the treaty were: Germany, France, Italy, the Netherlands, Belgium and Luxembourg.

1955—Conference in Messina, Italy: The foreign ministers of the six nations, presided over by the Belgian Paul Henri Spaak, met in a Conference in Messina, Italy. The agreements they reached meant a definitive step in the European construction.

March 25, 1957—The Treaties of Rome: These treaties established the European Economic Community (EEC) and the European Atomic Energy Community (EAEC or Euratom) by the six nations. "It was evident that economic integration was the only practical way toward a political union that should be achieved after a long time. The failure of the European Defense Community (EDC) had demonstrated that political and military union was still a utopian objective."[17]

Brussels and Luxembourg: Over time, Brussels became the selected site for the EEC to meet, while Luxembourg was the site where the ECSC met. These two committees evolved into the "working groups" that even today run the executive functions of the European Union.[18]

October 17, 1957—a European Court of Justice was Established: This was begun in order to settle regional trade disputes.

1960—The European Free Trade Association (EFTA) was Begun: Those nations who belonged were: Austria, Denmark, Norway, Portugal, Sweden, and Switzerland, and the United Kingdom.

1965—A Larger European Economic Community (EEC) was Established: To form the EEC, three established European communities were merged together: the original EEC, the European Atomic Energy Community and the European Coal and Steel Community. They were combined by a treaty of April 8, 1965, and came into effect July 1, 1967. The Council of the European Communities replaced the EEC and Euratom Councils, as well as the ECSC Special Council of Ministers, but the division of powers remained intact.

1968—The European Customs Union was Formed: This was a move toward abolishing duties at international borders and establishing a uniform system for taxing imports among EEC countries.

1978—A European Standardized Monetary System and Exchange Rate was Established: This was called the European currency unit (ECU) and exchange rate mechanism (ERM). The ECU was initially just used for travelers' checks and inter-bank deposits. However, this set the stage for the emergence of a common currency.

1986—The Single European Act was Passed: This modified the Treaty of Rome and set up a framework for a completely unified European market. Gradually, what began as a simple coal and steel agreement was transformed into a common market and a European Customs Union, laying the groundwork for a European currency.[19]

February 7, 1992—The Treaty on the European Union (EU) was Signed in Maastricht, Holland: This is what the politically correct website says about it, making it sound quite appealing and benign: "It [The Treaty on the European Union] created the Council of the European Union, the institution which represents Member States within the EU. The Council, in its composition of government representatives at ministerial level, is the main EU forum in which decisions are debated and taken. It is part of the decision-making triangle—Commission, Parliament and Council—and its powers concern the common policy domains covered by the Treaties establishing the European Communities. In addition, it plays a key role in the two areas of intergovernmental cooperation established by the EU Treaty, common foreign and security policy

(CFSP) and justice and home affairs, in which the European Parliament and the Commission play only a minor part."[20]

How Much Influence Does the EU Really Play? Is it only a minor part in the "justice and home affairs" of each member nation as this last sentence states? According to the previous mentioned author, Lindsay Jenkins, in her books *Britain Held Hostage and The Last Days of Britain,* she believes that is not true. The EU plays a very major part dictating to each member nation what they can and cannot do in their own country. She believes that the EU makes "80 percent" of the major decisions and the parliaments of the member nations merely "rubberstamp" what has already been decided (The rest of the quote is found on pages 21-22.):[21]

The EU Council: The politically correct article describes more about the powerful EU Council: The Council consists of all the heads of state of the nations that belong to the EU. The website article does mention that the Council, through various treaties, has been given "greater responsibility," increased "effectiveness and transparency," it also states that all of the Council's "deliberations are confidential." May I ask, how transparent are confidential meetings?

The Council also makes its decisions by "unanimous" vote. In other words, there is no one expressing any opposition or a contrary vote. They all have to be "lock-stock" together. That sounds like real "democracy" in action, doesn't it? I wonder how much arm twisting is going on to get that unanimous vote, or are the Council members so afraid to say anything different than what the leadership wants?

The article also states just how powerful the Council is. It "enjoys decision-making powers in its own right." "It is responsible, on its own, or with the European Parliament, for translating the general interest of the Community, as proposed by the Commission, into rules that are legally binding on all Member states."

The website states, "It has often been compared with an intergovernmental body, at which state representatives defend their national interests and seek a compromise." However, that is not the case. The Council is only interested in "Community" provisions and procedures," which "govern the organization and operation of the Council." In other words, individual nations are not their concern. The Council is only looking out for the "Community." (Notice, the word Community is always in capitol letters, as if it is some God, to be held up and worshiped.)

Some of the expanding responsibilities of the Council are: "the sharing of legislative and budgetary powers with the European Parliament; an increase in the number of domains in which decisions are taken by a qualified majority; the growing importance of the role of the Council in coordinating intergovernmental cooperation; public access to its deliberations and votes on legislative acts; or the definition of a policy on access to documents."

How the Council of the European Union Evolved and Became More Powerful: The politically correct article insinuates that the forming of the Council was done with the intention of giving the smaller nations more power against the "the Higher Authority," a "supernational decision-making body, with an intergovernmental committee." The article suggests that the Council was formed by "compromise." I wonder if the compromise did not include bribes and threats, as has occurred in recent years as the EU is forcing partnerships with other smaller countries, of which you will read later.

How did the Council originally operate? According to the article, issues relating solely to coal and steel were referred to the "Higher Authority." Other matters were only considered with the Council's agreement. The Council both "scrutinized and acted as an intermediary" between the common market and the national economies of Member States.

"In 1993, the Council of the European Communities became the Council of the European Union. They then had powers of decision-making and coordination in the three pillars of the Union: the Community pillar and the two intergovernmental pillars."[22]

January 1, 2002—The Euro was Introduced: The traditional currencies of the member nations were phased out with the exception of England, which is still using the pound. Switzerland, who has refused to join the EU, is still using its own currency. What effect has the euro had on the economy of the member nations? It is the same old adage that is behind all socialistic economic policies—redistribution of wealth. The original member nations who had a more stable economy are the ones who have to pay the way for the new third-world countries coming into the fold, and it is greatly affecting their economy. I know from talking to our German relatives, the cost of living has doubled or tripled in some cases. Everything is more expensive—from food, to clothes, to housing.

In the beginning of the January, 2010, the news was released that Greece was in such a serious financial condition that some are calling it bankrupt. Greece was seeking for China or the European Union to bail it out. Of course, this affects the rest of Europe's economy, because they all share in the Euro. (http://www. businessinsider.com/roubini-greece-is-totally-bankrupt-2010-1.)

2004—Expansion to 25 nations and Ratification of a New Constitution: The EU expanded from 15 members to 25 in 2004, making a new constitution necessary for practical governing. Before it could come into effect, the EU constitution had

to be ratified by all 25 EU member states, either through a referendum or by a parliamentary vote. Nine countries already had done so: Austria, Hungary, Italy, Germany, Greece, Lithuania, Slovakia, Slovenia and Spain. People were told that rejection by even a single remaining country would "supposedly" prevent it from taking effect in November of 2006.

Signing of the Constitution: The Constitution for the European Union was signed at Capitoline Hill, Rome, October 29, 2004, in the Appartamento dei Conservatori, Sala degli Orazi e Curiazi, before the bronze statue of Pope Innocent X by Alessandro Algardi.

The EU Flag: The official flag for the EU is shown hanging from the table on which the ministers are signing the EU Constitution. It has twelve white stars in a circle against a sky blue background. It became the official flag in 1985. The twelve stars do not represent member states, as some people would think. There would now have to be 27 stars if that were the case. They represent the concept of "unity, solidarity, and harmony among the people of Europe." (http://europa.eu/abc/symbols /index_en.htm.)

EU Passports: One can see from the new passports for member states of the European Union, how dominant the EU is. At first the EU passport supplemented the other nation's passports; now it has supplanted them. All member nations are carrying EU passports, with the European Union written in bold at the top and with the nation underneath, then the national seal and the word Passport. Ordinary EU member nations' passports are burgundy-red. It is interesting what the Wikipedia Encyclopedia article then adds "The European Union passport is a result of consensus, of recommendation rather than directive. It is the underlying nationality, not the passport itself, that yields Community rights."[23] (So according to this statement, the nationality itself is yielding its

Community rights through this passport. Did you notice the word Community, written again in capitol letters?)

More Comprehensive Intrusive Passports with Biometrics: According to other websites, there are discussions about adding biometric identifiers to the passports (such as RFID chips) just as is already being done in the new passports in the USA (since 2008).[24]

January 1, 2007, Expansion to 27 Nations with the addition of Bulgaria and Romania:[25] Turkey is the next nation that would like to join. Germany is very opposed. That would bring even more of a huge influx of Moslems into their nation with the borders essentially wide open.

The European Union is a Full-Fledged Regional Government: According to Dr. Jerome Corsi, the author of the *Late Great USA,* a book about the movement to form a North American Union, the purpose for the European union has been fulfilled:

> Over a period of fifty years, the internal borders between EU countries were largely erased so European Union citizens could live and work in the EU country of their choice. Over this same period of time, a professional bureaucracy sprouted and grew in Brussels and Luxembourg. . . Virtually gone is the ability of European countries to set their own policy direction, and the ultimate arbiter of justice is the European Court of Justice in Luxembourg, not the highest national court in each country. In short, Monnet's vision of a future where the nations of Europe would gradually surrender their sovereignty to participate in a regional government had been largely achieved.[26]

The European Union has all that is Required for a Federation: According to Chief Justice, Michael Kirby, of the high Court of Australia, who was promoting a similar union between New Zealand and Australia, he describes the EU as a federation:

> Although the F word (federation) cannot be uttered in Europe, and most especially in the United Kingdom, those who look at developments in that continent cannot really deny that a federal system of sorts is gradually emerging. There is a fundamental law to which the parts have subscribed (the Treaty of Rome). And there are

the three constituent parts of government: the European Parliament in Strasbourg; the European Commission in Brussels and the European Court of Justice in Luxembourg. It may not be a federation of the 1776 or 1901 type. There is no single head of state. There is no single language. There is no single allegiance. But who can doubt that out of the rather rapid developments in Europe stimulated by economics will come a kind of allegiance?[27]

The next chapter will tell of the deception and lies that were told to the people in the creation of the European Union and will give descriptions of the changes that have happened to the political structure and economy by Europeans having to live under its rule. There are also statements by the many groups of people who are opposing it and trying to rid their nation of it.

Chapter Four

**The Truth About the EU and Its Background,
People and Groups in Europe Who Oppose It,
The New EU Constitution Now Called a Treaty,
Latest Vote by Ireland and the New EU President,
Fifty Plus Reasons to Oppose the EU**

My friend Kitty Werthman, who is the Eagle Forum State President of South Dakota, grew up in Salzburg, Austria, where she experienced first hand what it was like under Hitler when he took over both Germany and Austria. She returned to visit her relatives in Austria in the summer of 2006. Now that the EU has taken over, she sees a great deal of similarity between the Austria of her youth under Hitler and what is going on today. She has spoken out against the EU on many radio programs. Edward Spalton of Derby, England, heard her being interviewed via internet with Dr. Stan Montieth of Radio Liberty. Spalton sent Kitty a copy of a speech that he gave on this subject, and she gave me a copy of it to use for my book. Mr. Spalton, as of 2009, was serving as Vice Chairman of Campaign for an Independent Britain (CIB), one of several groups in England opposing the European Union.

Now that you have read the politically correct version of the founding and progress of the EU in the last chapter, you can contrast it with the version that Dr. Spalton gives. He is a former member of the trade committee to bring the EEC (European Economic Community) to England. He gave this speech in 2006 to a class of 16-18 year old British students as part of a program organized by an independent think-tank called CIVITAS.

Excerpts from Dr. Eward Spalton's Speech, "The EU as Experienced— from Moderate Support to Outright Opposition"

The EU was Promoted by German Propaganda Taught to Young Students at an Early Age: Back in 1958, when Spalton was a young high school student, he was on a school trip to Germany, where he and other classmates stayed with

German host families who had children their same age. The British students were all told by the young German students the same thing, as if they had it memorized and rehearsed: "Have you heard about our '*Wirtschaftsgemeinschaft?* It will guarantee our living standard."

When the British students got back to England and asked their teacher about what that long German word meant, he translated it into "Economic Community" and told them that it was a new treaty between Germany, France, Holland, Belgium and Luxembourg that had been made the previous year. The British called it "the European Common Market." Spalton and all of the students thought it sounded like a good idea—"that countries were putting past enmities behind them and shaking hands in a rather British way." The teacher pointed out to them, "This shows the difference in tradition between here and Germany. You could never be taught a political opinion like that in a British school, as if it were a fact." In other words, the German students had all been given propaganda to persuade them to one line of thinking.

Spalton said that today things are different—the "European dimension" had been introduced to the British curriculum and the propaganda techniques have been employed to try to sell the idea of the EU to them as well, with only one viewpoint allowed.

The EEC Common Agricultural Policy (CAP) Used Unfair Trade Tactics; Products Were Overpriced; and It Was Forced Upon Member Nations by Bully Tactics: In the mid 1960s, Spalton was working in the animal feed business and spent a lot of time in Holland, studying their methods of calf rearing and animal feed production. He discovered that the prices for ingredients in the animal feed, such as milk powder and wheat, were three times higher in Holland than they used to be before they became part of The European Economic Community. The EEC bought up any surplus products at a fixed price. Heavy import levies ensured that no outside competition could undercut the higher prices. The feed manufacturer also got a large subsidy from the EEC as well.

Dr. Spalton asked the director of the Dutch company, with whom his British company was associated, why they had agreed to such a system? He answered, "Little Holland is the neighbor of big Germany, and the Germans wanted it." In other words, Holland had to give in to the big bully tactics of their big neighbor.

I am sure the Dutch remembered what had happened to them during the II World War when they had tried to stand up against big Germany. Their major cities were bombed, and many people were starving because food supplies had been cut off. Dutch people who had befriended and helped Jewish people were punished, and many of them also ended up in concentration camps.

The EEC was Sold to the British as a Free Trade Agreement—Nothing Mentioned About a Political Union or a Euro Currency: The propaganda machine in England spoke about nations cooperating more closely together in free trade and never having to suffer another major European war. That sounded really good to most people who remembered World War I and II. There was a feeling of optimism about the EEC that even Spalton began to feel.

In 1972, Mr. Spalton was appointed to a government committee of trade representatives whose job it was to meet with the Ministry of Agriculture and work out details for bringing the Common Market to England. Until then, Britain had enjoyed free trade at world prices for food products which had been kept fairly cheap since 1906. As his colleagues began to find out how the CAP worked, they were outraged. It was complicated and bureaucratic and meant that a new army of inspectors would be brought in to make sure that they only claimed the right amount of subsidies. They were told that the whole country would be better off, in spite of much higher food prices, because now Britain could sell their goods in mainland Europe without having to pay the high import levy (customs duty), which had been 30%.

The leaflet that the government put out to promote Britain being part of the EEC repeatedly referred to the trade advantages of the "Common Market" and never mentioned a political union. It also promised that there would not be any economic and monetary union (the euro currency). It was off the agenda forever. This is what the British people were also promised by the Conservative Leader, Edward Heath:

> *There is no question of eroding any national sovereignty; there is no blueprint for a federal Europe. There are some in this country who fear that in going into Europe we shall in some way sacrifice independence and sovereignty. These fears, I need hardly say are completely unjustified.* (Edward Heath, British Prime Minister in 1975)

At the time that Heath made these comments, Spalton and most people believed him. They could not imagine that a British Prime Minister would dare to tell such a barefaced fundamental lie about the direction he was taking the entire country. However, by 1989, Heath felt sufficiently secure to admit that "he had been lying his head off." As he remarked in 1989, "The project was always political. The means were and are economic."

The EU is not just an International Union, It is a Supranational Union: Dr. Spalton states they have since found out that this creation of a new state authority is above all the other member states, just as the American federal government is above all the 50 states that belong to it. But the member states of the EU, according to Spalton, have less control or democratic responsibilities than the American states. And they are losing more and more control and responsibilities as time goes on. As Spalton states:

> The aim of the Rome Treaty of 1957 was to create "an even closer union" between the people of Europe. So, it is always a 'work in progress.' Nothing stays still. It has been compared to a train moving along a railway line, and, as the Germans say, '*Die Weichen sind gestellt*,' the points are set.[28]

October 29, 2004, The First EU Constitution was Signed in Rome, Italy: The writing of the EU Constitution was an incremental process, continuing on for many years, starting with the Treaty of Rome in 1957, the Treaty on the European Union in 1992, in Maastricht, Holland, and an amendment added in Nice, France, in 2001. The negotiations and the wording of the Constitution were done "at foreign minister level with the participation of a representative of the Commission and two observers from the European Parliament." The negotiations were started under the six-month Italian Presidency and continued on under the Irish Presidency and closed June 18, 2004, when they finally had all agreed on the wording of the Constitution. Rome was chosen as the place for its signing since it was the city where the European Community was first established with the Treaty of Rome back in 1957.

However, for the Constitution to become official, it needed to be ratified by what were then 25 member states, either by referendum by a vote of the people of that nation or by its parliament, depending on the individual laws of each country.[29]

The French Rejected the EU Constitution: On June 30, 2005, the French vote on the EU Constitution took place, and the majority of the people voted NO by a 11% margin. With a large 70% turnout, the NO votes were 55.5 %, and the YES votes were 44.5 %. French President Jacques Chirac was very disappointed, for he had been pushing hard for a YES vote. He said, "France's decision inevitably creates a difficult context for the defense of our interests in Europe."

Here are some of the reasons people gave for voting against the Constitution: "I voted 'no,' because the text is very difficult to understand. Also, I'm afraid for democracy. The way the EU functions is very opaque. Many people there are not directly elected," said Emmanuel Zelez, age 32, a film editor. "I think that the constitution will destroy our political structure. It's just about economic interests," said Anne Le Moel, a 42-year-old professor of philosophy. Other opponents "feared it would strip France of its sovereignty and generous social system and trigger an influx of cheap labor."[30]

The Dutch Also Said No to the EU Constitution: With a wide margin of 23.2%, the Dutch soundly rejected the EU Constitution. Results showed that 61.6% of voters said NO to the charter, and 38.4% approved it. The turnout in the election was 62.8%. One of the leading people opposing the EU Constitution was Geert Wilders, who told reporters he had not expected such a "decisive result, which exceeded poll predictions." "If you realize that two-thirds of parliament supported the constitution, and two out of three people in the land are against, it means a lot is wrong in the country."

BBC's reporter Geraldine Coughlan in The Hague said many voters feel that "Brussels has too much power and that their national politicians are not protecting them enough." Some are disillusioned with the "single currency, the Euro, and some disagree on rapid EU enlargement." Some are "also afraid of Brussels interfering in their liberal policies on soft drugs and gay marriage." [As the reader will find out later in this chapter, the EU is promoting gay marriage.]

The Prime Minister, Jan Peter Balkenende, who had campaigned for a Yes vote, said he was "very disappointed," but he said his government would honor the vote, which was "consultative rather than legally binding."[31]

The NO Votes by France and the Netherlands Didn't Seem to Really Matter: What an interesting comment made by Mr. Balkenende. So, this whole voting process was just for "consultation" and was "not legally binding?" It was just for show and has no real merit as far as the progression of the EU is concerned? It appears that is exactly what he meant, and the EU continued on as if these negative votes by France and Holland never happened.

The Next Constitution Was Called a Treaty so No National Referendum would Be Necessary: The no vote by the French and Dutch, however, did cause the next try at a constitution to be done differently. Calling it a treaty meant that no longer would the people have to vote on it. Just the parliaments would vote, thus avoiding those "pesky people," who really are not too bright anyway. What do they know about what form of government is best for them? "Government always knows what is best, especially big government, and the bigger the government, the better," thus is the philosophy of those running the European Union. However, there are many groups forming who do not agree with them.

Groups that have Organized in England to Oppose the European Union and to Get Their Country Out of It: Edward Spalton is a member of several organizations in England fighting the EU. One that he thinks is having an effect is called **The British Declaration of Independence** (BDI). Information about it can be accessed at their website, *www.BDIcampaign.org.* This is what he wrote Kitty Wirthman in a letter:

> *So many things which you experienced in Nazi Austria are happening today in slightly different forms to us in Britain, as a result of our membership in the European Union . . . It is dreadfully hard slow work, getting people to wake up to what is happening to us, as the freedom and sovereignty of our respective countries are whittled away a little at a time.*

Spalton states that the BDI identifies members of parliament who "actually believe in the right of self-government," by getting them to sign a pledge to their electorate that they: "believe in the right of self-determination;" they will "assert the sole authority of the Westminster Parliament to initiate, pass and repeal all legislation and regulation applied to the people of the United Kingdom;" and they will assert "the supreme authority of the British judiciary in all law applied to the people of the United Kingdom."

There is also a BDI bill on which members of parliament are being urged to vote yes that will make it an Act that only the British Parliament will make the laws over the British people. They are having some success with some members of the Parliament getting them to sign the pledge, but the leadership of all the main parties, Conservative, Liberal Democrat, and Labor Parties, are in favor of EU membership and won't sign the pledge.[32]

"The Real Face of the European Union:" Another group in England that is working towards getting England out of the EU is "Campaign for Truth." They have produced a documentary DVD called "The Real Face of the European Union," with the director and narrator Philip Day. It is very well done. I saw it first online on "You Tube.com." It is a good warning to Americans that the same thing could happen here on our soil, also by stealth and deception, unless enough people are alerted and wake up to the transformation of America that is going on around us.

What Voting is Like in the EU Parliament: One of the people featured on the Campaign for Truth DVD is Nigel Farage, a member of the UK's Independence Party and a Member of the European Parliament (MEP). He describes his function:

> MEPs are here to vote and to vote often and to vote regularly. Sometimes we vote up to 450 times in the space of 80 minutes . . . Most of the MEPs don't know what is going on half the time. They can't read all the documents because they are so massive. They are simply given a list of items drawn up by civil servants with the number of each item, and next to it, they are told how to vote, "yes" or "no." And that is what they do. They vote and they vote exactly as directed. It's rather like paying monkeys. It is an absolute farce. It is a complete sham masquerading as democracy.

The Overhauling of the British Justice System: The documentary describes the most frightening part of belonging to the EU—the changing of the British system of justice to the EU "corpus juris," (meaning body of law.) The following parts of the British system will be scraped: trial by jury (Citizens will face an appointed judge who will pronounce them guilty or not guilty.); Habeas Corpus (a person can be arrested and held without charge for up to nine months.); "Innocent until proven guilty" will be done away with. (The accused will have to prove their innocence against the huge machinery of the state.)[33]

The Abolition of Britain: This is the title of a book written by British author Peter Hitchens, who tells of the state that Britain is now in today, living under the dictates of the European Union. Their country is suffering the loss of its own governance over "energy, trade, competition, agriculture, the environment, social policy, public health, employment policy, immigration, criminal justice, and foreign affairs." Hitchen's plea for the British people is to wake up and help halt this process:

Ann Shibler, in an article that she wrote for the *New American*, "What we can learn from the EU," adds the comments, "Existing for 900 years, with centuries of independence and sovereignty under its belt, it is hard to understand how it [Britain] could come to this point." [It is also hard to understand how America is coming closer and closer to the same point.]

A Divorce From the EU: The documentary, "The Real Face of the European Union," closes with a plan to get the British Parliament to literally divorce themselves from the EU and renegotiate a genuine free trade agreement with the countries of Europe. With enough political will they hope they can "work to vote for people who will not allow the continual surrender of our sovereignty to continue."[34]

What the Euro Has Done to the Economy and Living Standards In Europe: Perhaps it might be possible for England to free itself of its EU connection, because it has not yet allowed its currency to become intertwined in the euro, as has happened in the other 26 countries that belong. The following tells what has happened to the living standards for people both in Germany and Austria because of the euro. I am sure moving to an amero would will have the same affect on the United States and Canada, as we would be intertwining our currencies with that of Mexico, a 3rd world poverty stricken country.

Buying Power of Money has Become Devalued by Two-Thirds: My husband called a bank in Germany, in June of 2007, to check on a life insurance policy that his mother had established for him back in 1990. When she started it, it was worth 300,000 German marks. Kurt was told that because of the EU and the devaluation of the currency that the Euro has caused, the policy is worth one-third of its value—about 100,000 marks. The lady he spoke to was very upset, as well, with what has happened to the standard of living and quality of life of Germans today. This all shows how much promised "prosperity" the EU has brought to Germany.

Many Elderly People are Forced to Go into Public Housing and Rely on Food Stamps: The following is an interview I had with Kitty Werthman. She told me of her visit in April, 2007, to her native Austria and to Bavaria, Germany, where her husband is from. Everyone she spoke to from both countries, relatives, friends, business associates, even bankers, were very angry about the EU and the Euro and told how bad the living standards are now for them. Here is what Kitty said:

The people were lied to. They were given false promises of prosperity and security to entice the various countries into a European Union. Back in 2002, they were told, 'It will just take a little time to adjust everyone and your currencies into the euro, just be patient.' Well, about six months later, when their retirement pensions were adjusted to the euro, they noticed that they were cut in half. When they went shopping, they discovered the euro bought about half of what their former currency used to buy for groceries.

When I would go to a restaurant in Austria or Germany, I used to could get a good meal for about fifteen German marks. Now with the euro, it is the equivalent of 30 German marks. In other words, the cost of living has doubled but the incomes and the pensions have stayed the same.

With all the borders wide open and the huge influx of foreigners, the "free health care system" is so overloaded and abused; the average person can't get the care they need. Those who have the money to afford it are buying extra medical insurance and going to private health care facilities so they can get the treatment they need. However, they still have to pay a huge amount of taxes to help pay for the "free health care" that they do not benefit from. More than 50% of all incomes is taken in taxes by the government.

Many of the retirees, who used to be fairly well off, with their pensions giving them enough to cover their rent, groceries, and other basic monthly expenses and even allowing them to go on vacations once or twice a year, now with the devaluation of the currency under the euro, their living standards have been drastically reduced. Many now have to ask for food stamps; many have had to give up their apartments and move to public housing. There is immense poverty now among senior citizens. One can imagine the humiliation, the sorrow, and one can understand the anger these people feel. What they worked so hard for all of their lives, half of it has now been taken away from them.

One of the major problems in Germany and Austria is there is no conservative movement or conservative sources of information. Most of the people pay little attention to the inner workings of their government. There are no talk radio programs that discuss political issues, and the only news they get, coming from America, is CNN, which just gives them more of the liberal viewpoint. They also are not learning from history, so history is going to repeat itself.[35]

Polish People are Upset with the EU over Moral Issues: According to an article that appeared April 27, 2007, "EU Requires Adherence to Sodomy in Polish Schools: A Model for NAU?," the EU is trying to tell the Polish Prime Minister and the people that they are not allowed to object to teachers who are sharing their pro-homosexual views in the Polish schools.

> The Polish prime minister believes that teachers who push homosexual propaganda should be fired. 'What homosexuality has to do with math, science, history, and other appropriate classroom subjects, I do not know.' The EU, however, is aghast, and has dispatched investigators to examine 'the emerging climate of racist, xenophobic and homophobic intolerance in Poland.' Might the investigation itself be racist and xenophobic? The Poles aren't like the French, the Germans, or the Dutch with regard to homosexuality. The French, the Germans, and the Dutch want the Poles not to be like Poles, but to be like the French, the Germans, and the Dutch. And isn't that what the EU boils down to? A thuggish, centralizing, culturally imperialist body seeking to achieve through political machinations what its domineering member states failed to do through conquest?[36]

The EU's Attempt to Force Abortion on all Member States: Something else that conservative, pro-life member nations have to worry about is an EU resolution to get them to go along with "universal" abortion. According to the Catholic Family and Human Rights Institute (*www.c-fam.org*), the Council of Europe was pushing "universal" abortion as part of the Cairo Conference Anniversary, October 2, 2009. The Parliamentary Assembly of the Council of Europe (PACE) was to vote on a resolution at the end of October that calls on European states to achieve "universal access to comprehensive sexual and reproductive health services," including "safe abortion" by 2015.

UK parliamentarian and abortion advocate, Christine McCafferty, prepared a report and draft resolution in honor of the anniversary entitled, "Fifteen Years Since the International Conference on Population and Development Program of Action (ICPD). Her report called for increased funding for "sexual and reproductive rights," including "family planning, emergency contraceptives, safe abortion, skilled birth attendants and obstetric emergency care," which "must be accessible, affordable, appropriate and acceptable to all, irrespective of age, community or country."

The draft resolution goes farther in recommending: "sexuality and relationship information and education" in public schools; ensuring access to a variety of "modern methods of family planning services;" ensuring that European countries allocate 10% of their development assistance to "population/sexual and reproductive health and rights" and to start developing a European convention on sexual and reproductive health.

McCafferty's report tried to make the case that the resolution is necessary to reduce maternal mortality; "restrictive abortion laws" increase the incidence of unsafe abortion. The report leaves out the facts that the two countries in the EU with the most restrictive laws against abortion—Ireland and Malta—are also two of the countries with the lowest maternal mortality in the world, not just in Europe.

The report cites Moldova as a country where maternal mortality is high due to unsafe abortion. The truth is, according to the Center for Reproductive Rights, Moldova is listed as a country with some of the most liberalized laws in the world concerning abortion and other moral issues. Obviously, such liberal abortion laws do not protect the lives of women, but only hurt them.

The report pays meager lip-service to "state sovereignty" by mentioning that the legality of abortion still remains in the hands of national governments, but if the EU has their way, that will not last long. By 2015, if the resolution passes, abortion will be "universal" for all countries belonging to the EU.

Part of the Population Control Agenda: The European Center for Law and Justice (ECLJ) has released a memo against the draft recommendation and report. The ECLJ states that the Council of Europe has "no authority or competency to promote abortion." They express their concern about "the promotion of population control in general and abortion as a means of family planning . . ." According to the ECLJ, the recommendation and its explanatory memorandum go much further than a previous PACE resolution on Access to Safe and Legal Abortion in Europe, which actually stated "that abortion can in no circumstances be regarded as a family planning method" that "must, as far as possible, be avoided."

International Parliamentary Conference Hosted by The United Nations Population Fund: The Council of Europe's decision on the draft recommendation is necessary in preparation for an International Parliamentary Conference on the "Implementation of the ICPD Program of Action" meeting. According to the ECLJ, the conference was being organized by the United Nations Population Fund and was to take place in Addis Ababa, Ethiopia, at the end of October, 2009.[37]

One can see how closely the EU works with the UN. Could it be the EU really gets its marching orders from the UN as would all other unions, including a North American Union? As you will read later, the UN is now using the EU in the formation of other unions and in exercising control over them.

Angela Merkel Tried to Give the EU a Rosier Face and a Happy Birthday Celebration, Pretending it was 50 Years Old: An article in the *Bloomberg News*, March 23, 2007, "Angela Merkel Takes Place as Europe's Unifier," tried to portray a "politically correct and rosier" picture of the EU and of Merkel's "outstanding" job of leadership. It also gave an update of the 50th Birthday celebration (March 25) and the plans for a new Constitution in the works for the EU.

Even though the EU did not really officially exist until the Treaty on the European Union was signed in Maastricht, Holland, in 1992, or more legitimately until the signing of the first EU Constitution in 2004 and its ratification by member nations in 2005, Merkel and others are trying to make the EU more acceptable by giving it a longer life, pretending it is 50 years old. They are saying that its birthday was the signing of the Treaties of Rome, March 25, 1957, when the European Economic Community and the European Atomic Energy Commission were established, the forerunners to the EU.

Obviously, the March 25th birthday did not go over very well, so they are trying for a new one, making the EU to appear even older. On the same website that tells about the 12 stars on the flag is the statement: "The ideas behind the European Union were first put forward on 9 May, 1850, by French Foreign Minister Robert Schuman. So 9 May is celebrated as the EU's birthday." It is now called "Europe Day." (http://europa.eu/abc/symbols/index_en.htm.)

Amazing! European Union birthday history is now being rewritten according to the "ideas" in people's minds. What if we all celebrated our birthdays on the day that the "idea" for having a child first entered our parents mind. We certainly would all be much older, wouldn't we? I, for one, would not like that very much. I don't believe the new birthday is going to go over any better with the Europeans than the March 25th attempt. I think most people prefer honesty over political manipulations.

The *Bloomberg* article about Merkel was written by columnist Frederick Kempe, who was serving as President of the Atlantic Council, one of the many organizations that were created in the last century to enhance "trade" but also to further the globalist, one-world government agenda.

According to Kempe, the Chancellor of Germany, Angela Merkel, took her turn as the leader of the European Union Counsel. (Until the new constitution was ratified which gave the provisions for selecting an official president, who would serve 2 1/2 years, the various leaders of EU nations would take just short six month terms serving as president of the EU Counsel.)

Kempe mentioned some of the accomplishments to the EU he felt Merkel had made: She had gotten the EU's constitutional and institutional reforms back on track, advanced a freer trans-Atlantic market, hammered out a difficult EU budget deal between the UK and France, and brokered an agreement among 27 European nations to reduce carbon emissions by 20 percent by 2020. Kempe felt Merkel had gained the regard and trust of President Bush and Condoleezza Rice. She had reduced the suspicions of Israel and had helped in the "game of Middle Eastern peace."

A Poll Taken in Europe Regarding the EU: According to a FT/Harris poll that Kempe sites, 44% of the citizens of the five largest countries in the EU "believe it has worsened their lives." "Twenty percent of those surveyed said they would be better off if their countries got out of the club." The sad thing is this is no ordinary "club" of which you can just drop your membership. The EU has become very binding for member nations, especially when their finances are now part of the Euro and the EU is ruling on the majority of their laws. It would be very difficult, if not impossible, for a country to just drop out of it.

Merkel's Hope Was to Instill EU Pride: Kempe writes that Merkel hoped to reinvigorate public support for the EU. That was the goal with all the various birthday parties that happened March 25, 2007, in each of the 27-member countries, where they were "supposedly" celebrating 50 years since the EU first was "birthed." Merkel was in hopes these parties would instill EU pride, "like winning last year's soccer World Cup did for German self-confidence."

The New Constitution—The Lisbon Treaty

Merkel's "Secretly-Drafted" Constitution Did not Have the Input of Member Nations nor the Vote of the People: Merkel's goal was to push through a new constitution by 2009, which she said would be "a better read on European history and the future than the long-winded, uninspiring constitution that Dutch and French voters have rejected." Her constitution would be better, why? According to Kempe, it was drafted "secretly among only three signatories—herself, Europe's commission and parliamentary president." Merkel thus avoided "the numbing edits of 27 member countries."

Merkel and others also avoided any "numbing rejections" by not letting the people in each nation vote on the new constitution themselves as had happened with the first one and the people in France and Holland voted it down. The only exception was Ireland that has it written into their Constitution that even treaties have to have a vote by the people. Merkel avoided such an embarrassing vote from ever happening again by changing the name of the constitution to a treaty. That way only the ministers to the EU parliament from each country would vote on it.

Kempe ends his article with the following:

> Merkel has her problems. She has a dysfunctional governing coalition and a strangely self-satisfied country that resists necessary economic change. She is often overly cautious when leadership is required . . . I'll be wishing her well in promoting the real source of Europe's postwar successes: economic dynamism, individual freedoms, democracy and **trans-Atlantic common purpose.**[38] (As you will read later in this chapter "common purpose" has a double meaning.)

I am afraid most of the European citizens who are disgruntled with the EU would not agree with Kempe. The EU has not brought postwar successes. For most of the original seven member countries, which are now carrying the burden of cost for the third-world countries that have joined the "club," it has not brought economic dynamism (strength), just the opposite. It has been an economic disaster, costing them dearly. It has not brought individual freedom. They have had to give up much of their freedoms.

Yes, maybe the EU has brought more "democracy," if you believe in the original definition of "democracy," majority or mob rule. With such a large, encompassing, powerful government ruling over all of Europe, there is much more mob rule. But the rights of the minorities and the individuals are no longer heard or protected, as would be under a republic, based on a firm rule of law and small, local, representative government.

Kempe mentions the "trans-Atlantic common purpose," but does not elaborate on what that purpose is. Could it be that the purpose of both the European Union and eventually the NAU is to form large regional governments on both sides of the Atlantic that will be working towards the same objectives? You will be shortly reading about the Trans-Atlantic Network and Common Market that are already in the works.

Dec. 13, 2007, Lisbon Treaty Was Signed: The new constitution, which is 346 pages long, was signed in Lisbon, Spain, by representatives of 27 nations. That is why it is given the name the Lisbon Treaty, rather than the new constitution.

More Information On the New Constitution: In March of 2008, I met a lady from England, Fern Abbot, who is also doing her part to speak out against the EU. She was visiting friends and heard about our annual Eagle Forum of California Education Conference that was held in Santa Rosa, California, March 29, with the theme of "Protect American Sovereignty." She heard that Dr. Jerome Corsi, Phyllis Schlafly, and Dr. Stan Monteith would be speaking and that my talk was about "Laying the Foundation for a North American Union and its Parallel to the European Union." She and a friend drove all the way from Portland, Oregon, to attend. We met at the conference and have had several conversations since.

She told me that the new constitution would be called a "treaty," so it would not be necessary for the individual people in each nation to vote on it, just as we had suspected. Only the parliaments of the individual nations will have to approve it, and that has already taken place. Only one nation was still holding out and that was Ireland. It is written in Ireland's own constitution that their people must have the chance to vote themselves on such a referendum. The vote is worded in a very strange way. If you say no to the treaty then you are saying yes to having an EU army. If you vote yes on the treaty then you vote no on the army. She said those who have seen the treaty say it is essentially the same old EU Constitution, not much new.

She told me of several groups in England who are trying to fight the EU besides the ones I have already mentioned. She suggested the following website: Brits at their Best, *www.britsattheirbest.com*. She also said that much information can be found in video clips on U-Tube that she has helped post herself.

She said there are a few newspapers who are speaking out against the EU, such as the *Daily Telegraph*. But *The Guardian* and the *Observer* are government newspapers and the *BBC* is sponsored by the EU. Thank goodness for internet! That is how the British people are able to get the truth passed on, just as here in America. Thanks to talk radio stations, many American are able to hear the truth on these issues that would otherwise be kept secret.

June 12, 2008, "Irish Voters at First Reject EU Treaty" (the New EU Constitution): (However, I'm afraid, a year later they voted to accept it, as you will read towards the end of this chapter.) I received an e-mail giving me the exciting news that the Irish rejected the EU Treaty. The following is a summation of an article written about it by Sarah Lyall and Stephen Castle, June 13, 2008:

> Ireland rejected the Lisbon Treaty by a vote of 53.4 percent to 46.6 percent. The treaty was a 'painstakingly negotiated blueprint for consolidating the European Union's power and streamlining its

increasingly unwieldy bureaucracy.' Why did the majority of the Irish people reject the treaty? It was the result of a 'highly organized campaign that played to the deepest fears about the EU.' Many people feel the EU is 'remote, undemocratic and ever more inclined to strip its smaller members of the right to make their own laws and decide their own futures.'

What the EU Leaders Said About the Irish Rejection of the Treaty? They were frustrated, but "they would try to press ahead for a plan to make the Lisbon Treaty work after all and would discuss the matter when EU leaders gathered for a summit meeting in Brussels the next week." [Many believed they would have no problem, just as they did with the rejection of the French and the Dutch to the EU Constitution that took place in 2005. They just pretended that the rejection did not exist and went right on according to plan.]

What Other Europeans are Saying against the EU? They feel alienated, confused, and disillusioned with the EU. They have no passionate support for it. They feel it is bossy and running their lives—making 85% of the new laws passed in Europe every year. They don't want it to have a "blank check" anymore. In other words, they want restrictions placed upon it. Here are some comments about the EU coming from Irish political leaders:

> 'Many ordinary Europeans still feel alienated from the EU and confused by how it works. Europe as an idea does not provoke passionate support among ordinary citizens. They see a bossy Brussels, and when they have the chance of a referendum in France, the Netherlands or Ireland to give their government and Europe a kick, they put the boot in.' said Denis MacShane, a Labour member of the British Parliament and a former minister for Europe. Libertas [the main group opposing the treaty] and other opponents of the treaty capitalized on voters' confusion, their disillusionment with the government and their feelings of alienation from the institutions of Europe, which is the source of about 85 percent of the new laws passed in Europe every year . . . 'It's a pro-European country, but they didn't understand the treaty—why it was needed, what it was going to change. They just don't want to give Europe a blank check anymore.' said Michael Bruter, a senior lecturer in political science at the London School of Economics.

What Does the Lisbon Treaty Change About the EU? The treaty is described in the article as "dense and complex." Here are some of the provisions it would bring to the EU:

- For the first time a full-time president, but who would not be elected by the people, just appointed by the commission.
- A new foreign policy chief who, among other things, would control EU development aid (also appointed.)
- Reduce the number of members on the European Commission, the EU's executive body, rotating the seats so that each member country would sit on the commission 10 out of every 15 years.
- Change the voting procedures so that fewer decisions would require majority votes.

Who Were the Ones Who Voted For and Against the Treaty in Ireland? Those who were leading the yes vote on the treaty were the Irish "establishment," including the major political parties and most business groups, which had worked for its support for years.

Declan Ganley, a businessman, formed the group "Libertas" to campaign against the treaty. He argued that the treaty took power away from Ireland. He didn't want Ireland to drop out of the EU, however. He just wants the EU to be more "democratic." He wants the proposed president and foreign affairs minister to be elected by the people, rather than appointed. He said that the no vote would force the Irish Prime Minister, Brian Cowen, to renegotiate the treaty and secure a "better deal."

The EU is all About Redistribution of Wealth: It appears from the article, one of the ways in which the EU enticed Ireland's support in the first place was by pouring billions of dollars into the country in the late 1980's. Ireland was then transformed "from an insular, impoverished agrarian society to a European powerhouse with an enticingly low corporate tax rate and some of the world's largest pharmaceutical plants." But now that Ireland is doing well financially, it has to do its part to finance other poorer countries. That is one of the objections that many Irish people have to the EU. "Having been the beneficiary of European money for years, Ireland now finds itself having to help finance the newer, and poorer countries that have recently joined the Union."

Will Turkey Join the European Union? The EU permits its "citizens" to travel on EU passports and to work or live in any country in Europe that they choose to. Turkey's population is 77 million and 99 % of them are Muslims. Since Germany is the closest industrialized, fairly well off nation next to Turkey, the Germans are so afraid they will have a huge influx of Turks, and they will choose to stay in Germany. Many Muslims are already in some of the major cities such as Berlin. Germany is already paying enormous welfare for unemployed Muslims and providing for their many children.

Who is Promoting Turkey Being Part of the EU? Obama, of course! On his European tour he spoke to a group of European ministers in Prague and told them:

> "The United States and Europe must approach Muslims as our friends, neighbors, and partners in fighting injustice, intolerance, and violence. Moving towards Turkish membership in the EU would be an important signal of your commitment to this agenda and ensure that we continue to anchor Turkey firmly in Europe."

And what about the injustice, intolerance, and violence that the Muslim neighbors are showing to the Europeans as they sweep the continent, terrorizing Europeans, demanding their traditions, their Sharia law to be honored and demanding speech codes that have muzzled politicians. "That is why many Germans believe, "unfettered access to Europe's major cities for Turkish Muslims would be catastrophic."[39]

"Turks are Conquering Germany": From reading the above quotes and the following information, one can understand why most Germans are a little afraid of Turkey joining the EU, but it is, of course, politically incorrect to say so. A *"Bundesbank"* official, Dr. Thilo Sarrazin, a member of the executive board of the "Bundesbank" (the federal bank of Germany, similar to our Federal Reserve), was reprimanded and was under police investigation for speaking his mind as he saw what was happening to his nation of Germany. According to an article by Ambrose Evans-Pritchard, published October, 2009, in the BST, Sarrazin gave vent to a "wild outburst against Berlin's Muslim population, resorting to language reminiscent of Nazi race theory." Sarrazin told Europe's culture magazine *Lettre International* the following:

> Turks with low IQs and poor child-rearing practices were conquering Germany by breeding two or three times as fast. A large number of Arabs and Turks in this city, whose number has grown through

bad policies, have no productive function other than as fruit and vegetable vendors.

Forty percent of all births occur in the underclasses. Our educated population is becoming stupider from generation to generation. What's more they cultivate an aggressive and atavistic mentality. It's a scandal that Turkish boys won't listen to female teachers because that is what their culture tells them. I'd rather have East European Jews with an IQ that is 15 percent higher than the German population.

As one can imagine, such statements have created quite a ruffling of politically-correct feathers. Dr. Sarrazin has since apologized, but his comments may have breached Germany's anti-racism laws, and his job at the bank is now "untenable." Of course, his statements have had a reflection on the Bundesbank. The chief, Axel Weber, who attended the G7 summit in Istanbul, found Turkish newspapers in an uproar, and he had to have bodyguards to protect him.

According to the *Suddeutschen Zeitung*, Weber might be in difficulty himself, because he at first approved of Sarrazin's interview after calling for a few changes.[40]

Regionalization and Devolution to Further Divide and Conquer—"Perforated Sovereignty": According to a video clip, "The EU, UK and Regionalization" showing an interview with Edward Spalton, July 29, 2009, the EU is using devolution to split up its member nations and destroy feelings of pride or patriotism by establishing EU-designated regions within those nations. The EU is trying to turn the "United Kingdom into a disunited kingdom." Spalton calls it "perforated sovereignty."

Once the EU regions are established inside a country, then the EU only conducts its affairs and operates its funding directly with EU-appointed officials in those regions, bypassing counties and locally-elected government officials and even Britain's central government. Each of the regions then has a sort "mini-embassy" in Brussels with regional ministers pleading their cases to get more funding for their region. Spalton adds, "Obviously, the ones who can convince the authorities that they are the most enthusiastic supporters of the agenda of integration are going to be the most favored ones." [It kind of makes one think of dogs begging and competing with each other under the table of some high Lord for their little pittance of scraps.]

Spalton says that presently the regions inside Scotland and Ireland are getting more favorable treatment from the EU than the British. Could the reason be because there are so many groups inside Britain opposing the EU, including the one for which Spalton is the Vice President—"Campaign for an Independent Britain" (CIB)? The power over the funding that the EU now possess gives them the power to come in and interfere in local affairs. They are trying to squash any opposition by cutting off funds, money that Spalton said originated in Britain anyway and has been taken from them by EU taxes. One region getting more funding than another causes feelings of jealousy and bad feelings and turns regions against another, which Spalton believes is part of the plan.

Spalton believes that there is also resentment because England is so much larger in population than Scotland and Ireland. He does not believe the three countries can co-exist much longer as the United Kingdom, and there will soon be a breakup, which he believes has been the aim of the EU since its beginning. It is called "divide and conquer."

How Were the Regions Set Up? Spalton said that the EU has paid no attention to the 48 counties of England, some which have existed since the middle ages, but the regional boundaries were delineated in completely artificial areas with no historical existence in England. Obviously, this is one more attempt to break up long-standing traditions, customs and feelings of pride in one's county or homeland. Spalton said that the EU is putting regions in competition with each other, "essentially for "our own money, which if it weren't for the EU, would never have left the country."[41]

How Well is the European Union "Community of Nations" Working?
Does Europe really play the "leading role in the world," as Obama stated back in April, 2009, when he visited many European countries, praising Europe and making his customary disparaging remarks about the United States?

According to an April 20, 2009, article in *Newsweek*, called "The What of Nations?" by columnist George Will, he does not agree with Obama. He states, "Actually, Europe plays almost no leadership, even in Europe." Will believes the European Union is just a "geographical, rather than a political denotation."[42]

In other words, the various nations that belong to the EU are not marching along together, "speaking with one voice," as the poster supporting the European Union portrayed. Most of the people are proud of their own countries and want to speak with their own voice and their own language and be called citizens of their own country, not Europeans. However, I think George Will is going to be surprised someday to find out just how powerful the EU really is, not only on its own member nations but on countries throughout the world, as will be shown in the next chapter

September 8, 2009, the German Parliament Re-Ratified the Lisbon Treaty:
Even in Germany, which supposedly has always been so supportive of the
creation of the EU, the *"Bundestag"* parliament had to vote again to re-ratify
the controversial treaty. This was done after the German Supreme Court asked
for "extra safeguards" against the extension of EU powers in June.

According to an article in the *UK Telegraph*, "new legislation had to be
drafted to satisfy judicial fears that the Lisbon Treaty did not allow the EU 'to
exceed the powers given to it' by usurping national parliaments." Angela Merkel,
arguing for the re-ratification said, "It brings Europe closer to the people." "The
changes to the German law enacting the Lisbon Treaty require the government
to inform MPs as 'thoroughly and as early as possible' about EU decisions."[43]

**The 2009 Vote to Ratify the Lisbon Treaty by Ireland and Suspicion of
Voter Fraud:** I received an e-mail from Fern Abbot, in October, 2009, the same
British friend who has kept me up to date on the last Irish vote on the treaty a
year ago in 2008. It appears now the Irish have voted Yes to approve the treaty
by a wide margin, 67.1 to 32.9 percent of the 58 percent turnout. This was a
much wider margin than had been expected by recent polls which showed the
"No" side surging forward. Why? The financial crisis had hit the Irish hard, and
they were told that their lives would be improved if they would approve the
treaty and receive all the financial help coming with full-fledged membership
in the EU. They, therefore, buckled and voted for the treaty. That is what the
media was saying anyway.

I was very disappointed to hear that Ireland had ratified the treaty. Due to
the fact that I have part Irish ancestry, I was really proud of the "fighting Irish"
for holding out against the EU. However, I was informed by an e-mail, October
7, that there was a serious question of voter fraud in the election. Here is an
excerpt from the article, "The Irish Referendum is Null and Void" by Christopher
Story, October 5, 2009, printed in the *Sovereign Independent*:

> *Under Irish law, ballot boxes are required to be delivered by members of
> the garda (police) to the polling stations at 7:00 am on the date the election
> takes place. This legal requirement applies to ALL polling in Ireland,
> whether elections or referenda. On this occasion, however, the ballot boxes
> were delivered to the private residences of the polling/Returning Officers,
> 48 hours prior to the Referendum.*

According to Story, there were a number of honest officers who objected
to this "breach of procedure," possible "breach of security" and not following

"electoral legislation." But the officials dismissed the objections, saying that "the ballot boxes possessed no commercial value, so it would be in nobody's commercial interest to steal them." The officials avoided the main objection that since the Irish ballot boxes were delivered 48 hours early, someone could have 48 hours to stuff the boxes with YES votes, as Story says "routinely happens in places like the former Soviet Republic of Georgia."

Story believes that since the "electoral law was flouted," the outcome of the Irish Referendum should immediately be declared "fraudulent and null and void!" He also believes that three questions should be asked in conducting an investigation: One: What is the total number of registered voters in Ireland? Two: How many voters voted in the Referendum? Three: Was the total vote tally greater than #One above?

Story states further that "any operation to steamroll the Lisbon Treaty . . . will accordingly be fraudulent on this basis alone . . . It follows that all measures taken under the Lisbon Treaty will likewise be illegal." Story ends his article with the following about the illegality of the EU itself:

> . . . the European Union Collective is itself blatantly illegal, not least because the Treaty of Rome documents were never properly signed (given that several attendees signed blank sheets of paper because their translations were not available at the time of signing)[44]

Has anything come of Story's claim or protest? No, of course not! Just as voter fraud claims in the United States never seem to be investigated. The elite are too powerful and too much in control.

Powerful Influences on the Irish Vote both from Inside and Outside Ireland:
Columnist Sarah Foster wrote an interesting article in *NewsWithViews.com*, October 20, 2009, entitled "Ireland Says Yes to the New World Order." According to Foster there were many "powerful forces" that used "big bully" tactics and "intense pressure" on Irish voters "to get it right this time." She quoted several people who stated as such (emphasis added):

> Brendan O'Neill, editor of *Spiked-Online*, stated, "For those of us who believe in democracy, it is galling to hear officials in Brussels congratulate the Irish people for speaking with a 'clear voice' on the Lisbon Treaty. The Irish people have spoken, yes, but in the voice of someone **put into a headlock** by far more powerful forces."

Lorraine Mullally, director of the London-based think tank *open Europe*, which strongly opposes the EU, said "The Lisbon Treaty transfers huge new powers to the EU and away from ordinary people and national parliaments. EU elites will be popping the champagne and slapping each other on the back for **managing to bully Ireland** in to reversing its first verdict on this undemocratic Treaty. But most ordinary people around Europe will not welcome this news, as they were never given a chance to have their say on the Treaty."

Powerful Elite and Much Money Used to Sway the Irish Voters: Both Mullally and O'Neill mention that those who were backing the Yes vote were virtually "all government employees, the Irish Parliament, the entire Irish media, trade unions, the banking and financial community, the Irish bishops, and a slew of multinational corporations."

Christopher Booker, EU critic and columnist, added that "the European Commission poured **$1.5 million**" [**$2.2 million**] into an "unprecedented advertising blitz." EU Commission President Jose-Manuel Barroso (of Portugal), and an assortment of MEPs and officials came to Ireland personally "to promote the cause." And sorry to say, even the U.S. Chamber of Commerce got involved, "issuing a dire warning that a No vote would cost Ireland some 300,000 jobs."[45]

Tony Blair, Former Prime Minister of England, was Expected to be the Next EU President: According to an article that appeared in *TimesOnLine*, by Bojan Pancevski of Brussels, October 4, 2009, once Ireland ratified the treaty, it remained for the Czeck and Polish presidents to sign it. Their ratification of the treaty were the last signatures needed to allow two key positions to be created in the EU hierarchy: President of the European Council of Heads of State, popularly known as EU President, and High Representative for Common Foreign and Security Policy, in effect a foreign minister.

Most everyone in Europe was expecting Tony Blair to be "selected" the First President of the EU. [Notice there is no vote of the people for the president; he/she is appointed by the commission.] The writer insinuates that it would be with not much enthusiasm that Europeans would want Blair to assume this position.

Those supporting the EU were hopeful that if Blair became president that he could sway England to be more supportive of the EU. But as this article states, Blair is not that popular back in his own country. In an interview, October 3, 2009, William Hague, the Tory shadow foreign secretary said that appointing Blair would be "the worst way to sell the EU to the people of Britain."[46]

Being President of the EU for Tony Blair Would Have Been a Fulfillment of the Fabian Socialist Dream: As the reader will find out in Chapter Ten, Tony Blair belongs to a quasi-secret group that is over 100-years old in England known as the Fabian Society that has become very powerful and has taken over the faculty of major British universities, such as Oxford and Cambridge. They also have control of the labor party, which they founded in 1900. Former Prime Minister Gordon Brown is also a Fabian.

The motto of the Fabians is to "Remold It [the World] Nearer to the Heart's Desire." They have been doing that through socialist policies and practices ever since they began to have influence in government. Their ultimate goal is for a one-world government with them, of course, in charge. Tony Blair would have been a little bit closer to realizing that dream as head of the European Union. However, as you will read later, surprisingly, Blair was not selected.

November 3, 09, Czech President Vaclav Klaus Finally Signed the Lisbon Treaty: Caving into pressure from his own government advisors and also pressure from EU leaders outside Czechoslovakia, President Klaus signed the treaty. He signed, however, only if the EU leaders agreed to a last-minute demand for a Czech opt-out from the treaty's Charter of Fundamental Rights (since many of those rights are in contradiction to the morals of the Czech people).

What did Klaus' signing mean for the EU? It meant that the treaty was now ratified by all of its 27 member states. It was no longer just a treaty. It had become the law of the European Union, and the EU leaders were able to proceed forward on fast track.

The new posts that the treaty created, president and foreign minister, were filled within a week's time. They are appointed positions, so no one had to bother with an election.

What does that mean now for the referendum process in England? David Cameron, the Tory leader, who became the Prime Minister May 11, 2010, had promised the British that if he were elected, they would be able to have a referendum vote concerning the EU. Now, he is saying that it might be impossible. Cameron had also promised that if elected he would do his utmost to get an amendment passed to the European Communities Act of 1972 to prohibit by law the transfer of power to the EU without a referendum. He said,"that will cover not just any future treaties like Lisbon, but any future attempts to take Britain into the euro," to which he is also very opposed. Let us hope that Cameron will be true to his promise. (*BBC*, November 3, 2009)

Prime Minister of Belgium, Herman Van Rompuy Chosen as President of the EU: At the EU Summit held November 21, heads of state of all 27 EU nations unanimously chose Van Rompuy as the new president. He was a less controversial choice than Tony Blair and seemed to be well liked by most of the commission. It also made heads of state from smaller nations feel better to have a president coming also from a smaller country such as Belgium. Van Rompuy said he would give up his position as Prime Minister of Belgium to assume this new position, which is to be for 30 months (2 ½ years).

In his acceptance speech Van Rompuy mentioned "global governance" and "global management," as if they are something good and goals to strive for with the EU. Here is a quote from his speech:

> Two-thousand and nine is also the first year of global governance with the establishment of the G20 in the middle of the financial crisis. The climate conference in Copenhagen is another step toward the global management of our planet.

British Baroness Cathy Ashton was selected as the EU Foreign Policy Chief, primarily responsible for setting up free trade agreements with other countries and unions outside the EU. (You will read about the big bully tactics that are being used to set up those agreements and unions in the next chapter.) ("http://www.wnd.com/index.php?fa=PAGE.view&pageId=116823")

Many Reasons Why People in Europe Should Want to Get Out of the EU: (Based on research by David Noakes and others.) I received a You Tube Video Clip coming from the UK entitled "the Dangers of the EU," which gave 52 reasons for leaving the EU. It first showed an actor dressed in a simple costume of the 1600s portraying Lord Oliver Cromwell saying the following moving words—obviously the feelings of those fighting the EU:

> I will give this nation back its self respect. We will walk in this world with our heads held high. I will liberate man's souls from the darkness of ignorance . . . I will bring the law within the reach of every common man. There will be work and bread for all. This nation will prosper because it is a Godly nation and we walk hand-in-hand with the Lord. I swear by the name of the living God that I will see this nation properly governed, if I have to do it myself. Dear God, give me the strength to do it.

Fifty Plus Reasons why Britain Should Leave the EU:

1. The European Union's six constitutional treaties build a dictatorship.

2. The EU has the laws of a police state—enforced after the Lisbon Treaty is ratified.

3. The EU's 111,000 regulations will bring in a soviet style command economy and abject poverty.

4. Unelected EU dictators will control the nuclear weapons of former nations of Britain and France.

5. The EU's six treaties will compel us to hand over all of our armed forces to the EU.

6. Our armed forces and police have been told they will swear a new oath to the EU or be fired.

7. The EU's 111,000 regulations will rigidly control personal lives, more than any nation in history.

8. EU regulations now cost us 100 billion pounds a year (According to Better Regulations Commission Annual Report 2005)

9. When enforced, those regulations will destroy most of our 5.4 million small businesses.

10. Up to 13.5 million will be unemployed after EU regulations close small businesses.

11. The 111,000 regulations will make us subject to continual arrest (SOCPA 2005).

12. There are now 3,095 crimes against the EU State on the British Statute books.

13. We will be stopped on the street for continual checks of our EU ID cards after ratification.

14. The EU's Constitutional treaties replace the British Constitution after ratification.

15. The EU's treaties will close our Westminster Parliament when its 5 years expire on May 5, 2010.

16. The EU's road pricing and then ID chips will keep the state informed of our exact position.

17. Huge taxes/fines will be the result of road pricing, congestion charging and global warming policies.

18. The EU Regionalization Plan will abolish England and our 48 counties in favor of 9 EU regions.

19. The 9 EU regions will report directly to Brussels, not to Westminster, which will be a defunct EU regional council at best.

20. The EU Regionalization Plan will abolish our 19,579 councilors.

21. British Common Law was mainly replaced by EU Corpus Juris in 1992. [EU] government is now above the law.

22. Police have shot 30 innocent people dead and have not been successfully prosecuted.

23. [There have been] 1,100 deaths in police custody since 1992 and no successful prosecutions.

24. Police Shoot to Kill policy now in force; illegal under British Common Law, okay under EU Corpus Juris.

25. The EU was conceived in Germany, June 22, 1940, as the EEC—in a speech by Herman Goering.

26. The first EEC conference was Berlin University in 1942; 13 nation summit in Berlin in 1943, run by Von Ribbontrop.

27. After the fall of Germany, the Germans switched the EU from a Nazi to a communist basis in 1946.

28. Hitler's *Verteidungs Dienst* (DVD) (intelligence department) still controls EU development.

29. Edward Heath, Geoffrey Ripon, and Roy Jenkins were recruited by the DVD in 1958 as saboteurs.

30. The DVD has arranged finance to put pro-EU ownerships of British newspaper groups.

31. EU has been sabotaging Britain with German Frankfurt School techniques since the 1950s.

32. The EU's main subversive organization, Common Purpose,* was run from the ODPM [Office of the Deputy Prime Minister].

33. The EU's Common Purpose has trained 30,000 local leaders for the "post democratic era."

34. Common Purpose has been inside the NHS [National Health Service] for 20 years, controls it and has wrecked it.

35. Common Purpose has 400 staff inside the BBC censoring out anti-EU news and current events.

36. Common Purpose has hundreds of staff in local newspapers also censoring out anti-EU news.

37. Common Purpose is transferring power from councilors to the unelected council executives.

38. Common Purpose has the EU gravy trains inside local and national government.

39. Common Purpose has built most of Britain's 8,500 quangos* costing us 167 billion pounds.

40. These quangos bribe compliant pro-EU local officials and businessmen with 150,000 pound salaries.

41. EU quangos are the reason your council taxes are going through the roof.

42. The EU is utterly corrupt and cannot account for 95% of its expenditures (yes, 95% lost).
43. The EU has over 200,000 off shore bank accounts, from which it pays bribes.
44. We now lose 30,000 pounds trading with the EU.
45. Outside [before joining the EU] we had an even balance of payments.
46. The EU constitution is similar to the Soviets and EU Commissioners are similar to the Politburu.
47. The EU is a sham, with no real power, just like the old Soviet Parliament.
48. The leadership of the Conservative Party has been controlled by the EU since the 1960s.
49. The labor and liberal democrat leadership has been controlled by the EU for 20 years—that's why your vote doesn't count.
50. The Amsterdam Treaty gave the EU control of our immigration, now running at 2.6 million pounds.
51. Our infrastructure can't cope with the 10 million immigrants the EU has let in since 1997.
52. Around 380,000 highly qualified British people emigrate annually to escape from the EU and its overcrowding.[47]

*Common Purpose (CP) is the equivalent to what could be called communitarian law and "Community Organizers" in the USA. They are the new name for the old "Communist Party," for they have the same beliefs and use the same tactics. CP, in England, teaches and trains people in the "collective" mind set, prepares them to be "future leaders" and, of course, be more receptive to the EU and globalism. The following is what a group called "Common Purpose Exposed" says of them:"

> Common Purpose (CP) is a Charity, based in Great Britain, which creates 'Future Leaders' of society. CP selects individuals and 'trains' them to learn how society works, who 'pulls the levers of power' and how CP 'graduates' can use this knowledge to lead 'Outside Authority'.
>
> Children, teenagers and adults have their prejudices removed. Graduates are 'empowered' to become 'Leaders' and work in 'partnership' with other CP graduates. CP claims to have trained some 30,000 adult graduates in UK and changed the lives of some 80,000 people, including schoolchildren and young people.
>
> But evidence shows that Common Purpose is rather more than a Charity 'empowering people and communities.' In fact, CP is an

elitist, pro-EU political organization helping to replace democracy in UK, and worldwide, with CP chosen 'elite' leaders. In truth, their hidden networks and political objectives are undermining and destroying our democratic society and are threatening 'free will' in adults, teenagers and children. Their work is funded by public money and big business, including international banks.[48]

*A quango (an acronym for "quasi, autonomous, non-governmental organization")—an organization or agency that is financed by government but supposedly acts independently of it.[49] (The USA has many similar organizations—ACORN is one of them.)

Summary Statements Against the EU by Authors and Leaders in European Nations: The following quotes show that there are many prominent leaders in Europe who do not like the encroaching power that the EU is exercising over their nations, and there seems to be no way out.

Christopher Booker (UK author and columnist): *"Treaty by treaty, without most people recognizing its true underlying agenda—and leaving the nation states and their institutions in place as if nothing too dramatic was happening—this new government gradually took over the powers of national parliaments. It already decides far more of our laws and how we are governed than any mainstream politician ever dares admit."*[50]

Roman Herzog (Former President of Germany from 1994-1999. He stated in 2007): *"Eighty four percent of the legal acts in Germany stem from EU headquarters in Brussels, not from German legislature."* Herzog wonders if it's realistic to continue referring to his country as a *"parliamentary democracy."*

Vaclav Klaus (President of Czechoslovakia. He stated in 2003): *"There will be no more sovereign states in Europe and only one will remain."* He calls what is being built *"the European Superstate."*

Mike Nattrass (The leader of a splinter political party in Great Britain): *"The EU was sold to the British people as a trading agreement and has turned into a political union, which is changing our basic laws and traditions."*[51]

Miguel Angel (Spanish Foreign Minister): *"We are witnessing the last remnants of national politics."*

Lindsay Jenkins (Author of *Britain Held Hostage* and *The Last Days of Britain*): *"Today, over 80 percent of everything that goes through the House of Commons and the House of Rules, merely rubberstamps Brussels . . . We recently 'celebrated,' if that is the right word, our 40,000ᵗʰ directive coming from Brussels having attacked central government . . ."*

Edward Spalton (Former member of the European Economic Community (EEC) and now Vice Chairman for Campaign for an Independent Britain (CIB), written in the previous mentioned letter to Kitty Werthman, who had grown up under Hitler in Nazi Austria), *"So many things which you experienced in Nazi Austria are happening today in slightly different forms to us in Britain, as a result of the European Union . . ."*

The EU is Expanding Overseas: In spite of these very accurate statements and the protests of several groups against the EU, it continues full steam ahead. Their unlimited, encroaching power over 27 member nations does not seem to be enough. There is a bigger agenda. The EU is reaching across the ocean to America and other continents. The next chapter tells of the "integration" between the USA and the European Union in a Transatlantic Partnership. Coming on board in that partnership, are other countries of the Americas: Canada, the Islands of the Caribbean; soon South America will be included.

There are also plans underway for other unions in South America, Africa, Asia, the Pacific Islands, Australia/New Zealand, all the islands of the sea, and even combining North and South America. These unions are being encouraged as a way to compete in trade and commerce with larger countries like the USA and the European Union. Even before these unions are completed, the EU, like a giant global octopus, is already stretching out its tentacles to grasp onto and establish binding economic trade "partnerships"—"harmonizing" EU laws with these other nations as well, so as to later establish economic and political unions. Once the economic and political unions are firmly established, the final goal can easily be implemented—world government.

The European Union is the Soviet Model for the Rest of the World: As conservative author, columnist, and expert on the former Soviet Union, Charlotte Iserbyt, stated in an article written in February of 2005, *"The European Union (region) is the model for the rest of the world as it becomes regionalized (communized). Gorbachev referred to the European Union as The New European Soviet in a speech in London in 2002. President Bush [through his efforts promoting a North American Union] was implementing The New American Soviet in this hemisphere.*[52]

Chapter Five

"Transatlantic Economic Integration"—Binding the USA with the EU; Canada Coming on Board; "Economic Partnership Agreement;" Binding the Caribbean Islands and all of Latin America with the EU; The Union of South American; Other Unions Forming Across the Globe; Is Socialized Medicine "Nationalized Health Care" Part of the Plan?

As we learned with NAFTA, the North American Free trade Agreement, the elitists used the term "agreement" to avoid using "treaty," though NAFTA is in every sense of the word a treaty. Why did they do this? Because treaties require a 2/3 vote of the US Senate, and the elitists knew they could never get NAFTA through with that much of a vote. By calling it an agreement, they just needed a simple majority to pass it, which they eventually got.

Now with an even bigger "agreement" that should definitely be called a treaty, binding us with the European Union in a "transatlantic common market," the elitists are doing the same thing. However, this time they are even avoiding the word "agreement." They are using every other name they can think of—"integration, networks, common market, partnerships" not even allowing it to come before Congress for any kind of a vote. They are doing the whole thing "in a very quiet way," to use the words of Utah Republican Senator Bob Bennett, who served as the first Chairman for the Transatlantic Policy Network. They are trying to keep the whole thing hush-hush and avoid the radar of the public eye. Obviously, these people truly believe that we no longer have government "of the people, by the people and for the people." It is now government of the elite, by the elite, and for the elite, and they can do whatever they please. There is no stopping them.

Economic Integration Between the US and the EU: The large letters "EU-US" were displayed boldly on the back wall of the podium for the European Union Parliament Session, Friday, March 6, 2009.[53] Who was speaking at the lectern—none other than Hillary Clinton, Secretary of State for the USA.

What do these letters mean? Is the EU and the US combining in some sort of a merger? Why has the U.S. Congress and the American people not heard about this merger?

Again, stealth and deception are going on behind the scenes for this merger just as the one to form the SPP and a North American Community/Union. The people and the vast majority of elected officials are being kept in the dark.

Below are excerpts from an article written by Dr. Jerome Corsi about President Bush committing the US to an even more binding, "**deeper economic "integration**" with the EU in May of 2007. What is meant by deeper is not explained? How deep can the US go, without any money? We are already deep, deep in debt—trillions of dollars. Or do they mean deeper in our entanglements and commitment to global government?

Just as Bush did with the Security and Prosperity Partnership with Canada and Mexico, he signed on to this "integration" without any Congressional oversight. Do our presidents now regard themselves as kings that they can sign such binding commitments without any permission from Congress? Hundreds of major decisions are being made by "executive orders," no different than what a king would do. But America is supposed to be a Republic, not a monarchy? Sometimes one wonders why we even have a Congress or a Constitution, for that matter, if our presidents continue to ignore them?

Dr. Corsi refers to the document signed as an agreement, but President Bush, German Chancellor Merkel and European Commission President Barroso try to avoid using that term. Again they are using deception, trying to make what they are doing appear as innocent as possible. It is just called "integration" or a "plan." The following is what Corsi wrote in his article:

> President Bush signed an agreement creating a 'permanent body' that commits the U.S. to 'deeper transatlantic economic integration,' without ratification by the Senate as a treaty or passage by Congress as a law. The 'Transatlantic Economic Integration' between the U.S. and the European Union was signed April 30 at the White House by Bush, German Chancellor Angela Merkel—the current president of the European Council—and European Commission President José Manuel Barroso.
>
> The document acknowledges 'the transatlantic economy remains at the forefront of globalization,' arguing that the U.S. and the European Union 'seek to strengthen transatlantic economic integration.' The agreement established a new Transatlantic Economic

Council to be chaired on the U.S. side by a cabinet-level officer in the White House and on the EU side by a member of the European Commission.

The Leadership for the Transatlantic Economic Council: The leader chosen by President Bush to head up the TEC on the U.S. side was Allan Hubbard, assistant to the president for Economic Policy and director of the National Economic Council. The head on the European side, for the EU Council, was Günther Verheugen, Vice-President of the European Commission in charge of enterprise and industry.

What Is the Purpose of the Council? It was established to "create regulatory convergence" between the U.S. and the EU on some 40 different public policy areas, 'including intellectual property rights, developing security standards for international trade, getting U.S. GAAP (Generally Accepted Accounting Practices) recognized in Europe, developing innovation and technology in health industries, developing a science-based plan on bio-based products and establishing a 'regular dialogue' to address obstacles to investment.' Barroso said the Council is meant to be a '**permanent body with senior people on both sides of the Atlantic.'**

What Does Barroso Mean By Senior People? Does he mean top executive kind of people or perhaps those who are having a "senior moment"—those with dementia, whose memories are failing them, who can no longer remember what it means to be free and independent as a nation. Perhaps those with dementia are the kind of "senior" people that it takes to be willing to go along with such a "convergence," especially without any congressional oversight or voice of the people.

The Closer the U.S. is with the EU, the Better Off Our People Will Be? At a joint press conference, President Bush thanked the other two leaders for signing the "trans-Atlantic economic integration plan," and said, "It is a recognition that the closer that the United States and the EU become, the better off our people will be."[54]

And what judgment right does Bush or these other leaders have as to "how better off our people will be," when the people, themselves, or their elected representatives are not given any knowledge about this integration or any opportunity to vote on it? Perhaps some of us think things were much better off for our nation when we heeded the advice of our founding fathers and didn't have "entangling alliances" with other countries. George Washington stated, "It is our true policy to steer clear of permanent alliances with any portion of the foreign world." Thomas Jefferson added, "Peace, commerce, and honest friendship with all nations—entangling alliances with none."[55]

Implementing RFID (Radio Frequency Identification) Technologies: One of the purposes listed for the Transatlantic Economic Council is the regulation over the use of RFID chips. These minute chips will not only be used on goods, but eventually on all drivers' licenses and other forms of ID for all people in North America and in Europe. (As was already mentioned, they are starting to use RFID on passports for both regions.)

RFID, along with other biometrics, was suggested by Robert Pastor in his book, *Towards a North American Community*, published in 2001 (see Chapters 11 and 12). RFID was originally on the bill that became the Real ID Act of 2005, demanding that all state drivers' licenses have the same uniform biometrics, essentially turning drivers' licenses into national and international ID cards.[56] You will also read in Chapter 12 about the use of RFID for required (EDL) Enhanced drivers' licenses to be used on the borders; their use in clothing, shaving equipment, cell phones, the new digital televisions, in pets, farm animals and yes, even in humans.

Transatlantic Policy Network (TPN) and Economic Council: In April of 2007, President Bush met with Angela Merkel of Germany, and they signed onto a Transatlantic Economic Council. One of the purposes of the Council is to implement a Transatlantic Common Market between the EU and the U.S. by 2015 (again with No Congressional Vote!) In February of 2007, a Transatlantic Market Implementation Group put in place "**a roadmap and framework**" to direct the activity of the Transatlantic Economic Council to achieve the creation of the Transatlantic Common Market by 2015.

Membership of the TPN: According to their website, "TPN has grown into a broadly based multi-party group of EU and U.S. politicians, corporate leaders, influential think tanks and academics," whose goal is a "strengthened transatlantic partnership."

2009, February 18, A Transatlantic Strategy Forum was Added: Just as was said in Chapter One, by Richard Gardner, there will always be a lot of buzzing and confusion as the New World Order is under construction, " . . . *It will look like a great booming, buzzing confusion . . . but an end run around national* *sovereignty.* "So a new wing was added to the Transatlantic Partnership under the direction of the Czech President, who took his turn as the leader of the European Council. With the permanent president of the EU, Herman Van Rompuy, who was selected in November of 2009, there will probably be more booming and buzzing and additional wings added.

The forum's stated goal is to "build a transatlantic capacity with the best qualities of a think tank allied to the capacity to mobilize governments in Europe and the U.S. to identify and share strategic priorities." It is supported by its founding partners: the Atlantic Council of the U.S., the Transatlantic Policy Network (TPN), Chatham House, the Center for Strategic and International Studies (CSIS) and the *"Deutsche Gesellschaft für Auswärtige Politik (DGAP)"* (the German equivalent to the CFR, Council on Foreign Relations, which is written about in Chapter Nine).

Non-Governmental Network? When one googles TPN, several references popup all saying that this is a "non-governmental" network, but for both the EU and the USA, it is amazing how many members of government are part of it, both from the EU Parliament and the from U.S. Congress, both Democrats and Republicans. The first U.S. chairman was **Senator Bob Bennett** (R-Utah), who is now serving as its honorary U.S. president.

Other U.S. Senators Formerly and Presently Involved: Thad Cochran, (R-Miss); Chuck Hagel, (R-Neb); Gordon Smith, (R-Ore); Barbara Mikulski, (D-Md); Pat Roberts (R-Kan); and Barbara Mikulski (D-Maryland), Roger Wicker (R-Mississippi).

U.S. Representatives Who Are Members of the TPN Network: The Chairman of the U.S. Steering Committee is Jim Costa (D—California); Vice Chairman is Ron Kind (D-Wisconsin); Chairman of the U.S. Congressional Group is Devin Nunes; (R-California); other members John Boehner (R-Ohio); John Dingell (D-Mich); Kenny Marchant (R-Texas); F. James Sensenbrenner, (R-Wisc.); Gary Ackerman (D-New York); Shelley Berkley (D-Nevada); Marsha Blackburn, (R-Tennessee); John Boehner (R-Ohio); Rick Boucher (D-Virginia); Kevin Brady (R-Texas), Henry Brown (R-South Carolina), Eric Cantor (R-Virginia), Dennis Cardoza (D-California), Michael Conaway (R-Texas), Jim Costa (D-California), Joseph Crowley (D-New York), Susan Davis (D-California), John Dingell (D-Michigan), David Dreier (R-California), Jo Ann Emerson (R-Missouri), Eliot Engel (D-New York), Sam Farr (D-California), Bob

Goodlatte (R-Virginia), Doc Hastings (R-Washington), Bob Inglis (R-South Carolina), Jay Inslee (D-Washington), Darrell Issa (R-California), Steve Israel (D-New York).[57]

The TPN is Following the Blue Print of Jean Monnet: The Transatlantic Policy Network (TPN) is described on their website as a "**non-governmental organization**" headquartered in Washington and Brussels. It appears to be following the blueprint written in 1939 by Jean Monnet, the world-government advocate and architect of the European Union who "sought to create a Transatlantic Union as an international governing body." Monnet recognized that "**economic integration inevitably leads to political integration.**"

Integration and Harmonization of Rules and Regulations to be Completed "in a Very Quiet Way": One of the members of the TPN advisory board, Representative Jim Costa, D-California, writing in the Fall 2007 issue of the Streit Council journal, *Freedom and Union*, affirmed that the target date for implementation was 2015.

Why have we not heard anything about this? Jim Costa and Senator Bennett both stated that, since the framework has already been created with the Transatlantic Economic Council, "**the infrastructure would not require congressional approval, like a new free-trade agreement would.**" Bennett added that what has become known as the "Merkel initiative," would allow the Transatlantic Economic Council to **integrate and harmonize** administrative rules and regulations between the U.S. and the EU "**in a very quiet way,**" without having to introduce a new free trade agreement to Congress.

Amazing! Such a big agreement (much bigger than NAFTA), an inter-continental Common Market, and our Congress does not even get the chance to vote on it! This is another example of stealth and deception and how we the people are losing any say in our government. As Jerome Corsi writes:

> The Transatlantic Economic Council is an official international governmental body established by **executive fiat in the U.S. and the EU** without congressional approval or oversight. No new law or treaty was sought by the Bush administration to approve or implement the plan to create a Transatlantic Common Market. The U.S. congressmen and senators are involved only indirectly, as advisers to the influential non-governmental organization.

If you go to the TEC website, you can see the progress already made in the integration and harmonization in the following U.S. and European government agencies: "The Office of Management and Budget, the Food and Drug Administration, the Environmental Protection Agency, the Occupational Safety and Health Administration and the Securities and Exchange Commission." **A very revealing picture is at the bottom of the page showing the flag of the EU with its 12 circular stars against a blue background, blending in with the USA flag so that the stars begin to line up together.**[58]

The Streit Council—A Step Towards World Government: The Streit Council is named after Clarence K. Streit, who called for the creation of a Transatlantic Union as a step toward world government in his 1939 book *Union Now.* He was calling for an international constitution and a federation of the following 15 democracies: U.S., UK, France, Australia, Belgium, Canada, Denmark, Finland, the Netherlands, Ireland, New Zealand, Norway, Sweden, Switzerland and South Africa.

Senator Bennett Is Bringing Back the Streit Philosophy: Ira Straus is a globalist, a Fulbright professor of political science at Moscow State University from 2001 to 2002 and dedicated to bringing Eastern Europe and Russia into NATO. Straus states that **Senator Bennett has brought back Streit's philosophy seven decades later.** He felt Bennett was echoing in his writings the precise goals that Streit had stated back in 1939. One example is Bennett's claim that creating a Transatlantic Common Market would combine markets that comprise 60 percent of world Gross Domestic Product under a common regulatory standard that would become "the de facto world standard, regardless of what any other parties say." Similarly, Streit wrote in *Union Now* that the economic power of the 15 democracies he sought to combine in a Transatlantic Union would be overwhelming in their economic power and a clear challenge to Nazi Germany and the communist Soviet Union. Now Germany is one of the leaders of the TPN, and many countries of the former Soviet Union are members through their membership in the EU.

A Transatlantic Common Market will Lead to Political Integration: Another article that appeared in the Fall 2007 issue of the Streit Council journal was one by World Bank economist, Domenec Ruiz Devesa, who quoted Jean Monnet, **"that economic integration must and will lead to political integration, since an integrated market requires common institutions producing common rules to govern it."**

Congress Has No Say—But They Get to Pay: As has already been mentioned, those in charge of the TPN do not feel there is any need for any congressional oversight of their plans for a Transatlantic Common Market, but they do suggest that all the countries involved have the budget to pay for it. In their report in February, the Transatlantic Market Implementation Group wrote that their aim was "to remove barriers to trade and investment across the Atlantic and to reduce regulatory compliance costs." They further strongly suggested "that the respective governmental bodies [of all countries] involved have the necessary budgetary and organizational resources to work closely with each other."

Where did the Transatlantic Common Market Idea Originate and What Progress Has been Made? It started back in the Clinton era in 1995 when he joined the 1995 New Transatlantic Agenda with the European Commission. At the November 9, 2007, meeting, a joint report stated progress in the following areas: "removing barriers to trade and investment; easing regulatory burdens in various policy areas including drugs and disease control; the importation into the EU of U.S. poultry treated with pathogen reduction treatments; federal communication commissions allowing suppliers to create declarations of conformity for products; uniform standards for electrical products; and agreements on standards for pure biofuels."[59]

The Financial Meltdown Being Used as the Momentum to Further Transatlantic Partnership: It is interesting to hear again the expression of "partnership." The Brussels Forum, another branch of the transatlantic network, declared the following about this new partnership:

> Since the beginning of the financial crisis in the fall of 2008, the world economy has deteriorated at an alarming rate . . . **The U.S. and European governments must reassess the role of the transatlantic partnership in the global economy and re-ignite it as the catalyst of global economic recovery.**

James Perloff warns us of the threat to our Constitution as America pursues this "partnership:

> Experience has proven that if America moves ahead with the Transatlantic Partnership, the economic alliance will be converted incrementally into a **political merger.** The once-powerful nations of Europe are progressively finding themselves reduced to the status

of mere provinces of the European Union. Should America unite with the EU, we can expect to follow suite, **find our Constitution scrapped for international regulation, and ourselves—after over 200 years of the blessings of independence—little more than a colony of Europe.**[60]

Canada is Also Joining onto the Transatlantic Common Market: Canada's partnership with the EU is also happening by stealth and deception, with no parliamentary oversight or approval of the Canadian people, just as in the USA. I received an e-mail from Connie Fogal, the former head of the Canadian Action Party, the group that is leading the charge in Canada against the movement to a North American Union. Here is what she sent:

> As reported in the *Globe and Mail* on September 18, 2008, "Canadian and European officials say they plan to begin negotiating a massive agreement to integrate Canada's economy with the 27 nations of the European Union, with preliminary talks to be launched at an Oct. 17 summit in Montreal three days after the federal election." The article continues, " . . . a senior EU official involved in the talks described (them) as 'deep economic integration negotiations.' [What is meant by "deep?" Could it imply that the negotiations are deeply hidden from the general public or will delve deeply into the economy of Canada, or both]?
>
> "The proposed pact would far exceed the scope of older agreements such as NAFTA by encompassing not only unrestricted trade in goods, services and investment and the removal of tariffs, but also the free movement of skilled people and an open market in government services and procurement—which would require that Canadian governments allow European companies to bid as equals on government contracts for both goods and services and end the favoring of local or national providers of public-sector services."
>
> As has been stated, this "proposed pact would far exceed NAFTA," yet as with the transatlantic partnership of the USA with the EU, the Canadian parliament was given no opportunity to vote on this pact.

While the public has not been allowed to see the study or the draft text, apparently large corporations have. The article notes, "Proponents, including all of Canada's major business-lobby organizations, are in favor of the deal . . ."[61]

Update on Canada: According to Canada's *Financial Post*, March 5, 2009, the news about Canada joining a Transatlantic Common Market is leaking out and becoming more acceptable. Canada is ready to form a closer relationship with the European Union:

> Canada and the European Union have agreed to begin free trade negotiations . . . After months of 'scoping exercises' the two parties have come to an agreement on the areas they would like to negotiate, including trade in goods, services, and investments, and have now adjourned to prepare their proposals to take to the negotiating table ' . . . At long last, Canada is poised to realize the immense potential of a closer transatlantic relationship,' said Thomas d'Aquino, president of the Canadian Council of Chief Executives.

Mexico's Free Trade Agreement with the EU in 2002: Mexico has not been left out by the long-stretched tentacle of the EU. They were entrapped in a trade agreement with the European Union on their own back in the year 2002. And what has been the result? According to the website www.grain.org., that published in August, 2008, a "briefing" on the EU's "Agenda for Domination" on all of Latin America, Mexico has not benefitted in any way, but has been put into far deeper debt by their entanglement with the EU:

> In Mexico, the economic damage is even clearer. Its overall trade deficit increased from a little over U.S.$ 9 billion in 2002, when the country signed an agreement with Europe, to almost U.S.$19 billion in 2006.[62]

2008, October 15, An Economic Partnership Agreement (EPA) Was Signed—Binding Fourteen Islands of the Caribbean with the EU: A frightening article in the *New American* magazine written by John F. McManus, "EU Déjà vu in the Caribbean," tells of the dictatorial agreement that was signed onto by Antigua & Barbuda; Bahamas; Barbados; Belize; Dominica; Dominican Republic; Grenada; Jamaica; St. Lucia; St. Vincent & the Grenadines; St. Kitts & St. Nevis, Suriname, and Trinidad & Tobago.

The EPA is a very complex and binding agreement between the governments of these thirteen countries and the executive arm of the EU, the European Commission. The EPA replaces any previous trade-only pacts that existed. These countries are now linked in an economic union with the 27-member EU that promises to do to the Caribbean nations what the EU has already done to Europe.

Big-Bully Tactics Used by the EU: How were the Caribbean countries persuaded to go along with the EPA? According to the President of Guyana, Bharret Jagedeo, who initially refused to sign the agreement, he was immediately threatened by EU officials with punitive tariffs. Bruce Golding, Prime Minister of Jamaica and Owen Arthur, Prime Minister of Barbados, had both received a threatening letter from Jose Manual Baroso of Portugal, the President of the European Commission, which told them of "dire consequences" if their countries did not sign the EPA.

Jagedeo even appealed to the United Nations complaining about the bullying tactics of the EU. He pleaded for a renegotiation of the EPA but to no avail. He finally reluctantly agreed to go along with the rest of the Caribbean countries, and Guyana became the 14th nation that signed onto the EPA pact.

Only Haiti has not signed the EPA, mainly because the Haitian government was so overwhelmed recovering from the devastating 2008 hurricane that ravaged the country. Haiti was given until 2010 to join the EPA pact, but January 12, 2010, an even more devastating earthquake of 7 magnitude hit, so those plans were delayed again.

The "Prince of Darkness" was the EU Negotiator for the EU/Caribbean Arrangement: Peter Mandelson received the title "Prince of Darkness" by the British media, because of his ruthlessness in his communist youth. Mandelson obviously used some of the same ruthless tactics as he "bullied" the Caribbean leaders into signing the 2,000-page EPA document. When he had accomplished his task, he, unexpectedly, left his post and returned to England, where he served in the government of Prime Minister Gordon Brown. In June, 2009, Mandelson was appointed Britain's first Secretary of State.

What Does the EPA Document Demand of the Caribbean Governments? Each participating country will have to begin removing tariffs by the year 2011, but tariffs are the main source of revenue for these small nations. They will have to find some other source for funds to operate.

According to **Havelock Brewster**, a former ambassador of Guyana to the EU, who warned his country not to sign on to the EPA, it contained "non-binding," declaratory, general statements on the part of the European Commission, but very specific, time-bound, binding, "subject to sanctions' requirements" for the small Caribbean nations. He warned, "We should avoid entering into open-ended commitments."

Comments by Caribbean Leaders and Educators Against the Unfair, Dictatorial EPA:

Norman Girvan, Professor at the West Indies Institute of International Relations, former secretary-general of the Association of Caribbean States, stated, *"The final stages of the EPA were rushed to conclusion with little opportunity for the public to become familiar with its positions and to deliberate its implications . . . The region will have to live with the consequences indefinitely, consequences that may prove difficult to reverse . . . The EPA sets up an elaborate institutional structure of government . . . endowed with a degree of supra-nationality that [our existing] government does not possess."*

Dr. Clive Thomas, Economics Professor of Guyana, wrote in an article published by the *Caribbean Media Sphere,* that *"through a mixture of blatant bullyism, bribery, cajolery, deception, intellectual dishonesty, and plain bluff, the EU has worked a monumental deception on the region."*

Sir Ronald Sanders, Former Caribbean Ambassador to the World Trade Organization, said, *"The EPA may well return Caribbean nations to the state of plantation economies where the commanding heights are owned by foreign companies run by expatriate managers and the Caribbean people are merely workers."* He also warned that in any dispute arising over the agreement, *"individual countries will be up against the full force and resources of the EU as a whole. The potential for disaster is glaring."*

Dennis Partin, wrote in the Sept. 14, 2008, *Trinidad Guardian, "Europe is, no doubt, laughing and congratulating itself on how easy it, once again, divided, conquered and ruled the Caribbean."*

Christian Aid, a British-based charity group that works among the poor of 50 Latin American countries, urged the Caribbean leaders to not sign the EPA. Leaders of the Christian Aid stated that *the EU was pursuing its own mercantile interest, that the so-called partnership between the EU and the small Caribbean countries was really between the 'bully and the bullied,'* and that *European producers would flood the region and force local competitors out of business.*

Dr. Joseph Stiglitz, MIT professor, a Nobel Prize-winning economist, former chief economist for the World Bank. He spoke in Ghana and urged that small nation to not lose its identity. He pointed out that the EU's $12 trillion economy is "88 times larger" than all of the Caribbean nations put together, and they were being pressured into signing the EPA. Stiglitz had resigned (or got fired) by the World Bank, once he started speaking out against "extremely managed trade agreements" that undergird the world trading system. He had described the World Bank, the International Monetary Fund, and the World Trade Organization as *"interchangeable masks of a single governance system."*[63]

All of Latin America to be Partnered with the EU: The reader may remember a battle that conservatives were engaged in for the years 2005-6, stopping the FTAA, Free Trade Agreement of the Americas, that would have placed all the countries of the Americas, both North and South in a giant free trade agreement, similar to NAFTA, the North American Free Trade Agreement, which has proven to be such a detriment for all three countries involved in it.

Fortunately, a giant effort was launched by conservative groups all over the USA, and the FTAA never got the votes needed to pass. The FTAA was a vital step to the globalists; it was to be the next step after the passage of NAFTA, passed in 1994, and CAFTA (Central America Free Trade Agreement), passed in 2005 (by 2 votes in Congress). Had the FTAA passed, all of the Americas would have been linked to a giant free trade agreement with the USA.

As has already been stated, the globalists never gives up. If plan A fails, there is always a plan B. Plan B is that the "older and wiser bigger brother," the European Union, has taken over in the place of the little brother, USA, who failed to get the job done. The FTAA is going forward as planned, but now by stealth and deception. As with the Caribbean Islands, the various Latin American countries are being bullied and coerced to join in with a link to the EU, not to the USA.

Latin American Countries Report Devastating Experiences with the EU: The previously mentioned website *www.grain.org* gives a summary of statements from countries across Central and South America who have signed onto the FTAA with the EU. These statements show the tactics that were used to get them to sign on and what they have learned from their connection to the EU:

• **Secrecy:** The report states that all negotiations with the EU "have been conducted largely in secret, which prevents parliaments, citizens, and social movements from obtaining any relevant information." The secrecy is needed "to prevent the kind of social mobilization that helped scupper the FTAA" in the US Congress.

- **EU Bypasses Independent Nations and Negotiates with Regional Blocs of Nations**: They put pressure and threats on the regional bloc to put pressure on the independent nation who refuses to join in.
- **Agreements are Broad in Scope and Open-ended, Designed to be Extended:** The agreements cover much more than just economic matters. They are so written that the EU can continue to extend them and make up the rules as they go along. "The EU does not, therefore, need to sign the same agreement with all countries, because it can achieve in future reviews anything that it does not achieve in the first round."
- **Parliaments and Social Movements are Denied Any Chance to Reject the Changes the EU has Imposed on their Country:** This means countries are losing their "right to exercise national sovereignty."
- **Severe Consequences for Countries that do not Comply:** The EU takes the leaders of the country to a private tribunal whose decisions are binding. If the country does not comply with the tribunal's decisions, then the EU can take reprisal measures such as increasing tariffs the country must pay and banning imports from that country.
- **Countries Are Losing Control Over Their Own Resources**: For example, Chile has lost control over 70% of its mining exports. They are now handled by foreign companies.
- **Free Trade Agreements Do Not Have Any Economic Benefits—Countries Are Going Deeper in Debt:** As with the case of Mexico, already sited, their trade deficit went from $9 billion to $19 billion after 4 years being part of the EU free trade agreement.
- **Free Trade Agreements are "Instruments of Colonization and Domination,"** so stated President Evo Morales of Bolivia in response to a request by his fellow neighbor countries for him to join with them in an Andean Community of Nations negotiations with the EU.

What is the Ultimate Motivation behind the EU and their Free Trade Agreements? John McManus says it very well at the end of his article in *the New American*, "EU Déjà vu in the Caribbean:"

> . . . economic union precedes political union and will eventually
> mean loss of independency. If all nations can be made submissive

to several economic unions, and those unions are led by individuals
who gradually and deceptively convert them into political unions,
the path to world government will have been forged.[64]

Other Unions of Nations Forming: We no longer have just the European
Union to look at as an official union and as an example of "deeper integration."
There are unions forming on every continent. The following is a brief history
of some of those:.

South American Unions

Historical Background: Just as with the European Union, South American
Unions, did not just happen overnight. There had to be many steps, trade
agreements, councils and agencies set up to govern them to eventually lead to a
union. It is interesting to see how they seem to follow the same steps as with the
establishment of the EU. Could there be a "master plan" written for all nations
to follow in setting up unions? Here is a history of some of those steps:

There were several South American unions or "communities" that are
now being merged into one. Just as with the EU, these groups were first called
communities.

1) **The Andean Community (CAR):** It was started in 1969. It originally had
   four countries as members: Ecuador, Venezuela, Columbia, and later Peru
   joined them. It has an Andean Presidential Council, a Court of Justice, and
   a common market that was completed in 2005.

2) **The Caribbean Community (CARICOM):** It was begun in 1973, with
   13 nations of the Caribbean area as members. Later Haiti and Suriname
   joined it.

3 **MERCOSUR, the South American Common Market:** It was established
   in 1991 and consists of Argentina, Brazil, Paraguay, and Uruguay.

According to Robert Pastor, none of these communities were working very
well because of national rivalries and civil war. They finally agreed to have a free
trade agreement in 2005. [65]

Hugo Chavez, the president of Venezuela, was an example of the problems
going on between nations. He withdrew his membership in the Andean
Community because of their voting for the FTAA, and he joined MERCOSUR
instead. [67]

4) **UNASUR:** It was started May 23, 2008, and consists of the two communities
   of CAR and MERCOSUR merged together to form a big South American
   Union consisting of 12 countries.

What is the purpose of this merger? Again, it is the same old excuse being used for the forming of all the trade agreements and unions— "for a balance of power, to better compete in the global market place and to compete with bigger countries like the USA and the EU."

The following is the news report of this merger that took place in Brazil, (May 23, 2008, *Bloomberg News*). Notice that it will be a powerful trading bloc worth $2 trillion; It is being "modeled" after the European Union; it will have 12 nations involved and is planning on a "South American Parliament, and a President's Council."

The 12 nations who are members of UNASUR are: Argentina, Bolivia, Brazil, Chile, Colombia, Ecuador, Guyana, Paraguay, Peru, Suriname, Uruguay, and Venezuela:

> Brasilia, May 23 (*Bloomberg*)—South American leaders signed a treaty to create a continental bloc modeled on the European Union . . . The summit today in Brasilia marks the culmination of diplomacy Brazil started in 2004 to unite the region's two main trading groups—known as Mercosur [a sort common market of Argentina, Brazil, Paraguay, and Uruguay] and the Andean Community of Nations [CAR—made up of five nations]—into a single bloc with gross domestic product of about $2 trillion.
>
> It also follows other efforts, most promoted by Venezuelan President, Hugo Chavez, to strengthen regional economic ties and counter U.S. influence . . . The Unasur treaty sets goals for integration of energy and transportation networks and immigration policies . . . It also establishes a South American parliament in Cochabamba, Bolivia.[68]

Notice how similar the steps are for the formation of the South American union to how the EU was created: The countries all had trade agreements or common markets established among the nations. They all had a "community" of nations established, followed by a series of yearly summits, that the executives of each country attended. From those summits, a governing body was established. Slowly the governing body gained more power and morphed into a permanent body, with a parliament created, a Commission, and a constitution or a "treaty created."

The report did say that each nation's parliament would have to approve the "treaty." Then the official union could be formed.

That last step was what was left out of the movement to form a North American Union. The parliaments of Canada and Mexico and our Congress were never allowed to vote on this issue. It was kept in the dark from the beginning and is now even more in the dark. But as with most of these far left ideas, it is just waiting for the opportunity to raise its ugly head once more.

All the 12 nations involved in the treaty are: Argentina, Bolivia, Brazil, Chile, Colombia, Ecuador, Guyana, Paraguay, Peru, Suriname, Uruguay and Venezuela.

African Union

The African Union was formed on July 9, 2002, to succeed the Organization of African Unity (OAU). The OAU was formed during the decolonization upheavals of the 1960s and was criticized as being ineffective, just "talk and no walk," but others called it a "dictator's club."[69]

Again, notice that the African Union is loosely based on the European Union, with the same form of organization. It was formed to "promote trade, unity, cooperation, and integration, and deal with security and regional conflicts among the independent nations of Africa." It consists of 53 African nations and its headquarters are in Addis Ababa, Ethiopia.

The AU Organizational Structure:

- **The Assembly**, the main decision-making body, comprised of heads of state who meet at least once a year and elect a chairperson who serves one year. Libya's Muammar Qaddafi was chairman for 2009.
- **The Executive Council**, comprised of foreign affairs ministers of individual states. The Executive Council is responsible to the Assembly.
- **The Commission** consists of ten commissioners who manage the day-to-day tasks of the AU and implement policies and report to the Executive Council. The 2009 chairperson is Jean Ping of Gabon.
- **The Peace and Security Council (PSC)** can intervene in conflicts to protect the security of the continent. It has fifteen member states, elected for two or three year terms, with equal voting rights. The PSC is overseeing the establishment of a permanent African security force. It plans to have five or six brigades of 3,000 to 5,000 troops stationed around Africa by 2010.
- **Pan-African Parliament** debates continent-wide issues and advises AU heads of state. It currently has advisory powers only, but there are plans to grant it legislative powers in the future. It was begun in 2004 to "ensure the full participation of African peoples in governance, development, and economic integration of the Continent."

- **The Economic, Social and Cultural Council (ECOSOCC)** was established in 2005 to seek to build partnerships between African governments and civil society. It includes African social groups, professional groups, NGOs, and cultural organizations. The 150-member General Assembly was launched in September 2008, replacing the ECOSOCC's initial interim structure.
- **The Court of Justice**. In 2004, the AU agreed that the regional African Court on Human and Peoples' Rights would be merged with the Court of Justice. As of August 2009, the merger of the two courts was still in process.
- **The Financial Institutions**. The AU charter names three bodies: the African Central Bank, the African Monetary Fund, and the African Investment Bank. By 2009, only the African Investment Bank had been established, based in Tripoli, Libya.

The "incarnation" was conceived by Moammar el-Qaddafi, the Libyan leader. The union has grand plans for the future that include the establishment of a central bank, with a single currency by 2023, and a human rights court. President Jakaya Kikwete of Tanzania was the leader in 2009.[70]

East African Union

August 20, 2007: Perhaps, the big union was not working too well and not all African nations got along with each other. Thus in 2007, East African heads of state met to form an East African Community, with talks of an official union, a common market and a single global currency by 2012. They also spoke about joining with the **European Union** in an economic partnership.

The reason for doing this? The same excuse is given about being able to better compete with other large trade areas such as the USA. This is what Museveni, the chairman for the summit, stated:

> We are all now worshipping the USA instead of worshipping God. The Latin American Spanish colonies which after independence acted differently are now far behind the USA in all aspects of human endeavor. 'Europe which was the epitome of fragmentation, war, bigotry etc is also waking up," he asserted. "Some leaders are talking of a United States of Africa. Do not under-estimate this view. Eventually, small countries of West Africa have found out, from the experience of the last 50 years of independence that without unity they cannot manage. It is a good movement; it needs to be harnessed carefully,' Museveni warned.

The East African Union is working towards having its own currency by the
year 2012.[71]

Asian Unions

Union forming in Asia is much farther along than one could imagine. There are
several that have been formed. The third one, the largest, seems to be engulfing
all the others. There is also talk of a common currency, called the AMU, that
may be coming sooner than we think.

1. **Central Asian Union, called "Turkastan"**—Land of the Turks, proposed
    April 26, 2007, consisting of four Turkish republics, Kazakhstan, Kyrgyzstan,
    Turkmenistan, and Uzbekistan, plus it would include the Non-Turkish, but
    culturally similar, republic of Tajikistan.

    Why would they be forming? To compete with the other larger unions
    of Central Asia and the Chinese-Russian-led Shanghai Cooperation
    Organization.[72]
2. **The Association of Southeast Asian Nations (ASEAN)**—officially begun
    August 8, 1967 with the Bangkok Declaration: It originated with Indonesia,
    Malaysia, the Philippines, Singapore, and Thailand and was begun as a
    "non-provocative display of solidarity against Communist expansion in
    Vietnam and insurgency within their own borders." It now has additional
    members: Brunei, Cambodia, Indonesia, Laos, and Myanmar.

    It floundered for awhile but was revived again in 1991 with the Thai
    proposal for a regional "free trade area." In July of 2009, at the 42nd annual
    meeting of ASEAN Foreign Ministers, they had representatives in attendance
    from the EU, promoting the idea of forming a formal political union by
    2015. And yes, just like the USA, Canada, Mexico, the Caribbean, the
    Union of South America, the East African Union and all the other unions
    forming, ASEAN has formed a partnership with the EU called APRIS,
    ASEAN **European Union** Programme for Regional Support. Its main
    purpose is "to raise awareness of the benefits of economic integration."[73]

Is the reader noticing a pattern here? It appears wherever there is some
kind of an established free trade agreement, a common market, an economic
community, a partnership, some organization of nations working together, then
suddenly the EU octopus appears with its outstretched tentacle and entangles
the group in more international agreements and furthers them along to forming
an actual economic and political union.

(Just google EU partnerships and see what amazing "conglomerations appear: EU-African partnership, EU-Eastern partnership, EU-mediterranean partnership, etc. The EU is obviously very proud of the fact that they are having a finger in everyone else's pie!)

3. **Asian Cooperation Dialogue (ACD):** The largest group of nations is not called a union, or a community, or a partnership; it is called a "dialogue." (My, are these names becoming clever!) It was begun in 2003 and nations have been joining ever since. Taiwan is shown on the map as being part of the Dialogue [because China still thinks of it as part of mainland China], but that is just to look good on the map. Taiwan is not really a member and is not given any representation or voice.

     Member States: ACD presently has 31 member states. They are: Bahrain, Bangladesh, Brunei, Bhutan, Cambodia, China, India, Indonesia, Iran, Japan, Kyrgyzstan, Kuwait, Laos, Malaysia, Mongolia, Myanmar, Pakistan, Philippines, Qatar, Singapore, Thailand, Vietnam, Kazakhstan, Kuwait, Oman, Russia, Saudi Arabia, Sri Linka, Tajikistan, United Arab Emirates, Uzbekistan

     Non-Member States: The Asian/part Asian countries who have not joined are: Afghanistan, Armenia, Azerbaijan (partially Europe), Cyprus (EU member), Egypt, (partly in Africa—AU, AL member), Georgia (partially in Europe), Iraq, Israel, Jordan, Lebanon, (AL member), Maldives, Nepal, North Korea, Syria (AL member), Timor-Leste (partly reckoned in Oceania), Turkey (partially in Europe), Turkmenistan Yemen, Kingdom of Bahrain.

Why did ACD nations come together to form a "dialogue?" For all the same reasons given for the other unions or trade partnerships forming, plus a few more: for cooperation, for interdependence, to reduce poverty and quality of life, develop a knowledge-based society, to expand the trade and financial markets within Asia and make their countries more competitive in the global market, to become a viable partner for other regions, "to ultimately transform the Asian continent into an Asian Community . . . for mutual peace and prosperity."

A Common Asian Currency: Yes, they too are working on creating a common currency that would "help protect them in times of recession and depression." They are contributing to a $120 billion reserve fund of foreign currency towards that goal.[74]

Australia/New Zealand "Trans-Tasman Union,"
A Union with Asia, or an Oceanic Union:

At first there was talk of forming just a union of Australia and New Zealand, called a Trans-Tazman Union, with their own currency, the Anzac dollar, but that soon came to a standstill. Prime Minister Helen Clark was in favor of a common currency and a full economic union with Australia and harmonizing their laws, regulations, and programs. She wanted to unite for the same reasons as those being given for forming other unions, "to compete with bigger nations in trade and commerce."

Fortunately, as more people began to find out about the plans for merger in Australia and New Zealand and enough opposition was expressed, the union and common currency did not happen. But, the plans did not disappear. They were just waiting for another globalist prime minister to come along and get his new marching orders. That is what happened. Integration was tried again—this time under Kevin Rudd, the Australian Prime Minister, elected in 2007, and this time on a much larger scale—with Asia.

According to a *Bloomberg News* article, Rudd wanted a Europe-style union "to pursue trade agreements and boost cooperation on terrorism and resource security." The union would include Asia, Japan, India, Indonesia, and the Asia-Pacific Economic Cooperation.

Defense Minister, Joel Fitzgibbon, agreed with Rudd and told reporters, "We are part of the Asia-Pacific region and we must have deeper engagement with our friends and allies in the region. That delivers security for Australia through trust and confidence."[75]

However, Australia and New Zealand Were Rejected: A *Bloomberg News* article written by Darryl Mason, November, 21, 2007, told the story that Australia and New Zealand were locked out of the new Asian Union on orders of China. In spite of the fact that ASEAN secretary, General Ong Keng Yong, earlier had invited and insisted that India, Australia and New Zealand would be part of the plans to establish a "free-trade zone covering 16 nations who participate in the East Asia Summit," China demanded that only the Ten ASEAN Plus Three countries should be included in the community. "The Chinese refuse to accept the other three guys," General Yong said. "They have always maintained that the East Asia community is 13 countries." The writer sums up his article with the words, "China really is starting to rule the world."[76]

The Dominance of China: It is interesting to see the power that China wields over the other Asian countries, so much so that it is China who determines who can belong to their union and who can't. It is rather like the big bully in the neighborhood who gets to determine who is invited and who is rejected from joining the gang that meets in the tree house. Could it be because China is now building the tree house and furnishing it with most of its needed goods and services? And China is also holding most of the money with its immense trade with the other countries, while the other countries have great debt. Money speaks. Debt does not. The USA is finding that out.

Transparency of the Other Unions—Stealth and Deception of the North American Union: After finding out about all of the various unions forming around the globe, why would people be so shocked to find out such a thing is planned for North America? After all, it is now the fashionable thing to do. The only difference is the other unions seem to have made it in national and international news. The North American Union, or Union of North America, or whatever it will be called, has received no national news coverage, nor has the Transatlantic Partnership with the EU. We also seem to be the only group of nations left out in the decision process, with no vote by Congress or Canadian or Mexican parliaments, and no vote by the people. Integration is still very much a stealth campaign for North America.

Is Socialized Medicine "Nationalized Health Care" for all Nations Part of the Integration Plan? Beginning in the spring of 2009 and going on through March 2010, when it was finally signed into law, Obama's Health Care Plan was the topic of the day and being pushed heavily by the Obama administration. A good friend, researcher and member of our Eagle Forum Board for California, Nancy Thomson, raised the question of why Hillary and Bill and Obama all began so desperately pushing a "nationalized" health care plan so early in their administrations? Was that the plan that all of them received as their marching orders? Could it be because that is what is necessary for America to be successfully merged with Canada and Mexico in a North American Union? Is that what all nations must have to be successfully merged into a partnership with the EU and into a one-world health system dictated by the World Health Organizations (WHO)?

Canada already has a total socialized medicine system. According to an article that appeared in the *Arizona Examiner* by William Busse, August 24, 2009, Mexico was also working towards a total nationalized system, except for the wealthy elite, by the year 2010. The following is a summation:

Mexico's System of Health Care: Mexico has had a many-tiered system for health care: 1) The top tier consists of 3 million very wealthy people who pay for private insurance and get the best "state of the art" care with the best facilities, latest equipment and best doctors. 2) Fifty million salaried Mexicans pay into an insurance program administered through Social Security with a sliding scale based on their salaries. 3) About 17 million government employees receive health insurance through the Institute of Social Services and have their own separate clinics and hospitals. 4) The military also has its own program and separate health facilities. 5) About 40 million uninsured have been enrolling into the "public sector" national health care option called "Seguro Popular," which was implemented in 2003. To quote from the article: "The goal of the Mexican government is to have complete coverage for the uninsured by 2010 with eventual phase out of the other two public options."[77]

It is interesting to find out that the stated goal is the year 2010, the same year as the goal has been all along for the North American Union to be formed. Now that Obama Care has passed in the USA, perhaps we are still on schedule. More is written about Obama's socialized health care plan in Chapter 14 and how it will affect our nation.

Six Unions Promoted by a "Reformed" United Nations? On a strange website that I stumbled onto, supposedly part of the "reformed United Nations," are found suggestions for six unions to be formed to help heal and protect the earth.

The unions are: the already formed European Union, the African Union, plus an "Oceanic Union, consisting of all the islands of the Pacific Ocean, plus Austria and New Zealand; an Arab Union consisting of 23 Islam nations; an Asian Union, consisting of all the Asian nations; and then low and behold up pops an **Americas-Union**! Before describing that union, I will first quote what the website gives as the purpose for forming unions.

Purpose for Unions: To Help in "the elimination of poverty, corruption and war and the sustained improvement in the quality of life for every human being, it is proposed that six (6) great Unions of states shall be formed that in turn will also have special powers under the reformed United Nations (U.N.)"

Corruption in the UN Itself: As we have just found out in the last chapter, none of what is the stated desired purpose for forming unions has happened for those who belong to the European Union. Poverty has not being eliminated. Many people are now even poorer as the euro has greatly devalued their nation's currency. Corruption has not been eliminated. We read about the many corrupt, sneaky ways the EU is breaking up nations into regions, bypassing local governments and collecting money from the regions. Maybe declared war has been eliminated, but rebellions and terrorism is still going on, especially among Muslims in EU nations. Why would any of these proposed purposes work in new unions?

The UN does not have a good track record itself for the elimination of poverty, corruption and war. In the 64 years since its beginning, world poverty has only gotten worse. There is a great deal of corruption in the UN itself as millions of dollars have disappeared into private coffers. As you will read later in the Chapter on the UN, 141 new wars have started since 1945, the UN's birthday.

"Don't Worry, Forming Unions Has Nothing to do with World Government": The website pretends to be on the same side of the issue as people who are worried about the sovereignty of their nation being threatened. "Citizens of . . . Nation states rightfully should reject . . . motions to have their sovereign rights eroded in favour of . . . "global government.""

The website then tries to pretend that the forming of unions has nothing to do with promoting world government. Unions are just "a second layer" to assist sovereign states. A second layer of what? They do not explain. Could it be a second layer of harsh international government regulations and taxation? (As if federal regulations are not enough!) Then we can have even more of our rights, freedoms, and property taken away and pay even more taxes?

Scare Tactics: The one sure record that the UN has going for itself that we can always count on—is its ability to create environmental scare tactics to try to implement its policies. It seems the bigger the lie, the more it will be believed. There are three big ones given on this website to justify the formation of unions—all under the title of "healing and protecting the earth." From what does the earth need to be healed and protected? Of course, what they have been promoting for so many years—global warming or "climate change," all caused by evil mankind, especially those found in the USA, the "greediest nation on earth." And what would they hope to accomplish from these scare tactic?—redistribution of wealth on a massive scale; the shutting down of energy and resources in the United States; massive outsourcing of jobs and industry to other countries; bringing the USA down to a 3rd world country, destroying the middle class, all the goals you have already read about in the first chapter.

However, as you will read at the end of the chapter on the UN, the global warming hot air balloon had a big whole punched in it, just shortly before the UN Copenhagen Climate Change Summit, December 7.

On the Americas-Union website, two additional scare tactics concerning the whole earth are given: a possible "pole shift," and a possible hit from an incoming asteroid, which it portrays with a big colorful picture. And how will forming big unions better protect nations from such things? The website does not answer those questions.[78]

Americas-Union: It appears that whoever is promoting the aforementioned website does not think it necessary to wait for two separate American unions, North American and South American to officially become organized. The website already has both continents linked together in one big union. That was the original plan all along if the FTAA, Free Trade Area of the Americas had passed, which would have been a trade agreement over all the nations in the Western Hemisphere, except for Cuba. The promoters of the FTAA had been trying year after year from 1994 until 2005 to get it passed. But they were not successful.

However, perhaps that does not matter. NAFTA and CAFTA may be all that is needed to form an all-encompassing governing board and union over all of the Americas, especially now that they have the EU to act as the big bully to push it all through. We have already read about what the EU did to the Caribbean Islands and other nations in South America to get them to give in to the EU's demands.

It is rather disconcerting that someone or some group are bold enough to reveal this on a website, when before such efforts involving the USA in a union were kept top secret. Maybe the plans are much further along now and these people believe there is no stopping them.

Purpose for an Americas-Union? I was intrigued as to what the group promoting the website would give as the reasons why they want such an entity. What purpose does this all serve?

The website shows a huge picture of both North and South American continents. But there are no names of individual nations shown, no states, no provinces, and of course, no borders.

At the bottom of the picture is a rectangle telling you to "click here to view," If you do, then you get to see the charter that is already drawn up and ready to go. There is also a similar charter written for the other unions. None of them are called constitutions. That would be a little too bold, so they were given the name "charter" instead, but it is in every sense of the word, a constitution.

What are the nations of the Americas promised if we form such a union? We are promised permanent status in the general assembly of the UN and the Supreme Council. (Big whoopee!) We are promised our "future." The United States is promised that we can get out of our enormous debt and our living standards will increase:

"The future of the United States, Canada and every nation in North, Central and South America depends upon the success of creating a clear economic and social union. In doing so, it is not only possible but certain that the United States will be able to trade its way out of its massive debt and in turn guarantee that living standards can not only be maintained but will actually increase."

The words on the website insinuate that if the countries of North America and South America do not choose to go along with this idea, then it will, obviously, be the fault of the USA. It will be because of "the most powerful minority interests in the world, those that fund the campaigns of United States politicians." And who would they be? People like George Soros and other very wealthy democrats or progressives, who contributed to Obama's campaign to the tune of $750 million, more than any other presidential candidate in history? I would not call them minority interest. They are the majority.

The website continues, "For the sake of humanity and their own souls, it is hoped that these people will agree that it is time for the world to come together as one." Interesting, earlier we were told that the formation of unions has nothing to do with promoting a world government, now we are being told that it is the ultimate goal, and, if we do not go along with the idea, "our souls will be lost." There is nothing that explains why a world government would be better for humanity or for our souls.

If we do not go along with this idea, we are warned, "the UCADIAN model has provisions for the establishment of the most democratic political apparatus in history to ensure [that] candidates who truly represent the citizens of the United States and the World will be elected and those who continue to hold the world to ransom will be swept from office."[79]

What is the UCADIAN model? When you google it, several interesting websites pop up. It sounds like it is some new-age concept of "unique collective awareness."

Is this Really Part of a UN Plan for a Large American Union? When I first read the information given on the website, www.americas-union.org, it seemed so farfetched that, at first, I was just going to ignore it, but the more I read it, and the more I know about the new-age, earth worshipping leaders of the UN, I decided that maybe there is some truth as to what their plans for us really are, as spelled out on this website. Much of it sounds outlandish, but the vast majority of environmental treaties that the UN has already come up with also sound outlandish.[79]

In the next chapter you will see the Gomberg Map, drawn up in 1941 (published a year later), showing that the plan for forming large regional unions is nothing new. It was thought of long ago. It has just taken much longer than planned to gain enough power and control through their world organization, the United Nations, to indoctrinate government leaders and their people to the regional, global government concepts—to make it all possible. The map shows "The United States of the Americas," which includes all of North America and Greenland linked together in one big regional government. There is also a United States of South America and eight other large regional governments across the globe.

Chapter Six

Early Plans for Large Regional Governments;
World War I and II; the League of Nations; The Gomberg Map of
1942—The Nations of the World Already Divided into Regions;
Nationalization of Banks, Industries, and Infrastructures, All Part
of the Regional Plan

As you have read in the first chapters about the formation of the European Union, elitists were planning for European regional government long before it actually happened. The excuse given was to stop the tragedy and destruction of war by getting rid of what was causing it, that "evil thing called nationalism." As you will see from the Gomberg Map, globalists were planning regional government not only for Europe but for all the nations of the world clear back in 1942.

For the nations of the world to want to go along with these globalists' plan and agree to give up the sovereignty and pride of their own nationhood, they had to first experience for themselves the tragedy and horror of world war. The elitists also had to figure out a way to get America involved in Europeans' wars so we also would be more agreeable to regional and world government.

How Did America Get Involved in World War I? The majority of Americans were not interested in joining in European wars. Many still remembered the admonishment from George Washington's Farewell Address that warned us against "the insidious wiles of foreign influence . . . one of the most baneful foes of republican government." He also stated, "The great rule of conduct for us, in regard to foreign nations, is, in extending our commercial relations, to have with them as little Political connection as possible."[80]

Create a Crisis Involving American Citizens: It was, therefore, necessary to devise a crisis, an incident which would supply the provocation. That incident occurred when the German submarine sank the British ocean liner the Lusitania, on its way from New York to England, killing 1,200 innocent passengers, 128 of whom were Americans. This greatly aroused the anger of the American people against Germany. Thus, shortly after Woodrow Wilson was reelected under the slogan, "He kept us out of war," America found itself involved in World War I.

Certain facts were denied the American people, however, about the Lusitania. It was not your normal passenger ship. It was transporting six million rounds of ammunition, plus other war munitions, to Britain, which the Germans were made aware of. The Germans had even taken out large ads in the New York papers warning Americans not to sail on the Lusitania. Their navy would be forced to sink any ship carrying war supplies to England, just as the British navy was doing to them.

In a 1972 book, *the Lusitania,* British author and researcher, Colin Simpson, revealed that the Lusitania was a registered armed cruiser of the British fleet carrying military personnel and munitions and that it was sent at considerable reduced speed into an area where a German U-boat was known to be waiting. Then the escort ships for the Lusitania were withdrawn. The ship was deliberately sent to disaster. Because of all the ammunitions that the ship was carrying, it only took one single torpedo to set off an enormous explosion. The ship was sunk in just eighteen minutes.

Of course, none of this was revealed to the American people. They were told by the news media and politicians that Germany had attacked an "unarmed" innocent passenger ship. And because many of those on board were Americans, the people of this nation were outraged and decided that Germany should be punished. Congress and President Wilson declared war on Germany in April, 1917. In that war, 48,000 Americans were killed and 228,000 wounded. As Mr. Simpson states in his book, these innocent victims were "all pawns in this vicious scheme to further the globalists' agenda."

The truth about the Lusitania was suppressed in hearings investigating the disaster. President Woodrow Wilson ordered the original manifest, which listed the ammunitions, to be hidden away in the Treasury archives.[81]

The League of Nations—The First Attempt at World Government: In January, 1918, ten months before World War I ended, President Wilson delivered his famous "Fourteen Points" speech (under the guidance of his advisor, Edward Mandell House, who most researchers think wrote the speech). Wilson proposed a world government organization be formed called the League of Nations, that would prevent any future world wars from happening. However, the U.S. Senate rejected the idea in 1919.

This first attempt to get us involved in world government failed, but undaunted the globalist elite tried again, this time with a second world war, even bloodier and longer lasting than the first. Surely, then all the nations involved would want to form a world government organization.

How Did America Become Involved in World War II—Another Terrible Tragedy Occurred: Again, the American people did not want to get involved in a second world war. But, amazingly, history repeats itself. Conveniently, a second terrible tragedy occurred that changed their minds. This time it was the Japanese bombing of our navy base in Pearl Harbor, Hawaii, that caused the deaths of two thousand U.S. servicemen. Congress and the American people were so enraged they were willing to support President Roosevelt declaring war on Japan and its allies of Germany and Italy, and we entered into World War II. The following gives the details of how President Roosevelt was actually provoking the Germans and the Japanese to some actions against us, and he was informed well in advance of the Japanese Air force heading for Pearl Harbor. He could have alerted our navy to defend ourselves, but he, and the elitists advising him, again needed a terrible tragedy to turn the hearts of the American people to war, so Roosevelt allowed it to happen.

> In 1940, a Gallup poll found that 83 percent of the American people were against going to war in Europe. Something had to happen to change their minds. President Franklin D. Roosevelt, without any declaration of war by Congress, began to provoke Germany and the Axis powers by aiding Britain with 50 destroyers and hundreds of millions of rounds of ammunition. All German consulates were closed, and U.S. ships were ordered to sail into war zones and, in some cases, to depth-charge German U-boats. FDR also provoked Japan by enacting a trade embargo against any trade with Japan and freezing all Japan's assets in the U.S. The Panama Canal was also closed to its ships. An ultimatum was then issued setting stringent conditions in order for trade to resume. Eleven days later, December 7, 1941, the Japanese attacked Pearl Harbor, leaving two thousand American soldiers dead and eleven naval vessels sunk or damaged.
>
> It is now well documented that Roosevelt and his general, George Marshall, knew ahead of time that the Japanese were going to attack. They could have prepared the navy at Pearl Harbor and saved all of those lives. As it was, they stripped the island of most of its air defenses shortly before the raid and allotted it only one-third of the surveillance planes needed to detect approaching forces. They

wanted a crisis to occur that would so outrage the American people
that we would be willing to enter again into a world war, and that
is what happened.[82]

The Outcome of World War II: The war ended May 8, 1945, with the
surrender of Germany. Japan surrendered six months later on September 2,
after the terrible dropping of two atomic bombs on Nagasaki and Hiroshima
in August. The war left about 60 million dead, 35 million were civilians, 25
million soldiers—from Europe, Eastern Europe, Japan, and America. **American
lost 405,400 soldiers**.[83]

The Soviet Union greatly expanded its territory and Communism became
the new enemy. The Second World War was fought to supposedly stop the
Germans from taking over other countries like Poland. At the end of the war,
Poland was now taken over by the Communists, as was East Germany, most of
Eastern Europe and parts of Asia. Fortunes were made by international business
cartels, and the world was moved closer to a one-world government. The nations
of the world now agreed to a world government organization, this time called
the United Nations—exactly what the plan had been all along.

**The 1942 "New World Moral Order" Map: Showing the United States of
the Americas, Other Regional Governments and the Globalist Objectives
Striving for World Government:**

How I Obtained the Map: A concerned patriotic American, who had been
doing her own research and was an activist for more than 40 years, Bernadine
Smith, heard me speak about the background of the North American Union
on a radio interview. She contacted me and told me of the map that shows how
early on in history the elitists were already planning for world government. She
was very kind to send a copy of the map to me and all the information that goes
along with it. I am including the map on the next page. On the bottom of the
map is written "Our Policy Shall be This," and lists the 41 objectives the elitists
have as they are preparing for world government. They are speaking from the
viewpoint as if this is what the USA desires and we are promoting it.

Background Information of the Map: The map was actually drawn up in 1941
(but published in 1942), before Pearl Harbor had happened, before the United
States had entered World War II, before the war had ended and Germany had
lost. It was also before the United Nations had been established. The forty-one
objectives written at the bottom of the map sound like whoever wrote them

knew all of those things were certain to take place. Many of the objectives are the same as those of the UN.

Under the title "Outline of Post-War New World Map," is a sort of introduction explaining the map. Notice the word "moral" that is used supporting the belief system of those who believe in world government. They are convinced that world government is the "moral" thing to do. They truly have a different concept of "morality" than we do. You will later find out that their world government also includes a world religion, but it is not anything that would resemble the Judeo/Christian religion based on the Bible. The following is the map and the words that are written at the top to introduce it:

Outline of Post-War New World Map

As the USA, with the cooperation of the democracies of Latin-America, the British Commonwealth of Nations and the Union of Soviet Socialist Republics assumes world leadership for the establishment of a **New World Moral Order** for permanent peace, freedom, justice, security, and world reconstruction.

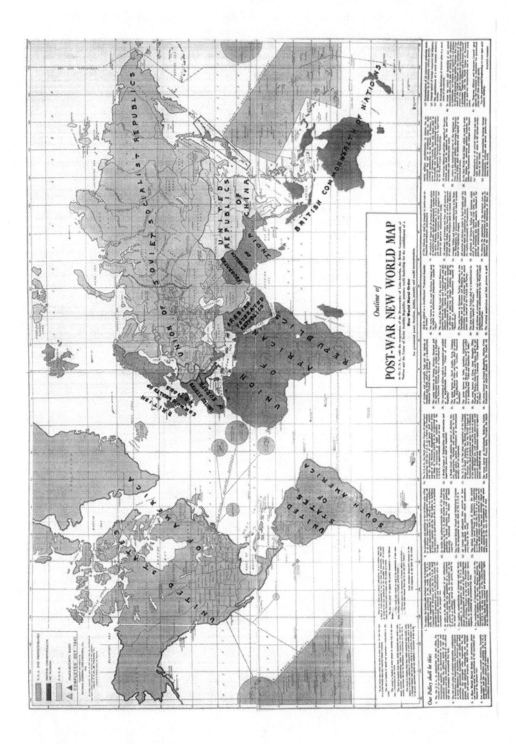

Black and White Version of the Gomberg Map Showing the Names of the Regions in Bold Print: The original map was in color with all the countries that made up a certain region of the same color. Notice there are no borders separating the United States from Canada or Mexico. In fact, the name Canada is no longer on the map. However, the provinces of Canada are still shown, as are the names of the states for the USA and the provinces of Mexico. South America just appears to be a group of united states rather than individual countries.

When I googled the Gomberg map, the following two articles appeared: the first coming from the *Observer*, a newspaper in England, which asks questions about who is behind this New World Order plan, and quotes two British men who believe strongly that such a plan for global government will someday become a reality. The second article has no name but describes the map and its objectives as something very positive, something that would be good for the world:

1) *The Observer*, **August 25, 1993:** *The Observer* has acquired a printed large color map prepared by a Maurice Gomberg in 1941. The map details a new world order plan that has redrawn the face of the globe. The United States is united with Canada, Greenland, Mexico, Cuba, and all of Central South American countries. (Is NAFTA now the tool to achieve their goal?)

Is the New World Order a select group of government people, acting in concert to impose their economic and military control over the nations of the globe, through a scheme that has existed since the turn of the century?

The *London Observer*, [what the Observer used to be called] of Sunday, Nov. 27, 1983, covered a speech by Lord Lothian, the wartime British Ambassador to the United States, entitled "Wings Over History, a New Civilization." In his speech he said:

'But though few yet realize it, the old anarchy of multitudinous national sovereignties is about to dissolve—and quickly at that. World unity is, of course, at present entirely out of sight. But that the world is going to fall into four or five main political and economic groups, each in great measure self supporting, each under the leadership of a great state equipped with modern military and air power, at any rate for a time, seems certain. Nothing that we can do can prevent it.'

Is the New World Order fiction? The more we search for the truth, the more we are convinced that this has been a long-range plan by influential men determined to change the world as we know it.

Are we Americans being used as pawns in the game of the wealthy Multinationals? H.G. Wells, considered by many the mentor of the men of the New World Order, wrote in his book *Experiment in Autobiography*: Chapter Nine, The idea of a Planned World: (p. 557)

'It will appear first, I believe, as a conscious organization of intelligent and quite possibly in some cases wealthy men, as a movement having distinct social and political aims, confessedly ignoring most of those aims. It will be very loosely organized in its earlier stages, a mere movement of a number of people in a certain direction who will presently discover with a sort of surprise the common object toward which they are all moving.

The consent of all the sovereign powers of the world to world pacifications is quite unnecessary. Indeed, as I point out—three or four powers alone could impose an enduring World Pax.' (H.G. Wells, p. 592)

When you click on the website mentioned below, an article pops up with no name for the article or for the author. The article not only explains the map and its ten regions but the concept of the New World Order as if it is ultimately "**for the good of mankind.**" Since the writer refuses to acknowledge who he is, I refer to him as "Mr. John Doe."

Mr. Doe also has some very snide comments about anyone who dares to look at this map disparagingly or disapprove of the New World Order. He tries to link such a disparaging person to the conspiracy-nut crowd who believe that small powerful evil groups are running government (and he lists all the possible groups). Here is how the article is named and found on the internet:

2) Article by Strange Maps (*http://strangemaps.wordpress.com/*) Published in Philadelphia in early 1942, this "Outline of (the) Post-War New World Map," created by Maurice Gomberg, shows a proposal to re-arrange the world after an Allied victory against the Axis forces. Its title refers to a **"New World Order,"** a vague concept, its many definitions often contradicting each other. At the core of the NWO, however, is always the notion that a small group of powerful individuals, institutions, industries and/or nations must lead the world in the right direction (i.e. towards 'unification'). This may be against the world's own will (and therefore done covertly, at least in some versions of the NWO-story), but **ultimately it is for its own good.**

One of the most recent references to the NWO by a major political figure was made by U.S. president George Bush (Sr), who explicitly used the NWO to refer to U.S. objectives in a Post-Cold War world. The term has a pedigree much older than the Cold War, or even both World Wars. Some might even say—and now we're straying somewhat prematurely into the field of conspiracy theory—that it goes all the way back to Roman times, as is attested by the (modified) quote of the Roman poet Virgil on the reverse of the U.S. Great Seal and (significantly or not, since 1935) on the back of the dollar bill: *Novus Ordo Seclorum*—literally: "A New Order for the Ages." [As the reader will find out in a later chapter, The actual literal translation from the Latin is a "new secular order"—meaning an order without God.]

Mr. Doe States the Concept of World Government is Nothing New and It Could be "the Best of all Possible Worlds:"

In a modern context, it was the British imperialist Cecil Rhodes (who gave his name to Rhodesia) who first proposed a federal world government to be imposed by the U.S. and the British Empire. U.S. President Woodrow Wilson was inspired by a similar concept to draw up his plans for a League of Nations in the aftermath of World War I. Most fascist regimes in the 20s, 30s and 40s of the twentieth century also proposed some sort of NWO—in fact, most styled themselves to be a "New Order." H.G. Wells—he of "*War of the Worlds*"—wrote *The Open Conspiracy* (1928) in which he describes his efforts to get intellectuals to back the idea of a World Social Democracy and "The New World Order" (1940), in which he details how a generation of struggle will be necessary to overcome the opponents of such a global government.

From this sketchy overview, it might be equally sketchily concluded that One World Government was the mostly benevolent projected outcome of an optimist, positivist, socialist and/or imperialist (or in some cases, *national*-socialist) world view, a kind of secular New Jerusalem, the best of all possible worlds . . .

Conspiracy-Minded People: Mr. Doe links together all those who speak out against a NWO as creating their own brand of conspiracies and tries to discredit them and make them appear ridiculous:

. . . Pick and Mix, and Create Your own Conspiracy: the Illuminati, the freemasons, the Council on Foreign Relations, the Trilateral Commission, the Jews, the Bilderberg Group, the G-8, the Nazis, the Bretton-Woods agreement, black helicopters, US-alien collusion, the Zionist lobby in cahoots with American Neo-Cons, those out to 'miscegenate' and dilute the white race, the House of Windsor, the Antichrist, a cabal of multinational corporations, extraterrestrial reptilians, the United Nations . . . I don't know whether **Maurice Gomberg**, of whom next to no information is traceable online, was an extraterrestrial reptilian, but he certainly has a Jewish surname, which would make him equally suspect in some circles. Not much more is known of him; it has even been suggested that this map was a Nazi forgery, to induce fear in America of a communist takeover of the world.

Mr. Doe sees nothing wrong with the map and thinks world reconstruction is a good idea:

But I think it's safer to assume that this map was an earnest attempt, out of the aforementioned benevolent socialist sentiments, to propose a reorganization of the world that would end war once and for all, and bring "permanent peace, freedom, justice, security and world reconstruction." Or at least let that be our working assumption in evaluating this map.

The Ten Regions that Mr. Doe calls "Building Blocks of the New World Order" are the Following:

1. **The United States of America (USA):** the US, Canada, all Central American and Caribbean states, most Atlantic islands (including Greenland and Iceland), most Pacific islands, Taiwan, Hainan, the Philippines and several now Indonesian islands, including Sulawesi. This was to be the dominant power in the world, military and otherwise.
2. **The Union of Soviet Socialist Republics (USSR):** the Soviets were to be rewarded with Persia (Iran), Mongolia, Manchuria, Finland, and all of Eastern Europe, which subsequently would form part of the Eastern Bloc (excluding Albania, but including the real-life maverick state of Yugoslavia, socialist but anti-Soviet). All of theses states were simply to become member-states of

the USSR. Austria and most of Germany, although 'quarantined' are shown within the Soviet sphere.

3. **The United States of South America (USSA):** including all South American states, with the three Guianas as a single constituent state and the Falkland Islands part of the USSA.

4. **The Union of African Republics (UAR):** All of Africa as a federation of republics.

5. **The Arabian Federated Republics (AFR):** covering Saudi and all other states now occupying the Arabian Peninsula, plus present-day Iraq and Syria.

6. **The Federated Republics of India (FRI):** Present-day Afghanistan, Pakistan, India, Nepal, Bhutan, Bangladesh and Burma (Myanmar).

7. **The United Republics of China (URC):** A federation including all parts of present-day China, Korea, the erstwhile French colony of Indochina (now Vietnam, Laos and Cambodia), Thailand and Malaya.

8. **The United States of Scandinavia (USS):** Norway, Sweden, Denmark.

9. **The United States of Europe (USE):** the Benelux countries, the German Rhineland, France, Switzerland, Spain, Portugal and Italy.

10. **The British Commonwealth of Nations (BCN)**, including Great Britain, Australia, New Zealand, Sri Lanka, Madagascar and most of Indonesia.

Smaller Entities Include: Eire (the whole of Ireland), **Greece** (including Albania), **Turkey** (excluding European Turkey), **Hebrewland** (the Holy Land plus Jordan) and **Japan**.

Enemy States were to be Quarantined: The three axis states (Germany, Italy and Japan) were to be "quarantined" until they could be readmitted into the family of nations.

Four Freedoms and A Moral Order: Mr. Gomberg possibly took his cue for this map from U.S. president Franklin D. Roosevelt's State of the Union Speech that was delivered to the 77th Congress, in which he spoke about the Four Freedoms and a Moral Order. Gomberg quotes these just before he gives his own statement about a New World Moral Order at the bottom of the map:

The Four Freedoms: The map contains a rectangular box that gives FDR's message to Congress on the Four Freedoms. As you will notice, "freedom from fear" includes a "world-wide reduction of armaments, something that is also mentioned in the 41 Objectives at the bottom of the map. FDR also mentions a "Moral Order" as does the map. These elitists seem to believe that world government is the "moral" thing to do for all of mankind. Could their definition of "moral" be different than ours? Could they be worshiping a different god, or no god at all? Here are the words of FDR written on the map. (Some people wonder if FDR is not the Mr. Gomberg who created the map?)

"The Four Freedoms" Franklin D. Roosevelt's Address to Congress on January 6, 1941:

In the future days, which we seek to make secure, we look forward to a world founded upon four essential human freedoms.

1. The first is freedom of speech and expression—everywhere in the world.
2. The second is freedom of every person to worship God in his own way—everywhere in the world.
3. The third is freedom from want—which, translated into world terms, means economic understandings which will secure to every nation a healthy peacetime life for its inhabitants—everywhere in the world.
4. The fourth is freedom from fear—w**hich, translated into world terms, means a world-wide reduction of armaments** to such a point and in such a thorough fashion that no nation will be in a position to commit an act of physical aggression against any neighbor—anywhere in the world. That is no vision of a distant millennium. It is a definite basis for a kind of world attainable in our own time and generation. That kind of world is the very antithesis of the so-called new order of tyranny which the dictators seek to create with the crash of a bomb.

    To that new order we oppose the greater conception—the moral order. A good society is able to face schemes of world domination and foreign revolutions alike without fear. Since the beginning of our American history, we have been engaged in **change**—in a perpetual peaceful revolution—a revolution which goes on steadily, quietly adjusting itself to changing conditions—without the concentration camp or the quick-lime in the ditch. **The world order** which we seek is the cooperation of free countries, working together in a friendly, civilized society.

    This nation has placed its destiny in the hands and heads and hearts of its millions of free men and women; and its faith in freedom under the guidance of God. Freedom means the supremacy of human rights everywhere. Our support goes to those who struggle to gain those rights or keep them. Our strength is our unity of purpose.

To that high concept there can be no end save victory. (From *Congressional Record,* 1941, Vol. 87, Pt. I.)

Gomberg's Concluding Remarks:

> . . . the USA with the cooperation of the Democracies of Latin-America, the British Commonwealth of Nations and the Union of Soviet Socialist Republics, assumes world leadership for the establishment of a **New World Moral Order for permanent peace, justice, security and world reconstruction.**[84]

World Reconstruction? Did you catch that last word? Isn't it interesting that just about every socialist, communist, Marxist, Fascist uses the same terminology—they want to reconstruct or rebuild the world according to their utopia pattern or agenda. Obama and his many czars want to reconstruct or transform America. Many of us prefer the old America. We don't want it reconstructed. We want it restored.

Protectorates and Peace-Security Bases: The world is to be divided up into regions as "protectorates and peace-security bases." That doesn't sound so bad does it? They are not really trying to break up nations and destroy their sovereignty. They are just establishing some nations linked together for protection, peace, and security, something like the "Security and Prosperity Partnership." You might fall for that until you read all 41 objectives which begin to sound pretty totalitarian, such as total disarmament of the world (except for the world army and those elitists in control).

The Most Disturbing of the Forty-One Objectives are the Following: (These are especially frightening when we see how close the elitists have already come in their attempts to achieve them.)

#5—Disarmament and Demilitarization: The USA (both North and South America), the Commonwealth of Great Britain and the USSR were to be the big bully nations that would **disarm and demilitarize** all the other nations.

#14—Re-education and Incorporation: Germany and Austria were to be re-educated and to be incorporated into the Soviet Union. (At the end of World

War II, the Soviet Union didn't quite get all of Germany, but they did get half, all of East Germany. What a sad socialist state they made of it.)

#16—A World Court and International Police: The UN was established with a world court and UN Peace Keepers, which are to eventually take the place of the military and police for all nations.

#s 31-38—Work Camps, Confiscation of Property, Quarantined Areas and Population Control: These objectives talk about the evil countries of Germany-Austria, Italy, and Japan, the losers of World War II. If the people could not be sufficiently reprogrammed, then their property was to be confiscated; they would be forced into work camps and other quarantined areas; and population control would be used on them so they could not produce anymore evil people. If a tyrannical one-world government is in place, plans for gathering up people and putting them in work camps could be for any group of people who are deemed "evil." Anyone who protests or opposes the elitists' objectives could be the ones who are gathered up and put into work camps, quarantined, and could be forced to have "population control," whatever form that will be—just depending on the whims of the elitists in charge. That is how government works under tyranny, by the whims of the tyrants in charge. They make up the rules as they go along, rather than following a firm rule of law.

 # 39—Nationalization of Resources, Banks, Industry, and Redistribution of Wealth: This is the most frightening of all the objectives, because we see so much of it already coming true under the Obama administration. This objective encompasses six separate goals and begins with the words "the following economic changes are imperative:"

a. **Nationalization of all natural resources and equitably distribution of same to everyone in the world.**
b. **Nationalization of all banks, foreign investments, railroad and power plants—everywhere in the world.**
c. **Nationalization of all armament producing establishments by all remaining military powers.**
d. **Federal control of foreign commerce and shipping.**
e. **The establishment of a world common monetary system.**
f. **World-wide limitations of interest rates to a maximum of two percent.**

Nationalization? A few years ago, you would never have heard this term used, or imagined it ever being used in a free-market country like America. If you even remotely hinted that our federal government might do such a thing, you would be laughed at, but now with the financial crisis and the federal "bailout" of banks, insurance companies, mortgage and investment companies, auto industry, states, private homes, etc., nationalization of all of the above is starting before our very eyes.

Perhaps there will be a new crisis affecting railroads and power plants causing them to face bankruptcy, thus the federal government will have to step in and nationalize these as well. They are already doing that with Amtrak. It could not make it on its own without the federal financial assistance.

Inter-Nationalization? Maybe such infrastructure might be "taken over by some other country—nationalized by them. Already, much of our infrastructure has been sold or leased to foreign countries. Remember back in April of 2006, there was a protest by the American people that a foreign company, Dubai, was planning to buy 22 Eastern and Gulf Port operations. The number was finally reduced to nine which Congress readily approved. From "Phyllis Schlafly's Report" of September 2006, we find out that nine is just a little drop in the bucket. "Homeland Security admits that 80% of our 3,200 terminals nationwide are operated by foreign companies and countries." Mrs. Schlafly describes much more of our infrastructure that has already been sold to foreign entities:

> In June [of 2006], a Spanish firm (CINTRA) paid $1.3 billion for a
> 50-year lease to operate a 10-lane toll road through the heart of Texas.
> The same month, an Australian company bought a 99-year lease on
> Virginia's Pocahontas Parkway. Also in June, an Australian-Spanish
> partnership paid $3.8 billion to lease the Indiana Toll Road for 75
> years. Last year [2007], Chicago sold a 99-year lease on the eight-mile
> Chicago Skyway to the same buyer for $1.8 billion, and the tolls are
> expected to double . . . The tolls from the U.S. side of the tunnel
> between Detroit and Windsor, Canada, belong to an Australian
> company . . . .

How Wise is the Selling of Such Infrastructures? These negotiations seem to be done hastily to remedy the immediate financial deficits that the states are having without looking at what revenue they will be losing over the long term. For example, Indiana legislators are concerned that the above mentioned Spanish firm could rake in $133 billion over the 75-year life of the lease for the Indiana Toll Road, for which Indiana received only $3.8 billion.

Mrs. Schlafly gives another example of how Orange County, California, had entered into a foolish contract with a French company to allow them to lease and set up a toll road on Route 91 for $130 million. When county officials found out that the fine print in the contract prohibited them from building more roads, it had to buy back the lease for $207.5 million. They lost $77.5 million in the deal. No wonder so many counties, cities, states are having financial problems.

How Did the Selling of American Infrastructure Ever Become Possible? Back in April 30, 1992, President Bush Senior signed Executive Order 12803, called "Infrastructure Privatization." It encouraged state and local governments to "privatize infrastructure assets" defined as "roads, tunnels, bridges, electricity, supply facilities, mass transit, rail transportation, airports, ports, waterways, water supply facilities, recycling and wastewater treatment facilities, solid waste disposal facilities, housing, schools, prisons, and hospitals. Bush's orders didn't put any restrictions on who the purchasers had to be, American or not, friend or foe.[85]

Nationalization of Resources and Armaments? Maybe there will be more environmental "shortage" scares and nationalization of all natural resources will follow "with equitable distribution of same to all nations everywhere in the world." Of course, because of riots that might happen, martial law could be called for with confiscation of guns and ammunitions. Then only government-owned factories will be able to make armaments and only government officials will be able to have weapons.

Federal Control of all Foreign Commerce and Shipping.: Does "Federal" really mean an all powerful world federal government that will control all foreign commerce and shipping? Could NAFTA (North American Free Trade Agreement) and now the Transatlantic Common Market between USA, Canada, and the European Union be leading up to such a world federal control?

World Common Monetary System: This would control all the banks of the world and limit the interest rates to no more than 2 percent. No longer could you choose to go to one bank over another because of their higher interest rate. All would be the same; all competition would be destroyed. This objective would seem so farfetched except for the fact that we already have in place the World Bank and the International Monetary Fund that regulate all the banks of the world. We have the Federal Reserve which sets the interest rates for all USA banks. There is no real competition between banks anymore. We see the European Union in full bloom with a common currency, the Euro, and we see the movement to a North American Union with talk of a common currency for Canada, Mexico and the USA—the Amero. Would it not be easy someday to just combine those major currencies into one big world currency?

Notice what is written at the very end after listing all of his scary 41 objectives: **"For this purposeful beginning we must fight until absolute victory."** That sounds pretty committed doesn't it? It doesn't say how long it will take, but someday they will have absolute victory! I personally believe they are getting very close. But, as the reader will see throughout this book, many of their plans have been thwarted or postponed as people became aware of what was really going on. There is hope that we can do it again.

The following are all 41 objectives written as they appear at the bottom of the map: (I have emphasized by bold letters what I feel are most ominous.)

Outline of Post-War New World Map by Maurice Gomberg, Philadelphia, 1942:

1) We, the U.S.A, in cooperation with out allies, for reasons of our national safety and in the interests of international morality, are determined to crush and completely destroy the military power of the Axis aggressors and their satellites regardless of cost, effort and time necessary to accomplish this task.

2) **The old world order** of colonial oppression, exploitation of dominions, rival imperialisms and mercenary balance of power diplomacy; of majesties, dictators, privileged minorities, plutocratic monopolists and similar social parasites; the corrupted order responsible for the present world cataclysm, endangering our national safety and peaceful progress, **shall never rise again.**

3) A **New World Moral Order** for permanent peace and freedom shall be established at the successful conclusion of the present war.

4) For reasons of history, economic structure, favorable geography and the welfare of Mankind, **the U.S.A. must, altruistically, assume the leadership of the newly established, democratic, world order.**

5) To reduce the burden and criminal waste of armaments expenditures everywhere in the world, the U.S.A., with the cooperation of Latin-America,

the British Commonwealth of Nations, and the U.S.S.R. shall undertake to guarantee peace to the nations which will be **permanently demilitarized** after the conclusion of the present war.

6) In order to be able, in fulfillment of our obligations, to effectively prevent the possibility of a recurrence of another world cataclysm, **the invincibility of the U.S.A. as a military, naval and air power, shall be the major prerequisite.**

7) For realistic considerations of strategy and our invulnerability, it is imperative that the **U.S.A. shall obtain relinquishment of controls of their possessions from all foreign Powers in the entire Western Hemisphere, its surrounding waters and strategic island outposts as outlined on accompanying map.**

8) For considerations of hemispheric defense and in the spirit and tradition of the new Monroe Doctrine of hemispheric solidarity and the "Good Neighbor" policy, **the U.S.A., with the consent of the Latin-American Republics, shall obtain control and protectorate rights of the relinquished territories.**

9) To strengthen our position in the Caribbean area which is of obvious importance to hemispheric defense, **all possible inducements shall be offered to our neighbors of Central America and the West Indies to facilitate their entrance as equal states of the U.S.A. as outlined on map.**

10) To fortify the politico-economic unity of the Western Hemisphere, **the U.S.A. shall promote and assist the unification of South America into a well organized, democratic, federated "United States of South America."**

11) **Their liberated British, French and Netherlands Guianas shall be recognized as one state of the U.S.S.A.**

12) **All Powers shall relinquish their controls of their colonial, mandate and strategic island possessions everywhere in the world.**

13) **The British Commonwealth of Nations**, the second military and naval Power of importance cooperating in a binding compact with the U.S.A. as a Power for freedom, shall **retain and acquire control of such territories, peace-seeking security bases and strategic island outposts for the maintenance of world peace and freedom of the seas as outlined on map.**

14) **The U.S.S.R.,** the third military Power of importance cooperating with the U.S.A. as a Power for freedom and the maintenance of world peace, **shall acquire control of the liberated, disorganized adjacent areas and those**

of Germany-Austria to be re-educated and eventually incorporated as equal republics of the U.S.S.R., as approximately outlined on map.

15) **A World League of Nationalities** with arbitration and supervision powers shall be organized.

16) **A World Court** with punitive powers of absolute boycott, quarantine, blockade and occupation by international police, against lawbreakers of international morality shall be organized.

17) The U.S.A. with the close cooperation of the United States of South America, the British Commonwealth of Nations, the U.S.S.R. and the World League of Nationalities, shall promote and assist in the unification of the relinquished territories and the areas at present unsoundly divided into well organized, democratic and **absolutely demilitarized** federated republics as approximately outlined on map.

18) The areas known as Netherlands, Belgium, Luxemburg, Switzerland, France, Spain, Portugal, the island of Corsica and eventually Italy and the islands of Sardinia and Sicily shall be unified as a **demilitarized, federated "United States of Europe**."

19) The areas known as Sweden, Norway, Denmark and the Spitsbergen islands shall be unified as a demilitarized, **federated "United States of Scandinavia**."

20) The continent of Africa shall be reorganized and unified as a **demilitarized, federated "Union of African Republics."**

21) The areas known as Saudi Arabia, Syria, Lebanon, Iraq, Hejas, Yemen, Aden and Oman, shall be unified as a **demilitarized union of "Arabian Federated Republics."**

22) The areas known as India, including Afghanistan, Baluchistan, Nepal, Bhuta and Burma shall be unified as a **demilitarized "Federated Republics of India."**

23) The areas known as China, Inner Mongolia, Tibet, Thailand, Malaya, Indo-China and Korea, shall be unified as a **demilitarized, federated "United Republics of China."**

24) The areas known as Greece, Macedonia, Albania, Crete, Dodecanese and adjacent islands in the Aegean Sea shall be unified as a **demilitarized "Federated Republic of Greece**."

25) The areas known as Eire and Northern Ireland shall be unified as a **demilitarized independent republic of "Eire."**

26) The area of the Holy Land of the ancient Hebrews, at present known as Palestine and Trans-Jordan, and the adjacent requisite regions outlined on map, for considerations of history and the imperative necessity to alleviate a

post-war refugees problem, shall be unified as a **demilitarized independent republic of "Hebrewland."**

27) The area known as European Turkey, adjacent to the Dardanelles, sea of Marmora and Bosporus, for considerations of realistic peace strategy shall be placed under **joint control of the U.S.S.R. and Turkey.**

28) The area known as Turkey shall be a **demilitarized independent republic of "Turkey".**

29) All problems of exchange, transfer and repatriation of populations shall be administered by the **World League of Nationalities**.

30) The criminal perpetrators and their partners in guilt of this hideous war shall be brought to justice and **unforgettable punishment administered**.

31) **All subjects of Japan** and all persons of Japanese origin of doubtful loyalty shall be **permanently expelled from the entire Western Hemisphere, U.S.A. protectorates and strategic island outposts and their property confiscated for post-war reconstruction needs.**

32) All subjects of Germany and Italy and all persons of German and Italian origin known as **active supporters of Nazi and fascist ideologies shall be treated similarly.**

33) **German, Italian and Japanese immigration to the Western Hemisphere, its protectorates and island outposts shall be indefinitely stopped.**

34) All persons of German origins in East Prussia and the Rhineland shall be transferred to inner Germany and the regions permanently **de-Prussianized**.

35) All persons of German, Italian and Japanese origin shall be **permanently expelled from their now conquered territories and their property confiscated for post-war reconstruction needs.**

36) To cleanse the population of the defeated Axis aggressors of the intoxication of military chauvinism; to effectuate the removal and destruction of their potential military establishments; to recover the accumulated loot and to re-educate them for their eventual membership in the Family of Nations, the areas of Germany-Austria, Italy and Japan shall be hermetically and **indefinitely quarantined** and administered by appointed Governors subject to supervision by the World League of Nationalities.

37) **All resources, industrial and labor capacity of the quarantined areas shall be employed for the post-war restoration and reconstruction needs.**

38) To reduce the numerical power of the aggressor nations, as a potential military advantage, a **Population Control Policy shall be elaborated and applied in the quarantined areas.**

39) In the **New World Moral Order** which we seek to establish, besides the essential political freedom, the following fundamental economic changes are imperative:

- **Nationalization of all natural resources and equitable distribution of same to all nations—everywhere in the world**
- **Nationalization of international banking, foreign investments, railroads and power plants—everywhere in the world**
- **Nationalization of all armaments producing establishments by all remaining military powers**
- **Federal control of foreign commerce and shipping**
- **The establishment of a world common monetary system**
- **World-wide limitations of interest rates to a maximum of two percent**

40) To retain the victory and leadership of our united democratic effort—the aim of which is not vengeance or exploitation, but freedom and security to all nations for peaceful progress—the unified "**Supreme War Command of the United Nations**" and the conclusion of the present war, shall **be reorganized and transformed into a permanent "Supreme Military and Economic Council" collaborating with the World League of Nationalities in post-war reconstruction and to enforce world peace.**

41) The "Supreme Military and Economic Council" shall appoint the Governors to administer the quarantined areas until their eventual parole.

> **For this purposeful beginning we must fight until absolute victory**. Maurice Gomberg

The Map Can Be Ordered from the Library of Congress or Found on Line: Write to the Library of Congress: Geography Map Division, Washington DC and ask for the 1942 world map. (Notice the benign sounding, nice words written about it): "Outline of post-war new world map" by Maurice Gomberg, Philadelphia, Feb. 25, 1942. **Shows protectorates and peace-security bases.** Includes quotes from President Franklin Roosevelt's message to the 77th Congress on the State of the Union, including the Four Freedoms and the Moral Order. SOURCE: Library of Congress DIGITAL ID: g3200 ct001256, URL: *http:// hdl.loc.gov/loc.gmd/g3200.ct001256* or *http://strangemaps.wordpress.com/http:// history.sandiego. edu/gen/maps/1900s/1942world4000.jpg* [86]

Is it not interesting that just a few years after this map and its objectives were published, even before World War II was ended, the groundwork was already being laid for a new form of world government—the United Nations? And many of these objectives are incorporated into it.

Part of the elitist plans to get nations ready for forming large unions is to break them up from within, to destroy traditional states or provinces and put them into large regions, with unelected officials in charge. The goal is to destroy local government and locally elected people, and, in doing so, to destroy the pesky 10th Amendment that has caused the Federal Government so much grief. As you will read in the next chapter, there was an attempt to destroy our state governments and put the USA into 10 large regions back during FDR's era. Again, this was done by "stealth," without the American people knowing anything about it.

Chapter Seven

Regional Plans to Break Up the United States,
A Map Dividing the Nation into Regions,
Plans to Abolish County and City Governments

In October of 2008, I received a large packet in the mail of material that made up two big binders, both about 4 inches thick. They were sent to me by the same kind, patriotic lady, Bernadine Smith, who had sent me the Gomberg Map. They were about "The Politics of Change in Local Government Reform," (TPOC) a "change" campaign that has been going on since the time of President Franklin Delenore Roosevelt and the "stealth and deception" used to bring it about.

The packet was a warning of what would be coming if Obama were elected and his same "Politics of Change" began to take over America. I am afraid not many Americans knew enough about Obama to be warned and many voted for his mantra of "hope and change." I am afraid we are now seeing some of the same socialist programs as FDR implemented under his "TPOC," especially since FDR is one of Obama's role models.

Secret Plans to Restructure the USA: The first binder contained information about the secret plans that were going on in 1935 to restructure the USA, to move the states into nine large regions (later ten after Alaska and Hawaii became states) and have regional rule instead of state government, thus creating a more powerful and all encompassing federal government, no longer held at bay by state's rights and the Tenth Amendment. The ultimate goal was to destroy or so weaken the Constitution that it would not have any more effect on limiting the power of the federal government.

National Resources Planning Board (NRPB): This is the organization created by FDR to restructure our nation and turn the states into regions. Why would FDR want to do such a thing? He was going along with the New World Order plan, preparing our nation for world government.

FDR's good friend, Joseph Stalin, had written a book, ***Marxism and the National Question***," which was published in 1942 (the same year as the Gomberg map.) In his book he made the following statement (emphasis added): *"Divide the world into regional groups as a transitional stage to total world government.* ***Later the regional groups can be brought all the way into single world dictatorship.***"

So, in preparation for our nation to be part of a regional government, such as the North American Union, FDR, and those behind him, figured we had to first get the people away from their feelings of any loyalty to their states and make them more willing to accept larger federal controls and eventually regional government. This preparation started back in 1935 with the following:

1935, April 21—Brainwashing at the Breakfast Table: On the back of one of the children's favorite breakfast cereal—Kix, appeared a map of the United States, all divided up into nine regions. (Later the map was changed to ten regions after Alaska and Hawaii became states.) The map was labeled, **"America's Regions, Explore the Great Land of Ours."** The regions were listed on the map as "departments" (making it sound very official, as if it were all ready a done deal). The departments were:

Department of New England—Maine, Massachusetts, New Hampshire, Vermont, Rhode Island, and Connecticut

Department of The Middle Atlantic—New York, Pennsylvania, New Jersey, Delaware, West Virginia

Department of the South Atlantic—Maryland, Kentucky, Tennessee, Virginia, North Carolina, South Carolina

Department of The Mississippi—Arkansas, Louisiana, Alabama, Mississippi, Georgia, Florida

Department of The Southwest—Texas, Arizona, New Mexico, Oklahoma, Missouri

Department of the Great Lakes—Michigan, Illinois, Indiana, Ohio

Department of The Prairies—North and South Dakota, Minnesota, Wisconsin, Nebraska, Iowa, Kansas

Department of The Rockies—Idaho, Montana, Wyoming, Utah, Colorado, Nevada

Department of The Pacific Coast—Washington, Oregon, California

A reporter for the *New York Times Magazine*, Delbert Clark, wrote an article that appeared April 21, 1935, that told of the proposal to abolish the states. Fortunately enough people became aroused, upset, contacted their Congressmen and got it "stopped." But not really stopped; these liberal socialists never give up. They just go underground for a while and continue on with their bad ideas. As you will see later in this chapter, the movement towards regionalizing the states is still going on, again by stealth and deception, but under the auspices of the United Nations. A copy of the 1935 map follows, followed by some of the highlights of Clark's article:

NINE GROUPS INSTEAD OF THE 48 STATES

1935 Map of the United States DividedUp into Nine Groups

"Nine Groups Instead of the 48 States" by Delbert Clark, *New York Times Magazine*, 4/21/1935:

There is a growing sentiment—it is still too inchoate to be termed a movement—among certain members of Congress with advanced social views and a willingness to break with tradition, in favor of drastic change in our form of government to facilitate nation-wide reforms frequently blocked by the very nature of our confederation. Since, obviously, there is a political dynamite in any proposal to abolish States, in so far as they provide a check upon the Federal Government, no one has yet dared to broach publicly the thesis that the abolition would be in the public interest and is, in fact, a distinct possibility in the somewhat distant future.

Clark interviewed one of the members of Congress who held such "advanced social views," Senator Wagner from New York. Clark then cited some of Wagner's reasons why getting rid of the States would be "in the public interest." (Clark also attributed these views as coming from FDR and his "New Deal." Wagner was the author of one of the New Deal's most socialist regulators of private businesses, "The National Industry Recovery Act," which was "originally intended as a measure of social and business reform.)

Reasons to Abolish the States:

1. To expedite Federal regulations of intrastate affairs, which are often blocked by States' rights. Clark gives examples of the "long, tedious process" of amending the Constitution and getting the states to ratify the amendments such as with the income tax, (Amendment 15), prohibition law (Amendment 18), right to vote for women (Amendment 19). Getting rid of states would allow the Federal government to move its policies much quicker.
2. To speed things up in times of emergency, when "traditional state sovereignty must be forgotten for the common welfare."
3. To bring about better "cohesion." There are social and economic changes that are caused because of the artificial barriers provided by state lines.
4. To get rid of the "troublesome commerce clause," with its words of "interstate and intrastate" that is confusing and interpreted differently by different states and by the courts.

Provisions of the Plans to Remove the States and Form Large Departments Instead:

1. **State Lines Would Still Exist but Would be Meaningless:** All state rights and government would be abolished. State lines would be left for sentimental reasons.
2. **Reapportionment of the United States into Ten Departments (Regions):** These would be (eventually) ten great departments, to be locally self-governed but without the power to hamstring the national government in its legislative acts. [In other words, the departments would not have the same states' rights to put any checks or balances on an all-powerful federal government.]

3. **The House of Representatives Would Be Left the Same:** They would still be chosen from the various state districts as now.

4. **The Senators Would be Chosen from the Ten Departments:** Each department would elect the same number of senators by popular vote. Each department could have ten senators, making 100 senators. [This would make the final count in the senate of 100 no different than today where each state gets to elect two senators.]

5. **The Governors Would Govern the Departments:** The governors would be chosen at large by popular vote from the departments they live in. There would only be ten governors that the Federal government then had to deal with and they would be responsible to the President.

6. **City Government and School Boards Would Still Exist:** Local autonomy would still be possible for the election of city councils, who would govern over police, fire protection, sanitation, etc. School boards would still be locally elected and govern over the schools.

7. **Taxation, Economics and a Uniform System of Banking Would be under the Federal Government**. A pro rata share of the national revenue would be given to each department to run their affairs. (It is interesting to see how close we are to this point with the control of all banks under the Federal Reserve and especially now with Obama's nationalization of major large banks. There are also ten designated federal reserve banks to match the ten regions.)

8. **General Social Regulations Would be Under the Federal Government:** This would include a uniform system of marriage and divorce, social insurance, labor regulations, and a uniform system for traffic regulations. [The social issues were left under the jurisdiction of the states, because our wise founding fathers knew that people in a certain area will have different religious beliefs, traditions, and social mores than others. They did not want the federal government dictating to the American citizens everything in their lives. That is why marriage, divorce, education, even traffic regulations including drivers' licenses were left up to the states. Can you imagine how different our nation would be today had the states been abolished back in 1935 and all of these social issues placed under the federal government? Without any state governments to stop them, it would have made it so much easier to impose socialist/liberal ideals on all Americans. We could have had abortion, same-sex marriage, socialized medicine, national ID cards for drivers' licenses, hate speech laws, regulations such as the "Fairness Doctrine" to drive out conservative

media, all sorts of other ills mandated for all of us. Thank goodness that never happened!]

9. **There would be Less Bureaucracy and Less Cost:** Senator Wagner stated, "It would not be any worse than it is now, maybe a little less, with less state governments to have to worry about. Thus it would be less wasteful, more efficient, and cost less." [I'm sorry, without state governments to reign in the power of a large federal government, the bureaucracy could be even greater. Look what is happening to Obama's administration already. Because there is no stopping him from Congress, which is top-heavy with Democrats, Obama has appointed 40 czars, only accountable to him, with no Congressional approval, and they are all receiving salaries around -$170,000 a year. He could go on appointing more and more czars with no stopping him. That is what happens when someone or some entity has unlimited power.]

10. **The Constitution:** According to Senator Wagner, it would not be abolished. There would still be the checks and balance on the Federal government that come from the other two branches of government, legislative and judicial.[87] [Would that really be true? States' rights have been very important for keeping a check on the overstepping power of the Federal government and to help preserve our Constitution. What if you have all three branches of government marching in sequence with each other, with the majority all from the same party, exactly what we have with the Obama administration? That is just one of the reasons the states are needed to protect and stand up for the Constitution when the President, Congress and the Judiciary system no longer are doing so. You will read an example of this in Chapter 18, which tells of many states standing up for their Tenth Amendment Rights against the overstepping power of the Federal government.]

11. [**Abolish the Military and National Guard:** This was not stated by Senator Wagner but I included it, since, according to Bernadine Smith, one of the main reasons FDR and his cronies wanted to abolish the states was to eliminate the National Guard over whom each state has jurisdiction. Eventually, the nation's entire military and all armaments would be eliminated (as was planned for all nations), so only the UN military would remain and would be armed. Why would they want to do that? The main reason for the military is to protect the borders of a nation. The elitists want to do away with borders.][88]

Pride of Statehood and Self Assertiveness Stopped the 1934 Plans for Regions: At the end of Clark's article, he stated that the biggest difficulty trying to implement such a "profound reorganization of our political system is sheer pride of Statehood:" [I add, thank goodness!]

> While generally stronger in the East than in the West, this sentiment is a powerful force. There has appeared of late a remarkable resurgence of State consciousness, a self-assertiveness on the part of States, some of which in the old pre-depression days hardly knew they had boundaries.

Liberal Judges—the Solution to Restructuring Government: However, Clark suggests that if the courts would just rule a little bit more along the line of "social change," maybe such a revision of government and states could be still possible:

> Whether the issue will ever be raised is a moot question. The revisionists may never be heard from publicly—especially if the Federal courts soon experience a miraculous transformation and begin, with unanimity, interpreting law in the light of social change.[89]

Obviously, Clark was of the same liberal mindset himself, or he would not have suggested such a solution to bring about a "miraculous transformation." We also hear the same words coming from Obama. He is all about "transforming" our government, and he is well on his way accomplishing his goals by socializing America. One of his goals is to also appoint liberal judges who will "interpret law in the light of social change." He succeeded in appointing Sonia Sotomayor, who believes in social justice and empathy rather than making decisions according to the Constitution and the Rule of Law. Again let me state, we don't need our government transformed. We need it restored.

Much of what Clark suggested about judges happened earlier with FDR. The liberal judges, whom he appointed and those who have followed them, have helped to transform our nation into a very different place today than what our Founding Fathers had envisioned. Some of the transforming decisions made by those judges were based on no prior precedent such as taking prayer and God out of public school in 1962 and making abortion legal in 1973.

The New Deal Built the New World Order: Such was the title of an article found on a website called "Global Gulag." The article states that "FDR Was the Supreme Socialist. His ideal was the total destruction of the balanced "Federalism" that shared power, affirmed states' rights, and respected individual Liberty." The article mentions all the socialist programs that FDR believed in and implemented during his 12 years as president: expansion of central planning, moving the U.S. towards a collectivist state, creating a huge variety of alphabet soup federal agencies that converted the free enterprise system into a federal despotic system of command and control. He packed the courts to get his socialist goals approved. He enacted social security, unemployment insurance, minimum wages and a 40-hour work week, and created the National Labor Relations Board to protect workers' rights to form unions and other major reforms. (It is the huge power of the unions that have helped to create the enormous debt of such companies as our auto industries that were ready to go bankrupt and have now been taken over by the federal government.)

What FDR Believed: He supported a bill to eliminate the right to bear arms. He told Churchill that "an unwritten Constitution is better than a written one." He did not believe in Constitutional checks and balances, that is why he wanted to destroy the states. He did not believe in representative government and said that Congress did not represent the will of the people and should be ignored. He did not believe in the rule of law and said to his top deputy, KGB agent Harry Hopkins, "I want to assure you that we are not afraid of exploring anything within the law, and we have a lawyer here who will declare anything you want to do legal." As the website states:

> The New Deal was a *coup d'etat* designed by plutocrats for installing an oligarchy, to achieve an autocracy, administered by quisling bureaucrats . . . FDR was a commie soul mate—liberal Democrat style—of Uncle Joe [Stalin].[90]

FDR Took Our Nation Off the Gold Standard: With no gold to back it, the fiat paper money of our nation has become greatly debased, lowered in value and purchasing power by more than 100%. A dollar bill used to say "redeemable in gold." After we were taken off the gold standard, a dollar bill used to say, "redeemable in silver." After we were taken off the silver standard under Nixon, then the dollar used to read, "backed by the full faith and credit of the United States." I just took a look at the money I had in my purse to get the exact words and they are no longer there. I looked at all of my paper money, a dollar, five dollar, ten dollar, and twenty dollar "Federal Reserve Note" and discovered the only words written on them are "This note is legal tender for all debts, public and private." There is nothing written anymore about being backed by the full faith and credit of the United States. Maybe that is because there is no more faith or credit of the United States. The government knows they are bankrupt. At least they are being honest with us with what is written on the currency now. Because of our enormous trillions of dollars of debt, there is nothing left with which to do any backing. In other words, our money is presently worth about as much as the paper on which it has been written. The only words that are left on the present day dollar that resembles the old dollar are the words still written "In God We Trust."

FDR Was the Original Father of the North American Union: Bernadine Smith adds more about FDR: He made 26 speeches in support of world government. His New World (Moral) Order was called the "New Deal." He was the original "father" of the North American Union, wanting to move all the nations of the Western Hemisphere into one government. By 1943, he had Ten Federal Regions operating in the United States, with named persons as chairmen, with funding coming from his National Resource Planning Board. (Thanks to one courageous governor of whom you will read below, this was stopped by Congress.)

FDR's Goal Was to Be the First President of the World: According to Bernadine Smith, FDR was behind the scenes in setting up the United Nations and in world management. He thought because of the important part he played he would be the one selected to the first president of the world. However, before the UN was officially founded in October of 1945 and before he could even sign the UN Charter, he died of a heart attack on April 12, 1945.[91]

FDR's Three Amigos in Charge of Abolishing the States: FDR hired three men to conceive the methodology and the techniques for the gradual step-by-step transformation of the United States into regions and to replace the Republic with a socialist world order. They were Luther H. Gulick, Charles E. Merriam, and Louis Brownlow, and they made up the President's Committee on Administrative Management, 1936-1937. The following is what Luther Gulick said, expressing his view about States:

> Is the state the appropriate instrumentality for the discharge of important functions? The answer is not a matter of conjecture, or delicate appraisal. It's a matter of brutal record: The American state is finished! I do not predict that the states will go. I affirm that they have gone!

The Three Amigos always referred to our Republic as a "democracy." In a book that Merriam wrote, *On the Agenda of Democracy*, he revealed what is really meant by democracy—"the adoption of communist/socialist principles and goals."[92]

1943—The Impact of One Person Standing for Truth—Governor Ralph L. Carr of Colorado: The clandestine plans for regional government were proceeding on schedule until one man spilled the beans and informed the American people of the approaching plans to break up the states by forming regions, destroy the Constitution, our form of government and property rights, thereby creating essentially a dictatorship. In his farewell address to the Colorado State Legislature, Carr warned them of these plans.

His speech was written up in the New York Herald Tribune and began to be the talk of Congress. Most Congressmen denied that they knew anything about these plans, which many found hard to believe because Carr's speech came seven days after FDR's National Resource Planning Board (NRPB) Report was issued to Congress. Carr based his speech on that report. The NRPB was pretending to be all about "protecting natural resources." What it would have done was destroy state government, states' rights and sovereignty. Individual property rights and the hopes and dreams of Americans would have been gone too, without any recourse on their part. The following is an excerpt from Carr's speech:

> There exists in this country today, a plan to commence the remodeling of the lives of American freemen, on a basis so dictatorial, so monarchistic, so bureaucratic, that its very exposition proves its hostility to our American form of government. I predict that, unless something intervenes to stop them, within six months the details will be made public of schemes which will first shock and then absolutely astonish the householders, the taxpayers, the entire American citizenry.[93]

Something did intervene to stop them. The impact of Carr's speech so shook up Congress that they refused to fund the NRPB, and it essentially disappeared from the radar screen. However, once Congress had rejected it, they turned to other matters. No further investigation of the plan took place. Did it die away? No, of course not! No liberal, socialist plan dies away. The plan was just hidden for awhile. The NRPB has continued on. It is no longer centralized from

Washington, but decentralized within the states, as you will read further in this chapter, regional governments are being pushed inside states to break up county and city governments, pretending government will be more "streamlined, and costs will be reduced." In some states, they have succeeded. Regional government is how planning and zoning policies are being forced upon rural areas, restricting and taking away property rights.

Incremental Regionalism by Stealth and Deception through UN Policies and the Environmental Movement: Bernadine Smith adds the following commentary:

> By keeping the people in utter ignorance, what was once a theory in the thirties, thus became an accomplished fact. Dual governments have been in operation since the United Nations Ten Regions were installed. Constitutional government hangs on a thin thread. As soon as our guns get taken away, our Constitution and individual land ownership will cease, which is a stated goal of the United Nations.[94]

1972, February 14: A New Regional Map with Ten Regions—Placing the United States Under the Administrative Control of the UN: By 1972, a new map was produced, this time including the states of Hawaii and Alaska and U.S. Territories. How did this happen? Did Congress vote for such regions to be formed and to be placed under the control of the UN? No, this happened by Executive Order coming from President Nixon, No. 11647. Here are the regions formed:

Region 1—Maine, Vermont, New Hampshire, Massachusetts, Rhode Island, Connecticut.

Region 2—New York and New Jersey (also includes the Virgin Islands and Puerto Rico)

Region 3—Pennsylvania, West Virginia, Virginia, Maryland, Delaware;)

Region 4—Kentucky, Tennessee, N. and S. Carolina, Mississippi, Alabama, Georgia, Florida;

Region 5—Minnesota, Wisconsin, Illinois, Indiana, Michigan, Ohio;

Region 6—Texas, New Mexico, Oklahoma, Arkansas, Louisiana;

Region 7—Kansas, Nebraska, Iowa, Missouri;

Region 8—Montana, Wyoming, Utah, Colorado, North and South Dakota;

Region 9—California, Hawaii, Nevada, and Arizona;
Region 10—Alaska, Washington, Oregon and Idaho

You will read in the chapter about the UN how the regional system is bringing about amazing environmental reforms. States have been forced to accept these regional changes; otherwise they would not get badly needed federal funding. There are regional planning boards that exist in every state, getting their marching orders from, not just the federal government, but from the United Nations. It is also interesting to find out (in the chapter about Robert Pastor) that there are also ten EU education centers located across the USA, to promote the acceptance of the EU, one in each region.

Attack on Local Government—Plans and Attempts to End County and City Governments: Not only are state governments a threat to limiting the all-encompassing power goals of the elitists in control of federal government, but so are the divisions of local control within the states. Thus, there has been an effort to destroy them as well. In the large packet of information that I received from Bernadine Smith were several newspaper clippings telling about attempts to abolish city and county governments and form large regional governments inside the states. Here are summaries of them: (The words "region, regional, or regionalization" are put in bold letters for emphasis.)

Fresno Bee, **September 27, 1987—"Brown Blasts Counties as Outmoded Idea:"** An Associated Press release reports on a speech Assembly Speaker Willie Brown gave to a group of his supporters in San Francisco in which he said, "Counties should be abolished . . . these political subdivisions are wasteful and inefficient." He labeled the counties as "historical accidents" that duplicate each other's services, such as jails, airports, ports and transit systems—agencies that could be "better administered by **regional** authorities."

The article mentions that the 58 counties in California were heavily lobbying Sacramento for additional funds, asking for more state tax revenues to be given to local governments. Brown was against this and was asking for a commission to be appointed by the governor to study this issue and to "revamp" local government.

Los Angeles Times, **October, 25, 1987—"Brown Seeks to Abolish Local Government:"** Again Willie Brown's objections to local governments are mentioned as he asked the Assembly Office of Research to "study his proposal to abolish city and county governments."

Hanford Sentinel, **March 22, 1996, Sacramento—"Ex-governors, Speaker Talk on State's Problems:"** This article was written nine years after Willie Brown first made headlines asking for local government to be abolished. By 1996, he was actually serving as the Mayor of San Francisco, and yet he still was preaching the demise of local government. (San Francisco, however, had already switched to a system where the separate county government had been abolished. They now have supervisors who run both the city and the county, and the mayor oversees all of it.) Here are quotes from the article:

> He [Willie Brown] also said the state needs to overhaul its system of local governments, making greater use of **regionalization** and redrawing counties. 'There clearly needs to be a reconfiguration and a look from a different perspective as to how local government can be financed and can finance themselves . . . . There is zero justification for the continuation of counties as we know them . . . Some are too small, some are too isolated, and some have almost no function at all.'

San Francisco Chronicle, **April 7, 1995,—"New Orange County Plan Would Eliminate Supervisors—Cities, State Would Take Over Most Services:"** (Notice the words "regional government" is not mentioned as to what would really take over most services, but one of the supervisors suggests it later in the article.)

Some residents and leaders of Orange County were so upset with their Board of Supervisors that they were ready to abolish the whole system of county government and just have city government. Why? The Orange County Supervisors had lost $1.7 billion on bad securities investments and had actually been forced to file for bankruptcy. The loss had forced large cutbacks in schools and almost every other public service.

A new interim treasurer, Tom Daxon, had spent three months helping to organize the recovery effort and had suggested that the county consolidate its 31 cities along the lines of Marion County, Indianapolis; Jacksonville and Duval Counties in Florida; and San Francisco City and County, where county supervisors have been eliminated and their authority given over to city council members. (In San Francisco, they are still called supervisors but they run the city and county.)

An aide, David Kiff, was also in favor of eliminating the supervisors. According to him, "The county would save $1.9 million" by doing so, but the biggest saving would be by eliminating county courts—$27 million for trial courts and $23.2 million for the marshal's office. General spending could be cut by about half the $275 million now proposed.

One of the supervisors, Marian Bergeson, a former state senator, was helping in the plan to eliminate the supervisors. She suggested a **regional** service board could take over, but it would probably require amending the state Constitution for that to happen:

> Representatives from cities and other agencies would sit on a **regional** service board to handle parks, sanitation, water, social services, public protection, and other "local" government jobs. A "mayor" would oversee it all. Agencies such as the county's 54 water districts would consolidate. Unincorporated areas would have to join a city or make one.

Other supervisors were not very pleased with the whole idea. Supervisor Roger Stanton said, " . . . the general concept of taking government away from the people—as with a joint powers authority—is cause for concern." Gacci Vasquez said he worried "the process would create new bureaucracies."

Did the elimination of the supervisors and county government ever happen in Orange County? No, thanks to some wise financial advice and help that was given by a sharp businessman, John Moorlach, the county was able to slowly rise out of their serious situation, and county government continued.

John Moorlach had run against Robert Citron, the incumbent county treasurer in the election of 1994, speaking out about the approaching financial crisis that would happen if the treasurer and county finances did not change course. However, the people did not heed his warning; he lost the election and everything he predicted came true in December of that very year. Citron resigned in disgrace. The interim treasurer that the article mentioned, Tom Daxon, was there only a few months. Fortunately his suggestion for dissolving county government was not heeded.

Moorlach was asked to become the official treasurer which he accepted. Moorlach was able to help the county get through Chapter 9 bankruptcy filing, restructure and they are still afloat as a county. They have a huge bankruptcy debt to pay back of $89 million a year. They are running a tight ship, but they are able to do it. Moorlach was elected in 2006 as a County Supervisor where he is the head of the financial department, so he can still oversee what is going on. He says his claim to fame is he predicted the biggest crash in county government finances, and he has participated in the biggest fiscal recovery of a county in U.S. history.[95]

The following is what was printed of Moorlach by the *Orange County Registrar* in 2003 when he was running for County Supervisor:

> Mr. Moorlach is well-known for having predicted in 1994 that investments by then-Treasurer Robert Citron were headed for trouble. His warnings weren't heeded, the county experienced a bankruptcy . . . Mr. Moorlach's predications came true, and Mr. Moorlach was appointed, then elected and re-elected treasurer . . . He retains his reputation as a white knight, someone known for his sound judgment and integrity. But Mr. Moorlach also is known for his wry wit, strong opinions and willingness to speak out about important matters, regardless of the political consequences. (*The Orange County Register,* July 24, 2003)

San Diego Union Tribune, **November 11, 1995, "Streamlined Regional Government Proposed, Study Group Suggests Election to Abolish City, County System" by Caitlin Fother:** Yet another attempt was reported at abolishing local government in California, this time in San Diego. Some of the same reasons were given as with other counties and cities, "too many layers of government," resulting in "gridlock, overlap, duplication, and redundancy." The solution? Get rid of the San Diego County Board of Supervisors and all of the city councils and switch to a "streamlined, **regional** government."

These "wise words" were being suggested by the "San Diego **Region** Citizens' Commission on Local Government Efficiency and Restructuring," which was submitted after their "20 months' study." I wonder what they were studying? It certainly wasn't the U.S. Constitution, or American History and the wonderful advantages that we have had in personal liberty because of local, representative government. Could their 20 months' study have been the before-mentioned book by Joseph Stalin, *Marxism and the National Question,"* which told how important regional government was as a transition to total world government? Perhaps they were studying FDR's plan for regional government?

The report recommends that restructuring be done one step at a time.

1) A **regional** board should be created to replace the county board of supervisors. It would be responsible for planning, policy making, delivery of services and evaluation of performance.
2) Second, community councils would replace city councils and would handle such things as land-use permits, park policies, and community policy.

The article does mention four things that the group had found in their "study" that are supposedly so serious that county and city government must be abolished: (My rebuttal to these four things are added in brackets.)

- The San Diego **region** is governed by more than 865 elected officials. [That is actually good for such a large county with a population of over 3 million. According to the US census website, as of 2008, San Diego county has 3,001,072 people.[96] Rounded off that means there is one representative for every 3500 people. If one believes in local representation, there should be a large number to represent so many people.]
- The trash system is at best, not a system—and at worst, is a shamble. [And large **regional** government is going to make that work better? What you need are more and smaller systems, so you can have competition, which always improves quality. A monopoly is just the opposite. It takes away incentives and quality goes down.]
- No single flood-control agency exists, nor is there much coordination, cooperation, or planning among the agencies that do operate. [And why should there be one single flood control agency? Is it not better to have many agencies who can respond quickly to the needs of their own local citizens in their own areas?]
- There is no comprehensive **regional** planning effort with regards to the homeless. [And why would such a thing be necessary? Again, many different local churches and relief organizations should be available for the homeless. Is that not better than one large, **regional** agency? Homeless people usually don't have any transportation. They need to be helped by people and agencies closest to them.]

Boston Herald, July 12, 1997, "Weld Signs Law Ending All County Government," by Maggie Mulvihill: According to this article, the Governor of Massachusetts, William F. Weld, signed into law a historic bill to abolish county government in Massachusetts, adding his own measure to ensure its elimination by 1999. Why was this happening? The governor said it was because "the counties have become obsolete, with inward-looking bureaucracies, with dozens of departments and department heads that serve themselves, and not the taxpayer." [And is state or regional government any less self-serving?]

Weld further states, "The legislation we are signing today is a good first step in eliminating vestiges of Massachusetts colonial government." (And what was so bad about colonial government? That was what helped launch our wonderful form of local government, getting things done closest to the people, exactly how representative government is supposed to be as envisioned by our founding fathers.)

Of course, the real reason for Weld's action was concerning money. Several counties were in great debt and were soon to declare bankruptcy, starting with Middlesex County that had defaulted on $4.5 million in bonds. Middlesex County would be immediately eliminated and the state would assume its debt. Worcester and Hampden Counties would be eliminated a year later or sooner if they defaulted on their payments. Weld said that "current inefficiency of the county government system, laden with patronage and poor fiscal management, had accumulated approximately $45 million in debt statewide."

Sections of the bill approved by the state legislature had been vetoed by the governor. These would have allowed ten counties to establish local commissions to rewrite their charters and go on functioning. No, Weld said that would only preserve a "bloated *status quo* and allow counties to continue to unnecessarily soak up taxpayer funds."

The article ends with the following quote from Governor Weld, "County government has been around Massachusetts as long as the Weld family, but while great-great-grandfather Weld's hunting jacket has not yet lost its usefulness, counties, I'm sorry to say, have."[97]

A Few County Governments Are Still Allowed in Massachusetts, Most Have Formed Regional Governments: I discovered a follow up article about Governor Weld and the law he signed abolishing the counties. According to the article, a few solvent counties were able to go on functioning:

> The law in Massachusetts still allows for communities to form
> **regional** compacts and governmental entities, but allowed a number
> of counties to continue. Traditional and modern County and **regional**
> governments still exist in Southeastern Massachusetts. Barnstable
> County, Massachusetts, which is Cape Cod, functions as a modern
> **regional** government and fulfills a number of **regional** services.

One county that was dissolved was Worcester. It exists today only as a historical geographic region. It has had no county government since July 1, 1998 [the year after Governor Weld signed his law into effect], when all former county functions were assumed by other governmental agencies. The article describes how Worcester functions:

There are vestiges of the old system: for example, county sheriffs are still elected but are under the state Executive Office of Public Safety. The office of district attorney is effectively a county-wide position even though the district may include one town from a neighboring county. There is not, however, a county council or a commissioner. Communities are now granted the right to form their own **regional** compacts for sharing services. The geographic area of Worcester County is covered by two **regional** planning commissions: Central Massachusetts (centered on the city of Worcester) and Montachusett (centered on the cities of Leominster and Fitchburg).

Why Did Massachusetts Abolish Most of Their County Governments? According to the article it was to save costs, but also since cities were so close together and densely populated, county governments were less essential. The states of Connecticut and Rhode Island have also gotten rid of their county governments.

Why City and County Governments Have Not Lost Their Usefulness and Are Still Needed: I personally think if Governor Weld's great-great grandfather was a loyal, patriotic American and proud citizen of Massachusetts, he probably was rolling over in his grave wondering what whacky idea had gotten into his great-great grandson's head to support and sign into law a bill to abolish county governments.

Grandfather Weld would be joined by countless others. So many of our brilliant founding fathers came from Massachusetts, such as John Adams and his cousin, Sam Adams. John Adams was the Second President of the United States. Sam was the one who instigated the Boston Tea Party. They would both be lamenting what was happening to local representative government, which they had worked so hard to establish for our nation.

Massachusetts had a great legacy as the birthplace for such government and for private ownership of property and the "free enterprise system." This is what had helped the Pilgrims to flourish and they passed it on to others who followed them.

Massachusetts was also the home of the Boston Tea Party, where the first stand was taken against an all-powerful tyrannical big government. The colonists had learned from Great Britain that the bigger the government, the more power is exercised over the people. That is why they wanted local government, strong states rights and a weaker federal government. Each state was divided into counties, and counties contained various cities. Our founding fathers strongly believed that the most efficient government and the one that provided the most freedoms and happiness was the one closest to the people. Local elected representatives for the county board of supervisors, city councils and school boards were far better than one big regional government, where the people would have little say in whom represented them or what policies were being passed.

Just as state governments have served as counterbalances and checks on the power of the federal government, city and county governments have helped reign in all-powerful state governments and central control. Governor Weld, however, decided he and his state legislators knew better; they could throw overboard the established wise policies of local representative government and establish bigger government, just as their founding fathers had thrown over the tea in protest against such big government—what irony!

Where Did Our Founding Fathers Receive the Inspiration for Limited, Local, Representative Government? More is written in greater detail in *The Incremental Chipping Away of the Once Great USA* about the research that our founding fathers did on what form of government they wanted for our country. To summarize, our founding fathers decided the only examples of true representative government that truly worked in history and what they wanted to duplicate for our nation were two: 1) what was established by Moses and his father-in-law, Jethro, to govern the vast number, about 3 million, of the Twelve Tribes of Israel after they left Egypt; and 2) the form of government that the Anglo-Saxons had brought to England back in 400 AD. Both were based on representative government closest to the people. A leader was chosen by the people over ten families; another leader was chosen over fifty families; another over 100 families; another over 1000 families. Those leaders would make the decisions for their jurisdiction. Only the most difficult and complicated matters were then brought to Moses, or to the Chiefs of the Anglo Saxons.

The Children of Israel and the people governed under the Anglo Saxons were the happiest and most content with their local representative governments. Their leaders were accessible, close by, problems solved quickly, and people were allowed to live in relative peace, freedom, and harmony. That is what our founding fathers wanted for our country and why they established our government as they did.[98]

Massachusetts State Senate Passed a Resolution for the USA to Become Part of a World Federation: Not only would the founding fathers from Massachusetts be rolling over in their graves about their great grandchildren passing laws to abolish the county system and form even bigger state government, but how about their forming the biggest government of all—world government? The following is a copy of a state senate resolution passed in Massachusetts, May 13, 1992 (at the same time that Governor Weld was in office) and signed by the President of the Senate, the Clerk, and the Senator proposing the resolution:

The Commonwealth of Massachusetts

RESOLUTIONS MEMORIALIZING THE CONGRESS OF THE UNITED STATES TO INITIATE THE CONSTITUTIONAL PROCEDURES TO ENABLE THE UNITED STATES TO PARTICIPATE IN A REPRESENTATIVE WORLD FEDERAL GOVERNMENT.

WHEREAS, GLOBAL TRANQUILITY REQUIRES AN INTERNATIONAL BODY ELECTED ON A REPRESENTATIVE BASIS FROM AMONG WORLD GOVERNMENTS; AND

WHEREAS, THE ESTABLISHMENT OF SUCH A BODY MAY REQUIRE AMENDMENTS TO THE CONSTITUTION OF THE UNITED STATES AND THE CHARTER OF THE UNITED NATIONS; AND

WHEREAS, ARTICLE V OF THE CONSTITUTION OF THE UNITED STATES EMPOWERS THE CONGRESS OF THE UNITED STATES TO PROPOSE AMENDMENTS TO THE CONSTITUTION; NOW THEREFORE BE IT

RESOLVED, THAT THE MASSACHUSETTS SENATE CALLS UPON THE CONGRESS OF THE UNITED STATES TO PROPOSE AMENDMENTS TO THE CONSTITUTION OF THE UNITED STATES WHICH WILL ENABLE PARTICIPATION IN A REPRESENTATIVE WORLD FEDERAL GOVERNMENT; AND BE IT FURTHER

RESOLVED, THAT A COPY OF THESE RESOLUTIONS BE TRANSMITTED FORTHWITH BY THE CLERK OF THE SENATE TO THE PRESIDENT OF THE UNITED STATES, THE PRESIDING OFFICER OF EACH BRANCH OF CONGRESS AND THE MEMBERS THEREOF FROM THE COMMONWEALTH.

Senate Adopted May 13, 1992

William M. Bulger, Senate President
Edward B. O'Neil, Senate Clerk
Senator Frederick E. Berry

Below is a copy of the signatures of the Senators who signed the resolution with the great seal of the Commonwealth of Massachusetts at the left.

SENATE, ADOPTED, MAY 13, 1992.

PRESIDENT OF THE SENATE

CLERK OF THE SENATE

OFFERED BY:

SENATOR FREDERICK E. BERRY

It is hard for most Americans to believe that elected officials would actually come up with such an idea—to propose that an amendment to our precious Constitution be added essentially destroying the Constitution itself and our nation—moving us into a World Federation.

You will also read in the end of Chapter 17 on "The Timeline Towards a Regional Merger," that there is a prediction by a respected Russian economist, there could be a breakup of the USA into regions as early as the spring of 2010. This would be caused by the financial crisis and the terrible conditions that some of our states are finding themselves in, such as California, with $42 billion dollar debt at the beginning of 2009 and rising. Some state governments will no longer be able to stay solvent, and the federal government will no longer have the funds to bail them out. He compares the condition of our nation to what was going on in the Soviet Union before it had its crash in December of 1991.

This is all part of the plan of devolution, that you read about in Chapter 4. England and other countries are being broken up into regions, and the EU will only deal with their carefully selected ministers from those regions for any funding, bypassing county and even central governments.

Obama's Executive Order Sets Up Ten Military Governors in Preparation for Martial Law: Just before this book was in its final stage for publication, I received an e-mail from my friend in Canada, Connie Fogal, telling me of an Obama executive order, signed January 11, 2010, "Section 1822, of the National Defense Authorization Act of 2008, Public Law 110-181," which can be found at the government website http://www.whitehouse.gov/sites/default/files/2010executive_order.pdf.

According to the article sent, this executive order is essentially creating a military structure underneath ten appointed governors that will coincide with the ten FEMA (Federal Emergency Management Agency) regions already established.

The governors will come under the direct authority of the Secretary of Defense and the Department of Homeland Security. Could this be another ploy to break us up into ten regions and get us away from state government with states' rights and state national guards, designed to protect the state structure?

The author of the article believes this will be used to "destroy the Constitution and the Bill of Rights and to render each American effectively into nothing more than a member of a work gang, subject to control of the Regional Military Governor, who is under the Secretary of Defense, who is under the President." Posse Comitatus will be dead, Habeas Corpus dead, the Bill of Rights dead, and only the whims and subjective decisions of the Regional Military Governor, as directed by the President will be "the Iron Fist Rule of the Land." This will, of course, be via the Secretary of Defense and Secretary of Homeland Security, as executed by Northcom troopers, who now include U.S., Canadian, Mexican, and other Foreign troops as well as mercenaries, the states' National Guards, Militias, and Police agencies all lumped together. (http://www.stevequayle.com/News.alert/08_Hawk/100112.Obama.EO.html; http://shutking.blogspot.com/2010/01/breaking-news-obama-signs-martial-law.html.)

As you will read in the next chapter, such plans have been in the works for a long time. Breaking up, dividing and conquering nation states, forming regional and eventually world government have been the agenda of the United Nations from the very beginning of its existence.

Chapter Eight

The United Nations

Its Founding, Structure and Ultimate Purpose; Treaties and Conferences Promoting Regional and World Government; Using the Green Movement for a "Green World Order"

From where is this movement to break up our nation, to move us towards a regional government coming? What has been trying for years, since its inception, to destroy our form of government, our Constitutional Republic, our free enterprise system, our property rights? What has been moving us closer to socialism, globalism and the destruction of our borders and national sovereignty? What was behind the movement to form the European Union, pushing it along from the beginning? That's right—the United Nations. The UN is really the power behind regionalism and globalism over the whole world.

As an example, I start off with a "Summit of the Americas," held April 22, 2001, in Quebec, Canada, where George W. Bush signed the "Declaration of Quebec City," pledging his "commitment to hemispheric integration" and his "commitment and adherence to the principles and purposes of the Charter of the **United Nations . . .**"

This was also where President Bush made an impassioned plea for the heads of the other 34 American countries to join him in trying to ram through the Free Trade Area of the Americas (FTAA), which would have been one large free trade agreement for all of north, south, central America and would have made it much easier to form a large American Union like the EU. Fortunately, enough people fought the FTAA in our nation and it was never passed. Here is what was written on the website about the "Declaration of Quebec City (emphasis added):

Declaration of Quebec City

We, the democratically elected Heads of State and Government of the Americas, have met in Quebec City at our Third Summit, to **renew our commitment to hemispheric integration** and national and collective responsibility for improving the economic well-being and security of our people. We have adopted a Plan of Action to strengthen representative democracy, promote good governance and protect human rights and fundamental freedoms. We seek to create greater prosperity and expand economic opportunities while **fostering social justice** and the realization of human potential.

We reiterate **our firm commitment and adherence** to the principles and purposes of the Charters of the **United Nations** and of the Organization of American States (OAS) . . . [99]

History of the United Nations—How it Got its Start

1940—The Commission to Study the Organization of Peace—The Ultimate Goal Was Kept Quiet: As World War II was drawing to an end, a commission was set up to plan the organization of an international society. Its purpose was to design a new world order, and to serve as a sort of information agency on world affairs for the general public. Its members, of course, would not tell the public about the goal for world government until they were properly prepared. One of its leaders was Quincy Wright from the University of Chicago. The following is a very revealing statement that he made to the *Daily Maroon*, the student newspaper at the University of Chicago. Notice the same attack on nationhood and sovereignty as those who were promoting the forming of a European Union:

> In order to establish permanent peace in the world, it is necessary to
> stop the clustering of all political loyalties around the same symbols.
> My point was that excessive loyalties to certain sacred cows, such
> as sovereignty, nationality, neutrality, and domestic jurisdiction is
> ruining civilization.[100]

August 14, 1941—The Atlantic Charter was Signed by President Roosevelt and Winston Churchill: This committed the two countries to a "permanent system of general security."

October 30, 1943—The Moscow Declaration was Signed: Russia joined the allies in declaring the necessity of establishing an international organization to maintain peace and security.[101] Notice it is exactly as the Gomberg Map Objectives stated—The USA, Britain, and the Soviet Union would be in charge of establishing a world organization "to guarantee peace to the nations."

July, 1944—Bretton Woods, New Hampshire, the International Monetary Fund (IMF) and World Bank Were Established (Forerunners to and Part of the United Nations): The announced purposes for these organizations sounded very admirable—the World Bank was to make loans to war-torn and undeveloped nations so they could build stronger economies. The IMF was to promote monetary cooperation between nations by maintaining fixed exchange rates between their currencies. How would they do that? An excellent book that gives much of the background on the IMF, the World Bank, and the Federal Reserve is *The Creature of Jekyll Isand*, by Edward J. Griffin. Griffin answers the question of how the IMF would maintain fixed exchange rates:

> Terminate the use of gold as the basis for their currencies and replace it with a politically manipulated paper standard. In other words, it was to allow governments to escape the discipline of gold so they could create money out of nothing without paying the penalty of having their currencies drop in value on world markets.

Politicians and bankers hated when a country was on the gold exchange standard. That meant the exchange rates of various currencies were determined by how much gold they could buy on the open market. The value of such currencies was set by supply and demand on the open market and was beyond what the politician and bankers could manipulate. By doing away with the gold standard, they could do what they had already done for the United States, but now on a global basis—create money out of nothing, a common fiat money, for all nations and then require them to inflate together at the same rate.

The Chief Architects of the IMF and World Bank: Harry Dexter White, Assistant Secretary of Treasury for the United States, and his assistant Virginius Frank Coe (who both turned out to be Communist spies working along with the Soviet Agent Alger Hiss), were the main players in the design for the IMF and the World Bank. They were joined by John Maynard Keynes, an economist and well-known Fabian from England.

The Fabians were an elite group of intellectuals who formed a semi-secret society for the purpose of bringing socialism to the world, but more slowly through propaganda and legislation, rather than a revolution as the communists would prefer. The Fabians never used the word socialism, but welfare, medical care, better working conditions, etc. To emphasize the importance of gradualism in promoting their cause, they adopted the turtle as the symbol of their movement. They have essentially taken over the entire Labor Party now in England.[102] (More is written about the beginning and history of the Fabian Socialists in a Chapter Ten.)

The Socialist, Revolutionary Agenda: Through the actions over the years, the true agendas of the IMF and World Bank are being revealed. They have been subsidizing global socialist revolutions for decades. Cato Institute researcher Doug Bandow pointed out in 1994 that all the countries which have been relying on IMF aid for more than 30 years are all socialist countries: "Chile, Egypt, India, Sudan, Turkey, and Yugoslavia, Bangladesh, Barbados, Gambia, Guinea-Bissau, Pakistan, Urganda, Zaire, and Zambia." Billions of money has also have been siphoned into former "communist" countries of Russia and its Warsaw Pact allies, which are still run by Communists, but who now call themselves "reformers."[103]

Funding Terrorism, Revolutions, and Organized Crime: Much of the money the IMF gives to each of these socialist nations has been funneled into revolutionary groups, terrorist organizations and groups like the Russian mafia, fueling massive criminal activities. A video put out by the United Nations called "Armed to the Teeth," is a propaganda piece against "small arms," vilifying guns that are being used for killing millions of people across the globe. The video never reveals where the countries are getting the money with which to purchase those guns or the training for their revolutionaries. The funds are coming from the IMF and the World Bank. Thus, the United Nations and its institutions, particularly the IMF and the World Bank, were the ones most responsible for the chaos and revolution portrayed in the bloody scenes of their own video.[104]

From Which Countries Does Most of the IMF Funding Come? "From each according to his ability, to each according to his needs"—this famous communist quote is certainly alive and well and is being practiced by the IMF. The IMF is funded on a quota basis by its member nations, almost two hundred in number. But, of course, the greatest share of capital comes from the more highly industrialized nations, such as: the United States, Great Britain, Japan, France, and Germany. The U.S. contributes the most, twenty percent of the total. In reality, that twenty percent represents about twice that amount, because most of the other nations contribute worthless currencies which no one wants. "One of the routine operations of the IMF is to exchange worthless currencies for dollars so the weaker countries can pay their international bills."[105] (I wonder what is planned as the value of the US dollar continues to shrink and approaches the category of "worthless currency?")

1944, August—Dumbarton Oaks, Georgetown, United Nations Charter was Created: Members of the state departments of the United States, Great Britain and the Soviet Union met for many days under a cloak of secrecy to work on the plans for a "postwar security arrangement for an organization that would prevent future wars." That's what had been told to the U.S. Congress, anyway. However, no one could find out if that was really true. Not even one American senator was allowed in, nor was the press allowed, except for the opening ceremonies. A year later the charter was sent out to nations of the world. Fifty nations signed it including the United States. In the U.S. Senate, only two votes were cast against it.[106]

The Vote by the U.S. Senate to Ratify the UN Charter Treaty was Done by "Fast Track:" The Senators were only given three days before they had to vote on the UN Charter Treaty. During those three days the senators were given much false information about the UN by John Foster Dulles, Secretary of State, and his crew of one-worlders who lied and mislead the senators. Dulles was a member of one of the top 13 American Illuminati families and was hand picked for this assignment by the elite Committee of 300. (You will read about both of these groups in a following chapter.) Dulles had the support of Senator W. Lucas, representing the wealthy Wall Street bankers in the Senate. [107]

What is the UN Charter Like? According to those in the know, the UN charter is purely a Marxist-Leninist blueprint. This is what was said of it by a former top Communist Party leader, Joseph Z. Kornfeder, who testified before Congress in 1955.

> . . . the UN blueprint is a Communist one. I was at the Moscow headquarters of the world Communist party for nearly three years and was acquainted with most of the top leaders . . . I went to their colleges; I learned their pattern of operations, and if I see that pattern in effect anywhere, I can recognize it . . . They [the master designers] and the Kremlin masterminds behind them never intended the UN as a peace-keeping organization. What they had in mind was a fancy and colossal Trojan horse . . . Its [the UN's] internal setup, Communist designed, is a pattern for sociological conquest; a pattern

aimed to serve the purpose of Communist penetration of the West.
It is ingenious and deceptive.

Even a former UN Secretary-General, U Thant, a Burmese Marxist and
winner of the Soviet Union's Lenin Peace Prize, stated that the aims of the
UN Charter were the same as those of the Communist leader Lenin: "**Lenin's
ideals of peace and peaceful coexistence among states have won widespread
international acceptance and they are in line with the aims of the UN
Charter.**" But what does "peace" really mean? According to author, Bill Jasper,
"It is of utmost importance to keep in mind that "peace" in Marxist-Leninist
terms, does not mean an absence of war, but an absence of resistance to
Communism."[108]

Here is what Dr. John Coleman adds about the UN Charter and its similarity
to Communist Documents:

> A critical examination of the UN Charter shows that it differs
> only very slightly from the *Communist Manifesto* of 1848, an
> unabridged, unaltered copy of which is kept in the British Museum
> in London.[109]

UN Charter Treaty Violates the US Constitution: According to Professor
Herman von Holst, in his book, *Constitutional Law of the United States,* the
power exists under the Constitution to make treaties with foreign countries.
The UN does not qualify; it is not a country. Nor can the Senate or House
give substance to a treaty that is creating an entity greater than Congress itself,
which the UN purports to be. Von Holst also writes that every treaty must be
consistent with a provision in the Constitution. If not, it is "not admissible; it
is ipso facto, null and void." Von Holst continues:

> The United Nations treaty violates at least a dozen provisions of the
> Constitution, and since a "treaty" cannot override the Constitution,
> each and every one of its Security Council resolutions, are null and
> void in so far as they affect the United States. This includes our alleged
> membership in this parasitical organization. The United States has
> never been a member of the United Nations, is not now, and can
> never be, save and except where we, the people agree to have the
> Constitution amended by the Senate and ratified by all the States,
> to permit membership in the United Nations.[110]

1945, October 25, San Francisco, CA—The United Nations Was Officially Founded: In spite of the unconstitutionality of the UN Treaty, the obviously misinformed U.S. Senators ratified it, as did governments of nations around the world. The UN Charter was ratified, the IMF and the World Bank were established; thus the official founding of the UN was just a mere formality. In San Francisco, the elitists celebrated the birth of their baby "behemoth" that was hoped would grow into a very powerful world government.

The Founders of the United Nations: In laying the groundwork for the UN, all of the U.S. members of the steering committee were from the state department and all were members of the (then) secretive Council on Foreign Relations (CFR) except for one, Secretary of State Cordel Hull. Later, at the founding day in San Francisco, October 24, 1945, all 43 of the U.S. delegates were members of the CFR, with the exception of one. (More is written about the CFR, its founding, goals, and the profound effect it has had on the chipping away of our form of government in the next chapter.)

Alger Hiss, One of the CFR Members Who Served as the Acting Secretary-General, Was Later Proven to be a Spy, a Secret Soviet Agent. He also played a key role, serving as the Executive in drafting the UN charter at the Dumbarton Oaks Conference in 1944.

President Harry Truman: Truman became President after FDR died and signed the United Nations Charter, "knowing full well that the U.N. was designed to become the government of the world."[111]

What is the Purpose of the United Nations? Children in the public schools are told that the UN was created as the "last best hope for world peace." They are told how "visionary men" from many nations came together after World War II to form an organization that would prevent such a war from ever happening again.

The truth is the UN was entirely a creature of socialists, communists, and other globalist who belonged to such quasi-secret organizations as the CFR, the Roundtable group and the Fabians from England. It was created for purposes entirely different than what is taught in our schools. It was created as a vehicle to accumulate and usurp power so that it eventually would become the vehicle for imposing world government over the entire world.

Propaganda promoting the UN is similar to what was used as the reasons for forming the European Union. "National sovereignty and nationalism create wars." Therefore, what is the solution to war?—Do away with nation states and form a one-world government. The UN was to be the nerve center, "coordinating the growth of a whole host of international organizations into bona fide instruments of world government." The creators of it "planned a world ruled and managed by them, using any means possible."[112]

What Ever Happened to the United Nations Ending all Wars—Isn't That the Reason for which the United Nations was Established? In the preamble to the UN Charter, there are several statements about their objectives to save people from war and to maintain peace. However, notice the last one cited:

> *"We the peoples of the United Nations determined—to save succeeding generations from the scourge of war, which twice in our lifetime has brought untold sorrow to mankind . . . to practice tolerance and to live together in peace with one another as good neighbors, and to unite our strength to maintain international peace and security, and to ensure . . . that armed forces will not be used, save in the common interest.*[113]

Most of these words in the preamble sound nice, words with which most people could agree, except for the last sentence—"**armed forces will not be used, save in the common interest**." Who gets to determine what the common interest is? What if the common interest of the United Nations is a communist dictatorship and world government—which it is—then, of course, armed forces can be used against any nation or community or group standing in the way of that "interest." The proof of the objectives of an organization is in their actions. Has the UN really prevented any wars? It appears to be just the opposite. According to the Wikipedia Website, there have been 141 wars across the globe since the UN was created back in 1945. Wars seem to be on the rise.[114]

Could it be that the UN was Actually Created to Foment War? Why? Because through war amazing changes can take place; governments can be toppled; central banks can be established, and socialist, communist, dictator regimes put in place. Such regimes are easier to control and easier to bring under one-world domination. As you will read in the chapter on the financial crisis, it is very important in the elitist's agenda for world government to first have in place a world central bank and economic dominion. Every nation needs to be under the control of a central bank, through which the World Bank can operate. Did you know that before the Iraq War, Sudam Husain refused to allow a central bank in his country? Now that the old regime is toppled, guess what Iraq has? A central bank.

And wars are very costly. The nations have to go to banks to borrow money; thus the wealthy bankers are very happy when nations are at war and they are happy to fund both sides to keep the wars going.

As you will read later, a belief in population control is shared by most of the elite who helped in the founding of the UN and continue in their support of it. War is a very good way to decrease the population. Millions of soldiers and many civilians are killed during war.

Support of the United Nations and World Government by the NEA, National Education Association: One of the founding members of the UN, who served as an education consultant, was William C. Carr, Associate Secretary of the NEA. A few months after the founding of the United Nations, the NEA began teaching the concept of world government to their teachers. Here is what appeared in the January, 1946, NEA Journal entitled "The Teacher and World Government," written by the editor, Joy Elmer Morgan:

> *In the struggle to establish an adequate world government, the teacher has many parts to play. He must begin with his own attitude and knowledge and purpose. He can do much to prepare the hearts and minds of children for global understanding and cooperation . . . At the very top of all the agencies which will assure the coming of **world government** must stand the school, the teacher, and the organized profession.*[115]

How the United Nations Moves Its One-World Government Agenda Forward: The UN promoters discovered that the world was not quite ready to give up their sovereignty, even after the terrible World War II. It was going to take longer and would have to involve more cunning strategies to promote world government. Those strategies have come through many different UN agencies and treaties (also called conventions) that are promoting the globalist agenda. Here is a summation of some of the most influential agencies and treaties since the UN was founded in 1945:

Influential UN Agencies and NGOs (Non-Governmental Organizations):

UNESCO (UN Educational, Scientific, and Cultural Organization)— Established in 1945: Its main purpose was to construct a world-wide education (or indoctrination) program to prepare the world for global governance. (Notice how they are using the word "governance" instead of government. It sounds a little less overbearing.) " . . . the Conference of Allied Ministers of Education called for a United Nations Bureau of Education." UNESCO became that bureau, essentially "the Board of Education for the world." Every nation was to have a national or federal department of education that would then be under the auspices of UNESCO. In total violation of the US Constitution, which leaves education (as coming under the 10th Amendment) under the jurisdiction of the states, the US finally succeeded in obtaining a Federal Department of Education under President Carter in 1980, as a payback to the NEA for their help in getting Carter elected.

Quotes by Government Officials and UNESCO Leaders against Nationalism and Sovereignty:

> We are at the beginning of a long process of breaking down the walls of national sovereignty. UNESCO must be the pioneer. (Spoken by William Benton, Assistant U.S. Secretary of State, at a UNESCO meeting in 1946.)[116]

> As long as the child breathes the poisoned air of nationalism, education in world-mindedness can produce only precarious results. As we have pointed out, it is frequently the family that infects the child with extreme nationalism. The school should therefore use the means described earlier to combat family attitudes that favor jingoism [aggressive foreign policy that might lead to war with other nations] . . . We shall presently recognize in nationalism the major obstacles to development of world mindedness. (Written in a UNESCO publication in 1949.) [117]

1. **IUCN (International Union for the Conservation of Nature):** The IUCN was established in 1948 by Julian Huxley and his good friend, Max Nicholson, both were members of the Royal Institute of International Affairs. The IUCN drew heavily from the 50 year old British "Fauna and Flora Preservation Society" for its leadership, funding and for its members. The IUCN was instrumental in the formation of the World Wildlife Fund (WWF) in 1961 and the World Resources Institute (WRI) in 1982. These three NGOs are using the excuse of protecting the environment and the world's resources to essentially do what Gomberg's Map, Objective No 39, suggests, the takeover of "all natural resources and equitable distribution of the same for all nations—everywhere in the world." According to Henry

Lamb, an expert on the pervasive takeover of private property rights that is coming from such UN programs, "These three NGOs [IUCN, WWF, and WRI] have become the driving force behind global governance."[118]

2. **UNICEF (UN International Emergency Children's Fund):** UNICEF was created in 1946 to supposedly provide emergency relief to the child victims of World War II. In 1950, it was reauthorized to shift its emphasis to programs of long term benefit to children in underdeveloped countries, and in 1953, it became a permanent entity of the UN. UNESCO's purpose was to educate the world; UNICEF became the fund-raising device to deliver the education to the children.

3. **UNEPTA (UN Expanded Program of Technical Assistance):** It was established in 1949. In 1959, its name was changed to the UNDP (UN Development Program). Its stated purpose is to "promote higher standards of living, full employment, and conditions of economic, social progress and development. More than $1 billion is spent annually on this program in developing countries. (One would think that if that is the case since 1949 or 1959, surely more progress would have been made helping these nations—$50 billion spent over the last 50 years. Much could have been done with that money. However, we have also found out that there is a great deal of corruption and fraud in the UN and much of the money is given to governments of these poor countries, and the poor never see a dime of it.)

Some of the Remaining 130 UN Agencies and NGOs: The following have been lumped together to show how varied their roles are and how vast: Their names explain pretty much what their various assignments are. They cover every aspect of "governance" one could ever imagine: UN Relief and Works Agency (UNRWA)—1949; UN High Commissioner for Refugees (UNHCR)—1951; UN Food and Agricultural Organization (FAO)—1946; UN International Atomic Energy Agency (IAEA)—1953; UN International Civil Aviation Organization (ICAO)—1947; UN International Labor Organization (ILO)—1948; UN International Maritime Organization (IMO)—1947; UN Universal Postal Union (UPU)—1948; The UN World Health Organization (WHO)—1948; The International Telecommunications Union (ITU); UN Industrial Development Organization (UNIDO)—1966; The World Intellectual Property Organization (WIPO)—1967; UN Environment Program (UNEP)—1973.

Important UN Declarations and Resolutions:

Universal Declaration of Human Rights (UDHR), Its Promotion in American Schools and the Degradation of the Bill of Rights: The UDHR was adopted by the General Assembly on Dec. 10, 1948. It is a list of 30 articles that "set forth the basic civil, economic, political, and social rights and freedoms of every person" . . . "that people are born free and equal in dignity and in rights." Its preamble states that the declaration is meant to serve "as a common standard of achievement for all peoples and all nations." The 30 articles listed sound very good, so good that they are being promoted in our public schools above the US Bill of rights. In most history and government classes in our public schools and universities, this document is taught as the major list of human rights and the U.S. Bill of Rights is ignored or hardly mentioned.

Usually, if the Bill of Rights is taught, it is taught as a list of negative rights, while the UN rights are positive. One UN biased textbook, from which I have had to teach, which has a version for both middle school and high school, is called *We The People, The Citizen and the Constitution*. It is funded by the U.S. federal government and written by a government-appointed and authorized group called "the Center for Civic Education," of Calabasas, California.

The text only partially mentions some of the Bill of Rights (the students never get to see all Ten Amendments), but the students do get to read all 30 of the UDHR, which is published in the Reference Section of the book. The text asks the question, "What is the difference between positive and negative rights?" It does state accurately that negative rights "are restraints on the power of government and prevent government from taking away rights that citizens already possess." However, it then states, "Positive rights require a government to actively secure benefits for its citizens such as economic security, health care, or a clean environment." In other words, governments should be promoting socialism and communism, where all is "supposedly" provided for the citizen. [119]

The Bill of Rights are also spoken of as out-moded, while the UN UDHR are more updated and closer to our time. " . . . the Bills of Rights is a document of the eighteenth century, reflecting the issues and concerns of the age in which it was written."[120]

The textbook later asks the question, "How do the rights listed in the Universal Declaration of Human Rights appear to reflect the history and experiences of the time in which it was written?"[121] Obviously, the students get the message that these rights are more up to date and closer to the time in which we are living, so more relevant. The fact that the entire document is also printed in the text book while the Bill of Rights is not, lets students understand that the UN Declaration should have greater importance.

The preferred right that is mentioned of the U.S. Bill of Rights is the First Amendment (mainly Freedom of Speech), which many teachers believe gives them the right to preach from their classroom pulpit whatever personal political opinion they would like to pass on to their students. In *We the People*, three whole chapters are devoted to the First Amendment, including Freedom of Speech, Religion, Assembly, Petition, and Association. The Fourth, Fifth, and Eighth Amendments are briefly mentioned in another chapter—how we are protected against unreasonable law enforcement procedures. [122]

What important amendments are left out and nothing written about them at all?—the Second Amendment (right to bear arms—own a gun) and the Ninth and Tenth Amendments (which tell about citizen and states' rights and sovereignty—whatever is not specifically mentioned in the U.S. Constitution as something over which the federal government is given jurisdiction, then those rights belong to the citizens and the states). Remember this is a federally funded textbook. The federal government would rather not have citizens know that there are such things as states' rights to put a check and balance against an all-encompassing federal government. In the 2002 version of the *US National Standards for Civics and Government*, which establishes the federal education curriculum, the First Amendment had 81 references; the Second, Ninth and Tenth Amendments had none, zip, zero, as if they had never been written.[123]

The Major Difference between the UN Declaration of Human Rights and the U.S. Bill of Rights: Yes, the U.S. Bill of rights is negative. It states all the things that government cannot do in trying to take away your God-given rights. Government cannot deny your freedom of religion, of speech, to petition the government, your freedom to assemble, your freedom to bear arms to protect yourself and your family, your freedom of privacy, and to be treated fairly before the law and yes, your freedom to have states' rights and states' sovereignty as mentioned in the 9th and 10th amendments. In other words, where God giveth, only God can taketh away, not government.

The UN Declaration of Human Rights does not believe the rights they mention are God-given. They believe all rights come from government. They list their 30 nice-sounding rights but then in article 29 (3) they state, "These rights and freedoms may in no case be exercised contrary to the purposes and principles of the United Nations." We have already learned that the real purpose of the UN is to move us to world government, so any rights that get in the way of that are hereby null and void. In other words, where the UN giveth, the UN can taketh away.

Resolution 1296 (passed in 1968)—Granted Consultative Status to Certain NGOs: One of the first NGOs to apply was the Lucis Trust, parent organization of the Lucis Press (originally named the Lucifer Publishing Company). It is an occult, new-age company started by Alice Bailey to publish her own books that were supposedly "channeled" to her by a spiritual guide, a dead Tibetan she called Djwhal Khul. The Lucis Trust used to be located at the UN headquarters in New York City. Why? Alice Bailey assumed the leadership of the New-Age Theosophical Society after the second leader Annie Besant, a Fabian Socialist, had passed away. She had taken over after the death of Madame Helena Petrovna Blavatsky, who was the founder of the Theosophical Society and revered as the "High Priestess" of the New-Age Movement. (More is written about her and the New-Age Religion in Chapter Fifteen.)

The Theosophical Society had many prominent members who helped found the United Nations. Some of its 6,000 members today include such prominent CFR members as Robert McNamera, Donald Regan, Henry Kissinger, David Rockefeller, Paul Volker, George Shultz, and other members of the CFR.[124]

The Convention on the Elimination of all Forms of Discrimination against Women (CEDAW): This is an international convention adopted in 1979 by the United Nations General Assembly. It came into force by those countries which ratified it on September 3, 1981. It is described as an international bill of rights for women, similar to the Equal Rights Amendment that Phyllis Schlafly successfully led the battle to defeat here in the United States. Fortunately, because many Americans have been sufficiently informed about the detriments to such a program, the USA has not ratified the CEDAW. We are the only developed nation which has not.

CEDAW is Promoting Radical Feminism: Some nations which did ratify CEDAW have written resolutions and objections against some of its provisions saying that CEDAW is demanding a radical feminist agenda, such as:—in Belarus, the CEDAW Committee tried to stop the "sex-role stereotypes" of "Mother's Day" and "Mother's Awards," which they said were "encouraging women's traditional roles." In other countries, CEDAW has supported the decriminalization of prostitution. Slovenia was criticized because only 30% of their children were in daycare. Colombia was told to liberalize its abortion laws and to inaugurate campaigns encouraging contraceptive use and "reproductive health awareness." CEDAW has also tried to promote all nations having an equal rights amendment passed as part of their constitutions. Many Islamic countries view the CEDAW as biased towards the cultures of Western nations and have placed reservations on the elements that they see as in fundamental contradiction with Islamic Sharia law. [125]

UN Convention on the Rights of the Child (CRC): According to an article written by Chris Carter, of January 9, 2009, of Family Security Matters, the CRC was signed by President Bill Clinton back in 1995, but was never ratified by the U.S. Senate. The Senate felt it was a threat to parental rights and the family structure. However, with such a liberal president as Obama and a liberal senate, it is feared that the CRC may be ratified. President Barack Obama has already expressed his support of the CRC and said that it was embarrassing to find ourselves in the company of Somalia, the only other UN nation not to ratify the CRC. If our government were to ratify the CRC, the UN would have the final say over what is in the best interests of the child. The following are some of the many ways in which the fundamental rights of parents to raise their children as they see fit would be undermined:

Pulling a child out of school to home school him, against the child's wishes, would not be allowed. Also home schooling and private Christian schools are frowned upon because schools must follow a "global curriculum," which most home school parents and Christian schools do not believe in. The child's wishes must prevail over the parents as to the kind of school he/she wants. We have already seen in Germany, which has signed on to the CRC, that home schooling has been outlawed.

Children will have the following "rights" granted to them: freedom of expression, thought, association, privacy, conscience, a right to rest and leisure, a right to view any kind of literature, even materials that parents would find unacceptable such as pornography. Children will have "freedom of thought, conscience and religion." Parents could not take their child to their church against his/her will, nor could they forbid him from joining a strange cult or gang. Full abortion and contraceptive rights are granted, even against the wishes of the parents. Any child under the age of 18 is protected from "degrading punishment" and "physical violence," ranging from spanking to rape.

The CRC even establishes a framework for the child to seek government review for every parental decision, what Chris Carter calls "a Pandora's Box of litigation." Can you imagine how many children could be suing their parents for every little thing they don't like? There are also provisions for national children's health insurance and other welfare programs.

Carter states that the treaty is open for however the UN wants to interpret it. When Australia, which had signed onto it, argued that spanking was not specifically banned, the Committee replied, "The Convention should be interpreted holistically taking into consideration not only its specific provisions, but also *the general principals which inspired it.*" The CRC committee is, thus, left with "wide" inspiration and interpretation. Carter quotes what Phyllis Schlafly states about the CRC:

> *Unlike our U.S. Constitution, which only mentions rights that can be enforced against the government, this UN treaty declares rights of the child against parents, the family, private institutions, and society as whole. Do we really want to give every child the legal right to say anything he wants to his parents at the dinner table? To watch television ("access to the media") instead of doing homework? To escape household chores because they interfere with his UN right to "rest and leisure"? To join a cult instead of attending his parents' church? To refuse to speak English in our public schools? I think not. The UN Treaty on the Rights of the Child should be rejected as contrary to American constitutional law and common sense.*[126]

Resolution 2997 (passed in 1972)—UN Conference on the Human Environment: The New-Age leader, Maurice Strong served as the Secretary General for the conference, which recommended the creation of the UN Environment Program, which began the next year. This conference helped launch the environmental movement, which was a whole new concept. Before the 1970s, most people believed in "conservationism," which meant that man was to be a wise steward over the earth, the plants, animals and resources, which were given to man by God; but man was not to worship those resources or the earth from which they came.

The environmental movement is just the opposite. It is based on New-Age beliefs, atheism, or pantheism, which is the worship of nature and "mother earth" or "Gaia." According to environmentalists, "man is no different or better than any other creature on earth" and should have his property and resources restricted or given to other creatures (especially "endangered" ones.) In fact, most modern environmentalists, who have been carefully groomed in the public schools and universities with only pro-environmental viewpoints, do not believe in property rights. They say such things as, "Our fragile earth, Mother Gaia, is not to be owned. She is to be worshiped and preserved and her finite resources carefully restricted and shared."

Most experts, who have researched and studied the environmental movement, describe it as a watermelon, "green on the outside but red on the inside." They can see a great deal of parallel between environmentalism and the radical communist movement back in the 1960s. The communist professors have just traded their red coats for green and are having far more success in taking property rights away and furthering other Communist agendas. Remember, the first of the Ten Planks of the *Communist Manifesto* is the "abolition of private property." (Read the many radical statements made by leading environmentalists in the last chapter on quotes if you have any doubts of their far-leftist leanings and agenda for people, our property, and our nation. They seem to forget that they are people too. But, of course, they are a different breed. They get to own the property and have all the benefits, because they are the "saviors of the earth," the average man is not.)

The Many Green, Global Programs Pushed Through by the United Nations in the Name of the Environment: Under the name of protecting the environment, a massive number of green programs started after 1970: A Regional Seas Program (1973); UN Conference on Trade and Development (1974); A Global Framework for Environmental Education; International Environmental Education Program (IEEP); Global Environmental Monitoring System (GEMS); World Conservation Monitoring Center at Cambridge, England. (The last four were passed in 1975.) Human Exposure Assessment Location Program (HEAL); UN Conference on Desertification (COD) (1977), Designated Officials for Environmental Matters (DOEM); and in 1980, World Conservation Strategies was published by a joint effort of the IUCN and the WWF; World Convention on the Law of the Sea—1981 (This would give taxing authority to the UN); (Fortunately the U.S. Senate has continued to vote this down. However, under Obama's administration, it is expected to pass); The Biodiversity Treaty was passed in Rio de Janeiro, 1992, but rejected by the U.S. Senate. However, in 1996 Clinton signed it into law by Executive Order. It is implementing Agenda 21 and the Wildlands Project, both highly restrictive on the rights of property owners. (More detail is written about Agenda 21 and the Environmental Movement in the *Incremental Chipping Away of the Once Great USA.*)

The Environmental Grantmakers' Association was Created in 1985: More than 100 wealthy heads of major foundations belong. They meet annually and decide to which worthy causes their grants will go. They are the ones who have greatly fueled the environmental scare tactics to convince the world that we are on the brink of disaster. Why would they do such a thing? What is their motive? They tell people that the only way this disaster can be averted is by:

> . . . *a massive transformation of human societies which would require all people to accept their spiritual and moral responsibility to embrace their common global heritage and conform to a system of international laws that integrate environmental, economic, and equity issues under the watchful, regulatory authority of a new system of global governance.*

International Centre for the Study and Planning of Information and Communications (1980): This center was created out of concern for "independent" news monopolies. They were not at all concerned by state controlled news. The commission that established this Center believed that "a new world information order was prerequisite to a new world economic order."

The Association for Progressive Communication (APC): This was the next step. It linked together networks in Brazil, Russia, Canada, Australia, Sweden, England, Nicaragua, Ecuador, South Africa, Ukraine, Mexico, Slovenia, and entered into a partnership with the Institute for Global Communications (ICG). This huge computer network now boasts 17,000 users in 94 countries. It has exclusive contracts with UN agencies to disseminate information about and from UN conferences (and, of course, to make sure only the politically correct version of the news will be passed on).[127]

Maurice Strong, the Behind-the-Scenes Head of the United Nations: According to Dr. Stan Monteith, it is Maurice Strong who actually runs the United Nations. He is the advisor to the Secretary General as well as to whoever is serving as the head of the World Bank. Strong reorganized the UN administrative structure in preparation for assuming power when the world government is established.

Just to give the reader an idea of the globalist that he is, here is a list of all the positions and organizations that he has belonged to (Most of these are new-age, radical environmental groups, and organizations that promote a one-world government and one-world religion): Chairman of the Earth Council; Chairman of the World Resources Institute; Co-Chairman of the Council of World Recovery Forum; Member of Toyota's International Advisory Board; President of the World Federation of the United Nations Association; Trustee of the Aspen Institute; Director of the World Future Society; Director of Finance for the Lindisfarne Association; the founding endorser of Planetary Citizen; convened the fourth World Congress, trustee for the Rockefeller Foundation; member of the Club of Rome; Secretary General of the First Earth Summit in 1972, of the Second Earth Summit in 1992; and of the Earth Summit Plus Five in 1997.

Radical, Environmental Beliefs: If one wants to have an idea of the true purpose of an organization, it helps to have an idea of the belief system of the people who head it. The Global Biodiversity Assessment Report represents the radical, extreme environmental concepts developed at the Second Earth Summit for which Maurice Strong served as the Secretary General. It basically called for the deconstruction of Western civilization. Maurice Strong was quoted as saying, "Frankly, we may get to the point where the only way of saving the world will be for industrial civilization to collapse."[128]

New-Age, Pagan Beliefs: According to Larry Abraham and Franklin Saunders, who are the authors of a book called *The Greening,* Maurice Strong owns a large piece of land in Colorado, called "the Baca:"

> *There Strong and his wife are establishing an international community of spiritualists, complete with monasteries, devotees of the Vedic mother goddess, amulet-carrying native American shamans, Zen Buddhists, and even Shirley MacLaine . . . They are not only promoting a one-world government . . . they are supporting a one-world religion to substitute for Christianity.*[129]

What the Green Movement Really Means—a Green World Order: The United Nations promotion of environmental organizations and causes goes right along with their agenda of world government, using environmental scare tactics as a way to get people to come on board. "We must unite under a world government to solve the threatening crisis. They are too big for any one nation to solve."

An excellent book on this subject is *Green Hell: How Environmentalists Plan to Control Your Life and What You Can Do to Stop Them,* by Steve Milloy. It reveals the real agenda behind "green"—total government control. The common denominator behind all green demands are: increased government regulations, reduced economic productivity, and a lower standard of living.[130]

The threat that the greens are putting great emphasis on now is "global warming," allegedly caused by man-made carbon dioxide. Even though over

31,000 scientists have signed a petition denying these claims (*www.petitionproject. org*), the greens refuse to allow any debate on the subject.

According to an article by James Perloff in *The New American*, "Exposing the Green World Order," which gives a review of Milloy's book, the greens are becoming so adamant in not tolerating any opposition to their global warming hype, that one of them, David Roberts, a writer for *Grist Magazine*, has called for "war crime trials" for those who deny global warming. James Hansen of NASA has stated a similar recommendation. He said that coal and oil company executives who cast doubts on global warming "should be tried for high crimes against humanity and nature." Whatever happened to the "scientific method" that allows for objective testing and examination of hypothesis? The greens have thrown that out the window. Why? They know that under true testing and examination, the scientific evidence is not there to support their claims. As Perloff states, "Greens' refusal to allow open discussion of global warming's validity—except by themselves—is virtually an admission that their viewpoint is indefensible."

There are enormous governmental controls, regulations, and money to be made behind the enforcements of green global warming policies. Greens certainly can't afford to give all that up for a silly thing like the "truth," that global warming does not really exist and what little rise in temperature that does sometimes exist is cyclical, caused by the sun, that mankind has nothing to do with it.

The Green Movement Involves Much Green Money: The Greens like to pretend that they consist of just concerned, small, poorly-funded "grass-root" groups. Perloff sites Milloy as stating that "The ten largest green organizations had revenues of more than $1.36 billion in 2007 and net assets in excess of $7.1 billion."

Perloff cites examples of governmental global warming regulations that exist or will soon exist in various parts of the world promising to bring into governmental coffers enormous amounts of money and greatly limit energy use and standard of living of most people. If businesses, factories, or people exceed their "carbon footprint"—their allotted amount of rationed energy—their energy will be cut off and they will have to pay enormous fines. The British government is conducting trials on "smart meters" that set off alarms when homes exceed allotted electricity limits. In Pennsylvania, Governor Ed Rendell has approved a law that will require utility companies to cut their customers' annual electricity consumption by one percent by May, 2011, or they will be fined up to $20 million. In 2008, San Francisco Mayor Gavin Newsome proposed any person who mixed their recyclables with their regular trash should be fined $1,000. In the city of Marburg, Germany, also starting in 2008, new homes were required to include solar panels or face fines of $1,500. (Even though the cost of solar panels and their upkeep may be more costly than what the homeowner can recoup in energy savings.)

Greens are Creating an Artificial Energy Shortage to Micro-Regulate Everyone's Lives: If Greens were truly interested in improving energy resources, they would allow for offshore drilling or viable alternatives such as nuclear power, which creates no carbon emissions. Some even oppose "renewable energy" such as wind, solar, and biofuels, claiming they each have some negative impact on the environment. Instead, as Perloff states, "Greens are creating an artificial energy shortage, drastically increasing the cost of energy and providing an excuse for the government to micro-regulate every home in Orwellian fashion."

Greens are Using Global Warming as Fear Tactics for Population Control: According to a letter that I received from Austin Ruse, the President of C-FAM (Catholic Family & Human Rights Institute), the United Nations announced a population control proposal at the December, 2009, Climate Change Conference in Copenhagen. The proposal said that every nation on earth should be forced to reverse "the disastrous global birthrate" and adopt China's "one-child-only" policy.

Al Gore, "Mr. Global Warming," himself, said that overpopulation fosters global warming. He suggested "that birth-control and abortion programs be expanded in developing countries to help reduce the environmental threat."

What about those who are not willing to comply and want to have more than one child? An Australian medical expert proposed charging couples who have more than two children a "one-time fee and then an annual fee to offset the effect of their greenhouse-gas emissions."

In summary, the UN green extremists think that children are nothing more than "carbon-emitting beings" that degrade the environment" and should not be allowed to be born.

Other Harmful Aspects of the Green Movement: The Green opposition to DDT, the most effective way to stop Malaria, has caused it to be banned across the globe and has led to millions of deaths due to malaria; DDT was the most effective way to kill mosquitoes. When it was allowed to be used, Malaria had almost disappeared.

However, due to the anti-DDT propaganda book, *Silent Spring*, written by Rachel Carson, published in 1962 and promoted by the Green movement, DDT is now banned in the USA and most other nations.

According to 2009 statistics, 60 million people have died since 1972, when the United States banned DDT and other nations followed our example; over 300 million people are now affected each year by malaria, over 1 and 1/2 million die from it and almost half of those are children. (http://www.microbiologybytes.com/introduction/Malaria.html)

Of course, that is exactly what most greens would like. Most of them advocate population reduction, so if millions now die each year from Malaria they think that is a good thing.

Other harmful effects of the green movement are: They want cars to run on alternative energy which causes cars to be built lighter reducing their safety and increasing their costs; Greens oppose cleaning out the underbrush in forests, resulting in an increase in large forest fires that have destroyed many homes and taken lives as well; In 2005, Greens even filed a law suit to stop the U.S. Navy from conducting exercises using sonar to detect enemy subs, saying that sonar disturbed whales and other marine animals. Fortunately, the Supreme Court sided with the Navy, but only by a 5-4 majority; the enormous Green indoctrination in our public schools is producing an army of green misled activists and causing many children to grow up depressed about the "doomed-planet" future. It is predicted that under Obama, "the green president," all of the green propaganda is going to get much worse.[131]

Greens are Controlling and Restricting the Use of Water: In 2001, 1400 farmers and ranchers of a very fertile area for farming, Klamath Falls, Oregon, had their irrigation water taken by the federal Bureau of Reclamation to "supposedly save" a sucker fish, a bottom feeder that really does not need much water. It does better in finding food in shallow water. Of course, the environmentalists said the coho salmon were also at risk and needed lots of water. Here is what *the Heartland Institute* reported about the government's taking of water:

> On April 7, the federal Bureau of Reclamation decided to allocate nearly all water in the Klamath Project for the benefit of the sucker fish in Upper Klamath Lake, and to the salmon in the Klamath River. Allowing farmers in the Klamath Water Basin to continue to irrigate their crops would jeopardize sustainable levels in the lake and river, concluded the Bureau.

The farmers went before a federal judge pleading for their right to use the water. However, on April 30, the District Judge, Ann Aiken denied their plea, citing treaty obligations to two area Native American tribes who are allowed to fish for the salmon and obligations under the Endangered Species Act. Judge Aiken denied a requested injunction against the federal government's decision, stating that the citizens were unlikely to show the federal government had violated the law in cutting off water to the farmers. As Judge Aiken stated, "**the interests of the fish outweigh those of the farmers.**"[132]

Who Asked the Fish? I personally don't believe anyone consulted the fish or the Creator of the fish as to know what their "interests" were. But since the judge seems to think she knows what the fish are thinking or speaking, I will add my own interpretation. Having grown up in Idaho and having gone fishing often for trout and salmon, I'm sure I speak "fish" as well as any judge. I'm sure I heard the salmon and sucker of Klamath Falls saying, "Please allow the farmers to use the water. We really don't require that much water to survive." I could add my testimony to that fact. We caught large trout and salmon in very shallow Idaho streams. They do not require a lot of water to live. And if some did die, would that be so bad? There are many other fish in the sea and in other rivers.

Would it not be better to save human life over fish? I am sure if it were Judge Aiken's life which was at risk or she was threatened with losing her job and watching her family go hungry verses the life of the fish, she would decide differently. Then the interest of the fish would not outweigh her own life. That is the biggest problem with many of the decision makers affecting thousands of other lives, they have forgotten "the Golden Rule—to treat others as they would want to be treated."

"The Bucket Brigade"—Protestors from Many Different States Came to Assist: In May of 2001, hundreds of people protested the judge's ruling by lining the streets of Klamath Falls to pass 50 buckets of water (representing the 50 states of the union) hand to hand to dump water from Lake Ewauna, near Veterans Park, to the A Canal near Klamath Union High School. This was listed in one paper as "a technical violation of the Endangered Species Act."

On August 21, another type of bucket brigade happened when people from many other states came to Klamath Falls to show their support for the poor farmers. About 4,000 gathered between the Klamath County Courthouse and the County Government Center across the street. They placed a 10-foot-high bucket (as a memorial of government abuse) in front of the Government Center where it still remains.[133]

A First-Hand Description of What the Klamath Falls Farmers Were Up Against: Devvy Kidd, author, activist, former Congressional candidate, went to Klamath Falls in July and September of 2001 to see what was really going on. In an article for *NewswithViews,* January 14, 2005, she described the abuse of power that she witnessed:

> *I went to Klamath Falls in July 2001. It was a shocking experience. I stood face to face with armed federal coppers standing guard over the canal denying the precious water to our farmers. It was quite chilling. I saw a federal sniper sitting up on the hill just watching to make certain these desperate people—and desperate they were—didn't attempt to tear down the barbed wire fence and measures the federal coppers had taken to keep anyone from getting to the canal controls. I looked into the faces of my fellow country men and women and saw despair and rage beyond anything I had ever experienced in my life. Words cannot describe what I saw and never would I have ever thought I would see this type of deliberate government destruction against her own people in these United States of America.*

Eventually, the Bush administration did make some meager show of hearing the many letters and pleas for help and some water did flow through the canal later in the irrigation season, but it was too late. The damage had already been done and the crops were lost. Devvy describes what her second visit was like in September talking with some of the farmers. She took with her a constitutional attorney Larry Becraft to let the farmers know what their legal options were:

> *What these beaten people were facing was a monstrous situation against a leviathan beast and ten or twelve different state and federal agencies—millions of dollars in legal fees. Money these people didn't have because the government had killed their ability to even grow their own food. That's right. The fields in the surrounding area were fallow with nothing but weeds growing; farmers were actually going hungry! Food was trucked in by caring Americans. Two days after I got home, 9/11 hit and any promise of help by the a few Congress critters and local politicians became dust in the wind.*[134]

The Klamath Farmers Lost Their Right to Water and their Livelihood over an ESA Ruling Later Proven to be Illegal: The 1400 Klamath farmers in the summer of 2001 lost their crops from their land which totaled over 220,000 acres. Most of them never recovered, meaning they lost their farms, ranches, homes, and livelihood. The loss of one summer's crops is too much for most farmers. They could never recover from such a loss. Many of them were forced into bankruptcy, and other businesses that depended on the farmers were also forced to close.

Devvy Kidd reported that on January 12, 2005, in Eugene, Oregon, a federal judge, Michael Hogan ruled that the coho salmon in the Klamath River Basin region had been illegally listed under the Endangered Species Act as a threatened species. The judge agreed with the Pacific Legal Foundation that the federal government violated the ESA when it failed to consider hatchery fish in its assessment of coho in southern Oregon and northern California rivers. The following is a statement from PLF attorney Russ Brooks:

> *This victory came too late for the farmers who were pushed into bankruptcy and the businesses that were forced to close to protect fish that were never endangered. Our rivers and streams are teeming with salmon, yet the Klamath community was practically destroyed because of environmental politics run amok.*[135]

2009 Summer Shutdown of Water for Central Valley, California, the Breadbasket of the Nation: The latest example of governmental abuse of power and the Green "war on water" is the attack on the Central Valley of California, where almost 900,000 acres have been affected. This is farmland that used to provide 12% of the food of our nation, once referred to as "the bread basket of our nation," now turned into a dust bowl. Farmers have been allowed only 10% of the water they need to grow their crops and fruit orchards, resulting in most of the land remaining dormant. Under the hot, dry sun, the land has turned into a dry desert, with no crops and, in some places, 40% unemployment.

Why was this done? Supposedly, it was to save the life of a little fish, "the delta smelt," that was being killed when the pumps would be turned on to pump the water into the delta, the canal that brings water from northern California to the desert area. The delta smelt, no bigger than three inches, looks exactly like its cousin, a minnow. In fact, it just might be a minnow, and there are plenty of minnows around. No one would believe that the minnow could be on the endangered species list. But by calling this little minnow a new name, "the delta smelt," the environmentalists have been able to get it on the endangered species list, and, use it as an excuse to shut down the farms of the Central Valley. Do they really value the life of a little fish more than that of farmers and the people, who would have eaten the produce from the Central Valley, or are there bigger agendas? Is this one more attack on wiping out the middle class, that includes many farmers and ranchers?

The Central Valley used to be the most fertile land and the biggest producer of cantaloupes, almonds, artichokes, olives, nectarines, peaches, grapes, strawberries, oranges, lettuce, nuts, etc. What are people now expected to eat—produce coming from third world countries like China, which does not have our same standards for growing food? Who knows what kind of soil and fertilizer is being used there. Is this one of the rewards for China bailing out our enormous trillion dollar loans? It now gets to be the bread basket of America?

July 1, Fresno Protest: An estimated 15,000 outraged farmers and farm workers held a protest march on the Fresno court house, July 1, against the federal government because of their not allowing the water to come through the Delta canal to grow their crops. The crowd held various signs, such as: "We need water for your food," which was also written on a streamer flying behind a plane overhead. Other signs had the following messages: "If you like foreign oil, you will love foreign food; Water = Jobs; Save fish, ruin humans; We can't afford any more change; The feds value fish over families; Farmers are the real endangered species."

Alan Autry, known as "Bubba," the former major of Fresno, was one of the speakers. He compared the endangered species act to acts of domestic terrorism. He received much applause from the crowd.

Valiant Efforts by Representative Devin Nunes, R, 21st District: Since the Endangered Species Act is a federal act (really a United Nations act being pushed on all the nations); states no longer have the right to have jurisdiction over their own land. The California legislators and the governor are not able to do anything about their own water being turned off. This battle has to be fought in Congress. Congressman Nunes, who represents several areas in the Central Valley, has tried for two years to get the Democrat Congress to pass some legislation to allow the water pumps turned back on, to allow water to come through the Delta to water the crops. In a speech he gave July 9, 2009, before Congress, that can be seen on You Tube, he showed a poster of 651 days—how long the government-imposed drought has lasted in the Central Valley, almost two years. Congress has done nothing while the vibrant economy of the valley has deteriorated to that of a third-world country. Unemployment in the San Joaquin Valley is reaching 20%. In some communities it is 40%. Despite this economic catastrophe, the Democrat leadership has remained silent and done nothing.

Nunes supported the Calvert Amendment, which would have restored the flow of water to the desperate areas of the Central Valley. This amendment was offered during a midnight session of the "Energy and Water Appropriations Markup," that Nunes told about: Thirty minutes of debate followed with "outrageous statements" made.

One of the members of the committee said that instead of the water being sent to the farmers, it was needed for salmon and other endangered species such as the killer whale. Congressmen Nunes pointed out on a map that killer whales live way up north, north of Washington. "What do they have to do with the water needed for land-locked farmers way down in the Central Valley of California?"

Another statement was made that the culprit in this debate is not the endangered species act, but climate change. Nunes asked what does climate change have to do with 40,000 people without jobs? Another statement was that the Calvert Amendment was a "wish amendment." Nunes replied, "Yes, wish is the right word to use. My constituents wish that the democrats in this body would do their job."

Other colleagues complained that it is California farmers who are putting fishermen out of work. Nunes replied that the truth is "the federal government put the salmon fishermen out of work. In fact, the federal government paid $100 million for the salmon fishermen not to fish. It doesn't take $100 million to solve the crisis in California. It doesn't even take a penny, just turn on the pumps and restore the water is all that we are asking."

Threatening Statements Made—Support for Water for the Central Valley Would Mean "Loss of Earmarks": Nunes stated that a member of the Energy and Water Committee, in that midnight session, threatened that if any member of the committee voted for the Calvert Amendment they would lose their "earmarks." Earmarks are essentially "bribes," special funding that Congressmen get to take back to their states for various pet projects to mainly ensure that they can be re-elected. Earmarks are obviously used to keep Congressmen in line and made to vote a certain way by threatening to take them away if they don't vote how they are told to. It almost sounds like Congressmen have become sheep with earmarks in their ears, following dutifully along, no longer free to vote according to their own conscience. This is one more example of how far our Congress has strayed from the Constitution. There is no mention of "earmarks" or anything similar in the Constitution.

Nunes pointed out in his speech before the House that "it is amazing what happens when the clock strikes midnight, and they think no one is watching what people will say." He stated, "My message to you is we are watching. I put the entire meeting up on you-tube for everyone in the world to see the pathetic excuses that were made in that committee that night."

"The Endangered Species Act wasn't Written by God; It was Written by Man." This was a quote made by Congressmen Simpson from Idaho during the committee debate on the Calvert Amendment. Simpson went on to say, "If we can't make exceptions to it when necessary, what kind of representatives are we." Nunnes, of course, agreed with Congressman Simpson. Nunnes ended his remarks stating, "My constituents don't want your welfare, they want the Democrat leadership and this body to do their job."[136]

People are Waking Up Across California to the True Agenda of the Environmental Movement: The one good thing that is coming out of the terrible abuse of government power and the sad condition that the farmers of the Klamath Valley and the Central Valley now find themselves in is—they are finding out the truth of environmentalism, that it really is just like a watermelon, green on the outside, but red on the inside. It is communism with a green coat of paint. The #1 plank of the *Communist Manifesto* is "abolition of property rights," and that is exactly what is going on.

Many of the tea-party rallies and town-hall meetings and protests that are going on across California and the nation are also because of environmental abuse of power. Some of those will be described in Chapter 18 about the good things that have happened as people are waking up—"There is Hope."

Sean Hannity's Television Show September 18, 2009, Filmed in the Central Valley: Hannity has been covering the serious situation in the Central Valley in California in many of his radio and television broadcasts. September 18, he flew to California and filmed his evening television show in the San Joaquin Valley to shed additional light on the seriousness of the unemployment and dust bowl conditions. He entitled the show, "The Valley that Hope Forgot."

One of the guests that Hannity had was an actor and comedian, Paul Rodriguez, who owns a farm in the Central Valley and serves as chairman of the California Latino Water Coalition. Rodriguez used to be a democrat and voted for Obama, but has since switched to being a Republican when he received no help from his democrat Congressmen over this water issue. Rodriguez read from a letter that he and every mayor in the valley had signed and sent to Obama pleading with him to turn on the water.

Mr. President, with all due respect, we pray that you will read our letter and look at our dilemma. We don't want you to give us a loan. We didn't do anything wrong. We did everything right. We grew more food than anybody else with less water. And for that, our reward was you cut the water off. Come on, what's up?

Rodriguez described what is now happening with once hard-working and productive California farmers. They have to wait in line at food banks to receive food grown in other countries because America's government will not allow them to use the existing water supply to grow crops that could feed much of the nation.[137]

What is Really Behind the Endangered Species Act (ESA) and Its Promotion over the Life of Mankind? In case the reader thought we had lost track of the UN, which this chapter is supposed to be about, you guessed it, the answer to the above question is the United Nations. The UN is what is behind the ESA and the promotion of radical environmentalism, regulations, loss of liberty, loss of use of property, loss of resources, loss of money, and the taking of water. This is all being done in the name of "protecting endangered species," which are really not endangered. The true endangered species is man and our rights and liberties.

Foresters in Washington, Oregon, and California will tell you that the original "endangered species," the spotted owl was never endangered. There were plenty of them. But millions of acres of forests are now closed to any logging and hundreds of logging mills have been closed down because of that one little species. Obviously the minnows and delta smelt are very plentiful. How many are needed in this world anyway? Only God knows how many creatures He created and how many He would like to have in any certain area. It is time for the environmentalists to stop playing God. He does a much better job at it and is not so costly. In fact He does not charge a dime for taking care of all the species in the world.

Through the years, the truth has been revealed about the environmentalists and their Endangered Species Act. It has nothing to do with their wanting to take care of species, it is all about money and control and taking away property. Because of the ESA and the green army of radical environmentalists behind it and their billions of dollars in funding, any silly little animal can be listed as endangered just depending on where it is located and what industry, plant, hospital, mine, or farming area the environmentalist would like to close down.

The ESA is all Part of the Scheme of "Redistribution of Wealth": When property is no longer able to be farmed or used, then it is greatly devalued and is sold at rock-bottom prices, which has happened with many of the farmers in Klamath Falls and the Central Valley. They have sold their land just to be able to pay off their debts and to try to start over someplace else. Who buys the greatly reduced property? "Benevolent" environmental groups such as the Nature Conservancy or the Sierra Club buy the property and then jack up the price and sell it to the federal government for some "reserve," or it is sold to a redevelopment agency. (More is written about redevelopment following.)

The ESA is all part of the scheme of "taking from those who have and giving to those who have not," not only in the USA, but in other countries across the globe.

How much of the billions of dollars that have gone into the ESA and its many costly regulations are actually used to take care of endangered species and get them off the list, or is that not really the goal or intention at all?

Since 1973 when the EPA was created, 1300 species have been listed as endangered. According to a "White Paper" report coming from UC Davis, 359 of those species listed as endangered or threatened are in California.

According to a Tom DeWeese Report, only ten species have ever been taken off the list, and most of those were removed because of a judge's ruling that they had been fraudulently listed in the first place.

One such specie was the tiny Bruneau hotsprings snail found on fertile farm land near Twin Falls, Idaho. The snail was put on the endangered species list officially in 1993. Many farmers thought this was a joke, since the snail is only the size of a pin point. They created a billboard saying, "Last one leaving town, don't forget to feed and water the snail."

However, when springtime came, and they tried to plow their ground and use their water, they discovered this was no joke. They had lost all rights to use their land.

The local farm bureau and the Cattlemen's Association banded together and raised money to go to court, suing for the snail to be taken off the list and for the farmers and ranchers to be able to use their land.

Fortunately, an honest federal judge heard their case. He hired some honest biologists to do the counting of snails, down on their hands and knees using magnifying glasses. From their report, the judge ruled that there were plenty of bruneau snails to go around, and the snail was removed from the endangered species list.

Why would environmentalists want to do such strange things as to list tiny little snails and other weird creatures on their enormous "protected" list? Again, when something does not make sense, follow the money trail. There are millions of dollars involved in the recovery plan for these species. There is much money involved when property can no longer be used for its intended purpose, and the land is greatly devalued in price. Some nice environmental agency can buy it at dirt cheap prices and then sell it to the federal government or some developer for a much higher price. Later, through mitigation, the new owner will have to pay for an equivalent area to be set aside as "endangered species habitat," and then he will be somewhat free to farm the land, again with lots of regulations and fees.

All this brings enormous money into the coffers of the ESA agency and other groups working with them. What is actually being done with that money, no one knows. Obviously, the little creature is not being put in some resort hotel and fed and coddled with all of the millions of dollars. Perhaps some two-legged bureaucratic creatures are, however.

Former Congressmen Richard Pombo from California tried to get a bill passed asking for the ESA to be audited to see how effective it was. The bill was not passed, and it probably cost Pombo his next election for daring to even question it. He was slandered and accused of trying to kill the ESA. Pombo found out the hard way that it is not politically correct or popular to question the "green" agenda.

Even President Nixon began to question and perhaps regret that he had signed into law the legislation to create the ESA. Shortly before his death in 1994, when the Bruneau snail was still in the news, he made the following statement: " . . . measures designed to protect endangered species such as bears, wolves and bald eagles are now being used to force Idaho farmers off their land for the sake of the thumbnail [actually pin-point]-size Bruneau hot springsnail."

The following information about the ESA is from Devvy Kidd, who reveals the UN connection and how it has all been done by international treaties.

> The Endangered Species Act (ESA) has always been one of the most heinous mechanisms being used against the American people and once again, its authority is derived from treaties. The Endangered Species Act of 1973 derives its authority and power from . . . international treaties most Americans have never heard of . . .

ESA treaties can be found in Section 2, paragraph (4) of the Endangered Species Act of 1973 under the statement: "the United States has pledged itself as a sovereign state in the international community to conserve to the extent practicable the various species of fish or wildlife and plants facing extinction, pursuant to: 1)migratory bird treaties with Canada and Mexico; 2) the Migratory and Endangered Bird Treaty with Japan; 3) the Convention on Nature Protection and Wildlife Preservation in the Western Hemisphere; 4) the International Convention for the Northwest Atlantic Fisheries; 5) the International Convention for the High Seas Fisheries of the North Pacific Ocean; 6) the Convention on International Trade in Endangered Species of Wild Fauna and Flora; and other international agreements.

Devvy Kidd mentions that few people have any knowledge of these destructive treaties. "This is how the one-world-order agenda is being implemented: circumventing the U.S. Constitution by having the counterfeit U.S. Senate ratify treaties." Mrs. Kidd states that few attorneys even understand the issue of jurisdiction and treaties and "whether enforcement under international treaties is incumbent upon domestic Americans." She suggests reading *Reid v Covert,* which retired Judge J.J. Boesel cited in his legal writings pinpointing why America's participation in the UN is unconstitutional.[138]

Redevelopment Robbery: Because of the Kelo decision by the Supreme Court in 2005, which gave a new interpretation to "eminent domain," perfectly good but older property is now labeled "condemned" or "blighted." Thus, it is devalued and sold at a greatly reduced price to redevelopment agencies, who will turn the property into housing, or shopping malls, or other businesses that will bring in much higher taxes for city or county governments. Who cares how many businesses and families are broken up because of this decision? It is all about the money.

Green Global Threats "Necessitate" World Government: As with the entire United Nations and all of its endeavors, the green agenda is no different. Its purpose is promoting global government as well, just with the nice color of green. It also uses threats and fear tactics to create supposed "crisis." Since global warming, energy shortages, water shortages, and other crisis are being promoted as global threats, they will, of course, necessitate a world government to solve them. This is stated by former French President Jacques Chirac in a speech he gave to promote the Kyoto Protocol, another UN treaty, which would have all countries, who sign on, promise to greatly reduce their country's carbon emissions down to an average reduction of 5.2% from 1990 levels. The target date when all this is to be done was the year 2012. Fortunately, the U.S. has not signed the treaty, but maybe with our new green president and his green democrat Congress, that will happen.

Here is the statement by Chirac: "*For the first time, humanity is instituting a genuine instrument of global governance, one that should find a place within the World Environment.*"

Global Warming Lies Exposed: In what has become known as "Climategate," the global warming hot-air balloon of lies and exaggerations had a big whole punched in it, November 23, 2009, just a few weeks before the UN Copenhagen Climate Change Summit was to begin, December 7.

Some computer hackers were able to discover thousands of e-mails that had been sent between several two important science professors that crucial data refuting the global warming theories had been hidden and not allowed to be published. UK Professor Dr. Phil Jones, of the University of East Anglia, headed up the prestigious Climatic Research Unit, which was the main source of information for the UN Intergovernmental Panel (IPPC) and for the world media on climate change." Jones had corresponded mainly with a professor at Penn State in Pennsylvania, Michael Mann, the creator of the deceptive "hockey stick" graph. *USA News*, December 1, 2009, reports Penn State is investigating Michael Mann's participation in "cooking the books" on global warming data as well. Michael was told by Jones to "delete certain E-mails" and hide valuable scientific facts that did not support the global warming theory.

In an e-mail back in 2004, Jones wrote that he and his assistant would keep information out of the next IPCC report, "even if we have to redefine what the peer-review literature is." There were many similar e-mails. Jones has since stepped down from his position at East Anglia.

I was in hopes that this scandal would put a big hole in the "hot air" emitted by international wind bags at the Copenhagen Climate Change Summit that took place starting December 7, but they did their best to ignore it and went right on promoting their scare tactics trying to get all the nations to agree to more draconian restrictions on energy and redistribution of wealth, taking from the wealthier nations to give to the poorer ones. Fortunately, they were not quite able to accomplish their objectives and will have to stage another big CO2 emitting conference in the future.

From a *Reuters* article, December 16, 2009, it was estimated that the "carbon footprint" of CO2 emissions that were used up at this summit was the largest in history. With all the commercial and private jets flying into Copenhagen, the private limos, etc. bringing hundreds of thousands of people from over 200 countries, the emissions were over 46,200 tons of CO2, which could have taken care of 660,000 Ethiopians for one year.

(http://www.redicecreations.com/article.php?id=9134) (For the complete story and for a factual report of what the truth is about CO2, I highly recommend the book, *Climate Gate,* by Brian Sussman, former weatherman and a talk show host for KSFO radio in San Francisco. The book can be ordered from www.wndbooks.com)

UN Control Over Food and all Health Supplements—UN's *"Codex Alimentarius"* (Meaning Food Code): This is a set of UN regulations over food and supplements "supposedly" to ensure their safety to the consumer and to ensure fair practices in international food trade. The UN *Codex Alimentarius* Commission was established in 1963 by the Food and Agriculture Organization inside the UN and the World Health Organization (WHO).

Through the years, the UN and WHO have been supporting the powerful and wealthy pharmaceutical companies, who want to encourage people to take their expensive drugs for whatever ails them. They do not want competition by natural supplements or vitamins or even herbal teas. In 1996, a German delegation to the UN put forward a proposal that no herb, vitamin or mineral should be sold for preventive or therapeutic reasons, and that supplements should be reclassified as drugs. Fortunately, there was much opposition to this proposal and it did not pass.

However, at the 28th Session of the Codex Alimentarius Commission, July 4-9, 2005, "Guidelines for Vitamin and Mineral Food Supplements" were adopted as global safety guidelines. These guidelines have been adopted by the EU and, due to the U.S. "transatlantic partnership" with the EU, as well as our membership in the WHO and the UN, it is feared these draconian vitamin standards will be forced upon us as well. We are being asked "to harmonize" our vitamin laws to the emerging restrictive international standard. These restrictions on vitamins and food supplements will severely limit their availability and dosages and greatly increase their costs.

Who and What are Behind the *Codex Alementarius, (Shortened to Codex)*? Along with the UN, the WHO, the multinational pharmaceutical cartels, there are international banks that stand to benefit as they loan money to these various groups. The first attempt to implement its guidelines through the FDA (Federal Drug Administration) in the U.S. was defeated, so it is being promoted as a free trade issue through the FTC, Free Trade Commission. Its campaign is being called "Operation Cure-All."

Real Goal of Codex? "International harmonization" of health codes sounds quite nice and benign, but, as with all that the UN has anything to do with, it is all about power, control and money. The goal is to outlaw health products, vitamins and dietary supplements, except for those under their control. As has already been mentioned, the elitists who started the UN and still lead it believe in population control. They do not want to prolong the lives of common people, nor have them healthy with the use of herbs and vitamins. They also do not believe in competition and want to drive out of business the lowly middle class. Herbs and vitamin supplements can be used by the elite themselves, but they were not meant for the common lowly serfs.

Codex Regulations Would Supersede U.S. Domestic Laws: The website that gave most of the above information added that these UN laws would supersede our own laws, and this would happen without any voice of the American people.

Codex Bill Being Pushed by Senator John McCain: As if we don't have enough to worry about fighting UN codex laws, low and behold, in February, 2010, Senator John McCain decided to sponsor his own version of Codex regulations, a bill called the Dietary Supplement Safety Act (DSSA), which would put the same controls over vitamins and supplements as the UN wants to do.

Using the excuse that there are too many athletes able to get steroids without a prescription, McCain would like to make it so that almost every supplement is now classified as a drug and would require a doctor's prescription. His DSSA would repeal sections of the Dietary Supplement Health and Education Act (DSHSEA) that protects two kinds of supplements: 1) those that have been in the food supply and not chemically altered; and 2) those that were sold as supplements prior to 1994, the year that DSHEA was passed. If a supplement fits these two categories then the present law says the FDA cannot classify it as a drug, and it would not require a prescription.

McCain's bill would wipe out even these minimal protections and give the FDA and pharmaceutical companies much more power over supplements. Just a small list will be allowed to remain without prescriptions. Supplements that require prescriptions will, of course, be sold at much higher prices. (http://www. anh-usa.org/new _site/?attachment_id=2282.)

UN Control of Food Used to Control People: UN officials know that people who are hungry enough will bend to the will of the UN to get food. This was boldly stated by Catherine Bertini, Executive Director of the UN World Food Program at the Beijing China Fourth World Conference on Women, in September of 1995. Here is the quote by Bertini put in bold: *"Food is power. We use it to change behavior. Some may call that bribery. We do not apologize."*

Quote from the UN Itself—"Mounting Ecological Dangers"—a Task for Global Governance:

> *To keep global resource use within prudent limits while the poor raise their living standards, affluent societies need to consume less . . . Population, consumption, technology, development, and the environment are linked in complex relationships that bear closely on human welfare in the global neighborhood. Their effective and equitable management calls for a systemic, long-term, global approach guided by the principle of sustainable development, which has been the central lesson from the mounting ecological dangers of recent times. Its universal application is a priority among the tasks of global governance. (Our Global Neighborhood, 1995, Chapter One, a New World)*[139]

Quotes That Reveal What the United Nations is all About—World government with Absolute Power, Control and Tyranny, Devised for War-Making not Peace:

Quotes by Barry Goldwater, Senator from Arizona, and Republican candidate for President. He was brave enough to speak about the UN's anti-freedom, Communist links, and lust for tyrannical power:

> *The time has come to recognize the United Nations for the anti-American, anti-freedom organization that it has become. The time has come for us to cut off all financial help, withdraw as a member, and ask the United Nations to find headquarter's location outside the United States that is more in keeping with the philosophy of the majority of voting members, someplace like Moscow or Peking.*
>
> *Now those who seek absolute power, even though they seek it to do what they regard as good, are simply demanding the right to enforce their own version of heaven on earth, and let me remind you, they are the very ones who always create the most hellish tyranny. **A government that is big enough to give you all you want is big enough to take it all away.***[140]

Quotes by J. Reuben Clark, Former Under Secretary of State in 1928 and Ambassador to Mexico in 1939, found in the book *An Enemy Hath Done This* by Ezra Taft Benson:

The [UN] Charter will not certainly end war. Some will ask why not? In the first place, there is no provision in the Charter itself that contemplates ending war. It is true the charter provides for force to bring peace, but such use of force is itself war . . . It is true the Charter is built to prepare for war, not to promote peace . . . The Charter is a war document not a peace document . . .

Not only does the Charter Organization not prevent future wars, but it makes it practically certain that we will have future wars, and as to such wars, it takes from us the power to declare them, to choose which side on which we will fight, to determine what focus and military equipment we shall use in the war, and to control and command our sons who do the fighting.[141]

Quotes by Dr. John Coleman, who used to be part of the British Intelligence MI6, similar to the CIA: He is a researcher and author of many books revealing the quest for power of government and the New World Order. He is also the editor of a quarterly publication called *World in Review*. These quotes are from his book, *Committee of Three Hundred*:

The United Nations is a war-making body (not a peace-making one). It strives to place power in the hands of the executive branch instead of where it belongs in the legislative branch . . . Why would the UN want to provoke wars when its stated goal is to be an instrument of peace? Because wars makes far-reaching changes to countries which could not be achieved by diplomacy.

The UN uses foreign aid as a means to get a foot in the door to the resources of a country. No pirate or robber ever had it so good. Not even Kubla Kahn had it as good as the Rothschilds, Rockefellers, Warburgs and their kin have.

If a nation should refuse to hand over its resources, as was the case with the Congo, the UN troops go in and "compel compliance," which resulted in murdering many civilians and the Congo leader, Patrice Lamumba.[142]

Quotes from Ezra Taft Benson, former Secretary of Agriculture under Eisenhower, author of an *Enemy Hath Done It*, which is primarily about the United Nations:

When one stops to consider the degrees of communists influence at the UN . . . it is no wonder that the UN has never performed a real anti-communist act. How could it? On the other hand, it has helped the forces of communism on many occasions—helped either by direct action, as in the Congo, or by total paralysis, as in Hungary, Tibet and Israel.

The UN record should start us thinking. Is it an accident? Is it planned—or merely the product of historical forces? It is both! It is the product of historical forces which were planned many years ago. These forces were made inevitable by the very nature and structure of the UN. Allowing members of the world's greatest peace destroying force to help a peacekeeping organization makes about as much sense as appointing members of the Mafia to a police commissioner's board to control crime in Chicago!

As long as communists are permitted to hold membership in and allowed to help direct the activities of the UN, it can never keep the peace, and it can never promote the ideals so glibly written into the Charter and the Declaration on Human Rights. We should get out of the UN and get the UN out of the United States.[143]

There are many organizations and agencies that support the United Nations, and through which the one-world government objectives are being furthered. The next chapter tells of two of the most powerful groups who were actually the chief architects of the UN, the Royal Institute for Foreign Affairs of England, and the Council on Foreign Relations of the USA. Of course, these groups have the same goals as the UN, for they were its creators.

Chapter Nine

The Chief Architects of the United Nations—
The Royal Institute of International Affairs,
And The Council on Foreign Relations (CFR)—
Their Beginning, Influence, and Purpose

1891—The Royal Institute for International Affairs: This was the front organization for the secret society called "Round Table Groups:" The Round Table Groups were started by a millionaire, Cecil Rhodes, with three close friends, Lord Alfred Milner, William T. Stead, and a man named Brett, who later became Lord Esher. With the help of the Bank of England and financiers such as the Rothschild Family, Rhodes had established a virtual monopoly over the diamond output of South Africa, and, after the Boer War, which he and his fellow conspirators helped instigate, Rhodes had a monopoly on the country's gold as well.

The major part of his fortune was used to set up Rhodes Scholarships, to advance the socialist philosophies of his mentor and professor, John Ruskin, at Oxford College. What were those philosophies? Ruskin felt that the vast superiority of the British race made them the only ones qualified to rule the world and that should be their obligation and destiny—to extend British culture to all the people of the world and unite them under an English monarchy.

Rhodes died in 1902. He left his vast fortune in the care of his good friend Lord Milner, who used part of the money to bring a group of young men to South Africa to rebuild the Transvaal, that had been laid waste by the Boer War. While there, Milner taught them about their obligations to unite the world in world government. They became known as "Milner's Kindergarten" and became the outer circle of the Rhodes secret society named "The Round Table Group." Like all secret societies, it had circles within circles and no one really knew of the other circles or who other members were.[144]

Milner also continued using the vast fortune for Rhodes scholarships. Since 1909, there have been over 4600 young men who have been recipients of those scholarships and sent to Oxford where they are indoctrinated into socialism and world government. Bill Clinton was one of those recipients, as was his roommate

Strobe Talbot. But Clinton did not finish at Oxford. During the winter vacation
of 1969-70, he was sent from England to Russia where Strobe preceded him. It
was there that they both received more instruction in Communist and globalist
philosophy.

When Clinton became the President of the United States in 1992, Talbot
served as his Deputy Secretary of State. Talbot later became the President of
the Brookings Institution, a globalist think tank. He was chosen as an advisor
to Obama, as he was to Clinton. They are both fellow CFR members. Talbot
wrote an essay back in 1992 for *Time Magazine,* entitled "The Birth of the
Global Nation," in which he longed for a future where "nationhood as we
know it will be obsolete; all states will recognize a single, global authority."[145]
Obviously, his Oxford training in world government is still deeply ingrained
in his philosophy.

By 1915, the secret Round Table Groups had spread to seven countries
including England and the United States. By this time, powerful and wealthy
bankers had become members and had gained control of the English parliament.
These men were influential in helping to start World War I and to get England
involved in the war. Why? Because when a nation is at war, it needs lots of money
and its leaders will go into great debt to get it. Collecting interest on debt is how
the bankers make their money. They do not show any allegiance to any certain
nation, they finance both sides of the war, and that is what the British bank did
during World War I and II (as well as the American banks). (The RIIA has its
own website found at http://www.chathamhouse.org.uk/.)

The League of Nations: In 1919, as a result of the Versailles Treaty, the League of
Nations was formed. It "supposedly" was to be an international group of leaders
of nations meeting together to help prevent any further world wars.

President Woodrow Wilson is one of its founders. He spoke about it in his
Fourteen Point speech at the signing of the Treaty of Versailles. Of course, it
was not his idea. It really was coming from all the conspiratorial groups such as
the Round Table, who had been planning for its creation for a long time as a
way to move the world closer to world government. They thought that World
War I would have made the nations of the world so sick of war that they would
readily accept and want to join a "world body for peace."

However, the U.S. Senate rejected the treaty. They recognized it as a threat
to our U.S. Constitution and to our sovereignty as a nation.

Without the support of the United States, the League of Nations died on
the vine. Did these sinister men who created it give up? No, they decided they
would have to find a way to circumvent the power of the U.S. Constitution—to

form a more prestigious sounding organization that could be a front group for the U.S. roundtable group and that only members of this organization, who shared the same one-world government goals, would be elected or appointed to public office. They would also have to create another war, this time worse than the first and another world organization for peace, this time called the United Natons.

President and Mrs. Woodrow Wilson
And Edward Mandell House

Edward Mandell House—The Man Most Responsible for the Founding of the CFR: House was the chief advisor for President Woodrow Wilson. House's father had represented the Rothschild banking family during the Civil War and emerged very wealthy. House was not only Wilson's top advisor, but he dominated the President and his cabinet. Wilson referred to him as his "alter ego." Many believe that it was actually House who was running the government from 1913 to 1921.

The Book Written by House

It was Edward Mandell House who planned for the United States to give up its sovereignty at the end of World War I by signing onto the League of Nations. However, that plan was thwarted when the U.S. Senate refused to ratify entrance into the League. Some 59 enlightened senators recognized that this document, sought to put the League of Nations above the U.S. Constitution, that it really was a "One-World Government document," and they refused to sign it. (It was nice that Senators thought about protecting the U.S. Constitution back then. Now they seem to totally ignore it.)

House was a Marxist and socialist who, in 1912, had written a book called *Philip Dru: Administrator,* that told of a conspiracy (the actual word he used) which gained control of both the Democrat and the Republican Party and used them as instruments in the creation of a socialist world government. His book called for the establishment of a state-controlled central bank and the passage of a graduated income tax as steps toward the goal of world government. Is it not interesting that the very next year after his book was published, 1913, our nation had passed legislation creating both a central bank (The Federal Reserve) and the 16th Amendment, creating the income tax?

House was disappointed with the defeat of the League of Nations, but he was not beaten. He told Sydney Webb, the leader of the Socialist Fabian Society, the foremost proponents of the League of Nations in Great Britain, that the only way to get around the U.S. Constitution was to permeate all future United States administrators with key Socialists who would take a bi-partisan approach to matters of major consequence."

The Plans for a Bi-Partisan Approach to Get Around the U.S. Constitution: On May 19, 1919, House hosted a dinner party at the Majestic Hotel in Paris for selected Fabian Socialists from England and American Socialists. Guests were Professor James Shotwell, Roger Lansing (Wilson's Secretary of State), John Foster Dulles, Allen Dulles, Tasker Bliss, and Christian Herter (the man most responsible for placing Mao tse Tung in power in China.) Leading Fabians from England were R.W. Tawney, Arnold Toynbee and John Maynard Keynes (whose socialist, "Keynesian"-economic theories are what are most prevalently taught in our high school and college economic classes today.)

The group decided that to get around the U.S. Constitution, it would be necessary to set up an organization in the U.S. similar to, and to work with, the Royal Institute of International Affairs (RIIA). The American branch would be called the "Institute of International Affairs" with the stated purpose: "to facilitate the scientific study of international questions." There would be similar branches established in Canada, Australia, Chile, etc. However, they decided later to change the name for the USA group to the "Council on Foreign Relations" to make it appear as if there was no connection to the powerful British group.

Myron Fagen, a playwright, has written an essay about the CFR and their link to the secret society, the Illuminati, which you will read about in the next chapter. He states, "The masterminds in control of the . . . conspirators were foreigners, but to conceal that fact, most of them changed their original family names to American sounding names." For example, the true last name of Clarence and Douglas Dillon, who were invited to be part of the group who planned the

CFR, was Laposky. Douglas Dillon later became the Secretary of the Treasury for John F. Kennedy.[146]

Founding Day for the CFR: On July, 29, 1921, the Council on Foreign Relations (CFR) was established in New York City with the help and influence of the Roundtable Groups of England. The CFR used to be a highly secretive group, but they have now gained such power and influence that they are quite open about their membership, activities and globalist philosophies, which you can read on their own website *www.CFR.org.*

Influence of the Powerful Rockefeller Family: The Rockefeller family donated the land for the CFR headquarters, located at the corner of Park Avenue and 68th Street in New York City. Little by little, they began to have more and more control and influence over the CFR and its membership. Major funding came for the CFR from the Rockefeller Foundation and the Carnegie Foundation. David Rockefeller became the Director in 1949 and the Chairman of the Board for 1970 to 1985. He continues to have enormous influence and power over the CFR.[147]

Who Were the First Members of the CFR? Its members were politicians high up in government, banking, and academia. Some of them were the same players you have already been reading about: Edward Mandel House, financiers J.P. Morgan, Paul Warburg, Walter Lippmann, Elihu Root, Herbert Hoover, Lional Curtis, John Foster Dulles, Herbert Lehman, Henry Stinson, Averill Harriman, educators James Thomson Shotwell of Columbia University, Archibald Coolidge of Harvard, and Charles Seymore of Yale. John W. Davis became its founding president.

The Purpose for the Royal Institute and the CFR: The following is a statement made by one of the members of the Royal Institute for International Affairs, Arnold Toynbee, a British professor, spoken before a similar "international" group in Denmark, in 1931. He reveals one of the Royal Institute's main objectives which is the same objective for the CFR: *"We are at present working discreetly with all our might to wrest this mysterious force called sovereignty out of the clutches of the local nation states of the world."*[148]

The Pretended Purpose: However, if you click on the CFR Website, you will find a very innocent-sounding mission statement. They are just a nice foreign affairs organization and center to help people better understand the world:

> *The Council on Foreign Relations is an independent, national*
> *membership organization and a nonpartisan center for scholars dedicated*
> *to producing and disseminating ideas so that individual and corporate*
> *members, as well as policymakers, journalists, students, and interested*
> *citizens in the United States and other countries, can better understand*
> *the world and the foreign policy choices facing the United States and*
> *other governments.*[149]

Their mission statement doesn't sound bad at all, does it? However, when
you read the statements below, some written by people who once belonged to
the CFR, you find there is a vastly different hidden agenda:

Hidden Agendas Showing the Real Objectives of the CFR:

- **Disarmament, Submerging U.S. into a Powerful One-World Government**:
  "This purpose of promoting disarmament, and submergence of U.S. sovereignty,
  and national independence into an all-powerful one-world government is the only
  objective revealed to about 95 percent of the CFR 1,551 members [the number
  of members back in 1975]." Rear Admiral Chester Ward, Judge Advocate
  General of the Navy from 1946-1960. (Written after giving up his 15-year
  membership in the CFR.)
- **Elimination of all Armed Forces and Armaments**: This statement is found
  in the 1961 State Department Document 7277, adopted by the Kennedy
  Administration. (All of the state department and President Kennedy were
  members of the CFR.) *". . . elimination of all armed forces and armaments*
  except those needed to maintain internal order within states and to furnish the
  United Nations with peace forces . . . by that time it (UN global government)
  would be so strong no nation could challenge it."
- **One-World Banking, Credit, Manufacturing System, Policed by**
  a One-World Army: *". . . The goals of the Establishment are somewhat*
  strange . . . At the central core is a belief in the superiority of their own skill to
  form a world system in which enlightened monopolistic capitalism can bring
  all of the diverse currencies, banking systems, credit, manufacturing, and raw
  materials into one government-supervised whole, policed of course by their own
  world army." Rear Admiral Ward.[150]
- **Dominate the Political Systems of Each Country and the Economy of**
  the World as a Whole: *Tragedy and Hope,* was published in 1966, written
  by liberal Professor Caroll Quigley of Georgetown University (who was Bill
  Clinton's mentor and to whom Clinton gave the most credit when he was

elected to the presidency). *Tragedy and Hope* is a history of the insiders and their activities revealing their intent to create a one-world government. It is from this book and an earlier one called the *Anglo-American Establishment,* that we get most of the information about Cecil Rhodes, Lord Milner and the Round Table Groups. The following is what Quigley said about the purpose of the CFR and other insider groups, " . . . *nothing less than to create a world system of financial control in private hands able to dominate the political systems of each country and the economy of the world as a whole.* "[51]

- **Do Away with U.S. Nationality:** In the 50th Anniversary issue of "Foreign Affairs" the official publication of the CFR was an article by Kingman Brewster, Jr. entitled, *Reflections On Our National Purpose.* In it he stated, **" . . . our purpose should be to do away with our nationality,** *to take some risks in order to invite some others to pool their sovereignty with ours. "*

- **Surrender the Sovereignty and Independence of the United States:** *"The most powerful cliques in these elitist groups have one objective in common: they want to bring about the surrender of the sovereignty and national independence of the United States."* Admiral Chester Ward, from the 1975 book that he co-authored with Phyllis Schlafley, *Kissinger on the Coach,* that reveals the inner workings of the CFR. Admiral Ward had belonged to the CFR, so he knew firsthand what they were all about.

- **Destroy Sovereignty Piece by Piece:** The CFR's *Foreign Affairs* magazine published an article by Richard Gardner (CFR) in 1974 in which he proposed: " . . . *an end run around national sovereignty, eroding it piece by piece; that will accomplish much more than the old-fashioned frontal assault. "* Gardner, former deputy assistant Secretary of State, was Bill Clinton's (CFR) campaign advisor on the United Nations and became Ambassador to Spain when Clinton became president.

- **Yield Some of our Sovereignty:** On September 29, 1992, Winston Lord (CFR) acknowledged *"to a certain extent we are going to have to yield some of our sovereignty."* President Reagan appointed him as Ambassador to China, and later President Clinton appointed him Secretary of State for East Asian and Pacific Affairs.

- **To Obliterate National Borders and Establish a One World Rule:** Senator Barry Goldwater described the CFR's belief in no borders, *"The Council on Foreign Relations . . . **believes national boundaries should be obliterated and one world rule established. "***

- **Eliminate Borders Between the U.S., Canada and Mexico by the Year 2010:** This plan is spelled out in detail in the Council on Foreign Relations (CFR) 59-page document called "Building a North America Community," written in May of 2005 by a task force of CFR members, one of which was Robert Pastor, known as the father of the North American Union. It describes a five year plan for" the establishment by 2010 of a North America economic and security community with a *common outer security perimeter"* (the northern border of Canada and the southern border of Mexico), thus effectively eliminating secured borders between the U.S. and Canada and the U.S. and Mexico.

The actual "building of the North American Community" had already begun two months before the publication of the CFR document with the launching of "the Security and Prosperity Partnership" of North America (SPP) on March 23, 2005 at a meeting in Waco, Texas, between President George Bush, then Mexican President Vicente Fox and then Canadian Prime Minister Paul Martin. A follow-up meeting was held in Ottawa on June 27, 2005, where U.S. representatives, including Homeland Security Secretary told a news conference, *"We want to facilitate the flow of traffic across our borders.*"[152] (Chapter Eleven tells more about the SPP meetings that have been held ever since 2005.)

- **To Exercise Enormous Influence on Government, especially the State Department:** When it was first established, the CFR was a quasi-secretive organization that very few people knew of, but it soon began to have enormous influence over U.S. government, especially foreign policy. By 1940, at the invitation of FDR, members of the CFR gained dominance over the State Department. They have maintained that domination ever since. As an example, read the following statement made by Hillary Clinton, the U.S. Secretary of State under Obama's administration. She was asked to give a report before the CFR, July 15, 2009, at their new office building in Washington D.C. After being introduced by Richard Haas, the CFR President, her opening remarks were:

> *Thank you very much, Richard, and I am delighted to be here in these new headquarters. I have been often to, I guess, **the mother ship** in New York City, but it's good to have an outpost of the Council right here down the street from the State Department. We get a lot of advice from the Council, so this will mean I won't have as far to go **to be told what we should be doing and how we should think about the future.***[153]

So, in other words, **The CFR is the "Mother Ship"** for the State Department and tells them what they "should be doing" and what they "should be thinking about the future." Thank you, Hillary—pretty revealing words, coming from our Secretary of State! I would add that it is not only the State Department that gets its marching orders from the "mother ship," but all the branches of our government.

- **To Exercise Enormous Influence on the Executive Branch of Government**: Beginning with President Franklin D. Roosevelt, it became customary that the final candidates running for presidency for both the Republican or Democrat Party would just happen to belong to the CFR. And for the presidency elected, at least one of the two, either president or vice president would be a CFR member. Eisenhower and Nixon were both CFR members, as were Democrats Stevenson, Kennedy, Humphrey, and McGovern. Since 1940, seven elected presidents have all been CFR members before they were elected. There are only three exceptions: Gerald Ford, Ronald Reagan, and George W. Bush, but their Vice Presidents were all members: Nelson Rockefeller, George Bush Sr., and Dick Cheney. Gerald Ford after his presidency became a member of the CFR.[154]

- **To Back Both Sides of an Issue and Back Both Candidates Running for Office**: That way whoever wins, the CFR always wins. Author Daniel Estulin's research reveals that "the Council on Foreign Relations creates and delivers psycho-political operations by manipulating people's reality through a 'tactic of deception,' placing Council members on both sides of an issue. The deception is complete when the public is led to believe that its own best interests are being served while the CFR policy is being carried out."[155]

- **To Act as Invisible Rulers:** Felix Frankfurter, Supreme Court Justice (1939-1962) said, *"The real rulers of Washington are invisible and exercise power from behind the scene."*

- **To Serve as the Foreign Policy Elite Who Prepare People for Top-Level Missions in Government:** In his book, *Men and Power*, Helmut Schmidt, former Chancellor of West Germany referred to the CFR as the "foreign policy elite" which prepared people for "top-level missions in government," and he noted, "it had a very silent but effective way of seeing to its own succession."

- **To Act as Another Form of Government—A Bureaucratic Elite, which has Little Regard for the Constitution**: Senator William Jenner warned in a speech, *"outwardly we have a constitutional government, but we have operating within our government and political system another body representing another form of government, a bureaucratic-elite, which believes our constitution is outmoded."*

- **To Act as its Own Secret Political Party—the Only One with Any Consequence**: In 1987, Professor Arthur Selwyn Miller, a Rockefeller-funded historian, wrote *". . . . the fact that the existence of the Establishment—the ruling class—is not supposed to be discussed. A third secret is . . . . that there is really only one political party of any consequence in the United States . . . . The Republicans and the Democrats are in fact two branches of the same (secret) party."*

- **To Act as a "Think Tank" for Foreign Affairs:** This is how CFR members are trying to portray themselves—as a small, innocuous "think tank." This is also how Rush Limbaugh now describes the CFR on his radio talk show. I heard him announce in the fall of 2007 that President George W. Bush would be speaking before the Council on Foreign Relations that day. He then added, *"If some of you do not know what that is—the CFR is kind of a "Think Tank" about Foreign affairs."*

The following is a very clever answer to the "think tank" label being used to describe the CFR. This is the last paragraph of a letter to the editor that was published in a Delaware newspaper by Allen Ide of Millsboro, Delaware. He was replying to an earlier letter to the editor that was defending the CFR and called it a "think tank.":

> *Your reader's view that the CFR is a think tank analogous with other think-tanks is like saying a row boat is analogous to a battleship because they both can float on water. The statement is true as far as it goes, it just does not begin to go far enough. It totally ignores the differences which are far greater than the similarities, thus creating a false impression.* [156]

2008 Election: Many of the original candidates running for presidency for 2008 were CFR members, such as Rudy Giuliani, Fred Thompson, John Edwards, John McCain, Hillary Clinton, (as is her husband Bill. They are also members of Bilderbergers, and Bill is a member of the Trilateral Commission, which you will read about in the next chapter.) Obama is not CFR but is a member of the Bilderbergers. However, he has strong affiliations with the CFR. One of the top CFR leaders was his advisor, Zbigniew Brzezinski, who just happens to be the co-founder of the Trilateral Commission. Obama's Vice President, Joe Biden, is a CFR member.

The candidates in the 2008 election who were not CFR members were not given much air time in the debates or real news coverage, with the exception of Mitt Romney. Romney had been asked to speak before the CFR and was accepted by them. It could have also been due to the many millions of dollars that he spent on his own campaign. He was hard to ignore. The conservative candidates running who were not CFR and not accepted by them, Congressmen Ron Paul, Duncan Hunter, and Tom Tancredo, were virtually ignored or ridiculed by the media. Mike Huckabee was treated a little bit better. Perhaps, it was because of his liberal views on immigration and high taxes when he was the governor of Arkansas. Those who ended up on the final slate, McCain and Obama, both have strong CFR connections.

Judges Who Are All CFR Members: The Roe v. Wade Case of 1973, that legalized abortion, was decided by nine Supreme Court Justices who were all CFR members: Burger (appointed by Nixon in 1969); Douglas (Roosevelt 1939); Brennan (Eisenhower 1956); Stewart (Eisenhower 1958); White (Kennedy 1962); Marshall (Johnson 1967); Blackmun (Nixon 1970); Powell (Nixon 1971); Rehnquist (Nixon 1971). If a vacancy arises, it is distressing to find out that the president of the nation is advised by CFR members on his cabinet as to whom the best selection for a Supreme Court justice should be. Is anyone surprised if the person selected just happens to be a CFR member too? As Daniel Estulin writes, "This not only compromises the American justice system . . . it also suggests that the final custodians of our individual rights are, in fact, looking after the interests of the CFR."[157]

Vast Majority of all Cabinet Members are Picked from the CFR: It is almost as if a president would not dare pick a cabinet member if he or she is not coming from this exclusive club. Take a look for example at our last five presidents: President Jimmy Carter, himself CFR, had 284 CFR members of his cabinet. Ronald Reagan, not a member of the CFR, who all the conservatives were sure would bring a change in policy, ended up with a CFR Vice President, George Bush, and 257 CFR members of his cabinet. By 1988, Reagan's CFR cabinet members had grown to 313.

President Bush Sr., who was not only a CFR member, but a member of the elite Trilateral Commission, (of which you will read later), led the number of CFR members in his cabinet with a whopping 382! Bill Clinton, a member of the CFR, the Trilateral Commission, and the Bilderburgers, three exclusive elite groups, was not to be outdone by any former president. At the end of his 8 year term as president, he had 548 members of his cabinet from the CFR.

George W. Bush, who does not belong to the CFR, picked a very powerful CFR Vice President, Dick Cheney, who also just happens to be a former director of the Trilateral Commission. At the half point in George W. Bush's first term, he had 516 cabinet members picked from the CFR. As one can see, it does not matter if the president is a republican or democrat, the CFR insider control continues on.[158]

Other Members of the CFR Prominent in Government and Media Positions: Dick Cheney, Condoleezza Rice, Paul Wolfowitz, Robert M. Gates, John D. Negroponte, Richard Perle, Colin Powell, Madeleine Albright, Zbigniew Brzezinski, Henry Kissinger, Jack Welch, Alan Greenspan, Paul Volker, George Sorros, Brent Skowcroft, George Shultz, Jimmy Carter, Warren Christopher, James D. Wolfensohn, Steven Weinberg, Barbara Walters, John Kerry, Angelina Jolie,

McCain and Obama, final candidates for the 2008 election; both have strong ties to the CFR.

Strobe Talbot, Casper Weinberger, Dean Rusk, Robert McNamara, Arthur Schlesinger.[159]

What About McCain and Obama? Would it have mattered much which one was elected in the 2008 election as far as the CFR Goes? McCain is a member. Obama is not, but they both had top CFR advisors helping them with their campaigns. Obama's advisor was not only a leader in the CFR, but the co-founder of the Trilateral Commission, Zbigniew Brzezinski. McCain had CFR Randy Scheunemann as his top advisor. He was the former aid to Trent Lott and Bob Dole, both CFR members, as was Elizabeth Dole. With every election since 1940, no matter who is elected, the vast majority of cabinet members will be CFR members and it will be the promotion of CFR goals and policies as usual.

CFR Members in Obama's Cabinet—Is Obama Really All About Change? Let's see how many new fresh faces he has picked or are they the same CFR retreads?

CFR Members in Obama's Foreign Policy/National Security Team: Hillary Clinton, Secretary of State, Robert Gates, Secretary of Defense (CFR); General James Jones, National Security Advisor (CFR); Governor Janet Napolitano, Head of Homeland Security (CFR); Susan Rice, US Ambassador to the UN (CFR). The only man on his new security team who is not a member of the CFR is Eric Holder as the Attorney General.

As Members of the Economic Team: Timothy Geithner, Secretary of the Treasury (CFR); Lawrence Summers, National Economic Council Director (CFR); Paul Volker (former Federal Reserve Chairman, member of the Trust Committee of the Rockefeller Group, and former Director of the United Nations Association of the USA), Now Head of Economic Recovery Advisory Board (CFR).

Other Members of the CFR on Obama's Team: Rahm Emanual, Chief of Staff; David Axelrod, White House Advisor. Other CFR advisors are: George Mitchell, Richard Holbrooke, Eric Shinseki, Ivo Daalder, Neal Wolin, Lael Brainard, Ashton Carter, and Michele A. Flourney. (Many of Obama's czars are members of the CFR. More will be written about them in the chapter on Obama.)

How Large is the Membership in the CFR Today? According to a writer back in 2004, the membership then was 4,200. Most of them are life members, but some are accepted for just a five-year membership. Membership in the Council is by invitation only: a potential member must be a U.S. citizen who has been nominated and seconded by other CFR members and elected by the Board of Directors.

Two-thirds of CFR members live in the New York and Washington, DC areas. Fully 31 percent (1,299 individuals) are from the corporate (business) sector, with another 25 percent (1,071 individuals) coming from varied academic settings (professors, university administrators, researchers, fellows). Nonprofits contribute 15 percent (640), government 13 percent (541), law 8 percent (319), the media 6 percent (248), and "other" 2 percent (74). Members pay a yearly fee on a sliding scale, depending on age, occupation, and residence.

Corporate Membership: There is also a special category of corporate membership: executives from 200 "leading international companies representing a range of sectors" participate in special CFR programs. Corporations representing capital in its most abstract forms-the financial sector, the largest commercial and investment banks, insurance companies, and strategic planning corporations-are most heavily represented in the Council. Petroleum, military, and media companies also have fairly close connections. A review of director lists of major corporations found that the following corporations have at least three of their directors who are also CFR members: American Insurance Group and Citigroup: Eight directors; J.P. Morgan Chase, Boeing: Six directors; The Blackstone Group, Conoco, Disney/ABC: Five directors; Kissinger-McLarty Associates, IBM, Exxon Mobil, Dow Jones, *Wall Street Journal*, Viacom/CBS, Time Warner: Four directors The Carlyle Group, Lehman Brothers, Morgan Stanley, Goldman Sachs, Merrill Lynch, Credit Suisse, First Boston. *Washington Post/Newsweek*, Chevron Texaco, Lockheed Martin, Halliburton, Alliance Capital: Three directors.

The CFR Uses Tax-Free Foundations for Funding Purposes: Thomas R. Dye stated that nearly 40% of all foundation assets were controlled by the top ten or eleven foundations, which in turn were controlled by the CFR. "The directors or trustees have great latitude in directing the use of foundation monies to underwrite research, investigate social problems, create or assist universities, establish think tanks, endow museums, etc."

Daniel Estulin in his book, *the True Story of the Bilderburger Book* (of which you will read more in the following Chapter), gives an example of a Tax-Free Foundation—the RAND National Defense Research Institute. It is a federally-funded Council on Foreign Relations "Think Tank," sponsored by the Office of the Secretary of Defense and headed by a CFR member, Michael D. Rich. Its leadership is interlocking between the trustees at RAND and those of the Ford, Rockefeller, and Carnegie Foundations, which Estulin describes as a "classic case of CFR/Bilderberg modus operandi." The Ford Foundation gave one million dollars to RAND in 1952, when the president of the Ford Foundation just happened to also be the president of RAND. RAND's clients include an impressive list of both government and private agencies and businesses: the Pentagon, AT&T, Chase Manhattan Bank, IBM, the Republican Party, the U.S. Air Force, The U.S. Department of Energy and NASA.[160]

Why Have Most Americans Not Heard About the CFR? Is it not amazing that one group is so powerful that it effectively controls national governments, and multinational corporations; it promotes world government through control of media, foundation grants, and education; and it controls and guides the issues of the day, and no one seems to know or question this?

Major Media Heads, who Belong to the CFR, Are Controlled by It: The following is a statement made by David Rockefeller where he thanked the media for their "discretion:

> We are grateful to the Washington Post, the New York Times, Time Magazine and other great publications whose directors have attended our meetings and respected their promises of discretion for almost forty years. . . . It would have been impossible for us to develop our plan for the world if we had been subjected to the lights of publicity during those years. **But, the world is now more sophisticated and prepared to march towards a world government. The supranational sovereignty of an intellectual elite and world bankers is surely preferable to the national auto-determination practiced in past centuries.**[161]

February 9, 1917, Statement Made by Congressman Oscar Callaway How Major American Newspapers Had Been Taken Over (as written up in the Congressional Record):

> In March, 1915, the J.P. Morgan interest . . . and their subsidiary organizations, got together 12 men high up in the newspaper world and employed them to select the most influential newspapers in the United States and sufficient number of them to control generally the policy of the daily press of the United States. These 12 men . . . found it was only necessary to purchase the control of 25 of the greatest papers. The 25 were agreed upon; emissaries were sent to purchase the policy, national and international, of these papers; an agreement was reached; the policy of the papers bought, to be paid for by the month; an editor was furnished for each paper to properly supervise and edit information . . . considered vital to the interests of the purchasers.[162]

So, the control of the newspapers has been going on since 1915. This control was used back then to persuade the American people to go along with the US entering World War I. How many other "persuasions" have been used by these same 25 newspapers over the year since to support the socialist, globalist agenda and portray it as something wonderful and beneficial?

Just How Wonderful Would a One-World Government Be? Is it going to be the heavenly "utopia" so many people have been programmed to think of, where there are no wars, only peace prevails, everyone is equal and all injustice and inequality has been done away with? If you have read the fictional books written by authors describing the future that they envision, such as: *Brave New World; 1984; Animal Farm; The Giver; Philip Dru: Administrator;* a one-world government will not be a heavenly place at all.

Playwright Myron C. Fagan Reveals the Truth about the CFR, the UN and The Plans for World Government: Myron C. Fagen became acquainted with John T. Flynn, the author of *The Roosevelt Myth, While We Slept,* and *The True Story of Pearl Harbor.* Flynn told Fagan about the CFR and about what was really going on in government. He invited Fagan to see some micro-films and recordings revealing the truth about Yalta and the plot of Franklin Roosevelt, Alger Hiss, Harry Hopkins, Stalin, Molotov, and Vishinsky to deliver the Balkans, Eastern Europe and Berlin to Stalin.

Fagan was so upset with how these powerful, deceptive people had kept the truth from the American people that he wrote two plays: "Red Rainbow," in which he exposed the Yalta plot and "Thieves Paradise," that told of the plot to create the United Nations as the "housing" for a Communist One-World Government.

At the same time, Mr. Fagan launched a "one-man" crusade to unmask the "Red Conspiracy," people who were involved in producing films to promote communism and a "one-world government." These people were not only producing films in Hollywood but also productions for television and radio.

Fagen created the Cinema Education Guild (CEG) in 1947. As a result of his work and the CEG, the Congressional Hearings began in which more than 300 of Hollywood's most famous stars, writers, directors and producers were unmasked as the chief activists of the Red Conspiracy. The worst of the group, the infamous "Hollywood Ten," were sent to prison.

Fagen spoke on a tape about all that he had found out—who was really behind the one-world conspiracy and what the final plans are. The tape is called "The Illuminati and the Council of Foreign Relations." Here is a quote from it:

> In the final phases of the conspiracy; the one-world government will consist of the king-dictators: the head of the United Nations, the CFR, and a few billionaires, economists, and scientists who have proved their devotion to the great conspiracy. All others are to be integrated into a vast conglomeration of mongrelized humanity; actually slaves.[163]

Yes, as shocking as that may sound, that is the goal. The elitists truly want to bring back the Dark Ages and the feudal system with them as the powerful lords, kings, and dictators and the rest of humanity as serfs or slaves.

The next chapter will tell of even more powerful secret societies who are working for the same goals as that of the RIIA and the CFR in support of the United Nations and world government. (For a listing of all the other similar groups to the RIIA and the CFR that exist in many other nations, go to http://www.isgp. eu/AppendixA.htm.)

Chapter Ten

More Support for the UN by Other Secretive Organizations Supporting Regional and World Government

This chapter gives a closer examination of other powerful secretive groups that wield great power and influence over the US government and the move to integration and world government.

The Bilderbergers

1954—The Founding of the Bilderbergers at the Hotel de Bilderberg in the Netherlands: Similar to the CFR, but very secretive, the Bilderbergers is a powerful international organization made up of men and women who believe in world government and who are the ones behind the scenes creating world policy even for the United Nations. Unlike the CFR, the Bilderbergers have no website and no membership list. They would like to remain secret and anonymous, but more and more people are finding our about them.

Their organization was started in Osterbrook, Holland in 1954, supposedly under the direction of the husband of the Queen of Holland, Prince Bernhard. There are several noteworthy facts about Prince Bernhard and his background and connections:

Prince Bernhard: Bernhard, according to several reports, was a member of the Nazi Party, the *"Sturmabteilung"* and was an officer in the Cavalry Corps called the *"Reiter SS."* He was also on the board of an I.G. Farben subsidiary, called Farben Bilder. The Prince later denied these well-documented memberships. But some believe it was from his association with Farben Bilder that he suggested the name of Bilderburgers instead of from the name of the hotel where they first met.[164]

Farben Provided War Materials and Funding for Hitler: I.G. Farben was the largest of the American industrial cartels that was invested in war industries—providing war materials to Hitler as well as the primary source of political funding for Hitler. Farben also staffed and directed Hitler's intelligence (spying) section and ran the NAZI slave labor camps as a supplemental source of manpower for Germany's factories. During the Allied bombing raids over Germany, the factories and administrative buildings of I.G. Farben were spared upon instructions from the U.S. War Department.

Wall Street was also Involved in Funding Hitler: Much of the capital for the expansion of I.G. Farben came from Wall Street, primarily from Rockefeller's National City Bank; Dillon, Read & Company; J.P. Morgan's Equitable Trust Company; Harris Forbes & Company; and the predominantly Jewish firm of Kuhn, Loeb & Company. As one can see, when it comes to making money, these elitists have no loyalty or patriotism to country or to ethnic roots. Keeping with tradition, they fund both sides of the war. War to them is just a big money-making enterprise. [165]

The Founding Members of the Bilderbergers: Joseph Retinger, a Polish socialist, is the one who master-minded the founding of the Bilderbergers and invited Prince Bernhard to host it. They were joined by Duncan Sandys, a British Eurocrat, and John J. McCloy, from the USA, who was serving as Chairman of the CFR as well as the U.S. High Commissioner to Germany after World War II. He had served as Assistant Secretary of War, during which time he had approved an order permitting Communist Party members to become officers in the U.S. Army. In a memo that FBI head, J. Edgar Hoover, had sent to President Truman, he had warned him of an enormous Soviet espionage ring in Washington . . . and identified McCloy, Dean Acheson and Alger Hiss, as worrisome for their pro-Soviet leanings."[166] McCloy was joined by his staff member, Sheppard Stone, and Robert Murphy, the U.S. Ambassador to Belgium, and Prime Minister of Belgium, Paul-Henri Spaak, who was the head of the movement to form a European Community or Union. He was affectionately known in Europe as "Mr. Socialist."

The Purpose of the Bilderbergers—Relinquish Nationalism to a World Government: As with the CFR and the Trilateral Commission, the two other quasi-secret groups, they all have a similar purpose—to move the nations of the world away from nationalism and closer to a one-world government. The following was said by the supposed founder **Prince Bernhard of Holland, "*It is difficult to re-educate people who have been brought up on nationalism to the idea of relinquishing part of their sovereignty to a supra-national body.*"** The following are the many ways in which the Bilderbergers hope to achieve their goals:

- **Move Europe in the direction of a European Union and to provide the funds to do so:** McCloy, as the U.S. High Commissioner in Germany, raided the huge pile of European currencies that had stockpiled as a result of the Marshall Plan aid, and he, Stone and Murphy "promptly and unhesitantly put ample funds at the disposal of Paul Henri Spaak" so he could use them towards creating a European Union. March 25, 1957, three years after the Bilderbergers was formed, the treaties took place that officially launched the European Union, the two Treaties of Rome. They created the European Community and the European Atomic Energy Community.[167]

- **Promote A Global Agenda and the Notion that National Sovereignty is Antiquated and Regressive:** According to an article about the Bilderburgers in *World Net Daily*, May 30, 2007, "The New World Disorder," their purpose today is the same as when it was first founded, "According to sources that have penetrated the high-security meetings in the past, the Bilderberger meetings emphasize a globalist agenda and promote the idea that the notion of national sovereignty is antiquated and regressive."

- **Erase the Sovereignty and Gain Control of the Economies of all Nations:** According to the same *WND* article, The Bilderbergers, along with the CFR and TC, *"have become a shadow government whose top priority is to erase the sovereignty of all nation-states and supplant them with global corporate control of their economies under the surveillance of "an electronic global police state."*

- **Use Scare Tactics such as the Threat of Nuclear War:** This will make countries more willing to submit their sovereignty to the control of a world body such as the United Nations.[168]

- **Create a Fascist One-World Empire:** Daniel Estulin, whose book about the Bilderbergers was mentioned in the chapter about the CFR, wonders how these supposed "humanitarian do gooders" such as "John Edwards, Hillary Clinton, the Rockefellers and every Royal House of Europe" can continue to attend these Bilderberger meetings and return home to happily go forward expanding the powers of the one-world government apparently knowing full well *"that the final objective of this despicable group of hoodlums is a fascist One World Empire?"*[169]

- **Create a Global Economy, World Government (Selected not Elected) and A Universal Religion:** Estulin quotes from Father William H. Shannon, who has researched much on the Bilderbergers:

> *"The Bilderbergers are searching for the age of post-nationalism: when we won't have countries, but rather regions of the Earth surrounded by Universal values—that is to say, a global economy, one World government*

(selected rather than elected) and a universal religion. To assure
themselves of reaching these objectives, the Bilderbergers focus on a 'greater
technical approach' and less awareness on behalf of the general public."

- **Centralized Control of the People:** Through modern technology and mind control, they plan to direct all humanity to obey their wishes. This is described in Zbigniew Brzesinski's book, *Between Two Ages: America's Role in the Technetronic Era*. He foresees under the New World Order, no middle class, only rulers and servants.

- **A Zero-Growth Society:** As has been mentioned before, population control has always been one of the objectives of the elite. I always thought it was because smaller populations are easier to keep track of and control. Estulin has a new take on the reasons for it that he has gleaned from reports at Bilderberger meetings—"to stop prosperity, progress, and production." These elitists are really ruthless.

> *In a post-industrial period, zero growth will be necessary to destroy vestiges*
> *of general prosperity. When there is prosperity, there is progress. Prosperity*
> *and progress make it impossible to implement repression, and you need*
> *repression if you hope to divide society into owners and slaves. The end*
> *of prosperity will bring an end to the production of nuclear-generated*
> *electic power and all industrialization (except for the computer and service*
> *industries.) The remaining Canadian and American industries would*
> *be exported to poor countries such as Bolivia, Peru, Ecuador, Nicaragua,*
> *where slave labor is cheap. One of the principal objectives of NAFTA*
> *will then be realized.*

- **De-Industrialize the World by Suppressing all Scientific Developments:** This is why the elite are so opposed to nuclear energy. It would generate enough cheap energy to bring third-world countries out of their backward state and make them less dependent on US foreign aid, which keeps them in servitude.

- **A State of Perpetual Imbalance so Apathy on a Massive Scale Can Be Created:** The elite do not like opposition. They prefer a confused, demoralized, and apathetic populace. Estulin describes how they purposely create apathy:

> *By artificially manufacturing crisis that will put people under continual*
> *duress,—physically, mentally, and emotionally—it is possible to keep*

people in a perpetual state of imbalance. Too tired and strung-out to decide their own destinies, populations will be confused and demoralized to the extent that "faced with too many choices, apathy on a massive scale will result."

- **Centralize Control of All Education:** In *The Incremental Chipping Away of the Once Great USA,* I write about the attack on education and reveal how centralized control is already a done deal in our nation. Now that we have national standards coming from the Federal Department of Education that receives its marching orders straight from UNESCO, the UN organization is essentially in charge of American education. (Of course, the Department of Education tries to keep that hush-hush. Not too many Americans would be happy to find that out.)

   Estulin writes that one of the reasons for the European Union, the North American Union, the Asian Union, the African Union and all the other regional governments that are being formed it to *"seek greater control of education in general and to allow one-world globalists to steralize the world's true past."* He says it is already working. *"Todays youth are almost completely ignorant of the lessons of history, individual liberties, and the meaning of freedom."*

- **Centralize Control of All Foreign and Domestic Policies:** Little by little, the powerful elite are exercising more and more control over foreign and domestic policies of all nations. It is a done deal for the Europeans under the European Union, and it will be the same for us if we come under a North American Union. We will have lost our own autonomy as the European nations have done.

- **Empower the United Nations:** The elitists are hoping to give the UN more and more power, to shape it into a *"de jure" (legal)* and then *"de facto" (actually existing)* world government and charge a UN tax on "world citizens."

- **Form Large Western Trading Blocs:** By expanding NAFTA throughout the Western Hemisphere including South America, a large American Union will eventually form similar to the European Union. (Of course, they can't call it an American Union as yet, just like they never called the EU a union until it was a done deal. They did not want to alarm the Europeans into any action that might have stopped the EU from forming.)

- **Expand NATO:** As the UN intervenes in more trouble-spots globally, as it is in Afghanistan now, NATO becomes the UN's world army.

- **Create One Legal System:** The International Criminal Court and the International Court of Justice are to become the sole legal system for the world. There will only be trial by a tribunal. The jury system will be gone.

- **Create One Socialist Welfare State:** The Bilderbergers envision a socialist welfare state, where obedient slaves will be rewarded and non-conformists will be targeted for extermination.[170]

The Bilderbergers are One of the Most Influential Groups on the Planet but No Press Coverage is Allowed: Many news directors are Bilderberger members but are not allowed to do any news coverage while they are in attendance. *World Net Daily* quotes from a 2003 BBC report about the Bilderbergers:

> 'It's officially described as a private gathering,' noted a BBC report in 2003, 'but with a guest list including the heads of European and American corporations, political leaders and a few intellectuals, it's one of the most influential organizations on the planet.'
>
> . . . Not a word of what is said at Bilderberg meetings can be breathed outside. No reporters are invited in and while confidential minutes of meetings are taken, names are not noted. The shadowy aura extends further—the anonymous answer phone message, for example; the fact that conference venues are kept secret. The group, which includes luminaries such as Henry Kissinger and former UK chancellor Kenneth Clarke, does not even have a website.'
>
> Those attending the Bilderberg meetings defend the secrecy by such comments, 'The secrecy is not evidence of a grand conspiracy, but only an opportunity to speak frankly with other world leaders out of the limelight of press coverage and its inevitable repercussions.'[171]

David Rockefeller Thanked the Directors of News Sources for their "Discretion" for Forty Years: Rockefeller made the following comments at the 1991 Bilderberg meeting held in Baden-Baden Germany:

> We are grateful to the Washington Post, the New York Times, Time Magazine, and other great publications, whose directors have attended our meetings and respected their promises of discretion for almost forty years . . . It would have been impossible for us to develop our plan for the world if we had been subjected to the lights of publicity during those years. But the world is more sophisticated and prepared to march towards a world government. The supranational sovereignty of an intellectual elite and world bankers is surely preferable to the national auto determination practiced in past centuries.[172]

How Does One Get Tapped to Become a "Bilderberg Person?" The group's steering committee decides whom to invite and their qualifications have not changed over the years. "Essentially, they look for a One-World Order enthusiast and a Fabian Socialist, who believes in control of society in all of its activities and control of the individual, which is best achieved through global government."[173]

Membership is Structured with an Inner Circle (or Core) and with Concentric Circles: Estulin believes that not all members are "bad" people. They are deceived, thinking it is some great honor to be invited to join the Bilderbergers. The membership is similar to so many "secretive" groups, including the CFR, with circles inside circles. It is only the inner core who really fully understands what the ultimate purpose of the group is. The exterior layer (secret team) protects the inner core and their identity. None of the different circles really know who are in the other circles or their objectives or roles. This is to protect itself from possible prosecution by denying its participation in the operation.

The Extent of Power In Membership—Both Sides of the Political Spectrum: Estulin points out that almost all of the presidential candidates for both parties have belonged to at least one of these organizations: many U.S. congressmen and senators; most major policy-making positions, especially in the field of foreign relations; much of the press; most of the leadership of the CIA, FBI, IRS, and many of the remaining governmental organizations in Washington. CFR members occupy nearly all White House cabinet positions. When one considers that most prominent members of mainstream media are also members of what Edith Kermit Roosevelt, granddaughter of Theodore Roosevelt called "this legitimate Mafia," how can we assert that Americans obtain their news from independent sources?

Likewise, when we consider the membership in one or more of these groups of almost every American president since the inception of these organizations, we can no longer pretend that any Democrat or Republican presidential candidate offers the American people an alternative to the ruling elite global hegemony.

Almost every famous player in politics and finance in the world is invited, and their political affiliations supposedly range from "liberal to conservative," for example: George W. Bush, George Soros, Gerald Ford, George McGovern, and Jimmy Carter.

If a True Conservative Is Nominated for Office, Who is Not a Member of the Elite, He is Labeled and Humiliated and Can't Possibly Win: Estulin gives the example of Barry Goldwater who shocked the establishment by winning the Republican nomination in 1964. Rockefeller and the CFR controlled media labeled Goldwater as "a dangerous radical who would abolish Social Security and drop atom bombs on Honoi." Of course, his opponent Johnson won by a landslide.[174]

The same has been true of the real conservatives in the election of 2008. Congressmen Duncan Hunter, Tom Tancredo and especially Ron Paul were virtually ignored. Even though Ron Paul raised millions of dollars and had a huge following—especially of young people, who agreed with him on so many issues—the media would not give him the time of day. He was, for the most part, ignored in the debates.

Some think there was also voter fraud going on in the primary elections concerning votes for him. Here in California, many people called in on talk radio the night of and the day after the February, 2008, primary election and said that when they went to vote, they were given a Democrat ballot even though they had been a Republican all their lives long, so they were not able to vote for the Republican they wanted to vote for. Many would have liked to have voted for Ron Paul. Brian Sussman, talk show host for KSFO radio in San Francisco, even called into the Secretary of State reporting these calls and asking for an investigation and a new election. The Secretary of State just passed it off saying, "There are always a few glitches in every election" and would do nothing more about it.[175]

The Bilderberg Members Today: *A World Net Daily* article tells of the meeting of the Bilderbergers in Turkey in 2007. Here are some of the elite who were scheduled to attend: Donald Graham, chairman and chief executive officer of the *Washington Post;* Richard N. Haass, president of the Council on Foreign Relations; Henry Kissinger, David Rockefeller, John Vinocur, senior correspondent of the *International Herald Tribune;* Paul Gigot, editor of the editorial page of the *Wall Street Journal;* Nicholas Beytout, editor-in-chief of *Le Figaro;* George David, chairman of Coca-Cola; Martin Feldstein, president and chief executive officer of the National Bureau of Economic Research; Timothy F. Geithner, president and chief executive officer of the Federal Reserve Bank of New York, now serving as Obama's treasurer; Vernon Jordan, senior managing director of Lazard Freres & Co.; Anatole Kaletsky, editor at large of the *Times of London* and General William Luti, the new "war czar."

Governor Rick Perry of Texas: One of the men attending the Bilderberger Meeting in Turkey in 2007 was the governor of Texas, Rick Perry. He left for the meeting just after he vetoed the bill the Texas legislators passed putting a two-year moratorium on public/private partnerships, trying to stop the Trans Texas Corridor from proceeding through their state. Perry deliberately saved his veto until the legislators were out of session. They only meet every other year so there was nothing they could do to stop the TTC at that point.

Who are the Directors of News and Media who Attend Bilderberg Meetings? According to author, Daniel Estulin, just about every mainstream news and media source has a director who belongs to the Bilderbergers: Katherine Graham, (now deceased) former owner of the *Washington Post*; Donald E. Graham, Publisher, *Washington Post*; Jim Hoagland and Charles Krauthammer, columnists for the *Washington Post*; Andrew Knight, News Corporation Director of *Knight-Ridder*; Arthur Sulzberger, *New York Times* editor and also CFR member; Robert L. Bartley, Vice President of the *Wall Street Journal* (CFR and the Trilateral Commission member); Mortimer B. Zuckerman, Chairman and Editor-in-Chief of *US News and World Report, New York Daily News*, and *Atlantic Monthly* (also CFR); William F. Buckley (now deceased), Editor-in-Chief of the *National Review*; Thomas L. Friedman, *New York Times* columnist; Bill Moyers, Executive Director of Public Affairs TV and former Director of the Council on Foreign Relations.[176]

Do We Have a Free Press or is there Media Control with so Many Members Belonging to the CFR, Bilderbergers or the Trilateral Commission? For example, The News Hour with Jim Leher is the cornerstone of PBS's programming. Leher is a CFR member, and when one examines the funding of the news hour by: Archer Daniels Midland (ADM) whose chairman Dwayne Andreas was a member of the Trilateral Commission; Pepsico, whose CEO Indra Krishnamurthy Nooyi is a Bilderberger and TC Executive Committee member; and Smith Barney which is interlocked with Citigroup, a global financial services company that is a member of the Bilderberg Group, the CFR, and the TC, what kind of "news" should one expect from Leher's News Hour? Consider also that many of the journalists on the News Hour: Paul Gigot, David Gergen, William Kristol, and William Safire are members of one or more of the three groups. "Would it be reasonable for us to suspect that PBS might not be quite as impartial in certain delicate matters of public interest . . . ?"[177]

The Connection Between the Bilderbergers, World Events and Other Elitist Groups: Daniel Estulin is a Madrid-based journalist and a gutsy investigative reporter who tells of some harrowing close calls he had while doing his 15-year research on the Bilderbergers, who obviously do not want to be researched. Estulin connects the dots between the Bilderberg Group, world events, notable politicians and corporate tycoons and the two other secretive groups of the ruling elite, the Council on Foreign Relations (CFR) and the Trilateral Commission (TC). Estulin was motivated to do his research because of his curiosity why the mainstream media has never covered any meetings of the Bilderbergers.

The Power and Influence of the Bilderbergers in Shaping the Events of the World: Phyllis Schlafly, in her first book, *A Choice Not An Echo,* published back in 1964, greatly shook up the Republican party leadership for she exposed pseudo-Republicans such as the Rockefellers for the traitors to our nation which they were then and continue to be. She wrote the following about the secret Bilderbergers, whom she discovered holding a meeting on St. Simons Island in Georgia, close to the neighboring island hotel where she was staying in 1957:

> *The most elaborate precautions were taken to prevent Americans from knowing who attended this secret meeting or what transpired there . . . The participants at the St. Simon's meeting were some of the biggest names in American politics, business and the press.*
>
> *As described by an eye-witness observer of the meeting, 'Those who came were not the heads of states, but those who give orders to heads of states'—in other words, the kingmakers . . .*
>
> *Officially called DeBilderberg group, the U.S. kingmakers were joined on St. Simon's Island by a similarly select assortment of foreigners with whom financial and political contacts are maintained . . .*[178]

Another Quote About the Power and Influence of the Bilderbergers:

> *A clique of the richest, economically and politically most powerful and influential men in the Western world, who meet secretly to plan events that later appear just to happen.* (*The Times of London*, 1977)

> *World events do not occur by accident: They are made to happen, whether it is to do with national issues or commerce; and most of them are staged and managed by those who hold the purse strings.* (Dennis Healey, former British Defense Minister)[179]

How Information is Leaked About the Bilderberg Meetings: The Bilderberg meetings are supposed to be top-secret. However, there are groups of people who somehow always seem to find out where they are and manage to find ways to get someone to tell them what their meetings are all about. Daniel Estulin is one of those. He goes to the hotel a few days before the Bilderberg members are coming. He makes friends with some of the waiters, bell boys, and other employees, tells them about the group who is coming and what their purpose is and asks for their help in just listening in to the conversations and the topics of discussion. If he finds a willing person, he arranges to meet them somewhere after the meeting and gets the information from them. His book also includes some close calls where his life was in danger. For example, the elevator had been tampered with, and he almost stepped into an empty elevator shaft.[180] He was also bribed to stop doing his research. In Spain he was arrested and held for questioning, but they had nothing on him and had to let him go.

A Cesspool of Duplicity, Lies, Blackmail, and Bribery: What Estulin has discovered in his research has had a marked effect on him. He describes the evil and corruption he has seen:

> *This parallel world remains unseen in the daily struggles of most of humanity, but, believe me, it is there: a cesspool of duplicity and lies and double-speak and innuendo and blackmail and bribery. It is a surreal world of double and triple agents, of changing loyalties, of professional psychotic assassins, brainwashed black ops agents, soldiers of fortune and mercenaries, whose primary sources of income are the dirtiest and most despicable government-run subversive missions-the kind that can never be exposed.*[181]

Where the Meetings Have Been Held Since the Beginning of the Bilderbergers:

- 1954 (May 29-31) at the *Hotel de Bilderberg* in Oosterbeek, Netherlands
- 1955 (March 18-20) at the *Hotellerie Du Bas-Breau* in Barbizon, France
- 1955 (September 23-25) at the *Grand Hotel Sonnenbichl* in Garmisch-Partenkirchen, West Germany
- 1956 (May 11-13) at the *Hotel Store Kro* in Fredensborg, Denmark
- 1957 (February 15-17) at the *King and Prince Hotel* in St. Simons Island, Georgia, USA
- 1957 (October 4-6) at the *Grand Hotel Palazzo della Fonte* in Fiuggi, Italy

- 1958 (September 13-15) at the *The Palace Hotel* in Buxton, England
- 1959 (September 18-20) at the *Çinar Hotel* in Yeşilköy, Istanbul, Turkey
- 1960 (May 28-29) at the *Palace Hotel* in Bürgenstock, Nidwalden, Switzerland
- 1961 (April 21-23) at the *Manoir St. Castin* in Lac-Beauport, Quebec, Canada
- 1962 (May 18-20) at the *Grand Hotel Saltsjöbaden* in Saltsjöbaden, Sweden
- 1963 (May 29-31) in Cannes, France
- 1964 (March 20-22) in Williamsburg, Virginia, USA
- 1965 (April 2-4) at the *Villa d'Este* in Cernobbio, Italy
- 1966 (March 25-27) at the *Nassauer Hof Hotel Wiesbaden* in Wiesbaden, West Germany
- 1967 (March 31-April 2) in Cambridge, England
- 1968 (April 26-28) in Mont Tremblant, Quebec, Canada
- 1969 (May 9-11) at the *Hotel Marienlyst* in Helsingør, Denmark
- 1970 (April 17-19) at the *Grand Hotel Quellenhof* in Bad Ragaz, Switzerland
- 1971 (April 23-25) at the *Woodstock Inn* in Woodstock, Vermont, USA
- 1972 (April 21-23) at the *La Reserve di Knokke-Heist* in Knokke, Belgium
- 1973 (May 11-13) at the *Grand Hotel Saltsjöbaden* in Saltsjöbaden, Sweden
- 1974 (April 19-21) at the *Hotel Mont d'Arbois* in Megeve, France
- 1975 (April 22-24) at the *Golden Dolphin Hotel* in Çeşme, İzmir, Turkey
- 1976 no conference. The 1976 Bilderberg conference was planned for April at *The Homestead* in Hot Springs, Virginia, USA. Due to the ongoing Lockheed scandal involving Prince Bernhard at the time, it had to be cancelled.
- 1977 (April 22-24) at the *Paramount Imperial Hotel* in Torquay, England
- 1978 (April 21-23) at the *Chauncey Conference Center* in Princeton, New Jersey, United States
- 1979 (April 27-29) at the *Grand Hotel Sauerhof* in Baden bei Wien, Austria
- 1980 (April 18-20) at the *Dorint Sofitel Quellenhof Aachen* in Aachen, West Germany
- 1981 (May 15-17) at the *Palace Hotel* in Bürgenstock, Nidwalden, Switzerland
- 1982 (May 14-16) at the *Rica Park Hotel Sandefjord* in Sandefjord, Norway

- 1983 (May 13-15) at the *Château Montebello* in Montebello, Quebec, Canada[13]
- 1984 (May 11-13) at the *Grand Hotel Saltsjöbaden* in Saltsjöbaden, Sweden
- 1985 (May 10-12) at the *Doral Arrowwood Hotel* in Rye Brook, New York, United States
- 1986 (April 25-27) at the *Gleneagles Hotel* in Gleneagles, Auchterarder, Scotland
- 1987 (April 24-26) at the *Villa d'Este* in Cernobbio, Italy
- 1988 (June 3-5) at the *Interalpen-Hotel Tyrol* in Telfs-Buchen, Austria
- 1989 (May 12-14) at the *Gran Hotel de La Toja* in Isla de La Toja, Spain
- 1990 (May 11-13) at the *Harrison Conference Center* in Glen Cove, New York, United States
- 1991 (June 6-9) at the *Steigenberger Badischer Hof Hotel, Schlosshotel Bühlerhöhe in Bühl (Baden)* in Baden-Baden, Germany
- 1992 (May 21-24) at the *Royal Club Evian Hotel, Ermitage Hotel* in Évian-les-Bains, France
- 1993 (April 22-25) at the *Nafsika Astir Palace Hotel* in Vouliagmeni, Greece
- 1994 (June 2-5) at the *Kalastajatorppa Hotel* in Helsinki, Finland
- 1995 (June 8-11) at the *Palace Hotel* in Bürgenstock, Nidwalden, Switzerland
- 1996 (May 30-June 2) at the *CIBC Leadership Centre* aka *The Kingbridge Centre* in King City, Canada
- 1997 (June 12-15) at the *Pine Isle Resort* in Lake Lanier, Georgia, United States
- 1998 (May 14-17) at the *Turnberry Hotel* in Turnberry, Scotland
- 1999 (June 3-6) at the *Caesar Park Hotel Penha Longa* in Sintra, Portugal
- 2000 (June 1-4) at the *Chateau Du Lac Hotel* in Genval, Brussels, Belgium
- 2001 (May 24-27) at the *Hotel Stenungsbaden* in Stenungsund, Sweden
- 2002 (May 30-June 2) at the *Westfields Marriott* in Chantilly, Virginia, United States
- 2003 (May 15-18) at the *Trianon Palace Hotel* in Versailles, France
- 2004 (June 3-6) at the *Grand Hotel des Iles Borromees* in Stresa, Italy
- 2005 (May 5-8) at the *Dorint Sofitel Seehotel Überfahrt* in Rottach-Egern, Germany
- 2006 (June 8-11) at the *Brookstreet Hotel* in Kanata, Ottawa, Ontario, Canada.

- 2007 (May 31-June 3) at the *Ritz-Carlton Hotel*, in Şişli, Istanbul, Turkey.
- 2008 (June 5-8) at the *Westfields Marriott*, in Chantilly, Virginia, United States
- 2009 (May 14-17) at the *Nafsika Aster Palace* in Vouliagmeni, Greece (near Athens)
- 2010 (June 3-6) at Sitges, Spain.

What Goes On in the Bilderburg Meetings? Some very important decisions are made in these meetings that have powerful consequences:

1. **Nations are Divided Up—Revolutions are Planned and Promoted:** Bilderbergers believe if they can get part of a nation to secede from the union, then it will be that much easier to take over the entire nation—"divide and conquer." An attempt was made at doing this to Canada. Remember back in 1996 when there was talk of the Quebec Province of Canada seceding from the nation? Supposedly, the reason was because they wanted the French language rather than English to be the official language. Guess who was fomenting and promoting the secession? It was the Bilderbergers. There was to be a Unilateral Declaration of Independence in Quebec to be launched in 1997.

    The hope was by fragmenting Canada and causing a financial crisis and unrest, it would make it much easier to bring Canada into a Continental Union with the USA. Their goal was to do that by 2000. Then the next step was to bring in Mexico and form a North American Union.

    Fortunately, some good patriotic Canadians got wind of it in time to alert some of the newspapers as to what was really going on and who was behind it. *The Toronto Sun* wrote an article about it May 30, 1996, blowing the cover of their secret meeting and the agenda for the meeting. A radio host, Dick Smythe, also got wind of it and began speaking out about it. When the principal news outlets began checking the information sent to them about the agenda of this secret meeting, "it became clear to them that Canada, one of the world's wealthiest countries, was scheduled to be ruthlessly partitioned by the Bilderbergers and the New World Order." Because of their news coverage, the people were alerted to this plan and it didn't happen.[182]

2. **Presidential Candidates are Created:** In 1991, Bill Clinton attended the Bilderberg Conference in Baden-Baden where Estulin asserts that Clinton was "anointed" to be the next U.S. president, and shortly thereafter, he took an unexpected, unannounced trip to Moscow. It appears, says Estulin, that he was sent there to get his KGB student-era, anti-Vietnam war files

"buried" before he announced his candidacy for president, which happened some two-and-a-half months later. Today, Clinton is a member of all three groups: Bilderberg, CFR, and TC. Hillary Clinton is also a member of the Bilderberg Group.

3. **Rulers and Presidents are Brought Down:** And what happens if the "anointed ones" become too autonomous and no longer fall in line? One chapter in Estulin's book, "The Watergate Con-Game," answers that question. Estulin suggests that Richard Nixon was brought down by the Bilderbergers and the Council on Foreign Relations, of which he was a member, because of his insubordination and unwillingness to submit to the shadow government. He refused to support the GATT treaty in direct violation of David Rockefeller's orders to support it. (Nixon felt that GATT, General Agreement on Tariffs and Trade, would greatly undermine American jobs and American sovereignty. It has proven to be true. Because of GATT, "we can trace the roots of the 1991 recession/ depression which . . . cost the jobs of 30 million Americans.") But his refusal to sign it cost the loss of Nixon's job. A few months after he publicly declared he would not sign the GATT treaty, "Watergate" had taken place, and so much opposition was mounted against him from his own cabinet (most of them CFR members), there was nothing left for him to do but resign. "Presumably, Nixon's demise was carefully crafted to demonstrate to subsequent Chief Executives the price they would pay for disregarding the agenda of those who anointed them."[183]

4. **International Laws are Created which the United Nations is to Administer:** This private club of world leaders and interlocking agencies continue to subjugate all free nations to their rule through international laws, which they manipulate and have the United Nations administer.

5. **The Elitist Members Run the Central Banks of the World and are Creating Billions of Dollars for Themselves:** The Bilderberg Group, the Council on Foreign Relations and the Trilateral Commission have set about to loot the entire planet:

> *Their members run the central banks of the world and are poised to control discount rates, money-supply, interest rates, gold prices, and which countries receive or do not receive loans. By manipulating money up and down the business chain, the Bilderbergers create billions of dollars for themselves. The ideology of money and the lust for power is what drives them."*[184]

6. **The Elitist Members of the Big Three Groups Want to Dismantle the Industrial Might of the USA and Bring the Collapse of the US Economy:**

Why? So they can then buy up the "train wreck" for pennies on the dollar and create a fast-track strategy for owning the world. Estalin gives a summary of the economic history of the twentieth century and tells how a financial collapse has been planned by the financial cabal starting back in the 1980s with "the leveraged buy-out junk bond operation functioning as a giant protection racket to the blown up real estate market." They were "destroying some as a way of collecting tribute from the rest."

> Hot money was poured into the real estate markets causing real estate prices to rise like hot air balloons. "The wealth created by these rising values provided more money to pump into the bubble." "The speculator went from being the enemy to being the role model. The old-style productive industry became the realm of losers, replaced by the hot new industries of finance and information . . ."

The effect of all of this deregulation and speculation has been the decimation of the economy of the United States. Over the last three decades, the productivity capacity of the U.S. economy has been cut in half, while at the same time, the cost of living for the American people continues to rise causing many to have to go into debt to meet their payments.

According to a 2009 CNN Money report, the average American household with at least one credit card, has nearly $10,700 in credit-card debt, with interest rates in the mid to high teens. They get their statistics from CardWeb.com.

7. **The Elitists Want to Wipe Out the Middle Class, Let the Poor Get Poorer and the Rich Get Richer:** The elitists are fulfilling their age-long desire to wipe out the middle class. We have always been a pain in the neck to them. We are the ones who have a little free time to keep an eagle eye on them. They want those of us who do not agree with their goals for a New World Order to be brought down to serfdom and high taxes, to be so poor that all we can do is eke out an existence and have no time for politics or anything else. As Estulin states, "This is the price the interconnected organizations of "international insiders" have exacted behind our backs. They have sacrificed our dreams, our independence, and our self-sufficiency at the alter of the New World Order."[185]

8. **Steal Governments from People and Replace them with Transnational Corporations:** Father William H. Shannon has written and researched much of what he calls the "Big Three," the CFR, Bilderbergers, and the Trilateral Commission. He is a priest of the Diocese of Rochester, a free-lance writer,

founder of the International Thomas Merton Society and professor emeritus at the Nazareth College in Rochester, New York. His quote follows:

> *In the final months of 2007 we are witnessing the stupendous success of the Big Three's strategy for planetary economic hegemony as the cacophony of their carefully engineered global economic cataclysm reverberates across America and around the world. It was never about buyers who didn't read the fine print when taking out liar loans. It was always about silver-tongued, ruling elite politicians and central bankers, anointed by the shadow government, who ultimately and skillfully stole and continue to steal governments from people and replace them with transnational corporations.*[186]

Note: It appears that the Bilderbergers have finally decided that since so much of their existence has been revealed to the world, they would actually create a small website about themselves portraying themselves in a more positive, innocuous light. The website gives the impression that their purpose is to bring "leading citizens" from Western Europe and North America together in "off-the-record" discussions of "common problems of critical importance." That's all. It then lists the many topics of their concern and even gives the locations for their once a year meetings. (The website is http://bilderbergermeetings.org/meeting2010.html.)

The Trilateral Commission

1973—The Trilateral Commission (TC) was Established: David Rockefeller and his fellow CFR friend Zbigniew Brzezinski were the founders of the TC, which is the third of the "Big Three" quasi-secretive groups. Maybe David and Zbigniew were bored. Perhaps they felt the groups already established to move us towards world government were not powerful enough or not moving fast enough. Or maybe they wanted to expand their own influence.

Real Purpose of the TC—To Control the CFR, the Bilderburgers, and the United Nations: According to an article by Will Banyon in *Nexus Magazine*, the reason the TC was created was for the expansion of power. David Rockefeller was enraged over President Nixon daring to go against his will, not only in regards to GATT but also Nixon created a New Economic Policy (NEP) and succeeded in freezing wages and prices to stop inflation, essentially rejecting Rockefeller's council and the liberal internationalist program. Nixon was a member of the CFR that David Rockefeller was head of, but that did not seem to mean anything to Nixon. Rockefeller also did not like the fact that the United Nations was increasingly dominated by radicalized Third World nations. So he decided to form a new organization to go over the heads of both CFR and the UN.

Other Purposes—Create a "New International Economic Order" and Gain More Control Over Governments: This is how Senator Barry Goldwater described the Trilateral Commission:

> The Trilateral Commission is international. Representation is allocated equally to Western Europe, Japan, and the United States. It is intended to be the vehicle for multinational consolidation of the commercial and banking interests by seizing control of the political government of the United States.[187]

Members of the TC, along with the CFR, and the Bilderburgers, (many of whom are all the same) began to establish a "headlock" on the Executive Branches of governments with so many of their TC members being elected or appointed as cabinet members.[188]

How the Trilateral Commission is Organized: It represents three areas of the world: North America, Europe and the Asian Pacific (mainly Japan). The American headquarters are in Washington D.C; the European in Paris, and the Asian in Tokyo. Each region has a chairman and a deputy chairman plus twelve more members, who constitute the executive committee. Committee members meet several times during the year to prepare their work and agenda. Thomas Foley has served as the North American Chairman since May 2001. Peter Sutherland is over Europe, and Yotaro Kobayashi is over Japan.

Tokyo, October 21-22, 1973, the First Meeting of the TTC was Held: Sixty-five people attended from North America; of those, 35 were members of the Council on Foreign Relations. Its membership quickly grew to over 300 powerful elitists from North America, Europe and Japan.

How is Membership Chosen? The Executive Committee selects the members. At any given time it has around 350 members, each serving a three-year term. Like the CFR and the Bilderbergers, the TC members are proverbial insiders, who come from the political, commercial, banking, and media sectors. There are past presidents of the US, like Carter and Clinton. There are ambassadors, secretaries of state, Wall Street investors, international bankers, foundations executives, think tank executives, lobbyists, lawyers, NATO and Pentagon leaders, wealthy industrialists, union bosses, media magnates, university presidents, and key professors, senators and congressmen, as well as wealthy entrepreneurs. The largest proportion of TC members come from global corporations: US 34%; Western Europe 39%; and Japan, 65%.

If TC Members are Elected or Appointed to Political Office they Must Resign their Membership in the TC: However, as with the CFR and the Bilderbergers, the fact that they are a member of the TC seems to be the prerequisite for them to be elected or appointed to office in the first place. As Estulin points out, they still retain the same TC socialists' philosophy during the time that they are serving in office. Most of them come right back and renew their membership once their time of service is up.

Publications: The TC puts out an annual Task Force Report and a journal called the *Trialogue*. They, like the CFR, have a website where articles are displayed.

Secrecy about their Goals and Operations: The TC members, as well as the CFR and Bilderbergers, are pledged to secrecy regarding their real goals and operations.

What Are Their Real Goals and How Does Their Policy Affect Us? Anthony Sutton, author of *Trilaterals over Washington,* examined six position papers that the TC released to the public called the *Triangle Papers.* He writes that "this group of private citizens is precisely organized in a manner that ensures its collective views have significant impact on public policy."

World Economic Controls: Gary Allen, after reading the *Triangle Papers* made a prediction that he included in his book *The Rockefeller Files,* "If the Triangle Papers are any indication, we can look for four major thrusts toward world economic controls:

1. **"Pursue a world monetary system**
2. **Loot U.S. resources for the further radicalization of "have-not nations"**
3. **Stepped-up trade with the Communists**
4. **Milk the energy crisis to gain greater international control"**
Daniel Estulin Gives Other Goals of the Trilateralists:
5. Force the Standard of Living to Decline: Paul Volcker, former Federal Reserve Chairman in the late 1970s, a member of the TC, who once worked for Rockefeller's Chase Manhattan Bank, actually had the audacity to say, "The

standard of living of the average American has to decline." During his term as head of the FED, he made sure that it did decline:

> Under his "fiscal austerity" program implemented during Jimmy Carter's administration, in October 1979, the Treasury Bill rate increased 6% in just a six month period. Interest rates soared from 5% in 1977 to 18% in 1980. The increase added further momentum to the inflation that sent the '80s' and early '90s' into an economic slump that was comparable to the Great Depression in the way that it restructured the global economy and eliminated industrial jobs.

6. "A Growing Interdependence and a Global Marketplace:" It is interesting to see that the TC is not trying to hide their goal of "interdependence" for nations, which essentially means giving up sovereignty and independence. This information is found on their own website.

7. Global Taxation? Brzezinski foresaw the international interdependence community being funded by a "global taxation system," the same thing that the Bilderbergers have been pushing since the 1990s. Isn't that amazing that they both want the same thing? Could it be because both groups were started by the same people?

There are various schemes for that global taxation, one is called LOST, Law of the Sea Treaty, that you will read about in chapter 17. Another scheme is a bill, originally presented by Senator Obama, to help get rid of the poverty of the world. Beware of both and keep an eagle eye on them. If they are defeated they keep coming back.

8. Erode Away National Sovereignty, "Piece by Piece": Richard Gardner, an original member of the TC, published his article in 1974, "The Hard Road to World Order," in the *Foreign Affairs Magazine* of the Council on Foreign Relations. In this article appeared the famous lines revealing how the elitists plan to accomplish their goal for a world order, " . . . an end run around national sovereignty, eroding it piece by piece, will accomplish much more than the old-fashioned frontal assault." His suggestion was to use treaties and trade agreements that would bind and weaken and supersede Constitutional law piece by piece. He also esteemed the role of the United Nations as a third-party legal body to erode the national sovereignty of individual nations.

Gardner predicted more controls over private property by the environmental movement, through "new procedures to implement the principle of state responsibility for national actions that have transnational environmental consequences, probably including some kind of international environmental impact statement . . ."[189]

Other Groups Who Support the United Nations and the Movement to World Government: These groups are not as well known as the CFR, Bilderbergers, or the Trilateral Commission, but they may wield just as much or even more power and influence in the agenda for world government.

Socialist International

A group that is almost unheard of inside the USA but is well known throughout the rest of the world is Socialist International (SI). They began in 1951, with the same one-world government objectives as the "Big Three," and they are not afraid to say so. One of their spokespersons stated in 1962 at an SI Congress in Oslo, Norway, "The ultimate objective of the parties of the Socialist International is nothing less than world government. . . Membership of the United Nations must be made universal."

Who belong to this globalist group? Many are leaders in government from around the world: Gordon Brown, Prime Minister of Great Britain; Kevin Rudd, Australia Prime Minister; Jacob Zuma, President of South African National Congress; Jose Zapatero, President of Spain's Socialist Workers Party; Daniel Ortega, President of Nicaragua's Sandinista Liberation Front; Michele Bachelet, President of Chile's Socialist Party; Hosni Mubarak, President of Egypt's National Democratic Party; Joseph Stiglitz, Chairman of the UN's Commission of Experts on Reform. He is also an economics professor at Columbia and a mentor to Obama for the rapid socializing of virtually all sectors of the US economy.

The SI, as of March 1, 2010, boasts that its membership includes 170 political parties and organizations world wide.

As with the UN, the Socialist International seeks to bring about world government by implementing "green" regulations through its "Commission for a Sustainable World Society" (CSWS).

Carol Browner is a former SI Commissioner and former member of the CSWS. She is now serving in Obama's administration as Director of the White House Office of Energy and Climate Change Policy. One can only imagine what green regulations will start coming forth under her watch.

According to Bill Jasper, who wrote an article about the SI for *The New American* magazine, March 1, 2010, the SI has powerful influence on both the global/financial leaders, but also the socialist/communist leaders of the world. They do this through controlling two different world summits: the World Economic

Forum (WEF), held in Davos Switzerland, for the rich and super rich, and the World Social Forum (WSF, held in Porto Allegre, Brazil, for the radical socialists, communists, Marxists, union activists, feminists, and environmentalists.

The WEF and the WSF appear on the surface to be opposing one another, but with the SI behind them both, they are both pushing for the same goal, "globalism," and the "development of the UN into an all-powerful world government." (Bill Jasper, "The Grasp of Socialist International," *The New American*, March 1, pp. 22-26)

World Federalist Association (WFA)

One can tell by their name what they believe in—a one-world federalist government. However, they use the art of deception to keep people from knowing who they really are and what their goals are. They have changed their name several times—depending on what continent you live on. They originally were called the United World Federalists (UWF). They dropped the United and were just called World Federalists. In Europe they are called "Citizens for Global Solution." In the USA, they are called "American Freedom Association." (That really sounds pretty good, doesn't it, like something you would want to belong to and support?)

Their Vice President, John Logue, told the Human Rights and International Organization Subcommittee of the U.S. House Foreign Affairs Committee that he believes that the U.N. must tax, make and enforce law "on the individual." Obviously, the American Freedom Association has a different concept of what "freedom" is. To the conservative American, freedom is less government and more individual responsibility, not more and bigger government. United Nations control is the biggest government imaginable. Logue stated:

> The United Nations must have taxing power or some other dependable source of revenue. It must have a large peacekeeping force . . . In appropriate areas, particularly in the area of peace and security, it must be able to make and enforce law on the individual.[190]

According to Gary Alan, author of *None Dare Call it Conspiracy*, the United World Federalists (UWF) (its original name) is one of the most important groups promoting the "world union" and is heavily interlocked with the CFR. Richard Nixon (CFR) wrote a letter to the UWF commending them for promoting world law: "Your organization can perform an important service by continuing to emphasize that world peace can only come through world law." Nixon also wanted a United Nations world supreme court and UN police force.[191]

Fabian Socialists

The Fabian Society was started in 1884. They got their name from a Roman General, Quintas Fabian, whose tactics were based on patiently waiting for the enemy to make a mistake and then striking hard. Their mascot is a turtle, also a symbol for patience and slow-moving change. They believe "the slower the system of change, the least suspecting will be the people."

There is a famous stain-glass window showing a picture of some of the original Fabian founders hammering on the world to remold it. At the top are the words etched into the glass in ancient-looking capital letters that read, "REMOLD IT NEARER TO THE HEARTS DESIRE." George Bernard Shaw, the famous playwright, a co-founder of the Fabians, was the designer of the window and is shown as one of the figures doing the hammering. The other man depicted is Sidney Webb, the other co-founder. E.R. Peace is shown holding the bellows to heat up the world so it can be more easily shaped. H.G. Wells, the famous author, is the first of a line of scholars at the bottom of the picture. Wells is making fun of the others who are kneeling and praying. To whom are the others praying? The picture shows them kneeling before a pile of the important literature of the day. In other words, they are worshipping the wisdom of man, not of God. They are worshipping secular humanism, which is the religion they believe in.

A coat of arms is portrayed hanging right above where the world is being hammered. It shows a black wolf in sheep's clothing. At least you have to admire the Fabians' honesty and boldness. They are not holding anything back as to what their motives are—deception, pretending to be innocent lambs, while they are really dangerous wolves.

The stain glass window was stolen from the Webb House in Surrey, England, back in 1978, but in 2005, it was discovered at a sale in Phoenix, Arizona. Someone from the Fabian Society purchased it and returned it to England. In 2006, Tony Blair, who was then the Prime Minister of England, and a fellow member of the Fabians, unveiled the stain-glass window and gave a speech about it in its new location at the London School of Economics and Political Science building.[192]

The Fabians were the foremost proponent of the League of Nations in Great Britain and now support the United Nations and its move for world government. They decided that the only way to get around the US Constitution was to "permeate all future United States administrators with key Socialists who would take a bi-partisan approach to matters of major consequence."

Fabians believe in creeping socialism. You don't have to have a major revolution to bring a nation to socialism, just the drip system will do the job. Three tactics that they use are: gradualism, penetration, and permeation. In England they have gradually infiltrated the universities and the labor party and other groups and corporations. They now are penetrating and permeating their doctrine. It is considered an honor to be chosen to belong to the society.

The Fabians have become very powerful in England; most of the labor party are members. The former prime ministers Tony Blair and Gordon Brown are both members. The new prime minister David Cameron (elected May 10, 2010) is not a Fabian, but he is surrounded by members of his cabinet and parliament who are.

The membership of the Fabians, according to a 2004 report, was 5,810 individual members, of whom 1,010 are young Fabian college students. There are 294 institutions that belong, 31 political groups: labor party, co-operative societies, or trade unions; 190 libraries, 58 corporations, and 15 other—making the total 6,104 members.[193]

The Club of Rome (COR)

The Club of Rome was founded in April of 1968, by Aurelio Peccei, an Italian industrialist, and Alexander King, a Scottish Scientist. Peccei's book, *Human Quality*, formed the basis of the doctrine adopted by the Club of Rome.

According to one website, the main emphasis of the Club of Rome is to help speed up the movement to a one-world order through scare tactics concerning the environment. One of their main objectives was to convince the world that it was overpopulated and running out of resources (by 1990) and it would take global government to solve all the problems. In 1999, their own website stated that their objective was, "to act as an international, non-official catalyst of change."[194]

In 1972, the Club of Rome published a book called *Limits to Growth*. It was written by a group of its members and supposedly supported by computer graphs. It was their attempt at creating a threat about over-population and running out of resources. The authors stated that there were only 550 billions of oil left on the earth and the world would run out of oil by the year 1990. The book sold over 30 million copies and was translated into 30 languages. It really helped to further the scare about over populations and curb the birthrate in countries across the globe. It didn't seem to matter that none of their predictions came true; 1990 came and went; there was and still is plenty of oil; plenty of other resources; but no one lost faith in the Club of Rome. It is still very popular and very powerful.

Its members consist of 300 elite, wealthy people, even some royalty from around the globe, such as the king and queen of Spain and the Queen of Holland.[195] Other members are or have been: Willy Brandt (former Chancellor of Germany), Richard Gardner (CFR member), Averill Harriman (CFR), Senator Claiborne Pell, Cardinal Joseph Rettinger, Maurice Strong (environmental, new-age, UN leader), Mikhail Gorbachev (former head of the USSR), Henry Kissinger (CFR), David Rockefeller (CFR, Trilateral Commission). It is amazing how many elitist organizations Rockefeller belongs to and was even one of their founders.[196]

According to Dr. John Coleman, who has written much about the Club of Rome, it operates under the cover of NATO, the North Atlantic Treaty Organization, and the majority of the COR executives were drawn from NATO. The Club of Rome formulated all of what NATO claims as its policies and through the activities of Lord Carrington, a member of the COR and the Committee of 300 (of which you will read at the end of the chapter), NATO was split into two factions, a political (left wing) power group and its former military alliance.[197]

If you check their own website, they list various classifications for membership: active members, associate, honorary, and institutional members. Some of the active members include bank presidents, ambassadors, university presidents, professors, economists, a UNESCO director, authors from around the world. In 2007, the President was Prince El Hassam of Jordan.[198]

Skull and Bones

No list of secret societies would be complete without including the Skull and Bones, the exclusive fraternity at Yale University that was begun back in 1832. According to Dr. Stan Monteith, who writes about it in his book, *Brotherhood of Darkness,* it was begun as Chapter 322 of a German secret society, which perhaps is a branch of the original secret society of Europe, the Illuminati, that was started in Germany. It has maintained its same bizarre occult traditions and secret oaths ever since.

The group is known by many names: "The Order, The Brotherhood of Death, The American Establishment." Members refer to each other as "Bonesmen." Only 15 men are inducted into the fraternity during their senior year. Once they are members, they become part of the ruling elite, the establishment for life. They are assured that they will get prominent positions in whatever chosen field they have selected. Many of them end up as leaders in banking, in industry or in politics. Many also become leaders in the other secret societies such as the CFR, the Trilateral Commission and the Bilderbergers.

Bonesmen help their sons to become members so it is kept in the family. For example, the Bush Family: Prescott Bush joined Skull and Bones in 1917; his son George H. Bush became a member a generation later, and his son George W. the next generation. Here are the names of other prominent families who have all had members in the Skull and Bones for generations: Whitney, Phelps, Bundy, Lord, Rockefeller, Harriman, Weyerhaeuser, Perkins, Stinson, Taft, Wadsworth, Gilman, Payne, Davison, Pillsbury, Sloane. "Many Bonesmen belong to the small clique that covertly rules the world."[199]

From Where Do all These Groups Receive their Marching Orders? As one sees the unity of purpose and how all these various secretive groups seem to be marching in sink together for the same objectives, one wonders if there isn't some super group over them telling them what to do. Whenever one begins researching secret societies, the first name that they will usually find is the Illuminati. Is this the "mother ship" so to speak? Or is it just a front group for another "supreme leader" or are they one and the same? I will first give information about the Illuminati and then write more about the other group.

The Illuminati

The Illuminati got its start back in the 1700s, by Adam Weishaupt, a professor at the University of Ingolstadt, in Bavaria, Germany. Weishaupt was Jewish, became a Jesuit Priest, and then turned his back on all religion and professed to be an atheist. Most researchers believe, however, that he did have a religion. He was part of the occult as were most of those who rose to be his fellow leaders. Funding for the Illuminati came from the wealthy Rothschild banking family, who some believe were the real founders of the group, using Weishaupt and others as the front men.

The Illuminati comes from the word "illumination." Its members believe that they are the truly "illuminated" ones, enlightened by their superior knowledge, intellect, and blood lines. Others say the name comes from the fact they are really worshiping Lucifer, and Illuminati is a Luciferian term meaning "keepers of the light.[200]

The official founding day for the Illuminati was May 1, 1776, the same year, just two months later that in America, The Declaration of Independence, was written, and the US declared their independence from Great Britain, July

4. It is interesting how often when something wonderful is about to be created, Satan has a counterfeit for it. Some believe that the Illuminati is not only the forerunner for many other secret societies but also for communism, because their objectives are so similar. It is also interesting that May 1 has been an important date in communist regimes ever since.

The Original Wolves in Sheep's Clothing: Similar to all the secret groups, the Illuminati believed in putting on an innocent, benevolent appearance, while, behind the scenes, they had very sinister plans. William H. McIlhany has done much research on the Illuminati. His article "A Primer on the Illuminati," was republished in the June 22, 2009, *New American.* He stated that Weishaupt's camaflouge for his subversive group was to maintain a public image of "a charitable and philanthropic organization." This image is what attracted many German clergy and educators to the order, convinced that it was "the purest form of Christianity, to make of all mankind one happy and prosperous family."[201]

It wasn't until the members had risen to higher positions in the order that they began to find out that this was not a Christian organization at all, but just the opposite. Its leaders were atheists or Satanists—out to destroy the Church and all existing governments and to replace them with their own members of the Illuminati to help usher in their utopian ideas for a new world order. By the time the members had come to this realization, usually their original high ideals and morals had been so compromised and so much was now "hanging over their heads," that they were afraid to leave the order and stayed, becoming much more a part of the evil schemes.

A Description of the Character of Weishaupt and Other Leaders of the Illuminati: John Robison, a Scottish Professor of Natural Philosophy at the University of Edinburgh, was invited to join the Illuminati. He had heard good things about it and was, at first, flattered by the invitation. However, being a scholar, he decided to first investigate it and read some of their writings. In doing so, he found out their evil intentions to destroy established governments and the church.

He also found out just what kind of "immoral" people Adam Weishaupt and other leaders of it really were. Robinson wrote a book about his findings to warn other people about them entitled *Proofs of a Conspiracy*, published in 1798.

In his book he described Weishaupt and his cohorts as involved in all sorts of occult rituals, criminal activities and sexual perversions. Robison had received a copy of a letter that Weishaupt (using the pseudo name of Spartacus) had sent to another leader (with the pseudo name of Cato), in which Weishaupt describes, in his own words, what a deplorable state of debauchery their immoral lives had gotten them entangled in.

Weishaupt was concerned that an influential, wealthy man, whom he wanted to impress and wanted to have join them, would find out the truth about them when he came to Munich (Athens).

"When the worthy man comes to Athens, what will he think? What a meeting with dissolute immoral wretches, whore-masters, liars, bankrupts, braggarts, and vain fools! When he sees all this, what will he think? He will be ashamed to enter into an association, where the chiefs raise the highest expectations, and exhibit such a wretched example; all this from self-will, from sensuality. . .

I tell you, we may study: and write, and toil till death. We may sacrifice to the Order, our health, our fortune, and our reputation (alas the loss!) and these Lords, following their own pleasures, will whore, cheat, steal, and drive on like shameless rascals;. . . and interfere in everything. Indeed, my dearest friend, we have only enslaved ourselves."

And was Weishaupt any different in character than the other Illuminati leaders whom he described? Robison adds in paranthesis, "(observe, Reader, that Spartacus writes this in August, 1783, in the very time that he was trying to murder Cato's sister.) Weishaupt had gotten her pregnant. All attempts to have her have an abortion had failed, and Weishaupt was afraid she would have the a baby and accuse him of being the father and ruin his "sterling" reputation. (*Proofs of a Conspiracy*, pp. 8-82.)

How the Existence of the Illuminati and Their Plans Were Revealed: A secret document revealing some of the Illuminati's subversive plans for fomenting the French Revolution, as well as some of the members' names was being carried by a Mr. Lanz, an Illuminati member and courier, who was traveling by horseback from Frankfort to Paris in 1785. Inside the borders of Bavaria, he was struck dead by lightening. The document was found and, because of its subversive contents, was delivered to the Duke of Bavaria, Karl Theodor Dahlberg, who, after reading the incriminating information written in it, began an investigation. One of the names mentioned in the document was Xavier Zwack. Zwack's home in Landshut was raided and his copy of Weishaupt's writings was taken.

Four professors were called on as witnesses in a court in Bavaria. They belonged to the same Masonic Lodge, St. Theodore, as Weishaupt and knew about the Illuminati because many of the Illuminati members had infiltrated the Lodge. The professors testified of the Illuminati objectives: worldwide revolution, destruction of Christianity and the family, destruction of established governments and kingdoms, elimination of private property rights, promoting atheism and a socialist world government. The Illuminati plans for fomenting a revolution in France were also revealed as a step towards achieving their goals. The professors said that members of the Illuminati like to preach "liberty and equality," but these words are not what they really believe in. They are used as "deception to win the masses to their side."

With the evidence from the witnesses, the courier's document, and the self-incriminating writings of Weishaupt, himself, the Duke issued an edict on March 2, 1785, outlawing the Illuminati and calling its members "enemies of the state." They were to be disbanded, bared from Bavaria, and all the Free Mason lodges they had infiltrated were closed. The Duke also sent copies of the most incriminating Illuminati writings to all of the monarchs of Europe as a warning to them to beware of this order in their own areas.

Did the Illuminati Come to an End? No, as we have seen from other examples of evil and cunning people, they never give up; they just change their names and go deeper underground. The Illuminati became "literary or reading groups." They also continued to join other secret organizations such as the Free Masons in other parts of Europe and (sorry to say) the United States. The following is a statement attributed to Adam Weishaupt that tells how the Illuminati members were to infiltrate other groups:

> For in concealment lies a great part of our strength. For this reason we must always cover ourselves with the name of another society. The lodges that are under Freemasonry are in the meantime the most suitable cloak for our purpose . . . As in the spiritual Orders of the Roman Church, religion was, (alas!) only a pretense, so must our Order also in a nobler way try to conceal itself behind a learned society or something of the kind . . . . [202]

Illuminati Influence on Beethoven: According to researchers, over 2000 very influential and gifted people in Europe became members of the Illuminati or were influenced by it. One of those was the famous composer Ludwig van Beethoven.

In the spring 2008 edition of the *Tuft University Magazine* was a very interesting article by Jan Swafford, "The Town that Made Beethoven." It tells of Bonn, Germany and of the humanist period known as the enlightenment, in German, "*Aufklarung*," that greatly influenced the people including Beethoven's musical instructor and mentor, Christian Gottlieb Neefe. Neefe was a member of the Freemasons and later joined the Illuminati. In fact, he became the head of the Bonn Lodge for the Illuminati. Swafford describes the political aspirations of the Illuminati that Neefe believed in:

> The utopian agenda of the Illuminati was to form a secret order of enlightened men who would infiltrate governments and influence them in progressive directions, until churches and aristocracies withered away and reason and justice reigned.

Did Neefe influence his prized pupil Beethoven in the way of the Illuminati? Swafford believes yes. "As an Illuminatus, Neefe had pledged to educate promising youths in the ideals of the order. Beethoven's mature thoughts bears traces of that influence." What were his "mature" thoughts? According to Swafford, members of the Illuminati were taught "only good, moral, intellectual and spiritual" principles to help them "remake the world":

> Each Illuminatus was to remake himself morally and intellectually by various spiritual exercises and ruthless self-examination, then go and remake the world . . . Neefe preached to his students a relentless sense of duty: his gifts were owed to the world . . .

According to Swafford, Beethoven believed that personal morality was fundamental. To be a good artist, you must first be a good person. Like an Illuminatus but entirely on his own, he was determined to better himself both artistically and morally, then to use his talent to serve the good, the true, and the beautiful.

Beethoven's Ninth Symphony Reflected Illuminati Idealism: One of Beethoven's most popular compositions, "the Ninth Symphony" with its climatic "Ode to Joy," according to Swafford, was the climax of Beethoven's idealism, influenced by Illuminati humanistic philosophy. Beethoven intended the Ninth Symphony as a sort of anthem that could help bring about "the pursuit of happiness and the brotherhood of humanity."

It is interesting to find out that "Ode to Joy" has been adopted as the anthem of the European Union, the goal for which many Illuminati in Europe have been striving.

Swafford does not believe that Beethoven ever officially joined the Illuminati or the Free Masons, even though he was surrounded by many of his friends who were members. Swafford felt that Beethoven was too independent.

Swafford adds "In any case, the Illuminati lasted only a few years."[203] Yes, that is exactly what its members wanted people to think. But, as has already been stated, after it was outlawed, it did not disappear; it went underground and infiltrated other groups, and it is still very much alive today.

How the Illuminati Attracted and Kept Its Members, the Same Techniques Still Being Used by Secret Groups Today: Adam Weishaupt and the other leaders of the Illuminati were very clever and understood well human psychology and the weaknesses of men. Whatever worked they would use to entice people to join their group. It is good to be aware of these techniques because they are still being used today to attract members into the various elitist groups of modern times.

1. Portray the society as being exclusive, only for the elite, the nobility, the scholarly, the highest in intellect. It would be a great honor to be asked to join. This is especially important for prideful people who are easily influenced by flattery.

2. For the people who appear to be sincerely pious, portray the society as one that promises a better life, a better world, with noble virtues, high moral and intellectual ideals. People were told that the Illuminati could be traced back to the Knights Templar, to Jesus Christ, to the Temple of Solomon, to Moses. (It was not until the person was deeply entrenched in the society that he would find out that the real source of "enlightenment" of the society is not Christ, but Satan.)

3. Portray the order in a cloak of mystery and intrigue. As Weishaupt stated, "The world is not quite ready yet for these high ideals and noble virtues, therefore, they must be kept secret at all costs." Weishaupt added, "Of all the means I know to lead men, the most effectual is a concealed mystery. The hankering of the mind is irresistible."

4. For the greedy and those who seek power, they were promised both: great riches, especially those with skills in banking and finances, and positions of power and prominence.

5. For those in the lower working class who showed promise, they were enticed to join to solve the problems of inequality and injustice in the world. They were promised that the society would change those injustices and make all people equal.

6. For the adventurous, they were promised high adventure, mystery, and intrigue. They were the ones who were sent on missions, as you will read in the following story.

7. Keep the members in the group by finding out secrets about them, that they would never want revealed, or by putting them in a situation where they are tempted to compromise their high ideals and there is a witness present to testify about this, or pictures are taken.

8. Keep the various groups small and exclusive. Never let the members know who is really in charge, who the real leaders are, or what the real objectives are, until they rise up higher in the ranks and can be completely trusted.

An Old Illuminati Journal Found: While my husband and I were visiting his parents back in Germany, in 1994, Kurt picked up a copy of a popular German magazine, *Focus,* that had a very interesting article in it about the Illuminati. Kurt translated it from German to English for me.

The article stated that an old journal had been discovered in Dresden, written back in 1799, by a leader of the Illuminati, a German author, Johann Joachim Christoph Boden. During Hitler's Third Reich, and after World War II when East Germany was under the control of the Soviet Union, the journal had been confiscated and locked up by East German authorities. After the Berlin Wall came down and East Germany was freed, the journal was found and revealed to the public.

Some of the entries in Boden's journal tell of the Illuminati's involvement in the occult. He describes a black mass and occult rituals that he was part of. He tells of the many members who belonged to the Illuminati, some in very high positions of aristocracy. He said that in 1799, there were 2000-2001 members throughout Europe: 17 were lords, 62 were counts, and 11 others held some other government position. Many were Free Masons, as was Boden, having become a Mason in 1761. He belonged to the Hamburg Lodge where he served as the treasurer. He wrote about a special secret mission and traveling to France by couch. He had a secret identity for himself, Emelius. (As has already been mentioned, the Illuminati liked to use Roman names. That was part of the mystery and intrigue. What irony that Weishaupt had chosen the name Spartucus for himself. Spartucus was the leader of a large group of Roman slaves and who led them to seek for freedom. Weishaupt was the leader of a large group that seeks just the opposite, to enslave all those who are not of the special, illuminated, elitist category.)

Boden was gone from May until August on his mission and wrote in his journal, "I have the pleasure to say that I did not work in vain."

The Illuminati and the French Revolution: And what was Boden's mission? The writer of the German magazine article, as well as many other researchers, strongly believe that the Illuminati were the ones instigating the French Revolution. The article states, "The bloody event of the millennium, in the Catholic center of Europe, was the work of the godless group from Germany." The Illuminati had three objectives in France: to attack the monarchy, the church, and the nobility, and they certainly achieved all three.[204]

What was France like after the French Revolution? It was left in a terrible state of anarchy, exactly what the Illuminati wanted. The Reign of Terror that began in 1794 not only destroyed civil government but the lives of over 300,000 Frenchmen; 297,000 of whom were of the middle and lower classes. The supposed "people's revolution" primarily victimized the people it was supposed to be helping. There were, however, 3,000 of the royalty and elite class who were killed, including King Louis XVI, who was killed by the guillotine. Many of the elite who were killed by the out-of-control mobs were members of the Illuminati themselves, such as the blood-thirsty Robespierre, who had presided over much of the terror.

The Attack on the Christian Church: According to William H. McIlhany, the church in France suffered greatly from the very onset until the end:

> . . . the clergy was singled out as an object of relentless persecution and eventual extermination. Churches were profaned and prostitutes were worshiped on the altars. The campaign to de-Christianize France included even the creation of a new calendar stripped of religious significance. Assaults were mounted against religious education . . .[205]

The English writer, Edmund Burke, sums up the terrible conditions in which France found herself:

> . . . Laws overturned; tribunals subverted; industry without vigour; commerce expiring; the revenue unpaid; the people impoverished; a church pillaged; and a state not relieved; civil and military anarchy made the constitution of the kingdom; everything human and divine sacrificed to the idol of public credit; and national bankruptcy the consequence.[206]

(More about the Illuminati and their influence on Communism, the Communist Manifesto, the Russian Revolution and the furtherance of Socialism and Communism is written in the accompanying book, *The Incremental Chipping Away of the Once Great USA.)*

The Free Masons

As was mentioned in the above information on the Illuminati, many of its members came from the Free Masons, and after the Illuminati was outlawed in Bavaria, the Masonic lodges were closed throughout the land as well. Why? Because the Masons and the Illuminati had so much that they shared in common, such as: they both appeared on the surface to be innocent, Christian-orientated service clubs; they have similar goals, secrecy, rituals, oaths, mystery, various levels that one aspires to; a hidden "elect" governing group who are the only ones who really understand what the true objectives are and whom the group is really worshipping.

How the Masons Are Organized: According to the website Christians Beware, "Freemasonry is a hidden fraternal order. . . defined. . . as a system of morality."

New members go through three steps or degrees in what is known as the "Blue Lodge." The first degree is called "Entered Apprentice," the second is "Fellow Craft," the third is called "Master Mason." Most men only go to the third degree, but if one chooses, he may advance higher, either through the York Rite or the Scottish Rite.

The Scottish Rite has thirty-three degrees. In each degree, the Mason pledges himself to a different Egyptian deity. The thirty-third degree is largely honorary.

The Shriners: When a man reaches the thirty-second degree, he has access to becoming a Shriner. As a Shriner, he now pledges himself to the pagan God Allah, which religion teaches that Jesus did not die on a cross, and that God has no Son. The Shriners wear the red hat with a picture of the moon God, Allah, on it.

By the time a person has reached the higher degrees of the Masonic Order or the Shriners, he, definitely has found out that this organization is not the Christian group he thought it was, but is really worshiping another god. (http://bibleprobe.com/freemasonry.htm.)

Dr. Stan Monteith writes much about the Masonic order in his book, *Brotherhood of Darkness:* He quotes from Manley P. Hall, the leading Masonic philosopher of the 20th Century, author of *Lectures on Ancient Philosophy,* and *The Lost Keys of Freemasonry.* [After Hall's death, the *Scottish Rite Journal* referred to Hall as "Masonry's Greatest Philosopher."] According to Hall's writings, Masonry has two levels, an outer "visible" fraternity, and an inner "invisible, august brotherhood of the elect" that has a very different purpose:

> Freemasonry is a fraternity within a fraternity—an outer organization concealing an inner brotherhood of the elect . . . it is necessary to establish the existence of these two separate yet interdependent orders, the one visible and the other invisible. The visible society is a splendid camaraderie of "free and accepted" men enjoined to devote themselves to ethical, educational, fraternal, patriotic, and humanitarian concerns. The invisible society is a secret and most august fraternity whose members are dedicated to the service of a mysterious arcanum arcanorum (a secret or mystery). In each generation, only a few are accepted into the inner sanctuary of the work . . . [207]

Arcanum Arcanorum: According to Webster's New Dictionary, (2003), arcane comes from the Latin word for hidden and means "secret or esoteric." Esoteric means—"intended for or understood by only a chosen few." In the Merriam Webster's Thesaurus, esoteric has as a synonym—"recondite," meaning—"beyond the reach of the average intelligence." So in other words, the hidden Masons, "the invisible, august fraternity, the brotherhood of the elect, the inner sanctuary" are dedicated to the service of a secret intended only for a chosen few—a secret that is beyond the reach of the average intelligence. (I wonder how that would make the average Mason feel if he really knew how the chosen elite felt about his intelligence?)

And what is that hidden secret? It is the secret that has been passed down through countless ages, through many different secret societies from the beginning of mankind. It includes all the occult symbols, signs, codes, rituals, oaths, philosophies and promised positions and powers. The new members of the Masonic order are given a hint at the secret, each time they go through a ceremony and advance to a higher degree and take an additional Masonic oath. To quote from Dr. Stan:

> During each ceremony the candidate is asked, "What do you desire most?" He is told to respond either "the Light" or "more Light," but

he is never told what the Light represents. Christians . . . know that when they invited Jesus into their heart, something happened, and their lives were transformed. In a similar manner, when an initiate kneels before his Worshipful Master and asks for the Light, something happens, and his world view changes. Unless he renounces his oaths, and leaves the Lodge, he will never be the same. What happens when an initiate asks the Light into his life?

Deception, Concealment, False Impressions: Dr. Stan quotes from Albert Pike, the leading Masonic philosopher in the 19th Century, who wrote a book called *Morals and Dogma,* originally published in 1871. On page 104, Pike wrote the following:

> Masonry . . . conceals its secrets from all except the Adepts and Sages, or the Elect, and uses false explanations and misinterpretations of its symbols to mislead those who deserve only to be misled; to conceal the Truth, which it calls Light, from them, and to draw them away from it.

Pike explains further, on page 819, the deception and false impressions deliberately used on the initiates, the first three levels in Masonry, referred to as "The Blue Degrees:"

> The Blue Degrees are but the outer court or portico of the Temple. Part of the symbols are displayed there to the Initiate, but he is intentionally misled by false interpretations. It is not intended that he shall understand them; but it is intended that he shall imagine he understands them. Their true explication is reserved for the Adepts, the Princes of Masonry.
>
> What is the Truth or "Light" that Only the Adept Are Able to Understand? Only the selected few, the "elect" reach the higher levels of Masonry, the 32 or 33rd degree. It is then when they fully understand the meaning of the symbols, the truth and the "Light," for which they have been asking and "desiring most." According to Pike, page 321, in *Morals and Dogma*, the source of Light that Masons seek most is:
>
> Lucifer, the Light-bearer! Strange and mysterious name to give to the Spirit of Darkness! Lucifer, the Son of the Morning! Is it he who bears the Light, and with its splendor intolerable blinds feeble,

sensual, or selfish Souls? Doubt it not! For traditions are full of Divine Revelations and Inspirations . . . [208]

Manly P. Hall shares his testimony about the power that comes into a Mason's life through the worship of Lucifer. "When the Mason learns that the key to the warrior on the block is the proper application of the dynamo of living power, he has learned the mystery of his Craft. The seething energies of Lucifer are in his hands . . ."[209]

Masonic Interpretation of the Story of the Garden of Eden in Genesis: Pike explains that the battle for good and evil began in the Garden of Eden, but that Bible-believing Christians and Jews have it all wrong. Masons of the higher levels are taught that the snake, Lucifer, was the Angel of Light, the good angel, who wanted to help Adam and give him light and knowledge of good and evil, so he could become like the Gods. The Lord is referred to as a demon and "the Prince of Darkness," who was the creator of Adam and Eve but then tried to prevent them from gaining knowledge. In the words of Pike:

> . . . the Prince of Darkness . . . made Adam, whose soul was of the Divine Light, contributed by the Eons, and his body of matter, so that he belonged to both Empires, that of Light and that of Darkness . . . the Demons forbade Adam to eat the fruit of "knowledge of good and evil," by which he would have known the Empire of Light and that of Darkness. He obeyed; an Angel of Light induced him to transgress, and gave him the means of victory; but the Demons created Eve, who seduced him . . . [210]

More Details of Who Masons Are Really Worshipping: William Schnoebelen was once a Satanist and a Mason, very high up in the Masonic Order. He somehow was able to break free of the tight hold that the occult had on him, became a Christian and has written a book exposing what his experiences as a Satanist and a Mason were like.

The book is called, *Masonry, "Beyond the Light."* He tells of the many degrees that he passed through, including some that American Masons are unaware of; such as the Egyptian rites of the Paladin.

During his initiation into "Palladium Masonry," William sadly admits to standing with fellow Masons and chanting: "Glory and love for Lucifer! Hatred! Hatred! Hatred! to God accursed! accursed! accursed!"

He says that drugs such as hashish provided some of their "illumination," which he believes was the same source of "light" for the "Illuminati" back in the 18th century, started by Adam Weishaupt.

During the Palladium initiation, William tells how Masons promised to surrender themselves, body and soul to Lucifer, usually for 7 years, and Lucifer promised to grant them all their worldly desires.

Through drugs and occult, they practiced opening the "Third Eye" which, when opened, flooded their brains with the "pure consciousness of Lucifer himself." William said this is Satan's counterfeit of the Christian's "being born again." One would then look at the world and people as Satan does.

As this degree progressed, the participants had conversations with the dead and experienced a ceremony where they would "marry" the dead, in which the demons ultimately possessed them entirely to a point that "there is no longer anyone home in the host body."

William describes his experience of being "linked mentally into a vast spider web of communication as part of an invisible army of slaves almost totally dependent on Satan." (http://bibleprobe.com/freemasonry.htm.)

What a twisted view of the world is taught to the very elite of the Masonic order! No wonder they have such a strange concept of morality, what is good and bad, right and wrong. No wonder such strange laws have been passed by Masonic legislators and signed by Masonic U.S. Presidents, and such twisted rulings have been handed down by Masonic U.S. Supreme Court Justices.

U.S. Presidents Who Have Been Masons: There are several websites that list the U.S. President who have been Masons. Since this book is mainly dealing with the events of the past 100 years, I only list the Masonic presidents starting at the turn of the century in 1900. Since 1900, we have had eighteen Presidents and ten have had Masonic affiliations. Seven of the presidential candidates who ran against some of these presidents were also Masons. Does that not seem a little bit unusual? Does membership in the Masonic order seem to be a prerequisite to run for office? Here is the list of presidents:

Theodore Roosevelt, 26th President, 1901-1909; William Howard Taft, 27th President, 1909-1913 (who later became the Chief Justice of the Supreme Court from 1921-1930); Warren G. Harding, 29th President, 1921-1923; Franklin Delano Roosevelt, 32nd President (and a 32nd degree Mason), 1933-1945; Harry S. Truman, 33rd President, 1945-1951 (He served as the Grand Master of Masons of Missouri in 1940 and obtained the 33rd Degree.); Lyndon Baines Johnson, 36th President, 1963-1969; Gerald R. Ford, Jr., 38th President, 1974-1977;

[William Jefferson Clinton, 42nd President, 1992-2000, was a senior member of the De Molays, a boys' club for Masons.]; And low and behold, Barack Obama, our 44th President, also turns out to be a Mason. (This is according to a DVD by Texe Marrs called "Rothchild's Choice." Obama is part of the Prince Hall Masonic Lodge of Chicago, where Jesse Jackson also attends.)

Here are the names of the other Presidential Candidates who were Masons who ran against some of the above presidents and lost: Thomas E. Dewey, New York Governor; Bob Dole, former U.S. Senate Majority Leader; Barry Goldwater, Former Senator from Arizona; Hubert Humphrey, Vice President of the United States; George McGovern, Senator from South Dakota; Harold E. Stassen, Minnesota Governor and George C. Wallace, Governor of Alabama.[211]

Monteith quotes from Paul Fisher in his book, *Beyond the Lodge Door.* Fisher gives examples of the damage done to the Christian heritage of our nation and traditional family values during the 30 years that Masonic Supreme Court Judges held a majority in the Court:

> President Roosevelt and President Truman packed the United States Supreme Court with Masons, and between 1941 and 1971, they [the Masons] controlled the highest court in the land. During that thirty-year period, they removed God, prayer, and the Bible from our schools in an effort to destroy the Christian heritage of our nation. They also centralized power in Washington D.C. in an effort to destroy our federal system.
>
> The leaders of Masonry are working to replace our republican form of government with an authoritarian system, create a nonsectarian religion, and unite the world under their control.[212]

It was also in 1973 that the Supreme Court, still dominated by Masons and CFR members, passed Roe vs Wade, which legalized abortion. Since 1973, close to 50 million babies have been aborted in our nation. What a terrible legacy to a nation that has written in its Declaration of Independence that we believe in the unalienable rights granted by our creator of "life, liberty, and the pursuit of happiness."

A One-World Religion: Although the Masons profess to not be a religious organization, Albert Pike reveals in his book, *Morals and Dogma,* that "Masonry is a worship." On page 219, he states, "That Rite raises a corner of the veil, even in the Degree of Apprentice; for it there declares that Masonry is a worship."[213]

We have already found out in previously mentioned writings who the "Light" is, whom Masons are really worshipping. Now we find out from a 1950 article in their monthly publication, originally called *The New Age Magazine*, that their goal is for us all of us to be worshipping the same "Light," in a one-world religion. When they speak of God in this quote, it is, obviously, their God—Lucifer, "The Great Light," not Jesus Christ (emphasis added):

> God's plan is dedicated to the **unification of all races, religions and creeds.** This plan, dedicated to the new order of things, is to make all things new—a new nation, a new race, a new civilization and **a new religion, a nonsectarian religion that has already been recognized and called a religion of "The Great Light."**[214]

Masonic Religious Symbols that Have Become Part of the U.S. Government: Have you ever wondered why we have an unfinished pyramid with a scary "all-seeing eye" on the back of the American dollar bill? How did it ever get there, and what does it really mean? Influential Masons had become part of our government early in American history, though many of them were of the lower levels and probably were clueless as to what it was really all about. George Washington was a Mason but was inactive for more than 30 years. According to one author, 53 of the 56 signers of the Declaration of Independence were Masons.[215]

Some of the more enlightened Masons were able to wield their influence on the symbols that were finally chosen for the United States Great Seal. They chose a symbol which depicts their desired destiny for our nation. In 1789 it was put on one side of the Great Seal of the United States, but it was kept hidden. (It was a little too revealing for most American back then.) Only the side of the Great Seal showing the eagle was ever displayed.

Finally in 1940, Henry Wallace, part of FDR's cabinet, convinced Roosevelt to put both sides of the Great Seal on the back of the dollar bill. The front side would still show the picture of George Washington. Both Wallace and FDR were 32nd degree Masons. They felt it was time for the world to become acquainted with the pyramid and the all-seeing eye—the important Masonic symbol.

The All-Seeing Eye and Unfinished Pyramid: What does it mean? All Masons are told that the all-seeing eye is that of the "Great Architect of the Universe." New members and members of the Blue Degrees suppose this phrase is referring to God, the Creator of all things, as most Christians also believe when they look at the dollar bill. However, the "all-seeing eye" over the pyramid is a pagan symbol found in many pagan religions. It is best known as the eye of the pagan God Isis or Horus. Masons of the highest levels, the elect brotherhood, understand the truth of what the eye really represents. It is the eye of the "Great Light," Lucifer, whom they are really worshipping. The pyramid itself is a symbol of power and was used by ancient cultures and religions as an initiation chamber. Manly P. Hall says the following of the symbol:

> On the reverse of our nation's Great Seal is an unfinished pyramid to represent human society itself, imperfect and incomplete. Above floats the symbol of the esoteric orders, the radiant triangle with the all-seeing eye . . . There is only one possible origin of these symbols, and that is the secret societies which came to this country 150 years ago before the Revolutionary War.[216]

The Number 13: Throughout both sides of the Great Seal, the number thirteen is used thirteen times—in the number of the stars, clouds around the stars, stripes, arrows, leaves and berries in the olive branches, feathers in the tail, layers of stones in the pyramid, number of letters in E Pluribus Unum, which is found above the eagle, and the numbers of Annuit Coeptus, found above the pyramid.[217]

What does the number 13 represent? To the ancient Egyptians, who also had pyramids with 13 layers, it represented "spiritual completion." That would go along well with the pyramid on the great seal, to be capped some day with the all-seeing eye, when the new world order is in place. Those promoting one world government believe this will bring "spiritual completion" to the earth and to the willing inhabitants still left on it.

Some also believe the number 13 represents rebellion against authority. This comes from the Old Testament, Genesis 14:4, where the people served their king, 12 years, and in the 13th year they rebelled. It was Judas, the 13th apostle, seated at the table with Jesus at the Last Supper, who rebelled against him. There were 13 colonies who rebelled against Great Britain.

Latin Translations: Above the eagle on the Great Seal are found the words, "E Pluribus Unum," which means "Out of many—one." Most people think that means out of the thirteen original colonies, one nation has been formed. It could also mean in the broader sense—which is the ultimate goal of all of the secret societies—"out of many nations, one world." "Annuit Coeptus" means "Announcing the birth of"—finished by the phrase found under the pyramid—"Novus Ordo Seclorum"—"A New Secular Order."

Announcing the Birth of a New Secular Order: Secular means nonreligious, without God, at least not the Christian God. It also means the elevating of human interests over all things—in other words, secular humanism. The secular humanists believe government is the primary instrument of implementing "the good of human interests" over all things; therefore, they are the primary advocates of big government, world government, totalitarian government. The #12 plank of the "Humanist Manifesto II" states, "Support the ending of nationhood and national sovereignty and advocate a "world community.""[218]

So the pagan all-seeing eye and the pyramid are announcing to the world the birth of a new secular order—the birth of secular humanism, which is advocating the ending of nationhood, national sovereignty and one-world government. What a nice statement for our nation to have on our Great Seal and our dollar bill, handled by millions of people daily around the world!

What do the Masonic Symbols Stand for of the Compass, the Ruler, and the Capitol G?: When one enters a Masonic Lodge, one sees their most famous symbol of a compass over a ruler on the wall. It is also shown on the aprons worn by their Grand Masters, whose pictures hang on the walls.

There is always a compass and a ruler lying on top of an open Bible. One assumes that the compass and ruler stand for exactness and correctness and choosing the right course, especially as they relate to the Bible, that the Bible should be interpreted and measured according to these measurements.

However, according to many scholars they have a very different symbolism. As with most secret societies, there is a sexual connotation. The compass stands for the male symbol and the ruler or square stands for the female. (http://bibleprobe.com/free masonry.htm.)

The G in the Masonic Symbol: Between the two legs of the Masonic compass and above the ruler lies a large Capitol G, which most people assume stands for God. But according to Masonic scholars, as the Mason moves up to another level, they are told the G stands for Geometry, used by the "Grand Architect of the Universe."

But others say the G really stands for Gnosticism, which is an offshoot from early Christianity, bringing in mysticism, ancient Greek and oriental philosophy. Gnostics believe that "spiritual knowledge" or "enlightenment" brings salvation, not faith. Is it Gnosticism, then by which the Bible is to be interpreted? That would give an entirely different meaning to the Bible.

The fourth interpretation of the G goes along with paganism and the sexual symbolism of the compass and ruler. Mason Shaw, who is an ex-33 degree

Mason, says; "In reality, this letter [G] represents the "generative principle" of the worship of the pagan Sun-god, Osiris, and the "worshipped phallus. . . " The G in its position (along with the square and compass) on the east wall over the chair (throne) of the Worshipful Master, represents the Sun, worshipped since antiquity by pagans while facing the East. (*The Deadly Deception,*" page 144 http://bibleprobe.com/freemasonry.htm.)

"A Thousand Points of Light": This is a Masonic slogan that refers to the day when they believe Satan's one-world religion will be ushered in and in full swing across the globe. It is what "enlightened" Masons think of when they look up at the sky at night and see a thousand stars shining.

Neither of President Bush Sr. or Jr. were Masons, but they both used the term often, "Thousand Points of Light." President George H. Bush used it when he was speaking about his "Thousand Points of Light Initiative," involving Americans in charitable efforts. His son George W. spoke of the "Thousand Points of Light," as he launched, by Executive Order, his "Faith-Based Initiative," giving Federal funding to different charities, many of which were religious organizations.

Some people were concerned and opposed to this, saying that this was setting churches up to get used to federal funding and would put them more under the control of the Federal government.

"So as Above, So it is Below:" This is one of the Masonic slogans that was portrayed by the Masonic architects who helped lay out the city of Washington D.C. Every monument has a reflecting pool in front of it that shows the monument reaching into the heavens with a reflection down on earth. This has two meanings: "We down here on earth need to ascend into our heavenly consciousness, get in touch with our spiritual masters and become our own God through enlightenment." Masons believe the greatest curse of mankind is ignorance. They worship Satan because he was the angel of light who rebelled against God to bring knowledge and enlightenment to Adam and Eve, which he told them would make them wise and become as the Gods. (This is explained on a DVD called "The Riddles in Stone, the Secret Architecture of our Nation, The Capitol," written and directed by Chris Pinto. It is available at Radio Liberty, 800-544-8927)

"So as Above, So it is Below" also has a connotations that goes back to the War in Heaven, that is spoken of in the Book of Revelations, 12:7, when Satan and his followers were cast down on the earth. Masons believe that for peace and unity to be on earth, there must be peace and unity between heaven and earth. Therefore, they believe it is time to declare that the war in heaven is over, and the time of hell is now over also. Heaven and hell can now be unified, and Satan can be welcomed back and regain his throne as the "true god of heaven and earth." This is stated on a website that is promoting a United Nations one-world religion called "one-faith-in-God." (http://one-faith-of-god.org/covenant/one_faith_0010.htm.)

A Canadian website, cites an interesting scripture in the Old Testament which gives a good answer to these Masonic beliefs. It could refer to any group or religion exalting itself or their God above the true God, either here on earth or in the heavens: **"Though thou exalt thyself as the eagle, and though thou set thy nest among the stars, thence will I bring thee down, saith the Lord."** Obadiah 1:4 (http://www.scoreboard-canada. com/babylon-lightfoundation. htm, August, 28, 2007)

1962—the Pivotal Day in American History—Christianity Taken Out of our Nation's Schools, Secular Humanism Ushered In: As has already been mentioned, at the same time FDR and Wallace were adding the Masonic pagan symbols to our U.S. dollar bill, they were stacking the Supreme Court with Masons, who were also bent on ushering in "a New Secular Order" to our nation by removing prayer, the Bible and any reference to God in our public schools.

Secular Humanism—the Religion of all the Secret Societies: Remember the stained glass window that describes the goals of the Fabian Society? At the bottom of the picture, it shows a stack of books in the middle, with the famous Fabians of the year 1910 shown kneeling to the books and worshipping their religion—"Secular Humanism—" man's great intellect and knowledge. They have been doing their part ever since, "molding the world" towards that religion, just as the Masons have and the members of other secret societies.

The New Secular Order: Masons and others believe that when the pyramid is totally built, with the cap on it, that is when the "New World Order" will be ushered in—what Masons, Illuminists, and all the other secret groups have been anxiously striving for—a one world government, of course, with them in charge.

A Zionist Conspiracy? Some writers and researchers try to put the blame on the movement towards a one-world government on the Jews and say that it is a Zionist conspiracy. Dr. Stan Monteith writes in his book, *Brotherhood of Darkness,* that, yes, many of the wealthy bankers, politicians, journalists, and insiders who are involved in the all of the secretive groups are Jewish, but many are also of other religions. He believes that there is a greater link that connects them all through their "Masonic," CFR, Bilderberger, Trilateral, World Federalists, Fabian, Club of Rome, Bonesmen, Illuminati, etc. affiliations than anything else. He believes they have tried to use the Jews as a "scapegoat"—even when they are Jewish themselves—to keep people from finding out the truth as to who and what organizations are really behind the movement to socialism, communism, regionalism, integration, and a one-world government.

"Protocols of the Learned Elders of Zion": Some people refer to a document that appeared back in 1905 in Russia called the "Protocols of the Learned Elders of Zion" (which you can easily find on line), as proof that there is a Zionist conspiracy. The "Protocols" give a series of 24 steps for taking over and assuming power over the world. They were supposedly found by a Russian, Sergyei Nilus, who began circulating them in Russia in 1905. He said that they had been written at a secret session of a Zionist Congress in Basel, Germany.

The Protocols claims that the Zionists were responsible for the French and Russian Revolutions, planned on creating other wars and desired to eventually seize control of the world. Articles began appearing in Russian newspapers quoting from the Protocols. Word also leaked out that Jacob Schiff, a wealthy Jewish banker in the U.S., had provided $20 million to finance the Bolshevik Revolution. (Schiff's own nephew testified the same about his uncle.) Many Russians believed the Protocols and began to persecute the Jews and to destroy their property. The Protocols were also circulated in Europe and led to more Jewish persecution, culminating in the horrible atrocities during Hitler's 3rd Reich and the holocaust.

A Hoax: An appraisal by John S. Curtiss, who is familiar with Jewish habits of thought, finds the Protocols very suspicious for several reasons: The Bible is only mentioned once. If they had been written at a true Jewish congress, they would have quoted from the Bible often. The New Testament is quoted in Latin. Jews do not use Latin in their religious services, only Catholics do. Nor do Jews use the New Testament. They do not regard it as scripture. The main language used at the Basal Congress would have been German. A German Bible or a Hebrew-translated Bible would have been better suited for the Protocals had they been authentic, written by a Jewish author.[219]

Dr. Stan Monteith also believes the Protocols to be a hoax. He examined Colonel Edward Mandel House's papers at Yale University and discovered a copy of the Protocols among them. He believes that House was either the writer of the Protocols or had much to do with their distribution.

Myron Fagan, who delivered on tape a long essay about the Illuminati and its link to the CFR, back in the 1960s, believes the Protocals were actually written by Weishaupt and the Rothschilds (who were Jewish themselves) and were used much earlier to deflect attention away from themselves and the real conspirators. He stated on the tape:

> *And at this point let me stress a prime feature of the Illuminati plans. When and if their blueprint for world control, the Protocols of The Elders Of Zion, is discovered and exposed, they would wipe all the Jews off the face of the earth in order to divert suspicions from themselves. If you think this is farfetched, bear in mind that they permitted Hitler, a liberal socialist himself, who was financed by corrupt Kennedy, the Warburgs, and the Rothschilds, to incinerate 600,000 Jews.*[220] [Originally, the number of the Jewish people who were killed by Hitler in the concentration camps was estimated at much less than the six million that it was later stated to be.]

Monteith gives other examples of those involved in secret societies, such as J.P. Morgan (CFR) and Henry Ford (a 33rd degree Mason), who were the real ones who helped fund the Nazis and the Bolsheviks, but who put the blame on the Jews. Ford built automotive factories for both the Nazis and the Communists and even received an award from Hitler. Ford wrote the *International Jew*, which claimed that Jewish bankers financed Bolshevism.[221]

Hitler, who was part Jewish himself, of course, blamed the Jews for all the ills of Germany, when it was his own henchmen who were doing most of the evil deeds, themselves, such as setting fire to the parliament building, the Reichstag. Through his propaganda campaigns, Hitler turned many of the German people against the Jews so they did not mind when the Jews were rounded up and taken to "work camps" or "concentration camps." Most Germans had no idea what horrific things were really going on in those camps until World War II had ended and the truth was revealed.

Committee of 300—the Mother Ship of Secret Societies:

According to researcher and author, Dr. John Coleman, who used to be part of the British Intelligence and worked for MI6 (similar to the CIA), and has done extensive research into all the secret societies, there is a more powerful group, which is above all the others and gives all the other groups their marching orders (and for whom the others are probably front groups). It is called the "Committee of 300." He believes the RIIA, the CFR, the Round Table Groups, the Bilderbergers, The Trilateral Commission, the Club of Rome, the Fabians, the World Federalists, the Illuminati, the Masons and all the other groups are circles within circles of the Committee of 300. Just as the Illuminati, this powerful group existed much earlier than at the time of Cecil Rhodes, and played a major role in much of the wars and revolutions of the world before 1890.

The Common Threads: According to Coleman, there are many common threads that the Committee of 300 shares with all the other secret societies that it controls: a hatred for Christianity; to bring about a socialist/communist form of government, where freedom of religion and other freedoms are greatly curtailed (if not destroyed); to destroy vast numbers of people (since they believe the world is over-populated anyway); to take away private property, natural resources, and nationalize them; to take over education in public and private schools, so students will only be taught "correct" indoctrination; to establish eventually a one-world government, with a world economy and a world religion (which will be a new-age, earth-worshiping, pagan religion—definitely, not Christian); and to put the world back under the control of the naturally superior, British royal blood line, as it was supposed to be before the "foolish" Americans fouled things up and defeated the British in the Revolutionary War and again in the War of 1812. But since there are many noble Anglo-Saxon blood lines in America, the Committee of 300 is allowing some elitist Americans to help them out in their quest for world dominion.

***The Open Conspiracy* Gives More Sinister Plans**: Coleman cites a member of the Committee of 300, one of its senior spokesmen, who was also a leader of the Fabian Society, H.G. Wells, who wrote a book called *The Open Conspiracy: Plans for a World Revolution,* in which he describes the world the elitists envision.

Along with the above mentioned objectives, Wells' books lists a return to the feudal system of the Middle Ages, in which a one-world population will exist, where euthanasia of the sick and elderly will take place, and parents will be restricted to only two children (from then on abortion will be mandatory). Children will be removed from home at an early age to be brought up as wards of the state, as state property. Marriage will be outlawed; family life, as we know it, will cease, and free sex will become mandatory; diseases, wars and famines will take care of "excess population," until only one billion people, who are useful to the ruling class in areas strictly and clearly defined, will remain. There will be no middle class, just rulers and servants.

The U.S. Constitution will be abolished and forbidden to be read. National pride and racial identity will be stamped out. One will be punished severely for even mentioning one's racial origin. All laws will be uniform under a world court, backed up by a one-world police force and military, where national boundaries will no longer exist.

Mind-control drugs will be expanded and used in compulsory "treatment," where "rebellion or disorderly behavior" is detected. Such drugs will be given in food or water supplies, without the knowledge or consent of the people.

One-World Government employees will run drug bars, where the slave-class will be able to spend their free time. In this manner the non-elite masses will be reduced to a level of behavior of beasts, with no will of their own, easily regimented and controlled.

Each person will have an ID number marked on [or in] the person, readily assessable, and the number will be in a master file at the NATO Computer in Brussels, Belgium. [As you will read in the chapter about "Big Brother Watching Over Us," the ID number is already becoming a reality—used on drivers' licenses, passports, and other forms of ID containing RFID (Radio Frequency Identification) chips. Some people, such as police officers in London and Alzheimer patients in the U.S., already have these chips inserted in their wrists or other parts of their bodies. In a few years, such chips could be required for all people.]

The master files of the CIA, FBI, state and local police, IRS, FEMA, Social Security and similar agencies in other lands will be expanded and will be the basis for a personal record kept on every one. The system will be on the basis of a welfare state, and each person will be indoctrinated to understand that he or she is totally dependent upon the state for survival. The following is an excerpt from Coleman's book:

> . . . those who are obedient and subservient to the One-World Government will be rewarded with the means to live; those who are rebellious will be simply starved to death or declared outlaws, thus a target for anyone who wishes to kill them. Privately owned firearms or weapons of any kind will be prohibited. Industry will be phased out, nuclear energy systems shut down. Only the elitists in control will have access to any of the earth's resources, including agriculture, with food production strictly controlled. Large populations in cities will be forced to move to remote areas; those who refuse to go will be exterminated. [222]

Many of these Plans Have Already Been Set Into Motion: According to Coleman, the Committee of 300 was the real instigator of The French and

Russian Revolution, as well as the African Anglo-Boer War [as well as all wars that followed]. The aftermath of all of these wars was that in Christian nations, Christianity was either greatly weakened, or destroyed, as in France and Russia; a socialist or communist government was soon well established; enormous genocide of millions of people took place (vast population control); countries and history were altered drastically. In the case of the Boer War, natural resources of South Africa (especially diamond and gold mines) were also seized. Ultimately, a world body to bring us closer to world government was established—the United Nations.

Quotes that Reveal the Existence of Such a Powerful Secretive Group: Here is a statement by President Woodrow Wilson, who Coleman believes found out about the Committee of 300 shortly after his wife's death. Perhaps, he felt death was soon eminent for himself, as well, and wanted to clear his conscience:

> *Some of the biggest men in the United States, in the field of commerce and manufacture, are afraid of somebody, are afraid of something. They know that there is a power somewhere, so organized, so subtle, so watchful, so interlocked, so pervasive, that they had better not speak above their breath when they speak in condemnation of it.*

Dr. Coleman also discovered this same fear and attitude in the intelligent circles, of which he was once a part. No one dared speak of the "Olympians," the controlling executive body of the "300," or when they did, it was in hushed tones and with great awe. Coleman quotes from an article written by H.G. Wells called, "An Open Conspiracy," in which he reveals many of the objectives of the Committee of 300 [Notice the highlighted words talking about a one-world religion and the reference to "a thousand points." H.G. Wells was not a Mason, but he used many Masonic symbols in his writings. (http://freemasonry.bcy.ca/fiction/wells.html.)]:

> *The political world of the Open Conspiracy must weaken, efface, incorporate and supercede existing governments. The Open Conspiracy is the natural inheritor of socialist and communist euphemisms; it may be in the control of Moscow before it is in the control of New York. The character of the Open Conspiracy will now be plainly displayed. It will be a **world religion**. This large, loose, assimilatory mass of groups and societies will definitely and obviously attempt to swallow up the entire population of the world and become a new human community.*

*The organization of this that I call the Open Conspiracy, which will ultimately supply teaching coercive and direct public services to the whole world, is the immediate task before all people, **a planned World State is appearing at a thousand points**. When accident (or crisis) finally precipitates it, its coming is likely to happen very quickly. Sometimes I feel that generations of propaganda and education may have to precede it. There must be a common faith and law for mankind.*[223]

The British Superiority of the Committee of 300: As was mentioned, one of the objectives of the group was to promulgate a worldwide British plutocracy [government ruled by a wealthy class], with, of course, them in charge. Why? They were British, with noble blood running through their veins. They were the most capable, most intelligent, far superior in every way to the common man, and they had the money to prove it. It didn't matter how dishonestly they had obtained that money; as long as they had it, it showed their vast superiority to other creatures.

Along with millionaire, Cecil Rhodes, one of the leaders of the group was the wealthy banker Lord Nathan Rothschild, who headed up the Rothschild Banking dynasty in England. Here is what Cecil Rhodes said about the superiority of the British:

I contend that we are the finest race in the world and that the more of the world we inhabit the better it is for the human race. Just fancy those parts that are at present inhabited by the most despicable specimen of human beings, what an alteration there would be in them if they were brought under Anglo-Saxon influence ... I contend that every acre added to our territory means, in the future, birth to some more of the English race who otherwise would not be brought into existence.

One of Their Goals—Expansion of the British Empire (found in Rhode's first will and testimony):

The extension of British rule throughout the world, the perfecting of a system of emigration from the United Kingdom and of colonization by British subjects of all lands wherein the means of livelihood are attainable by energy, labour, [sic] and enterprise ...

He then lists all the countries that Britain should occupy. Notice their plans for the United States that I have put in bold. They wanted the U.S. back as a colony.

. . . the entire continent of Africa, the Holy Land, the valley of the
Euphrates, the islands of Cyprus and Candia, the whole of South America,
the islands of the Pacific, the whole of the Malay ArchiCopelago, the
seaboard of China and Japan, **the ultimate recovery of the United**
States of America as an integral part of the British Empire.

The British elite never could get over the fact that they had lost the
Revolutionary War and The War of 1812, and that the USA no longer belonged
to them. It was very humiliating for them, and they do not like to be humiliated.
They even helped support the Southern States in the Civil War, hoping to break
up our nation into two factions, thus so weakening us that they could have war
with us again and easily take us back under their rule.

The Second Goal—the Creation of a Powerful Empire, an Imperial
Parliament with Colonial Representation and (Supposedly) the End of All
War. In the words of Cecil Rhodes:

> *. . . the consolidation of the whole Empire, the inauguration of a system*
> *of Colonial Representation in the Imperial Parliament which may tend*
> *to weld together the disjointed members of the Empire and finally the*
> *foundation of so great a power as to hereafter render wars impossible and*
> *promote the best interests of humanity.* "[224]

Bill Clinton's favorite professor and mentor when he was attending
Georgetown University was Carol Quigley, who, in his book, the *Anglo-American*
Establishment, wrote the following:

> *. . . what is not so widely known is that Rhodes, in five previous wills,*
> *left his fortune to form a secret society . . . And what does not seem to be*
> *known to anyone is that this secret society was created by Rhodes and his*
> *principal trustee, Lord Milner, and continues to exist to this day.*[225]

This Secret Society Would End all Wars and Absorb the Wealth of the
World.: Dr. Dennis Cuddy quotes from an 1890 letter that Rhodes wrote to a
close friend, W. T. Stead:

> *Please remember that the key of my idea discussed with you is a Society,*
> *copied from the Jesuits as to organization . . . an idea which ultimately*
> *[leads] to the cessation of all wars and one language throughout all the*

*world . . . The only thing feasible to carry this out is a secret [society],
one gradually absorbing the wealth of the world to be devoted to such an
object . . . Fancy the charm to young America . . . to share in a scheme
to take the government of the whole world!* [226]

The Committee of 300 Works Through Deception to Bring About Change:
They employ a vast number of specialists in deception, teachers, leaders, whose
sole task is to dupe as many people as possible into believing that major change
just happens, so, of course, should be accepted.

Coleman's Chart on the Committee of 300: Dr. Coleman put together a chart
showing the hierarchy and inner workings of the Committee. At the top are
the most powerful players showing lines of authority and control underneath
them. It shows that a variety of different agencies, organizations, and political
persuasions are under the Control of the Committee of 300 and are supporting
the United Nations. They are not all British. (They, obviously, will use and work
with lesser human beings if it helps fulfill their objectives.)

Committee of 300

The United Nations				
Zionism Communism Fabianism Liberalism Socialism, fascism Right Wing Parties		Royal Institute for Int. Affairs	Member Nations Kings of Saudi Arabia Sheiks of Dubai, UAE British Intelligence -MI6 Other Intelligence Agencies, CIA, Mossad	
Rhodes/ Milner Group Round Tables	Terrorism	Tavistock Institute of Human Relations	Petroleum, Banking, Mining, Insurance, Commerce, Industry	Religious Organizations OWG (One-World Government) Church Foundations
Freemasonry, Other Secret Societies, 9 Unknown Men	Club of Rome NATO		Executive Arm of the RIIA—CIIA (Royal Institute for International Affairs and the Canadian Institute for International Affairs)	
Drug Trade	U.S. Military		Trilaterals	Bilderbergers
British East India Company Hong Kong London Council Madellin Cartel Cali Cartel	Institutions SRI MIT IPS Rand Hudson Wharton		Council on Foreign Relations	
			U.S. Government	Media Control
			Education Environment Abortion Gun Control Parliamentary System FEMA	ABC, CBS, NBC, BBC, CNN, NYT, UPI Washington Post, etc.

**(Based on Coleman's Chart of the Committee of 300,
Printed with his Permission)**[227]

The United Nations or World Government: The UN is, of course, at the top of the chart. Even though, we are not quite there yet, world government is the goal and has been from the inception of the UN, and it continues to be the goal of all the secret societies that helped create the UN and continue to support it. Some of those are shown underneath on the chart.

    Directly underneath, are all the member nations that belong to the UN. To the right of them are the various Arab kings. To the far left are the various liberal creeds or "isms" that are promoting world government. (Notice how both the far left-wing and the far right-wing groups are lumped together. Coleman believes they all lead eventually to the same end of world government. Maybe that is because extreme right-wing groups do not believe in any government control at all, which leads to anarchy. Anarchy leads to chaos, which eventually leads to a police state to establish order by the biggest bully who can take charge, which leads to tyranny, a dictatorship and to world government—exactly what the other isms on the far left are striving for.

The Royal Institute for International Affairs, RIIA: According to Dr. Coleman, the RIIA, the real creators of the CFR and the United Nations, has enormous power and influence, which is shown by the black line stretching from it out over all the other organizations and institutions under it.

Under it are: the Rhodes/Milner Group, otherwise known as the Round Table; the Free Masons and other Secret Societies; and Nine Unknown Men, who are the leaders of the secret societies. Terrorism is shown all by itself. As has already been mentioned, terrorism is a vital part of the whole plan for keeping subjects willing and compliant.

British Intelligence: To the right of the RIIA, underneath the member nations, is shown the British Intelligence; underneath it are the various other intelligence agencies for other nations. Specifically mentioned are the CIA for the United States and the Mossad of Israel.

Does that mean that all of these intelligent agencies are really working together under the direction of British intelligence? Here we thought they were all spying on each other. Could they all be promoting the same cause of world government? How would they do that? Could they actually be creating, training, and promoting common enemies? Could these enemies be used as the excuse for a war on terror? Could the war on terror be used to create fear in the hearts of the people? Could that fear be used to take more freedoms away, freedoms which people would never have been willing to give up before?

Dr. Stan Monteith believes that the answer to all of these questions is yes. Most of our enemies are really created and trained by these agencies, such as the Taliban, who were trained by the CIA to fight against the Russians in the first Afghan war. Monteith calls it "the best enemies money can buy."

Why would a government create their own enemies? Monteith believes that governments always need some kind of "bogyman" or "hobgoblin" to keep the people in line, to make them constantly afraid, so they are more pliable and willing to give into the demands that keep taking their liberties away and move us closer to world government.

The enemy used to be communism and the cold war with the Soviet Union. Now it is terrorism, with constant threats from the Taliban, Al Qaeda, Hezbollah and other terrorist front groups. (From a personal telephone interview with Dr. Monteith, March 8, 2010)

Industries and Businesses Under the Control of the RIIA: At the right are listed various industries and businesses: petroleum, banking, mining, insurance and commerce. We have already found out that so many of the leaders of these companies belong to either the RIIA, or the CFR, or their equivalent organizations in other countries. That explains why these groups are all marching to the same globalist tune.

One-World Government Church: At the far right under the arm of the RIIA are religious organizations. Just as there is to be a one-world government, a one-world bank and economy, a one-world military, and a world court system, there will also be a one-world religion, of course, under the auspices and control of the world government. And we know what kind of a church it will be, definitely not Christian. (You can read more about the one-world religion in Chapter Fifteen.)

Foundations: Under the one-world church, is listed foundations. These are all the tax-exempt foundations that are very wealthy and powerful and donate money to various leftist causes to keep them going and keep them in line. Some of the most powerful and influential foundations are Rockefeller, Ford, Carnegie and PEW Charitable Trust.

Executive Arm of the RIIA—CIIA: Under the powerful arm of the RIIA and its counterpoint in Canada, the CIIA, comes all the other secretive groups, the Trilateral Commission, the Bilderbergers, and the CFR, Council on Foreign Relations. It is interesting to see on the chart that under these arms comes the U.S. Government, as if it is just one more puppet on the string of the powerful elitists. Could that really be true?

As has already been written, it appears that a person cannot even be nominated as a candidate for president or vice president unless he or she first belongs to or has the approval of these powerful groups. CFR, Trilateral and Bilderberger members make up the majority of a president's cabinets, as well as many other appointed judges and elected officials.

Coleman's chart also shows the media— with all of its many branches of newspapers, radio and television news— as another group that is under the direct control of the elite. As has already been mentioned, just about every head of every major news station, newspaper, and magazine is a member of at least one of the powerful groups shown above. Can we call that a free press?

At the bottom of the chart are shown the many other systems and institutions that are under the control of the powerful elite: education, environment, abortion, gun control, parliamentary system (in Britain and Canada and other countries that have such a system) and FEMA, Federal Emergency Management Agency.

Tavistock Institute of Human Relations: Directly underneath the Royal Institute for International Affairs is Tavistock. It is also in the same large bold lettering to show it is very important to the RIIA.

What is Tavistock? According to Dr. Coleman, it is a mind-control institute, founded by a brilliant technician, John Rawlings Reese, who developed techniques for controlling society from individuals to millions, through "brain-washing methods. This was the mind-control technique used on American prisoners of war in Korea, what the "Manchurian Candidate" movie was based on. Coleman believes Tavistock has such power in our world today, that he has written a whole book about it, *Tavistock Institute of Human Relations.*

The Tavistock Mind Control Technique: It includes breaking down a person's morale through a strategy of terror and confusion; keeping the person hazy as to where he stands and just what he may expect, and who his real friends are or his enemies. It includes isolation, frequent vacillations between severe disciplinary measures and promises of good treatment, the spreading of contradictory news. Soon the person is unsure if a particular plan would ever lead towards or away from his goal. Under these conditions, even those who were strong in their morale originally and were ready to take risks to accomplish their goals, become paralyzed by severe inner conflict as to what to do.

According to Dr. Coleman and Daniel Estulin, the author of *The True Story of the Bilderberg Group,* this technique of confusion was what was used on President Nixon to force him to resign after the Watergate scandal, to teach him a lesson and to be an example to any other president of the United States who would dare to not follow orders. The man responsible for using the Tavistock method on him was his "loyal" friend, Henry Kissinger, (CFR and Bilderberger), who had first served as the National Security Advisor and later as Secretary of State for Nixon. As Coleman states this was a warning for all would-be aspirants for the White House, from the Committee of 300 that "Nobody is beyond our reach."[228]

The technique used on society includes keeping them bombarded with confusing news, chaos, terrible stories about the decline of society, to make them feel that to be accepted they must also be part of that society and participate in its ills: pre-marital sex, abortion, pornography, etc. Of course, none of this helps them feel better about themselves. They feel worse and often turn to drugs or alcohol to numb their feelings.

When people feel demoralized, confused, lacking self-esteem, unsure of the future, they are more willing to welcome the sudden appearance of a "Messiah," and a New Order that promises them a better world, a well-ordered society, in which people will live in peace and harmony.[229]

Today, the Tavistock Institute operates a $6 billion a year network of foundations in the US, all funded by taxpayers' money. Ten major institutes are under its control, with 3,000 other study groups and think tanks that originate many types of programs to increase control over the American people. The Rockefeller-funded **Rand Institute** is one of the biggest. Rand, other American foundations and the Rockefeller-financed Tavistock Institute in England all have a single goal in mind—"to break down the psychological strength of the individual and render him helpless to oppose the dictators of the New World Order."[230] According to Estulin, "Rand is also referred to as the U.S. Brainwashing Institution, for its experiments in methodology for social planning and psychological response to stress."[231]

Institutions: According to Dr. Coleman, Tavistock has psychological training grounds and networks at many major institutions and universities both in England and the United States. Coleman lists some of these on the bottom of his chart and others are found on a website, Committee of 300—Source Watch: University of Sussex; SRI, (Stanford Research Institute); MIT, (Massachusetts Institute of Technology); Georgetown; IPS (Institute for Policy Studies—founded by the Rothschilds and James P. Warburg, and bolstered by British Fabians such as Bertrand Russel); Rand (mentioned above); MITRE Corporation, Hudson Institute; Wharton School of Economics (located at the University of Pennsylvania). He also lists a network of "secret groups:" the Mont Pelerin Society, Trilateral Commission, American Ditchley Foundation, and the Club of Rome, which give instruction in the Tavistock methods.[232]

The Club of Rome: Directly underneath the Tavistock Institute on the chart is the Club of Rome. According to Dr. Coleman, the Club of Rome is a conduit in the instructions of the Tavistock Institute. It is through the Tavistock techniques in brainwashing that the scare tactics concerning the over population of the world and the environment could be spread.

NATO, North Atlantic Treaty Organization: Underneath the Club of Rome comes NATO. Why? What does it have to do with the Club of Rome or the RIIA and how does it support the UN? According to the *World Book Encyclopedia*, NATO was established in 1950 to "provide unified military leadership for the common defense of 16 Western nations . . . against a possible attack from Russia or any other aggressor. Twelve nations signed the original treaty. They were: Belgium, Canada, Denmark, France, Great Britain, Iceland, Italy, Luxembourg, the Netherlands, Norway, Portugal, and the United States. Greece and Turkey signed the treaty in 1952, and West Germany in 1954. Spain signed on in 1982.[233]

NATO's Connection to the Club of Rome? According to Dr. Coleman, NATO was actually created by the Club of Rome and its founder Aurellio Peccei, who really had the most control of NATO and formulated its policies. Obviously, Peccei was getting his marching orders from higher up, since the NATO policies are also in accordance with the UN.

It is interesting to find out that the the countries that belong to NATO are the ones who are most responsible for the funding of UN programs to carry out the depopulation efforts that the Club of Rome was calling for. According to a United Nations report, "The UN Fund for Population Activities is the largest multilateral source of external funding for population action programs in developing countries." Between 1969 and 1978, UNFPA provided over $250 million in support of more than 1,200 population projects in more than 100 countries. In 1977, the Fund's annual budget exceeded $100 million. The major donors were NATO nations. The US has provided about 30% of the total UNFPA funding.

NATO headquarters in Brussels, Belgium, is the place where a super computer is located where data is stored and retrieved on the earth's population, but the data is also used for surveillance purposes.[234]

NATO's Connection to the United Nations and World Government: According to Elmo Roper (CFR member) and a member of the Atlantic Union Committee, which also helped establish NATO, their objective for NATO from the very beginning was moving us towards world government through the military:

> For it becomes clear that the first step toward world government cannot be completed until we have advanced on the four fronts: the economic, the military, the political and the social . . . the Atlantic pact [NATO] need not be our last effort toward greater unity . . . It can be one of the most positive moves in the direction of One World.[235]

According to John F. McManus, author of *Changing Commands, The Betrayal of America's Military,* NATO was actually created by the UN; it is to operate "at all times" under the auspices and watchful eye of the Security Council of the UN. One of its main purposes is to get US soldiers used to fighting under the command of a foreign entity, to bring us one step farther away from national sovereignty to world government:

NATO has always been a creature of the United Nations. Formed under the UN Charter's Chapter VIII (headlined "Regional Arrangements"), NATO is required to adhere to Article 54 of the Charter: "The Security Council shall at all times be kept fully informed of activities undertaken or in contemplation under regional arrangements or by regional agencies . . ."

McManus believes strongly that the forces of world government within our government caused us to take another step away from sovereignty with the creation of the North Atlantic Treaty Organization (NATO). Its effect on national sovereignty and our nation's men at arms has been enormous.

McManus quotes John Foster Dulles (one of the CFR founding members), who served on the Senate Foreign Relations Committee when discussion about NATO was going on. Dulles urged the passage of the treaty to authorize NATO and told the committee that NATO should be operated, "not as a military instrument but as a step in a political evolution." He knew that the treaty also included a commitment for "economic cooperation," making it a clear path to regional and world government.[236]

U.S. Military Under UN Command? Underneath NATO on Coleman's chart is written the U.S. Military, with a line going up connecting it to all the entities above it. When one first reads this, one thinks, no, that couldn't be. Our military is autonomous, standing alone. It only takes orders from and is under the control of our own government and our Constitution, to which all the military take a pledge to defend. We could not possibly be getting our marching orders from NATO, Club of Rome, Tavistock, RIIA, and at the top—the United Nations—or could we? For the last few wars that the U.S. has gotten involved in, where did Presidents Bush Sr., Clinton, and Bush Jr. go for permission to declare war? It wasn't to the US Congress as is supposed to be according to Article 1, Section 8, "The Congress shall have power to . . . declare war." These presidents went first to the United Nations. Obviously, they think the UN is the entity under which our U.S. military is now getting its marching orders.

UN Grants Permission for USA to Declare War: The precedent began with President Bush Sr. and the Gulf War. The following was written in the CFR Journal, *Foreign Affairs*, 1991, essentially praising Bush for this bold move:

Never before in American history was there a period quite like it. For 48 days the United States moved inexorably toward war, acting on authority granted by an international organization. On November 29, 1990, in an unprecedented step, the United Nations Security Council authorized the use after January 15, 1991, of 'all necessary means' to achieve the withdrawal of Iraqi forces from the territory of Kuwait.

"New World Order" and the United Nations: John McManus states that President Bush Sr. then used the Gulf War as a way to further the role and power of the United Nations. As a member of the CFR and the Trilateral Commission, Bush shared the same UN world government goals. He began giving many speeches shortly after he went to the UN and during the Gulf War supporting and praising the UN and the New World Order. Here are four quotes from them:

September 11, 1990, Televised Address: *'Out of these troubled times, our fifth objective—a new world order—can emerge . . . We are now in sight of a United Nations that performs as envisioned by its founders.'*

January 7, 1991, Interview on U.S. News and World Report: *'I think that what's at stake here is the new world order. What's at stake here is whether we can have disputes peacefully resolved in the future by a reinvigorated United Nations.'*

January 9, 1991, Press Conference: *'And that world order is only going to be enhanced if this newly activated peace-keeping function of the United Nations proves to be effective. That is the only way the new world order will be enhanced.'*

August, 1991, National Security Strategy of the United States, signed by George Bush: *'In the Gulf War, we saw the United Nations playing the role dreamed of by its founders . . . I hope history will record that the Gulf crisis was the crucible of the new world order.'* [237] (More quotes by Bush and many others about the new world order are found in the last chapter.)

What Ever Happened to the United Nations Ending all Wars? As was already mentioned in the chapter on the UN, according to the Wikipedia Website, there have actually been 141 wars going on across the globe since the UN was created back in 1945.[238] Why would the UN want to foment war? War can cause amazing changes to take place, such as: governments can be toppled; central banks established, socialist, communist regimes can be put in place. Such regimes are easier to control and easier to bring under one-world domination.

As we have already seen with the propaganda put out by the Club of Rome, which many of the same elite belong to, population control is also what they believe war is good for. Millions of soldiers and many civilians are killed during war.

And wars are very costly. The nations have to go to the banks to borrow money, thus the wealthy bankers are very happy when nations are at war and are happy to fund both sides to keep the wars going.

Another Sinister Reason for War—to Use Soldiers as Human Guinea Pigs—"Gulf War Syndrome:" Many soldiers came home from the Gulf War with a strange sickness, which also has happened to soldiers returning from the Iraq war. The Pentagon blamed it at first on "post traumatic stress disorder" (PTSD). Ailing veterans were sent to psychiatrists and generally prescribed "Prozac" as the treatment of choice. But there were far too many soldiers who had the same symptoms. This was an actual physical illness, and they were passing it on to their wives and children. One cannot do that with PTSD. The Pentagon then tried to blame the sickness on exposure to chemical and biological warfare, but very few of the soldiers had been near such places where such weapons had been used. Eventually the truth began to surface. The one thing that all these soldiers had in common was a risky and untested vaccine that they had been forced to take when they entered the military.

Captain Joyce Riley, Associate Director of the American Gulf War Veterans Association, and a retired reserve Captain, is one of the most vocal former soldiers who is speaking out about the cover up of the vaccine. She, herself, was made sick by a Mycoplasma infection, that she believes came from the contaminated military vaccines. There is a video that her group puts out, "Gulf War Syndrome: The Spreading Epidemic Cover-Up."[239] The CIA was forced to make an apology and, supposedly, there is some compensation that soldiers with Gulf War Syndrome are able to receive from the government.

Depleted Uranium and Chemical and Biological Experimentation: I recently watched a DVD called "Beyond Treason," a Power House Production produced by William Lewis. It shows veterans from the Gulf and Iraq Wars testifying of the terrible illnesses that they now have because of serving in Iraq. Not only was it from the experimental Anthrax vaccines, but also from exposure to chemical and biological weapons and depleted uranium, which was being used for ammunition. The radiation is now in their bodies and in their sperms. Their children have been born with severe malformations. The soldiers are receiving no medical help. In fact, their medical records are being destroyed and the authorities are saying that these men are not sick.

According to the DVD, 200,000 veterans are now disabled and 10,000 have died from the after affects of these illnesses. What are the illnesses? They have respiratory problems, increased risk of cancer, severe skin rashes, chemical toxicity, kidney problems, neurological problems, and, of course, their emotional health is greatly affected. Many are severely depressed and feel they are losing their minds. Of course, this has caused divorce rates to rise among these veterans, as well as crime rates. A medical doctor, Dr. Doug Rocky, who served as the doctor for one of the brigades, is also sick with the same illness. He stated that the depleted uranium causes the cells of the body to malfunction.

Joyce Riley is also shown on the DVD. Both she and Dr. Rocky testify that our soldiers are being used as guinea pigs, as "pawns in a chess game," that the government is knowingly allowing our soldiers to be harmed.

In Iraq, the winds blow the depleted uranium around so Iraqi citizens are also affected. The DVD shows pictures of Iraqi babies that have been born also with terribly deformed bodies, bulging eyes or only one eye, heads without brains, missing limbs, etc. Of course, none of this is being shown on major media television or other media sources. The government does not want anyone to know about the way in which our soldiers and the Iraqi people are suffering.

No Weapons Allowed for Veterans Who Have PTSD: What is also interesting, the Department of Homeland Security has made a ruling that any soldier who has returned from war who shows signs of PTSD (which is now one in five), is no longer able to use a weapon the rest of his life. They are labeled as psychological risks. The government is afraid they might stress out and kill someone. So, many of our most highly skilled veterans in the use of weapons, who would be able to protect their families against some criminal or against tyrannical government, are not able to posses or use weapons.

One young man, named Eddie, wrote the following on a blog commenting on a *LA Times* article, "Gun Rights Fight isn't Over, 6/27/08: "Are our soldiers returning home with PTSD to be denied the right to defend themselves? I wonder how many would serve in the military if they were told if they return home with PTSD, they'll have less rights than the criminals and the police?[240]

The Canadian Institute for International Affairs: This is the Canadian counterpoint to the RIIA and the CFR in the USA. It also has a line connecting it to Interpol, the British Intelligence (M16), and, of course, the United Nations.

The Mexican Counsel on International Affairs (Consejo Mexicano de Asuntos Internacionales): This is the Mexican counterpart to the RIIA and the CFR. It is not shown on Coleman's chart, but I mention it here, for their members are very much a part of the movement to form regional government and the NAU.

The Drug Trade (Opium and Cocaine): At the very bottom of Coleman's chart, on the left side under the heading of "Drug Trade," are shown several groups which are bringing drugs into England, the USA and other countries, and their connection to China and India. These are: the British East India Company, the Hong Kong London Council, the Madellin Cartel, and the Cali Cartel. Dr. Coleman devotes 47 pages in his book to a chapter entitled "The Unbridled Drug Trade." There are also vast fortunes coming from the Caribbean from their drug dealings. Coleman said that under the guise of importing "tea," the British East India Company is really in the business of importing vast supplies of opium.

Major Swiss banks and their off-shore branches are also involved in "multi-billion dollar drug money laundering." Coleman says that the Bank of International Settlements and the IMF (International Monetary Fund) are also in on the drug money. "Let me say without hesitation that both these banks are nothing more than bully-boy clearing houses for the drug trade." If the country, which they are trying to intimidate to go along with their "asset stripping," refuses to negotiate, then the IMF threatens to cause a run on the country's banks by using "narco-dollars." Of course, the country cannot allow that to happen and soon complies. The following is a statement by Coleman that tells how long the connection of the Chinese economy has been tied to the opium trade and to Great Britain.

> The Chinese economy is tied to the economy of Hong Kong, and we don't mean television sets, textiles, radios, watches, pirated cassettes and video tapes: we mean opium/heroin. Without the opium trade, which it shares with Great Britain, the economy of Hong Kong would take a terrible beating . . . The oldest of the British families, who were leaders in the opium trade for the past 200 years, are still in it today.[241]

Drugs Make People More Compliant and Apathetic About a New World Order: For those who desire to usher in a one-world government, Coleman says drugs play a very important two-fold purpose: "first to garner colossal incomes for the oligarchs and plutocrats . . . and second to turn a large part of the population into mindless drug zombies who will be easier to control." This was recognized by a Venezuelan ambassador to the United Nations who said the following:

> *The problem of drugs has already ceased to be dealt with simply as one of public health or a social problem. It has turned into something far more serious and far-reaching which affects our national sovereignty; a*

*problem of national security, because it strikes at the independence of a
nation. Drugs . . . denaturalize us by injuring our ethical, religious, and
political life, our historic, economic, and republican values.*

Of course, the drug trade and the vast money to be made is supported by
U.S. banks, as well, with the importation of mainly cocaine and heroin—a
derivative of opium. According to Coleman, not only are American bankers
involved, but also the CIA. Why? "There is ample evidence that the CIA and
the British intelligence MI6 have already spent at least a decade working towards
this goal . . . to bring about a state where people will no longer have wills of their
own, neutralized in the One World Government." Coleman believes eventually
all governments will legalize drugs, so they can have a monopoly and better
control, regulate, and use them to control society. This is supported by the Club
of Rome in the following statement:

> . . . *having been failed by Christianity, and with unemployment rife on
> every hand, those who have been without jobs for five years or more, will
> turn away from the church and seek solace in drugs. By then, full control
> of the drug trade must be completed in order that the governments of
> all countries who are under our jurisdiction have a monopoly in place
> which we will control by controlling supplies reaching the market . . .
> Drug bars will take care of the unruly and the discontented. Would-be
> revolutionaries will be turned into harmless addicts with no will of their
> own . . .*[242]

Other Less Known Secret Societies: Dr. Coleman mentions several other
secret societies and fraternities that are not as well known, again all circles inside
the bigger circle. Some of these are: Rosicrucian Order, Order of St. John of
Jerusalem, the Venetian Black Nobility, the Mont Pelerin Society, Hellfire Clubs,
The Knights of Malta, and the Inter-Religious Peace Colloquium.

The Good Club: As if all this vast conglomerate of elitist secretive brotherhoods
is not enough, May 5, 2009, another exclusive group was organized. According
to a *Sunday Times of London* article by John Harlow that appeared May 24,
"Some of the America's leading billionaires have met secretly to consider how
their wealth could be used to slow the growth of the world's population" and to
take on the task of overcoming "political and religious obstacles to change."

The group met at the Manhattan home of Sir Paul Nurse, a British Nobel
prize-winning biochemist and the President of the private Rockefeller University.

The meeting was called a "summit," and the attendees were invited by Bill Gates, the Microsoft co-founder. Who were some of the attendees? According to the *Times* article, they included: David Rockefeller Jr., "the patriarch of America's wealthiest dynasty;" financiers Warren Buffet and George Soros; Michael Bloomberg, the mayor of New York City; and the media moguls Ted Turner and Oprah Winfrey.

Patricia Stonesifer, former chief executive of the Bill and Melinda Gates Foundation, which gives more than £2 billion a year to good causes, was also in attendance. She said the billionaires met to "discuss how to increase giving" and they intended to "continue the dialogue" over the next few months.

Another unnamed guest said they decided to name their group "The Good Club," because they believe they are all involved in good causes. There was no vote but "a consensus emerged" that one of their most important causes would be to back a strategy in which population growth would be tackled, as a potentially disastrous environmental, social and industrial threat. He continued:

> *This is something so nightmarish that everyone in this group agreed it needs big-brain answers. They need to be independent of government agencies, which are unable to head off the disaster we all see looming.*

When the guest was asked why all this was a secret meeting without any press present, he answered, "They wanted to speak rich to rich without worrying anything they said would end up in the newspapers, painting them as an alternative world government."[243]

"The New Jacobin Elite:" William Jasper wrote an article about the "Good Club" in the *New American* magazine, July 6, 2009, and named them "the new Jacobin elite." If the reader remembers, the Jacobins were another name given to the Illuminati or the Committee of 300 and given credit for the French Revolution. Their purpose in causing the mass killing of over 300,000 people was also under the mantra of "population control" and getting rid of "political and religious obstacles" to change and doing it all under the name of saving the "environment." The Jacobins were the environmentalists and the New Age group of the 1780s.

Had their plans succeeded, not just 300,000 French people would have been killed, but between 8-18 million, one-third to two-thirds of the French population back in 1789. The Jacobins wanted to depopulate France and turn its people from Christianity, from worshiping the Creator, to the pagan New Age religion of worshiping nature, the creation. Their mantra was "Perish forever the memory of the priests! Perish forever Christian superstition! Long live the sublime religion of Nature."

Just as with the new Jacobin elite, the old Jacobins were made up of some of the wealthiest, privileged members of society, people such as: Louis Phillipe II, Duc d'Orleans, (who hated his cousin, King Louis XVI, and his wife, Marie Antoinette. She had rebuffed his sexual advances and caused him to be banished from the court). Others were: Duc de Biron, the Marquis de Sillery, the Vicomte de Noailles, the Baron "Anarcharsis" de Cloots, the Comte de Mirabeau, the Marquis de St. Hurge, the Vicomte de Segur, and the infamously perverse and cruel Marquis de Sade, who loved to hurt people for the pure pleasure of it. It is from him we get the expression "sadistic." These wealthy Jacobins are the ones who funded the revolution and unleashed their agents to "terrorize, de-Christianize, and depopulate France, in the name of their deceptive mantra, "Liberty, Equality, and Fraternity."

Christianity was outlawed. The de-Christianizing of France included: closing and desecrating churches, desecrating and trampling on crucifixes. Catholic Mass was forbidden, priests and nuns were butchered, exiled or forced to apostatize. The mass killings of the 300,000 people included not just men, but many women and children. They were killed by the guillotine, by mass drownings, shootings, and mass hackings with swords.

Jasper ends his article telling how the new Jacobins, the Good Club, have already been achieving their purpose of population control and de-Christianizing of the world:

> These are the folks who have been the leading private financiers of the global depopulation and de-Christianization campaigns, the promoters of abortion, homosexuality, and New Age environmentalism. And in Barack Hussein Obama they have found their Camille Desmoulins [a young, handsome, influential leader in the French Revolution], a handsome young lawyer with oratorical skills to push their agenda—all the while declaiming against the rich and the powerful.[244]

The next chapter tells of a similar, influential, well-spoken, intellectual man who has been most responsible for promoting the ideas of integration for the countries of North America. He is also a member of the elite CFR, the modern-day Illuminati. He is known as the "Father of the North American Union," Robert Pastor. The chapter also tells of the stealth and deception campaign under his leadership and that of the CFR and other secretive groups to create a North American Union.

Chapter Eleven

NAU Stealth and Deception A Go-Go!

CFR's Robert Pastor—the "Father of the NAU;" Pastor's Background and Objectives; The Security and Prosperity Partnership (SPP); Many Secretive Organizations and Forums Supporting NAU Integration; NAU Propaganda at Universities— NAU Mock Parliament Sessions; National and Multinational Corporations Promoting Integration, North American Summits, Pastor's and CFR's Latest Stealth Campaign

What has been going on for many years secretly "under the table", by stealth and deception, promoting the transformation of our nation and a North American merger, is what inspired the title of this chapter. The more one finds out about the secrecy, the intrigue, the many government agencies involved, the banks, the businesses, the multi-national corporations, even universities involved, and how far these plans have progressed without any congressional oversight or vote of the people—it truly is "Stealth and Deception A Go-Go!"

This chapter will also examine the background, the objectives, the writings and statements of Robert Pastor, known as the "Father of the North American Union." We will see how many of the provisions he has suggested are already being implemented. We will also see how one of his suggestions—to promote the NAU in our universities—was being done in the examples of American University and Arizona State. We will also examine the "globalist indoctrination" speech given by Prime Minister Gordon Brown at Harvard.

This chapter will also take a look at the many North American Summits that have taken place for the leaders of all three countries, and it will reveal Pastor's and the CFR's latest stealth strategy—"play dead."

Robert Pastor, "Father of the North American Union": Back in 2001, Robert Pastor, a long-time CFR member, authored a book entitled *Towards a North American Community*. This book, plus the other many articles that Pastor has written promoting a community or union of North America, has given him the title of "Father of the North American Union."

In 2002, Pastor became a professor and Director of the Center for North American Studies and Vice President of International Affairs at the American University in Washington D.C. Holding these positions, Pastor was able to indoctrinate many students into his North American viewpoints. He also had his students participate in "mock parliament" programs where US, Canadian, and Mexican college students would come together to learn how to participate in parliament sessions. These are similar to what college and high school students across our nation have been participating in through "Model UN" sessions. The whole purpose for these sessions is to indoctrinate better acceptance and need for the UN among students. Pastor has had the same purpose in promoting "mock Parliament" sessions for a North American Union. He was promoting better acceptance of a North American Union in young susceptible minds.

Why was Pastor and the CFR promoting "mock parliament sessions," rather than "mock Congress sessions" as the form of government they would want for a North American Union? Obviously, our form of government, a Republic with our Constitution and Congress, is not what is planned for when integration with other countries is to take place. Since the ultimate goal is world government and all the rest of the world seem to have the parliamentary system, the global elitists think American youth need to get used to the idea of parliaments as well.

Background on Robert Pastor, the Father of the North American Community or Union: According to Dr. Jerome Corsi, who has done extensive research and writing about Mr. Pastor, if anyone deserves the title of "Father of the NAU," he does. Pastor has a decade-long history of "viewing U.S. national interests through the lens of an extreme leftist, anti-American, globalist political philosophy." The following are some of the groups that Pastor worked with and positions he has held:

1977—Pastor Served on an Ad Hoc Working Group for the Institute for Policy Studies (IPS): According to a former communist, now conservative author, David Horowitz, the IPS is "America's oldest left-wing think-tank," that has long supported communist and anti-American around the world. It has been a place for KGB agents from the Soviet embassy in Washington "to convene and to strategize."[245]

The "Working Group on Latin America" of which Pastor was a member produced a 1977 report entitled, "The Southern Connection: Recommendations for a New Approach to Inter-American Relations." This report argued that the U.S. should abandon our anti-communist allies in Latin America in favor of a more "ideological pluralism," essentially telling the U.S. to accept all the revolutionary, terrorist, Communistic forces that were developing in South America, such as the Sandanistas in El Salvador.[246]

1975-1977— Pastor was the Executive Director of the Linowitz Commission on U.S./Latin American Relations: The Commission got its name from Sol Linowitz, who was a registered foreign agent of the Communist regime of Salvadore Allende of Chile. The commission advised President Carter to turn the Panama Canal over to Panama.

1978— Pastor was the Director of the Office of Latin American and Caribbean Affairs in the National Security Council in the Carter Administration: He served as Carter's point man in convincing the Senate to narrowly vote for the Carter-Torrijos Treaty on April 18, 1978. That is the treaty that would give control of the Panama Canal to Panama, which took place in 1999.[247]

1989—Pastor Co-Authored a Book with His Communist Friend: His long-time friend, Jorge G. Castaneda, who is a member of the Mexican Communist Party, wrote a book with Pastor *The book was* entitled *Limits to Friendship* about promoting integration between Mexico and America, that integration is good for everyone, that *"The United States . . . should demonstrate to the left . . . that it can live with genuine social change or revolutionary regimes."* Castaneda went on to become an aggressive pro-illegal immigration minister under President Vicente Fox.[248]

1993—Pastor was Appointed by President Bill Clinton to be Ambassador to Panama: However, he was not approved by the Senate, mainly because of Senator Jesse Helms, who blamed Pastor for the give away of the Panama Canal, what Helms and many considered, "the most disastrous and humiliating period in the history of the U.S. involvement in Latin America." Helms also claimed that Pastor bore responsibility for what Helms saw as "a Carter administration cover-up of alleged involvement by Nicaragua's Sandinista government in arms shipments to leftist rebels in El Salvador."[249]

2001—Pastor's book, *Towards a North American Community,* was Published: Pastor followed the lead of Jean Monnet, the father of the European Union, by never referring to the merger of the U.S., Canada and Mexico as a union. He always spoke of it as a "community," as did Monnet. The words are not so alarming sounding as "Towards a North American Union" would be, but as with the deception behind the EU, they essentially mean the same thing.

Pastor wrote a chapter in his book asking the questions: "Is a North American Community Feasible? Can Sovereignty Be Transcended? He answered the questions: of course, in the affirmative. Trilateral thinking is "contrary to habit, but essential." He also talks about "Reorganizing Governments."

Pastor has a section on infrastructure and transportation; on customs, borders, perimeters, immigration. He suggests a national and international ID card for all citizens.

Pastor advocated setting up a commission, education centers and using universities to promote the concept of a NAU; the creation of a common NAU currency, the Amero, as first proposed by Canadian economist, Herbert Grubel. (One can access Pastor's book and read it on line just by googling *Towards a North American Community* or Robert Pastor's Name. It is 234 pages.)[250]

Pastor's Recommendations in His Book *Towards a North American Community* that Would Create the Structure for a North American Government: He suggests three institutions to be established, which are similar to an executive branch, legislative and judicial. The names of these institutions copy almost exactly their EU Counterparts:

1) **A North American Commission (NAC)** would consist of 15 "distinguished individuals," five from each nation; they would hold summit meetings and start working groups with two offices: Office of North American Statistics, and North American Planning Office to analyze the data that the other office receives. These would be independent of the governments of the three countries. The leaders would meet every six months to implement NAC recommendations.

2) **A North American Parliamentary Group (NAPG)** would be composed of legislators from the Canadian Parliament, the Mexican Congress and the U.S. Congress. This group would replace separate bi-lateral groups that were organized back in 1960, a bi-lateral U.S.-Mexican, and U.S.-Canadian inter-parliamentary groups. The NAPG would propose North American policies that each country would have to follow with uniform laws and regulations.

3) **A Permanent North American Court on Trade and Investments.** NAFTA Chapter 11 tribunals would be upgraded to a permanent court with appointed judges serving extended terms.[251]

The NAC Would Be Doing the Following: work with appropriate ministers in the three governments, as well as with universities and research centers; draft papers on ways to improve cooperation and facilitate integration; consider an explicit "regional policy" to reduce disparities within North America; educate the public on the existence and potential of the region and seek to instill a sense of regional identity; try to alleviate anxieties about integration among certain groups and device policies that respond to NAFTA related problems.

Centers for North American Research and Studies: Pastor recommends education centers, funded by all three countries. These centers would be similar to the ten European Union Centers that the EU funds inside the United States: centers for NGOs (non-governmental organizations), business and labor groups, partnership groups between cities, states, provinces and universities.

2002—Pastor Began His Career at the American University to Further His Objective to Educate (Indoctrinate)Young People about the NAU: He became Vice President of International Affairs, and Director of the Center for North American Studies in the Office of International Affairs. The university was offering a bachelor's and a master's degree in North American studies.

Pastor started mock parliament sessions for college students at the university to teach them how to run a North American parliament. He was able to personally implement one of the provisions of his book—to get education centers and universities involved. The other university that was already involved was Arizona State in Tempe, Arizona.

2002 The North American Forum on Integration (NAFI) was Started: (More is written on NAFI in the chapter on the NAFTA Superhighway, where they are playing a major role.) The first two years NAFI hosted conferences to educate leaders, businessmen and educators promoting North American integration. In 2005, they started hosting a "Triumvirate," for college age students from all three countries. It was "the only North American Model Parliament." Robert Pastor was on its board of directors as was M. Stephen Blank, Ph.D., who was the founder and Director of the "North American Center for Transborder Studies" at Arizona State University.

The Triumvirate is similar to the model United Nations that exists at many colleges and even at some high schools. One hundred university students attend from Mexico, Canada, and the United States. Why would they be holding model parliaments for a North American union if that is not what is planned?

The students play one of three different roles: lobbyists, journalists, or legislators. The website gives a description of what these roles are: "Students participate in an "international negotiation exercise in which they will simulate a parliamentary meeting between North American political actors. The legislators will debate themes of a political, economic and environmental nature, while lobbyists will attempt to influence the legislators' decisions and the *TrilatHerald* journalist team analyses the evolution of the debates." According to their website, the main objectives of the model parliament are:

- To raise awareness among future North American leaders regarding regional integration issues.
- To allow participants to familiarize themselves with the functioning of democratic institutions.
- To help participants better understand NAFTA's political, economic and social realities.
- **To develop their sense of a North American identity. [Obviously, this one is the primary goal.]**
- To encourage intercultural exchanges and to promote the creation of North American academic networks.
- To inform the current decision makers of the priorities and the concerns of North American youth.[252]

I have put #4 in bold because I think that is the major reason for holding these mock sessions. Those in charge truly want to promote the indoctrination in young malleable minds to think of themselves as North Americans and get over their pride in nationhood. Raymond Chretien, the president of the Triumvirate and the former Canadian ambassador to both Mexico and the U.S., was quoted as claiming "the exercise was intended to be more than academic."

When and where the Triumvirate Mock Sessions Have Been Held:
May, 2005—Ottawa, Canada, the Senate Building, under the presidency of former Ambassador, Raymond Chretien
May, 2006—Mexico City, Mexico, at the Senate Building, under the president, Senator Enrique Jackson
May, 2007—Washington D.C., at the Inter-Development Bank and the American University, where Robert Pastor was a professor and the head of the Department on North American Studies (Incidentally, the cost for each attendee at this session was $845! Quite a lot of money for a poor, struggling student!)

May, 2008—Montreal, Canada, at the City Hall
May, 2009—Querétaro, Mexico, at the Campus of ITESM (which stands for
the Monterrey Institute of Technology and Higher Education)[253]

What Are the Topics the Students at the Triumvirate Discuss? At the
2007 meeting, they were learning about "creations of a customs union,
water management, human trafficking and telecommunications in North
America."[254]

At the Montreal, Canada, 2008, meeting, the four themes that were
discussed and debated were: 1) Fostering Renewable Electricity Markets; 2)
Countering North American Corporate Outsourcing; 3) Western Hemisphere
Travel Initiative that would requires all travelers to present a passport or other
equivalent documents denoting identity and citizenship when entering the
U.S., Canada, or Mexico, Bermuda, and the Caribbean; (The reader will learn
more about such drivers' licenses in the next chapter). 4) NAFTA's Chapter 11
on Investments: "An international tribunal was established to resolve disputes
in which NAFTA investors claim national, state, or local laws in any one of the
three countries adversely impacts NAFTA investments."[255]

**2004—Robert Pastor Wrote an Article for CFR's *Foreign Affairs* Publication,
Entitled "North America's Second Decade,":** Pastor stated that the U.S. would
benefit by giving up its national sovereignty. " . . . evidence suggests that North
Americans are ready for a new relationship that renders this old definition of
sovereignty obsolete."

**2005, March 23, Pastor's NAU Dream Began to Happen, the Security and
Prosperity Partnership (SPP) was Formed:** (At Baylor University, Waco Texas)
The heads-of-state of all three countries, President Bush, Vicente Fox of Mexico,
and Prime Minister Martin from Canada, met for a summit.

*Canadian Prime Minister Paul Martin, right, and Mexico's President
Vincente Fox, left, shake hands as U.S. President George W. Bush, center,
looks on following their meetings and a joint news conference at Baylor
University in Waco, Texas, Wednesday, March 23, 2005.* (Notice the
SPP logo on the wall behind them, showing all of North America
with no separation into countries.) (AP Photo/J. Scott Applewhite),
Range Magazine, Spring 2007.

The Purpose of the SSP: The press release issued in each country stated the
purpose for this partnership:

> We will establish working parties led by our ministers and secretaries
> that will consult with stakeholders in our respective countries. These
> working parties **will respond to the priorities of our people and our
> businesses,** and will set specific, measurable, and achievable goals.
> They will outline concrete steps that our governments can take to meet
> these goals, and set dates that will ensure the continuous achievement
> of results. Within 90 days, ministers will present their initial report
> after which, the working parties will submit six-monthly reports.
> Because the Partnership will be an ongoing process of cooperation,
> new items will be added to the work agenda by mutual agreement
> as circumstances warrant.

Response to the Priorities of the People and Businesses?: Notice the second
sentence of the press release that I put in bold. The goals set by the working

parties were to be "in response to the priorities of the people and businesses of each country." Who determines what the people consider their priorities? Did anyone ask us? No, the majority of the people in each country, including our elected representatives in Congress, did not even know until much later that such an entity as the SPP or the movement to build a North American Union was even happening. None of this was presented to Congress for their approval. It was only done by the executive branches of government by each country. Most elected officials only found out about it because their constituents were writing or calling and complaining to them and asking for some congressional investigation and oversight. (In Chapter Eighteen, the reader can see what progress was made fighting this by outraged citizens, state legislators, and some Congressmen willing to take a stand against it.)

Businesses in Favor of a North American Union: Yes, the press release of the SPP did mention that they would respond to the "priorities of businesses." I'm sorry to report that there are some businesses who are in favor of essentially "selling out American sovereignty, independence, the free-enterprize system and our form of government—all for a "mess of pottage," for monetary gain. Many of these businesses like the idea of having a NAFTA Superhighway, a way of speeding the delivery of foreign-made cheap goods coming mainly from China.

Some of these companies are mentioned later in this chapter as those supporting the "North American Project," as taught at Arizona State University. Wal-Mart and Ford Motors are examples of American companies. Canadian companies are the Bank of Canada and those involved in trucking and railway.

The Joint Statement on the SPP: It was described as an initiative to: "establish a common approach to security to protect North America from external threats, prevent and respond to threats within North America, and further streamline the security and efficient movement of legitimate, low-risk traffic across our shared borders."[256]

The SPP was Under the U.S. Department of Commerce: It worked in virtual secrecy for three years. There were no public reports released on their activities and no release of names as to who were on their "working groups."

Perhaps no one would have even known about the SPP had it not been for Phyllis Schlafly who discovered a report about it by the Council on Foreign Relations on the state department's website, back in the summer of 2005. She wrote about it in her Phyllis Schlafly Report, June of 2005:

There were memorandums of understanding and trilateral declarations of agreement covering the following issues: energy, transportation, financial services (including loan and foreign aid policy), communications, technology, environmental policy, border and immigration policy, and the means for multiple governmental agencies to interact . . . President Bush denied that there was any secrecy, yet he continued to refuse to give the names of those in the working groups or any reports of their activities.

Judicial Watch, another good conservative organization, through a Freedom of Information Act request, was able to get more information about the SPP on their structure and activities. Throughout the SPP documents one could read the words, "convergence, harmonization and integration" of laws and policies. How do you converge, harmonize or integrate our U.S. Constitution with two socialist countries? You obviously would have to get rid of our Constitution, something some of these elites have been plotting to do for a long time.

Go to *www.SPP.gov* **and Search Yourself:** Mrs. Schlafly suggested that you go to the actual government website and do your own research. That was four years ago, and supposedly now the SPP no longer exists. I was afraid the website would be gone, but it is still there. The heading states "SPP, a North American Partnership," then adds: "Going forward, we want to build on the accomplishments achieved by the SPP and further improve our cooperation." It gives the important dates of all that happened starting in 2005 when the SPP began and continues on to the 2009 summit meetings, listing the following that took place on 08/10/09:

> Joint Statement by the North American Leaders; Press Conference by President Obama, President Calderon of Mexico, and Prime Minister Harper of Canada; North American Leaders' Declaration on H1N1; North American Leaders' Declaration on Climate Change and Clean Energy.

The website also shows the original logo of the SPP, a world globe showing all of North America and the words Security and Prosperity Partnership of North America written across the globe. At the bottom of the website are the words, "This website is an archive for SPP documents and will not be updated from now on."[257]

2005, March 29, Mexico, USA, Canada Agree To Review NAFTA and Change Name to the SPP: According to a Mexican publication, "*El Financiero,*" the executives of all three countries were pretending that the SPP was just a new name for NAFTA. The governments of Mexico, the United States, and Canada agreed to an "in-depth revision," but not a renegotiation, of the North American Free Trade Agreement (NAFTA), which even includes a name change. Thirteen years after it was signed, the trade agreement between the three countries is now called the Security and Prosperity Partnership of North America (SPP):

> Without so much as mentioning or addressing the thorniest bilateral issues for Mexico, such as migration, the three presidents stated the priority of the new partnership as "the security of North America," basically from "external threats" such as terrorism, drug trafficking, organized crime, trafficking in persons, and smuggling.

Primarily addressing the issues that the United States found most pressing, President Vicente Fox, President George Bush and Canada's Prime Minister Paul Martin promised to "conclude the first stage" and bring in "a new era" of the trade agreement that includes—despite the recognized differences and incompatibility of the countries' regulatory frameworks—a common energy strategy.[258]

2005, May 17—A Paper Was Published Entitled "Building a North American Community"—Report of the Independent Task Force on the Future of North America: This was issued by the task force after they met three different times, once in each country. Many of the recommendations in this paper were almost the same as those given by Robert Pastor in his "Modest Proposal" back in 2002. They are essentially a five-year plan for the implementation of a North American Union. Here are some of the recommendations: (President Bush has denied any connection of these to what the SPP is doing and their documents, but according to Tom DeWeese, they have proven to be identical.)

- adopt a common external tariff;
- adopt a North American Approach to Regulation;
- establish a common security perimeter by 2010;
- establish a North American investment fund for infrastructure and human capital;
- establish a permanent tribunal for North American dispute resolutions; hold an annual North American Summit meeting that would bring the heads-of-state together for the sake of public display of confidence;

- establish minister-led working groups required to report back within 90 days and to meet regularly;
- create a North American Advisory Council;
- create a North American Inter-Parliamentary Group."[259]
- create a North American Military Defense Command;
- create a North American Development Bank.[260]

2005, May—Pastor Admits the Report "Building a North American Community" was the Blueprint for the SPP: Pastor was the CFR Co-Chair and Principle Editor of the report. In his June, 2005, testimony to the U.S. Senate, Dr. Pastor informed the Foreign Relations Committee that his report was not only the "blueprint" for the goals of the SSP, but also the steps the three countries should use to achieve them. Some of those goals are: the SSP should create a NAU "community" by 2010; the North American Aerospace Defense Command (NORAD) should be expanded into a North American military command; a North American Development Fund should help pay for Mexico's economic development; a North American Union Court should be established to resolve disputes; A North American Advisory Council should serve as the NAU executive branch; a North American Inter-Parliamentary Group should act as the NAU lawmakers. And the borders between the three countries should be erased, with only an outer security "perimeter."[261]

If one does not think this sounds like a union being formed exactly like the European Union, with its own executive council, legislative parliament, judicial court, and even a military, they just aren't paying any attention. And most Americans are not.

2005, June—Pastor Spoke before the U.S. Senate Foreign Relations Committee Suggesting E-Z Border ID Cards for all North Americans: Pastor entitled his report, "A North American Community Approach to Security." Notice the use of "North Americans," already replacing the designation of Americans, Canadians, and Mexicans, just as one hears the term Europeans being used more and more for residence of the EU, rather than the country they reside in. The ID cards will all have RFID chips so the drivers can be scanned and their identity known without having to stop. (More is written about that under Real ID in the next chapter.)

> Instead of stopping North Americans on the borders, we ought to
> provide them with a secure, biometric Border Pass that would ease

transit across the border like an E-Z pass permits our cars to speed through toll booths.[262]

2007—Robert Pastor Published His Very Revealing "Working Paper"—"North America: A Partial Eclipse and a Future Community":

It was published at the American University. In his paper, he is very blatant and forthright. Anyone reading this cannot doubt that the plan was for a "union" for all three countries from the beginning of NAFTA, which is described as the "first draft of the constitution of North America."

Pastor mentions a North American Union, a North American Customs Union, a North American Investment Fund, a North American Advisory Council and centers to promote "North American studies."

He talks about reducing the income gap between developed and undeveloped countries if we want to reduce the flow of illegal "migrants. (Kind of sounds like "redistribution of wealth," exactly what Obama believes in too. We are certainly busy reducing this gap in the USA now with our financial crisis, huge debt, loss of jobs, loss of homes, and huge rise in unemployment.)

Pastor talks about a "**reconfiguration of the North American political system.**" One wonders what kind of a political system he has in mind? It would definitely not be what the USA presently has—a Republic. Students are already being trained in the parliamentarian system, SPP working groups have been "harmonizing" our laws with those of Canada and Mexico, and a new North American constitution has been drafted (as you will read about at the end of Chapter 17). Pastor's language also reminds you of Obama's desire to "transform America."

I have summarized the main points of Pastor's "Working Paper" and included some of his direct quotes. I have emphasized in bold his most blatant points:

Robert Pastors Main Points of his Working Paper:

- **"NAFTA was the First Draft of a Constitution of North America":** NAFTA was "the center of a unique **social and economic integration** process" . . . "an effort to redefine the relationship between advanced countries and a developing one," . . . "The **flow of people**, cultures, food, music, and sports across the two borders **have accelerated** even more than the trade in goods and services . . .
- **"The Income Gap Must Become Narrow to Reduce the Flow of Migrants":** Pastor stated that "proponents of NAFTA argued erroneously that free trade would reduce the flow of migrants, but the opposite

happened." " . . . Surveys suggest that roughly **90 percent of all Mexican illegal migrants leave jobs to come to the United States; they seek higher wages. Illegal migration is unlikely to shrink until the income gap begins to narrow.**

- **North America's New Agenda—A North American Community, "One State or a Union":** Pastor wrote, "It is time to stop debating NAFTA and start addressing North America's new agenda. We need to begin by articulating a vision of a North American Community." Pastor discussed Canadian, Mexican, and U.S. citizens' opinions about formation of a "North American Union," "one state or a union," "a union in a new North American entity," **"continental political union,"** and **"reconfiguration of the North American political system."**

- **"A North American Community is an Idea so Compelling It will Sooner or Later Emerge as a Frontier Issue":** "The underlying basis of a community exists. Provided people are not threatened by a loss of culture or identity, and incentives for productivity and improvements for standard of living are evident, the three peoples of North America are ready to listen to ideas, including political union, on how to accomplish those ends."

- **North American Customs Union:** "To compete against China and India, the three leaders need to help North American businesses to become more efficient by negotiating a Customs Union in five years." This would eliminate costly "rules of origin" procedures and needless inspections . . .

- **North American Investment Fund To be Used to Build Interconnecting Roads:** North America is different from Europe, but it should learn from their experience, and establish a "North American Investment Fund that would invest $20 billion per year for a decade to build roads to connect the south and center of Mexico to the United States. Mexico should provide half of the funds; the U.S., 40%, and Canada, 10%. The funds should be administered by the World Bank.

- **North American Advisory Council:** The three leaders [of Mexico, Canada, U.S.] should hold annual summits, but to make sure the meetings are not just photo-ops, "a North American Advisory Council should be established. Unlike Europe's Commission, the Council should be lean, independent, and advisory. It should prepare the agenda with proposals on North American transportation, the environment, education, and other issues. The Europeans provide about $3 million each year to support 10 EU [European Union] Centers in the U.S., but the three governments of North America provide no support for North American studies anywhere."

Statistics of "Supposed" Surveys and Polls of People of all Three Countries:
Questions were "supposedly" asked of Americans, Canadians and Mexicans,
back in 1990 and again in 2000, about erasing the border, forming a North
American Union and sharing a common currency. We are not told what people
were surveyed or how many of each country. Perhaps it was students of the
universities that were already going through an indoctrination program in
support of a North American Union. Or perhaps it was members of the Council
of Foreign Relations and their equivalents in each country or other liberal, elitist
groups. Or maybe statistics were just pulled from the sky, as is often the case
with liberals, where "ends justify the means, and they are willing to do whatever
it takes to achieve their "ends." The following is what Pastor says are the results
of the polls (Emphasis added in bold):

> **Erasing the Borders: In 1990—one-fourth of the Canadian and
> Mexican population** were in favor of erasing the border with the
> United States, and nearly half (**46 per cent**) of Americans favored
> eliminating the Canadian border.
>
> **In 2000—about 50 per cent of Americans** were in favor of
> doing away with the Mexican border. The Mexicans agree with the
> Americans on this issue.
>
> **Forming a North American Union:** "When Mexicans,
> Canadians, or Americans are asked whether they are prepared to give
> up their cultural identity in order to form one state or a union, all
> overwhelmingly reject the proposition. *But when the question is asked
> whether they would be prepared to form a single country if that would
> mean a higher quality of life for their country, **a majority** of the people
> in all three countries answer affirmatively.*
>
> **Forty-three per cent of Canadian think it 'would be a *good
> thing*** to be part of a North American Union in ten years,' and only
> **27 percent think it would be a bad thing**. Moreover, *nearly one-half
> (49 per cent) think North American Union is likely to happe*n. As with
> the **Mexicans, Canadians** are much more **willing to contemplate
> a union in a new North American entity** than to be part of the
> United States. A majority (**57 percent**) would oppose joining the
> United States while only **23 percent** would consider it."
>
> **Survey about a Common Currency:** "When asked whether
> Canada and the United States should have a common currency,
> the **Canadian public split 45 per cent in favor, and 44 per cent**

opposed. This suggests that Canadians are much further along than their leaders in thinking about some of the practical, but sensitive, questions of integration."

For the American public, a relatively higher percentage favor continental political union than is true of Mexicans and Canadians. Support for union soars when the contingency options e.g., if that would mean a better quality of life, etc. are included. *In 1990, 81 per cent of Americans said they would favor forming one country with Canada if it meant a better quality of life, and 79 per cent agreed if it meant the environment would get better.* These numbers declined a bit in 2000 but remained relatively high; 63 per cent approved of forming one country if it would improve the quality of life, and 48 per cent if the environment would get better, but they remained high. When one disaggregates the data, younger and wealthier Americans are readier to contemplate political union than older or poorer citizens.

What Should One Conclude from This Data? *First, the majority of the people in all three countries are prepared to contemplate **a reconfiguration of the North American political system** provided they can be convinced that it will produce a higher quality of life and handle problems like the environment more effectively than if these are done by each country. Secondly, the principal motive is economic, the approach is pragmati*c, and the main drawback is the fear of its effect on culture and identity. To the extent that people perceive their cultures at risk, they resist integration. Third, **younger people are more connected and ready to experiment with new political forms,** and so the prospects for future integration are likely to get better. Fourth, as Karl Deutsch predicted a half century ago, more contact and trust among peoples can facilitate integration, which, in turn, can increase trust. In disaggregating the data on a regional basis, one finds greater support for integration among those regions with the most contact—i.e., the southwest of the United States and the northern part of Mexico and on the Canadian border.[263]

What Should One Really Conclude from this Data?—That it is totally Fraudulent! How it is that "the majority of the people in all three countries are prepared to contemplate a reconfiguration of the North American political system . . ." when the vast majority of all three countries have yet to even hear of it? We are being deliberately kept in the dark on these issues. I would say that probably 95% of the people in America, Canada and Mexico still do not know anything about an NAU.

How about actually putting it up for a vote before all three countries? Then you would really get the accuracy of a true poll; of course, that is, if there are honest elections without voter fraud allowed.

Harvard University—Gordon Brown Promotes Globalism and Rejection of National Sovereignty: Harvard invited British Prime Minister, Gordon Brown to speak at their campus, April, 2008. Due to the fact that Pope Benedict XVI was visiting the United States at the same time, Mr. Brown's speech did not get much press coverage. Perhaps, it was planned that way, since his speech would be a little too revealing and shocking for most Americans. As has already been demonstrated with the forming of the European Union, one of the deceptive tactics is to keep people in the dark until the union has already taken place.

What Brown was saying sounds amazingly similar to what a North American Union would be all about—exactly like the European Union. Brown started off by demanding that the USA issue a "Declaration of Interdependence." Here are some of the highlights of his speech as stated by Phyllis Schlafly and her reply to him in her April 30, 2008, column:

Global Interdependence with "Global Obligations:"
> . . . His speech used the word global 69 times, globalization 7 times, and interdependence 13 times . . . Brown rejected the traditional concept of national sovereignty, which means an independent nation not subservient to any outside control, telling us to replace it with "responsible sovereignty," which he defined as accepting what he calls our global "obligations." Hold on to your pocketbook!

New Global Rules with Massive U.S. Cash Handouts and "Transcending Borders:"
> Brown admitted that his "main argument" is that we must accept "new global rules," "new global institutions," and "global networks." Brown's global rules include massive U.S. cash handouts and opening U.S. borders to the world. Brown warned us that his vision of the globalist future is "irreversible transformation." He wants to "transcend states" and "transcend borders" as he builds the "architecture of a global society."

Americans Must Think Inter-continentally and Have a Global Religion with Similar Ideals:

Brown even slipped in an attempt at thought control: "Americans must learn to think inter-continentally. We are all internationalists now." . . . Brown peddled the nonsense that the peoples of the world "subscribe to similar ideals." He tried to tell us that all religions (Christians, Jews, Muslims, Hindus, Sikhs and Buddhists) have "common values" and "similar ideals." No, they certainly do not.

Global Trained "Civilian Experts" and Military under the United Nations: Brown wants to increase the power of the United Nations to become the source of "an international stand-by capacity of trained civilian experts, ready to go anywhere at any time," and even be able to exercise "military force." Americans do not intend to cede such authority to the corrupt UN.

A Global Society is Advancing "Democracy" across the World: This statement is true if you believe democracy to be mob rule and the precursor to socialism and communism. But, if you believe democracy to mean allowing the people to have a say in their own government, then this statement is not true at all. As you have already read, Gordon Brown and the other heads of state of European countries did not even allow their people to have a say in the latest constitution for the EU. They called it a treaty, "the Treaty of Lisbon," instead of a constitution. That way they could bypass the vote of the people. As Phyllis Schlafly explains, Brown's global society would require:

> . . . all signers to surrender their sovereignty and democracy to unelected bureaucrats in Brussels and judges in Strasbourg. It takes away their rights to pass their own laws, and to surrender any vetoes of EU decisions, and gives the EU bureaucracy and tribunals total control over immigration policy. Instead of a self-governing nation whose democratic system was developed over centuries, England is now ruled by what Margaret Thatcher called 'the paper pushers in Brussels.'

The New World Order?—In his speech, Brown kept repeating the words "The New World Order." The elite think this term will mean some great utopian system, of course with them in charge. They try to portray it as something wonderful that we should all be working towards, even sacrificing for. What would the NWO really mean for the average American citizen? It would mean just the opposite of a utopia. It would be a one-world tyrannical system of government, with a one-world planned economy, no free enterprise system, no free anything. The government will dictate all that you do, including what you can become. We will have a greatly reduced standard of living. American workers will be in a common world labor pool with billions of workers across the globe who subsist on very low wages—like $2 a day.

A March Forward to Globalism: Gordon Brown invites the students at Harvard and all those who read his speech, to march forward to globalism "where there is no path." Phyllis Schlafly ends her column saying:

> He's correct that there is no path on which we can expect globalism to lead us to a better world; in fact every path toward global government is a surrender of our liberty and our prosperity. Gordon Brown should go back home and study up on how Americans refused to accept orders from King George III.[264]

Arizona State University Announced "Building a North America Project": As mentioned, the other university which had already gotten on board with the "education" part of Pastor's recommendations is Arizona State University. Its business school was pushing for "integration" with Mexico and Canada back in the year 2000, even before Pastor started teaching his classes at the American University. One would think with the enormous problems that the state of Arizona is facing and has experienced from the millions of illegal aliens coming over their border from Mexico, they would not be in favor of integration with such a third World Country with its high crime, drugs, gangs, and disrespect for laws. However, that is not the case with ASU.

In 2007, one was able to go their website to see what the Arizona State North American Project looked like. It was very revealing. (*www.asu.edu/clas/nacts/bna/who.html.*) Now, 2009, you can find references about the website, but it is no longer there. Here is what it used to say (emphasis added):

> The "**Building North America**" project began with a website, originally launched in 2000 and hosted by the American Society-Council of the Americas, which provided links (with editorial comment) to hundreds of sites of interest to the growing community of "**North Americanists**."
>
> This site was inspired by the notion that **economic integration in the NAFTA Triad (Canada-U.S.-Mexico)** was advancing despite the lack of press and public attention it received, and that a presence on the web would allow those of us in the Triad countries, and beyond, to "link up" to a growing body of research and, by extension, to one another as professional colleagues in the academic, business, and policy worlds.

In this same vein, the PanAmerican Partnership for Business Education launched a consortium of four North American business schools to promote a new generation of entrepreneurs with a deep knowledge of these integration trends in the region, while also generating more research and case studies regarding how businesses, governments, and organizations were shaping, and adapting to, the evolution of a shared economic space.

Nearly a decade later, and more than a decade after NAFTA, we are now bringing together the fruits of this research endeavor in a new, updated and redesigned "**Building North America**" website, generously hosted by the North American Center for Transporter Studies (NACTS) at Arizona State University and with the cooperation of our Partners, the Americas Society-Council of the Americas, and the Kansas City, Missouri International Affairs and Trade Office. We are still faced with a **regional integration process** that advances and deepens without the kind of attention—either within the academy or in government circles, let alone the general public—enjoyed in Europe; at the same time, we are betting on the continued existence of scholars and policy practitioners who would benefit from a site which would consolidate the research and data we are all generating, and thereby build community among us.

ASU's Partners: The website showed the logos of some of the partners with whom the Arizona State Business School North American Project was working: ASU North American Center for Transborder Studies; Americas Society-Council of the Americas; Kansas City, Missouri, City of Fountains, Heart of The Nation; Canada-US, Fulbright.

Goals: The website clearly stated what the goals of the North American Project are—promoting the acceptance of integration among university students of the three nations (emphasis added):

The links, documents, and other materials on this site have been selected, organized, and in some cases designed **to advance teaching and research on North American regional integration.** In particular, we hope to expand teaching materials available to university professors, both those who teach courses with "NAFTA content" and those in a variety of disciplines such as political science (international relations, international political economy), economics (international economics), and business (international business, international finance, international marketing) for whom a module on some dimension of **North American integration** would illuminate an important theory or operational issue. At the same time, the site also aims to **benefit the broader community of North Americanists**, within the academy and beyond, by putting at our collective fingertips—or mouse-reach—the kinds of current and historical material that will benefit research into, and understanding of, **North American integration—past, past, present, and future.**

National and Multi-National Businesses and Corporations Involved: Another amazing link the ASU website provided was a list of all the companies and corporations that were involved in supporting the North American Project and provided teaching modules to be used by university professors at ASU:

Pradeep Gopalakrishna, Wal-Mart in the NAFTA Market Case, Teaching Note

Angel Maas, H-E-B Expansion into Mexico Case, Teaching Note

Patrick LeBlond, Canadian National Railway Company (CN) Case. Company Fact Sheet, Teaching Note

Loris Apse, North American Film Production in Québec, Teaching Note

David Descoteaux, Quebecor World and the Benefits of the North American Platform, Teaching Note

Rolando Gonzalez, Quebec and the Biotech Industry in North America, Teaching Note

Alexandra Perez and Mathieu Jolicoeur, The Importance of Quebec Companies in the North American Economy—Jean Coutu (PJC) Case, Teaching Note

Philip Rosson, Mad Science, Teaching Note

Guy Stanley, Magna International (and teaching note), Magna International, Power Point back up

Stephen Handelman, Bombardier Case, Teaching Note

Noushi Rahman & Saima Prodhan, The Rise and Fall of Vincor, Teaching Note

Stephen Handelman, Ford Case Ford 2006 Annual Report, Teaching Note

Annette Hester: Iogen: The Ingenious Path of a Biotech Leader, Teaching Note: (Guy Stanley)

Stephen Handelman, Canadian Cross Border Trucking, Teaching note by Guy Stanley

Bank of Canada Income Trusts, CTA Key Issues 2007

Unfinished Business Brooks and Kymlicka

Government Websites for North American Integration: Another link that the Arizona State University Website gave was a list of all the government agencies in all three countries that are involved—a very revealing statement of how deep the North American integration is in government of all three countries and probably has been for a long time:

Canada-U.S. Relations, Department of Foreign Affairs and International Trade Canada /Affaires étrangères et Commerce international Canada (DFAIT-MAECI)
http://www.dfait-maeci.gc.ca/can-am/main/menu-en.asp

Canadian Border Services Agency / Agence des services frontaliers du Canada, (CBSA-ASFC)
http://www.cbsa-asfc.gc.ca/

Citizenship and Immigration Canada / Citoyenneté et Immigration Canada
http://www.cic.gc.ca/english/index.html

Comisión Internacional de Límites y Aguas entre México y Estados Unidos (CILA;

International Water and Boundary Commission, Mexican Section, Ciudad Juárez, Chihuahua, Mexico, *http://cila.sre.gob.mx*
Connect2Canada, NewsCan Service, Canadian Embassy, Washington, D.C., *http://www.connect2canada.com*

Industry Canada, Information by Subject, including: Business and Industry; Economy; Environment; Trade and Investment, among others. *http://www.ic.gc.ca/cmb/welcomeic.nsf/ICPages/Subject*

Instituto para Mexicanos en el Exterior (IME; Institute for Mexicans Abroad), Secretaría de Relaciones Exteriores (SRE; Mexican Foreign Ministry) *http://portal.sre.gob.mx/ime*

Instituto Nacional de Migración (INM; National Migration Institute) Secretaría de Gobernación (Mexican Interior Ministry) *http://www.inm.gob.mx/principal.asp*

International Boundary and Water Commission (U.S.-Mexico), U.S. Section, El Paso, Texas
http://www.ibwc.state.gov/

International Joint Commission (IJC-CMI), U.S.-Canada Forum for Cooperation on Boundary and Transboundary Waters *http://www.ijc.org/en/home/main_accueil.htm*

Mexican Embassy, Washington, D.C. *http://www.embassyofmexico.org*

North American Aerospace Defense Command (NORAD), HQ Peterson Air Force Base, Colorado; bi-national U.S.-Canada aerospace defense organization *http://www.norad.mil/*

North American Commission for Environmental Cooperation, Montreal
    http://www.cec.org/home/index.cfm?varlan=english
North American Commission for Labor Cooperation, Washington, D.C. *http://
    www.naalc.org/*
North American Development Bank (NADBank) *http://www.nadbank.org/*
NAFTA Secretariat, Trinational Site *http://www.nafta-sec-alena.org/DefaultSite/
    index.html*
Partnership for Prosperity (P4P), U.S.-Mexico initiative, launched in Sept. 2001.
    http://www.p4pworks.org/p4p_us.php
Policy Research Initiative (PRI), Government of Canada: North American,
    Linkages Project (Cross-Border Regions, etc.) *http://www/policyresearch.
    gc.ca*
Secretaría de Economía (SE; Ministry of the Economy), Mexico; covers Trade
    and Industry, Trade Negotiations, and Foreign Investment *http://www.
    economia.gob.mx/*
Secretaría de Relaciones Exteriores (SRE; Mexican Foreign Ministry. (Subsecretaría
    para América del Norte (Undersecretariat for North America) does not have
    its own site *http://www.sre.gob.mx*
Security and Prosperity Partnership of North America *http://www.spp.gov/*
U.S. Citizenship and Immigration Services (USCIS)—part of Department of
    Homeland Security (DHS); administers naturalization procedures *http://
    www.uscis.gov/graphics/index.htm*
U.S. Customs and Border Protection (CPB)—part of Department of Homeland
    Security (DHS); administers border security and facilitation of legal
    cross-border commerce, *http://www.cbp.gov/*
U.S. Department of Commerce, *http://www.commerce.gov*
U.S. Department of Homeland Security (DHS)—Immigration and Borders
    Page *http://www.dhs.gov/dhspublic/theme_home4.jsp*
U.S. Immigration and Customs Enforcement (ICE)—part of Department of
    Homeland Security (DHS); responsible for enforcing immigration and
    customs laws. *http://www.ice.gov/*
U.S. Trade Representative (USTR)—Chief trade negotiating office of the U.S.
    federal government *http://www.ustr.gov/*
Western Hemisphere Travel Initiative: Canadian Border Services Agency, *http://
    www.cbsa.gc.ca/agency/whti-ivho/menu-e.html* [265]

Why is Arizona State's Website for "North American Project" now Missing?
Perhaps the above information was too revealing and the university was getting
a lot of criticism. As you will read at the end of this chapter, the same thing has

happened to Robert Pastor's department at American University. It no longer exists either, and Robert Pastor no longer has his position there.

Arizona State, however, still has its other department through which the North American Project was working, the "North American Center for Transborder Studies (NACTS)." NACTS was founded by Steven Blank, who worked with Robert Pastor in the "mock parliament sessions" for college students. He served as its founding director, but is now serving as the Senior Research Analyst. He also writes for its quarterly newsletter called "North American Crossroads."

If you click on its website, it shows the other universities that it is working with in promoting a pro-North American viewpoint: three Mexican universities: "*El Colegio de la Frontera Norte (COLEF)* (Translated—College of the Northern Frontier);" *Instituto Technologico Autonomo de Mexico (ITAM)* (Technological Institute of Mexico;" *Tecnologico de Monterrey—Centro de Dialogo y Analisis sobre America del Norte* (Technological Institute of Monterrey—Center of Dialogue and Analysis About North America).

Stephen Blank and Other North American Connections—"North America Works (NAW)": Along with Robert Pastor, Blank is also a member of the CFR. He is also part of "North America Works," another group that holds conferences to promote "North Americanism," with the emphasis on trade. It is defined as "a national forum on trade policy."

"North America Works" was organized by the David Rockefeller-created "Council of the Americas." Stephen Blank is very influential in their conferences. In fact, he is known as the "driving force behind them." He was one of the speakers at the one held in Kansas City in November 4-6, 2009. In his bio as written on the program, it states that he is a Senior Fellow at CIGI (Center for International Governance Innovation—an "international think tank").

Blank is Co-Chair of the North American Transportation Competitiveness Research Council. He recently retired as a professor of international business and management at Pace University's Lubin School of Business. Previously, he served as director of the Lubin Center for International Business Development and founded the Pan American Partnership for Business Education, an alliance of four North American business schools. His bio also states that Dr. Blank is Chairman of the Board of Directors of NAFI—the North American Forum on Integration.[266]

2009, February 19—NACTS Sent a Report to President Obama on "Seizing North American Opportunities" and Praising NAFTA: The report was sent to Obama shortly before he left for his first summit meeting with the

Canadian Prime Minister. It was prepared by "a consortium of leading experts and universities in the U.S., Canada, and Mexico." They state that they had spent more than a year of "intensive consultations" to prepare the report. They urged Obama to "strengthen U.S. partnerships with its neighbors on challenges ranging from border security to global competitiveness and environmental protection."

NACTS's new director, Rick Van Schoik, urged the president to not lose track of the "urgency next door," and "unprecedented North American opportunities for enhancing our nation's competitiveness, security and sustainability." He told the president that we should not "undo NAFTA and praised it for the "40 million jobs that it has created in the U.S., Canada, and Mexico between 1993-2007." I will now reply to that outrageous claim about NAFTA.

The Truth about NAFTA: Where is Mr. Van Schoik getting these statistics about NAFTA creating 40 million jobs? Who knows? He's probably getting them at the same place that Robert Pastor got his statistics of those in support of a North American Union—out of thin air! Perhaps NAFTA has created a few service jobs and the need for more government workers, especially "border patrol" agents, because of the enormous illegal alien problem that has actually been exasperated by NAFTA. But according to several writers, NAFTA policies have caused enormous job losses and the outsourcing of millions of jobs in all three countries.

Lou Dobbs, the former, gutsy CNN television journalist, was one of the few television newsmen to report about the SPP and the clandestine movement towards a North American Union. On November 12, 2009, Dobbs shocked the nation and announced that was his last CNN broadcast. He had resigned and was able to end his contract early. CNN was probably very happy to be rid of their only conservative reporter. But conservatives were not at all happy to see him go. Many thought he was the best reporter on CNN, and they miss his show.

In 2006, Dobbs wrote a book called *War on the Middle Class,* in which he states that by 2006, NAFTA had caused the loss of **1 million jobs** in the USA. Instead of helping Mexico, NAFTA had caused Mexican manufacturing wages to fall 25 % by 1998. Of course, by 2009, it is even worse. Many farms and farmers also have gone under, not able to compete with the "fair trade" of NAFTA. More than half of the Mexicans now live in poverty, which, of course, has caused an even higher increase in illegal immigration to the USA, exactly opposite of what had been promised by the proponents of NAFTA.

Dobbs also cites a 2004 report from the University of California-Berkeley that as many as **14 million** jobs are at risk of being outsourced.[267]

William Norman Grigg, in his book, *America's Engineered Decline*, quotes from the *Christian Science Monitor*, who wrote the following about NAFTA on its 10th anniversary, 2004, "while opening doors for U.S. exports and helping Americans get low-cost consumer goods . . . NAFTA has displaced American workers and devastated entire towns . . . It's evident from the job-training centers in southern Texas to the 'NAFTA ghost towns' of North Carolina with their shuttered textile mills."[268]

Many factories and plants, textile mills, steel mills, have closed up and died away or they were outsourced to other countries. Many were important jobs for the survival of a nation to be self sustaining, such as manufacturing, steel and textile. These jobs were relatively high-paying as well.

***Wall Street Journal* Also Reveals Harmful Effects of NAFTA:** In a front page article, "Pain From Free Trade Spurs Second Thoughts," March 28, 2007, Alan Blinder, economist professor at Princeton, revealed his warning of how bad the "deeper downside" of NAFTA will probably become. Blinder used to be a former Federal Reserve vice chairman and advisor to several presidents. He used to be a strong supporter of "free trade, globalism and open borders" but now he is predicting that NAFTA will probably put another 30 to 40 million American jobs at risk, mostly from outsourcing.

Professor Blinder, who has a Ph.D from MIT and is considered a very prestigious economist, finally took a good look at the facts about NAFTA and job loss, and the facts changed his mind. He ranked 817 occupations to identify how likely each one is to go overseas. The most vulnerable jobs are bookkeepers, accountants, computer programmers, data entry keyers, medical transcriptionists, graphic designers, financial analysts, and even economist. Blinder says that the millions of American jobs that have already gone to Asia are "only the tip of a very big iceberg."

The Wall Street Journal article also cites Nobel laureate Paul Samuelson, the author of many economist textbooks, who has gone public with his reservations about NAFTA. He now is criticizing "over-simple complacencies about globalization" and says "rich-country workers aren't always winners from trade." He made that point in a 2004 essay that stunned colleagues.[269]

NACT's Report to the President Continues Support for North Americanism: Continuing on with the NACTS's Report to Obama, other points supporting "a North American strategy for the 21st century" by NACT's director, Rick Van

Schoik, were: "economic development and job creation for all three nations;" [We can't even handle our own rising rate of unemployment—which is estimated to be much higher than what reports say—closer to 20% of our nation.]

Have smart infrastructure investments for "faster and greener trade; increase global competitiveness with other trading blocs; **combat "the security threats to North America from the** "narcoinsurgency" waged by Mexican organized crime, fuelled by guns and cash from the U.S." [sounds like Van Schoik thinks the U.S. is responsible for the organized crime going on in Mexico.]

And, of course, there has to be a little "green agenda" thrown in—"rapidly accelerating climate change that underscores the need to not only deal with emissions, but also water shortages and lost biodiversity;" Van Schoik continues:

We could achieve "energy security next door, not an ocean away, if we do a few things right . . . and right now;" Mexico "offers a vital window of opportunity that simply must be supported, as potential risks and benefits extend far beyond its borders."

Van Schoik adds that the President needs to: strengthen "maximize bipartisan U.S. support and Mexican consensus . . ." and "energize the North American Trilateral Leaders Summit by **expanding involvement by the three federal legislatures and other key stakeholders;**" [Amazing, he is actually suggesting to let Congress and the parliaments from the other two countries be part of this instead of keeping them in the dark. Could it be that Van Schoik thinks our Congress is more liberal now and under Obama's leadership, they will be more supportive of forming a North American Union?]

Other suggestions in the report were: "designate a North America/borders authority;" "prepare for **enhanced joint defense** and better management of **natural and human-generated catastrophes;**" develop a "**North American trade and transportation plan;**" create a "joint, revolving **fund for infrastructure investments;**" implement "a North American **greenhouse gas exchange strategy** to promote **energy independence and climate security**; establish a joint, practical assessment of progress on key North American issues.[270]

NACTS Report is Reinventing the Wheel: All of the above have already been done by the SPP "working groups." They were at it for many years. I do not believe all their work is now dead and buried just because we have a new administration, even though that seems to be what the elite would like us to believe.

2008, January—Pastor's and the CFR's New Tactics—Pretend All Movement to A North American Union is Dead: Surprisingly, at the beginning of 2008, out of the blue, Robert Pastor resigned his position at the American University and announced that he was going away to work on some books and to be part of a global think tank, called the "Global Elders." In an interview with Dr. Jerome Corsi, Pastor said he resigned to begin a one-year sabbatical to work on three books, one would be about North America. Corsi found out later that the new permanent university President, Neil Kerwin, had decided to shut down Pastor's Office of International Affairs. Could that have been the real reason why Pastor resigned?

Pastor said that he is going to be working with the "Global Elders," a globalist-minded, conflict-resolution group of 13 world figures, including Nelson Mandela, Desmond Tutu, Kofi Anan, and Jimmy Carter. The Elders website states, "We are moving to a global village and yet we don't have our global elders. The Elders can be a group, who have the trust of the world, who can speak freely, be fiercely independent and respond fast and flexibly in conflict situations."[271] (I don't know about the "trust of the world" part, but all the members definitely fit the category of "elders" and are of the same liberal, globalist, Marxist ilk as Pastor. He should feel right at home among them.)

2008, July—Pastor Stated that the SPP was Having Its Last Hurrah: Pastor wrote an article entitled "The Future of North America," published in the July/August issue of the Council on Foreign Relations magazine, in which he said that the SPP April Summit will probably be their last hurrah. He thinks the new U.S. president will probably discard the whole idea. The executives of all three countries will still have meetings, but the term SPP will no longer be used. He believes the reason why the SPP is failing is because of the decision policy to keep the SPP below the radar of public opinion. " . . . keeping the issues away from public view has generated more suspicion than accomplishments."

Amazingly, a little bit of truth eventually comes out. Will this experience cause government policy to be less secretive and more open and "transparent?" Not when it comes to moving Americans towards regional or a one-world government. The elitists know that the vast majority of Americans would be outraged at such an idea. That is why they have tried to do it under the radar screen.

Is Pastor's Dream Really Dead and Buried? Don't believe it for a moment. The elitists have been at this plan far too long; too many multi-national corporations are behind it, too many governmental policies are already in place, ready to go at a moment's notice, when the right "crisis" comes along.

As has been the modus operandi with many liberal plans before, when the opposition begins to find out what they are all about and mounts a strong attack, the liberals just fake defeat, "play dead." They are hoping that the patriotic Americans who have been fighting the SPP and the movement to an NAU for so long will all breathe a sigh of relief and go back to normal life, while the elitists move forward with even "deeper integration and in an even more "quite way."

Perhaps, the plan is to simply bypass the North American Union and move right on to the "Transatlantic Partnership" with the EU that was written about in Chapter Four. Or the plan could be to use that Partnership to draw attention away, while they go full steam ahead with the NAU or UNA, the Union of North America (another possible name change).

They can also be using the financial crisis, loss of jobs, loss of money, loss of homes, or Obama's Cap and Trade, and controversial health care bill, etc. to hold people's attention, while they go deeper with their secret plans for regional government.

As you have seen, the mock parliaments for the students are continuing; the 2009 one was held in Mexico in May. Other conferences such as "North America Works" are continuing, and the summits of the executives from all three countries are continuing. Here is a report of the one for 2009 that took place in August, also in Mexico.

2009, August 9-10, U.S.-Canada-Mexico Summit in Guadalajara, Mexico: President Obama met with Mexican President Felipe Calderon and Canadian Prime Minister, Stephen Harper at the *Cabanas Cultural Institute*. The main topics for the summit meeting were the "now-global swine flu epidemic," as well as drug trafficking, security issues, clean energy, the economic crisis, commerce and trade across the borders and the ban on Mexican trucks.

As Robert Pastor predicted, the meetings of the three executives from each country are now called "Summits." The SPP is no longer used, no mention of it, as though it never existed. Notice what was written about the 2009 summit. No mention of a name change, as if they have always been called "North American Leaders Summits." The article insinuates that from the onset back in 2005, these trilateral summits have never been of much concern, no need to pay attention; they are rather boring, "sleepy affairs." The article was written by Jennifer Loven, AP White House Correspondent:

President George W. Bush kicked off the trilateral tradition in 2005 with the first summit held near his Texas ranch. They typically are rather sleepy affairs—no splashy news, little attention. Despite the lofty name of North American Leaders Summit, it lacks a defining cause and is usually more a progress report on commercial and security integration than an action-packed headline-grabber.[272]

Name Changes Were Suggested by the Hudson Institute: According to the *Phyllis Schlafly Report* of September 2009, the suggestion to change the name of the SPP to "North American Leaders Summit," came from the Hudson Institute, another international "think tank" similar to the CFR and the Center for Strategic and International Studies, who have been working together in promoting the movement towards a North American Union. Other words that have been dropped are "union, amero, illegal aliens, even guest workers." All these words had become embarrassing. "Economic integration" and "integrated economies" are the acceptable words to use instead when referring to any movement to form a North American Union. "Labor mobility" is now to be used when speaking about illegal aliens.

"Unlimited Labor Mobility" and "Free Access for Mexican Trucks": These were what was demanded of President Obama by President Calderon in the summit talks. Calderon stated that it was "unthinkable" for the United States to function "without the contribution of the Mexican laborers and workers." He also demanded "U.S. citizenship" for all Mexicans living illegally in the United States.

Obama's response? He promised to "continue to work to fix America's broken immigration system," which Mrs. Schlafly believes are the "code words for amnesty for illegal aliens." The one good thing, Obama did not give in to Calderon's demand to open our roads to Mexican trucks. Congress passed a law banning the trucks and it still stands. According to a Rasmussen pole, 66% of Americans still oppose lifting the Congressional ban. Mexican trucks still do not meet our safety standards, nor do their drivers.[273]

According to Jennifer Loven, in her AP story, Obama has pledged to "renew immigration overhaul efforts, including a **citizenship path for illegal immigrants.**"[274]

Mexican Drug War: In the summit talks, John Brennan, Obama's Homeland Security aid, mentioned the large number of people who have been killed in the drug war—11,000 since 2006. Obama wanted to give $100 million to Mexico to help in the drug war, but it was held up over concerns in Congress over abuses by the Mexican military.

Obama said he wanted "to stem the illegal southbound flow of American guns and cash that helps fuel this extraordinary violence." In other words, Obama was back at his old game of blaming America for all the ills of the world—this time for the Mexican drug violence. Mrs. Schlafly writes, "most of the guns found at the Mexican crime scenes are not American, and U.S. taxpayers are already generously footing the bill to train Mexicans to fight the drug war."

Climate Change Pledge: Canada's Prime Minister Stephen Harper asked for all three executives to pledge to work together "on a North American focus against climate change in order to assure and guarantee a new international covenant that is efficient and truly global."

Obama reaffirmed his commitment to pass the "Cap and Trade Bill," so as Mrs. Schlafly writes, he could be "be hailed as a hero at the upcoming United Nations climate-change conference in Copenhagen (that took place in December, 2009, in Copenhagen, Denmark)." He promised the other two executives that he would "take the lead by reducing U.S. emissions by 80% by 2050" and to work with other nations to "cut global emissions in half."[275]

Swine Flu Talks: AP White House Correspondent Jennifer Loven reported that the leaders also expressed their concern for the upcoming possible swine flu epidemic. John Brennan said that the talks between the three leaders were "timely and crucial," that they need to link up health officials and ready vaccine and antiviral supplies and they must publicly reinforce a determination not to panic when cases arise. He warned that there will be people who will get very sick and die. The leaders need to try to keep the severity and reach of the illnesses to a minimum, but they need to do everything possible to "ensure the continuation of commerce, transportation and trade between the three countries . . ." especially in this time of a "limping economy."

Brennan praised NAFTA, as if it were something all three countries should be proud of—"The largest free-trade zone in the world." The borders must be left open. Closing the borders would be very costly for families and businesses on both sides of the borders.[276]

A New Crisis Involving All Three Countries as the Impetus for a Union?
A new crisis could happen, such as a bigger epidemic of swine flu affecting all three North American countries. Or the financial crisis will get so bad, the U.S. dollar so devalued, people's lives so devastated, so many people out of work, state

government could collapse, with such chaos and anarchy reigning, that some new remedy will have to be found.

A new currency for all three countries could then come to the rescue—the amero. Of course, there will have to be government agencies over the amero and order once more established. What a good time to introduce the new government already set up ready to go: a North American Union, with its inter-Parliamentary Group, its Judicial Branch, and its executive branch, a North American Defense Command—to establish order, and a financial institution, the North American Development Bank—to save the day and to usher in the amero.

With the excuse of having to work with "deeper integration" to preserve lives, to establish order, Canada, Mexico, and the USA could be moved into a union together. Perhaps, as planned, this could happen by 2010, the original goal as the following quote states.

> "the Security and Prosperity Partnership signed by President Bush and Vicente Fox of Mexico and Martin of Canada, on March 23, 2005, should become **by 2010**, an official North American economic and security community, the boundaries of which would be defined by a common external tariff and an outer security perimeter, within which the movement of people, products, and capital will be legal, orderly, and safe.[277]

More information on all that has transpired in laying the foundation for a NAU is found in Chapter 17, the Timeline to a North American Merger. The next chapter continues with a vital part of Robert Pastor's plan for a North American Union, to have "biometric border passes," essentially national ID cards that will be used by all three countries. Pastor and the CFR and other elitists wanted the use of RFID in these cards so people could always be tracked. The government would always know where all of their subjects are at all times.

Chapter Twelve

"Big Brother" is Watching You:
East Germany Visit—What Life is Like Under a Police State;
Attempts at National ID Cards and Data Bases in the USA; The
Patriot Act; The Department of Homeland Security; The Real ID
Act of 2005; The Western Hemisphere Travel Initiative; The Pass
ID Bill; RFID Chips and Implants—All Part of the Merger Plan

A society whose citizens refuse to see and investigate the facts, who refuse to believe that their government and their media will routinely lie to them and fabricate a reality contrary to verifiable facts, is a society that chooses and deserves the Police State Dictatorship it's going to get. (Ian Williams Goddard, a free-lance writer and artist)

Pastor's Recommendation for an International ID Card for all Three Countries: As you read in the last chapter, the SPP is "supposedly" dead, (or has been given a new name and gone deep under cover) but one of Pastor's important proposals is definitely not dead and is going full steam ahead—to have a national ID surveillance card, containing biometric identifiers, for all three countries which would give the citizens of each country easy access across each others' borders. The data collected would also be shared between the three countries and other countries like the EU. This chapter tells how far we have come in fulfilling Pastor's proposal.

I begin with two personal stories that my husband and I experienced while traveling in East Germany that gave us a glimpse into what life was like under Communist tyranny, where "big brother" was constantly watching over you; precious freedoms and privacy were gone.

Personal Visits to East Germany—What Life was Like for People Living Under a Police State under Communist Rule: During the summer vacation of 1970, my husband and I served as tour guides for an organization called World Academy for a six-week trip to Europe. We were in charge of 55 high school students and ten parents. Part of the tour included West Berlin, but to get there we had to travel by train through East Germany. What an experience that was! We witnessed firsthand the sad state of a country that had been taken over by a communist dictatorship and separated from the rest of Germany by an enormous wall. They were prisoners inside their own land.

The Train Ride Through East Germany: Before we could board the East German train, all of our luggage and purses were opened, searched and any American magazines, books, literature, or Bibles were confiscated. The Stasi police did not want American "propaganda" coming into East Germany to expose the people as to what life was really like in the United States, nor did they want Bibles. The people were only allowed to receive the news reports and propaganda the government wanted them to receive and they did not like people to have religion, especially Christianity. Christian churches were persecuted in East Germany just as they were throughout the rest of the Soviet Union.

We had been warned that our American literature and Bibles might be taken. I was pregnant with our first child, and before we had to give them our luggage, I borrowed one of my husband's belts, went into the restroom and strapped my Bible on top of my stomach with his belt. It was hidden underneath a loose hanging, obvious maternity blouse. Fortunately, the police did not look there and I was able to smuggle my Bible on board with me.

Most of us were pretty frightened as we boarded the train. Each compartment had its own stern looking East German soldier standing with a rifle in his arms. My husband had the nerve to go talk to the one in our compartment to find out more about what life was like in East Germany. The soldier was surprised to find a fellow German among our group of Americans. But he was pretty tightlipped. He told how many people were in his regiment and where he was from and that was about it.

Gazing out the window of the train, we were struck by the sharp contrast between West and East Germany. It was like going from bright day to somber night. West Germany was prosperous and thriving with beautiful cities and villages, painted homes, immaculate, manicured lawns, gardens and fields; the paved roads and highways in good repair; modern cars and buses; the people were dressed in fashionable clothes and bright colors and looked busy, industrious and happy.

Traveling through East Germany, we saw just the opposite. Most of the houses and buildings were in sad shape, in great need of repair, brown and grey with no paint on them. We could see where patches of stucco had crumbled away and the inner wire and wood were showing. We saw row after row of gray, drab rectangular apartment buildings made out of cement, looking all the same, with no flowers in the windows. The fields were full of weeds. The roads were in great need of repair with big potholes here and there.

The only cars on the road were the tiny, East German-made Trabants, which resembled the match-box cars little children play with. There was only room for two in the front and two in the back.

When the train stopped at various cities and towns, we could get a closer look at the people. Even though it was summer time, the clothes the people were wearing were shades of gray, black, and brown. It takes more money to dye clothes, and since the government owned all the textile and clothes manufacturing, obviously no dyes were used. These colors and materials were all they were offering. The people's faces matched their clothes. They looked very sad and somber.

West and East Berlin: The city of Berlin before World War II was the seat of government for all of Germany. Four years after the end of the war, Russia took over East Germany, where Berlin was located. In 1949, Berlin was divided in half. The Russians controlled East Berlin, which became the capitol of East Germany. West Berlin was still allowed to belong to West Germany, but it was like an island surrounded by East Germany. The capitol of West Germany was moved to Bonn.

East Germans did not want to live under a dictatorship. They had already experienced enough of that with Hitler. Millions began leaving their homes and possessions, fleeing to the west in large numbers. Most of them came through Berlin. By 1961, 3 1/2 million East Germans had fled to the West.

The Berlin Wall: The Communists decided they had to put a stop to the East Germans fleeing. They built a wall right through the city and beyond to keep the people in. It was built in 1961 and remained until 1989. It was 12 feet high, 3.9 feet wide and stretched 26 miles between the two sections of the city. It then was continued on to section off all of East Germany from West Germany. It stretched 87 miles, with 302 watch towers where guards would stand to keep anyone from trying to dig under it or climb over it. They also had barbed wire in front of it to prevent attempts to cross it.

Our Arrival in Berlin: Because of the free enterprise system and freedoms that exist in West Germany, West Berlin was also a thriving and prosperous city and looked just like the rest of West Germany. We were all so happy to arrive there and breathed a sigh of relief to be off the East German train.

Trip to the Berlin Wall: The next day we went by bus to see the Berlin Wall. It was an enormous high gray cement wall. It seemed much higher to me than just 12 feet. As we got off the bus, the bus driver told us that every afternoon at this time—2:00, an elderly lady would come and climb up on a platform so she could see over the wall and wave to her sister. That was the only contact they had with each other and how they knew each other was still alive. No letters or phone calls were allowed between East and West Berlin. That is how dictatorial Communist Russia was over the East Germans.

We waited and sure enough we saw the lady come and climb up on the platform to look over the wall and we saw her wave. There were tears in many of our eyes watching. After the woman had descended, a few of us at a time also climbed the platform so we could see what East Berlin looked like.

East Berlin: Again what a contrast! Looking from West Berlin to East Berlin was like looking from brightness to darkness. We saw lots of cement buildings, some old monuments in need of repair. We saw the same cement cinderblock apartment buildings with no flowers. We saw drab streets and sidewalks in need of repair, very few cars, people dressed in somber colors. It almost resembled a city that was in mourning. I'm sure that is how most of the people there felt. They were in mourning for their loss of freedoms.

Visit to Dresden, East Germany, in March of 1990: Kurt and I and our good friends, Dian and Richard Tashjian, were visiting his parents in Southern Germany for their 50th wedding anniversary. It was just a few months after November 9, 1989, the day that East Germans were finally allowed to be free and to visit West Germany, and the Berlin Wall began to be chipped away. (October 3, 1990, East and West Germany were officially reunited as one country again.)

Like many tourists, Kurt and I and our friends decided this would be a good time to travel on to East Germany and see what it was like. We also drove to Berlin and were able to chip away at the wall and get a few pieces of it.

In Dresden, East Germany, we rented a room from a couple because all the hotels were filled. The couple, Mr. and Mrs. Wagner, were very hospitable and stayed up until late in the night answering our questions and telling us what life had been like for them since 1961, when the Berlin Wall had been erected, and they were no longer free, but were like prisoners under the rule of the Soviet Union over East Germany.

Mrs. Wagner had warned us about not drinking any tap water as soon as we arrived. She said all the streams and water supplies were polluted throughout the land. They could only drink bottled water. Sorry to say, our friend, Dian, had already drunk some of the water. The next day she ended up with Bells Palsy. One half of her face was partially paralyzed the rest of the trip.

Questions and Answers about the Life in East Germany under Communism: Here are some of the questions that we asked of the Wagners and their answers. The description they gave of what had happened to their country under Communist rule can serve as a warning to us in the United States as we see some of the same things happening in our nation as government becomes more powerful and more like a police state. My husband and I would translate for our friends from German to English. [The questions are in bold, the answers are in italics.]:

What happened to all the rivers and the water supplies? Why are they polluted? *Under Communist rule, the government owns and controls all factories and plants and can essentially do whatever they want. If they decide to dump all the refuse into the streams and rivers they can and they did. All the fish were dead and, of course, the underground supply of water had also become polluted.*

Why is the sky so gray and smells so bad? *The government-owned factories burn black coal for their energy supply. The smoke stacks are dumping black smoke into the skies. Again, since the government owns and operates the factories, they make the rules and there is no stopping the pollution.*

Why are the roads and highways in such bad condition? *The government does not have much incentive for repairing them. Plus there is only one government-owned company that does such work and their equipment is very old and breaks down a lot.*

We saw a man using an old rusty push mower to cut his grass. Do you not have any modern lawn mowers? *I have not seen any. They would be very hard to maintain and repair because we don't have the tools, also gasoline is very expensive. Most people just have to go on using their rusty old lawn mowers.*

Why do we see so many of the little Trabant cars broken down on the side of the road? (I had counted 25 in one day.) *There is only one government-owned and run manufacturing plant that makes cars and all they produce are the Trabant. The plant is very old and the cars are not very well made, nor are very many made each month. But since no competition is allowed, there is no incentive to improve the design or the plant or to increase production. There are very few places that repair the cars and not very many decent tools. Most people have to learn how to repair them themselves. The cars are also very expensive. You have to pay for them ahead of time and then wait several years before you get yours. Most people rely on bicycles instead.*

Why are the houses in such bad need of repair, with no paint on them? *Paint is usually the last on the list of what people need on which to exist. Food and clothing are more important. Plus the paint is very expensive and very limited in supply.*

What have the East Germans been able to do for recreation? *Not much. We don't have much extra money. We go on little trips if the car is working, if you have a car, or small trips by bicycles. Most of the forests that we used to go walking* *in were closed to us, because that is where the Russian army was storing their tanks and equipment.*

Kurt finally asked the most important question—How could the people just stand by and allow all this to happen, how a once beautiful country and hard-working German people could be brought to such a state—all their freedoms and their incentives lost? Mr. Wagner told us, "*The government controlled the people by fear and intimidation and by rewarding stool pigeons. If anyone dared to complain about the government, even sometimes to their own family members, that person would snitch on them to the Stasi police. There were great rewards for snitching. The person would be able to get his car immediately without having to wait for it for years or they would get money. When times are tough and people need money to feed their families, they are more inclined to be a stool pigeon. After awhile, the brave people who were willing to speak out were all gathered up and put in prison or exterminated. Others, seeing what had happened to them, were so intimidated that they became silent too.*

There were also many people who tried to escape either over or under the wall. Very few would ever make it. The walls were lined with barbed wire which the people could not make it through. There were too many watchtowers with guards and the people would be shot. Some places under the wall were mined and the people would be blown up if they stepped on them.

Mr. Wagner's own father was the chief of police. He had put many people in jail for criticizing the government—people who been turned in by their neighbors or even family members. Mr. Wagner said that just a few weeks earlier, now that East Germans were allowed to leave their country, his parents made a trip to visit West Germany. His father returned home and tried to commit suicide. He had discovered all the evil things that he had been told about the west were all lies, just propaganda to keep the East Germans from knowing the truth about what freedom can do for a country, and he felt so guilty for having been a part of that lie and for all the people whom he had put in jail for speaking the truth.

Before we went to bed that night, Mr. Wagner played his guitar and sang a beautiful song for us that he had composed. We have it on video tape. The song asked the question what is the most beautiful thing in the world? Some people would say a lovely woman, others would say beautiful scenery. His answer was music. With music he could soar over walls and boundaries and imagine what it was like to be free. We all had tears in our eyes listening to him sing.[278]

I have always remembered these two experiences and what my husband and I learned about life under communist tyranny and a police state. It made me very grateful to live in a nation that is free.

However, our visit with the Wagner Family was in 1990. Twenty years later, America has become very close to a police state, herself. Compare what is going on in modern day Russia and what is going on here with our huge Department of Homeland Security, the Patriot Act and the movement to a National ID card, with RFID chips attached, and socialized medicine passed into law.

All is in place for invasive and constant snooping into private citizens lives—exactly how secret police operate under tyrannical governments. The following makes me believe we are even closer to what people were experiencing in East Germany.

How to Recognize Living Under Nazis and Communists: Kitty Werthman grew up living in Austria, seven years under Hitler, and after World War II ended, she experienced three years living under communism, after the Soviets took over Eastern Austria. She and her husband now live in South Dakota. She has often spoken on radio programs telling about her experiences. I recently heard her speak at a national Eagle Forum Conference, September 26, 2009, in St. Louis, Missouri. Her message is even more meaningful, because she says under Obama, she is seeing so much coming to our nation that she experienced under Hitler and communism. Here are some of the highlights of her speech:

The Poor Conditions in Austria After World War I: Kitty Werthman said that conditions were really bad among the 8 and 1/2 million people in Austria after World War I. One-third of the workforce was unemployed. There was 25% interest on loans if you borrowed money. There was anarchy and unrest. Every day her mother would bake bread and fix a big kettle of soup to feed the hungry people who would come to their door.

The people began to hear of the good working conditions in Germany since Hitler had taken over: People had jobs; they were building massive autobahns and fixing up the cities; they had full employment and everyone appeared happy. Hitler promised the Austrians that if they would vote to be annexed to Germany and have Hitler as their ruler as well, that they also would have full employment and everyone would be happy. The desperate Austrians fell for it. In March of 1938, they voted 98% to have Hitler as their "*fuehrer*" (supreme leader) as well. They then believed everything would be fine.

Amazing Social Changes: Hitler's promise for full employment came true. Everyone had a job in some public works, mainly building projects such as autobahns. Germany and Austria had an Equal Rights Amendment. The German and Austrian women, who by tradition were homemakers and enjoyed being at home raising their children, now had to put their babies and little children in government-run day cares or public schools and go to work. The babysitters at the day care centers were actually women highly educated in child psychology.

Everyone had to work; otherwise you were considered a parasite. There were guaranteed incomes, subsidized housing, food stamps; everyone's income was equalized.

Changes in Local Government: Regionalism was put in place. The seven provinces were merged into four regions. By breaking up the provinces into centralized regions, it destroyed local control. There were no more elections; everyone was appointed. Kitty added that in South Dakota where she now lives, they tried to do the same thing, to merge their counties into larger regions. She testified at the state hearings and told them that is exactly what Hitler had done in Austria, and the proposal "went down in flames."

Nationalization Began: The first thing that happened, everyone got free radios so they could hear the daily broadcasts coming from Hitler. Hitler nationalized all radio stations, so his broadcasts were the only ones that could be received. He then nationalized all the banks; he nationalized the auto industry; he turned the auto industry mainly into a defense industry to manufacture tanks and machinery for war. He nationalized the health industry, education, and he nationalized the churches.

How the Health Care Changed: Now that all health care was "free," the Austrian excellent health care was ruined. It became "practicing medicine on a conveyer belt." Doctors were salaried by the government, and their salaries went down to nothing. Many doctors left the country. Research stopped. People would sometimes have to wait 12-18 months to get a hospital bed.

Education was also Nationalized: Before Hitler, prayer was allowed in school. After Hitler, there was no more prayer. The crucifixes were taken down and Hitler's picture was put in their place. There was no more religious instruction allowed, they had P.E. instead. The children had to go to school on Sunday. The two hours that they would have had church on Sunday, they had political instruction instead. The rest of the day was fun sports. The children received free sports equipment and had so much fun. It was much more fun than going to church.

Fortunately, Kitty's mother could see what was coming in the future with such an education. She recognized it as a school of propaganda and frivolity. She wanted her daughter to get a good education which would include religious instruction. She pulled her out of the public schools and sent her to a private Catholic convent school. Kitty really resented it at first, but her mother told her some day you are going to thank me. Years later, Kitty was grateful and did thank her. She observed that her friends who stayed in the public school and were indoctrinated never went back to their religious roots. Everyone in the public and private schools were told what they could study and what they could become. Her husband wanted to be a forester but he was told he had to become a doctor, which he did and later learned to like it. She was told she had to become a teacher.

Nationalization of the Churches: Hitler gave the excuse that there was not enough money coming in to the churches. He would help them out by taxing the people just a little more, 2%, for a church tax and give 2% to the churches. Once he got the churches used to that money, he began to control what the ministers could say or not say. If they spoke out against him or any of his policies, they could lose their funding.

The Welfare System: They had a huge welfare system. To support it, taxes skyrocketed up to 70% of your income. Hitler wrote a book, *Mein Kampf,* which means "My Struggle." No one read it. The young people were too involved in sports and having fun. The older people were too involved in working hard. If only we had read it because it told exactly what Hitler had planned for us all.

Regulations: With the new government came 100% regulations, especially in agriculture. They told the farmers how much they had to produce and what they could grow and could not grow. "They even told the chickens how many eggs they had to lay." There were many stringent safety regulations such as restaurants having to have round tables instead of square. Small businesses could not afford all the regulations and were forced to close down. Only the big businesses could survive.

Eugenics: Abortions were illegal because Hitler wanted lots of children for his Hitler's Youth, but there were selected abortions. Hitler wanted to develop his Aryan race, what he considered to be a superior race of people with blond hair, blue eyes, and higher intelligence. Children who were born with handicaps were disposed of and women who were obviously retarded were not allowed to "breed" or were forced to have abortions.

For Kitty's last year of teaching school, she was sent to a small village. There were fifteen mentally retarded people there. They were good workers but could not read or write. One day a van from the health department came. All fifteen were gathered up and taken away in the van. Their families had been told that the government had a program for them where they would be taught to read and to write. However, "as time passed, letters started to dribble back saying that all fifteen of these people had died a natural, merciful death. The villagers were not fooled. They knew that their loved had left in excellent physical health and all had died within 6 months. "We called this euthanasia." Twenty thousand children, who were physically handicapped and in a children's hospital in Vienna, were also euthanized. "They were considered useless eaters."

A Federal Police Force, the Gestapo: As things got worse and worse and Hitler began his propaganda campaign against the Jewish people, the Gestapo would be seen taking people away. People were disappearing all the time. They had no idea what happened to those people. They did not find out about the concentration camps until after the war was over.

People were Rewarded for Snitching: Food was rationed. You had to turn in a coupon to buy food. If you didn't you would be arrested. However, if you promised to snitch on your neighbor, then you would be allowed to go free. It began to get so bad that in her home, her family would only whisper, afraid someone would over hear their conversations.

Gun Control: Hitler told the people the best way to get rid of any criminals was to know where all the guns are, so the people all had to register their guns. Then they were told, that there were still too many criminals, so they would have to turn in their guns. If they didn't, they would be arrested. The gestapo already knew where all the guns were anyway. It would have been useless to fight them.

ID Cards: Everyone had to have an ID card and number and you had to have it on you at all times. If you were asked for it and didn't have it, you would be arrested. If you moved to a new area, you first had to go to the local police and register. They had to keep track of all of their citizens at all times. When Kitty first moved to the United States, she went to the local police stations to register. The officer asked what she was trying to do. He told her that was not necessary in the USA. She said she walked out of the station and realized for the first time that she really was free. "This is what it feels like."

Borders were Closed: Nobody could come in and nobody could go out. Everyone was afraid of the government. There is a famous statement, "When the people are afraid of the government, that is tyranny, when the government is afraid of the people, that is liberty."

NAZI means Nationalization. That is what is now happening in the United States. It is bordering on Marxism. Kitty told how she came to the United States. Her parents were aware that eventually all of Europe would fall under communism, which is essentially what is happening. The European Union is the first step. They had her apply for a visa and she was able to come to America, where she met her husband, who is from Germany. He had left when the practice of medicine had become so unbearable under socialized medicine in Bavaria. Kitty is asked often to speak at the Tea Party Rallies and has her story on CDs which are a popular item at the rallies. It is alarming to see the nationalization and similarities of what is now going on under Obama's administration.

Obama's Whitehouse Asked for Informants to "Rat Out" Critics of Health Care Bill: In August of 2009, I received several e-mails quoting what appeared on the Whitehouse website encouraging people to send in a report if they heard anything "fishy" about what people were saying about Obama's health care bill. Amazing how similar Obama's administration is becoming to the practices in Soviet Russia and East Germany. Here is the quote that appeared on the Whitehouse website. It is coming from Linda Douglass, communications director for the White House Health Reform Office:

> *"Since we can't keep track of all of [the disinformation] here at the White House, we're asking for your help. If you get an email or see something on the web about health insurance reform that seems fishy, send it to **flag@ whitehouse.gov**."* [279]

Here is one reaction to what appeared on the Whitehouse website: "I am shocked and dismayed that Barack Obama's White House is now monitoring email traffic nationwide if it opposes his government takeover of healthcare." Mathew Staver, Founder and Chairman of Liberty Counsel. He continues:

> *Barack Obama has turned his White House "Health Reform Office" into a Chicago-style political hack machine. Right on the White House's website, Obama's team admits that it is openly monitoring web and email "disinformation" opposing ObamaCare. What is happening in America? Now the White House wants everyone to rat out their friends and Internet contacts if they don't happen to agree with everything the President says about the biggest socialist scheme in American history! Meanwhile, the liberal elites in Congress are doing their best to undermine and discredit the building grassroots opposition to Obama-Care. The White House must be pretty rattled if it is asking Americans to "inform" on personal e-friends and contacts! (As revealed by Laurence & Kelleigh, radio talk show hosts)* [280]

Cybersecurity Act of 2009—Would Give the President, In Case of Emergency, Total Control of the Internet: Here is one more really "big brother" attempt. As has been mentioned, there really is not much "free press" in our nation anymore, with the owners, producers, editors of our top newspapers, radio and TV stations all belonging to the CFR and other elitist groups from where they get their controlled media sources. Consequently more and more people have turned to the internet for their news. It has become for many their "free press." If this bill goes through, internet freedom of the press and free speech will be coming to a halt as well.

August 27, 2009, Senator Jay Rockefeller's revamped bill, Cybersecurity Act of 2009, was presented in the House again. His original bill had been sharply criticized by Silicon Valley, the "heartland of the telecommunications industry," as a "dangerous government intrusion." According to FOX news, there could even be a "kill switch" to shut down online traffic by seizing private networks—"a move cybersecurity experts worry will choke off industry and civil liberties."

Larry Clinton is president of the Internet Security Alliance, which represents the telecommunications industry. He is very opposed to such legislation. He said that the original bill empowered the president "to essentially turn off the Internet in the case of a cyber-emergency." The bill does not define what kind of an emergency that could be—that is left up to the president.

Clinton said the new version of the bill is improved from its first draft, but the "troubling language" that was removed has been replaced with "vague language" that could still offer the same powers to the president in case of an emergency. "The current language is so unclear that we can't be confident that the changes have actually been made."[281]

Could the cyber-emergency be that too much opposition is circulating on the internet about Obama's health care bill or other of Obama's socialistic policies? Could it be because his approval rating keeps going down and the poll numbers are broadcast on the internet? Could Obama create an imaginary emergency about some pervasive "virus" that has hit the internet and consequently shut it down? All sorts of things are possible when such power is given to the president with nothing stopping him.

The Globalists Dream—Robert Pastor's Objectives for a National ID: As was stated in the previous chapter, one of the provisions that Robert Pastor was calling for in his various proposals for a "North American Community" was to have a national/ international ID card with biometrics (the preferred biometrics is RFID—Radio Frequency Identification Chips), so North Americans can be tracked, traced, and have a data file on them that can be shared with all three countries.

A national ID is not only Robert Pastor's objective, but is that of the CFR behind him, and has been the goal of those who believe in tyrannical government throughout history. This chapter will mention not only what has occurred with a national ID system in NAZI Germany, East Germany, Communist China, the former Soviet Union, and now modern day Russia and India, and a history of the attempts that have already been tried here in the USA to force a national ID upon American citizens.

The reader will find out what is happening with the Real ID Act of 2005, the Western Hemisphere Initiative, and the latest legislation—Pass ID, as well as the attempts to force RFID upon us all—not only in drivers' licenses and passports, but credit cards, personal purchases—such as shavers, shoes, clothes, cell phones, televisions, guns, ammunition, pets, farm animals, and lastly—implants within people themselves. This chapter will reveal how far the US has come in fulfilling the dreams of the powerful elite for a National ID card and why RFID is such a vital part of that plan.

As you have read in Chapter Four, RFID regulations are also part of the Transatlantic Partnership between the US and the European Union. Their excuse is for trade—to keep a better track on the shipment of goods and services, but, of course, also for protection and safety issues.

The excuse given for such a card is for people's own protection and safety—to identify the true North American citizens from illegal aliens; for uniformity, for ease and convenience in crossing borders; for health safety against outbreaks of diseases, epidemics, etc.

What In Actuality a National ID Would Be Like: All Americans would be forced to carry "The Card" (whatever it will be called), linked to a federal database, to drive a car, get a job, board a plane, enter a hospital emergency room or school, enter a federal building (which includes a post office), check out a book, have a bank account, cash a check, buy a gun, or have access to government benefits such as Social Security, Medicare, or Medicaid.

As Phyllis Schlafly writes, "Putting all that information on a government database means the end of privacy as we know it. Daily actions we all take for granted will henceforth be recorded, monitored, tracked, and contingent on showing 'The Card.'"[282]

"Liberty vs. Totalitarianism": was the name of an article written by Phyllis Schlafly in her July, 1998, Phyllis Schlafly Report, where she told of the mechanisms used by the dictators of police states to maintain control and keep a check over people—"the file, the database, and the internal passport."

Hitler's subjects of Nazi Germany had to have a number and their "papers" with them at all times. The Jewish people who were forced into concentration camps had a number tattooed on their arms. The Communist Chinese have a *"dangan,"* a cumulative file on every individual from childhood through adulthood, showing their performance and attitudes in school and in work, plus other information about their health, family, religion, any dangerous political ideas, etc. Citizens in police states have to carry "internal passports" or "papers" that have to be "presented to the authorities for permission to travel within the country, to take up residence in another city, or to apply for a new job."

In such police states, there must also be efficient watchdogs—"an army of bureaucrats fortified by a Gestapo, a Stasi or KGB." It used to be that these watchdogs had to commandeer an unlimited supply of paper and file folders on all their subjects, but now with modern technology, "the task of building personal files on every citizen, and tracking our actions and movements, [is] just as easy as logging onto the internet."[283]

Mrs. Schlafly wrote her article in 1998. Since that time the use of RFID technology has become far more advanced and has made her last statement about the ease in tracking citizens much more of a reality. With the use of RFID, building a personal file can be instantaneous, as well as keeping track of our every action and movement. The tiny chips are capable of holding enormous amounts of information, much more than any Gestapo, Stasi, KGB, or Red Chinese official ever dreamed possible. And what Mrs. Schlafly wrote about the "internal file," may become exactly that—internal—as more and more people become willing [or are forced] to take an implanted RFID chip, which is written about at the end of this chapter.

Communism, the Secret Police, and Invasion of Privacy in Modern Day Russia: Now that we have had a glimpse of the past in how Communism ran East Germany, part of the Soviet Union, let us take a look at what is going on in present day Russia. Even though the Soviet Union is disbanded and the communist regime is supposed to be over, according to many sources, communism is still alive and well. Many of the same old Communist bosses are back in leadership roles; the new secret police that has replaced the KGB, called FSB, Federal Security System, is still just as powerful and secretive and is still snooping into private lives.

Theoretically, modern Russia does not have any laws requiring people to carry a proof of identity. However, in practice, it is mandatory that at the age of 14, everyone must carry a passport at all times. This is especially true in Moscow, as lack of an ID during ad-hoc police checks is sufficient grounds for detention.[284]

Author and investigative reporter, William Norman Grigg, has written about the modern Russian system of intelligence gathering in his book *Liberty in Eclipse, the War on Terror and the Rise of the Homeland Security State.* Russia now has the FAPSI, Federal Agency for Government Communications, which has combined all of the national security, police, intelligence gathering, the FSB, all under one large head, similar to what the US has created with our huge Department of Homeland Security, DHS. FAPSI was given power by executive decree by Boris Yeltsin back in 1995, Decree 334—to "license all computer encryption software available in Russia, including that of all banks." Thus, no Russian bank can guarantee their customers confidentiality in their bank information.

The Russians also have SORM I and SORM II, equivalent to our Patriot Act I and Patriot Act II. SORM I allows the FSB to track every credit card transaction, e-mail message, or visit a website without the user knowing he is being watched. SORM requires every ISP (Internet Service Provider), as well as every telephone company and other communication services to allow the FSB to install an eavesdropping device that would provide the secret police with unlimited, covert access to communications. It would be connected directly to police headquarters through a dedicated high speed line. It could be directed at the discretion of the FSB without a court order.

SORM II allows the FSB to tap cell phones, land lines, and pagers, as well as the internet. So as we see, even though the Soviet Union is no more, the same control and surveillance of subjects is still alive and well in modern Russia.[285]

[As you will read at the end of the chapter, the USA is not far behind, or maybe even more advanced, for FAPSI was the role model for the DHS, as was the Russian SORM for the Patriot Act. And it was former members of the Russian KGB and East German Stasi who served as advisors for the creation of both of these, as well as for the Real ID Act and the Western Hemisphere Travel Initiative, another attempt at national ID cards.]

Modern China and Their People-Tracking Network: Mrs. Schlafly mentioned the "*dangan,*" which China has had in place for many years—their "cumulative file on every individual from childhood through adulthood." Now with the use of ID cards containing RFID chips and digital cameras, they are going to have a much better way of keeping track of all of their billions of people. According to an article that appeared in July, 2008, China was planning to use the city of Shenzhen, a Southern port city, as their pilot-people-tracking program. They would be using 20,000 digital cameras, ID cards containing RFID chips to keep track of 12.4 million people who live in the city:

Data on the chip will include not just the citizen's name and address but also work history, educational background, religion, ethnicity, police record, medical insurance status and landlord's phone number. Even personal reproductive history will be included for enforcement of China's controversial "one child" policy. Plans are being studied to add credit histories, subway travel payments and small purchases charged to the card. One of the most startling aspects of the plan is that this project is mostly made possible by an American company with solid venture funding. [286]

India's "Biggest Big Brother" Project: The last dictatorship country that we are going to take a look at and learn from is India. Their government declared in July, 2009, that they are going to be issuing national ID cards with biometric indicators (RFID) to their 1.2 billion subjects. According to a *Timesonline* article, written by Rhys Blakely in Mumbai, India, it is the "biggest big brother project yet conceived:"

> *India is to issue each of its 1.2 billion citizens, millions of whom live in remote villages and possess no documentary proof of existence, with cyber-age biometric identity cards. The Government in Delhi recently created the Unique Identification Authority, a new state department charged with the task of assigning every living Indian an exclusive number. It will also be responsible for gathering and electronically storing their personal details, at a predicted cost of at least £3 billion.*
>
> *The task will be led by Nandan Nilekani, the outsourcing sage who coined the phrase "the world is flat," which became a mantra for supporters of globalization. "It is a humongous, mind-boggling challenge," he told The Times. 'But we have the opportunity to give every Indian citizen, for the first time, a unique identity. We can transform the country.'* [287]

The Use of RFID Linking Each Card to a Data Base: The article mentions that RFID chips will be on each card—containing "personal data, proofs of identity, fingerprints, iris scans, and [possibly] criminal records and credit history. According to Mr. Nilekani, "Cards will be linked to a ubiquitous online data base and accessible from anywhere." [Accessible is a nicer sounding word than tracked or traced.]

The People Had No Vote and No Say: There are probably many of the 1.2 billion people in India who would like to go on living in their remote villages and have no proof of existence, just for the sake of being free and not yet identified. Maybe they do not relish having all their personal details gathered and electronically stored on an RFID chip. Maybe they don't want a "unique identity," linked to a gigantic data base that any government snoop can have access to across the globe; and maybe they don't want their country "transformed." But they have no choice about it. There was no vote taken by the people, because India is a dictatorship and the people are not free.

Why the Indian Government is Creating a National ID: The article does give the politically correct reasons that the government is imposing such a system on their people—of course it is for the people's own "safety and benefit:" to make information more uniform so that each province won't be issuing a different ID card requiring different information; if a poor person moves to a different province, he could get lost in the shuffle and not receive the state handouts that he needs to survive; it will close bureaucratic loopholes; it will fight corruption; it will identify illegal aliens; and it will track terrorists.

(Amazing how the same reasons have been used here in America to try to implement such a system. I wonder if the same language has been used wherever a national ID has been proposed and created. Again, we wonder who is writing the script for all the same propaganda used for "big government, big brother" proposals that are appearing in so many nations.)

How Many Nations Now Have a National ID System? According to the writer, Rhys Blakely, more than 100 countries already have compulsory national ID cards including France, Belgium, Greece, Luxembourg, Portugal, Spain, and Germany. Blakely adds that German police can detain people who are not carrying their ID card for up to 24 hours.

Large Countries That Do Not Yet Have National ID Cards: National ID cards are not yet used in USA, Canada, England, New Zealand, or Australia. (Blakely mentions that in Australia, people were out in the street protesting and forced the Government to abandon its plans for such a card back in the 1980s.) The Irish Republic and the Nordic countries still do not have national ID cards.[288]

England Backed Down on a Mandatory ID Card for all Airport Workers and Pilots: According to another article, England was starting to mandate that all airport workers and pilots get such a card, but there was such a protest that the government backed down. They are letting people do it on a volunteer basis now.[289]

Since England, the Irish Republic and the Nordic countries all belong to the EU, one can only imagine that the time will come when they will be forced to go along with the other countries that already have National ID for the sake of uniformity. However, since the EU passports already contain RFID chips, the EU officials already have a source for these countries international surveillance data base. Maybe the benevolent EU can pretend to offer them some "independence and liberty" on this issue.

Why Americans Historically Have Been Opposed to a National ID Card: Now that we have taken a look at what has gone on with national IDs in tyrannical countries, and what is presently going on with over 100 countries, let us see what has been the history of ID cards in our nation. Why has America had such a long history holding off such a card and why should we still be opposed to it today? There are mainly two reasons based on American heritage and beliefs:

The First Reason is Our Unique Judeo-Christian Heritage that Gives Us the Understanding and Belief that Rights Come From God, Not Government: There are words in our founding documents that no other nation has. The Declaration of Independence tell us that our basic rights come from God: "We are endowed by our Creator with certain unalienable rights, among these are life, liberty, and the pursuit of happiness." (This was mainly written by Thomas Jefferson, and signed by 56 others.)

If one reads the writings of our founding fathers, they explain their belief in "natural rights," which they had learned about by reading the essays of John Locke, a 16th century professor at Oxford, who even had to flee to Holland for a time to escape imprisonment for his views. Locke, in his essays, decried the "divine right of kings" to rule over man. He instead believed that man was sovereign himself and endowed with natural rights that come from God, not rights granted by a king or by government. These were very radical views for his day. But they had a profound effect on both Englishmen and our founding fathers in believing they had the divine right to the independence and liberty they were seeking in breaking all ties with England and starting a new nation.

Our founding fathers believed that natural rights from God were those we needed to "pursue our own happiness" and to maintain liberty—the right to own and take care of our own property, freedom of speech, religion, freedom to assemble, freedom to bear arms to protect ourselves and our families, freedom to have our privacy protected—essentially all the rights that are listed in the Bill of Rights. And like John Locke, they believed it was the duty of government, and its main purpose for existence—to protect and secure those God-given rights.[290]

Before 1962, when God was removed from the public schools with the Supreme Court ruling of separation of church and state, most American children were taught that God was very much a part of our nation and the above-mentioned rights came from Him. It logically follows then, that if rights come from God, they do not come from government and government should not be allowed to take them away.

The Second Reason is Our Belief that the Constitution was Inspired of God. It was to be a Beacon of Hope to the Whole World: Biblical scholars and historians who have studied the Constitution believe it to be truly an ingenious, inspired document, specifically designed to preserve, protect, and maintain the

God-given rights and freedoms we enjoy and have enjoyed for over 200 years. They believe that the God who inspired the Constitution is a God of liberty and wants his people on earth to be free—free over the whole earth—not just in America. That is why the U.S. Constitution used to be a beacon of light and hope of liberty to other nations as well—that is, back when it used to be obeyed, honored, and upheld with respect by U.S. presidents and other elected officials, instead of essentially being ignored as it is today.

In spite of the many graduates of American schools and universities today (including—obviously—many elected officials), who have never studied (perhaps not even read) the Declaration of Independence, the Constitution, or the Bill of Rights, there are still enough Americans who have read them and have been taught correct principles about them. Those people recognize when their God-given rights are being trampled on. They get very upset and contact their elected officials and protest.

The Fourth Amendment—The Right to Privacy is a God-Given Right: The right to privacy and to be secure in our own homes is one of the natural rights that is necessary for us to maintain life, liberty and property and pursue our own happiness. The 4th Amendment states, "the right of the people to be secure in their persons, houses, papers and effects, against unreasonable searches and seizures, shall not be violated." The rest of the 4th amendment states that if there is a probable cause, a search warrant must be issued before a government official can go into a private home to search.

A national ID card, which would contain a person's personal information in various forms of biometrics (especially RFID), stored in data bases, and able to be shared nationally and internationally, is definitely a violation of his/her God-given right to privacy.

Conflict of Two Different Belief Systems: However, many people believe we now live in a post-modern world, which they describe as post-Christianity—with Christianity not having much of an effect on our nation anymore. President Obama is one of those. As was mentioned in the Preface, on Obama's trip to Turkey, he announced to the audience of mainly Turkish officials, that "America is no longer a Christian nation."

As the reader has discovered throughout this book, the elitists who have gained control of our government—both elected and unelected—for the most part, have a post-modern belief system. Some may profess to be Christians, but "by their fruits, ye may know them." They are either atheists, or secular humanists, which is essentially the same thing; or new-age, or worship an entirely different god, Satan—one who does not believe in freedom and liberty, but believes in totalitarianism.

If one does not believe in God, then one does not believe in or honor the Judeo-Christian heritage of our nation; nor does one believe that we have God-given rights. And without a belief in God, where do rights come from? The only answer is from government, of course. "And where government giveth—government can taketh away," as you read about it in the United Nations Declaration on Human Rights. Article 31 essentially says that if the government deems any of these articles are not in keeping with the purposes of the UN, they are hereby null and void.

People with a post-modern world concept perhaps agree that government has the right to deprive citizens of their right to privacy, or any other right that government deems fit. These concepts may prevail until their own rights are trampled on by big government and they no longer have those rights.

History of a National ID in the USA—When Government Was Opposed to Such a System: Fortunately, over the years, the Christian world view has prevailed enough in the U.S. to ward off various attempts by the elitists in government to achieve their goals. Here is summary of all the times our government officials said no to the concept of a national ID:

1936—The Date When the Social Security Number was First Implemented: Americans were worried that this was going to some kind of a national ID number, but they were promised by the government, "This number will not be used for identification." My, has that changed over the years!

1971—The Social Security Administration Task Force: The task force again rejected the extension of the SSN to the status of ID card.

1973—Health Education and Welfare Secretary's Advisory Committee on automated Personal Data Systems concluded that a national identifier was not advisable.

1974—A Privacy Act was Passed: It stated, "It shall be unlawful for any Federal, State, or local government agency to deny any individual any right, benefit, or privilege by provided by law because of such individual's refusal to disclose his Social Security number."

1977—Even Liberal President Carter's Administration Agreed: The Social Security Number was not to become a national identifier for American citizens.

1981—President Reagan was Explicitly Opposed to the Creation of a National ID Card: When U.S. Attorney General William French suggested a "perfectly harmless" national ID system as well as to tattoo a number on the forearm of each American, Reagan responded with, "**My God, that's the mark of the beast,**" ending all discussion on the issue. Reagan was referring to Revelations 13:16-18, which many Christians believe will be the final act of tyrannical government to control its subjects—a mark required inside the right hand or the forehead of all people.

History of Big Government Promoting the Concept of A National ID in America: With the present renewed efforts for a national ID—implemented either through transportation, drivers licenses or health care, notice what other attempts have been tried in the same thing. History keeps repeating itself, especially among those with a "big brother" complex:

1986—The Commercial Motor Vehicle Safety Act was Passed: This is the first act that included provisions for the use of biometrics. Since that time, the American Association of Motor Vehicles (AAMV) and the International Civil Aviation Organization (ICAQ) have been promoting the use of biometrics, the creation of linked databases, and the sharing of information globally. (Sorry to say, this slipped by under President Reagan's watch.)

1992—The Clinton Era Began: Under President Bill Clinton, we had all sorts of attempts at implementing a national ID—actually 8 bills that were tried and made it through various stages in Congress. Some did get passed. Of course, deceptive, nice-sounding names were given to each of the bills:

1993—Health Security Plan: This was part of Hillary's ill-fated plan to provide universal health insurance and socialized medical care. It asked for a **national medical ID card,** referred to as **"The Card"** with a "**unique identifier number**" and would have set up a **national health data base with a National Health Board**, responsible only to the President. This board would have had extraordinary rulemaking powers to "assure uniformity" and to decide what may and may not be spent on health care by each provider. Physicians and other providers were to be required to report every medical service to the national database. It was sold to the public as "as each individual's personal key to free health care," as a means of "health care planning" and as a way to "eliminate fraud among providers."

Since much of this is being tried again under Obama's health care plan, including a national ID, read what Mrs. Schlafly had written about Hillary's bill. It is a good warning for what we can expect with Obama Care.

> *Allowing the government to collect and store personal medical records, and to track us as we move about in our daily lives, puts awesome power in the hands of government bureaucrats. It gives them power to force us to conform to government health care policy, whether that means mandating that all children [or adults] be immunized with an AIDS vaccine [or*

swine flu, or any kind of a vaccine] when it is put on the market, or
mandating that expensive medical treatment be withheld from seniors.

Once all medical records are computerized with unique identifiers
such as Social Security numbers, an instant check system will give all
government agencies the power to deny basic services, including daycare,
school, college, access to hospital emergency rooms, health insurance, a
driver's license, etc., to those who don't conform to government health
policies.

Fortunately, the American people recognized the national ID health card, the "unique identifier number" and the database as bringing an end to medical privacy. They did not want federal control over what health care we would be permitted to receive, with ultimate rationing by bureaucrats or gatekeeper and they so bombarded their congressmen with outraged letters and phone calls that Hillary's bill was soundly defeated.[291]

1993—Comprehensive Child Immunization Act: This was authorized by the Secretary of Health and Human Services (HHS) "to establish state registry systems to monitor the immunization status of all children." HHS sent $417 million of taxpayers' money to the states to set up these databases. This money had been supplemented by millions of dollars from the Robert Wood Johnson Foundation. It launched the "cradle to grave" aspect of government trying to spy on us from birth to death.[292]

1993—Brady Act: This act provided for an instant background check for prospective handgun buyers. They had to be screened against a database of convicted criminals. The FBI plans to keep a record of prospective handgun buyers for 18 months. A national registry of gun owners is illegal in our nation, but we are coming closer to it with laws such as the Brady Act.

1996—Health Insurance Portability and Accountability Act (HIPPA) (also known as the Kennedy-Kassebaum Act): This was intended to reduce the costs and administrative burdens of health care by making possible the standardized, electronic transmissions of administrative and financial transactions that were before this time only on paper. It was also calling for a **"unique health care identifier,"** essentially a **national ID number,** for every individual, employer, provider, and health plan. Everyone would have to submit an identification document with a "unique number" on it in order to receive health care, or the provider would not be paid. The bottom line was to require computerized reporting and to gather more and more information on government databases.

However, that was so egregious to most Americans and the uproar Congress received about it caused them to pass a bill for four straight years prohibiting the funding for the development of a "unique health-care identifier." (Section 513 of HR 3061)[293]

1996—The illegal Immigration Reform and Immigrant Responsibility Act: This law was supposedly intended to stem the tide of so many illegal aliens coming across the borders. It would not allow any state driver's license to be used after Oct. 1, 2000, unless it contains SSN as a "unique numeric identifier that can be read visually or by electronic means."* (Section 656(b) This Act also authorized the Federal Department of Transportation to establish uniform national requirements for birth certificates, so such information could be used on drivers' licenses.

The illegal immigration law ordered the Attorney General to conduct pilot programs in at least 5 states where the state driver's license includes a "machine-readable" Social Security number. (Section 403(c)) The law also orders the development of a "Smart Card" that "shall employ technologies that provide security features, such as magnetic stripes, holograms, and integrated circuits." (Section 657(a))

A "smart card" with these technologies can contain a digitized fingerprint, retina scan, voice print, DNA print, or other biometric identifier (such as a RFID chip) and will leave an electronic trail every time it is used.

The law also orders "consultation" with the American Association of Motor Vehicle Administrators. According to Phyllis Schlafly, the AAMVA is "a pseudo-private, quasi-government organization, [that] has long urged using drivers' licenses, with Social Security numbers and digital fingerprinting, as a de facto national I.D. card that would enable the government to track everyone's movements throughout North America."[294] (As you will see from the 2002 proposal that AAMVA suggested for a national ID card, Mrs. Schlafly is very accurate in her evaluation of them).

*Fortunately, in 1999, Congress repealed the controversial provision in this act so that the driver's licenses do not have to include Social Security Numbers.

1996—The Personal Responsibility and Work Opportunity Reform Act (also known as The Welfare Reform Law): Remember back in 1936, when the Social Security Number Program was started and we were told that it would never be required for identification, well things have certainly changed. This law demanded that states, in order to receive federal welfare funds, must collect SSN from applicants for any professional license, occupational license, or "commercial driver's license." (Section 317)

1997—The Balanced Budget Act of 1997: The writers of this law, under the guise of making "technical corrections" to the Welfare Reform Law, deleted the word "commercial," thereby applying the requirement to all driver's license applicants, and even added "recreational" (hunting and fishing) licenses. Another provision requires employers, since Oct. 1, 1997, to transmit the name, address, and SSN of every new worker to a Directory of New Hires. This is supposed to help track deadbeat dads, but the information is collected from all new workers (regardless of whether they are deadbeats or even dads) and maintained for 24 months.

1997—The Kidcare Bill: The mantra of this bill was **"just for the kids."** It was sponsored by Orrin Hatch, a Utah Republican, and Ted Kennedy, Democrat from Massachusetts. It was essentially socialized medicine but done through the back door through the children. It would have given five million children health insurance with tax payers paying for it. There was also a health care card associated with it. Neither the American Hospital Association or the American Medical Association were backing it. Fortunately, it was filibustered and did not pass.

1998—Child Support Performance and Incentive Act (known as Deadbeat Dads Act): It established a federal "instant check" new-hires directory. Employers are now required to "screen" every new employee or job applicant against the government database of child support orders. However, it also asked for a medical card that would keep track of your medical history plus everything else about you (such as if you are a dead-beat dad) or a Smart Card that would serve as your bank card and all sorts of other information.

2001—September 11, 9/11, the Terrible Tragedy Occurred: In New York City, close to 3000 people lost their lives, including 343 firefighters, as the Twin Towers Trade Buildings were hit by two planes, which were (supposedly) piloted by Muslim suicide bomber terrorists from Saudi Arabia.

The impact (supposedly) created enough burning jet fuel fire to reach the temperatures hot enough to melt the steel framework of the buildings and brought them down in a "free-fall" in just 15 seconds, pulverizing the cement and steel and turning everything in the buildings into fine particles of dust.

A few hours later, building #7, that had just a small fire blazing on the 12th floor, also came collapsing down in a free-fall acceleration in just seven seconds, with all of its cement and glass pulverized.

It is the downing of building #7 that has caused many people to start to question the government's official story of what happened to the buildings. No building can come down that quickly, and straight down, without harming any other building on either side of it, with every bit of it pulverized, supposedly, because of just a small fire burning on its 12th floor?

More and more experts are beginning to speak out that Building 7 was a planned demolition implosion. And if that is the case, then what about the twin towers that also came down in a matter of seconds once the implosion began, and again with everything pulverized into fine dust?

There is a large group of architects and engineers, who are skilled in designing and building steel buildings, who now are questioning the official story. They have over 1000 signatures on a petition asking for a new investigation into the truth of 9/11. It is spearheaded by Richard Gage, an architect of San Francisco. (Their website is www.AE911Truth.org.)

They are joined by scientists and physics professors, such as Dr. Steven Jones, formerly of Brigham Young University. Dr. Jones has carefully examined under a powerful microscope the tiny particles of dust that were left from the downing of the twin towers and Building #7. He has found nano-particles of red and black thermite, highly explosive materials in the dust.

The group of architects, engineers, and scientists are also joined by "Firefighters for 911 Truth," led by Eric Lloyd, who said there are many firemen who testified that they heard the sounds of explosions going off and saw flashes of explosives on each of the floors as the Twin Towers and Building 7 were imploding. Many testified it was the same as if the buildings were "pulled," the term used for when a demolition job is being done. (Their website is wwwfirefightersfor911truth.org.)

There are also pilots and members of the airforce who are questioning the official story. They are wondering what happened to all the airforce planes that should have been available to protect the skyways of New York City and Washington D.C. in case of any kind of an attack?

Why was it that every plane that very day had been called away to participate in a "mock terrorist drill," so no single plane was left to protect our own cities?

There are also questions about the "insider" trading that was going on the day before and the morning of 9/11 in both American Airlines' and United Airlines' stock, as if someone knew that something was going to happen that would greatly devalue their stock.

What does this all mean? It has some very serious implications. It means that people high up in the government were very much involved in the planning of 9/11, that explosives had been already placed in the buildings, just as in any other demolition job. Why would the government want such a thing to happen, and how could they do this to their own people? (Remember, this is not new. Such tactics were involved in getting the American people more willing to enter into World War I and II, seeking revenge for the many Americans who lost their lives with the sinking of the Lusitania and when Pearl Harbor was bombed.)

Governments always need an enemy, a way to keep their people full of fear, so they will fall into line and be more willing to give up essential freedoms. Dr. Stan Monteith calls it "the best enemies money can by." It had been planned, even before 9/11, for the US to be once again involved in a war in Iraq. Bush Jr. was to finish what his father had started; 9/11 made that war more justifiable. (I could never figure out, however, if the terrorists who "supposedly" had flown the planes into the twin towers were from Saudi Arabia, why were we seeking revenge against them by going into Iraq? That question never got answered. There are still many more unanswered questions.)

(Much of this information was taken from a DVD called 9/11: Blueprint for Truth and from a press conference given by the Architects and Engineers for 9/11 Truth, at the Marine's Motel, San Francisco, February 19, 2010.)

Because of the 9/11 tragedy and the "War on Terror" that followed, enormous strides have been made in taking away personal freedoms and the privacy of American citizens, things that would have been inconceivable before 9/11. For a little security, as they suppose, more and more Americans have been willing to give up personal freedoms. Consequently, the same security measures which have been passed in modern Russia, which have turned it once again into a police state, are happening here:

2001, September 14—Foreign Intelligence Surveillance Act (FISA) was Passed: Is it not just a little bit suspicious that in spite of the shock and numbness that had paralyzed the nation after the terrible tragedy that had just occurred three days earlier, Congress miraculously had a bill ready for just such an occasion and immediately got it passed. This bill allows the president of the United States—in acute threatening circumstances—to order a search or surveillance operation [such as wiretapping] in the interests of national security, and then, after the fact, can ask for a search warrant from a secret judicial body that rarely, if ever, turns down such a request.

One Courageous Judge Questioned the Constitutionality of Such An Act as FISA: After five years of secret surveillance operations going on, with, at least, 30 times when the President ordered "secret" wiretapping to take place, one judge was courageous enough to speak out against the Constitutionality of this law, U.S. District Judge Anna Diggs Taylor. In a scathing 43-page decision, she ruled that the administration's secret electronic eavesdropping program, which had begun right after 9/11, was flagrantly unconstitutional and incompatible with America's Constitutional history. She ordered the administration to desist immediately!

What happened? The Bush administration reacted in characteristic fashion of those who seem to believe in the "divine right of kings." It asserted the authority to ignore the ruling, filed an immediate appeal, and continued with the program as if the ruling had never happened. Attorney General Alberto Gonzales stated, "We're going to do everything we can in the courts to allow the program to continue."

A three-judge panel of the 6th Circuit Court of Appeals threw out a law suit against FISA and said that the plaintiffs could show no "standing," meaning that they could not demonstrate an injury to their rights sufficient to justify a lawsuit. In making their decision, they ignored what Judge Taylor had written in her Constitutional analysis. The powerful executive branch seems to assume the right to toss aside the other branches of government, the Constitution, the Bill of Rights, as old-fashioned relics of the past.

Judge Taylor then made the following statement, which describes the new prevalent viewpoint of the office of the president.

> *The government appears to argue here that . . . because the President is designated commander-in-chief of the army and navy, he has been granted the inherent power to violate not only the laws of Congress but the First and Fourth Amendments of the Constitution, itself . . . However, the presidency is not a self-created, autonomous entity, but one with a specific and limited constitutional mandate. The office itself was created, with its powers, by the Constitution. There are no hereditary kings in America and no power not created by the Constitution. So all "inherent power" must derive from that Constitution.*[295]

The "*Fuhrerprinzip*":—You will see this principle more in the next chapter for it is greatly exemplified by Obama. However, it started years ago; the same belief that the Germans had about Hitler is becoming more prevalent among Americans. It is the belief that the leader can do no wrong and should have unlimited executive powers. He has become the embodiment of America itself. Anyone who would dare to oppose him would not only be opposing the "dear leader" or the "*fuhrer*," but they would be opposing America as well.

2001—October 26, The USA Patriot Act Passed: It passed just a month and a half after 9/11. It contained 342 pages and was passed by Congress, sight unseen, five minutes after it was presented. It was in the middle of an anthrax scare.

Congressmen were threatened that if anyone voted against it, the next terrorist attack would be on their hands.

Again one wonders how a bill that resembles almost exactly a law that has been already functioning in Russia for many years, could suddenly be written just in one month's time after 9/11. Obviously, it was in the works long before 9/11.

According to one website, it was very similar to a bill that had been presented back in 1995, written by Joe Biden, but was never passed. In fact, Joe Biden, himself, drew parallels between his 1995 bill and its 2001 cousin. According to *The New Republic*, Joe Biden said when the bill was being debated, "I drafted a terrorism bill after the Oklahoma City bombing. And the bill John Ashcroft sent up was my bill." *The New Republic* described Biden as "the Democratic Party's de facto spokesman on the war against terrorism."[296]

According to Utah Senator, Orinn Hatch, in an article that he wrote for *USA Today*, May 14, 2003, the Patriot Act is similar to an anti-terrorism bill that he presented in 1996. Of course, he was all in favor of it and voted for it.

Connie Fogel, the past president of the Canadian Action Party, told me in a conversation in September of 2008, that Canada also suddenly came up with a similar bill to the Patriot Act, shortly after 9/11. It was also very lengthy and had to have been written long before. It greatly increased the government's ability to spy on its own citizens as did ours.

The USA Patriot Act gets its nice sounding name by taking the first letter of each word of the following long title: **U**niting and **S**trengthening **A**merica by **P**roviding **A**ppropriate **T**ools **R**equired to **I**ntercept and **O**bstruct **T**errorism Act of 2001. Wikipedia writes the following about it:

> The act increased the ability of law enforcement agencies to: search telephone and e-mail communications and medical, financial and other records; eased restrictions on foreign intelligence gathering within the United States; expanded the Secretary of the Treasury's authority to regulate financial transactions, particularly those involving foreign individual and entities; and enhanced the discretion of law enforcement and immigration authorities in detaining and deporting immigrants suspected of terrorism-related acts. The act also expanded the definition of terrorism to include "domestic terrorism," thus enlarging the number of activities to which the Patriot Act's expanded law enforcement powers can be applied.[297]

Some of the Most Offensive Provisions Of the Patriot Act: One of the few to vote against the Patriot Act, Congressman Ron Paul, Republican from Texas, and former conservative candidate for President 2008, writes of some of its scary provisions in an article entitled "Privacy and Personal Liberty:

- Expanded the federal government's ability to use wiretaps without judicial oversight;
- Allowed nationwide search warrants non-specific to any given location, nor subject to any local judicial oversight;
- Made it far easier for the government to monitor private internet usage;
- Authorized "sneak and peek" warrants enabling federal authorities to search a person's home, office, or personal property without that person's knowledge;
- Required libraries and bookstores to turn over records of books read by their patrons.

Congressman Ron Paul tried to get legislation passed to repeal the Patriot Act. It is his strong belief that "the Constitution was written to restrain the government, never to restrain the people."[298]

"Surveillance A-Go-Go:" Tom DeWeese believes the Patriot Act is just one more step to what he refers to as "surveillance a-go-go in full swing." In an article he wrote called "Total Surveillance Equals Total Tyranny," he stated, "*In the name of fighting terrorism, our government has gained the ability to see our every movement, inspect our every transaction, and walk into our homes without our knowing it.*"[299]

When you compare the provision of the Patriot Act with SORM I and II of Russia, they are not very different. If you call modern-day Russia a police state, what can be said of the USA today?

2002, January—the American Association of Motor Vehicles Administrators (AAMVA) Devised Proposal #0151: This proposal was also making use of the terrorist attack of 9/11. Senator Richard J. Durbin, Democrat of Illinois was supporting their proposal and was going to create a bill for if. According to critics it would have essentially changed state drivers' license into "de facto" national ID cards—demanding uniformity in all state drivers' licenses, and demanding that the license be used as an ID for purchases and transactions. The system would use bar codes and biometrics such as fingerprints and would have linked databases that would allow states to share information. The data from these transactions would then be collected at a national data base in Washington D.C.

Barry Goleman, who helped the motor vehicle administrators association create a national commercial driver's licenses database, said, "The concept of a unified system is not alien at all." Back in 1986, Congress authorized a commercial database system, which was put into place to prevent commercial drivers from hiding poor driving records through multiple licenses.[300]

"ID Cards Through the Back Door:" Phyllis Schlafly wrote an article against the bill, (1/30/02) saying, "Thus government busybodies would have access to your entire life history"—your traveling, banking, medical care, renting or buying a house, attending school or college, and even getting a job. The giant data base would not be foolproof. It would be subject to abuse, error, computer glitches and hacking as have many government data files such as the IRS and Social Security. It was also revealed that this data would be available to many other agencies, credit card companies, gun shops, auto dealers, colleges, and law enforcement agencies.[301]

The AAMVA is an International Organization: It was the intent of the American Association of Motor Vehicles Administrators that the data on the ID cards would be shared with Canada and Mexico as well. How could that be? Isn't the AAMVA strictly a US agency? No, it turns out that "American" to them stands for all of North America; Canada and Mexico are also members of the AAMVA, just one more part of the movement to bring all three countries closer together in some sort of a union. Fortunately, enough people expressed their outrage against the AAMVA proposal and it was defeated.

2002, July—The Department of Homeland Security (DHS) was Formed: Again, because of the fear of terrorism left over from 9/11, Congress hastily approved the bill authorizing the agency. How is it structured? It is very similar to the Russian FAPSI, with all the agencies dealing with security and intelligence gathered under one roof. It is the third largest department in government with 200,000 employees.

"**Homeland Insecurity:**" It bothers many Americans that so much power is all under one organization. They consider it a threat to the Bill of Rights and the Constitution. Tom DeWeese is one of those. He wrote an article in his *Tom DeWeese Report* called "Homeland Insecurity, Deconstructing the Constitution," (Nov. 14, 2002). He stated:

> This isn't homeland security. It is homeland insecurity for every American who still thinks the rule of law will protect him against surveillance and the demand that they turn over all aspects of their daily lives to the approval of the government.

Tom De Weese also read the fine print of the original Homeland Security bill where it called for "suggested minimum standards for state drivers' licenses." He recognized that language to be the same as what the defeated AAMV bill had called for, again another attempt to change state drivers' licenses into national ID cards.[302]

Others in Congress must have had that same fear, so they changed the language making it clear that the agency could not create a National ID system. Even Tom Ridge, the first head of the Department of Homeland Security, acknowledged, " . . . the legislation that created the Department of Homeland Security was very specific on the question of a national ID card. They said there will be no national ID card." So, what was needed was to create some other form of legislation that could somehow be slipped through Congress and passed without much attention or any debate. And that is exactly what happened.

2005, May 11, the Real ID Act was Passed By Stealth and Deception with No Debate: The Real ID started off as H.R. 418, which passed the House and then went stagnant. Representative James Sensenbrenner (R) of Wisconsin, "supposedly," the author of the original Real ID Act, attached the bill, as a last-minute rider, onto an omnibus (all encompassing) military spending bill (H.R. 1268), which included funding for the Iraq war, the Global War on Terror, and also money for the victims of the terrible Tsunami that had killed so many people and done so much damage in Indonesia. The bill passed 368-58 in the House and 100-0 in the Senate. "There was no debate whatsoever" on the Real ID piece of legislation. President Bush signed the whole thing into law on May 11, 2005.[303]

The Real ID had nothing to do with funding wars or Tsunami relief. It is amazing how some members of Congress are able to get away with attaching last minute riders onto bills that are totally unrelated and get them passed.

The Real ID Was Promoting Robert Pastor's Common "North American" ID Card: Title II of the Real ID Act calls for new federal standards in drivers' licenses. States were to comply by 2008. These new federal standards include biometric identifiers, which were recommended in Robert Pastor's CFR publication "Building a North American Community." As was mentioned in the chapter about the Transatlantic Partnership between the U.S. and the EU, the ultimate goal is to have every ID card include a small RFID (Radio Frequency ID) chip that could contain enormous amounts of information about a person's private life and be used for tracking purposes wherever they and the card were. This information can then be shared with other nations.

A Closer Look At the Real ID: I was so concerned about the Real ID Act of 2005 and its link to a national ID card for all citizens of American, Canada, and Mexico that I wrote a two-page, talking-point handout against it which I gave to each of my state legislators. Those two pages eventually grew into an 80-page booklet entitled *A Closer Look at the Real ID, Giving Up a Whole Lot of Freedom for a Little Bit of False Security,* which I also gave a copy of to key state legislators. However it was to no avail. I'm sorry to say, the liberal California legislators far outnumber the conservatives and they passed SB 60, which said yes that California was willing to be compliant with the Real ID, but, at the same time SB 60 was also saying that the bill would grant drivers licenses to Illegal Aliens—exactly opposite of what the Real ID's purpose was supposed to be all about. Fortunately, Governor Schwarzenegger vetoed the bill in 2008, however in 2009 the same bill was presented. The following is essentially my two-page write up about the bill in 2008.

The Real ID Act of 2005—Turning Your State Drivers' Licenses into National ID Cards: Not very many Americans are familiar with a little known federal bill that was passed into law in 2005 called the Real ID Act. This law was supposedly going to help prevent illegal aliens and terrorists from getting drivers licenses and make it easier to detect them. However, in reality it is infringing on the rights and privacy of all American citizens and turning our state drivers' licenses into national ID cards, where information on all of us will be collected in a national data center and that information can be shared with Mexico, Canada, and other countries such as the European Union.

Big-Bully Tactics Used by the Department of Homeland Security to Try to Get States to Comply? In the year, 2008, by May 11, states were to come up with legislation or resolutions saying yea or nay concerning the Real ID. Michael Chertoff, the head of Homeland Security, under Bush said in a press release January 11, that if states refused to go along with the Real ID Act, their citizens would not be able to board airplanes or enter a federal building with their regular drivers license.

In Spite of the Bullying Tactics, Many States Passed Legislation Against the Real ID: Eight states passed legislation against it in both houses and seventeen states had legislation pending. These states believe it was an infringement on their states' rights and their state sovereignty, plus most states simply can't afford its implementation which would cost millions of dollars. (It is estimated the cost for the entire nation to be between $8-11 billion!)

Why would it be so costly? The drivers' licenses will have to be completely redone with "biometric identifiers" added: barcodes, finger prints, picture ID, iris scan. What the federal government eventually wants is RFID (radio frequency identification) chips on each license. Then the government can more easily track everyone. Wherever we go and whatever transaction and purchase we make will be recorded in the national data base.

California Real ID Act Bill—SB 60: For the years 2008 and 2009, a bill was presented by Assemblyman Gill Cedillo, saying essentially, "Yes, California agrees to be compliant with the Real ID Act." However, it was also asking for all illegal aliens to be granted drivers' licenses, which would be defeating the "supposed" whole purpose for the Real ID Act in the first place—to crack down on illegals because they would be the ones without the drivers licenses. The bill was passed by the liberal legislators in 2008, but vetoed by Governor Schwarzenegger. Undaunted, a similar bill was presented for 2009, again authored by Gill Cedillo, who has tried to get drivers licenses for illegals every year that he has been in office. He is known as the "one bill Gill." Let us hope that whoever the future governor is that he or she will continue to veto such bills if they get passed.

California's AJR Resolution 51: A resolution was sponsored by Assemblyman Pedro Nava in 2008, that was saying no to the Real ID. It was a well-written resolution with the exception of the second paragraph from the end, where it states:

> "RESOLVED, That the California Legislature urges the California Congressional delegation to support measures to repeal Real ID, or at least delay its implementation until such time as its implementation costs are federally funded and amendments are made to reduce its costs and administrative burdens and to preserve essential states rights and civil rights and liberties . . .

We do not want the Real ID Act even if the implementation costs are federally funded and if the costs and administration burdens are reduced. The whole concept of a national ID with national data being collected on US citizens is wrong and contrary to the 4th Amendment that protects out privacy and it is a violation or states rights and state sovereignty.

Talking Points Against the Real ID Act of 2005

1. **The Real ID Act of 2005 was never an act of the people;** there was no discussion, no debate, no hearings and no input from constituents. It was attached on at the last minute to an omnibus appropriations bill, mainly

granting aid to the Tsunami victims and also money for the Iraq War. Anyone voting against it would appear heartless. (Only 3 Republicans voted against it.)

2. **It would be turning your state drivers' license into a national ID card**, where every drivers license will have the same information and the same biometrics which will be scanned and all that information will be collected in one large national data collection center.

3. **It would be an infringement of the federal government on state's rights and state sovereignty.** Drivers' licenses have always been left up to each individual state.

4. **It would put a huge financial burden on each state to implement with little or no funding coming from the federal government.** It has been estimated by the National Governors Association to be as high as $11 billion dollars for all of our states to fully implement it.

5. **It would be turning each state's Department of Motor Vehicles into federal immigration officers with enormous administration burdens.** They would have to copy, store, and verify as many as four different documents to grant each individual drivers license and put them in machine readable format.

6. **The security of the card is questionable with heightened risk of identity theft.** If a hacker can break into a national system, everyone's security is at risk. With each state having a different system, there is better protection of privacy.

7. **The data can be shared with other countries, especially Canada and Mexico.** That is what the original bill stated and the Canadian and Washington state websites state that is what the Real ID is mandating.

8. **It would grant unlimited power to the Department of Homeland Security**. DHS can also define and expand their purpose and power as they see fit.

9. **It would create a threat to our second amendment rights.** Whenever you would use your drivers' license as identification for a purchase of guns or ammunition, the new Real ID drivers' license would be scanned and your purchase recorded in a national data base. It would thus be creating a national registry for the purchase of guns and ammunition, something which is presently against the law.

10. **Commend your governor for vetoing any bill** that comes across his desk asking for compliance with the Real ID Act and commend any legislators who vote against such a bill and urge them to continue to do so each year if it comes up again, no matter if there is funding or not.[304]

Is it the End of the Real ID? By October of 2009, 25 states had passed legislation or resolutions saying no to the Real ID. Janet Napolitano, the Head of Homeland Security, said maybe she will just stop trying to push it through. So, have conservatives won? No, the Federal Government has many other forms of ID to fall back on such as the Western Hemisphere Travel Initiative, which has been moving steadily forward all along anyway, while all the attention was focused on the Real ID. And there is already another bill in Congress to replace it—PASS ID (written about later).

2007, January 23—The Western Hemisphere Travel Initiative (WHTI) was passed and was to be implemented by January 31, 2008. Just as with the Real ID Act, there is another phase coming later, with even more requirements. Again, the Department of Homeland Security (DHS) gets to make up the rules as they go along. The web site states, "At a later date, to be determined, the departments will implement the full requirements of the land and sea phase of WHTI." The website mentions the term "Notice of Proposed Rulemaking, (NPR)" which essentially means the DHS has been given "carte blanche" authority to change the policies, or add to them, as they see fit, just as they were given the same "NPR" with the Real ID Act. Here is how the website describes what the WHTI is:

> It is the result of the Intelligence Reform and Prevention Act of 2004 (IRTPA), requiring all travelers to present a passport or other document that denotes identity and citizenship when entering the U.S . . . the goal of the initiative is to strengthen U.S. border security while facilitating entry for U.S. citizens and legitimate foreign visitors by providing standardized documentation that enables the Department of Homeland Security to quickly and reliably identify a traveler. It is for all persons traveling by air between the United States and Canada, Mexico, Bermuda, and the Caribbean region. They are required to present a passport or other valid travel document to enter or re-enter the United States . . . (By June of 2009, these requirements were implemented. All people seeking to cross the borders between the above mentioned countries have to have a form of ID with an RFID chip attached, either a passport, EDL-enhanced drivers' license or a NEXIS card.)

E-Z Pass Permits Proposed by Robert Pastor for the Western Hemisphere Travel Initiative: Notice how the rules are already changing for the WHTI. Originally, the whole idea was presented as a way of having tighter and more secure border crossings. Next Pastor suggested that the WHTI passes be made like E-Z cards on a toll road, so the cars can speed through as if there is no border there at all.

Pastor testified before the Senate Foreign Relations Committee on June 9, 2005, just one month after the Real ID passed. The committee was discussing the next step—the Western Hemisphere Travel Initiative. Pastor was invited to give a report by an Independent Task Force on the Future of North America sponsored by the Council on Foreign Relations. The task force consisted of 31 people, ten from each country, Canada, Mexico and the USA. Pastor was the co-chair from the USA. The report was called "Building a North American Community." It offered a blueprint of the goals that the three countries of North America should pursue and the steps needed to achieve those goals. One of those goals was what kind of card should be used for the WHTI.

> The subject for the hearing today—whether passports should be required to cross our two borders—is symptomatic of the problem. We are thinking too small. We need to find ways of making trade and travel easier while we define and defend a continental security perimeter. Instead of stopping North Americans on the borders, we ought to provide them with a secure, biometric Border Pass that would ease transit across the border like an E-Z pass permits our cars to speed through toll booths.[305]

Western Hemisphere Travel Initiative Enhanced Drivers' Licenses: It appears that all that Robert Pastor and the rest of his 31-member team proposed back in 2005 is being totally implemented. While most of the state legislatures were busily occupied debating what to do about the Real ID, border states were being told that they had to hurry up and comply with the Western Hemisphere Travel Initiative that demands, "for security reasons and ease in crossing the borders" citizens must get their expensive "EDL—Enhanced Drivers License," that contains an RFID chip. Of course, they may also use other chipped traceable identification devices, such as a passport, if it is one issued after January of 2008, which also contains an RFID chip.

2009, July—("Try, Try, Again") Security in States' Identification Act of 2009 or The Pass ID Act, Senate Bill 1261: The liberal legislators behind a national ID never give up. Since 25 states have rejected the Real ID Act of 2005, they have come up with a new attempt, the PASS ID, Here are some of the provisions as written in the bill: S. 1261 would repeal title II of the REAL

ID Act of 2005, and it would amend title II of the Homeland Security Act of 2002 to supposedly "better protect the security, confidentiality, and integrity of personally identifiable information collected by States when issuing drivers' licenses and identification documents."

The Pass ID Act does use language that "pretends" to be concerned about the protection of the privacy of citizens. That is nice to hear, but as Jim Harper, a writer for the Cato Institute, said in a July 7, 2009, article he wrote, "Does the Pass ID Protect Privacy," "**Creating a national identity system that is privacy protective is like trying to make water that isn't wet.**" Such an attempt to protect privacy would be an impossibility, especially since the whole purpose of such a card it to pry into the private lives of the card holders.[306]

The bill is no different than the Real ID in specifying "minimum document requirements and issuance standards for the licenses and cards," thus imposing uniform federal standards on the states. And it states, as did the Real ID, that any state issued drivers' license or ID card, that is not "materially compliant" with the "minimum standards of the Pass ID Act," will not be accepted by any federal agencies. So, if the state is not willing to change their drivers' license to the necessary uniform biometrics, then a person holding that driver's license will not be allowed into any federal building, such as a social security office, a post office, nor can he/she pass security to board an airplane.

However, PASS ID does have a "benevolent" provision that will allow for people to use their old driver's license or ID card that was issued "pursuant" to the Pass ID Act to board commercial aircraft. But, of course, once those cards expire, then they must have the updated card that must be in compliance with the PASS ID.

The following are other provisions stated in the bill: It directs the Secretary of Homeland Security to enter into the appropriate aviation security screening database information on persons who have been convicted of using a false driver's license at an airport; It makes it unlawful for a person knowingly and without lawful authority to copy or resell information from a driver's license or identification card.

Provisions to Entice States to Get on Board—A Grant Program for EDL Licenses: The bill states that there will be a "state-to-state one driver, one license demonstration program." So the Department of Homeland Security will come into each individual state and give a selling pitch—a personal demonstration of just how convenient and easy to use these new updated drivers licenses will be and how important it is to have them all uniform so someone moving from one state to another will not be confused by new or different requirements on the license and will actually not need a different license.

The scariest provision was thrown in among the many in hopes no one would pay too much attention. PASS ID would establish a "state drivers' license **enhancement** grant program."[307]

The states will be tempted to be compliant with the PASS ID by applying for a federal grant. If they receive the grant then the federal government will pay for all the expensive costs of implementation. But notice—it is a grant only for "enhanced driver's license" or EDL. Whenever you hear the term "enhanced drivers' license," a red flag should go up! Enhanced means it has an RFID chip attached. That has been the ultimate goal behind the federal government's attempts for a national ID card all along, to get an RFID (Radio Frequency Identification) chip on the drivers' license, so a person can be more easily tracked and traced every time he or she uses their license.

Let us hope that this bill will be defeated, but if it should be passed by the liberal Congress and signed into law by Obama, let us hope that enough states will refuse to be compliant with it, just as with the Real ID. If you have half of the 50 states refusing to go along, the federal government can't very well implement a national ID drivers' license. Let us hope enough pressure will be placed on state legislators by their constituents that they can be strong and continue to refuse any form of a national ID card.

Is any of this Constitutional? Government, according to the 4th Amendment to the Constitution, is to protect privacy rights—"the right of its citizens to be secure in their persons, houses, papers, and effects," not to snoop into their daily lives, trace their every purchase and track their every move and hold a large data base on them. Such things occur in police states not in a nation that is supposed to be free.

According to Mark Lerner, who heads up two groups fighting the Real ID and the PASS ID, there was an amendment made to the PASS ID in a Senate committee, that makes it no better than before.

Lerner is concerned that while all the attention is being paid to so many other bills that get attention from the media every day, such as the Health Care, and Cap and Trade, that the PASS ID bill will be attached at the last minute as a rider onto some other bill, just as the Real ID Act was, and will be snuck past the Senate without any debate and will be voted into law. (Please go to his website for updated information on this issue—stoprealidcoalition.com)

2009, August—Obama's Health Care Bill Contains A National Health ID Card: Just as the Hillary Care Bill did back in 1992, Obama's bill has the same language about a national ID card—complete with government access to your personal information and even your bank accounts. The only difference is, instead of Obama holding a sample of the card in front of the television cameras and bragging about it as Bill Clinton did, Obama is keeping this national ID very quiet, as he is with many other aspects of his bill. He was hoping to get the total 1100 (or 2000 pages, depending on which version of the bill one looks at) passed on Fast Track without Congress really reading it as he did the Stimulus Bill. (The Health Card is mentioned on Pg 58: SEC. 163. ADMINISTRATIVE SIMPLIFICATION HC Bill. Pg 59: SEC. 163, states the Government will have direct access to your bank account for electronic funds transfer.)[308]

It was revealed just a few weeks after Obama's health care bill was passed in March, 2010, there is a provision in the bill not only for a national ID health card, but by the year 2013, the information on the card will be inserted on an RFID chip into everyone's arm. This is for "health and security" reasons, of course. They are only thinking of our "best interests" at all times. If they can't get us with a national ID on our drivers' licenses, they try again with a health card. This time they have been successful. Do you think this was one of the main reasons why they wanted to get the health care bill passed, but no one would talk about this aspect of it? (More is written about the health issues in Chapter Fourteen about Obama's Socialized America.)

Comprehensive Immigration Reform Act for America's Security and Prosperity Act Contains a National ID Card: (Notice the words "Security and Prosperity." That makes one a little suspicious of this bill right away.) As has been mentioned, the leftists never give up. If they can't get an ID card through one way, they will try another. The 2010 legislation for immigration, H.R. 4321/S contains language to implement a national ID card for all workers.

The Senate Version of the Immigration Bill: In a press release that came out March 11, 2010, Senators Lindsey Graham and Charles Schumer revealed their plans for the Senate version of the immigration bill. They would like it to contain a national ID card, which they refer to as "a biometric Social Security Card," supposedly, to ensure that illegals will not be able to get jobs.

My comments to this bill is, "Illegals have been able to get around such laws and such required ID before. Many have false SS cards and numbers. Many have false drivers' licenses and go by fictitious names. They are very clever and skilled at what they do. That is how they got here, and why they are called illegal."

The main purpose for the biometric social security cards will be to make it possible for the government to keep an eye on every resident of the USA, both citizens and non-citizen. It will be one more attempt to pry into our privacy, and keep tabs on us, wherever we are and whatever we are doing, and chip away at our freedoms and privacy rights."

The following is from researcher Vicky Davis. She believes that a national ID card will be used to keep tabs on the workers and meets the requirement for national management of the labor force as established by the e-government initiative of Al Gore, which was to redesign government systems.

Tech industry contractors did the redesign, which is essentially a corporate personnel system for the country. It merges education and work history for a "cradle to grave history and tracking system."

A "certification" national personnel system was designed by John-Hopkins, not because it's required for the jobs, but it will be used as a "trade authority" to assess the need for "guest workers" based on the number of available Americans relative to the number of jobs. The Labor Secretary could then allow visas either to fill shortages or to lower wages.

All employers will be required to list jobs online so that full and complete data is available: workers, jobs, rates of pay, etc. (Sent March 9, 2010 by Vicky Davis <eyeswideopen@ yahoo.com>.)

Obama Administration's Attempt to Take Over and Snoop Into Private Computers: Here is one more outrageous attempt by the federal government to pry into the privacy of U.S. Citizens. After enticing American car dealers to turn in their old cars at the DoT CARS system to be crushed for money—the "Cash for Clunkers," program, the following message appeared on the government website:

> *This application provides access to the DoT CARS system. When logged on to the CARS system, your computer is considered a Federal Computer system and is the property of the US Government. Any or all uses of this system and all files on this system may be intercepted, monitored, recorded, copied, audited, inspected, and disclosed to authorized CARS, DoT, and law enforcement personnel, as well as authorized officials of other agencies, both domestic and foreign.*

We assume since Obama has nationalized the auto industry, that he thinks that entitles him to take over and control all car dealers computers, especially if they are getting money from the federal government in the "Cash for Clunkers" program. Let this be one more warning to the America people—federal government money comes with many strings attached. Fortunately, after exposure on the Glenn Beck program, July 31, the above message on the website remarkably disappeared—was "scrubbed" over the August 1st weekend.[309]

Before leaving this subject of government snooping into our lives, there are two other important acts that we need to address, which greatly affects our right of privacy and increase the possibility of an American Police State. They are the Military Commissions Act and John Warner Defense Authorization Act of 2007. These acts essentially abolish two very important protections of our freedoms, habeas corpus and posse comitatus.

2006, October 17, Military Commissions Act (MCA) was Passed and Signed into Law by Bush: This act suspends habeas corpus guarantees and fatally undermines our conventional criminal justice system. It started out as an act that would just suspend habeas corpus for a non-citizen detained by the federal government, either at home or abroad, but it has since expanded to include citizens as well.

What is habeas corpus? It means that a person cannot be held or imprisoned without a trial or legal recourse. It is part of the long-standing Anglo-Saxon tradition passed down for 800 years for "due process under the law," and it used to pertain to anyone within the borders of England or the United States, whether citizen or non-citizen. Here is what Thomas Jefferson had to say about it: "The habeas corpus secures every man here, alien or citizen, against everything which is not law, whatever shape it may assume."[310] The MCA has destroyed that long standing guarantee.

Originally, the law did only pertain to non-citizens, but according to William Norman Grigg, it is now pertaining to citizens as well. He cites two Supreme Court decisions where it was ruled that these citizens were not protected by habeas corpus—Padilla v. Rumsfield and Padilla v Hamdi. He also cites a statement made by Alberto Gonzales, President Bush's Attorney General, who seems to believe that it is government that gives rights, therefore government can take them away, including habeas corpus:

> *The Constitution doesn't say that every individual in the United States or citizen is hereby granted or assured the right of habeas corpus . . . It simply says the right shall not be suspended—unless Congress does so in the event of insurrection or rebellion.*[311]

So all we need is the right insurrection or rebellion to come along or to be "created" or "caused" by government, and anyone participating or declared to be participating could have their habeas corpus rights suspended. Governments have been known to create their own crisis and then to blame it on others in various times in history, as we read about in Chapter One when Hitler caused the Reichstag building to be set on fire by his own men and blamed it on people he wanted to get rid of. History could repeat itself in our nation. We are not above such a thing happening here. Martial law could be declared and then, not just habeas corpus, but all of our rights could be suspended.

Imprisonment by Executive Decree: The MCA and the Bush administration has made it possible now to go back to the old unjust practice that pre-dates the Magna Carta—what was executed by the worst of dictators—imprisonment on the whim of the magistrate or the executive. That was one of the reasons why the Magna Carta came into existence was to stop such unjust imprisonments. Because of an uprising of his noblemen, King John was forced to sign the Magna Carta pledging that no free man should be imprisoned, dispossessed, outlawed or exiled save by the judgment of his peers or by the law of the land. It was the judges of England who developed the writ of habeas corpus to preserve what had been pledged in the Magna Carta and to have a check on the power of the magistrate.

However, in the face of constant threats to our security, Americans are forgetting all about history or the traditions upon which are nation was built, and we are allowing our Constitutional rights to be chipped away. Once one right is chipped away, others will follow. As Mr. Grigg states:

> *Once the fabric of constitutional rights is torn, the tear will continue to expand. Consequently, the government that rules citizens will eventually do to citizens what we permit it to do to innocent non-citizens.*[312]

2007, October 17, John Warner Defense Authorization Act of 2007 was Passed and Signed into Law by President Bush: This act was another one of those sneaky last minute "riders" added to the defense bill with little study. It effectively abolishes the Posse Comitatus Act, which forbids the use of the military as a domestic law enforcement entity. The President of the United States is now allowed to invoke and seize control of the National Guard units from each state in the event of a natural disaster or a threat to homeland security.

Where does the Posse Comitatus Act originate and why would it be so terrible if this act is abolished? It was signed into law after the Civil War in 1878 to end the "reconstruction period," the post-war military occupation of the southern states, which was in reality 12 long years of barbarism and terror. The south had been divided into clusters ruled by what became known as "carpetbaggers and scalawags"—petty dictatorships supported by the military. These dictators ruled with no consideration of the U.S. Constitution or the rights of the people. They ran up huge public debts and engaged in wholesale private plunder. Political rights were withdrawn from thousands of Confederates. Some 100,000 white voters were stricken from the polls and not allowed to vote. Southerners by the thousands were expropriated and disenfranchised, often reduced to poverty.

After 1878, when the Posse Comitatus Act went into effect, the military were pulled out, and the little dictatorships toppled. The South could then finally begin real reconstruction under the protection of the Constitution, the rule of law, and not under the arbitrary whim of dictators supported by military garrisons. From that time on, no military was to be used for the purpose of executing the law, absent specific authorization from Congress. Military were to be used for defending our nation against invasion. Law enforcement was left to local sheriffs and police.

According to the Posse Comitatus Act, if there were a dire emergency and the president would need to "federalize" sufficient militia [National Guard], he would need first a petition from the state government, or to show that domestic turmoil had effectively shut down the state government, before the president could act on his own and order the military intervention. However, that is now changed.

The 2007 Defense Authorization Act, Section 501, Gives the President Unprecedented Power to Act on his Own: The decision to intervene militarily within a state is now left up to the president and to him alone, redistributing enormous power from the states into the hands of the federal executive. Such an unprecedented structural change in our government should have been considered important enough to be an amendment to our Constitution, instead of slipped through as a rider on the end of a defense bill.

Before this bill was passed, there were letters of protests from the governors of all 50 states and territories stating that the measure would "expand the President's authority during natural and man-made disasters and could encroach on our constitutional authority to protect the citizens of our states." Rather than clarifying chain of command issues, as proponents of the act were stating, the governors felt this dramatic expansion of federal authority would cause confusion in the command-and-control of the National Guard during emergencies.[313]

2008, March—Attempt to expand FISA, Foreign Intelligence Surveillance Act of 1978: The House amended (FISA) to expand the government's ability to monitor our private communications. This measure will result in more warrantless government surveillance of innocent American citizens. Though some opponents claimed that the only controversial part of this legislation was its grant of immunity to telecommunications companies, there is much more to be wary of in the bill. In the House version, Title II, Section 801, extends immunity from prosecution of civil legal action to people and companies including any provider of an electronic communication service, any provider of a remote computing service, "any other communication service provider who has access to wire or electronic communications," any "parent, subsidiary, affiliate, successor, or assignee" of such company, any "officer, employee, or agent" of any such company, and any "landlord, custodian, or other person who may be authorized or required to furnish assistance." The Senate version goes even further by granting retroactive immunity to such entities that may have broken the law in the past.

The new FISA bill allows the federal government to compel many more types of companies and individuals to grant the government access to our communications without a warrant. The provisions in the legislation designed to protect Americans from warrantless surveillance are full of loopholes and ambiguities. There is no blanket prohibition against listening in on all American citizens without a warrant.

We have been told that this power to listen in on communications is legal and only targets terrorists. But if what these companies are being compelled to do is legal, why is it necessary to grant them immunity? If what they did in the past was legal and proper, why is it necessary to grant them retroactive immunity?

In communist East Germany, one in every 100 citizens was an informer for the dreaded secret police, the Stasi. They either volunteered or were compelled by their government to spy on their customers, their neighbors, their families, and their friends. When we think of the evil of totalitarianism, such networks of state spies are usually what comes to mind. Yet, with modern technology, what once took tens of thousands of informants can now be achieved by a few companies being coerced by the government to allow it to listen in to our communications. This surveillance is un-American.

We should remember that former New York governor Eliot Spitzer was brought down by a provision of the PATRIOT Act that required enhanced bank monitoring of certain types of financial transactions. Yet we were told that the PATRIOT Act was needed to catch terrorists, not philanderers. The extraordinary power the government has granted itself to look into our private lives can be used for many purposes unrelated to fighting terrorism. We can even see how expanded federal government surveillance power might be used to do away with political rivals.

The Fourth Amendment to our Constitution requires the government to have a warrant when it wishes to look into the private affairs of individuals. If we are to remain a free society we must defend our rights against any governmental attempt to undermine or bypass the Constitution.

The following is what Congressman Ron Paul stated before congress against of H.R. 3773, the FISA Amendment:

> *Just today (March 14, 2008), we read in the news that the federal government has massively abused its ability to monitor us by improperly targeting Americans through the use of "national security letters." Apparently some 60 percent of the more than 50,000 national security letters targeted Americans, rather than foreign terrorists, for surveillance.*
>
> *This is what happens when we begin down the slippery slope of giving up our constitutional rights for the promise of more security. When we come to accept the government can spy on us without a court order we have come to accept tyranny. I urge my colleagues to reject this and all legislation that allows Americans to be spied on without a properly issued warrant.*[314]

Many Examples of How America is Already Resembling A Police State: Will Grigg devotes a chapter in his book giving examples of how the military have already been used for unlawful domestic affairs that ended in cruel violations of civil rights and carnage of human lives. Two of the most well known incidents were at Ruby Ridge, Idaho, under the direction of President Bush Sr. and at Waco, Texas, under President Bill Clinton.

August, 1992—Ruby Ridge Incident: Ruby Ridge is a mountain in a remote part of Idaho, near Bonners Ferry, where the Randy Weaver family had a cabin. The family consisted of Randy, Vickie, his wife, a 16-year old daughter, Sarah, a 14-year old son, Samuel, a daughter Rachel, 10 years old, and a baby girl named Elisheba. They also had a fatherless young boy living with them, whom the family had essentially adopted, Kevin Harris, age 16.

Randy Weaver, a former Green Beret, refused to follow the FBI's orders and serve as a federal informant on his neighbors who were part of the Aryan Nation, an unusual religion that the FBI was investigating.

The FBI tried to force Randy to do the informing by pinning a rap on him of selling a sawed-off shotgun—an illegal weapon—requested by an undercover FBI agent. Randy was told that if he would consent to do the spying they would drop the charges. Randy still refused and also refused to show up for his court date on the "illegal firearm" charges. (It was found out later that he had been deliberately given the wrong date anyway.) Randy withdrew to his cabin, hoping they would leave him alone. For sixteen months he and his family just lived off the land, never coming down the mountain, and whenever they left the cabin it was with a weapon.

All the time, men who were part of a U.S. Marshal's Special Operating Group (SOG) were watching the Weavers with jet reconnaissance overflights of Ruby Ridge and the placement of high-resolution video equipment that recorded all of their activities from sites one and a 1/2 miles away. The report was given that Randy Weaver was "extremely dangerous and suicidal."

Perhaps, the FBI were going to use Randy as an example, so no one else would have the audacity to refuse to obey their orders, or maybe it was because of their Christian religion. The Weavers did not consider themselves part of the Aryan Nation, but they had attended a few of their meetings, and they did share their same belief that we are living in the end times, and we need to be prepared for whatever difficult times are coming our way. They believed in being self-sufficient, in keeping guns and knowing how to use them, and in home-schooling their children.

Maybe the FBI just wanted to use the Weaver family as a practice paramilitary drill. Whatever the reasons were, under the direction of President Bush Sr., and Larry Potts, assistant director of the FBI's Criminal Division, an attack was called for.

August 21, 1992, six U.S. Marshals, heavily armed, received the orders to go up the mountain. The Weaver's yellow lab dog, Striker, heard the men and was barking. Randy, Kevin, and Sammy, all carrying guns, came out of the cabin to see what Striker was barking about.

It ended up that the dog was shot and killed; Sammy, who was running back to the cabin was shot in the back and killed. Kevin shot one of the marshals, who later died, William Degan.

The shooting then stopped and Kevin heard a truck drive away, so he thought it was safe to go back to the cabin. He helped Randy and Vickie carry the body of their dead son to an adjoining shed.

After this initial confrontation, that evening and the next day many reinforcements were brought in: agents from the Boundary County Sheriff's Office; the U.S. Border Patrol; the Idaho State Police; the Idaho State Police Critical Response Team ("CRI"); the Idaho National Guard Armory; the FBI Hostage Rescue Team "HRT," a specialized full-time tactical team, based at the FBI Academy in Quantico, Virginia, and another group of the Marshal's Service

SOG units. There were probably about 400 men in total—against a family now of 6, one a baby of ten months.

In a second federal assault, that happened the next day, as Randy, Sara and Kevin were going out to the shed to pray over the body of Sammy, FBI sniper Lori Horiuchi shot and wounded Randy in the arm. Randy shouted to his wife, "I've been hit." Vickie quickly held the door open for them to run back into the cabin. As they were entering the cabin, a second shot rang out, and a bullet hit Vickie in the middle of her forehead. She sank to her knees and collapsed still holding her baby. The shot that killed her actually passed through her head and hit Kevin behind her in his arm and chest.

What did the government then do? They hollered with a bullhorn for Randy to give himself up, and since he didn't, they began bulldozing all the sheds and structures around the house, including the shed where the body of Sammy was.

The media began reporting on this siege, and it was getting nation-wide attention. People began to gather at the base of the mountain, outraged at what 400 armed men were doing to a poor family.

Finally, after seven days, Colonel James "Bo" Gritz, who had also been in the U.S. Army Special Forces, and whom Randy had much respect for, was allowed to speak to him and promised him that he would get a good attorney for him, Gerry Spence, who had a reputation for defending the "under dog" and winning. Bo brought with him his close friend Jack McLamb, a retired police officer from Phoenix, whom Randy also had heard of and respected. They were able to convince Randy to allow his wife's body to be taken out, as well as Kevin who was in great need of medical help. Finally the next day, Randy gave himself up, and he and his daughters were brought out of the cabin.

As soon as they stepped outside the cabin door, federal agents handcuffed Randy, and his daughters began to cry. As they were escorted down the driveway, they noticed snipers and camouflaged agents everywhere coming out of their hiding places, multiple armored carriers, helicopters flying overhead and a massive tent city at the base of the mountain. Sarah said, "All this for one family," as tears ran down her face.

Kevin was put on trial for killing William Degan, but all charges were eventually dropped. Randy was not found guilty of any federal felony counts, but was found guilty of failing to appear in court and violating his bail conditions. He had to serve four months in jail. After he was free, he filed a wrongful death suit against the federal government for the death of his wife and son.

In an out-of-court settlement, he was granted $100,000 and each of his three daughters was given $one million.

And what happened to the various FBI officers and U.S. Marshals who caused this horrendous abuse of power and cold-blooded murder? They received letters of "censor" and were suspended for 10-15 days. Lori Horiuchi, the sniper who did the shooting of Kevin and the killing of Vickie, received no punishment whatsoever.

April 19, 1993—The Waco, Texas, Massacre: For 51 days, under the direction of President Bill Clinton and his Attorney General, Janet Reno, the Bureau of Alcohol, Tobacco, and Firearms (ATF) and the FBI had a siege against a religious community called the "Branch Davidians" at their Mount Carmel retreat outside Waco. There were various reasons given for this siege. The group was stockpiling weapons and food. The head of the religious sect was supposedly abusing small children. Well, if any of that was true, it was nothing compared to the abuse these children and all the adults suffered at the hands of the federal government.

Because the Davidians would not come out and give themselves up, the government used military tanks to punch holes in the walls, pipe in gas into the compound and then set it on fire. Eighty people were killed in the inferno, including seventeen very small children. It is interesting to find out that all military records were soon destroyed after this horrible incident of genocide.[316]

Federal Paramilitary Forces Receive Impunity in Their Exercise of Lethal Force: In both of the above cases, the federal agents and military involved received no punishment for their genocide on fellow Americans. Lori Horiuchi had been the FBI sniper involved in both of these genocides. In a June, 2000, 9th Circuit Court of Appeals ruling, Horiuchi was acquitted of any charge of manslaughter in his slaying of Vicki Weaver and in his involvement in Waco. The court cited "supremacy clause immunity" as their rationale for dismissing the charges against Horiuchi. So, in other words, a federal agent is supreme, above the law, and immune to its regulations.

One dissenting judge, Alex Kozinski, in a scalding rebuke, denounced the court's decision stating that they were creating a "007 standard—"a license to kill." He warned that this new standard would now apply to all law enforcement agencies—federal, state and local.[317]

William Grigg cites many examples since this ruling where that standard has been embraced by police across the nation. Many do seem to believe that they are now supreme, immune and have practically an "unlimited license to kill."

"Militarizing the Thin Blue Line": Grigg gives examples where the police are developing more paramilitary units—over 50,000 in our nation as of 1999. The paramilitary units conduct training exercises with Army Rangers and Navy Seals. SWAT teams are deployed more than 40,000 times a year. The police are using combat equipment, uniforms, and gear, "surplus" supplies granted to them by the Pentagon. Much of this has come about because of the "war on drugs," and now even more so with the "war on terror." He also mentions that because the police are receiving so many supplies from the Pentagon, a federal agency, that the federal government is assuming more control over the police. "That which is funded by Washington is controlled by Washington. "As Grigg states:

> *Accordingly, as local police have become militarized, they have simultaneously become federalized—thereby being transmuted from a local force of peace officers into an army of occupation. So much for the Third Amendment, intended to prevent the emergence of a standard army 'quartered among us.* [318]

Federal Police: I was looking at a You-Tube video of a July 1, 2009, protest march by 8,000 farmers and ranchers in Fresno, California, who were protesting because they were not allowed to have any water to grow their crops because of a "supposed" Endangered Species, the Delta Smelt. I noticed what the man taking the video also noticed, two police cars marked "Federal Police, Department of Homeland Security." I thought to myself, we were never supposed to have federal police. Police are to be left local and under local control. What is happening to our nation? We are so vastly different than our founding father ever intended.

International or NAU Police?: There is a You Tube video clip that shows private security officers with badges on their right arms that show a picture of the continents of both North and South America. The writing on the badge says "Command Center, Private Security." On the back of their uniform is marked "Command Center, Private Officer." The You Tube clip asks are these North American Union police? *(http://www.youtube.com/watch?v=wJBZSzIh5Fo&feature=related)*

Private National Police Taking Control Over a Town? There have been private security agents hired for private corporations, businesses, schools, and universities, but national police taking over a town? I received an e-mail supposedly coming from a small town of Hardin, Montana, sent September 28, 2009, stating that the private police were hired by the city council, and they had fired their sheriff. The private police were there to take control of a newly built prison but also the town. They came into town with their black cars already marked with Hardin

Police signs on them. One of the things the police were doing was making sure everyone received their mandatory flu shot. If they refused, they would be taken and put in the prison, which would then be quarantined. It also said the police told the people that their guns must be taken and marked, and they seemed to know how many guns every resident had. This all seemed too hard to believe, and I dismissed it as a fictional story.

But over the next few weeks, parts of the story began to make national news, both on television and talk shows. A television station in Billings Montana, KULR-8 did a series of reports about it, but they never mentioned mandatory vaccines, nor was there anything about guns being gathered up and brought in to be marked. It appears the e-mail that was sent out was disinformation, or was it?

According to the television news broadcasts, the little town of Hardin had never had a police force, just a local sheriff. In an effort to raise money for the town, the city council had allowed a large prison to be built two years ago as a source of revenue, but it had never been used. The city council found a private police force that promised to fill the prison and to help take care of it and offer protection to the town. On September 28, they arrived in a series of Mercedes cars with "Hardin Police" stenciled on them and started patrolling the town.

Officials from Two Rivers Authority, the city's economic development agency, said "having APF patrol the streets was never part of their agenda." Until now, the Big Horn County Sheriff's Office was responsible for patrolling the city. However, numerous Hardin citizens have testified that APF mercenaries were patrolling Hardin's streets and speaking with strange accents that sounded like Russian.

"Ravenwood" Comes to America: Pastor Chuck Baldwin wrote an October 9, 2009, article about Hardin, in which he compared what is going on there to a TV series called "Jericho," where private police called "Ravenwood" had taken over a small town.

The Description of Hardin's Empty Jail: Baldwin describes the jail that the APF are supposed to be in charge of:

> *The Hardin jail is an interesting situation, all by itself. Completed in September 2007, the 464-bed facility has sat totally empty (which begs an investigative analysis as to how and why the facility was built in the first place). APF promises to fill the jail (with whom is not clear) and also intends to build a 30,000-square-foot military-style training facility and a 75,000-square-foot dormitory for trainees. Costs are to be covered by Ravenwood's—excuse me—APF's "business activities," which includes*

security and training, weapons and equipment sales, surveillance, and
investigations.[319]

According to the Billings TV news coverage, the city began to find out some
very strange things about this police force. They found out that the crest that
was on their website was an exact replica of a Serbian Coat of Arms. When the
Serbian government got wind of it and began to complain, the crest was changed
by the captain, Michael Hilton, who said he had chosen that crest because it was
one his grandfather had had. Captain Hilton spoke with a thick foreign accent,
had a felony background, had been in prison himself, and had many different
names that he has used in the past.

Though their website said that the American Police Force had many years of
experience and that the U.S. government was their biggest client, investigators
found out that was not true. They have only been in existence since February of
2009 and their "supposed" headquarters in California and Washington D.C. do
not really exist.[320] This all is described even more in Chuck Baldwin's article:

**Other Troubling Parts to this Story—A Private National Police Force
is Against the US Constitution:** As Chuck Baldwin writes, "Any kind of
national police force is not only unconstitutional; it is anathema to everything
American law and jurisprudence is built upon. Law enforcement is clearly and
plainly the responsibility of the states and local communities. That a mercenary
organization would take the moniker 'American Police Force' is, by itself,
disconcerting." Because of the many complaints about this, the APF changed
its name to American Private Police Force, (APPF) hoping that would solve
the problem.

Either They are a Fraudulent Group or Very Top Secret: On its website
APF brags about itself as being a national police force, saying that it provides
security and investigative work to clients in "all 50 States and most Countries."
It boasts about having "rapid response units awaiting orders worldwide, that it
can field a battalion-sized team of Special Forces soldiers "within 72 hours," and
that it "plays a critical role in helping the U.S. government meet vital homeland
security and national defense needs."

Yet, as the Billings TV news report mentioned and from an Associated Press
search of two comprehensive federal government contractor databases, there was
no record of an American Police Force. Representatives of security trade groups
said they had never heard of APF. Alan Chvotkin, executive vice president and
counsel for the Professional Services Council, said, "They're really invisible."

APF Might Be a Spin Off or a Front Group for Blackwater: The attorney
for APF, Maziar Mafi, who has since resigned, said the company was a spin-off

of a major security firm, but declined to name the parent company or give any other details. One source reports, "American Police Force, the paramilitary unit patrolling a small town in Montana, has been exposed as being a front group for the disgraced private military contractor Blackwater, now called 'Xe.'"

APF is Very Well Funded: The fact that they arrived with a fleet of Mercedes cars and in spiffy new uniforms with Hardin Police already written on their badges, and they were prepared financially to do all that they had promised, made it appear that they, obviously, were well paid by someone."

Criminal Record of Michael Hilton: Hilton has served several years in jail for fraud. He had many different names in his past records and still had to appear in a California court over an outstanding judgment in a fraud case. This has caused the Two Rivers Authority (TRA) to step back from the APF deal. And at the time of this writing, the future of the agreement between TRA and APF was uncertain.

International Police Force? Hilton is Serbian and many of his personnel are likewise Serbian. Residents also state that they were told "seventy-five percent of the security officers that were coming to be trained would be international."

This Might Be a Violation of Montana Law: Montana Attorney General Steve Bullock has launched an investigation into the Hardin matter. According to the AG's office, the investigation is predicated upon concerns that the company might be violating the Montana Unfair Trade Practices and Consumer Protection Act.

The Growing Trend of Private Security Exercising Police Powers: Baldwin quotes an article written by Jim Kouri, a retired police officer, who tells of an "American Society for Industrial Security" report which gives the number of private security forces compared to local police officers in our nation:

> There are more than one million contract security guards, with perhaps another million guards who are proprietary security officers who are hired directly by businesses and institutions. On the other hand, there are about 700,000 sworn law enforcement officers working for towns, cities, counties, states and the federal government.

Kouri adds that most of these "private police" mercenaries are military-trained, and they are also the ones providing most of the military-style training to America's various law enforcement agencies. He gives the examples of Lexington's (Kentucky) Police Department who contracted with Blackwater Security international to provide "homeland security training," and in New Orleans mercenaries openly patrol city streets. Blackwater officials have said they are on contract with the Department of Homeland Security and have been given the authority "to use lethal force if necessary."[321]

Baldwin asks the question, "Is this what we have to look forward to: foreign mercenaries—employed by international corporations and backed by the federal government—being used to police American cities?"

Could Hardin be a Test Run for A Civilian National Security Force?
Baldwin reminds us of the promise Obama made when he was running for office. It was made on July 2, at Colorado Springs, Colorado. *WorldNetDaily* has the exact quote. Obama said, *"We cannot continue to rely on our military in order to achieve the national security objectives we've set. We've got to have a civilian national security force that's just as powerful, just as strong, just as well-funded."*[322]

United Nations International Police Task Force (UNIPTF): Baldwin states that the potential problems concerning a national security force only intensify when we realize what the United Nations is doing. Perhaps Hardin was a test run for a UNIPTF:

> . . . in 1995, the United Nations' International Police Task Force (UNIPTF) was created. Ostensibly, the UNIPTF was formed to 'carry out programs of police assistance in Bosnia and Herzegovina.' Then, in 2003 the Civilian Police International (CPI) was created. This was a joint venture between the U.S. State Department and such notable private companies as Wackenhut and Kellogg Brown & Root (a Halliburton company; and, by the way, so is Blackwater. But this is just a coincidence, right?). The stated purpose was for "international law enforcement and criminal justice programs." Inertia for mercenary-style (backed by the federal—or even international government) law enforcement has been growing ever since.

Baldwin ends his article with the following: "In the CBS TV series, JERICHO, residents resisted the federal government's mercenary force, Ravenwood, and fought ferociously for their freedom and independence. At the time the show aired, it all seemed like fantasy. But if you talk with the residents of Hardin, Montana, today, they might say that fantasy is fast becoming reality. Stay alert, America: your town could be next."[323]

I include the above story as an illustration of just how much closer our nation is coming to a police state, where all the other things this chapter has informed us about could come true. Could the day shortly come when federal or private police or international police may be brought into your town and replace your local police or have jurisdiction over them? These could be police who are foreigners, who maybe have grown up in a culture where they have been taught to hate Americans, who have no relationship to the citizens of the community and would be willing to do things against the citizens that a local sheriff and local police would not do. It is important to think about these things and have some idea of what you could possibly do to prepare yourself for such a day. (Chapter 18 gives more information on what we can do to be prepared.)

Explorer Boy Scouts Being Trained to Fight Terrorism: (Could they be a part of Obama's future Civilian National Security Force?) I received a *New York Times* article written by Jennifer Steinhauer, May 13, 2009, telling of Explorer Boy Scout units who were being trained in all the skills of paramilitary police or border patrol agents.

The Explorer Scouts program is an affiliate of Boy Scouts of America started 60 years ago that is co-ed, so both boys and girls are involved in this paramilitary training. The article describes a group, in Visalia, California, of fourteen teenage scouts, the youngest only 14, who were involved in a training exercise conducted by Border Patrol agents. The scouts were preparing to storm a "hijacked" bus. In the mock exercise, they are described dressed in military gear, and with pellet guns drawn. They faced a mock scenario of "tripwire, a thin cloud of poisonous gas and loud shots—BAM! BAM!—fired from behind a flimsy wall." One of the young scouts then shouts, "United States Border Patrol! Put your hands up!" and the suspect was subdued.

As Steinhauer writes, "It is all quite a step up" from the good old days when Boy Scouts were learning how to tie square knots:

> The Explorer program . . . is training thousands of Explorer Scouts
> in skills used to confront terrorism, illegal immigration and escalating
> border violence—an intense ratcheting up of one of the group's
> longtime missions to prepare youths for more traditional jobs as police
> officers and firefighters."

Steinhauer quotes A.J. Lowenthal, a sheriff's deputy in Imperial County who is very devoted to the Explorers' events that he helps run. He said, "This is about being a true-blooded American guy and girl . . . It fits right in with the honor and bravery of the Boy Scouts."

The Explorers Program Has 35,000 Scouts Involved in Paramilitary Training: Scouts can choose from 12 career-related programs, including aviation, medicine and science, but of the 145,000 Explorer scout members, 35,000 have chosen to work with the 2000 law enforcement posts across the country.

The scouts meet weekly and work on their law-enforcement techniques in preparation for competitions. On weekends, there are often competitions with other posts (sometimes in other states), where the whole family travels to watch the competition. "Just as there are soccer moms, there are Explorers dads, who attend the competitions, man the hamburger grill and donate their land for the simulated marijuana field raids."[324]

I am a proud mother of five sons who grew up very active in Boy Scouts of America. Three of my sons made it all the way to be Eagle Scouts. I also was very involved in scouting, serving seven years in various positions from Den Mother to a position on the District Boy Scout Committee. I have a great respect for scouting, the camping and survival skills, and the good moral codes that the scouts are taught. I agree that Boy Scouts should be trained to be true-blooded Americans and show honor and bravery.

I just have a hard time with the paramilitary training, especially when the picture in the article of the "hijacked" bus showed, on the side of the bus, the official government crest of "Department of Homeland Security." I wonder how much of the government is involved in the backing of all this? It makes me think of Obama's plans for his own style of young "brown shirts"—his "Civilian National Security Force. Could much of the force be made up of paramilitary trained Boy Scouts?

Who are Now Classified as the New Terrorists? Will the Explorer Scouts be trained in the new definition of "terrorists," which may include many of their own conservative or Christian parents, who might be a little unhappy with Obama's administration and are part of a Tea-party group or some other "right-wing" group speaking out against Obama?

On April 7, 2009, Janet Napolitano, the head of the Department of Homeland Security, released a report warning law enforcement officials about who, essentially, the new "terrorists" are. The report leaked out to some news media and soon went out all over the internet. The following information is coming from *Reuters* in the UK, from an article written April 14, entitled, "Recession Fueling Right-Wing Extremism, US Says."

The report did not mention "Islamic extremists, Islamofascists or jihadists" any more. It seems that Obama is replacing "war on terror" with "overseas contingency operations," for fear of offending Muslims, but he apparently has no fear of offending Christians and conservatives. The new terrorists are now "right-wing extremists," defined essentially as anyone who is disgruntled and speaking out against the government.

The DHS report stated that right-wing extremists, anti-government extremists and militia movements are gaining new recruits by "exploiting fears about the economy and the election of the first black U.S. president." The report also warned that military veterans returning from Iraq and Afghanistan with combat skills could be recruitment targets, especially those who are having trouble finding jobs or fitting back into civilian society. The right-wing extremists might attempt to "recruit and radicalize returning veterans in order to boost their violent capabilities."

The report added that extremist groups are preying on fears that President Barack Obama would restrict gun ownership, boost immigration and expand social programs for minorities. It also said such groups were exploiting anti-Semitic sentiment with accusations that "a cabal of Jewish financial elites" had conspired to collapse the economy.

The trend is likely "to accelerate if the economy is perceived to worsen," as it did in the 1990s until the recession was over. "To the extent that these factors persist, right-wing extremism is likely to grow in strength," DHS said.

DHS spokeswoman Sara Kuban said the report was one of an ongoing series of threat assessments aimed at "a greater understanding of violent radicalization in the U.S." Supposedly, a similar assessment of left-wing radicals was completed in January, 2009, and distributed to federal, state, and local police agencies at that time. "These assessments are done all the time, this is nothing unusual," she said.

The report used the violent death of 168 people in April of 1995, caused by the bombing of a federal building in Oklahoma City by Army veteran Timothy McVeigh, as an example of right-wing extremism and of the "lone wolf" mentality to look out for. [The report did not mention that Timothy McVeigh did not act alone, but was accompanied by two mid-Eastern men, whom many testified that they had seen with him on several occasion before the bombing and the morning of.]

"Despite similarities to the climate of the 1990s, the threat posed by lone wolves and small terrorist cells is more pronounced than in past years," the report said. Because of the Internet, it is now easier to locate specific targets, communicate with like-minded people and find information on bombs and weapons. (Reporting also by Randall Mikkelsen in Washington, editing by Jim Loney and Alan Elsner)[325]

It is now Politically Incorrect to Refer to Islamic Murderers as Terrorists: Ever since Obama was elected, "the war on terror" seems to be over. It appears it is no longer correct to use the word terrorist referring to a Muslim, no matter how violent or terrible the act. This was definitely portrayed by the media coverage of the mass murder of 13 soldiers and the wounding of 30 others by the devout Muslim, psychologist "Major" Nidal Malik Hasan, at the Fort Hood Army base in Texas, November 5, 2009.

Hasan, armed with two guns, opened fire on a large crowd of unarmed soldiers, who were gathered at a center on the base where they are processed before they go overseas. Hasan probably would have killed more had he not been shot himself by a policewoman, Kimberly Munley, who had been directing traffic when she received word of the shooting. As she got out of her car, she spotted Hasan, brandishing his weapons and chasing a victim. She raced towards him and shot him. He turned and fired at her hitting her in both legs. Munley shot four times at Husan. They both went down with several bullet wounds. Munley has since recovered, but so has Hasan. He will live to stand trial for what he has done.

Those, who knew Hasan well and have been willing to talk, say that he had been saying some very strange things from when he first entered the base in July about his conflict with the wars in Iraq and Afghanistan, that they really were anti-Islam wars and it is against the Koran for a Muslim to kill another Muslim. (But the killing of non-Muslims, fellow Americans and fellow soldiers seems to be perfectly fine?) Hasan was soon to be deployed and was disturbed about having to go to battle against his fellow Muslims, so he staged his own battle against his fellow soldiers.

In spite of Hasan's attending services at the same mosques where radical Islam terrorists attended and hearing messages from radical imams, and in spite of his performing the same kind of evil deeds as a radical terrorist would perform, not once did you hear the word "terrorism" used by any report by any major media. Some reports even tried to pull the "victim card," that the major was a victim of having been teased for being a Muslim. Did that justify his killing so many innocent people, many of whom did not even know who he was or his religion?

In President Obama's talk at the funeral service held for the 13 victims, November 10, he only referred to Hasan as the gunman, not even calling him by name. Could it be because Hasan is too much of a Muslim sounding name? Of course, Obama never used the word terrorism or terrorist. He would like to be known as the president who ended the "war on terror." He could not acknowledge that it is still going on. (http://www.nytimes.com/2009/11/07/us/07police.html?_r=1.)

Where are the Policies Coming From That Make America Resemble More and More a Police State? Should it surprise the reader to find out that these ideas are coming from police states? Several authors have eluded to the fact that "expert advice" was brought over from former KGB and Stasi agents who helped create the Patriot Act, the Department of Homeland Security, the Real ID Act, the Western Hemisphere Travel Initiative, The Military Commissions Act, and the Defense Authorization Act, and all the other acts and procedures that make us resemble a police state. Here are quotes from several reputable authorities stating as such:

Links between the USA and the Soviet Union: Charlotte Iserbyt, conservative author and columnist, served as Senior Policy Advisor in the Office of Educational Research and Improvement (OERI), U.S. Department of Education, during the first Reagan Administration. She had papers coming across her desk showing how the education curriculum was being changed and put under federal control. Charlotte knew that this was not correct. She knew the Constitution well and knew that whatever is not specifically mentioned in the Constitution was to be left under local and state control. Education was one of the things deliberately not mentioned. Our founding fathers wanted education to be left up to the parents and local control. It should not be tampered with by federal government.

Charlotte also saw papers coming across her desk showing the link between education in the Soviet Union and the USA. She began copying those papers and many others and later used them for writing her book, *The Deliberate Dumbing Down of America*.

The Real ID was Designed by Former KGB Chiefs: In February of 2005, Charlotte wrote an article about the Real ID Act, before it was passed, and before it was given the name, Real ID. It was first called H.R. 418. Her article is entitled "Refuse the National ID Card" and was published in *NewsWithViews. com* and *rense.com*. 2/13/05.

> The drivers' license . . . legislation (H.R. 418) . . . is more serious than one may think due to the fact it was designed by two ex-KGB Chiefs, one of whom, Yvgeny Primakov, was the President of totalitarian Russia in the late nineties.

Charlotte stated in her article that not only Primakov, but another former KGB chief, General Alexander Karpov, were invited to help in the design of the internal passport that later became the Real ID. As shocking as this information sounds to most Americans, it was not shocking to Mrs. Iserbyt. Such joint ventures between the two countries have gone on for some time. When she had served in the Federal Department of Education, she found out that at the same time that our education system was being linked to the Soviet Union, in 1985, there was a merger of the KGB and the FBI when President Reagan had signed numerous agreements with Gorbachev.

She also found out about an agreement that was signed between the Soviet Police and New York City Police, which allowed Soviet policemen to assist in the arrest of people who were not paying their fares in the New York City subway system. Charlotte states that "these activities, unknown to most Americans, represent just the tip of the U.S.-Soviet exchange agreements iceberg." After the Berlin Wall went down and the Soviet Union was dissolved and Communism was, "supposedly," dead, those exchanges did not end, but escalated in partnerships between Russia and the U.S.

USA and Russians—"We Are Partners Now": Such were the words of Yuri Kobaladze, chief spokesman of the Russian Intelligence Service, after a meeting of Russian and American intelligence agents. The quote and a description of this new partnership come from an article that appeared in *Time* magazine, 7/5/93, entitled "A New World for Spies."

> *The Chairman of the Senate Intelligence Committee, D. Concini, and CIA Director Woolsey, met with Yvgeny Primakov, head of the Russian Foreign Intelligence service (KGB), over a period of several days. Members of the House and Senate Intelligence Committees were present. Woolsey and Primakov discussed how their organizations can cooperate and share information on worldwide threats, such as terrorism, the spread of weapons of mass destruction, and drug trafficking. Former head of the CIA Gates visited Moscow in October, 1993 . . .*

The Times article does say that not all CIA members would have been happy about this new partnership: "Were he still alive, James Jesus Angleton, the CIA's consummate cold war spook, would have launched a full-scale internal investigation condemning a conversation of any substance between Primakov, a long time Kremlin Middle East expert and Woolsey, as treasonous."

Mrs. Iserbyt also casts suspicion on how much trust we are to put in our new partner, Primakov, whom she states was in Baghdad just two weeks prior to our invasion of Iraq, "advising Saddam Hussein on how to deal with the Americans!"

Russia-China-USA Partnership?: Mrs. Iserbyt mentions in her article that Russia has also formed a partnership with China: "The Soviets and Chinese have joined together formally and have submitted joint agreements to the United Nations in which they spell out, in detail, their plans to lead the forthcoming communist world government."

So if we are partners with Russia, and Russia is a partner with China, what kind of a relationship does that make between the USA and China? Are we partners too? We might as well be—they practically own us, because they are holding most of our $ trillions of debt. (However, usually when you are so indebted to someone else to such a huge extent, they call it "servitude," or "bondage" rather than "partnership.")

My, how things have changed since the "supposed" end of the cold war and the new "war on terrorism!" The old Communist terrorists, who have mass murdered millions of their own people, are now are new partners in fighting the war on terrorism! Doesn't that all make perfectly good sense and make us all feel warm and cozy and much safer? Or does the world seem to have gone stark raving mad!

Explanation for the Madness—all Part of the One-World Deceptive Plan: Mrs. Iserbyt explains how this plan to pretend that the Soviet Union is no more and Communism is now dead—so, therefore, we can all be happy "partners" together—was actually laid out back in the 1950-60s, many years before these events happened. They did not just happen spontaneously, as we were all led to believe, after President Reagan told Gorbachev to "tear down that wall!"

Iserbyt cites several different books and reports that give evidence of these deceptive plans, two that were written by a Russian, Anatoliy Golitsyn, a former KGB agent, who had defected to the United States in 1961. His first book, *Perestroika Deception—The World's Slide Towards the Second October Revolution*, tells about the deception of Gorbachev's supposed "*Perestroika*," (meaning in Russian "detant or peace")—that it was all a pretense.

In Golitsyn's second book, *New Lies for Old*, he tells how the Communists have told the same old lies and done the same old tactics for years, taking one step backwards while they take two steps forward, feigning weakness, while gaining strength. The USA and other countries of the Western world have believed this deception, have let down our guard, and, as Mrs. Iserbyt puts it, we are "in a fast fall toward world Communism." This is what Mrs. Iserbyt writes about Golitisyn:

> In the late fifties, Anatoliy Golitsyn, a Soviet official, sat in on high level
> meetings in the Kremlin, during which the grand deception of the West
> was planned. This deception, which included the planned phony demise

of Communism, succeeded in hoodwinking Prime Minister Margaret Thatcher and President Ronald Reagan, resulting in their enthusiastically endorsing Gorbachev's Perestroika. It was Golitsyn who provided sensitive documents, over many years, to the CIA warning it of the merger . . . It was Golitsyn who warned President Reagan not to attend his scheduled visit to Moscow in 1988.

James Jesus Angleton, the Director of CIA's Counter Intelligence, was one of the few CIA agents who believed Golitsyn. Because of that, Golitsyn dedicated his second book to him and wrote these words: "In Memory of Jim Angleton, founder and outstanding chief of the Central Intelligence Agency's Counter-intelligence, a man of vision and courage, a warrior and comrade-in-arms, who recognized the dangers of the Soviets' new strategic challenge."

Support for the Accuracy of Golitsyn's Predictions: Another book that Mrs. Iserbyt cites is the *Wedge: The Secret War between the FBI and CIA,* written by Alfred A. Knopf, New York, 1994. Knopf writes of Mark Riebling, who carried out a methodical analysis of Golitsyn's predictions in *New Lies for Old.* He credited Golitsyn with "an accuracy record of nearly 94%" in his predictions, many years ahead of the events, of the phony "break with the past," the supposed "demise of Communism" that took place in Eastern Europe and the Soviet Union in 1989-1991.

Out of the Horse's Mouth: Of course, the best proof of the Russian collaboration in creating the Real ID Act, as well as, the other acts almost identical to the Russian systems—the Patriot Act and the Department of Homeland Security—is the statement made by Primakov himself, who was quoted having said the following in a press conference back in Russia: (My thanks to John W. Spring, a former radio host, who first made me aware of the Russian collaboration in the Real ID Act and told me of this shocking quote.)

The establishment of the State Security Citizen Threat File was just one of the many steps being prepared by the U.S. Government to tighten security. When the National Identity Card Act [the Real ID] is passed, the Posse Comitatus Act is overturned, and other items of repressive legislation [the Patriot Act and Department of Homeland Security] are approved by Congress, the White House [the executive Branch of the US government] will have acquired greater control over the American people than the Kremlin could exert over the Russian people when Stalin was alive.[326]

Other Reports that Give Evidence of Russian Influence in Homeland Security, the Real ID Act, and Other "Repressive Legislation": There are several other sources that substantiate the report that it was Primakow and Karpov who were asked to work with the Department of Homeland Security to help in the development of the Real ID Act and all the other subversive acts that are prying into American lives and turning our nation more into a police state.

Here is a summary of the various sources: 1) An article in the April 2003 issue of Soviet Analyst (*www.sovietanalyst.com*) entitled "Architect of Soviet Middle East Terror to 'Advise' Washington—"Convergence Acquires New Meaning" by Christopher Story, a researcher and author with offices in London and New York City; 2) May 15, 2003 issue of *The Howard Phillips Issues* and Strategy Bulletin in an entry entitled "GWB Names Kremlin Spymaster Primakov as Consultant to U.S. Homeland Security Team;" 3) *www.NewsWithViews.com*: "Former KGB Heads to Help Spy on Americans," 4/24/03 and "Former USSR/Russian Premier to Work for Homeland Security," 4/22/03, by Charlotte Iserbyt; and 4) *American Free Press*, "Get Ready for the Sovietization of America," 4/21/03 by Al Martin, *www.almartinraw.com*, a former intelligence agent.[327]

Report of Reece Committee on the Investigation of Tax-Exempt Foundations: A report that Mrs. Iserbyt cites, as well, gives evidence of the Soviet-American link that goes back to the 1950s. It is by the Reece Committee of 1953. Senator Reece headed up a Congressional Committee to investigate tax-exempt foundations. They had heard that some of the money that was being used by these left-leaning big corporate foundations was going to suspicious causes. The Research Director of the committee, Norman Dodd, had an interview with the President of the Ford Foundation, Rowan Gaither. He asked Mr. Gaither what their money was primarily used for. Here was the reply:

> *Mr. Dodd, all of us here at the policy making level of the foundation have at one time or another served in the OSS [the Office of Strategic Services, the forerunner of the CIA] or the European Economic Administration, operating under directives from the White House. We operate under those same directives . . . The substance of the directives under which we operate is that we shall use our grant making power to so alter life in the United States that we can be comfortably merged with the Soviet Union.*

Mr. Dodd was stunned and replied, "Why don't you tell the American people what you just told me, and you could save the taxpayers thousands of dollars set aside for this investigation?" **Gaither responded, 'Mr. Dodd, we wouldn't think of doing that.'**[328]

Mr. Dodd gave his report back to the Reece Committee, and what did they do with it? Nothing. They knew their hands were tied if they could get no witnesses from the tax-free foundations to ever confess and tell the truth before the committee as to where their money was going and the directives they were receiving from the White House. The Reece Committee was closed down shortly thereafter.

The Four Prong Approach: Mrs. Iserbyt, in the same article, tells how the deceptive merger has been happening between the soviets and the USA. She calls it the "Four-prong-Devil's Fork" approach:

> *(1) gradualism, called for by the Fabian socialists, which calls for the making of controversial changes over long periods of time, so people don't recognize what is happening; (2) semantic deception (use of traditional-sounding labels to sugar-coat evil intentions and programs); (3) endless supply of taxpayers' hard-earned money; and (4) use of the Hegelian dialectic, the deliberate creation of problems: poverty, wars, depression, etc. to induce concern/panic amongst the population in order to get the public to accept, often at the polls, the pre-determined freedom-destroying sugar-coated solution, which it would never have accepted had the problem not been deliberately created.*[329]

Other Examples of the Soviet American Link Involving Education, Military, Disarmament, and Many US Presidents, Both Democrats and Republicans:

1934—Education: *Conclusions and Recommendations for the Social Studies* **was Published:** This report was funded by the Carnegie Corporation of New York and compiled by the American Historical Association. A philosopher of British socialism, Professor Harold Laski, said of the report: "At bottom, and stripped of its carefully neutral phrases, the Report is an educational program for a Socialist America." Here are a few examples of what the socialist recommendations were: (I have put the words mentioning the age of collectivism and a world order in bold print.)

> *. . . consider the condition and prospects of the American people as a part of Western Civilization merging into a **world order** . . . that in the United States as in other countries, the age of laissez faire in economy and government is closing and a **new age of collectivism** is*

emerging . . . Organized public education in the United States . . . is
now compelled . . . to adjust its objectives, its curriculum, its methods
of instruction, and its administrative procedures to the requirements
*of the **emerging integrated order** . . . . If the school is to justify its*
*maintenance and assume its responsibilities, it must recognize **the new***
***order** and proceed to equip the rising generation to cooperate effectively*
in the increasingly interdependent society and to live rationally and well
within its limitations and possibilities.

1958—Agreements with the Soviet Union by President Eisenhower:
In the peak of the "Cold War," Eisenhower was the first U.S. President to sign
agreements with the Soviet Union, which was supposed to be our enemy. These
agreements related to joint efforts in education, space, the arts, medicine, etc.

1961, September 26—President John F. Kennedy signed the Arms
Control and Disarmament Act with the Soviet Union: This is referred to as
Public Law 87-297 and State Department Publication 7277 "Freedom From
War: The United States Program for General and Complete Disarmament in a
Peaceful World" which states in part:

The manufacture of armaments (including personal firearms) would be
prohibited except for those of agreed types and quantities to be used by
the U.N. Peace Force and those required to maintain internal order. All
other armaments would be destroyed or converted to peaceful purposes . . .
The disbanding of all national armed forces and the prohibition of
their reestablishment in any form whatsoever other than those required
to preserve internal order and for contributions to a United Nations
Peace Force.

There is a provision that asks for the creation of an agency such as the
Department of Homeland Security (on page 3). The Program also provides for
an internal order system (a military government) with global control systems
instituted over its "homeland." During this period America will be moved
from a sovereign nation into full blown "global government communitarian
management."[330]

1985—Education Agreements signed by Presidents Reagan and
Gorbachev Merging the Two Systems: Not only did education agreements
take place between the two presidents, but, during the same year, the Carnegie
Corporation of New York also signed agreements with the Soviet Academy
of Science. Thus began the changing of the U.S. education system from one

focused on academics and individual achievement to one focused on "school to work"—filling quotas for certain jobs requiring work-force training (performance/outcomes-based) for a "planned international socialist economy." This merger was going on when Charlotte Iserbyt was working in the Federal Department of Education. This is what she writes about it:

> *This failed socialist economic system which calls for communist "free trade" as well, is being implemented right now, under our very noses. This failed system is of benefit to a very small percent of the world's population known as "the elite" which benefits from socialist subsidies and the elimination of competition. What we are looking at in the United States today is the redistribution of wealth as well as the redistribution of brains, and nobody, not even a rocket scientist, seems to understand what is going on.*[331]

1993, April—The Former Presidio Army Base in San Francisco was Turned Over to Gorbachev for his Environmental Headquarters, Green Cross International, Gorbachev Foundation, and "State of the World Forums": The nation's number one military installation now belongs to a former Soviet President, former KGB, who has publicly stated that he is still very much a Communist. Gorbachev just traded his red coat for a green one, but underneath the green all is still red—just like a watermelon. It is not only red but very "new-age," as well. Yet today the former Soviet leader is wined, dined and lauded in the U.S., where he receives hefty speaking fees for spouting his pro-marxist doctrine on university campuses, business gatherings, and even Republican fundraisers. For example, October 16, 1990, Gorbachev was the keynote speaker for a Republican fundraiser in Des Moines, Iowa.And November 9, 1993, he spoke for a Republican Senatorial Committee and was given a $70,000 honorarium for his Gorbachev Foundation.[332]

"**State of the World Forums**:" In Jim Keith's book *Black Helicopters*, written in 1997, he states that there have been many "green," New Age, State of the World Forums, sponsored by the tax-exempt Gorbachev Foundation, which obtains much of its funding from the other tax exempt, one-world, "green" foundations—the Rockefeller Brothers Fund, the Mellon Foundation, the Ford Foundation and the Pew Family trusts.

Participants in the forums include New Agers, Communists, Eastern Religion advocates and one-worlders. Barbara Marx Hubbard spoke in 1995 and reiterated her belief that one-fourth of mankind must be eliminated. Other speakers and attendees have been Ted Turner, Carl Sagan, Shirley MacLaine, Bill Gates, Nelson Mandela and George Bush Sr.

According to Keith, Gorbachev wants global governance with a synthesis of New Age Eastern Religion. He believes the old beliefs and political systems must be abandoned.[333]

Then there is Gorbachev's "Earth Charter" which he believes would be a "kind of Ten Commandments for the Environment, something no one would be allowed to violate." (More is written about the Earth Charter in Chapter Fifteen, which tells of the movement to a one-world, earth-worshiping religion, essentially what the Earth Charter's principles are all about.)

2002, May—President Bush Jr. said the EU's role is to Help Converge the United States and the Soviet Union: According to a June, 2002, *New American* article, Bush was speaking before the Bundestag (Parliament) in Germany and described the EU as a "House of freedom—its doors open to all of Europe's people, its windows looking out to global challenges beyond." Mr. Bush discussed the EU's role in accelerating the convergence of the United States and the former Soviet Union. He stated, "Another mission we share is to encourage the Russian people to find their future in Europe, and with America."[334]

2002, May 24—Partnership Renewed with the Signing of Treaty Of Moscow: President Bush and Vladimir Putin signed what the *Associated Press* called the "Biggest Arms Reduction Treaty in History." As they signed, Bush and Putin proclaimed "a desire to establish a genuine partnership based on the principles of mutual security, cooperation, trust, openness, and predictability." According to President Bush, the treaty-signing ceremony "ended a long chapter of confrontation and opened up an entirely new relationship between our countries."

Putin added, "Together, we will counteract global threats and challenges. We're going to form a stable world order in the interests of our peoples and our countries."

The treaty committed Russia and the U.S. to reduce their strategic nuclear arsenals to 2,200 warheads each by December 31, 2002. Bush and Putin also signed an eight-page agreement pledging U.S.-Russian cooperation on "economic matters, the Middle East peace process, nuclear proliferation and missile defense and the war against terrorism."[335]

2003, April 10, What Kind of a Trusted Partner is Russia? Just ten months after signing the disarmament treaty with Bush, Putin was already announcing a new generation of Russian nuclear weapons—with multiple warheads and long-range capabilities—which would replace Russia's old stock. Mr. Putin said, "These are . . . terrible missiles, of which we have dozens with several hundred warheads. These weapons are even now ready for use."[336]

FBI and KGB Collaboration: Since 1994, plans have been in the works for ex-KGB agents to be brought over to work with FBI agents.

One of the places where they are working together is at the Center for Counterintelligence and Security Studies, a consulting service in Alexandria, Virginia, that has the following website (*http://www.cicentre.com*). *The New York Times*, in an article dated 8/24/03 entitled "Former Top Russian Spy Pledges Allegiance," stated that the above Center "provides expertise and advice in counterintelligence, counterterrorism and security for the government and companies." [Notice there is nothing mentioned about the **security of American citizens**—just government and companies.]

The hiring of these ex-KGB agents is a result of FBI/KGB collaboration, which *The New American*, wrote about in an article entitled "Community Policing, East and West." July 30, 2001:

> *Among Louis Freeh's supposedly commendable achievements as FBI director, according to Robert S. Bennett, was the realization of his vision of a 'global FBI.' It was in pursuit of that vision that Freeh traveled to Moscow in 1994, and—on the fourth of July—signed an agreement creating a framework for FBI/KGB collaboration. 'We can honestly say that our two nations have more in common than ever before,' declared Freeh at the ceremony, which took place after a tour of the KGB's Lubyanka Square headquarters. 'We are united in purpose and in spirit.'"*

The "unity" between Russian and USA law enforcement that Freeh speaks of had actually been going on for several years before his trip to Russia. "Cultural exchanges" for law enforcement had been signed between Reagan and Gorbachev the last year of Reagan's presidency. An example was written about in a *New York Times* June 19, 1991 article, entitled "Week in the Subway as Cultural Exchange." It told of the joint police activities in the New York subway, which surprised many Americans wondering what was going on?

> *A hapless fare-beater was arrested today in the Chambers Street subway station, and he was suddenly surrounded by six Moscow police officers. This was not a scene out of a Cold War nightmare. The Soviets were not taking over the United States. This was a cultural exchange.*

Former Russian Spy, KGB, Now US Citizen and "Trusted" Consultant: Another *New York Times* article entitled "Former Top Russian Spy Pledges

New Allegiance," 8/24/03, tells of Oleg Kalugin, a retired KGB general and son of a member of Stalin's secret police, who is now a United States citizen, working as a consultant at the Centre for Counterintelligence and Security Studies. He has a very interesting "anti-American" past and one wonders just how committed he will be as a new citizen. As a young KGB, trainee, he was sent in the late 1950s as a "U.S.-Soviet education exchange" foreign student to Columbia University. There he recruited American students to serve as spies working for Moscow. One of the greatest spies Kalugin later recruited was John A. Walker, Jr., a navy warrant officer, recruited in 1966 and paid more than $1 million before the FBI caught him in 1985. As Mrs. Iserbyt states of Kalugin, "And we 'sheeple' trust this new United States citizen to promote what is in our nation's best interest?"

Just as the "sheeple" in our media were so enraptured with Gorbachev, they also regarded Kalugin as a trusted advisor. He was a frequent TV commentator and regular guest on Fox News.

European Union is the Model for the Rest of the World in Implementing Soviet System: Mrs. Iserbyt is aware that we are following the same pattern as that of the European Union, which is also implementing national ID cards for all the nations that belong to the EU. The EU is following the communist pattern of having an "internal passport" for all citizens. She wrote:

> The European Union (region) is the model for the rest of the world as it becomes regionalized (communized). Gorbachev referred to the European Union as "The New European Soviet" in a speech in London in 2002. President Bush is implementing The New American Soviet in this hemisphere. The new drivers' license (internal passport) will extend throughout this hemisphere.

Refuse to Accept A Driver's License that Has Become An Internal Passport or National and International ID Card:

> All Americans, who cherish their freedoms guaranteed under The Bill of Rights, MUST refuse to accept this totalitarian identification card which will contain information, lifelong, on all aspects of our persons, what we have written, associations, and actions, past, present and future, and which will be used to identify and penalize those who disagree with government policies.[337]

Enhanced Means RFID: As was mentioned earlier in this chapter, there is a bill to replace the Real ID act with the PASS ID. The PASS ID has a provision to entice states to apply for federal grants so that they can get money to pay for Enhanced Drivers' Licenses. Whenever you hear the word "enhanced" it means RFID chips are added to the license. That has been the whole goal all along. Robert Pastor, the CFR, and all the globalists behind national/international ID cards want RFID chips added which makes for much better tracking of people. The following information about the use of RFID lets you know how far we have come with this technology.

RFID Tracking Devices for Digital Televisions: Remember back in 2008, when we were told that all American televisions had to be changed from analog to digital televisions by 2009. We weren't sure why, but it was for some technological reason, and since most Americans don't really speak techno-eese language, we just let it go without really questioning it. Well, according to a retired IBM employee, Patrick Redmond, who worked for 23 years for IBM, in Toronto, Canada, switching to digital televisions was for a much different reason. It was "to free up frequencies and make room for scanners used to read implantable RFID microchips," so people and products can be better tracked throughout the world. Redmond added:

The increased use of RFID chips would require the increased use of the UBF-UHF spectrum. That is why governments, in both the USA and Canada, required that televisions could no longer use those frequencies, but had to go digital. The UBF-VHF analog frequencies then could be freed up for only RFID signals.

Redmond said the governments planned to sell these frequencies to private companies and other groups who would use them to monitor the chips.

The Alarming Growing Use of RFID Chips: According to an article that was published in the *American Free Press* and has appeared on internet, Redmond has given talks, written a book and produced a DVD on the alarming growing use of passive, semi-passive and active RFID chips, which can be implanted in clothing, in Gillette Fusion blades, and in many other products that become one's personal belongings and go where the person goes. The chips are also embedded in all new U.S. passports, some medical cards, a growing number of credit and debit cards and so on. More than two billion chips were sold in 2007. The chips can be as small, or smaller, than the tip of a sharp pencil. It is all part of nanotechnology.

To verify the story about the RFID-DTV link, the *American Free Press* reporter interviewed Katherine Albrecht, radio host and author of the book, *Spy Chips*, which is all about the use of RFID chips. She told *AFP* that while she's not totally sure whether there is a rock-solid RFID-DTV link, it sounds very plausible, "The purpose of the switch [to digital] was to free up bandwidth. It's a pretty wide band, so freeing that up creates a huge swath of frequencies."

How RFID Works: In a DVD-recorded public lecture in 2008, Redmond spoke to an audience made up of Canadian Catholic patriots known as the Pilgrims of Saint Michael. He explained that the active, semi-passive or passive, "transponder chips" can be accessed or activated with "readers" that can pick up the signal given off by each chip and information gleaned from it. Depending on design and circumstances, the information can be picked up from far away and the identity and whereabouts of the product or person can then be tracked and data sent to a large data base in Washington D.C.

> . . . the active chips have an internal power source and antenna; these particular chips emit a constant signal. "This allows the tag to send signals back to the reader, so if I have a RFID chip on me and it has a battery, I can just send a signal to a reader wherever it is.[338]

Use of RFID Already Being Used on Pets and Animals: According to Redmond, over a million pets have been chipped, and farm animals are increasingly being chipped. Redmond does not mention this in the article, but I write about it in my book about the Real ID. There is a program in the U.S. called NAIS, National Animal Identification System, which is trying to make it mandatory that every farm animal and pet will be chipped (pretending that this is for health and security reasons, in case of an epidemic such as the Mad Cow disease, or swine flu, or bird flu, etc). However, most farmers and ranchers are protesting NAIS because of the high cost of the chips and the constant regulations and hoops that they then will have to jump through. The cost and regulations will put many farmers and ranchers out of business.[339]

Use of RFID Chips for Tracking People: According to Redmond, 31,000 police officers in London have in some manner been chipped as well, "much to the consternation of some who want that morning donut without being tracked." London also has put RFID chips on public transportation passes linked to the customer's name. If someone wants to know the whereabouts of a person using a bus or the subway, he can be found immediately because of the RFID chip in his pass. "John Smith, he can be found on subway car 32," Redmond said.

License Plates in Canada Have Been Chipped: While in the U.S., many states are still fighting the Real ID, not wanting drivers' licenses to become traceable-national ID cards, Redmond states that in Canada, drivers can be traced through their license plates, which have already been quietly chipped.

The chips can contain much information: work history, education, religion, ethnicity, reproductive history, political party, etc.

As of June, 2009, to "tighten security and speed the flow of traffic," all people, both Canadians and Americans crossing the border between Buffalo and New York, were required to have one of three IDs that contain RFID: either a passport, an enhanced drivers' license, or a NEXUS card. Then they can simply flash the card as they cross the border; it will be scanned and they can speed on their way. Not only the driver, but everyone in the car have to show such a card. (http://www.youtube.com/watch?v=1J4eE7K84o8&NR=1)

Prediction for the Future in Tracking People: Redmond added, "Nigel Gilbert of the Royal Academy of Engineering said that by 2011 you should be able to go on Google and find out where someone is at anytime from chips on clothing, in cars, in cell phones and inside many people themselves."

Hospital Patients: "Some 800 hospitals in the U.S. are now chipping their patients; you can turn it down, but it's available." Redmond added: "Four hospitals in Puerto Rico have put them in the arms of Alzheimer's patients, and it only costs about $200 per person."

Redmond Predicts Widening Use for People in the Future: Redmond says that "Chipping children to be able to protect them is being promoted in the media." After that, he believes it will come to: "chip the military, chip welfare cheats, chip criminals, chip workers who are goofing off, chip pensioners—and then chip everyone else under whatever rationale is cited by government and highly-protected corporations that stand to make billions of dollars from this technology."[340]

VeriChip, the Major Chip Manufacturer for Implantable Chips: One of the companies that is hoping to make billions from this technology is VeriChip. By going onto their website you can read the following description of the company, the chip and how it is implanted:

"About twice the length of a grain of rice, the device is typically implanted above the triceps area of an individual's right arm. Once scanned at the proper frequency, the VeriChip responds with a unique 16 digit number which could be then linked with information about the user held on a database for identity verification, medical records access and other uses. The insertion procedure is performed under local anesthetic in a physician's office and, once inserted, is invisible to the naked eye. As an implanted device used for identification by a third party, it has generated controversy and debate." (Information on website in 2008)[341]

"VeriChip Corporation, headquartered in Delray Beach, Florida, has developed the VeriMed™ Health Link System for rapidly and accurately identifying people who arrive in an emergency room and are unable to communicate. This system uses the first human-implantable passive RFID microchip, cleared for medical use in October, 2004, by the United States Food and Drug Administration. To complement its healthcare division, VeriChip Corporation established VeriGreen Energy Corporation in March, 2009, to focus and invest in the clean and alternative energy sector." [They also mention on their website that the Stimulus Bill is giving $79 billion towards developing renewable energy. Could it be that VeriChip has its eye on tapping into some of that money? What are they going to try to do? Come up with a green chip?]

[The information on their 2009 website, adds the following, obviously because people are starting to question and are concerned about the tracking capability]: "The microchip itself does not contain any other data other than this unique electronic ID, nor does it contain any Global Positioning System (GPS) tracking capabilities. And unlike conventional forms of identification, the Health Link cannot be lost, stolen, misplaced, or counterfeited. It is safe, secure, reversible, and always with you."[342]

How Secure is the Information on an RFID Chip? Many experts have demonstrated how easy it is to hack and then clone the e-passports that contain the chips. People have rigged devices that can swipe information from a passport from a distance of 8-50 centimeters. They then can relay the information to a second device up to 50 meters away.

British computer security expert Adam Laurie, of Bunker Secure Hosting, compared the ultra-secure e-passport system to "installing a solid steel front door to your house and then putting the key under the mat." Laurie, himself, has created a device that could be hidden inside a bag and could be used to read and clone a passport from a person seated next to him on the busy London Underground or on the monorail.[343]

UK National ID Card Was Cloned in 12 Minutes: In an article in *ComputerWeekly.com*, by Ian Grant, August 6, 2009, it was reported that a national ID card for the UK was put to a security test and failed. The *Daily Mail* newspaper also hired computer expert Adam Laurie to test the security that protects the information embedded in the chip on a card that is being issued to foreign national. Using a Nokia mobile phone and a laptop computer, Laurie was able to copy the data on the card and cloned it in just 12 minutes.

Laurie then rewrote data on the card, reversing the bearer's status from "not entitled to benefits" to "entitled to benefits." He then added fresh content that would be visible to any police officer or security official who scanned the card, saying, "I am a terrorist—shoot on sight."

According to the *Daily Mail*, Home Office officials said the foreign national's card uses the same technology as the UK citizens' card that will be issued from 2012. (Home Office is the same as the U.S. Department of Homeland Security.)

Guy Herbert, general secretary of the privacy lobby group *NO2ID*, said it was a mistake to assume that the Home Office cared about the card, or identity theft or citizens' benefit. He said that Home Office was just interested in the central database to record citizens' personal details in one place for official convenience to store in Whitehall. (Whitehall is the administrative center of the government for the UK, located in London. There is a massive computer there used for storing all data on citizens.)

> *It is that database which will deliver unprecedented power over our lives to Whitehall, and make the Home Office king in Whitehall. The card is an excuse to build the database. If the card is cancelled, it already intends to use passports as a secondary excuse.*[344]

How Safe would be an Implanted Chip? Little information is ever revealed about the harmful effects of implanted chips, but where VeriChip RFID has been implanted in some mice, rats and dogs, tumors have formed around them—as high as 10% in a study of 177 mice in a lab in Ridgefield, Connecticut. However, the chairman of VeriChip Corp., Scott Silverman, insists that the chips are perfectly safe and were approved by the FDA (Federal Drug Administration) and the HHS (Health and Human Services.)

When the FDA approved the device, it noted some risks: The capsules could migrate around the body, making them difficult to find and to ever extract. They could interfere with other implants such as defibrillators, or be incompatible with MRI scans, causing burns. The FDA did warn that there could be "adverse tissue reaction," but did not specifically mention tumors or malignant growth in animal studies.[345]

When the Department of Health and Human Services (HHS) approved of VeriChip, Tommy Thompson was serving as the head of HHS. Two weeks after the chip's approval, Thompson left the HHS, and a few months later turned up as a member of the Board of Directors for VeriChip with a large bonus and stock options. VeriChip also contributed with a large sum for his campaign when he was thinking of running for President in the 2008 election. Does that sound a little suspicious— like maybe some conflict of interest was going on?

When Thompson was interviewed on television and asked about the safety of the chip, he stated that it is so safe that all Americans should get chipped as a way to be linked to their health records. He also said that VeriChip could be used in the place of military dog tags. He was asked if he would take a chip himself in his arm. He said, "Absolutely, without doubt!" But as of the publishing of this book in 2010, he has yet to be chipped.[346] Does he know something about these chips that he does not want the rest of us to know?

Why is RFID so Important in the Plans for Integration and the New World Order? What better way for those who believe in absolute control and desire to keep a constant "all-seeing eye" upon their subjects at all times and at all places, than with this tiny chip that sends back radioactive signals that can be read and tracked. The tiny chip is capable of holding enormous information about each person, such as: an ID number, bar code, physical description, picture, finger prints, iris scan, name, address, educational background, occupation, books read, movies watched, what the person looks at on internet, his/her every purchase, political party, religious beliefs, health record, and of course, bank transactions and bank account number.

In summary, the RFID can reveal whether or not a person will be a compliant subject for the new world order, or perhaps it is best to put him/her away in a "work camp" or just be eliminated before he or she can influence too many others.

An Additional Warning to Refuse to Take a National ID Card and Any Card Leading the Way to RFID Chip Implants: A friend sent an e-mail message to check out a *You-Tube* video clip. I did and felt that what was portrayed was so important and answers many questions as to the real underground reasons for national ID cards and RFID implants. The video clip tells of Aaron Russo, a film maker, who, at one time, was friends with the Rockefeller family. He was having a conversation with Nickolas, one of the lesser known brothers of the infamous billionaire family. They were talking about the "War on Terror." Nickolas told Aaron that the war on terror was to be an eternal war—with no end to it. "By having this war on terror, you can never win. It can be an eternal war and you can keep taking people's liberties away."

Russo asked, "Why would you want to do that? You have all the money you need, all the power? What is your ultimate goal?"

Rockefeller answered, "The goal is to get everybody in the world chipped with an RFID chip. Then you get all their money and everything else about them on that chip, and if they don't like what we do, we turn off their chip."

The video clip then shows a picture of the Real ID drivers' license and says that this is the first step to getting a bar code on us and eventually an RFID chip onto our cards. The video shows a picture of the new U.S. passports that already has an RFID chip on it, but so tiny, you cannot even feel it.

Monitored, Centralized One-World Economy and Cashless Society: As Nickolas Rockefeller goes on to explain to Russo, "Everybody will be locked into a monitored control grid, a centralized one-world economy." This new system of doing our shopping and financial transactions will be portrayed as so modern, convenient, and secure. Just swipe your right hand over the counter or allow your forehead to be scanned and purchase your goods, do your banking transactions, go through airport security quickly. You won't have to worry about carrying your driver's license, passport, credit cards, or money around with you anymore, or any of it being lost or stolen. Your personal ID number, all the background information about you, your bank account number, how much is in your account, will be on your little chip implanted inside your right hand or inside the top of your forehead. Your wages from your job will go right into your account. You will never see any cash. It will truly become a cashless society. No cash will be printed. Since banks will no longer be places to hold your actual deposits as cash, most of our banks will no longer be needed and can be eliminated.

However, as Rockefeller already warned Russo, somehow the government will have total control over that little chip and the information about you inside it, and if you aren't towing the politically correct line—if you should dare to speak out or write something against the government—they can just "turn off your chip." Your bank account would be wiped clean. You would no longer be able to do any financial transactions or buy any food, clothing, or pay your mortgage. If your boss still wanted you to work for him, he might have his chip turned off too, so he would have no other option but to fire you. Besides, he could not pay you, not "even under the table." There would be no cash with which to do such things. In other words, the government could make it so you essentially no longer exist—all record of you would be wiped clean.

People will be Waiting in Line for the Chips: Because so many people in the United States and other nations are no longer professing to be Christians, are no longer reading their Bibles, they are unaware of the prophecies in the Book of Revelations that warn us against receiving these little "marks" or implants in the right hand or forehead. According to the narrator of the video showing

Nicholas Rockefeller speaking to Aaron Russo, "These chips will not be forced upon them, they will demand them."[347]

Warning About Taking the Chip and World Government from the Book of Revelations: Perhaps the reader has never read the Book of Revelations, the last chapter in the New Testament, especially Chapter 13, 14, and 16, which give us clear warning not to take an implanted chip. Therefore, I am going to quote the specific verses and explain how they pertain to what the government would like to force upon us. These verses are according to the King James version of the Bible:

> *Revelations 13: 16-17: And he [the anti-Christ] causeth all, both small and great, rich and poor, free and bond, to receive a mark in their right hand or in their foreheads; And that no man might buy or sell, save he that had the mark, or the name of the beast, or the number of his name.*

The "Mark" will be Necessary to Buy and Sell: In light of what Nickolas Rockefeller told Aaron Russo about the whole world being "locked into a monitored control grid, a centralized one world economy," and about everyone being forced to have an RFID chip implant for identification and for doing any kind of business, it makes it more understandable and believable what John the Revelator is prophesying. If you do not have that implanted chip, then you will not be able to buy or sell. You will be locked out of the system.

For Convenience or to be Part of the "In" Group: At first, the chips will be promoted as the convenient and "cool" thing to do. Many people, who have not been forewarned, or some who have, but could care less, will fall for the "cool" advertising and get the implants. It is much easier to not have to worry about where a purse or a wallet is, especially if the person is off to a nightclub for an evening of dancing in skimpy, tight-fitting clothes where there are no pockets.

An ad for Verichip, that can be seen on internet, shows pictures of young people at various Baja Beach Clubs in Europe being given the chip in their upper arm. They are all smiling and happy. The clubs are in Barcelona, Spain; Rotterdam, Netherlands; and Glascow, Scotland. Club goers like the idea of not having to carry a wallet or a purse that could be easily lost or stolen. It's much easier to allow their arm to be implanted with an ID chip that contains their name, private ID number, bank account number, etc. When they want to purchase a drink or food, all they have to do is extend their arm for scanning. As the Verichip ad promoting this idea states, "Get chipped, then charge without plastic. You are the card."

The picture and information comes from a religious website that is trying to warn us against falling for this idea. These implants are the "mark of the beast" and will have serious consequences on those who take them. (http://www.ridingthebeast.com/articles/verichip-implant/.)

Somewhere on the chip will be a unique number to identify each person, but that number will also include 666, the number for the beast, to show that you belong to him. The following scriptures are a warning of what will happen to those who take the implanted number:

> *Revelations 14: 9-10: . . . If any man worship the beast and his image, and receive his mark in his forehead, or in his hand, the same shall drink of the wine of the wrath of God, which is poured out without mixture into the cup of his indignation; and he shall be tormented with fire and brimstone in the presence of the holy angels, and in the presence of the Lamb.*

> *Revelations 16:2: . . . and there fell a noisome [foul, or bad smelling] and grievous sore upon the men which had the mark of the beast, and upon them which worshiped his image.*

Could the noisome and grievous sore be describing the cancer that some animals have growing around the RFID chip that is implanted at the back of their necks? Could eventually that same cancer be found growing around the implanted chip in humans? Would this be part of the punishment that will come for accepting the mark of the beast, signifying that the person was willing to pay homage to and worship the anti-Christ?

The Chip Could Also be Implanted Through Deception: People will be told that "the chip has nothing to do with the Mark of the Beast. That is just a silly religious superstition. The chip is for convenience sake, to make life easier for you." Or people could be told "they are not receiving a chip at all." They could be getting a flu shot or some other shot and not even know that the chip has been implanted. With new technology, the chip is so tiny now, even smaller than a grain of rice, that it could be easily slipped into the flu vaccine.

At first, receiving the chip may be voluntary, but after awhile, as the whole world becomes part of the one-world economy and cashless society, you will be told, if you do not receive it, you will not be able to buy or sell, receive medical treatment, receive your social security payment, your job wages. You will no longer be able to do any bank transactions; you will not be able to board a plane;

you will not be able to make payments on your home or pay the utility bill and thus could be evicted. You truly will be locked out of all systems.

However, for a Christian who reads and believes the above verses in Revelations 13 and 14, he will know that by receiving the implant, he is essentially "worshiping the beast" and turning away from and denying his belief in the God of the Bible and his Lord and Savior Jesus Christ. (More is written about this in the chapter about a One-World Religion.)

Obama's Police State—U.S. Placed Under International Police, Interpol, Granted Full Immunity: December 18, 2009, in the middle of the night, with little press coverage, Obama placed the U.S. under the authority of Interpol, an international police organization, based in Paris, France. Obama did this by amending an already existing Executive Order 12425. His amendment grants Interpol full immunity to operate within the U.S. They are thus immune from the reach of our own law enforcement and any oversight of the FBI, and they do not have to respond to any Freedom of Information Act. In other words, there are no checks on their power. Andy McCarthy, of the *National Review*, asks the following questions about this secretive Obama order:

"Why would we elevate an international police force above American law? Why would we immunize an international police force from the limitations that constrain the FBI and other American law-enforcement agencies? Why is it suddenly necessary to have, within the Justice Department, a repository for stashing government files which, therefore, will be beyond the ability of Congress, American law-enforcement, the media, and the American people to scrutinize?"

"At least one answer to these questions is very clear. A coup is underway in the United States of America, the goal of which is to establish complete, unquestioned authority over the citizens, a 'fundamental change' to the United States where citizens have no legal recourse against an authoritarian central government." (Anthony G. Martin, "U.S. Placed Under International Police-State," *Columbia Conservative Examiner*, December 26, 2009.)

The "Panty Bomber" of Christmas Day, 2009, Takes Violation of Privacy Issues to a Whole New Level: Umar Farouk Abdulmutallab is the Muslim Nigerian citizen who attempted to detonate explosives hidden in his underwear on Christmas Day, December 25, 2009, onboard a Northwest Airlines Flight 253, headed for Detroit, Michigan.

It was very strange how Umar, who was actually on a terrorist-watch list, whose father had even warned the CIA about his son's radical terrorist connections, was able to get on the plane with no passport. Some people think this was actually an inside job, that the well-dressed man in the suit who accompanied Umar at the airport in Amsterdam and made up the story that Umar was a political refugee, was really part of some government agency and had clearance to get him on the plane.

Could this have been some ploy with the end result to impose more restrictions and threats to the privacy of airline passengers and their willingness to take it because of elevated security threats? Many people are expressing concerns over the amount of radiation coming from the "electro-magnetic" waves of the scanners. Even though we are told that the amount of radiation is less than a cell phone, still for those who have to fly often, that amount of radiation begins to build up and could cause cancer. Others are expressing concern over the fact that the scanner can see them in their nude, the ultimate in evasion of privacy. We are being told that the face is not seen clearly, but I have seen other pictures where that is not the case. The facial features were very visible. What a perfect job for TSA employees who are hooked on pornography. Now they can be paid for looking at nude pictures.

Could the panty bomber incident be a ploy to get more airports to implement the expensive full-body scanning machines that cost about $250,000 each? Could some government agencies or agents benefit if more of these machines were sold? Many questions need to be answered. (http://www. theprovince.com/ technology/space/Naked+full+body+scans+coming+Canadian+airports+report /2408122/story.html.)

This incident makes the before-mentioned statement by Nicholas Rockefeller to Arron Russo even more believable, that the war on terror will be "an eternal war," so they can "keep taking people's liberties away."

Obama Health Care to Mandate the Use of RFID Chips: I received a phone call from my friend John Spring telling me that the health care bill has a section mandating implantable RFID chips. I then received an e-mail from another friend verifying what John had told me.

On page 1001, Subtitle C - "National Medical Device Registry," it states "The Secretary shall establish a national medical device registry (referred to as "the registry,") to facilitate analysis of postmarket safety and outcomes data on each device that. . . is or has been used in or on a patient. . . "

(2) Effective Date—It tells the date of when this is to be implemented—36 months after the bill is signed into law.

It also states that this will be implemented by the Secretary of Health and Human Services under section 519 (g) of the Federal Food, Drug, and Cosmetic Act, as added by paragraph (1)

And what does 519(g) state? The title alone is enough to let you know what it is all about. It was written, Dec. 10, 2004, "Class II Special Guidance Document:

"Implantable Radiofrequency Transponder System for Patient Identification and Health Information" (A ten-page document can be found at the FDA website --http://www.fda.gov/downloads/MedicalDevices/ DeviceRegulationandGuidance/GuidanceDocuments/ucm07219.pdf.)

I was also sent a You Tube video clip of an ABC Channel 7 news report entitled, "Human ID Chip," with Jay Adlersberg showing how easily the little chip is put into your arm, and how easy it can be scanned and your entire medical history will then appear on their computer.

Dr. John Halamka had a chip put in his right upper arm, because he wants to be assured that in case of an emergency and he might be unconscious, that the doctors would know how best to take care of him. He was quoted as saying, "I am a rock climber and I believe that if I fall off a cliff and you find me unconscious, the comfort knowing that you could scan me and figure out who I am, outweighs my concern for privacy."

The report said that about 80 centers around the country have the device that can detect and read the chip, and they expect many more people to be asking for them. [That will certainly be true now that we know that Obama Care will be mandating them.] (This video clip and other clips on RFID implants can be seen at www,youtube.com/view_play_list?=615A8CDAC8F4CC88.)

In the next chapter you will read about the financial crisis that hit the US and the world in the fall of 2008 and has become far worse in 2009. You will read how the crisis came about, who is really behind it, what the agenda is and what we can do to prepare for even worse times ahead.

Chapter Thirteen

**"The Financial Crisis," America's Central Bank,
Nationalization of Banks and the Auto Industry,
Plans for an Integrated North American Economy,
G-20 Global Summit—A One-World Economy,
World Central Bank and a World Currency**:

*I believe that banking institutions are more dangerous to our liberties
than standing armies. If the American people ever allow private banks
to control the issue of their currency, first by inflation, then by deflation,
the banks and corporations that will grow up around [the banks] will
deprive the people of all property until their children wake-up homeless
on the continent their fathers conquered. The issuing power should be
taken from the banks and restored to the people, to whom it properly
belongs.*

- Thomas Jefferson

"The surest way to overthrow an established social order is to debauch its currency."
(Vladimer Lenin, 1910, one of the founders of the Russian Communist Party
and the Soviet Union).

Could the financial crisis have been part of a plan to bring down our
nation and overthrow a once vibrant economy and free "social order," as Lenin
suggested? In this chapter you will find out that is exactly what has happened.
You will read about that plan and who and what have brought our nation to its
present financial disaster.

Not heeding the above warning of Thomas Jefferson, Congress allowed for
the creation of America's Central Bank, the Federal Reserve. Ever since 1913, our
free enterprise system and competition among banks has slowly morphed into a
centrally planned, no-competition banking system, with the all-powerful "Fed"
exercising total control over the finances of our nation. The economy has been
deliberately depressed, just as that of Europe's has. Over the years, our currency
buys less and less, as the cost of housing, food, oil, gasoline, and transportation
continually goes up in price.

Because of NAFTA and what it has done to the trade of our nation as well as that of Mexico and Canada, most of our textile, manufacturing plants, and steal companies have been closed down or have been outsourced to other countries. Since NAFTA was passed in 1996, we have lost an estimated 3 million jobs. Many family farms have been forced to close. Every day on the news we learn of more people losing their jobs and their homes.

The middle class of our nation is become smaller and smaller, exactly what the goal is as you read in Chapter One. Before going into the crisis, first look at the many statements that have been made asking for an end to national currencies and pushing for a global economic system and currency on page 634 of the last chapter. Could a global financial crisis be the ultimate step forcing such a system on us? Would there first be large political regions established and regional currencies that could then be much more easily brought together into a one world currency?

October-November, 2008, The Financial Crisis—Perfect Timing—Just Before the Presidential Election: In the fall of 2008, came the financial crisis, supposedly caused by high risky mortgage lending. Hundreds of thousands of Americans were losing their homes, and many banks, that had lent them the mortgages, were going under. As has already been mentioned, the timing could not have been more perfect. The polls were starting to go up for McCain once he selected Sarah Palin as his running mate. But once the financial crisis hit and Obama began to blame it on Bush, saying that McCain would just do more of the same, then Obama's poll ratings began to go up again, and he won the November Presidential election. It was still not a landslide victory. He only won by 53%.

"Bailout" or Nationalization of US Banks, AIG, Auto Industries: In October, 2008, Congress passed TARP, a $700 billion "bailout" of our nation's major banks, insurance companies, and two of our biggest auto industries. This was no bailout; this was the beginning stages of a take over, a nationalization of all of the above, implementing or fascism, or socialism, even progressing to communism. No one seems to understand these forms of government any more. They no longer are taught in our public schools or universities, at least not the way they should be, using their true definitions. Let me define them according to the *Thorndike Barnhart Dictionary, Webster's New Dictionary* and the *World Book Dictionary.*

The Definition of Fascism—*Thorndike Barnhart* states, "Any system of government in which property is privately owned, but all industries and business are highly regulated by a strong national government." *Webster's New Dictionary* gives the definition as, "A system of government characterized by dictatorship, belligerent nationalism and racism, militarism, etc." The *World Book* adds labor to the list that is regulated and includes these comments, "all opposition is rigorously suppressed." It is usually headed by a dictatorial leader.

The Definition of Socialism—*Thorndike Barnhart* and *Websters* gave similar definitions: "A theory or system of ownership of the means of production and distribution by society rather than by individuals." *World Book* added, "a theory or system of social organization by which the major means of production and distribution are owned, managed, or controlled by the government (state socialism), by associations of workers, (guild socialism), or by the community as a whole. "A system of social organization by which the major means of production and distribution are owned, managed, or controlled by the government." How does socialism differ from communism? Not by much.

The Definition of Communism—Thorndike Barnhart states, "A system by which the means of production and distribution are owned and managed by government, and the goods produced are shared by all the citizens." Such a definition does not sound so bad, does it? It sounds like just what a loving, benevolent, sharing society would want. This is what most of our public schools and universities are teaching about communism. There is nothing taught about the oppression, the lack of property rights, the lack of freedoms and basic rights. The "sharing" is only sharing in poverty. The wealth goes to the dictatorial leaders and their minions who support them and keep them in power.

There is also nothing that is taught about the millions of people who have been killed by their own evil rulers, such as Stalin in Russia and Mao Tse- Tung in China.

New Websters makes communism sound even better. It states, "Any theory or system of common ownership of property." However, it also gives a second meaning, "2. socialism as formulated by Marx, Lenin, etc. In other words, socialism and communism are pretty close.

At least the *World Book* gives a little bit more truthful view of communism: "A political, social, and economic system in which the state, governed by an elite party, controls production, labor, distribution, and largely the social and cultural life and thoughts of the people."

Fascism, Socialism, and Communism all Seek the Same End: The *World Book* goes on to say, "The classic difference between the systems lies in the different means they take to establish themselves." Communism uses armed forces or outside intervention; socialism uses more peaceful means, through elections and legislation. Thus communism is on fast track; fascism and socialism are slower methods, but they essentially want the same end results—that of total nationalization and control of property, the economy, production and industry and the enslavement of the people.[348]

I will leave it up to the reader to decide which system we are coming closer to. It is definitely no longer the free-enterprise system, where people actually had the freedom to do with their property what they wanted to, and put their goods and services on a free market, with very little regulation or none at all. In Chapter Fourteen, you will learn more about these systems as they are being implemented by Obama.

How Did the Financial Crisis Happen? The History of "Sub-Prime Borrowing": There are many different groups, financial lending banks and US Presidents, who have played a part in causing the crisis. The real culprit, however, is the Federal Reserve.

This chapter traces the history leading up to the financial crisis and shows that none of this has happened by chance. It has been carefully planned over many years and incrementally manipulated.

Most people like to blame the financial crisis on the Bush administration. Yes, he is partly to blame, but the history of sub-prime borrowing goes back to the big government-administrations of Jimmy Carter and Bill Clinton. Carter signed into law the Community Reinvestment Act of 1977. Before this time, banks followed the sound fiscal policy of only loaning money for mortgages to people who could at least pay 20% of the home purchase price. Jimmy Carter helped promote the "politically correct line" that banks were "redlining" loans for inner-city neighborhoods, refusing to help the poor buy homes. The CRA declared that banks have "an affirmative obligation" to meet the credit needs of the communities in which they are chartered. Federal regulators would then rate the banks on this basis when merger requests were filed. "The CRA rating became more important to banks than the quality of their loans. In fact, sound lending practices were considered to be racist."[349]

Under Presidents Reagan and Bush Sr., the Community Reinvestment Act was essentially ignored and not promoted. However, under Bill Clinton, tougher CRA ratings were issued in 1995. Banks had to demonstrate that they were investing more money in the poor, higher risk neighborhoods if they wanted to merge.

ACORN's Influence: ACORN is a very left-leaning organization, inspired by socialist/communist radical Saul Alinsky and got its start back in the 1970s during Carter's administration. Its purpose is to promote all sorts of social justice issues such as getting more poor and underprivileged on the voting records and into public housing. ACORN stands for "Association of Community Organization for Reform Now." ACORN agitators prided themselves in making sure mortgages were given to the poor, those who had no or very bad credit and no means to pay. ACORN helped launch the terms "sub-prime and alternative loans." Sub-prime mortgages are made to people who have bad credit history and alternative loans are made without any verification that the borrowers earn a decent income, have assets or even hold a job.

Freddie Mack and Fannie Mae's Role in the Crisis: Fannie Mae was started back in the 1930s under FDR's "New Deal" to provide banks with money to lend for mortgages. Its real name is the Federal National Mortgage Association. Freddie Mack was created in 1970 so Fannie Mae would not have a monopoly. They have marched in concert with each other ever since. Since they are both chartered by the government as GSEs (government-sponsored enterprises), it was assumed that they would have a guarantee forever by the federal government and could not go under.

A massive swindle began taking place through Fannie Mae and Freddie Mack in the name of profits. Their government handlers told their directors, Franklin Raines and Jim Johnson, to record profits, growth, and success no matter how risky. So they did. They bought up loans, no matter what quality, just to show them on the books. For awhile they had a trillion and a half dollars in assets. However, their combined debt was also in the trillions.

AIG and How European Banks Got Involved: AIG, supposedly the most credible insurance company in the world, was making what Fannie Mae and Freddie Mack were doing seem legitimate. It was offering unregulated insurance contracts, known as credit default swaps. AIG wrote a policy that guaranteed the sub-prime loan for the bank against default for five years. Since these contracts were "unregulated," AIG did not have to put up any capital as collateral on its swaps, as long as it maintained a triple-A credit rating. European banks especially liked these swaps, since they could maximize the spread between what they must pay for deposits and what they could earn by lending. Since, throughout history, prior to all this insanity, few loans had ever defaulted, the European banks were able to assure its regulators it was holding only Triple A credits. AIG was able to post hundreds of millions of dollars in profits that only existed on paper, while never having to post any collateral. Analysist Porter Stansberry reports, "An enormous amount of capital was created out of thin air and tossed into global real estate markets."[350]

Other Banks Got In On the Fraud: Lehman Brothers, Goldman Sacs, Merrill Lynch, Bear Stears, Washington Mutual, City Bank and so many more banks also followed the example of the Fannie Mae and Freddie Mack.

The Massive Bubble Was Helped by Low Interest Rates: Interest rates were hard for the poor to pay, so they were lowered as well. For awhile it took less cash to buy a house than to rent an apartment. Everyone was encouraged to buy a home. The stock market soared as the housing industry recorded record profits. It formed a massive bubble, all the way to 14,000 points.

Warnings Issued: This is what was said by Republican Representative Richard Baker of Louisiana, who chaired the House subcommittee overseeing Fannie and Freddie: "The taxpayers are living under an enormous rock suspended by a single rope. Once it breaks, there's no recovery." The *Economist* publication labeled Fannie and Freddie "arguably the most worrying concentrations of risk in the global financial system." "The *Wall Street Journal* editorial board likened Fannie and Freddie to failed energy trader Enron, attacking the two companies' exploding debt and "terrible" financial disclosure. Risk managers, hired by Freddie Mack and Fannie Mae, raised warnings about the dangers of investing in the sub-prime and alternative mortgage markets. But the warnings were ignored. (Taking these risks, however, had proved very lucrative for the CEOs of Fannie Mae and Freddie Mack. They made over $30 million between 2003 and 2007. Two prior CEOs, Franklin Raines and Leland Brendsel, were fired several years ago over accounting scandals. Later CEOs, Daniel Mudd and Richard Syron, were fired in September, 2008. They all knew that the train was going to crash, but they did nothing to stop it. Did any of them have to give their millions of income back? No, of course not. That would be too unreasonable.

The Bubble Had to Eventually Pop, the Chickens Had to Come Home to Roost, the House of Cards Had to Come Tumbling Down: Most economists understood that the financial real estate lending bubble, the huge rise in the stock market and the rise in consumer debt, would some day have to burst, that there would have to be a day of reckoning. It could not just go on and on. That day finally came and the chickens came home to roost, mainly during the years of 2007 and 2008.

The Federal Reserve decided to raise the interest rates "to reverse the inflation it had caused by flooding the market with worthless paper money." (That was the reason they gave.) There was also a huge rise in gas prices, sometimes doubling what people used to have to pay. Trucking firms had to increase costs; grocery costs went up; other companies failed; more jobs were lost. People who lost those jobs were already in great debt and had no money set aside to sustain job loss.

Just like a domino effect, the rise in interest rates raised the loan payments on mortgages; the sub-prime borrowers, who had no money in the first place, began to default on their loans. Banks, that were going under, looked to AIG to honor its insurance policies. But AIG had no money to repair the damages. And so, AIG, the world's largest insurance company, was suddenly downgraded by all the major credit-rating agencies, and AIG was ready to file bankruptcy. One by one, other banks were following suit. Freddie Mack and Fannie Mae lost $12 billion. Together they owned or guaranteed about $11.5 trillion in home loan debt nation-wide. Traditionally, they had backed 30-year fixed rate mortgages, among the safest of loans, before standards were lowered.

What Happened to Lehman Brothers? The same thing was happening to Lehman Brothers as other banks. They had huge debt on their balance sheets, $5.4 billion, and the assets that were supposed to balance the debt were becoming worthless with the rising default rate and the drop in housing prices. The banks had to pay interest on that debt, but they did not have the corresponding cash flow to be able to pay the debt. Lehman, for example, only had $2.3 billion in income. One writer, who is suspected of being a Lehman Brothers' employee, but wishes to remain anonymous, explains it very well in the following:

> When you can't pay your debt obligations, that's called being insolvent. Many people think that bankruptcy is caused by having more liabilities than assets, but that's not true. It's caused when you can't make good on your debts, so the repo [repossess] man comes and claims your assets in order to make up for it. When that happens, you have to file for bankruptcy in order to make sure that people get paid in the correct order, because otherwise different creditors are going to be suing you to make sure they get what you owe them.[351]

For some reason, Lehman Brothers was allowed to fail, to go bankrupt while other banks were allowed to be taken over by other banks or were given bail out money. Was it their own choice, or were they being used as an example of the downfall of the Free Enterprise System or to frighten other banks into being compliant?

Was Lehman Brothers the Sacrificial Lamb Used To Frighten Other Banks into Taking the Bailout Money? Attorney and author Ellen Brown asked the question in the title of an article she wrote September 7, 2009, "Economic 9/11, Did Lehman Brothers Fall or was it Pushed?" She quotes from a book by Larry McDonald, *A Colossal Failure of Common Sense,* which was published in July, 2009. He believes Lehman Brothers was not in substantially worse shape than other major Wall Street banks. He says Lehman was just "put to sleep." Why? Those plotting the financial crisis and the nationalization of major banks needed a sacrificial lamb to make all the other banks fall in line and accept the bailout money.

As the article points out, not only did this happen to Lehman Brothers, but it had also happened to a British bank exactly on the same day the year before, September 11, 2007. Northern Rock was the UK's fifth largest mortgage lender but it was allowed to fail. Chancellor Alistar Darling had something to do with both situations. He was supposed to be the one that would help Lehman Brothers but delayed until it was too late and then backed out. He had done the same thing with Northern Rock, with the same result.

> " . . . the bankruptcy of Northern Rock changed the rules of the game. Britain's major banks too would now be saved at any cost, in order to avoid the loss of customer confidence, panic and bank runs that could precipitate a 1929-style market crash."

Even the Judge who presided at the bankruptcy proceedings of Lehman Brothers, believed Lehman Brothers "did not just fall over the brink but was pushed." Judge James Peck said, "Lehman Brothers became a victim, in effect *the only true icon to fall* in a tsunami that has befallen the credit markets."

Who Was Behind the Sacrifice of Lehman Brothers? Some critics point to Henry Paulson and his cohorts at Goldman Sachs, Lehman's arch rival. Goldman certainly benefited by Lehman's demise. But there were others who were involved as well, more global players. The month after Lehman collapsed, Gordon Brown and the EU leaders called for using the financial crisis as an opportunity to radically enhance the regulatory power of global institutions. Brown spoke of "a new global financial order," restating what David Rockefeller said in 1994: *"We are on the verge of a global transformation. All we need is the right major crisis and the nations will accept the new world order."*

Richard Haas, President of the CFR, also stated in 2006: *"Globalization . . . implies that sovereignty is not only becoming weaker in reality, but that it needs to become weaker."* So, in other words, let's give sovereignty a little shove in the right direction to hurry its demise with "the right major crisis."

Gordon Brown put it like this: *"Sometimes it takes a crisis for people to agree that what is obvious and should have been done years ago, can no longer be postponed . . . We must create a new international financial architecture for the global age."*

The Collapse of Lehman Brothers Was the Perfect Crisis and "Shock Therapy" to Precipitate the Bail Outs: Representative Paul Kanjorski spoke on C-SPAN in January, 2009, and announced that the collapse of Lehman Brothers back on September 11, 2008, had precipitated a *$550 billion* run on the money market funds on Thursday, September 18.

This was the dire news that Treasury Secretary Henry Paulson presented to Congress behind closed doors, and despite their "deep misgivings" Congress approved of Paulson's $700 billion bank bailout. It was the needed "shock therapy" discussed by Naomi Klein in her book *The Shock Doctrine*, in which "a major crisis prompts hasty emergency action involving the relinquishment of rights or funds that would otherwise be difficult to pry loose from the citizenry."

April 2009—G20 Summit: Gordon Brown and Alistair Darling hosted the G20 summit in London, with the primary focus on the financial crisis. An "international Financial Stability Board" was established with a global regulator, to be based in the "controversial" Bank for International Settlements in Basel, Switzerland. A global currency was discussed and approved.

Columnist Ellen Brown states: "The international bankers who caused the financial crisis are indeed capitalizing on it, consolidating their power in 'a new global financial order' that gives them top-down global control."[352]

The Blame Placed on the Free Enterprise System and Not Enough Regulations: Amazingly, the system that has kept our nation free and out of bondage and helped us to have (at one time) the strongest economy in the world is now what is blamed for the financial crisis. Even Greenspan and President Bush both blamed the free enterprise system as the culprit and said that there was not enough government regulation. My, how politicians love to twist things! We haven't had a true free enterprise system in operation for many years now. If we did, none of this would have happened. We have had a central planned economy/socialistic system, with high regulations that did not allow for a free market or free economy. That is what NAFTA was all about, too many regulations, which caused the loss of 3 million jobs. (Now, because of the financial crisis and Obama's socialist policies, several million more people have lost their jobs.)

The Three Rs now Missing in our Nation: According to an excellent editorial in the *Wall Street Journal* by Dan Henninger, it is not deregulation or the free-market system that is too blame. It is the missing three Rs that our nation used to have in its business dealings, as well as what guided Americans every-day lives: Those Rs are: responsibility, restraint and remorse. They are the ballast that stabilizes the free market system with its risk and reward. Why are these missing from our nation? Henniger believes it is because of another R that is disappearing, that of religion, which kept us with some sense of morals and conscience, which kept us more willing to follow rules and guidelines. Henninger states:

"Responsibility and restraint are moral sentiments. Remorse is a product of conscience. None of these grow on trees. Each must be learned, taught, passed down . . . It has been my view that the steady secularizing and insistent effort at dereligioning America has been dangerous. That danger flashed red in the fall into subprime personal behavior by borrowers and bankers, who after all are just people. Northerners and atheists who vilify Southern evangelicals are throwing out nurturers of useful virtue with the bathwater of obnoxious political opinions.

The point for a healthy society of commerce and politics is not that religion saves, but that it keeps most of the players inside the chalk lines. We are erasing the chalk lines . . . Get ready for Mad Max."[353]

President Bush and Congress Erased the Chalk Lines: What did President Bush and Congress do about the Financial Crisis? Did they let natural consequences happen so these financial institutions could accept their responsibility, exercise restraint, show remorse, go bankrupt, restructure, right themselves and start again? No, of course not. That was not the objective.

October 3, 2008—TARP, Troubled Asset Relief Program, Was Passed: Bush called for an emergency session and congress voted to "bail out" these banks and institutions to the tune of $700 billion. They were all "too big to fail." "A terrible domino effect would happen if they were allowed to fail." A new office of Financial Stability was created under the Department of the Treasury to manage TARP. Freddie Mack and Fannie Mae were immediately given $100 billion each and essentially "nationalized" by the federal government. Already $350 billion had been spent, but still many banks were in danger of failing. So another $750 billion was added to the second half of TARP, adding up to $1.1 trillion of taxpayer dollars going out the door.[354]

Was any talk of responsibility, restraint or remorse asked of the CEOs? The CEOs were asked to appear before a House Oversight Committee and were given a bawling out mainly by Chairman Henry Waxman, but they received no other punishment.[355]

No Lessons Learned: According to Tom DeWeese, the same old failed policies are now proceeding with Fannie Mae and Freddie Mack. The new government handlers are demanding the same "show a profit on the books" no matter what, which can only result in taking more bad loans.[356]

Who is Really Bailing Out Whom? In spite of the nice name being used of a "bailout," it is really a take over, a nationalization of our financial institutions by the federal government with a financial czar appointed to be in charge. And who is really doing the bailing out? The American tax payer. We are left holding the bag. According to former talk show host, Lou Dobbs, on his December 17,

2008, radio show, because of this bailout, the estimated debt each American will be carrying as soon as he is born into this country is $40,000. Yet, we have no say in the matter. Isn't that kind of like "taxation without representation?" (After the passage of Obama's Stimulus Bill, putting our nation into another $785 billion debt, of course, Dobb's estimate is now more than doubled. Everyone will now be born with close to $100,000 debt hanging around his neck.)

Where Does the Money Come From? How could we suddenly come up with another $787 billion when our nation is trillions of dollars already in debt? The Federal Reserve comes to the rescue and does what it has done before and what it was designed to do. It authorizes the printing of vast sums of fiat paper money, or with modern technology, it creates the sum with a stroke of a finger on the computer. Either way the money is pulled down from the sky and is essentially worthless, backed up by nothing. Years ago, we were taken off any gold or silver standard, that used to back up our currency and gave the paper dollars value. What the Fed is doing is creating enormous inflation and a greatly depressed value to the dollar.

We can look to the example of Weimar Germany after World War I to see what happens when currency is mass produced and hyperinflation sets in. Germany had enormous war debts to pay off after World War I. To pay those debts, the Weimar government mass printed German marks, greatly devaluing them to almost nothing.

It took a wheelbarrow full of money to buy a loaf of bread. If people did not have their own gardens or source of food, they starved to death.

Who is Ultimately Behind this Crisis? As has been mentioned, lots of fingers are in the financial crisis pie, but ultimately the blame should be laid at the feet of the "benevolent organization," who is supposedly there to solve all financial woes—The Federal Reserve. "The Fed" (the nickname by which it has "affectionately" come to be known) is neither federal, nor a reserve. It is a secretive "international cartel of wealthy bankers," whose purpose was, from its beginning in 1913, to do away with competition among banks, to create a monopoly, and to create a central bank for our nation as well as to encourage the same for all other nations. That is exactly what the Federal Reserve is—a Central Bank, but the bankers got away with their plan by disguising themselves under the cloak of a nice-sounding name, "the Federal Reserve." All other U.S. banks are under their control.

A Clever Scheme to Shift the Losses from the Owners of the Banks to the Tax Payers: The schemers who created the Federal Reserve designed the amazing new "smoke and mirrors magic show." The federal government's role was to be an agent shifting the inevitable losses from the owners of the banks to the taxpayers. Over the years, Congress has given the Federal Reserve the power to control the entire monetary system of the United States. And what is interesting, the Fed has never had a real outside audit. No one seems to have power over them to oversee what they are doing. The only power the President has is to appoint a new chairman of the Federal Reserve every 14 years.

We Can See How Successful the Control by the Fed has Been: They have taken our nation off from the gold and silver standard, thereby being able to create fiat money out of thin air with no real value backing it; they have increased government control and intervention of the housing industry; stifled the free-market in residential real estate; caused the resulting crisis in the S&L industry; and the bailout of that industry with money taken from the taxpayer. This game called "bailout" had already happened with the Penn Central Railroad, Lockheed, New York City, Chrysler, Commonwealth Bank of Detroit, First Pennsylvania Bank, Continental Illinois, Long Term Capital Management, BCCI, Bear Stearns and President Bush's gigantic bailouts with the TARP bill of $700 billion to a wide variety of banks and lending agencies, and who knows where else the TARP money went, and where the Stimulus money for an additional $787 billion has gone? There is not a lot of accountability attached to the "bailout game." Even though most of the major banks were having serious financial problems and had lost billions, they were not allowed to fail, file bankruptcy or restructure. They were instead rewarded for their incompetence. Of course, the bailouts always have massive strings attached. The banks will now be highly regulated by the federal government. Essentially, they have become nationalized.

The Secret Meeting of Bankers Who Created the Federal Reserve: Back in 1910, representatives from some of the top banks, met secretly at a private resort owned by J.P. Morgan on Jekyll Island—off the coast of Georgia, and devised the creative scheme for the Federal Reserve (our American version of a central bank): The banks who were involved in the creation of the Federal Reserve were: Kuhn-Loeb, National City Bank, First National Bank, Bankers Trust, Guaranty Trust and J. P. Morgan. Many of these same banks are involved in today's credit crunch.

It is also interesting to find out that former British Prime Minister Tony Blair has now joined JP Morgan as a senior advisor. JP Morgan is closely associated with the Rothschild's, who are the originators of the concept of central banking and own vast interests in central banks around the globe.

How the Federal Reserve Bill Got the Support of Congress: The powerful bankers who met at Jekyll Island and created the plans for the Federal Reserve knew that they could not get it passed in Congress if people knew that bankers were the ones who designed it. They could not let the people know that what they were creating was a powerful central bank that would control the economy of the nation and exercise enormous control over all the other banks.

So how did they hide their plans from the American people and from Congress? They avoided any reference to a "Central Bank." They came up with the creative name of "Federal Reserve" and pretended that its purpose would be to highly regulate the big banks and not allow them to have a monopoly over the other banks. It would also stop the "busts and booms" that had happened over the years and make sure there could never be a big run on the banks, nor could there ever be a big "depression."

To make the American people fall for their hoax, they pretended to wage a war against the top powerful bankers, and those "bankers" (who were really themselves) waged a war back. Articles appeared in the major newspapers written by the bankers against the Federal Reserve legislation. This quieted the fears of the people and Congress. They thought the Fed must be a good thing if the bankers were against it, and it was passed.[356]

The Five Objectives of the Federal Reserve: According to G. Edward Griffin, author of *Creature from Jekyll Island*, the goals of the powerful cartel who created the Fed were the following: 1) stop the growing competition from the nation's newer banks; 2) obtain a franchise to create money out of nothing for the purpose of lending; [To do this the Fed had to get our nation off the gold and silver standard, which used to be necessary to establish the worth of the currency]; 3) get control of the reserves of all banks so that the more reckless ones would not be exposed to currency drains and bank runs; 4) get the taxpayer to pick up the cartel's inevitable losses; and 5) convince Congress that the purpose was to protect the public. (p. 23)

Global Monetary Links and Global Crisis: Because the Federal Reserve is an international cartel, and because the U.S. is linked to the IMF, the international monetary fund (as all nations are), what is going on in our financial crisis is, of course, affecting all other banks and nations. The world has already been integrated economically, from national accounting rules, clearing and settlement, and regulatory laws to global accounting rules, systems, and regulatory laws.

Global crises are now possible because the barriers between all the nation-states have been torn down: the economic, financial, political, trade, legal, and intelligence barriers. Now it is possible to bring down the value of all the stock exchanges at once instead of one at a time. Think how expedient that is for those who are in positions of this kind of power? No longer will any one government have any type of power to stop them!

The Income Tax Passed Shortly After the Federal Reserve: Both the Federal Reserve and the Income Tax were passed the same year of 1913. Both were never anything our Founding Fathers intended for our nation. Our Founders did not want us to have a central bank, for they knew that gave the government too much central control over money, inflation and interest rates and destroyed competition, the basis of the free enterprise system.

Nor did the Founding Fathers want us to have a federal income tax. Before 1913, our nation received what it needed for funding by tariffs on trade and sales taxes, and we were doing fine with little national debt.

Where did the idea come from for a central bank and a federal income tax? It is straight out of the Ten Planks of the Communist Manifesto: #2 "A heavy progressive or graduated income tax" and #5 "Centralization of credit in the hands of the State, by means of a national bank with State Capital and exclusive monopoly."

Senator Nelson Aldrich, from Rhode Island, was one of the most powerful men in Washington D.C., was the political spokesman for Wall Street and the father-in-law of John D. Rockefeller. It was on board his private railway car that all the creators of the Federal Reserve were transported to Jekyll Island. Senator Aldrich was the one who authored the bill that became the Federal Reserve Act.

Aldrich was also the author of the bill that became the 16th Amendment that "authorized" the income tax. There was a sneaky vote that happened late on Christmas eve when many people had already left for home. (It sounds like the same tactics have been repeated since with so many presidents getting controversial legislation passed.)[357]

As you will read below, the Federal Reserve and the Income Tax need each other to work effectively as a "mechanism for control over the economic and social life of society."

How the Federal Reserve and the Income Tax Work Together: The following was sent by a friend and amazing researcher Vicky Davis:

> Boiling it down to the essence, the Federal Reserve Act provided an open line of credit to the U.S. government. A consortium of banks provided the initial capital in exchange for being able to print and control the value of the currency by controlling the quantity in circulation.
>
> Taken together, it's easy to see that the income tax was the collateral for the open line of credit provided by the Federal Reserve Banks and the International Banksters. The system of federal financing

by tariffs wasn't in the interest of these Internationalists because it gave them no leverage to steal the fruits of American productivity and wealth. A tax on domestic labor and business was the method of turning the American people into chattel—beasts of burden to repay the debt. (Vicky Davis, eyeswideopen@yahoo.com., Sept. 21, 2009.)

Quotes about the Dishonesty, Corruption, and Abuse of Power of the Federal Reserve: The following quotes are by people who were in government and saw for themselves what the Fed was planning and doing:

> *The financial system has been turned over to the Federal Reserve Board. That board administers a finance system by authority of a purely profiteering group. That system is private, conducted for the sole purpose of obtaining the greatest possible profits from the use of other people's money. This (Federal Reserve) Act establishes the most gigantic trust on Earth. When the president signs the bill, the invisible governments by the monetary power will be legalized. The people may not know it immediately, but the day of reckoning is only a few years removed, the worst legislatives crime of the ages perpetrated by this banking bill . . . From now on, depressions will be scientifically created.* (spoken in 1922)
>
>   *. . . Under the Federal Reserve Act, panics are scientifically created; the present panic is the first scientifically created one, worked out as we figure a mathematical problem.* (spoken in 1923 by Minnesota Congressman Charles A. Lindbergh, the father of the famous pilot.)[358]

> *We have in this country, one of the most corrupt institutions the world has ever known. I refer to the Federal Reserve Board. This evil institution has impoverished the people of the United States and has practically bankrupted our government. It has done this through the corrupt practices of the moneyed vultures who control it.* (Congressman Louis T. McFadden, Chair of the House Banking Committee, 1932)[359]

> *Most Americans have no real understanding of the operations of the international money lenders. The accounts of the Federal Reserve have never been audited. It operates outside the control of Congress and manipulates the credit of the United States.* (Senator Barry Goldwater, Republican from Arizona)[360]

Institutionalized Usury: G. Edward Griffin adds, *"Charging interest on pretended loans is usury, and that has become institutionalized under the Federal Reserve. . . Modern money is a grand illusion conjured by the magicians of finance and politics. We are living in an age of fiat money, and it is sobering to realize that every previous nation in history that has adopted such money eventually was economically destroyed by it."*[361]

December, 2008—Nationalization of Nation's Auto Industries: The current heads of Detroit's Big Three automakers appeared twice before Congress asking for bailouts to the tune of $25 billion. Later they asked for $34 billion. They first arrived in their private jets, costing an enormous amount of money to their companies. Because of much criticism by the media, their second time appearing before Congress they came by car, costing much less. They also were willing to compromise for a $15 billion proposal instead.

This time at least the majority of Senators voted no. They believed that natural consequences should take place. Let the companies go bankrupt and reorganize and get rid of their debt themselves. Let them get rid of the heavy influence of the labor unions on the car manufacturing and the huge compensation plans for retired workers. Some Senators agreed with their constituents, "Why should all tax payers have to suffer because of someone else's negligence?"

December 19, 2008, President Bush decided to bypass the Senate and approved the bailout himself by Executive Order, with very little fan fair or opposition. Bush gave the auto industries $17.4 billion "in assistance" with a few requirements such as: auto workers must agree to lower wage and benefit concessions that will bring them in line to nonunion workers. However, executives don't have to cut their big salaries, nor do they have to stop the outsourcing of jobs overseas.

Nobody seemed to ask if Bush had the authority to do such a thing, nor to question if all this is Constitutional? Is anything written in the Constitution that the federal government should be bailing out anyone or nationalizing banks and companies?" No! However, as already mentioned, nationalization is written in Objective 39 of the globalists who created the Gomberg map and "abolition of property" is #1 of the Ten Planks of the *Communist Manifesto*. Number 5 states "centralization of credit in the hands of the State, by means of a national bank with State capital and an exclusive monopoly." Doesn't that sound like what has happened with the takeover of our banks?

Did the Nationalization (or Bailout) Help? Rush Limbaugh's radio program mentioned December 17, 2008, that 3 million industrial jobs are now gone from America. According to the *Washington Times*, November produced another

553,000 layoffs and in their report of December 15, the unemployment rate rose to 6.7%, the highest it had been in decades. (In California, unemployment rose to—8.4%) People filing for unemployment benefits rose to the highest in 26 years. The average American has $8,000 credit card debt. More homes were foreclosed. One in 10 American families were on food stamps.

NBC radio reported December 24, 2008, that there was a five-month long decline in personal spending—the greatest drop in 50 years. It was a bleak Christmas for most shops and businesses. It was also predicted that many would be going out of business in the new year. (That prediction came true. Every month, we heard of more businesses going under and hundreds of thousands of employees being laid off.)

One would think that President Obama would have learned something from Bush's TARP bill, how putting out nation into such enormous debt does not help the economy and does not work, and he would have not tried to duplicate it.

However, what if these insider presidents and those behind them, who are giving them their marching orders, have a different agenda for our nation? What if they deliberately want to bring down the economy even more; they want to nationalize even more industries, they want to put the American people into even greater debt, destroy jobs, destroy the middle class, and give the international bankers even more billions in interest on our loans, then the TARP bill was a great success, and we need something similar to it. That is exactly what Obama came up with.

2009, February 17—Obama's Stimulus Plan for $787 Billion, "American Recovery and Reinvestment Act of 2009, was Signed into Law: During the first month of Obama's Presidency, he continued to use "fear tactics" about the economy (mentioning the word "crisis" and "catastrophe" 25 times in one speech). He used doom and gloom and promised worse conditions, more loss of jobs, more loss of homes, if his Stimulus bill did not pass. And Congress buckled to all those fear tactics and did pass the 1,071 page-bill by a vote of 246-183 in the House and 60-38 in the Senate, with all Republicans except for 3 Senators voting against it.

Four days later Obama and Joe Biden flew to Denver, Colorado, to sign the bill into law. They first toured the Museum of Nature and Science's solar panel installation project. Before the crowd assembled to watch him sign the bill, Obama said, "The stimulus plan would help create up to a half a million so-called "green" jobs in the field of alternative energy and investments that will have long-term growth." (Of course, Obama did not tell us of the jobs that would be lost and millions of people layed off, which happened, in total contradiction of what Obama had promised with his Stimulus Bill.)

No newspaper article mentioned the huge amount of energy and its cost that Obama used up flying with members of his cabinet to Denver on Airforce One and that of Joe Biden who always has to fly on a separate plane.

On Glenn Beck's radio show that morning, Beck mentioned that it would take 10,000 gallons of jet fuel to fly to Denver from Washington D.C. for both planes, costing $20,000 an hour x 2 = $40,000 an hour. The trip would take 4 hours, costing $160,000 x2 = $360,000. All that to just go sign a bill? Just think how many green jobs or regular jobs that could have been created and salaries paid with that kind of money! (*Reuters*, San Francisco, Dec. 18, and the Glen Beck Show, Feb. 17, *www.GlenBeck.com.*)

The Federal Government is now in the Auto Business: Were the auto dealers helped by the big bailouts given to them by the Bush administration? Obviously not. They had to come with open hands asking for more from President Obama. As has already been mentioned, "bailouts means nationalization."

Some people are saying that "GM now stands for Government Motors." According to a news report May 31, 2009, the day before the big hearing about bankruptcy and reorganization of General Motors, 70% of GM would now be owned by the federal government. Over 400 franchises were being forced to close, with the car dealers left holding the cars.

What is very remarkable about the closing of the franchises—the one thing that the companies "chosen" to be shut down had in common was—they all supported McCain in the election with sizable funds. Those who supported Obama were allowed to stay open. Amazing what happens when government now runs companies, isn't it?

Brian Sussman of KSFO Radio in San Francisco reported on his June 1, 2009 broadcast that 789 Chrysler dealerships were being shut down. Ninety percent of them were owned by people who gave substantial amounts to Republican candidates including McCain. The first franchise that was told it had to close was owned by Vernon Buchanan, a Republican Congressman from Florida. He gave $2300 to McCain and has given $150,000 to GOP candidates since 2007.[362]

Student Loans Nationalized: Now that many of our banks have been nationalized, the auto industry has essentially been taken over, what other industries will follow suit? In September, 2009, I heard that Congress was considering a bill saying that the federal government would be the only organization able to give out student loans. According to Congressman Michele Bachmann, that is exactly the case. In a blog she posted, September 17, "Government to take over all student loans," she wrote:

> Today, the House will complete consideration of the Student Aid and Fiscal Responsibility Act of 2009, otherwise known as the public option for higher education (not to be confused with the public option for health care—but the similarities can't be overlooked). Advocates like the President maintain that if passed, this bill will bring a "level playing field" between government and private options. Sound familiar? However, history tells us that when it's all said and done, the only one left standing on the "level" playing field tends to be the government.
>
> Ending private sector competition in the student loan industry and making the Direct Loan program the sole provider will kill jobs, and greatly expand the control of the federal government. The Federal Family Education Loans (FFEL) program has been the overwhelming choice for student and parents for the past 40 years. In fact, 78% of all new federal student loans from 2007-2008 were administered through this program. Yet, the government wants to end it. It doesn't make any sense. If nothing else, this bill tells us one thing—if the government can't succeed on its own merits, they'll eliminate the competition. That should concern us all.[363]

Student Loans Snuck in as Part of the Health Care Bill: Perhaps, Obama and supporters of the student loan bill knew that it would not pass on its own, so guess where it ended up? It was snuck into the final version of the health care bill before its March 21 vote.

Obama and his accomplices gave a sort of exclusive "franchise" to a bank in North Dakota. It will be the only bank that will be allowed to handle the student loans. That was the way that they could bribe and win over one more vote for the bill coming from Senator Kent Conrad, who chairs the Senate Budget Committee, through which any reconciliation bill must pass. Of course, with this new bribe, he voted yes on the bill and was very helpful in supporting it.

Costs Could Rise and Only Politically Correct Students Will Receive Student Loans? If the federal government is in charge of student loans, all competition will stop, and the prices for those loans could be raised to whatever the government wants. Having seen what the Obama administration did with the auto industry—closing down first the franchises that did not vote for him—some of us are a little concerned that the same thing could happen to our students. Those who voted against him, or have donated money to the Republican party, or have written or vocally expressed their opposition to Obama and his policies, could be denied student loans.

The Health Industry: Obama's chief prize to nationalize was the health industry. Of course, he and his administration are not calling it nationalizing, nor are they calling it socialized medicine, but that is exactly what it will be. (More is written about the Health Care battle and its final outcome in Chapter Fourteen about Obama's Fast Track to Socialism.)

How about States? Will they be nationalized? In November 2008, we were told in California that our debt was $42 billion. The governor was saying that our state was facing "a financial Armageddon." In 2009, the state had to cut back on many services and salaries, but they still had to ask the federal government for stimulus money bailout, and they probably will again if the state hopes to stay afloat. The debt in 2010 was stated as $22 billion, but that is not counting the unfunded liabilities such as $500 billion for pensions.

Other states are following the example of California and asking for federal stimulus money. According to CNN, February 13, 2010, 46 states are requesting bail out money to mainly help with their medicaid payments, education and infrastructure projects. These states have a high rise in unemployment, with many of their people not able to pay taxes. One of the highest rates of unemployment is in California, 12.6% as of April, 2010.

According to Elizabeth McNichol, senior fellow at the Center on Budget and Policy Priorities, "the stimulus funds should plug in about 40% of the deficit in most states. . . totalling $144.6 billion." (http://money.cnn.com/2009/02/13/news/economy/stimulus_states/index.htm.)

Wow! Forty percent is a very high number! Does that mean that the federal government will now control almost half of each state taking the bailouts? As we have already found out, the bailout money does not come as a free gift. There are lots of strings attached. Perhaps this is why California does not seem to have control over her own water any more.

Former talk show host, Lee Rodgers, would often quote on his morning radio show on KSFO in San Francisco, a statement by his favorite history teacher, "If you're on my gravy train, you do what I tell you to do." We are going to see more and more states having to give in to all the demands of the federal government if they hope to stay on the dole of the high-priced "gravy train."[364]

Nationalization of Everything: Will anyone or anything be denied, or is that part of the plan to nationalize and control everything as the Gomberg Map Objectives called for back in 1942? In February, 2009, economist and former U.S. Senator Robert G. Torricelli, made the shocking statement in an article for *PolitickerN.J.com* that the federal government should not only nationalize Citibank, but partially nationalize every foreclosed home and take over ever health care and retirement account for the auto dealers. Back in February, he thought such action might appear aggressive, but by September he predicted it will be "standard international procedure."[365]

Did you notice that he said "international?" Is he on the inside of what the globalist plans are for all nations?

In fulfillment of what Torrecelli predicted concerning the government taking over foreclosed homes, a TV news broadcast, November 5, 2009, stated that the government was coming to the aid of the many poor people who were losing their homes. The government will take them over, and the people can pay rent to the government instead of being forced out of their homes. Amazing, just as Torricelli predicted! Of course, this will be made to appear so kind and benevolent by the government, and very few will question the "nationalization" of private homes.

Nationalize Gun Manufacturing and Armaments: The last item listed on objective #39 of the Gomberg Map was armaments. If the government nationalizes and controls all weapon and ammunition manufacturing, could they now say who gets to buy those weapons? Could they only allow police or military to possess weapons? Could the government say that the average citizen can no longer buy bullets? Maybe they could say that because of environmental laws against using lead, bullets can no longer be manufactured. Would that end our 2nd Amendment rights to protect ourselves and our families against unjust government intrusion? Remember what has happened in history. Before dictators have taken over in every country, guns were first outlawed and confiscated.

What Does Nationalization Mean? Former talk show host, Lou Dobbs, reported on his radio show early in December, 2008, about the humorous but wise words he had heard on Jay Leno's evening show concerning the bailouts. I don't know if I have the words exactly as stated but here is the jest of it: "When Castro took over Cuba and announced that he was a communist, and Cuba was going to become a communist country, he said that he was now nationalizing all banks, businesses, etc. In the US, we are doing the same thing, but we call it a bailout."

Isn't it interesting that what Castro and other communist dictators did in their nationalization, they did by revolution and by force. Here in the USA, the banks and auto industries came to Congress and begged to be taken over—for "bailouts." Did they not understand what that meant? I am sure the CEOs understand, for the vast majority of them are also members of the CFR. They know perfectly well that what ever the government funds, it controls. They like that idea because they believe in big government and eventually world government.

Nationalization May be Very Successful—for the Government: If you consider one of the elite's goals is control, then yes, nationalization will be very successful. Controlling huge auto industries and huge banks is going to be very lucrative for the federal government, done with tax payers' dollars. And, as has already been mentioned, nationalization is one of the major objectives of the Gomberg Map and the world control the elitists have in mind.

China and the American Dollar: Jason Lewis, talk show host from Minnesota, who took the place of Rush Limbaugh on his radio show December 24, 2008, predicted that China was going to dump the dollar, which would, of course, devalue the dollar even more. He also predicted that many 401-Ks would be wiped out.

Rowin Scarborough, who was a guest on Lee Rodger's KSFO Radio show, April 4, 2009, said that China has us over a barrel. If they don't buy our treasury notes, then we can't support our huge debt. Our only playing card is that they need us to buy their goods, but for how much longer?

More than 100 Banks Closed in 2009: On a CBS sixty minutes TV show, May 31, 2009, it was reported that 30 banks had closed. By November, 2009, it had risen to over 100 banks.

"Save the banks at all costs; they are too big to fail," was the mantra that both Presidents Bush and Obama gave for passing their unbelievable legislation, the TARP Bill and the Stimulus Bill. Obviously, with over 100 banks now closed, they were empty promises.

An International Financial Crisis: As has already been mentioned, European banks were also deeply involved in accepting the credit default swaps with AIG. They have also been greatly affected by the financial crisis and many have gone under.

International Car Manufacturers are also Being Affected: According to the news on ABC radio, December 22, 2008, Toyota was in hopes that the problems with the American Big Three Auto dealers would not affect them, that maybe their sales would continue to sore, but that is not the case. Toyota began suffering with sales falling. Of course, sales became especially bad for Toyota in the beginning of 2010, because of a recall of over six million cars due, supposedly, to a sticky gas pedal, or perhaps it was electrical computer problems. Whatever it was, it was causing accidents and deaths. There were even hearings in Washington D.C., where the leaders of Toyota were raked over the coals. (I am wondering if things could get so bad for Toyota, that, at least, the American branch could have to ask for a bailout, so they can be "nationalized" too.)

The San Francisco Chronicle, Dec. 21, 2008, reported that Canada was also having to aid its car companies with "emergency loans" to the tune of $4 billion (worth $3.29 billion in American dollars.) However, Ford Motor Company Canada is following the example of its parent company in the USA and is not asking for any bailout, just a line of credit to draw upon if necessary. Great Britain is also suffering financially as are most of the major industrial countries, even China is being affected by the financial crisis. All the stock markets are being affected.

Is His Miracle Pill "Stimulus Plan" Working? Is it solving all the problems that the savior Obama had promised? No, not at all! How could putting a nation into even greater trillion-dollar debt solve a financial crisis? The stock market plummeted the very day the Stimulus Plan was signed into law. Many companies and businesses continue to close down or go bankrupt. Thousands of people continue to loose jobs, averaging about 500,000 a month since Obama took office. Thousands are still losing their homes. Many financiers predicted the approach of another Great Depression, much worse than the one in the 1930's and longer lasting. It will have even a worse effect on the American people, mainly because we are so much less prepared, less self-sufficient, and in greater debt than people were back in the 1930s, and more Americans are being forced to rely on government handouts for even the bare necessities. In such a state, with little hope, they are feeling in a state of "great depression" themselves.

Unemployment—10% or 15.8%? According to Lee Rodgers Radio Talk Show, of KSFO Radio, San Francisco, May 28, 2009, unemployment would soon be at 10%, and the service on our enormous debt will be 100% of our GDP. A nation can no longer survive under such circumstances.[366] Obviously, none of these bailouts and enormous debt has helped our nation at all. According to the Washington Post, also a May, 2009 article, by reporter Frank Ahrens, the actual unemployment rates are much higher—more like 15.8 %:

This morning's news that U.S. unemployment has hit 13.7 million, pushing the rate to 8.9 percent, tells only half the story of this recession. The total number of Americans who are not working full-time but ought to be is actually about 22 million, or 15.8 percent, according to the **Bureau of Labor Statistic**s. Who are those other 8.3 million Americans? Call them the unofficially unemployed.

The article points out that many unemployed are not counted because of several reasons: The labor department cannot rely on unemployment compensation for their count because the records are not always accurate or up to date; some people are so discouraged they have simply given up and are no longer "marginally attached to the labor force"—some have not looked for work in 12 months—a large portion of these are young people, blacks, Hispanics, and men; some are sick or unable to work. Could the last reason be that the government does not want a higher report to show just how bad things really are in our nation under Obama's Stimulus Plan—that is not stimulating anything except big government?

Where does the labor department get the statistics for their monthly report? According to Ahrens, they contact about 60,000 households to determine the unemployment picture and have them represent the entire workforce, about 154 million Americans. Doesn't sound like a very accurate method, does it? The article goes on to say:

> The 15.8 percent figure is the highest since the bureau began keeping these figures in 1994. Excluding the current recession, the highest previous rate came in January 1994, when it hit 11.8 percent. The number was 8.7 percent in December 2007, when the current recession began. That means the number of the unofficially unemployed has shot up 7.1 percentage points since then. By comparison, the official unemployment rate has risen 3.9 percentage points since December 2007. This suggests that a greater percentage of people are becoming disenfranchised from the workforce than are getting laid off.
>
> By the way, in February, the White House predicted unemployment would top out at 8.1 percent this year, a figure that was blown through the following month. It has made no call on how high the unofficial unemployment rate will go.[367]

By November 2009, unemployment for the nation had risen to more than 10%, which many were saying was more like 18% figuring in those who were no longer even looking for jobs. According to the *Chicago Tribune's* Washington

Bureau, called "the Swamp," (a very fitting name), in an April 1, 2010, interview with Timothy Geithner, he stated that 8 million jobs were lost in the recession. ". . . this was the worst economic crisis since the Great Depression. . . a huge amount of damage was done to businesses and families across the country. . . and it's going to take us a long time to heal that damage."

Unemployment in California: As of September, 2009, unemployment in California had risen to 12.5 %, and in some parts of the Central Valley, such as the San Juaqin Valley, unemployment was at 40%, because of the farms no longer having any water and unable to grow crops. Other parts of the Central Valley are also pretty bad and not getting better. According to the *Berkeley Daily Planet,* in a March 25, 2010, article, Kern County had 16% unemployment rate and Kings and Tulare Counties both have 17%. Watsonville, which is not in the Central Valley, has even higher unemployment at 27%. So obviously the unemployment is affecting all parts of the state.

Obama's Administration Fudging on How the Stimulus Money Created Jobs: According to Lee Rodgers KSFO Radio Sunday rebroadcast, January 10, 2010, Obama's administration made the claim that $6.4 billion had been used in creating new jobs in 440 different congressional districts across the country. The problem is when one checks the various districts, they don't exist. Supposedly, millions of money was sent to zip codes in New Mexico to create jobs. However, those zip codes do not exist in New Mexico.

This report was verified by the normally very liberal, pro-Obama AARP (American Association of Retired Persons) publication, which stated in an on-line article November 30, 2009, that the first job reports appeared October 30, on the federal government's website, www.recovery.gov, which was where people could go to track job creation and the money spent. According to the AARP article:

"Millions of dollars went to congressional districts that don't exist. Nearly 4,000 reports did not show how any money was received or spent but listed more than 50,000 jobs that were created or saved. And more than 9,200 reports did not show any jobs but included expenditures approaching $1 billion, according to news articles and a report by the U.S. Government Accountability Office."

Congressman Todd Platts, (R) York County, Pennsylvania, called it "very unacceptable" that the information being reported is "so clearly flawed." He said that the best analysis of whether the stimulus money has worked or not is according to the federal unemployment rate, which was supposed to be kept under 8% by the passing of the stimulus plan. It has clearly not worked.

The national unemployment rate was 10.2%, in November, 2009, when the AARP article was written. (http://bulletin,aarp,org/states/pa/2009/48/articles/ stimulus_money_tracking_turns_up_errors_confusion.html.)

A New International Economic Order Implemented without a Fight: Would it not be logical for world leaders to say that the only way to solve the serious financial crisis is to come up with a new economic order, even a new currency to solve all of our nation's and other nation's woes and debts? Probably, many people who—earlier would have opposed any of this—but are now suffering so from the financial crisis, will breathe a sigh of relief and think this is a wonderful idea—anything to have some semblance of financial order restored![368]

As has been mentioned in prior chapters, the ultimate goal of the elitist insiders who belong to the CFR, the Bilderbergers, the Trilateral Commission, the Fabian Society and the other quasi-secretive groups, is to bring about a one-world government, a new international economic order and a one-world currency.

Regional Currency? Some people think that regional currencies will first be ushered in, such as the amero for Mexico, Canada and the USA, as the euro is already for the European Union. There are possible designs already being made for the amero. (Just google amero and you can see those designs. Written on them are UNA—Union of North America instead of NAU. I think it essentially means the same.) The following are news reports that tell of the amero and explain the concept of regional monetary integration:

1999—A Noted Canadian Economist, Herbert G. Grubel, Coined the Term Amero and Suggested it for a North American Monetary Union: Even before the euro became the currency for the European Union, academics in Canada and the United States were busily plotting a similar currency for North America. One of those was Herbert G. Grubel, of the Fraser Institute in Vancouver, British Columbia, who wrote a paper called "The Case for the Amero: The Economics and Politics of a North American Monetary Union." Grubel argued that such a union "would eliminate the costs of currency trading and risk, furthering the development of a North American common market along the model of the European Common Market." He proposed a plan to convert to the amero by 2010 and believed this could be done without changing the value of the three countries' present currencies:[369]

On the day the North American Monetary Union is created, Canada, the United States, and Mexico will replace their national currencies with the amero. On that day, all American dollar notes and coins will be exchanged at the rate of one U.S. dollar for one amero. Canadian and Mexican currencies will be exchanged at rates that leave unchanged their nation's competitiveness and wealth. In all three countries, the prices of goods and services, wages, assets, and liabilities will be simultaneously converted into ameros at the rates at which currency notes are exchanged.[370]

The Benefits of a Common Currency for the North American Countries? Grubel suggested that the amero would: "reduce the size and risk of foreign-exchange operations engaged in by banks, firms, and travelers as part of their routine economic activities." The United States, Canada, and Mexico would then constitute an "optimal currency area," which gives them a higher rating according to economists.

(Okay, maybe a common currency would be convenient for trade and banking between the three countries, but the risks to the sovereignty, autonomy, independence and loss of freedom of the three nations far outweigh any advantage. Plus, having witnessed what switching to the euro did to the German mark, devaluing it by 2/3rds, I can't imagine that the value of currency for the three countries would stay the same. I have heard that our dollar will be one-tenth of its value if changed to the amero, and that was before our present financial crisis. Some are thinking switching to a new currency can stop the terrible devaluation that is already happening to the dollar because of our enormous debt, but according to Grubel, each nation would take their debts (liabilities) with them and that would be converted to the amero.)

Grubel Proposed a North American Central Bank: A NA Bank would replace the national central banks of the three countries and would have a board of governors representing the "economics and population" of three countries. The language Grubel uses suggests that the NA Bank would have supremacy over the U.S. treasury and the treasures of Canada and Mexico.

2002, November 1-2—Robert Pastor Delivered a Speech to the Trilateral Commission Recommending the Amero: Pastor proposed that Canada, the USA, and Mexico all have a common currency and used the term amero. He felt it would not harm the value of the nations' present currencies. He thought the people of the three countries would be more willing to accept a new unified currency that to enter into a new "regional government." "The three governments remain zealous defenders of an aging concept of sovereignty."[371]

2006, November 27—The Amero to Become the Currency for the North American Community: This was reported by Steve Previs, a vice president at Jeffries International Ltd., in London, who told CNBC that "the amero is the proposed new currency for the North American Community which is being developed right now between Canada, the U.S. and Mexico." He cited, as his source of information, a Canadian economist, Herbert G. Grubel, who is given credit for coining the name "amero."

2007, May/June, "The End of National Currency": An article by Benn Steil, was published in the CFR *Foreign Affairs* Newsletter and on line. The CFR members are getting bolder in their statements of what they intend for our nation and all nations—**"abandon monetary nationalism"**—no national currency, just one big global currency. Here is a very revealing quote from his article:

> **The right course is not to return to a mythical past of monetary sovereignty**, with governments controlling local interest and exchange rates in blissful ignorance of the rest of the world. Governments must let go of the fatal notion that nationhood requires them to make and control the money used in their territory. National currencies and global markets simply do not mix; together they make a deadly brew of currency crises and geopolitical tension and create ready pretexts for damaging protectionism. In order to globalize safely, countries should **abandon monetary nationalism** and abolish unwanted currencies, the source of much of today's instability.[372]

2007, June 6—Financial Services Integration of the SPP: Judicial Watch is a conservative watch dog group that investigates government corruption, and has been revealing much of the hidden information about the SPP by demanding the truth through the Freedom of Information Act. Among the documents it obtained was a 10-page partnership "Work Plan for the Financial Services Working Group," which detailed 24 specific "deliverables" by officials from the U.S. Treasury, Finance Canada, BANXICO, the Federal Research Board-Atlanta, and regulatory agencies.

The work plan revealed that there would be improvements made to Mexico's infrastructure, paid by U.S. and Canadian taxpayers. There would also be "cross-border" cooperation in the areas of car insurance, Social Security totalization for Mexico, banking and the Federal Reserve's "Directo a Mexico" remittance program. The "totalization" program would allow any Mexican worker who has as little as 18 months of employment history in the U.S. to end up qualifying for Social Security retirement benefits, a cost that could reach into the billions.[373]

2007, November—*Regional Monetary Integration* was published by the CFR and the Cambridge University Press. It was written by two professors at the American University, Peter B. Kenen, Adjunct Senior Fellow for the International Economics, and Ellen M. Meade, Associate Professor of

Economics. American University is the same place where Robert Pastor was a professor and where a "Model North American Parliament" meeting was held in 2007 for students from Canada, USA, and Mexico to learn how to run a NAU parliament. (The elite have obviously already decided that we will not have a congress for the new government. Everyone must be the same in all countries with a parliament.)

Obviously, with this text book being used at the American University, the students were being taught about regional currencies such as the Amero that was planned to be used for the NAU. Here is a summary written about the book. Notice they are asking for a "single central bank, the globalists' dream come true:[374]

This book surveys the prospects for regional monetary integration in various parts of the world. Beginning with a brief review of the theory of optimal currency areas, it goes on to examine the structure and functioning of the European Monetary Union, then turns to the prospects for monetary integration elsewhere in the world—North America, South America, and East Asia. Such cooperation may take the form of full-fledged monetary unions or looser forms of monetary cooperation. *Regional Monetary Integration* emphasizes the economic and institutional requirements for successful monetary integration, including the need for a **single central bank** in the case of a full-fledged monetary union and the corresponding need for multinational institutions to safeguard the bank's independence and assure its accountability. The book concludes with a chapter on the implications of monetary integration for the United States and the U.S. dollar.

One Currency: Phyllis Schlafly writes the following about the planned currency for all three countries, all part of the economic integration for the North American Union:

When Larry King asked Mexico's Vicente Fox about plans for a "Latin America united with one currency," Fox answered in the affirmative. He said that one currency was part of the "vision" of the Free Trade Area of the Americas that Bush agreed to in the Declaration of Quebec City in 2001.

So now we know why the Bush Administration won't build a fence to interfere with "labor mobility" across open borders. Now we know why Bush won't pardon Ignatio Ramos and Jose Compean, while winking at the prosecutor's deal to give immunity to a professional drug smuggler. [Bush finally did do something to help Ramos and Compean, as he was leaving office. He didn't pardon them, but just reduced their sentence so they were both freed in 2009.]

Now we know why Bush thumbed his nose at the overwhelming congressional votes (411-3 in the House and 75-23 in the Senate) to exclude Mexican trucks from U.S. roads. Now we know why Bush has been more persistent in pursuing "totalization" to put illegal aliens into Social Security than to promote his proposal to privatize a small part of Social Security for American citizens. This is no conspiracy. It's all part of the "economic integration" of the North American countries that's been openly talked about for years.[375]

April 2, 2009, London, England—G-20 Global Summit—the "Launching Pad" for One-World Economy, World Central Bank and a World Currency: One of the many foreign trips that President Obama made in the first few months of his administration was to attend the G-20 London Summit (involving the top 20 leaders of the world) to try to solve the "financial crisis." According to William F. Jasper, a reporter for *the New American*, who attended the conference, the results were the following—all promoting more power and control to globalists over the finances of the world:

1) **'Global Financial Architecture Reform'**—code words for transforming or "supersizing" the IMF, International Monetary Fund, into a world central bank or a 'global Federal Reserve System.' The IMF would have vast new monetary and regulatory powers, assume a central role in the monitoring and regulation of global financial markets, and expand Communist China's influence in the IMF structure.

2) **Huge New Infusions of Cash:** Up to $1.1 trillion will have to be provided—principally, as usual—by the citizens of the United States, Japan, and Europe. (One wonders how the U.S. can possibly provide our expected donation when we are $trillions in debt ourselves?)

3) **Replace the Dollar as the World's Reserve Currency—with a new IMF Currency, with the IMF's Special Drawing Rights (SDRs):** At a CFR meeting, U.S. Secretary of Treasury Geithner stated he was "quite open to that suggestion" to increase the IMF's special drawing rights. He did add, "But you should think of it as rather evolutionary, building on the current architecture . . . rather than moving us to global monetary union." (A transcript and video of Geithner's statement are available at the CFR's website—*www.cfr.org.*)

4) **'Global Governance Stimulus':** This is a code word for the transfer of powers from nation states to institutions that are part of the United Nations system, such as: the IMF, World Bank, and regional development banks, "financial sister institutions to the UN," that were "created by many of the same architects who designed the UN." The WTO, World Trade Organization, will also be given enhanced powers so it can better enforce the G20's announced commitment to "fight all forms of protectionism and maintain open trade."

5) **Establish Regulations to Bring all Nations Closer to World Government:** According to author Bill Jasper, French President, Nicolas Sarkosy, is a closet socialist, who is pushing hard to scuttle what little sovereignty remains for nation states in the European Union." Sarkosy threatened to walk away from the G-20 Summit "if concrete global governance 'deliverables' on financial regulation are not met." The host of the summit, British Prime Minister Gordon Brown, ended the summit with the concluding words, announcing to the world the ultimate agenda, "a new world order is emerging."

6) **The G-20 Summit is a Launching Pad for Future Summits:** Dominique Strauss-Kahn, the managing director for the IMF, stated that the London Summit is going to be an "on-going process . . . completed over time with several rounds. He is hoping to shorten the period from 2013, the original goal to have all systems launched, to the year 2011.

Words of Warning: Bill Jasper sums up the G-20 Summit's frightening goals with the following:

> We are witnessing the demolition of our constitutional system and the piecemeal replacement of it with world government. Over the coming months, the architects of this new global system intend to wring every opportunity possible out of the current economic crisis to bulldoze through our constitutional checks and balances that stand in the way of empowering the IMF, the WTO, and the United Nations.

If the IMF is empowered with global monetary and financial regulatory powers, along with the ability to issue a global currency and bonds, it will no longer have to ask its member states for funding. Nor will the UN. The IMF will be able to provide the UN with the revenues it needs to become an actual world government, completely unbridled by any constitutional constraints, accountable to no one but the 'very powerful cabal' . . . running the show. (Bill Jasper, *The New American*, April 3, 2009, http://www.starsoverwashington. com/2009/03/purposes-of-g20-summit-april-2009.htm.)

What Can We Do As We Face Very Uncertain Times Financially? We can prepare for some form of definite hyper-inflation where the American dollar is going to be greatly devalued. All of the financial experts are expecting such and are warning the American people to invest in gold or silver that will give you something of value to barter with when the dollar has so shrunk in any value. Ever since Bush and Obama have put our nation into trillions of dollars of debt, the dollar has begun to be mass produced to try to pay down those enormous debts. Mass production of currency brings down the value of that currency.

Examples of Hyper-Inflation—Could This Be Happening to the USA? Some are saying that hyper-inflation in the U.S. could be as bad as the Weimar Republic after the end of World War II or even worse—as bad as Zimbabwe is today. During 1920-1921, the German government started cranking out an enormous amount of marks to pay off their huge war debts. The German mark went from a value of 60 marks per one U.S. dollar to 8,000 marks per dollar by December 1922. It took a wheelbarrow of paper money to buy a single loaf of bread. The paper marks became so worthless, some people were using them instead for insulation in their homes against the cold. Others were using them for wall paper to cover the cracks on their walls. If the German people did not have their own gardens or fruit trees, some source of their own food, they would have starved, which many did.

An article in the March 30, 2009, *New American* magazine, "From Riches to Rags," written by Warren Mass, tells of the enormous hyper-inflation in Zimbabwe (formerly known as Rhodesia). The nation's annual inflation rate rose from 1,000 percent in 2006 to 12,000 percent in 2007. In 2008, inflation was so out of sight, it was no longer measurable. A June 27, 2008, article in the United Kingdom *Times* reported the inflation rate at five sex-tillion percent, or 5,000,000,000,000,000,000,000,000.

Gideon Gono, appointed by Mugabe as the head of Zimbabwe's Reserve Bank, is known as the world's most "disastrous" central banker. He finally knocked 12 zeros off their dollar in an attempt to bring the currency back from the realm of fantastical. None of the computers, calculators or people could cope with all the zeros. Now the street value of one Zimbabwean dollar to an American dollar is 250, instead of 250 trillion. But essentially the money is worthless. However, Gono still wants to print more.

How did this happen to a once-prosperous area that had such rich soil, good farms and used to be a large contributor to the bread basket of Africa? In 1980, a Communist dictator, Robert Mugabe, took control of Rhodesia; its name was changed to Zimbabwe, and little by little, communism began to be imposed on the nation. Nationalization of all banks, industries and farms followed as did persecution of any land owners, especially those who were white.

There were not many white farmers. They represented less than one percent of the entire population. However, they were very hard working and good managers. They were responsible for 25 percent of all employment in the country and 40 percent of what the nation earned with exports. Under Mugabe, all that has come to a screeching halt. The farms have been seized without compensation and taken over by the government. The farmers were killed if they tried to remain on their farms and fight for their property. To save their lives, their only recourse was to flee, mainly to South Africa. Now the farms lie in ruin, the food is not produced, there is high unemployment and many people in Zimbabwe are going hungry, as are people in other parts of Africa, who had depended on the food that used to be exported from the once, very productive Rhodesian farms. *The New American* article ends with this profound statement:

> In today's troubled economic times, Americans can follow the examples of Germany or Zimbabwe and spend trillions of dollars to "stimulate" the economy, keeping the printing presses running day and night to pay the bills. Over time, the result will be hyperinflation and a ruined economy. Or Americans can return to fiscal sanity, balance the budget, abolish the Federal Reserve, restore sound currency, and return to the prosperous economy and free political system our nation enjoyed during much of the 19th Century.[376]

At the conclusion of this chapter on our financial crisis, the following wise quote sums up what the basis of the problem is and the solution. How well it describes what is going on in our nation today:

You cannot legislate the poor into prosperity by legislating the wealthy out of prosperity. What one person receives without working for, another person must work for without receiving. The government cannot give to anybody anything that the government does not first take from somebody else. When half of the people get the idea that they do not have to work because the other half is going to take care of them, and when the other half gets the idea that it does no good to work because somebody else is going to get what they work for, that my dear friend, is the beginning of the end of any nation. You cannot multiply wealth by dividing it. (Adrian Rogers, a famous Baptist Minister and Author, who lived from 1931-2005)[377]

On a radio interview on the Lee Rodgers morning radio show, KSFO, with Professor Hendrickson of Grove City College, Nov. 10, 2009, he stated the following profound statement: "Money is just a medium of exchange. It is not real wealth. Real wealth comes from production." Many people believe that Obama now has a war on production. He wants the people to be dependent on him and on government for all that they have, no longer on their own productivity.

As you have read in this chapter and preceding chapters, the plan is for regional and then global economic integration and a one-world currency. Is that going to be changed by President Obama's administration or just more of the same? I think the reader will discover that Obama's mantra for "hope and change" is really just "smoke and mirrors," the same movement to bigger government and socialism, except that it is moving on "fast track."

Chapter Fourteen

Obama's Fast Track to Socialism; His Questionable Background and Eligibility to be President; Attack on the American Dream, His Radical Czars; Scary Bills such as Health Care Bill; More Summit Meetings to Promote North American Merger; Is this Really the Hope and Change Americans Wanted?

"Government is instituted for the common good; for the protection, safety, prosperity, and happiness of the people; and not for profit, honor, or private interest of any one man, family, or class of men." - John Adams, a Founding Father, 2nd President of the United States

The reader has learned in prior chapters about the RIIR, the CFR, the Trilateral Commission, the Bilderbergers, and all the other secretive societies and their globalist agenda—to destroy national sovereignty, national solvency, and to bring a nation closer to regional and world government.

Such a government would be in direct contrast to the above quote by John Adams. No longer would government be for the benefit or for the happiness of the common man. It would only be for the benefit of the rulers, the rich and the powerful, who would be supported in their lavish lifestyles by the taxes of the poor, beleaguered, lowly common folk.

Establishing a Socialist or Communist state in a nation speeds up the process to world government and makes the transition much easier. Obama is the perfect president to help bring about the socialist transformation of the USA, for his whole background has been in preparation for such a job.

This chapter will explain Obama's background, how he was trained by some of the best communist experts in the field. It will list some of his cabinet members and his many czars and their globalist or Communist connections. It will tell what he has accomplished so quickly to bring us even closer to the socialist/communist/globalist goals.

Fascism/Socialism/Communism: I would remind the reader to again read the definitions of socialism, fascism, and communism given at the beginning of the last chapter. Remember they are striving for the same end, the eventual government ownership or nationalization of the economy, industry, commerce, private property and total control of the people. Socialism and fascism just work at a slower pace while communism is on fast track.

What Socialism and Communism Do to the Work Ethics of a Nation: A joke that was circulating during the 2008 campaign told of Obama speaking before a large audience. In his talk he said, "If I am elected, I promise you that the government will make sure you all will have adequate housing." (There were loud cheers and applause.) "We will help you pay your mortgage." (More cheers and applause) "I promise you that you will have free health care." (More cheers and applause.) "And I promise that everyone will have a job." (There was silence.) One man raised his hand and asked, "Why would we need a job?"

That is what socialism and communism do. They take away people's desire to work. If people are on welfare and get all sorts of free handouts and services, why work? Socialism and communism take away incentives and motivation to achieve. That is why the productivity of such nations is so low.

When I was substitute teaching in a high school in Santa Rosa, CA., the assignment was to have the students write down where they wanted to be ten years from that date. What kind of a job they would have, where they would be living, etc? This was a class composed of mainly Latino students, which was not unusual, because that is what most of the public schools are becoming in California.

One boy was not writing anything. I asked him what the problem was? Did he not have any goals or plans for his future? What kind of a career did he want? He told me he was just planning to be on welfare as his mother was, no other plans than that. I asked if he did not want to have a wife and family? He said yes, but they would be on welfare with him. Pretty sad!

I noticed his grades in the teacher's roll book. He had never turned in anything. He had total Fs. I went back to him and asked him if he was not planning to graduate? He said no. He was just waiting to turn 16 so he get out of school. I asked him if this is the kind of life that he would want for his child, if he were to become a father? Did he not want anything better for his son? Someone needs to break this cycle of welfare and not carry it on from one generation to another. I told him just for his own benefit, try to imagine that he had grown up in a different life, he had a bright future before him, he could become whatever he would like to become. I told him to write down what that would be and what life would be like for him in ten years. I don't know if that helped him any, but maybe just to get me to be quiet, he started writing and came up with a career for himself as a professional soccer player and at least he had a much brighter future.

That experience has stayed with me, and I have often reflected on it. As a teacher, I see more and more of the same kind of students: the bored, expressionless faces, no excitement about life, and no motivation to work. At some high schools, I have seen kids just outside wandering around the campus instead of attending classes. They know they have to show up to school, but instead of being inside a classroom, motivated to work hard, they, too, are just waiting until they are 16 and can quit.

What kind of a life will such dropouts then live? They will probably be part of the same welfare system as their parents and grandparents before them. Many will be involved in a life of drugs, alcohol and crime, as is so often the case with people who have dropped out of school, with no bright future, little education, and no skills to get a decent job.

WJR Radio Station Interview with Welfare Recipients in Detroit, Michigan Wanting "Obama's Stash:" Rush Limbaugh played a segment from some interviews that had been sent to him by an affiliate station, WJR radio in Detroit, Michigan. The interviews were done at the Cobo Center in Detroit, where 65,000 people were lined up to receive applications for a portion of $15 million in stimulus money, October 8-9, 2009. Only about 3,500 people out of those 65,000 were able to receive the money. But about 15,000 were allowed to get an application and apply for the money. The rest had to be turned away. There were scam artists outside the Cobo Center selling fake applications for $20 apiece for those who had been turned away.

A WJR reporter, Ken Rogulski, asked some of the people waiting in line the following questions and received some very revealing answers as to what people on welfare think where the money they receive is coming from. (His questions are in bold; the answers are italicized.)

Interview I: Rogulski asked Woman #1, **"Why are you here?"** She answered, "*To get some money.*" **"What kind of money?"** *Obama money.*" **"Where's it coming from?"** "*Obama.*" **"And where did Obama get it?"** "*I don't know, his stash. I don't know.* (laughter) *I don't know where he got it from, but he givin' it to us, to help us.* Woman #2: "*And we love him.*" Woman #1: *We love him. That's why we voted for him!* Both Women: (chanting) *Obama! Obama! Obama!* (laughing) **Interview II:** Rogulski: **"Did you get an application to fill out yet?"** Woman: "*I sure did. And I filled it out, and I am waiting to see what the results are going to be.*" Rogulski: **"Will you know today how much money you're getting?"** Woman: "*No, I won't, but I'm waiting for a phone call.*" Rogulski: **"Where's the money coming from?"** Woman: "*I believe it's coming from the City of Detroit* *or the state.*" Rogulski: "**Where did they get it from?**" Woman: "*Some funds that was forgiven (sic) by Obama.*" Rogulski: "**And where did Obama get the funds**?" Woman: "*Obama getting the funds from . . . Ummm, I have no idea, to tell you the truth. He's the president.*"

That was the end of the interview. You then heard the words of the reporter signing off, "In downtown Detroit, Ken Rogulski, WJR News."

I think most of the listening audience were equally shocked and saddened by these interviews—to think that the hard-earned money from American taxpayers is going to support people like this on welfare, to put our nation into even greater debt, and these people don't have a clue where the money is coming from! They think it is Obama's "stash!"

Rush Limbaugh's Commentary: Rush gave a very moving commentary about these two interviews. He said, "How sad it is that such things are happening in the United States of America." He added that if he were the president he would be embarrassed that there were people lining up thinking they were getting money directly from him. It would frighten him about the condition and future of the country, and he would really wonder what's gone wrong with our education system. He stated:

> These are poor black people. And when you listen to them they're out there having a good time talking about Obama, but look what they're doing? . . . They're lining up for so little money that it's insignificant. I'd be embarrassed that my policies, that my administration had created this kind of destitution, this kind of hopelessness. It's really, really sad ignorance.

Rush was in hopes that President Obama would hear of this, and he would be embarrassed at the people's ignorance. Rush was afraid instead that Obama "likes it." "He enjoys this kind of dependency on him and the federal government." Obama will look at this event in Detroit and think that as long as the people are so totally dependent on him that he will have "the next election sewn up." These people will never vote against him or the democrat party. Rush adds what saddens and sickens him even more is:

> . . . futures are bleak, futures are being destroyed all because of the narcissistic power and desire for that power held by the president and his advisory team. It really is sad, folks, when you boil all the pictures of it away. How about all that hope and change?[378]

What Has Happened to the American Dream? It used to be that anyone, if they had the desire and wanted to work hard could fulfill their American dream, to make a success of whatever career they wanted to pursue. You were rewarded for working hard. Now it appears that under Obama's plan the American dream will become an impossibility. If you work too hard and earn too much money, you will be looked down upon as the "greedy rich" and punished. The money will be taken away from you in higher taxes and given to the poor, to those on welfare to keep them there. It appears that instead of a war on terror, Obama has started a new war—a war on prosperity!

What will such a system do to the hard working people who want to achieve and provide jobs for others? Pretty soon they will work less, because they do not want to be labeled "rich" and pay the higher taxes. They will not be able to hirer as many people; the work productivity will decrease; the prosperity of the nation will go down, just as it does in all other socialist/communist nations.

"Do You Believe in the American Dream?"—Joe the Plummer's Question of Obama: It was Sunday, October 12, 2008. Obama had arrived in Ohio to do some campaigning and to attend a rally in Toledo. He thought he would first stop off at the small town of Holland and do a little campaigning and get some good photo ops. He would just walk down one of the streets and ask people to please vote for him—a good way to show that he was a simple man, just one of the people. He chose the small town of Holland, probably because it was a big labor community and most of the people belonged to labor unions and were Democrats. However, Joe Wurzalbacher, a plumber, was one of the exceptions.

Joe was outside playing catch with a football with his son. He heard all the commotion that was going on with neighbors coming out of their houses and gathering in the street, so he and his son went to see what was happening. There they saw Obama. They went closer and Joe hollered out his question, "Senator, do you believe in the American Dream?"

A conversation followed. Joe told Obama that, after working as a plumber for 15 years, he was going to purchase his own business. But the business was worth more than $250,000, and Joe was afraid that he would be punished for his hard work and taxed more for "fulfilling the American Dream," under Obama's plan.

Obama made several attempts to explain his tax plan, but the bottom line was always that Joe would suffer from increased taxes. Obama then made the following statements that were pretty shocking, made national news and revealed the true socialist that he was.

*I'm gonna cut taxes a little bit more for the folks who are most in need . . .
for the 5% of the folks who are doing very well—even though they've
been working hard and I appreciate that—I just want to make sure
they're paying a little bit more in order to pay for those other tax cuts . . .
It's not that I want to punish your success—I just want to make sure
that everybody who is behind you—that they've got a chance at success
too . . .* **I think when you spread the wealth around, it's good for
everybody.**[379]

Is Money Spread Around Really Good for Everybody? Obama's last
sentence reminds me of a line from the 1969 musical, "Hello, Dolly," where
Dolly says, "Money, pardon the expression, is like manure. It's not worth a thing
unless it's spread around." Does Obama equate money to manure, as well? The
way he and Michelle are shoveling through tax-payers money in their extravagant
trips and spending makes it appear that may be the case. The enormous salaries
that are being doled out to his 40 plus czars and Michelle's 26 assistants make
it appear that way as well.

Is manure or money really "good" for everything or everybody when it's
spread around?" I'm sorry, but that is not the case. Having grown up on an
Idaho potato farm, I know that too much manure put in the wrong place can
actually kill a plant. Welfare money does the same thing. Money—given to those
who do not work for it, have no real appreciation for it, and do not even know
from where it is coming—is not good. Welfare money just keeps people in the
same state: hopeless, unmotivated and on the government dole from generation
to generation. But maybe to the socialist elite mindset, like Obama, that is
considered "good." Socialist leaders would like everyone—but themselves—to
be lowly serfs, dependent on government for their every need.

Obama's "spreading the wealth around" statement is what made national
news and made many Americans wake up and realize that Obama is a classical
"Robin Hood" socialist, who truly believes in "taking from those who have and
giving to those who have not—in other words, "redistribution of wealth," one
of the strongest planks of socialism and communism.

Third Presidential Debate—Joe the Plummer Was the Winner: Thanks to
the news coverage that had already come out about Obama's conversation with Joe
the Plumber, most of the Third Presidential debate, held October 15th at Hofstra
University in Hempstead, New York, was about Obama's plans for taxation, taxing
the rich and redistribution of wealth. Joe's name was mentioned 25 times. Some
news broadcasts said that Joe the Plummer was the real winner of the debate.

After his encounter with Obama, and especially after the debate, Joe began to get hundreds of calls for interviews on radio, newspapers and television. He even ended up writing a book about his belief in the American Dream and the free enterprise system, not socialism. His book is called *Joe the Plummer, Fighting for the American Dream*. He was assisted in the book by Thomas N. Tabback, a journalist.[380]

I had the opportunity to hear Joe speak at a national Eagle Forum meeting September 25, 2009. It was exciting to meet him in person and to hear his passion about the American dream, how it used to be, and what we must do to try to restore it. He spoke about the four things he strongly believes in to keep the American Dream alive: accountability, responsibility, education, and the Constitution. At the end of his talk, he was presented with the "Golden Wrench" and the "Golden Plunger" awards.

How Far Are We On the "Socialist Path" Under Obama's Rule? Glenn Beck used to open his television show portraying us all driving along on our socialist path to the end. You would see the large block letters "Free Enterprise System" crumble as we drove by. You would then see the block letters "Socialism" standing before us, but they too would crumble as we drove by and then the end result was standing boldly in front of us—"Communism" in big red letters! Glenn Beck then would don his "Communist"-sounding deep voice and address us all as "Fellow Comrades" to give us the latest report of how our nation had done that past week on our road to the end. It was done in jest, but it was also done to warn us how far we have come. It is obvious that Glenn Beck is equally concerned about where our nation is headed.

The Plunge to Socialism/Communism: One cannot even use the term "road to socialism" with Obama. It is more like a giant plunge that has happened so fast. In just the first month of his presidency, he put our nation into $787 billion dollars debt with his Stimulus Plan, so he will now have all the money he needs to carry out his many socialist/communist programs and pay the huge salaries to his many czars. By the second month he had succeeded in nationalizing major banks (putting many other smaller banks out of business); nationalizing the largest insurance company—AIG; and nationalizing two major parts of the auto industry—GM and Chrysler; and he was well on his way to nationalizing our entire nation's health care, the nation's sixth largest industry. It took a little longer than he, expected—a whole year, but by March 23rd, 2010, he was able to sign the Health Care bill into law. (You will read a little of the unbelievable shenanigans that it took for that to happen later in the chapter.)

How Much of Our Nation Has Already Become Nationalized: In an interview on the Lee Rodgers' Radio Show on KSFO Radio, San Francisco, October 22, 2009, Congresswoman Michele Bachmann from Minnesota said that presently 36% of our nation has become nationalized. If the health care bill passes, that will bring it up to 48%. If Cap and Trade passes, that will make it so that 56% of our nation will be under the control of the federal government. How much more socialism will it take at that point to call ourselves a socialist nation?

Obama's Leftist/Socialist/Communist Background: Some Americans might be a little surprised at how fast Obama is taking us on this downward plunge, but if one does just a little research on his life, it is not surprising; that is how he was raised. If his mother and father and grandparents were not card-carrying members of the Communist party, they certainly associated with those who were and shared their philosophy.

His Feminist, Leftist Mother, Stanley Anne Dunham: Obama described his mother as the original "feminist," an atheist, very passionate in her leftist opinions and arguments. She had her own brand of "New Frontier" liberalism and wanted to blaze her own trail. "She was a lonely witness for secular humanism, a soldier of the New Deal, Peace Corps, position-paper liberalism."[381]

His Leftist, Narcissistic, Drunken Father, Barack Obama Sr.: As more information is revealed about Obama Sr., it appears that he was a true example of narcissism, only interested in himself, in fulfilling his needs and no one else's. He ended up with four wives and eight children, but he but abandoned one family after another.

A London newspaper, the *Daily Mail*, in a January, 2007 article, revealed much about Obama Sr. that his son did not want the public to find out about. In the article entitled, "A drunk and a bigot—what the US Presidential hopeful hasn't said about his father," Obama Sr. was described as a black foreign student from Kenya and a "slick womanizer", who was attending the University of Hawaii when he and Stanley Ann met. She was 18 and very naïve. Obama Sr. was 23.[382]

Obama Jr. was supposedly born August 4, 1961, in Hawaii. (There is much evidence that he was actually born in Kenya as you will read later.) Obama Sr. abandoned the family soon after his son turned two years old and went off to Harvard to study. His excuse for not taking his wife and son with him was there was not enough money in his scholarship. But according to information that Dr. Jerome Corsi discovered that is written in his book on Obama, there was another scholarship offered from another source, the New School for Social Research in New York, which would have given Obama Sr. plenty of money for his family.[383] Obama Jr. leaves that fact out, as well, in his autobiography that he entitled *Dreams of My Father.*

The Daily Mail reports that when Obama was around three years old, his mother divorced his father when she discovered he had a bigamous relationship with a wife back in Kenya named Kezia and a son there as well. (Of course, in the Islam religion, that is not considered bigamy. Most Muslim men have more than one wife, but it would have been nice if Obama Sr. would have told Stanley Ann about his other wife before they were married. Perhaps that would have changed her mind.)

While at Harvard, according to *the Daily Mail*, Obama Sr. had an affair with yet another American woman, Ruth Nidesand, whom he also later married after she followed him back to Kenya. Back in Kenya, Obama Sr. returned to his first wife, Kezia and fathered two more children. Ruth also bore him two sons, but eventually she left him when his drinking became so bad that he would fly into a whiskey rage and brutally beat her.

He had a very good job as a Harvard-trained econometrician in the newly independent government of Jomo Kenyatta, but eventually he lost his job after a drunken driving accident which left him with both legs severed at the knees. In spite of his condition, he fathered his eighth child by yet another woman.[384]

Shortly after Obama Jr.'s 21st birthday, he received word that his father had been killed in another drunken driving accident. Some believe it was really a form of suicide. Obama Sr. did not have much to live for with no job, no legs, and severe poverty.

Obama only met his father once when he was age 12. His father spent a week in Hawaii when Obama was living with his grandparents. Obama was not too impressed with his father, who, on first meeting him, scolded him for not studying harder. Obama did not feel that this absentee father should have any right to give him a scolding or any advice at all. He wrote in his book, "After a week of my father in the flesh, I had decided that I preferred his more distant image, an image I could alter on a whim—or ignore when convenient."[385]

Four years after his father's death, Obama Jr. visited Kenya and discovered the truth about his father's many wives and that he had seven half-siblings. However, Obama leaves out these sordid details and also his father's drunkenness in his book *Dreams of My Father.* Instead he makes his father appear as a sort of hero, a brilliant student who won scholarships to first the University of Hawaii and later Harvard, the most prestigious U.S. university. Obama also portrays his father as a victim, which he seems to think all blacks must be, and blames "racism" on anything that went wrong in his father's life, such as the breaking up of his parents' marriage.

In Obama's book, he quotes the sister of his father, Aunt Zeituni, whom he met in Kenya. Whatever she told him about his father, he only reports the good things, such as: "The problem with Obama Senior was that his heart was too big . . . he had taken on too large a burden trying to help his family in Africa and lift Kenya into a modern economic age."[386]

However, *the Daily Mail*, says just the opposite. He had a very small, selfish heart, not interested in anyone but himself. "We have discovered that his father was not just a flawed individual but an abusive bigamist and an egomaniac, whose life was ruined not by racism or corruption but by his own weakness . . ." This testimony came from Obama Sr.'s own relatives and family friends.

Why did Obama write his book and try to portray his father as a hero? Churcher in her *Daily Mail* article writes, that Obama probably wanted to "have a pre-emptive strike on those sure to pose the awkward questions that would inevitably face a serious contender for the White House."[387]

It sounds much better to say that Obama was the son of a brilliant foreign student who: was the first of his tribe to leave Kenya and to, study in America; who received scholarships to the University of Hawaii and Harvard; and who wanted to help his country and elevate them to higher standards—than to say that Obama was the son of a womanizer, bigamist, liar, egomaniac, abusive wife beater, drunk, who ended his own life jobless and in abject poverty.

Obama's Stepfather, Lolo Seotoro, Also a Heavy Drinker: His mother married a second black man, an Indonesian, Lolo Seotoro, whom she also met at the University of Hawaii campus. She moved with Lolo and her son to Indonesia, where Obama attended elementary school.

Both his stepfather and his real father were involved in leftist politics. Both became disillusioned and turned to drinking, which eventually took both of their lives. The drinking of Lolo greatly affected the marriage and family, so his mother sent Barack back to Hawaii to live with his grandparents, Stanley and Madelyn Dunham.

Barack started fifth grade at a prestigious college prep school in Hawaii. A year later his mother (now separated from Lolo) and his stepsister, Maja, joined him in Hawaii for three years while his mother finished a post graduate degree in anthropology. She and Maja then returned to Indonesia. Obama refused to go with them. He had had enough of Indonesia. He moved back in with his grandparents and finished high school.

During this time, Obama was suffering from feelings of abandonment by, not only his father, but also his mother, who was too busy with her own studies and career. Obama was also struggling with feelings of being unaccepted because of his race. According to his autobiography, he turned to drugs and alcohol.

He states, "I got high for . . . something that could push the questions of who I was out of my mind, something that could flatten out the landscape of my heart, blur the edges of my memory."[388]

Communist Mentor, Tutor, Influences from Communist Authors: At this time in his life, Barack was introduced to and tutored by a close friend of his grandfather, Frank Marshall Davis, a black poet and radical Communist leader. Stanley Dunham and Barack would visit Davis, drink with him, and listen to him recite his poetry. Barack would go to Davis alone for advice when he was unhappy with questions about his race and about his relationship with his grandparents. Davis was his mentor and, of course, shaped Barack's political ideas. Barack even refers to Davis as a father figure and once wrote a poem to him entitled "Pop."

During his teenage years Barack also read many books authored by black authors, who just happened to be communists as well. His favorites were Langston Hughes and Richard Wright. Hughes is most famous for a poem, "The Negro Speaks of Rivers." Hughes admitted before the Senate Permanent Subcommittee on Investigations in 1953 that he was a communist sympathizer and that many of his books were authored to "follow the communist line." Richard Wright, author of the 1940 novel, *Native Son*, had formerly served as the Harlem editor of the communist newspaper *Daily Worker* until 1937.[389]

Obama's College Education and Law School: Because all of Obama's records are sealed, all that we know is that he attended Occidental College in California, Columbia University in New York and Harvard Law School. None of his grades, the papers he wrote, his thesis, his Harvard Law Review articles, or his scholarly writings from the University of Chicago are available to see. Everything is sealed. Is that not a little bit suspicious? Maybe his papers were a little bit too revealing of his socialist/communist mindset, or perhaps they revealed where his real birth place was, or that he was attending school as a foreign student. Hopefully, some day the truth of Obama's background will be revealed.

Other Liberal/Socialist/Communist Influences on Obama's Life: He got his start in Chicago as a community organizer working for such groups as ACORN. Obama represented and won a voting-rights law suit for ACORN. He also ran its leadership training sessions and benefited from its financial support in his campaigns. Obama was well trained in the "community organizing techniques" of Saul Alinsky, who was also an avowed radical communist.

In Chicago, Obama was taught in person by another radical Communist, former terrorist, founder of "The Weather Underground," Bill Ayers, whom many people believe actually did the writing of his book *Dreams of my Father*, or at least greatly contributed, because it is Ayers style of writing.

Black Liberation Theology: In Chicago, Obama also spent 20 years listening to the racist/anti-American sermons of his pastor, Jeremy Wright, who preached "black liberation theology," a belief that Jesus Christ was really black and was oppressed by the ancient Romans, as well as by the white imperialists of that period who were colonizing Israel. Black-liberation theologians teach that Christ's message was really a radical one of "overthrowing white imperial oppression in order to achieve liberation."

Today, the liberation-theologians teach that America is the evil imperialist nation, with a "history of enslaving black people and colonizing them in modern ghettos of urban poverty." The black Christ would want his black people "to rise up and overcome" such an evil nation.

In one of Wright's sermons, he even was so bold as to say "God damn America." After the terrible tragedy of 9/11, Wright had the audacity to say that America had brought it on herself, "America's chickens are coming home to roost."

Liberation theology also teaches the Marxist "redistribution of wealth," taking from those who have and giving to those who have not.

The irony of all this, Jeremy Wright has actually done very well for himself in this nation which he considers so oppressive to blacks. He retired to a 10,340-square foot, four bedroom mansion and secured a $1.6 million mortgage for the home purchase and attached a $10 million line of credit for reasons unspecified in the paperwork.[391]

What effect on Obama's life have these many left-leaning Marxists, communists, and radicals had, either family members, friends, mentors and ministers? As my mother used to say, "The twig does not fall far from the tree." In other words, the character and philosophy of a child is not very different than the parents and others who raised him/her. Obama is not about to change his socialist/communist stripes now that he is elected President. He will go on believing and doing exactly what he has done before.

His Campaign Funds: Obama shattered all records with campaign fundraising, with total contributions of $750 million. But because he is a democrat, there will be no talk by the Democratic-controlled House about any campaign finance reform legislation. That only happens if it is a Republican who is elected and had high fund raising.

Barack's Questionable Birth Certificate and Eligibility to be President: Our founding fathers wanted to assure that the president of the United States would be a loyal American and not have strong ties to any other country. That is why they put in the clause in the Constitution that a person elected to President had to be "natural born Citizen" and, at least, for "fourteen years a Resident of the United States." (Article II, Section 1, U.S. Constitution) The framers of the Constitution excluded dual citizens from qualifying as natural born.

In spite of the media trying to avoid this issue or pooh-poohing it, more and more articles are coming out about it and several law suits have been filed, demanding to have the truth of Obama's birth clarified. Where is his birth certificate proving that he was born in Hawaii as he claims? The only thing he has is a certificate of live birth, which not even a soccer coach will accept as evidence of a child's birth and his real age. All of Obama's records now in Hawaii are sealed. Why would that happen unless there is something to hide?

Kenyan Birth Certificate for Obama: Obama's Kenya grandmother states that she was at Obama's birth in Kenya. The hospital where he was born, Coast General Hospital in Mombasa, Kenya, is very proud to have been the hospital where an American president was born.

There is even a picture of a Kenyan birth certificate for Obama circulating on the internet and an article about it by *worldnetdaily.com*. It shows his parents as Barack Hussein Obama and Stanley Ann (Dunham) Obama. He was born at Coast General Hospital, Aug. 4, 1961. No doctor is listed, but it shows signatures, certifying deputy registrar of Coast Province, Joshua Simon Oduya. It was allegedly issued as a certified copy of the original in February, 1964, and has an official Kenya seal. The *World Net Daily* article states that "*WND* was able to obtain other birth certificates from Kenya for purposes of comparison, and the form of the documents appear to be identical."

The birth certificate came from California attorney Orly Taitz, who has filed a number of lawsuits demanding proof of Barack Obama's eligibility to serve as president. Because of the birth certificate, Taitz has filed a new motion in U.S. District Court for the Central District of California for its authentication.

Taitz's motion "requests the purported evidence of Obama's birth—both the alleged birth certificate and foreign records not yet obtained—be preserved from destruction." She asks for permission to legally request documents from Kenya and seeks a subpoena for deposition from Secretary of State Hillary Clinton, so both the Kenya authorities and Clinton will be forced to authenticate the birth certificate.

Before, she was told you don't have anything backing your claims. Now she has more than Obama's certificate of "live birth" that he had posted on his website when he was running for office. She says the birth certificate she has posted coming from Kenya actually has signatures.[391]

Well, if that is true and Obama was born in Kenya, that's not so bad is it? His mother was American so wouldn't Obama automatically take her nationality when he was born? Yes, if she were of age; but, remember back in the year that Obama was born, one had to be at least 21 to be considered an adult and be able to vote. Stanley Ann needed to be 21 for Obama to receive her citizenship. She was not. There is also the question of his Kenyan father. At the time of Obama's birth, Kenya still belonged to the jurisdiction of United Kingdom. That would make Obama fall under the UK for his citizenship or if his mother were of age, he would have dual citizenship. Would that be all right? No, our founding fathers excluded dual citizenship from qualifying as natural born.

Over a Million Dollars Spent to Keep Obama's Past Hidden: Obviously, there are important secrets to hide if one is going to such expense and efforts to keep them hidden. What are some of the other records hidden? His kindergarten records, his adoption records; his high school and college records; and papers that were written such as those from Punahou High School in Hawaii; Occidental College in California; Columbia University in New York; his Columbia Thesis; his Harvard Law School Records; his Harvard Law Review articles; scholarly writings from the University of Chicago; his passport; his medical records; his files from his years as an Illinois State Senator; his Illinois State Bar Association; even his baptism records.[392]

Why are all of these records kept hidden? It is suspected that his adoption records, his baptism records, and all the various schools that he attended and even the papers he wrote would have some reference to the fact that his parents were divorced and he had been adopted by his second father who was Indonesian, He would be enrolling as a foreign student from Indonesia, which is where he went to elementary school.

There are records at the elementary school in Indonesia that Obama must not have gotten to in time. They state that since he had been adopted he was an Indonesia citizen. The records also state that he is of Muslim faith as were both his real father and his step father. During his college years, he traveled to Pakistan with a friend. Pakistan would not allow an American in at that time, but Obama was able to enter the country because he had an Indonesian passport.

Democrats Failed to Certify Obama's Constitutional Eligibility in 49 of the 50 States: According to an article by Drew Zahn of *WorldNetDaily* posted September 27, 2009, the Democratic National Committee used two separate forms to affirm Barack Obama's eligibility to be president in not only the November 2008 election, but also the primary elections. The first form included the language affirming his eligibility, filed in Hawaii, where state law requires the specific language. The other form filed in the rest of the 49 states, omitted the language.

Drew Zahn was getting his information from a writer for the *Canada Free Press*, JB Williams. Williams wrote, "It appears that the DNC never certified constitutional eligibility for Barack Hussein Obama, despite their many claims of proper vetting and certification, all of which we now know to be false."

Williams believes that all three Democrat signers of the eligibility certificate knew that what they were signing was not a true certificate. One of those was Nancy Pelosi, Speaker of the House, who would never respond to *WND* though they called her office many times. The White House also refused to respond.

Have Obama's Records in Hawaii Been Amended? An excellent article by Devy Kidd appeared in *NewswithViews*, September 23, 2009, entitled "Obama's Ineligibility: How Deep Does the Corruption Go?" She reviews much of what I have written above and includes the investigation of even more people. One is an attorney in New Jersey, Leo Donofrio, who's case against Obama was the first to be scheduled for conference by the U.S. Supreme Court, but "it was kicked to the curb without any hearing on the merits of the case. Not a single case brought to date has ever been heard on its merits."

Donofrio is now representing a lady in Hawaii who refers to herself as TerriK, who believes that there is proof that Obama's vital records have been amended. Donofrio is filing litigation in Hawaii in the circuit court to get those records that have been denied by Hawaii state officials from the Office of Information Practices (OIP) and the Department of Health (DoH).

The American People Deserve the Truth: Devvy sums up her article with the following statement:

> *Who would ever have thought anyone would be so brazen as to try to pull off what Obama/Soetoro has—so far. Americans relied upon the RNC and DNC to vet their candidates as to constitutional qualification. If they did, it is now a cover up of mass proportions because, clearly, Obama/Soetoro was never eligible. There can be no question (except to those who simply refuse to believe this slick flim-flam man is a pathological liar) Obama/ Soetoro, has covered up every single record of his life except a few scraps here and there that make him look good. There can only be one reason and that is Obama/Soetoro has always known he is constitutionally ineligible for the office of the president.*
>
> *It won't work. We the people deserve the truth and the longer this usurper remains in office, the worse it will be as far as legislation he has signed into law. You can thank every member of the Electoral College*

*and Congress for allowing this fraud to continue. We the people by the
hundreds of thousands did everything humanly possible to stop the vote
in Congress. If there was any question Obama/Soetoro was never eligible,
an investigation should have been initiated and the first ones to be put
under oath would be Nancy Pelosi and Howard Dean.*[393]

California Judge Scheduled Trial January, 2010, Over Obama's Eligibility:
U.S. District Judge David Carter, an ex-Marine, had set a trial for the case on
January 26, 2010. Had it taken place, it would have been the first time the merits
of the case would have been argued in open court.

According to a phone interview with Dr. Jerome Corsi, who has written
much about Obama's eligibility in his articles for *WorldNetDaily.com,* Corsi said
that the case was dismissed, as have all the cases against Obama, with the judge
stating that "there is no standing." In other words, the plaintiffs have not been
able to prove that they have "suffered a concrete and particularized injury" from
Obama's eligibility or not.

Personally, I believe the entire nation has suffered enormously through the
giant plunge to socialism that Obama now has us on. We could have a class
action law suit—*Citizens of the United States of America vs. President Obama!*

WND founder, Joseph Farah, launched a campaign to raise contributions
to post billboards asking, "Where's the birth certificate," and he produced an
excellent DVD documentary, "A Question of Eligibility."[394]

**Possible Class Action Law Suit by Military Who are Refusing to Follow the
Command of an Illegal Commander in Chief**: Another story that made no
national news (other than on the internet) tells of men in the Armed Forces who
were refusing to go to Afghanistan on the claim that Obama was not legally their
President and had no authority as their Commander in Chief. Did you hear about
it in the news? No, of course not, not with our controlled liberal media!

According to *World Net Daily,* Attorney Orly Taitz was representing Major
Stefan Cook, whose order to deploy to Afghanistan was revoked when he
challenged Obama's eligibility to hold office. That case was re-filed in a federal
court in Florida. The suit saught damages and a declaratory judgment. Named as
defendants were: Simtech, Cook's former civilian employer, and several officials,
including Col. Louis B. Wingate and Secretary of Defense Robert Gates. In an
interview Major Cook stated:

*"As an officer in the armed forces of the United States, it is [my] duty to
gain clarification on any order we may believe illegal. With that said,*

if President Obama is found not to be a 'natural-born citizen,' he is not eligible to be commander in chief."

As previously reported by *World Net Daily*, a judge in Georgia had dismissed Cook's case when the government suddenly revoked his orders to report to Fort Benning for deployment to Afghanistan. However, he and his attorney were trying again. His case raised the possibility of a class-action law suit among members of the military, that their orders weren't valid because of questions surrounding Obama's constitutional eligibility. As the article states, "Without proof that there is a legitimate commander in chief, the entire U.S. Army becomes 'merely a corps of chattel slaves under the illegitimate control of a private citizen.'"

The new complaint says it seeks Cook's reinstatement with his civilian employer, Simtech Inc., as well as protection from the Department of Defense and president "from further retaliation for plaintiff's challenge to the president's constitutional authority." Attorney Orly Taitz told *WND* she plans to file additional paperwork with the Florida court adding the alleged Kenyan birth certificate to Major Cook's case.[395]

Media Blackout Concerning Obama's Eligibility for President: In the chapters on the CFR, the Bilderbergers, the Trilateral Commission and the other elitist groups, the reader has already read about their power over government, as well as the media. The media is only allowed to reveal what the elitists tell them they can. Other things they are forbidden to talk about at peril of losing their jobs or other threats.

Two reporters from Canada, Douglas Hagamann, a private investigator and founder of Northeast Intelligence Exclusive, and Judi McLoud, founding editor of *Canada Free Press*, wrote a joint article entitled "Media Blackout on Obama Eligibility Dates Back to November," 8/4/2009. They interviewed several prominent USA journalists, very high up in news organizations who told them of the threats, manipulation, and disinformation used on them way back before the election in November to keep them quiet on this subject. They were told it was just a "fringe" matter and of little importance. However, these reporters knew that the eligibility to hold the highest office in the land was more than just a "fringe" matter. The very heart of the U.S. Constitution is at stake. Do we go on ignoring this part of it? Then what about other parts that don't necessarily fit our agenda? Hagamann and McLoud state that the first evidence they have are documents from a prominent U.S. talk show host that includes a stunning written admission:

. . . he was threatened with his career—or worse—should he talk about the issue of Barack Hussein Obama's birth records to a national audience. This document was obtained on December 10, 2008, and provides explicit detail of a "gag order" imposed on this host before and immediately following the national election last November.

The talk show host gave the reporters a signed document, giving the exact dates and times when he was forbidden to discuss any aspect of the birth certificate controversy. It reveals: who the people were threatening him, where the orders originated, and confirms that failure to adhere to the order would likely end his career in that industry. He also confirms that other, less specific, but more menacing threats were implied during other conversations with those making the subject off limits.

Hagamann and McLoud and the organizations they represent decided they needed more evidence before they could go public with their information. In the months since, they have found others who are also willing to talk and expose the media blackout that is going on. And they found others who were afraid. As one source stated, "I've got a career and family to think about." Here are two other sources:

1) An administrative assistant of a cable network news station in New York City. She provided detailed information of a 2008 meeting between the top network executive and four-well-known news anchors. She is the one who drafted the memo to the various hosts to notify them of the date, time and location of the high-level meeting at the request of the network's top executive. She was also present at the meeting and verified of the official warnings by the network official to the news anchors "to avoid any on-air discussion of the birth place, eligibility, and news accounts of litigation compelling Obama to produce a legitimate copy of his birth certificate." She also was asked to arrange a conference immediately following the meeting between the network executive and an attorney closely associated with Obama, who was acting on his behalf.

2) A corporate secretary for a major news network, who wrote a statement confirming the existence of a one-page inter-office memo, bearing the markings "confidential" and "not for dissemination." It was addressed and distributed to "news anchors and on-air talent" that specifically instructed the recipients to avoid any discussion pertaining to the Obama birth certificate controversy. The memo was written and distributed in October, 2008, and specifically instructed on-air talent to "advise guests, as necessary, to refrain from citing any news story, legal proceedings, internet 'blogs' or other sources

that pertain to the ongoing eligibility controversy of future President Barack Obama." (Amazing that they already were referring to him as the "future president." This was a month before the November election. Is this also evidence that our elections are rigged?)

The article states that "there is a wide-spread cover up that began at the earliest stages of the Obama campaign." The cover-up traces back to some of the most powerful and influential people in the U.S., . . . the top people. We are not talking about mid or upper level management—this is from the very top in all cases. The article ends with the question, "If there is nothing to the birth certificate issue and the question of eligibility, why the secrecy?"[396]

Could This Be the Smoking Gun? I received an e-mail just before the printing of this book showing an article coming from a popular Kenyan newspaper, called the *Standard* with the headlines, "**Kenyan-born Obama all set for U.S. Senate.**" The date was Sunday, June 27, 2004, when Obama was running for the Senate seat from Illinois. This must have been one of the few articles that he could not get to—to have sealed or deleted from some newspaper files.

The article does not give any more details about Obama's birth in Kenya. It focuses instead on the fact that the Obama's main rival, Jack Ryan, had just dropped out of the race because of a "furor over lurid sex club allegations", that his ex-wife, actress Jeri Ryan, had said her husband would take her to. Rather than have the scandal revealed, Ryan dropped out of the race.[398]

Surely if this article was not true, if Obama were not born in Kenya, he would have protested this newspaper article and tried to correct it, but that was not the case. Perhaps his plans were not yet laid to run for president someday, so he did not worry about this article.

The article was sent on to the attorney Orly Taitz. Hopefully, it can be used if the court cases against Obama are ever allowed to come to trial.

Obama's Cabinet and Czars—Is This Really Hope and Change?

What Are the Globalist Connections of Obama's Cabinet? Obama promised in his campaign to have change with new players in the game. Sorry to say, he has brought in cabinet members with the same old globalist elite connections as previous administrations. Even before the end of the inauguration month, President Obama has appointed eleven members of the Trilateral Commission to chief positions in his cabinet. They are: Secretary of Treasury, **Tim Geithner;** Ambassador to the United Nations, **Susan Rice;** National Security Advisor,

Gen. James L. Jones; Deputy National Security Advisor, **Thomas Donilon;** Chairman, Economic Recovery Committee, **Paul Volker;** Director of National Intelligence, Admiral **Dennis C. Blair;** Assistant Secretary of State, Asia & Pacific, **Kurt M. Campbell;** Deputy Secretary of State, **James Steinberg;** State Department, Special Envoy, Richard Haas: **Richard Haass;** State Department, Special Envoy, **Dennis Ross;** State Department, Special Envoy, **Richard Holbrooke.**

As previously stated in the Chapter about the elite organizations, Obama was groomed for the presidency by key members of the Trilateral Commission, **Zbigniew Brzezinski**, co-founder of the Trilateral Commission with **David Rockefeller,** who was Obama's principal foreign policy advisor. Patrick Wood ends his article with the following:

> *The Obama presidency is a disingenuous fraud. He was elected by promising to bring change, yet from the start change was never envisioned. He was carefully groomed and financed by the Trilateral Commission and their friends . . . In short, Obama is merely the continuation of disastrous, non-American policies that have brought economic ruin upon us and the rest of the world. The Obama experience rivals that of Jimmy Carter, whose campaign slogan was "I will never lie to you."* [399]

Obama and his Many Czars: On July 16, 2009, Fox News reported that Obama had appointed 34 Czars. A month later, it was up to 40 czars and rising. These "advisors" to the president earn enormous salaries, ranging from $150,000 to $170,000 a year. They exercise control over various parts of the federal government, the economy, and our lives, but they are only answerable to the president, with no "vetting," no congressional approval or oversight. (Out of the entire list, only two were approved by the Senate.) Supposedly, these Czars report to a Cabinet Secretary or to Vice President Biden. No one really knows except for Obama. Where's the transparency that Obama promised in his administration? I wrote the following article for our summer 2009 edition of the Eagle Forum of California newsletter, *the Sentinel,* comparing what is going on to a play I directed back when I was teaching school full time.

"Ali-Obama and His Forty Thieves (Czars)": My first year of teaching was in a middle school in Idaho Falls, Idaho, where I taught speech, drama and journalism to seventh, eighth, and ninth graders. The musical we chose to put on that year was "Alibaba and the Forty Thieves," selected mainly because of type casting—I had the perfect thieves right in one of my classes, my 3rd period, 7th grade class, consisting of 22 "swashbuckler" boys and 2 frightened girls.

My first day of teaching, while I was writing on the blackboard and my back was turned, someone in the 3rd period class stole my purse. With the help of the principal, we got it back, but, of course, the money was missing. The second day, in the same class, my car keys were stolen. Fortunately, whoever took them was either too scared to drive or decided my old clunker was not worth stealing. The keys showed up back on my desk at the end of the day.

Eventually, my third period class and I began to develop a working relationship; it happened on the day that I locked my keys in my car and asked for some of their assistance. The leader of the "pack" was very skilled in getting an old coat-hanger wire with a hook on the end down through the top of the window. Very quickly, he pulled up the lock and gave me my keys.

When I told this class about the musical we had selected, they were delighted and excited to play the parts "legitimately" of thieves, and they all did a very believable job. Not only did they have fun, but it turned out to be a very good learning experience for them. They found out that stealing does not really turn out well in the end. The forty thieves in the story all ended up being boiled alive in burning hot oil.

The Ali-Obama Robber-Baron: There is a remarkable similarity between the famous *Arabian Nights* story and our present day USA, not only in its title and the name of our present President, but in his robber-baron philosophy of "redistribution of wealth." The forty czars (thieves), whom he has selected as his assistants, share his philosophy and are sharing in the wealth, with some very nice salaries, over $150,000 a year.

The robber in the play had collected a huge cave full of treasures, a vast fortune in gold, jewels, precious diamonds and rubies. Ali-Obama and his czars have done the same. They have a $3 trillion budget and $787 billion tucked away in their Stimulus Package Cave, used for "kind, benevolent bailouts." This is robber-baron language for "nationalization," or "take-over" of large banks, insurance companies (like AIG), auto industries, and even states. In March of 2010, Ali-Obama added the American health industry to his vast collection of "nationalized treasures," in spite of 60% of Americans opposed to it.

Eleven billion dollars was given as a bailout to California to help with our $42 billion debt. Perhaps, more has since been given. Other states are also receiving large bailouts, but nothing like what has been given to California. Of course, this has been kept very hush-hush. Ali-Obama understands that residents of states would not be very pleased to find out their state is becoming nationalized.

Whatever has been given bailouts or nationalized has been added to the vast treasures of what the robber baron kingdom now owns and controls. The banks, insurance companies, auto industries, and states have essentially lost their own autonomy, freedoms, and their ability to direct and control their own lives. As you have noticed, Ali-Obama has appointed his own czar over the banks, another czar over the auto industry, etc, and they get to make all the rules now including lowering the salaries.

And from whom is this vast fortune of money in his Stimulus Package Cave really stolen? Yes, it has been borrowed from China and Japan and wealthy banks and individuals, but who gets to pay the huge debt back to China with interest? The American people will pay and our children and grandchildren for generations to come. It is as if we have become serfs in the Ali-Obama fiefdom, no longer a free people, with a great burden of debt hanging over our heads.

Our Form of Government Has Been Stolen: The greatest theft is the stealing of our Republic, once known as a free country—the United States of America. It is now becoming a robber-baron reich or a fiefdom, with a robber and his forty cronies at its head. Our founding fathers worked very hard to create a balance in power between the executive branch, the legislative, and the judicial, so no one branch would ever get so powerful it could rule and reign over the others without any checks and balances. However, that has all come to a screeching halt.

In the March 30, 2009, addition of the *New American* is found an article entitled, "A Presidency Fit for a King." It states that under Obama, we no longer live under the Constitution and its three branches of government. Rather, we live under the administrative law of an administrative state.[339]

These various bureaucracies, led by czars, are all under the control of the president, with no checks or balances from other branches. The czars do not have to be approved by Congress; they are considered "all-knowing experts," who seem to be above the law and traditional constitutional restraints. They only answer to the president. Obama can issue an order to one of his czars; policy can be changed immediately and rights and laws can be impacted across the country. That does not sound very different from a monarchy does it? (*The Sentinel*, Eagle Forum of California, Summer, Santa Rosa, CA, 2009, pp. 1-2)

Where Did the Idea for Presidents to have Czars Originate Anyway? The idea started back with Obama's role model, good old FDR, who called the ones he appointed "dictators." President Nixon thought that was a little too blatant and changed the name to czars. Most presidents have had one or two or three; George W. Bush had much more, but Obama takes the cake with forty plus.

Why is Vetting by the Senate so Important? The appointments of president's advisors first having to be approved by the Senate is part of the Checks and Balances the founding fathers established as such a vital part of trying to hold back the Executive Branch from turning into a powerful "monarchy." It is also to prevent radical, extreme, communist czars from being appointed, such as Van Jones who has since resigned, under pressure. Had he first had to pass scrutiny by the Senate, even as liberal as our Senate has become, he probably would have never been appointed. Perhaps the car czar, Steven Rattner, would have never been appointed either, and his embarrassing resignation in the midst of a scandal would not have happened.

Many Appointees Had Not Paid Their Taxes: Of course, it is far less embarrassing for President Obama, if his appointees do not have to be vetted or given a thorough investigation. Look at the number who had a tax evasion problem, even the man who is now the treasurer, Tim Geithner, and Kathy Sebelius, a former Governor, who is now the head of Health and Human Services. She had to pay over $8,000 in back taxes. Senator Tom Daschle, the first nominee for the HHS, ended up removing his name; performance officer Nancy Kelleher, Labor Secretary Hilda Solis, and U.S. Trade Representative Ron Kirk all had tax evasion problems as well.[400]

Obama's Many Czars in Alphabetical Order (Those not yet filled are highlighted):

1. Abstinence Czar—(TBA) (Begun by George W. Bush. Obama will probably not fill it. It is a position he does not agree with)
2. Afghanistan Czar—Richard C. Holbrooke,
3. Aids Czar—Jeffrey Crowley
4. Auto-recovery Czar, Auto-worker czar—Ed Montgomery
5. Bank Bailout (TARP) Czar—Herbert Allison (was approved by the Senate)
6. Behavioral science Czar—
7. Border Czar—Alan Bersin, an assistant secretary of homeland security
8. Car Czar—formerly Steven Rattner—now Ron Blume
9. Climate Czar—Carol Browner
10. Cyber Czar—TBA
11. Disinformation Czar—
12. Domestic violence Czar—Lynne Rosenthal
13. Drug Czar—Gil R. Kerlikowske, former Seattle police chief
14. Economic Recovery Advisory Board—Paul A. Volcker
15. Energy and Environment Czar—Carol Browner
16. Economic Czar I—
17. Economic Czar II—
18. Faith-based and Neighborhood Partnerships Czar—Joshua DuBois
19. Food Czar—
20. Government performance Czar—Jeffrey Zients
21. Great Lakes Czar—Cameron Davis
22. Green Jobs Czar—Formerly Van Jones
23. Guantanamo Base Closure Czar—Daniel Fried
24. Health Reform Czar—Nancy-Ann DeParle
25. Information Czar—Vivek Kundra
26. Intelligence Czar (Director of National Intelligence)—Dennis Blair
27. Iran Czar—Dennis Ross
28. Manufacturing Czar—Ron Bloome
29. Mideast peace czar—George J. Mitchell
30. Pakistan czar—
31. Pay Czar—Kenneth R. Feinberg
32. Performance Czar—Jeffrey Zientz
33. Political Affairs Director Czar—Patrick Gaspard
34. Regulatory Czar—Cass R. Sunstein (Was approved by Senate)
35. Safe-schools czar—Kevin Jennings
36. Science Czar—John Holdren
37. Stimulus Oversight Czar—Earl Devaney
38. Technology Czar—Aneesh Chopra
39. Terrorism Czar—John Brennan
40. Urban Affairs Czar—Adolfo Carrion, Jr.
41. War Czar—Douglas Lute (appointed by Bush and kept by Obama)
42. Weapons Czar—Ashton Carter
43. White House Political Affairs Director—Patrick Gaspard
44. WMD Policy Czar—Gary Samore
45. Weatherization Czar—Gil Sperling (Held over from Bush administration)[402]
46. White House Communications Director—was Anita Dunn, who resigned after she and Obama received much flack after she revealed in a commencement address that one of her favorite political philosophers was Mao Tse-tung, Chinese dictator, who caused the death of millions of his own people.

Radical Background and Views, Connection to ACORN, of Many Czars and Cabinet Positions:

Rahm Emanual—White House Chief of Staff: Rahm has a very interesting political background, having served with Bill Clinton as his assistant for political affairs and his advisor on policy and strategy. He was demoted because of Hillary.

He then was appointed by Bill Clinton to serve on the board for Freddie Mac, for 2000-2001. During 2000, Freddie Mac misreported its net income by 30.5%. In 2001, it misreported by 23.9% and in 2002 by 42.9%. This failure of Freddie Mac to report honestly its true income is regarded as one of the events leading to the financial crisis.

In November of 2008, Emmanual made his famous statement, "You never want a serious crisis to go to waste. And what I mean by that is an opportunity to do things you could not do before." [Could those things include nationalizing the major banks, mortgage companies, auto industries, etc.?] Read more: (http://www.politico.com/news/stories/0310/34697.html" \l "ixzz0jRqHGN4s)

Patrick Gaspard—White house Political Affairs Director's Ties to ACORN and Big Labor: Gaspard holds a very high position in the White House, the same position formerly held by Karl Rove under the Bush administration. Ashley Martella of *Newsmax. TV* reported on September 28, 2009, that Gaspard, before this appointment, was a long-term Acorn operative and the political and legislative affairs executive for the radical left wing union (SEIU) Service Employees International Union—hospital division.[402]

David Patten wrote an article printed in *NewsMax.com*, September 28, 2009, that goes into greater detail about Gaspard's background. He served until 2003 as the New York political director for Bertha Lewis, ACORN's CEO and "chief organizer." He also worked for 8 years as the political director of SEIU (Local 1199), a hospital workers local, according to the *Village Voice*, a free weekly "alternative" newspaper in New York City.

There is a close connection between ACORN and SEIU. SEIU Local 880 and the SEIU Local 100 is headed by Wade Rathke, the founder of ACORN. These SEIU locals are listed as "part of the ACORN network of organizations." They used to be on ACORN's Web site, but the references recently were removed.

Rathke described in May, 2009, on his blog, *ChiefOrganizer.org*, how Gaspard and other officials of the SEIU teamed up with HealthCare Reform Czar Nancy-Ann DeParle to pry big price concessions from private health firms. Speaking of the advantage that comes from having powerful friends in high places, Rathke wrote: "If Patrick Gaspard didn't reach out from the White House and help make that happen, then I'll tell you to take some remedial classes in 'politics 101."

The *Spectator* described Gaspard as "ACORN's Man in the White House." It also reported that he was national field director in 2004 for American Coming Together (ACT), a get-out-the-vote organization, which also had a fraudulent record like ACORN. The Federal Election Commission (FEC) fined ACT with a $775,000 fee for campaign-finance violations—one of the largest FEC fines ever. The ACT reportedly ceased operations in 2005.

ACORN's History of Dishonesty, Embezzlement, Fraud, Support of Prostitution and Tax Evasion: ACORN, the community-organizing group, for which Obama was a spokesperson and attorney, does not have a very good track record for honesty. In 1999, the founders, Wade and Dale Rathke, who also kept the books for ACORN, were under indictment for embezzlement of $1 million, which supposedly has been paid back. It now appears that the amount was more like $5 million (details below). The organization is under investigation nationwide for voter registration fraud. And in September, 2009, a series of videos were released showing ACORN workers at various centers across the nation caught on a hidden camera giving willing advice and support to a young girl posing as a prostitute and to a man posing as her pimp.

The advice given to the couple included changing the name of their occupation as prostitutes to "performing arts," so they could get a mortgage on a house; changing the name of under-age 13-year old prostitutes that would be coming from San Salvador to "dependents;" and if they had a hard time paying their income taxes on this illegal income, they were told "just don't pay them." (Of course, the later advice seems to be quite normal with many of Obama's choices for czar or cabinet positions found guilty of tax evasion.)

ACORN Funding Stopped: After the release of the videos and the coverage of ACORN on the Glenn Beck show television show and on many conservative talk radio programs, the end of September, 2009, the House and Senate finally voted to stop the funding of ACORN. How much money was stopped?

In an article entitled "Exactly how much taxpayer money has gone to ACORN?" Chris Moody quotes economist Chris Edwards that from the years 2003 to 2007, more than $12.5 million has gone to the support of ACORN.

However, according to Edward, ACORN's share of overall federal subsidies is small compared to thousands of similar organizations that have become hooked on the federal trough. There are 1,800 different federal subsidy programs, with a powerful lobbying force has been created that propels a $3.6 trillion spending juggernaut.[403]

ACORN Embezzlement was Really Five Million: Robert Travis Scott wrote an article October 4, 2009, on NOLA.com, telling of a new larger embezzlement that has taken place inside ACORN. The Louisiana Attorney General Buddy Caldwell says after a new subpoena and an internal review by the ACORN board themselves, the embezzled money taken by (supposedly) just one of the Rathke brothers, Dale, was really closer to $5 million, not $1 million. From 1999-2000, Dale Rathke had taken nearly $1 million in improper credit card charges.

Why is the Louisiana Attorney General involved in this investigation? ACORN got its start in New Orleans and it was there that the embezzlement took place at the original location on 1024-26 Elysian Fields Ave. ACORN has since moved its headquarters to Washington, D.C.

In the subpoena, it was unclear if some of the missing $5million was embezzled from state, federal or private funds. Caldwell said the subpoenas were focusing on possible ACORN violations of state employee tax law, obstructing justice and violating the Employee Retirement Security Act. The subpoena also requests documents from Citizens Consulting Inc., which assisted ACORN, and from various accounting and legal consultants in New Orleans.

Even though, ACORN Chief Executive Officer Bertha Lewis was part of the review board that found the missing additional $ millions at a board of directors meeting Oct. 17, 2008, she denied everything and said the accusations about the embezzlement are "completely false." The Rathke brothers could not be found for comments.[404]

Congress Voted to Cut off the Funds for ACORN: After all the bad publicity ACORN was getting after the release of the videos showing their promotion of illegal activities, both the House and the Senate voted that there would be no more funding for ACORN. Obama refused to support ending federal funding for ACORN, however, telling ABC: "It's not something I'm paying a lot of attention to."[405]

According to Congresswoman Michele Bachmann, the funding was only stopped for the month of October, 2009. In November, it started again, and ACORN was right back at its same questionable activities.

Cass Sustein is the Regulatory Czar: According to Talk Show Host, Sharon Hughes, who devoted her radio program, September 28, 2009, to a closer look at his life, Cass Sustein would like a new Bill of Rights to our Constitution, and he wants it by the year 2020. His Bill of Rights is based on one that FDR had but was never presented. It would be a socialist Bill of Rights demanding certain rights for all people such as the right to a useful job, a decent home, a good education and free medical care for all.

Sustein is a Harvard professor who has written 35 books about changing U.S. laws. He is against gun rights and says the 2nd Amendment is being misinterpreted. He also believes that in the U.S. court system, "animals should be permitted to bring suit, with human beings as their representatives," against people who are harming them. He also said that an adult dog or horse is more 'rational' than a baby. (I wonder if he would like the dog or horse to act as the attorney in the cases.) With such liberal views, one wonders what radical regulations the "regulatory czar" is going to produce for our nation.[406]

Kevin Jennings—the Safe School Czar: Obama appointed Jennings to be the head of the Safe and Drug-Free Schools, part of the Federal Department of Education. Jennings is anything but what most people would consider "safe" for their children. He is a former teacher and principal, who is a gay activist and author of pro-gay books for schools. In 1990, in Massachusetts, he founded and was the first president of GLSEN, the Gay, Lesbian, Straight Education Network, which, according to one of their websites, now has over 5000 schools (both high school and middle school) participating in the GLSEN- supported "Day of Silence." (This is a day in April, set aside to essentially "honor" those students who perceive themselves to be homosexual and those who support them, by giving them a special school day, in which they are to remain silent—signifying the "supposed" many years of "silence" that gays had to endure before they were able to come out of the closet and be recognized and accepted.) GLSEN tries to force its liberal pro-homosexual viewpoint on all American schools, teachers, and students through many radical books, videos, publications and presentations.

Jennings has published six books on gay rights and education. One of the most well-known is about gay teachers telling their stories, *One Teacher in Ten: Gay and lesbian educators tell their stories,* Kevin Jennings, ed., (Alyson Publications, 1994). One of the stories in the book tells of his own experience giving advice to a 15-year old gay student brought to him by an advisee. Here is what he wrote on p. 25:

> Toward the end of my first year, during the spring of 1988, Brewster appeared in my office in the tow of one of my advisees, . . . to whom I had been "out" for a long time. "Brewster has something he needs to talk with you about," she intoned ominously . . . On a hunch, I suddenly asked, "What's his name?" Brewster's eyes widened briefly, and then out spilled a story about his involvement with an older man

he had met in Boston. I listened, sympathized, offered advice. He left my office with a smile on his face that I would see every time I saw him on the campus for the next two years, until he graduated."

So, what do we learn from this story? Jennings, who was appointed to be the head of a federal office over the safety of our nation's school children, would do nothing himself to protect the safety of an under-age minor from being sexually exploited by an older man, something that is considered a felony in probably every state across our nation including Massachusetts, where this event took place. Instead of preventing the sexual exploitation, Jennings actually encouraged the relationship so he could see "a smile on the boy's face." His only cautionary advice to Brewster was for the boy to use a condom.

Other Reasons Why Parents Should Be Concerned About Jennings: Not only does Jennings support and promote homosexuality in schools, but he has a past drug abuse problem, has expressed his contempt for religion and his support for Harry Hay, of NAMBLA, "North American Man Boy Love Association." (NAMBLA's motto is "sex before eight, before it's too late.") In a transcript of a 1997 speech, Jennings said, "I was inspired by NAMBLA's Harry Hay, who started the first ongoing gay rights groups in America." Jennings did not mention that Harry Hay was a communist, who also founded such awe-inspiring groups as "The Radical Faeries" and the "Mattachine Society," a homosexual activist group that began in 1948. The name comes from a "Medieval French secret society of masked men who, through their anonymity, were empowered to criticize ruling monarchs with impunity."[407]

The Office of Safe and Drug-Free Schools (OSDFS): This office was started by the Bush Administration in 2002. According to its website, one of its primary functions is to "provide financial assistance for drug and violence prevention activities and activities that promote the health and well being of students in elementary and secondary schools, and institutions of higher education."

Jennings was appointed to the position largely because of his longtime record of "working to end bullying and discrimination in schools."

Background on GLSEN—the Shocking Books and Information to Promote Homosexuality and Promiscuity for School Age Children: Mission America has called GLSEN "a child corruption group." On their website, *www. missionamerica.com*, they expose some of the sexually graphic books GLSEN recommends for students. Most of the books still remain on the GLSEN web site: Children at Risk: GLSEN, Corruption and Crime (a survey of books recommended by GLSEN); How GLSEN Encourages Student Experimentation

With Homosexuality; Translating GLSEN's Deceptive Language about Homosexuality.[408]

Van Jones—the Former Green Czar: Because of negative exposure that Van Jones received on mainly the Glenn Beck television program, which revealed his radical, communist past, Jones resigned in August of 2009. It is still good to look at his background, however, to ask why Obama would ever appoint such a man, an avowed communist radical who just changed his red coat to green.

Sharon Hughes spoke on the subject of Obama's many czars for our Eagle Forum 8th Annual Constitution Breakfast, September 12, in Santa Rosa, Ca. Here are some of the interesting things she said about Van Jones, the former Green Czar, who, even though he was forced to resign, still has much influence on Obama's green policies. Jones referred to Obama as not only the first black president, but also the first green president. If Obama's green views are as radical as Van Jones, we have much to worry about.

The Radical/Revolutionary/Communist Groups Van Jones Was Connected to: The first group Jones was part of was "The October 27 Coalition," an anti-police organization whose mission was drawn up by leaders of the Black Panthers, another anti-police group. Van Jones signed and helped circulate a petition sponsored by the October 27 Coalition against police across the nation, accusing them of using the 9-11 attacks to carry out policies of torture.

Jones is a member of the "Revolutionary Communist Party USA." On their website he calls on participants to resist "so we will not be crushed." He is also speaking on a video they produced, asking for a "Theology of Resistance and a Theology of Liberation" aimed at "transforming America."

Jones was the founder and leader of a radical, communist revolutionary group called STORM, "Standing Together to Organize a Revolutionary Movement." He staged a vigil on September 11, 2001, entitled "People of color groups gather together in solidarity with Arab Americans and to warn the East Coast dead." That sounds a little bit radical and scary, doesn't it? He has also stated. "We agree with Lenin's analysis of the state and the party and also we have found inspiration in the revolutionary strategies developed by such third-world revolutionaries like Mao se Tung." For a long time, Van Jones was a member of the board of the Apollo Alliance, another extreme radical group

He warns us of some environmental crisis—"Might I humbly suggest Noah and his wife. Why Noah? Because we have a crisis coming. There has got to be an ark and it has got to be able to accommodate diversity on a massive scale."

Mellisa Harris Lanswell, part of the environmental justice movement, said that Jones, resignation is a "setback for environmental justice." She says the environmental justice movement, which started more than three decades ago, was created to help solve "racial injustice."

What is Environmental Justice? Environmental justice is the same as "social justice," which can be translated as the same old "Marxism" but with a new name. How do the proponents of environmental justice get their message out? They become "community organizers," another new, modern name for the old Marxists.

Environmental justice can be summed up as "redistribution of wealth"—taking from those who have and giving it to those who have not. That sounds good to the "have-nots" until they do a little research and find out that wherever "redistribution of wealth" has occurred in communist countries throughout history has not worked out the way the have-nots have been promised. The have-nots remain equally poor, while the wealthy and elite become even wealthier and more elite.[409]

Jones background and affiliations in Communist, radical groups, as well as many of his Marxist, green statements were cited on Glenn Beck's television show and other talk shows. It became obvious that Jones he was a little too Marxist and extreme and was reflecting negatively on the Obama administration. On September 6, he resigned. (http://www.cnn.com/2009/POLITICS/09/06/obama.adviser.resigns/index.html.)

Car Czar Steve Rattner and the Strange Closing of Chrysler Dealerships: Once the federal government had nationalized the auto industry, Obama appointed his friend Steve Rattner as the Car Czar, even though he had never held any position in the auto industry. Chrysler and General Motors were told they would have to close down many of their dealerships. Obama appointed the Automotive Task Force with Steve Rattner as the CEO.

According to Sharon Hughes, most people thought it was the Chrysler Corporation that decided which dealerships would have to be closed. No, it was the Automotive Task Force that made that decision and on what basis? Of the 789 dealerships that were closed, 788 had donated to Republican political causes. Only one had not. Rattner's wife had worked for the DNC, Democrat National Committee and had access to the information about donations given by the American people in the 2008 election.

The "Cash for Clunkers" Program: President Obama signed into law June 24, 2009, a bill that became known as "Cash for Clunkers," or the Car Allowance

Rebate System, or the federal scrappage program. It was intended to stimulate the slumping auto industry by encouraging consumers to trade in older, less fuel-efficient vehicles for new cars that would get better fuel economy by providing a credit of either $3,500 or $4,500. Credits would also be available for large vans, SUVs and pickup trucks irrespective of their fuel economy.

This idea was supposedly modeled after programs that had been successfully implemented in Europe. The official starting date was July 1, but the processing of claims did not start until July 24. By July 30, the $1 billion was already used up. Congress had to okay an additional $2 billion. The program was supposed to end on November 1, 2009; however, it was cut short on August 24 due to concerns that the money was running out.[410]

How Successful was the Program?: According to Wikipedia, the Department of Transportation, August 26 reported that the program resulted in 690,114 dealer transactions submitted requesting a total of $2.877 billion in rebates. However, the dealership that sold the most cars was Toyota, a foreign company. At the end of the program Toyota accounted for 19.4 % of sales, followed by General Motors with 17.6 %, Ford with 14.4 %, Honda with 13.0 %, and Nissan with 8.7%. It led to a gain in market share for Japanese and Korean manufacturers at the expense of American car makers, with only Ford not taking a significant hit. The Department of Transportation also reported that the average fuel efficiency of trade-ins was 15.8 mpg, compared to 24.9 mpg for the new cars purchased to replace them, translating to a 58% fuel efficiency improvement.[411]

Washington Has Bad Credit and Too Much Red Tape: According to an article in the *Washington Times*, "Dealers End Cash for Clunkers Before Government," many dealers chose to end their program long before the government decided to shut it down. Why was that? Two-thirds of all dealers that enrolled in the Cash for Clunkers program were still waiting for their first disbursement from the government clear into October, 2009.

Dealers also complained that the Cash for Clunkers was "tedious, unreliable, slow and nonsensical." It took 21 days just to review the submitted claim. Then if there was anything you forgot to fill in, such as a date, you had to resubmit everything. There were dealers all over the country that had 50 or 100 cars sitting in their storage area, just waiting for government approval and the disbursement of the $3500 or $4500 dollars. If you multiply 50 cars x $4,500 that equals $225,000 that the poor dealer was still waiting for. From a business perspective, that is a lot of cash to have to float for who knows how long. Thousands of car dealers across the nation were facing the same problem. They all learned firsthand that the federal government is not a very good business partner.[412]

Sneaky Takeover of Car Dealership's Computer Program: (This was also mentioned in the chapter on Big Brother is Watching You.) A little known part of the Cash for Clunkers program that no one knew about was revealed by the Glenn Beck show. When the dealerships would go on to the cars.gov website, they were told that their computer and everything on it now is the property of the federal government, and anyone in any agency can now have access to their computer, both domestic and foreign. Because Glenn Beck exposed it, it caused the federal government to remove the wording. However, we don't know if they ever removed the technology that allowed them to capture what was on the computers. I guess the Obama administration assumes that since they are essentially the owners of the American car industry, they should own all the computers involved in the dealerships as well. This is one more example of the bad effects of government takeover or nationalization or socialism in action.

If you go to *www.GlenBeckcars.govprogram*, you can see a You Tube clip of his show, July 31, 2009. It shows the exact language that was on the government website. A car dealer also sent in a YouTube video clip of his computer screen verifying the same language. Many busy dealers probably just glossed over it, did not pay much attention, clicked the button to submit their transaction so they could register the car and get their money back. Little did they know that their computers were now under ownership and control of the federal government! Here are the words that used to pop up on the website *cars.gov*:

Privacy Act and Security Statement

> *This application provides access to the DoT cars system. When logged on to the CARS system, your computer is considered a Federal computer system and is the property of the U.S. Government. Any or all uses of this system and all files on this system may be intercepted, monitored, recorded, copied, audited, inspected, and disclosed to authorized CARS, DoT, and law enforcement personnel, as well as authorized officers of other agencies, both domestic and foreign."*

On the You Tube broadcast of Glenn Beck's program, July 31, after exposing the above words on the government website, we heard comments from his two guests, Kimberly Guilfoyce, *Fox News* Anchor, and Jonah Goldberg, syndicated columnist. Kimberly said that the government has much modern technology that could be used for tracking the car dealerships' computers and their every transactions, files, etc. She said it is perfectly legal, once they have clicked on and agreed to register the car that needed to be "clunked." She described the government system as a giant octopus that "keeps rejuvenating its many tentacles every five seconds." Goldberg added that if the dealership has a phone system connected to his computer, then the government can legally listen to their phone calls as well.

Beck warned the television audience that if they went to the same website and clicked onto the same government program, their computer would also be subject to government tracking, even if you are not a car dealership. Glenn Beck added, "These czars seem to think that they are smarter than us and need to take care of us and take care of what they need to take care of because it is better for the collective."[413]

Resignation and Scandal: On July 13, Steve Rattner also resigned. He was under investigation by New York Attorney General Andrew M. Cuomo, for a million dollar pay-to-play scandal involving the Quadrangle Group that Rattner co-founded. Rattner may be under investigation also for a pay-to-play scandal for the closing of the Chrysler and GM dealerships as well.[414]

The Outsourcing of Auto Dealerships—Bringing the USA Down to a Third World Country: Now that the auto industry has been nationalized, essentially paid for by U.S. taxpayers, and GM is now Government Motors, what does the federal government, the new owner, plan to do to help the struggling auto industry? The plans are for closing their companies here in the U.S. and building plants overseas, in China, India, and Finland. Outsourcing is essentially another form of Marxism—"destroying the working class in order to distribute the wealth overseas."

What other reason would our president give a U.S. company to a foreign country? What other reason would the U.S. government loan Al Gore's Finland company millions of dollars to produce cars in another country? What other reason would U.S. auto companies close plants in the U.S. putting thousands out of work, and build new plants in foreign countries with billions of U.S. dollars? What other reason for employing thousands of foreigners? What other reason for all of the above unless the goal is to reduce the U.S. economy to that of a third-world country?

We're averaging a half million new unemployed every month, and the U.S. major auto companies are building new plants in foreign countries to employee foreigners? Nothing makes sense anymore unless you realize this is deliberately being done to destroy the middle class of our nation.

Check out the following articles, "General Motors Opens New Plant in China," *The Wall Street Journal;* "Ford to Build Third Car Assembly Plant in China," *The Wall Street Journal;* "Chrysler to build new India plant by 2009,"

(*http://in.reuters.com/article/businessNews/idININdia-29413020070908*); "Al
Gore's car company gets $528 million government loan to produce cars in
Finland," (*http://johnrlott.blogspot.com/2009/09/al-gores-car-company-gets-528-
million.html*); You Can't Do this to people, (*http://freedominourtime.blogspot.
com/2009/09/you-cant-do-this-to-people-robin.html.*)

Another Marxist Czar Resigned: Anita Dunn, who served as the White House
Communications Director, was exposed on the Glenn Beck show, October 15,
2009, for her love of the Communist dictator and mass murderer, Mao Tse-tung.
Beck unearthed footage of a talk that Dunn gave at a Catholic high-school
graduation June 5, 2009, where she said that Mao Tse-tung was one of her two
"favorite political philosophers." The other was Mother Teresa.

On a You Tube clip showing her speech, one could see a Christian cross
standing next to her at the side of the lectern. Yet, there she was admiring a man
who was the total opposite of Christianity, a man who was an avowed atheist,
who thought that religion was the "opiate of the people." And worst of all, he
was a man who had brutally killed 70 million of his own people, some of whom
were Christians and Christian missionaries.

After Glenn Beck's exposure of Dunn's communist leanings and the public
outcry and criticism that both she and Obama received, Dunn resigned November
11. She did not admit that Beck's show had anything to do with her resignation,
however. She said it was so she could spend more time with her family.

The Czar Accountability and Reform Act of 2009: Many Americans have
been writing and calling their Congressmen expressing their concern and outrage
about not only the communist leaning czars but the huge number appointed by
Obama. At the large Tea Party Express Rally that filled the Freedom Plaza with
over 2 million people in Washington D.C., September 12, some of the signs
read, "Czars belong in Russia."

In response to that concern, Representative Jack Kingston (R-GA) introduced
H.R. 3226, the Czar Accountability and Reform (CZAR) Act of 2009. According
to Kingston's press release some of the czars' salaries are as high as $172,000. In
addition, there are the costs for their staff, office supplies, travel expenses, etc. (If
you round off all the costs to $200,000 a month per czar multiplied by 40 that
equals $8 million a year.) Congressman Kingston sees Obama's many czars as a
growing problem that is costing tax payers millions that we cannot afford.

After Van Jones resignation, Rep. Patrick T. McHenry (R-N.C.) called
for Obama's czars to testify before Congress about their "authority and
responsibilities." Jones's "ability to slip into a position of power without due

congressional diligence only further underscores the necessity for a confirmation process," McHenry said. In a speech on the Senate floor, Senator Lamar Alexander (R-Tenn.) called the growing number of special policy advisers "antidemocratic."

To address the matter, Kingston introduced legislation which would withhold funding from any czar not confirmed by the Senate. Kingston stated:

> *While the Constitution may be inconvenient to the Administration, Article II, Section 2 clearly requires the 'advice and consent of the Senate.' Why won't the President use transparency and have these people come before the Senate and undergo the constitutionally-mandated process? In 300 years, czarist Russia had just 18 czars. It's taken just seven months for President Obama to nearly double that number.*[416]

Yes, there were a few czars in previous administrations, but nothing like Obama's: Ronald Reagan had 1, George Bush had 1, Bill Clinton had 3 and George W. Bush had 4 (one article said 36). Congressman Kingston is also concerned with not only the large number of Obama's czars but the speed in which they are being appointed, the vast policy areas they govern and their accountability to no one but Obama.

> *At this rate, we'll have 272 czars by 2012 . . . It seems President Obama is in the midst of forming a parallel government to push his policies. Not only do they duplicate existing Senate-confirmed positions, they are completely unaccountable. I serve on the Appropriations Committee which is responsible for overseeing every dollar spent by our government, but I've yet to see a single one of Obama's czars.*[416]

Michelle Obama and Her 26 Czar-ettes (Personal Assistants): It sounds like we also need a bill to try to stop the salaries for the many assistants of the first lady, which I have labeled "Czar-ettes." Michelle now has 26. That number may keep rising, similar to the number of czars for her husband. Wasn't she the one that told us she was trying "to give back to the country?" In one of her speeches she said, "In my own life, in my own small way, I have tried to give back to this country that has given me so much. See, that's why I left a job at a big law firm for a career in public service."

This quote makes it sound like Michelle is also willing to "tighten her belt" and sacrifice for her country, as Obama has asked all of us to do in this time of recession/depression. But in reality, it appears Michelle has had second thoughts about leaving the law firm salary she was receiving and has decided to take on a staff that is earning about as much as the entire firm at taxpaying dollars expense. It is amazing what some people are willing to do with other people's money!

President Obama gets a salary of $400,000 a year. The first lady does not receive a salary, but this hasn't deterred her from making sure her friends do. She has hired an unprecedented number of staffers to cater to her every need.

In July, it was reported that she had a staff of 22, more than any other first lady has ever had and their combined salaries are around 1 ½ million dollars—$1,495,700 to be precise. At the end of August, four more had been added. The grand total of what they earn is now $1,750,000 without taking into account the lavish benefit packages afforded to all of them. As one writer put it, "Little did American voters realize that the call for "change" would result in the establishment of an Obama oligarchy." (Oligarchy means rule by a small group of elite).

How does that compare to other first ladies? Mary Lincoln, the wife of Abraham Lincoln, was criticized for purchasing new china for the White House during the Civil War. Mamie Eisenhower had to pay for her own personal secretary out of her own money. Granted things have steadily gotten worse as more and more elected officials and their spouses are usurping power and money from the public trough, both Republicans and Democrats. Laura Bush had 17 staffers with a combined salary of $1.28 million.

Who are all of Michelle's Assistants? Chief of Staff Susan Sher gets the top salary of $172,200. Here are the salaries, names and titles of the rest: (The salaries have been highlighted.) $140,000—Frye, Jocelyn C. (Deputy Assistant to the President and Director of Policy And Projects For The First Lady); $113,000—Rogers, Desiree G. (Special Assistant to the President and White House Social Secretary); $102,000—Johnston, Camille Y. (Special Assistant to the President and Director of Communications for the First Lady); $102,000—Winter, Melissa E. (Special Assistant to the President and Deputy Chief Of Staff to the First Lady); $90,000—Medina, David S. (Deputy Chief Of Staff to the First Lady); $84,000—Lelyveld, Catherine M. (Director and Press Secretary to the First Lady); $75,000—Starkey, Frances M. (Director of Scheduling and Advance for the First Lady); $70,000—Sanders, Trooper (Deputy Director of Policy and Projects for the First Lady); $65,000—Burnough, Erinn J. (Deputy Director and Deputy Social Secretary); Reinstein, Joseph B. (Deputy Director and Deputy Social Secretary); $62,000—Goodman, Jennifer R. (Deputy Director of Scheduling and Events Coordinator For The First Lady);

$60,000—Fitts, Alan O. (Deputy Director of Advance and Trip Director for the First Lady); $60,000 Lewis, Dana M. (Special Assistant and Personal Aide to the First Lady); $52,500—Mustaphi, Semonti M. (Associate Director and Deputy Press Secretary To The First Lady); $50,000—Jarvis, Kristen E. (Special Assistant for Scheduling and Traveling Aide To The First Lady); $45,000—Lechtenberg, Tyler A. (Associate Director of Correspondence For The First Lady); Tubman, Samantha (Deputy Associate Director, Social Office); $40,000—Boswell, Joseph J. (Executive Assistant to the Chief Of Staff to the First Lady); $36,000—Armbruster, Sally M. (Staff Assistant to the Social Secretary); $36,000—Bookey, Natalie (Staff Assistant); $36,000—Jackson, Deilia A. (Deputy Associate Director of Correspondence for the First Lady). The salaries do not include the benefit packages which are the same as members of the national security and defense departments.

The list does not include makeup artist Ingrid Grimes-Miles and "First Hairstylist" Johnny Wright, (both of whom travelled aboard Air Force One to Europe.) Nor does the list include the regular White House servant staff or the Secret Service detail assigned to the first family, nor Michelle's own mother who lives at the White House with the family.[418]

First Lady Michelle Obama

According to one source, most of the people who have been appointed to these various first-lady assistant positions had a role in supporting democrat or liberal causes and in helping to get Obama elected. This is their payback time. Perhaps all of Obama's czars and Michelle's czar-ettes are part of the "shovel ready" jobs that Obama promised us in his campaign. Most Americans did not realize these jobs would all be paid for with their tax dollars.

Michelle and Obama's Many Expensive Extra Perks: Obama and the first lady have been criticized for various "extravagances" at tax payer's expense.

Jan. 19, The Inauguration: It started with their elaborate inauguration that cost $150 million. According to Yahoo news, part of that enormous sum was raised by the inaugural committee and fundraising, which paid for $41 million. But that still left $109 million paid by taxpayers' funds.

Feb. 17, Signing into Law of the Stimulus Bill in Denver, Colorado: Obama couldn't just stay at the White House to sign the enormous bill that was putting our country into such great debt for $787 billion. Of course not! He had to fly off to sign the bill in Denver, Colorado. Joe Biden went as well, but he always has to fly in a separate airplane for security reasons. The cost of both planes, the gasoline, the pilots, the secret security, etc. was probably close to $400,000—all that to sign a bill that is supposed to stimulate the economy. Wouldn't it do more for the economy to use that money to help people regain their jobs they have lost or to create some jobs for them—$400,000 could go a long way for several people for a whole year's salary.[419]

May 31, Date Night to Dinner and a Broadway Play: According to a UK publication, the Obama's May 31 "date-night" to celebrate his presidential victory with dinner and a Broadway play in New York City, actually cost about $1 million. (The American press said it was just $30,000. Even that is extreme for a date!) The costs were for: the private helicopter for Obama and Michelle; the use of three jets in which the secret security staff flew; the limousines to travel in once they all arrived in New York City and the wages for the security staff. The security accompanied the Obamas all the way from Washington to dinner in Manhattan and to the Broadway play. Obama did pay for the dinner and the cost of the Broadway tickets himself. That was very "generous" of him.

The play they saw was Joe Turner's "Come And Gone", which about poor black workers 100 years ago.[420]

What irony! It took an outrageous sum of money for the rich and famous black folks to go watch a play about poor black folks. Just think how many poor black folks a million dollars could have helped? And what candidate was it in the presidential campaign who promised to help the poor rise above their poverty by redistributing the wealth of the rich and famous? Obviously, Obama is exempt from those rich and famous. It will come from the others, the rich white folks, not him. He is above them all.

European Trip for the Whole First Family: The first lady, her mother, and their children followed Obama on his trip to Europe the first week of June for a family vacation. As the president went on to his speaking engagements, the family spent a few days shopping and touring, starting with a shopping spree on Sasha's birthday, June 5, which turned out to be an international affair, involving the president of France. All the stores in France are closed on Sunday. No problem, the Obamas contacted French President Nicolas Sarkozy, who bent the nation's laws and asked the boutiques to open just for Queen Michelle and her family. One wonders if this preferential treatment would have happened for any other "royalty," but maybe the Obamas are considered even a notch above most royalty.[421]

The Costs of the Trip? Katie McCormick Lelyveld, Michelle Obama's press secretary, stated: "All personal travel and expenses incurred were paid for personally." However, the cost of security for the 20 taxpayer-funded Secret Service vehicles and the costs of transporting the security overseas on their jet airplanes probably added up to much more than the $1 million date night in January. But the Whitehouse is keeping the information hush-hush on just what the costs were.

Leslie Paige, a spokeswoman for Citizens Against Government Waste, told the Boston Globe that few Americans would begrudge the first family some presidential perks—as long as the expenses don't grow to be indulgent on the taxpayer's dime. Paige did, however, criticize the White House for failing to report how much Americans paid for the first lady's vacation. "I doubt we'll see the true cost of the trip to Paris. Not keeping his promise to run a transparent government has been a disappointment, to say the least."[422]

Trip to Copenhagen, Denmark in Two Separate Jets, September 30—October 1: Obama and Michelle decided they would both fly to Copenhagen to appear before the International Olympian Committee (IOC) to plead for their bid to have the summer Olympics in their home town of Chicago, Illinois. For some reason they could not fly together. Michelle went two days earlier in Air Force Two with her good friend Oprah Winfried as a traveling companion. Obama came two days later in Air Force One. In Michelle's talk she said their trips were a "sacrifice for the kids of Chicago."[423] If only all of us could experience such a "sacrifice!"

What Were the Costs of All This? Nobody seems to want to even give a rough estimate. One author, Jim Clark, writing for the Post Chronicle, at least gives us the cost of fuel and operating Air Force One for one hour of flight—$40,243. Air Force Two must be the same because they are both 747s. Clark states that in the current presidency, the two planes have become "His" and "Hers."[424]

Why they needed to go in two separate planes? Just as their separate trip in June to Europe, they seem to like to squeeze as much "bang for the bucks" out of American tax-paying dollars as long as they can. There is, of course, all the additional expenses—secret service, special vehicles, additional assistants and their salaries. If you figure the trip to Denmark was around 10 hours there and 10 hours back. If you multiply $40,243 times 20 hours, that is $804,860 for one plane to fly to Copenhagen and back. The cost for two would be $1,609,760. If you add the costs of the two air force jets that are always supposed to accompany the president as protection when he flies, then you have an additional cost of twice that amount for those two planes equaling $3,211,520, plus the private cars, private security when they arrived. The whole thing could have been close to $3,500,000.

October 1, Obama and Michelle Returned from Copenhagen Defeated—Having Lost the Chicago Bid for the Olympics: Chicago did not even make it into the second voting by the IOC. It was the first city eliminated. It was pretty humiliating for the Obamas. What a sad waste of an enormous amount of money! Where is such expense even budgeted for in the federal budget? Is this why Obama needed to pass the Stimulus Bill—to "stimulate" his and Michelle's enormous desire to travel across the globe and spend lots of money for whatever silly excuse they come up with?

The next day Rush Limbaugh said in his commentary, October 2, "The Ego Has Landed." Obama couldn't convince the IOC to give Chicago the Olympics, but he's going to convince Iran to give up its nukes? "This is a clueless child with a Mars-sized ego."[424]

Those who heard the various speeches by the competing countries to the Olympic Committee have a good idea why Michelle's and Barak's speeches didn't persuade the IOC judges. They were all about them: their sacrifices, their family, their wants, their desires. It appears that they truly believe the whole world revolves around them, or it should. The other speakers promoted their country, the city where the Olympics would be held and the benefit it would be to the Olympics.

Has Obama ever promoted his country in any speech he has ever given, at home or abroad? Why would the judges want to hold the Olympics in the USA after all the apologies Obama has made for his country? He has made it clear to the world that the US has made numerous serious mistakes and is not a very nice place. Why would they want to come here? And if they have been paying attention to the news over the years, they were already well aware that Obama's home town of Chicago is really not a very nice place either. It has a history of corruption and vice, highlighted by the former governor, Blagoyovich, who wanted to sell Obama's senate seat to the highest bidder.

What Can We Possibly Do To Reign In the Out of Control Spending of Our President, First Lady and their Many Czars and Assistants? Our Republic was designed so that the Supreme Court could rule that what an out-of-control President is doing is unconstitutional. He could be tried and impeached by the House and confirmed by the Senate. The House, which is in charge of the budget, could reign in an out-of-control president by tightening the purse strings, by not allotting any funding for a certain project, nor for a new bureaucracy created. The House could refuse to pay the salaries for the new czars. They could tell the president no more silly trips overseas in two separate jets for you and your wife.

However, the president has already seen to it that he will have plenty of money for whatever projects and czars he wants. Using continuous scare tactics, he passed his enormous $787 billion Stimulus Bill the first month of his presidency and passed his even bigger $3 trillion budget the second month. The democrat-run House and Senate, obviously, are lock, stock and barrel, marching behind the president. The Supreme Court is also tipped toward the left side. They will not be trying to put any checks or balances on Obama. The Republican Congressmen do not have enough votes to do any reigning in of Obama or tightening any purse strings.

It looks like our only hope is for the American people ourselves to take back our country. The rating of Obama keeps going down in the polls. The Tea Party Rallies and Town hall meetings that started in the spring of 2009 and continued to gain momentum throughout the remainder of the year and on through 2010. Both conservatives and liberals, Republicans and Democrats were turning out in large numbers protesting together and waking up our elected officials to the fact that the majority of American people are not at all happy with what is taking place in our federal government. Maybe our elected officials will finally start listening and voting the way we ask them too. Perhaps they are a little bit concerned about being reelected. (Chapter Eighteen gives many ideas of what we can still do. There is still hope.)

Some of Obama's Scariest Socialist Legislation, Cap and Trade, Hate Crime Bill, Health Care Bill:

Cap and Trade: The Heritage Foundation put out a video clip entitled "Cap and Trade—Will it Save the Earth? It explains what the Cap and Trade bill is all about and answers the question—no, it will not save the earth, but it will create a much more expensive earth, and it will especially hurt the middle class and low-income households. It would be just one more attack on the middle class and another attempt to redistribute wealth.

What Does Cap and Trade Mean? Cap means a government imposed limit on carbon emissions. Trade means a government created market to buy and sell greenhouse gas credits. However, as the video points out there is going to be a huge tax imposed on energy usage. Some people call this bill "Cap and Tax" instead. The video starts off asking a very important question—will the cost of reducing emissions with tax and trade legislation be worth it?

In a series of "man on the street interviews," the video shows what the typical "indoctrinated" answers are to many questions concerning Cap and Trade. One woman stated she thinks that if the bill passes and emissions are reduced then her life expectancy will be longer. David Keutzer, PH.D scientist, and senior policy analyst at Energy Economics and Climate Change, says no. This bill will not add years to anyone's life and it will make no difference to the world's temperature. He says, basically, this is just an excuse for a huge tax. Companies and the consumers will have to pay an enormous tax because green technology costs so much more to produce and will have to be supported by raising taxes on anything to do with energy.

The atmospheric scientists who speak on the You Tube video teach the following about Cap and Trade: It will not reduce carbon dioxide. "The tiny affect that Cap and Trade would have to reduce CO2 would be so minuscule, it would not be worth measuring."

Thousands of scientists have signed statements that they disagree with the consensus and do not believe in global warming, and, especially, the myth of "man-made" global warming. "Cap and Trade will make no difference in the world's temperatures."

Will Cap and Trade Have any Affect on Carbon Dioxide? A young lady answered yes, that it would reduce it. According to another scientist, Ben Lieberman, who is a senior policy analyst at Energy and Environment, the answer is no. Carbon dioxide is a natural part of our life on earth. It is a natural part of respiration. We breathe it out of our lungs; plants absorb it and give out oxygen for us to breathe in. CO2 is a natural part of photosynthesis; it's what makes plants green. Maybe it is increasing a little because of fossil fuels, but that is good for the earth and does no harm to human health. The tiny affect that Cap and Trade would have to reduce CO2 would be so minuscule, it would not be worth measuring.

Should Future Generations Have to Foot the Bill? One man's answer was yes, "If we don't pass on the cost to future generations and don't do something now, then we will pass on the problem to them."

Dr. Lieberman stated the following about the deceptive bill: "This is a massive energy tax in disguise. It will raise electricity prices, gasoline prices, natural gas prices, by significant amounts over time. The impact on a household, especially low-income households, will be very substantial and will make everything else more expensive because energy goes into the costs of producing goods and services. It will be a real burden on all households, but low income households particularly."

An Environmental Police State Based on Carbon Control: What is looming on the horizon if the U.S. Cap and Trade bill passes and is signed into law, and if the UN Copenhagen World Conference December, 2009, Carbon Control proposals are accepted worldwide, we could have a nanny police state ushered in that would fulfill every globalist's dream.

Mark Mareno, of *www.climatedepot.com*, who is an expert on the subject of the truth about "climate change," was interviewed by Lee Rodgers on KSFO radio, November 13, 2009. He quoted Hillary Clinton who stated "to regulate carbon we need to control every aspect of everyone's lives." Mareno believes the plan is to use the excuse of carbon control to usher in a nanny police state, with increased regulations, controls, energy costs, and a global government. It makes no difference if any of this is based on true science or not, if there really is any warming or not, it is "all about politics, ideology, and a new religion."

Should Congress Raise Taxes to Reduce Emissions? Continuing with the Heritage Foundation video clip, a young man said he would feel okay about paying more taxes if he knew where the money was going and that it was being used wisely.

Dr. Kreutzer responded with, "I wish I could promise you that the trillions of dollars in new taxes that Cap and Trade would impose on the American economy would be spent wisely. Unfortunately, we can be much more certain of the exact opposite. The liberal *New York Times*, a big supporter of the Obama administration, says this about Cap and Trade, 'It is almost perfectly designed for the buying and selling of political support.' This will just be lobbyists gone wild with your tax paying dollars.[425]

California's Version of Cap and Trade: Just as we can learn from the Massachusett's version of socialized medicine that it does not work, and it is not what we want for our nation, we can learn from California's version of Cap and Trade which has been a disaster for our state.

In 2006, Governor Schwarzenegger proudly signed AB32 into law. It is called "California Global Warming Solutions Act," and is essentially California's attempt to show our obedience to the draconian demands of the UN Kyoto Treaty, something prior Senators have refused to ratify [of course, it is all different with Obama. That is why he is pushing the federal version of Cap and Trade.]

"Brave California" is tackling this "noble" endeavor all on her own and promising that by 2020, we will have reduced our carbon emissions by 30% to the 1990 level that the treaty is asking for.

In 2007, AB 32 began to be implemented. Each year since, more restrictions and regulations have come into play. These have been so bad and so costly that many jobs have been lost and businesses have been driven out of the state.

According to State Senator Robert Dutton, in a recent poll, a new poll came out showing voter support for AB 32 has dramatically declined. Only 40% approved of it and 56% disapproved, much different than it had been in 2006, when it first became law. The numbers were then 58% approved and 27% disapproved.

Why is the opposition increasing? Reality is setting in, and people are finding out the following facts about AB32: According to an article by Bill LaMarr, Executive Director of the California Small Business Alliance, written February 5th, 2010:

1) With all of its restrictions and regulations, AB32 will not have any measurable impact on reducing global warming. California's greenhouse gas (GHG) emissions are tiny, and reducing them by 30% or even by 100% won't make any difference. [Of course, more and more Californians are also waking up to the fact that global warming does not really exist, that it has all been a big con job based on fraudulent science, as the reader will soon read. People are remembering what they learned in elementary science that CO_2 is actually good for the environment. That is what makes plants turn green and grow.]

2. AB 32 has an enormous price tag, costing billions of dollars because of higher energy costs and hidden tax increases;

3) It is already having a huge impact on jobs. It is estimated that 1 million jobs have already been lost in California because of AB32, and another million will be lost each year due to all the costly regulations.

The Small Business Roundtable did a study on the costs of AB32 and found out that it would cost the average small business in California about $50,000 per year, because of increased costs for just about everything small businesses need: Electricity will increase by 60%; natural gas by 8%; gasoline and diesel fuels will increase in costs (to nearly $4 billion a year); and commercial office, industrial space, equipment and raw materials would all cost more because of AB32.

The California Air Resource Board (CARB) is planning to approve a system that imposes an "auction tax" on companies and public agencies that emit more than 25,000 tons of GHG a year, which would total $143 billion between 2012 to 2020 at $60 per ton. That's the equivalent of increasing gasoline prices by 53 cents per gallon or increasing a family's electric bill by hundreds of dollars per year.

Costs will be imposed on food processors, electric producers, airports, ports, universities, fuel producers… more than 500 companies in all. However, small businesses and consumers will ultimately pay the bill.

CARB would be doing an end run around the state Constitution by imposing this AB 32 Auction Tax without a two-thirds vote of the Legislature. (http://foxandhoundsdaily.com/blog/bill-lamarr/6396-voter-support-ab-32-shrinks.)

A petition drive started in March of 2010 to get an initiative on the ballot in November so that Californians, who are older and wiser now, can put a halt to the implementation of AB32 until California can get the unemployment rate down to 5%.

Global Warming Hot Air Balloon Punched Through with Big Hole: In what has become known as "Climategate," the global warming hot air balloon of lies and exaggerations had a big whole punched in it, November 23, 2009, just a few weeks before the UN Copenhagen Climate Change Summit was to take place, December 7. Some computer hackers were able to discover e-mails that had been sent between two important science professors that crucial data, refuting the global warming theories had been hidden and not allowed to be published. Professor Dr. Phil Jones of the University of East Anglia headed up the prestigious Climatic Research Unit, which was the main source of information for the UN Intergovernmental Panel (IPPC) and the world media on "climate change."

Jones had corresponded with a professor at Penn State in Pennsylvania, Michael Mann, who also was implemented in the deception. According to the *USA News*, December 1, 2009, Penn State is investigating Michael Mann's participation in the exaggerating or fabricating of global warming data. Michael was told by Director Phil Jones to "delete certain E-mails" and hide valuable scientific facts.

The following is what Phil Jones had written on one e-mail back in 2004, "I can't see either . . . being in the next [IPCC] report. Kevin [Trenberth, his assistant] and I will keep them out somehow—even if we have to redefine what the peer-review literature is." There were many similar e-mails.

According to the *UK Guardian*, December 1, 2009, because of this scandal, Phil Jones stepped down from his position as head of the Climatic Research Unit, while the whole matter is further investigated. What effect would this have on the Copenhagen summit and further legislation based on faulty science? It is hoped that there will be a world-wide outcry against this because of the deliberate falsifying of scientific evidence.[426]

Hate Crimes Bill Passed by Sneaky Tactics: October 8, 2009, the controversial expanded Hate Crimes bill, HR 1913, which could not have passed on its own merits, was attached onto a broad $681 billion Pentagon "2010 Defense Authorization Bill," a bill that most Congressmen felt was necessary to pass. It authorizes military pay, benefits, weapons programs and other essentials for the armed forces. Of course, the bill did pass by a margin of 281 to 146. Most of those who voted against it were Republicans who were willing to risk voting against a defense bill, to get rid of the Hate Crimes Bill.

Why Could the Hate Crimes Bill Not Have Passed on Its Own Merits? There were too many who objected to the bill's its expanded definition of federal hate crimes—crimes committed against a victim's "gender, sexual orientation, and gender identity." In other words, anyone who speaks out against or writes against "homosexuality" could be labeled as guilty of hate-crime violation. This would probably also pertain to same-sex marriages. What happened in passing Prop 8 in California in support of traditional marriage, would now be labeled "hate-speech."

The way the Hate Crimes Bill was written made it possible that other forms of "sexual orientation" would also be protected such as "pedophiles." When that was revealed, much opposition came against the bill.

The bill also aroused much opposition from the many people in America who still believe in traditional marriage and traditional families. They consider homosexuality and same-sex marriage as abnormal, unhealthy, immoral and a threat to traditional society.

Many ministers in America still preach against homosexuality in their churches, quoting scriptures from the Bible that refer to it as: "an abomination, sin, lust, abuse of self, defiling of self," (Leviticus 18:22, Isaiah 3:9, Romans 1:27, I Cor. 6:9, 1Timothy 1:10). With the Hate Crimes Bill, will ministers no longer be allowed to read these scriptures from their pulpits or they will be accused of Hate Crimes violation? Such things are already going on in Canada and Sweden where hate crimes laws exist and ministers have been arrested for reading such scriptures from their pulpits.

Some believe this bill will be an effort to prosecute "thought crimes," where the motivation of the attacker has to be discerned.

Statements by Republicans About the Sneaky Tactics Used to Pass the Bill: Even Republican members of the Armed Services Committee, who had helped write the Defense Authorization Bill, said they would oppose it solely because of the hate crimes proposal. One of those was Todd Akin of Missouri, who said: "We believe this is a poison pill, poisonous enough that we refuse to be blackmailed into voting for a piece of social agenda that has no place in this bill."

Representative Mike Pence of Indiana was concerned that the measure could "inhibit freedom of speech" and "deter religious leaders from discussing their views of moral traditions for fear of being caught up in the law." He added "It is just simply wrong to use a bill designed to support our troops to reverse the very freedoms for which they fight."[427]

HR 3200—Health Care Bill Would Implement a Costly Socialized Medicine: The following information is taken from a talk that I was asked to give at a public forum in Napa, California, on the Health Care Bills, September 6, 2009. The page numbers that are given are the pages in the bill from where the information is coming.

Now that Obama has been able to nationalize mortgage companies like Fannie Mae and Freddie Mack, banks, insurance companies like AIG, the auto industry, and student loans his goal is to nationalize the 6th largest industry in our nation—health care.

After finding out about the enormous amount of tax paying dollars being used to pay for the salaries for Obama's 40 czars (about $6 million) and for Michelle's 26 assistants (about $1,700,000) and about their extravagant spending on their dates and trips, how could we possibly trust what Obama says about "saving money" on a national health care system? If he and Michelle can't control their own wasteful spending, how can we believe they or the federal government could save money on such a huge national system?

Obama is promising us that government health care will produce "reduced costs, guaranteed choice, and quality care for all." But based on all our experience with government programs, government-managed health care will be just the opposite—much higher costs, the absence of choice, and inferior care for all.

Federalized Programs Do not Have a Good Track Record: Is there any system that the government has federalized and made it work better or more efficiently? Look at the mess they have made of education once it became under the control of the federal government? Our schools are no better, our children are not better educated, and we are losing many good teachers because they cannot make it on such low salaries. Education has to go through eight layers of bureaucracy before federal funding makes it down to local schools and teachers. No wonder it is hard to entice good teachers to go into the profession. All the money is siphoned off by layers of bureaucracy before it gets to the classrooms and to the students where it was "supposedly" intended.

The Various Health Care Promise that All Americans will Have Health Care: How can that be achieved? Employers will have to contribute to the costs. Many employers are barely surviving now without paying any health care for their employees. Such a system will force them out of business.

In the Kennedy Bill, the government insurance program will subsidize premiums for people with incomes up to 500 percent of the poverty level ($110,000 for a family of four), and private insurers will have to pay out a specified percentage of their premium revenues in benefits. Kennedy's bill doesn't give a clue as to how this could possibly be financed. No doubt it would be the same way the Stimulus Bill and the TARP Bill and all the other outlandish bills are being paid for—by printing an enormous amount of money and by tacking more debt on younger generations.

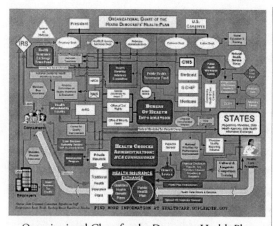

Organizational Chart for the Democrat Health Plan

Democrat Health Care Plan Flow Chart—Showing Just How Complex and Complicated the Health Care Structure Would Be and How Expensive: A chart was put together by some Republican Congressmen showing that 31 new federal programs, agencies, commissions and mandates would be created by Obama Care. They called it a "health care nightmare." Instead of money staying with local doctors and hospitals, it would first have to flow through nine layers of bureaucracy from the federal level to the state level. Before the money can then make it to where it is needed for local doctors, hospitals, and patients, it would first have to go through another four state levels.

No wonder there would be such little incentive for doctors even to go into medicine. By the time any money comes to them, so much has been siphoned off, there would be hardly anything left to pay for their expensive medical schooling. Who would want all those layers of bureaucracy over their heads telling them what they can do and can't do anyway? The chart can be seen more clearly at http://gopleader.gov/News/DocumentSingle.aspx?DocumentID=137304.

There are Abortion and End of Life Provisions: New concerns also surround the President's health care reform legislation that it would allow mandatory taxpayer funding of abortion. During mark-up of the Kennedy-Dodd health care bill, the Senate Health, Education, Labor and Pensions Committee approved provisions to **require** insurance plans to contract with organizations that perform abortions.

Several amendments were rejected that would have preserved states' laws regulating abortion, that would have prohibited federal funds being used for abortions, and provided protections for health care providers who refuse to perform abortions on moral and religious grounds.

How to Reduce the Costs of the Nation's Health Care Bill: A cartoon by Jim Davis depicts the future of what life could be like if the health care bill passes. It shows an elderly couple getting their mail and the wife reading a letter written to all seniors from America's Health Care Industry. It tells them what they can do to reduce the nation's health care costs—in large bold letters are the words written, "Drop Dead!"

The cartoon is referring to a provision in the bill that some people are calling a "death panel." Seniors must submit to "advance care planning consultation" (a.k.a. end-of-life discussions) every five years, or more often if there is "a significant change in the health condition of the individual, including diagnosis of a chronic, progressive, life-limiting disease, a life-threatening or terminal diagnosis or life-threatening injury." Will these consultants advise seniors to hurry up and die because they are costing too much money? (pp. *425* & *429*)

To deal with escalating health care costs, the government will follow "comparative effectiveness research." This means that government bureaucrats will assess all health treatments to determine whether or not they are "cost-effective and can be approved for payment." The not-so-polite word for this is "rationing." Life or death decisions will be made by bureaucrats on the basis of treatment cost and patient age, rather than by medical diagnosis.

That's the way health care works in Socialist Canada, England, and most of the nations of the European Union, but it's not the American way. Free-market competition, health savings accounts, and letting individuals spend or save their own money are the best ways to cut health care costs and allow doctors, hospitals, insurance companies to have the freedom to make their own decisions and to provide the best care for their patients.

The Health Care Bill and the Race Card: Obama spoke before Congress September 9 to promote his Health Care Bill. When he stated that "extending health care to all American who seek it would not mean insuring illegal immigrants," South Carolina Rep. Joe Wilson shouted, "You lie!" Wilson had done much research on that subject and knew that the health care legislation does not require any proof of citizenship, so any illegal alien could receive it just as any American. Wilson realized, however, that he was out of line in shouting out to the president and offered an apology after the speech was over, which the president accepted.

President Jimmy Carter was interviewed before NBC Nightly News September 16 and asked about Wilson's outburst. He replied, "I think an overwhelming portion of the intensely demonstrated animosity toward President Barack Obama is based on the fact that he is a black man, that he's African-American."

The next day he was speaking before Emory University in Atlanta, Georgia, and expounded more on that claim. "I think people who are guilty of that kind of personal attack against Obama have been influenced to a major degree by a belief that he should not be president because he happens to be African American."[428]

Conservative Attorney Ken Connor wrote an excellent article about this race card issue, "Pounding the Table: Health Care and the Race Card," 9/25/09. He stated:

> *There's an old adage popular among lawyers: If your case is weak on the law, pound the facts. If it's weak on the facts, pound the law. If your case is weak on the facts and the law, pound the table. Democrats—frustrated by the public's resistance to their grand scheme to federalize health care and desperate to discredit legitimate opposition by changing the terms of the debate—are pounding the table, invoking allegations of racism as the motivation for the opposition.*[430]

That has always been the case. When the opposition is weak in their arguments and can't really attack the message of their opponent, then they start attacking the messenger. They discredit their opponent by attacking him personally. The race card is now the preferred attack weapon whenever anyone speaks out against Obama's policies. We will see it being pulled more and more in the future.

Talking Points Against Obama's Health Care Bill: While Members of Congress were complaining that the health care bill was far too long and too complex to grasp, grassroot Americans were reading the bill and what they discovered was absolutely shocking!

A Summary of Scary Things the House Version of ObamaCare Contains: Healthcare rationing; Mandated audits of the books of private companies; A National Health ID card—complete with government access to your personal information and even your bank accounts; Government decisions about what healthcare benefits you can receive, even from your private employer; Employers will be required to auto-enroll all employees in ObamaCare with no options;

Death panel—end-of-life-care counselors could advise patients to just end it all now and go onto a happier life. There could also be a mandate that parents could have no more than two children, maybe even one as in China. They could also mandate that all doctors must be trained and willing to perform abortions.

Senate Version of ObamaCare Will Make Criminals of Non-Participants and Ration Care to Seniors: According to the American Family Association, the Senate version presented by Senator Baucus from Montana, called "America's Healthy Future Act," has some frightening mandatory requirements that will fine Americans up to $1,900 if they do not purchase health insurance, and if they refuse to pay the fine, they can be thrown in jail for a year or fined $25,000. And the IRS would be the government agency coming after you to collect. Dennis Smith is a senior fellow in healthcare reform at The Heritage Foundation's Center for Health Policy Studies. He says that penalty is just one of the many "hidden, unknown consequences" in the legislations.

The plan will also force severe rationing of health care to seniors by penalizing the 10% of doctors who submit the most in reimbursements to Medicare. This inevitably will pressure doctors to prescribe fewer and cheaper treatments just to avoid being the one doctor in 10 whose pay will be docked.

Since there will be a top 10% every year, doctors are likely to severely restrict treatment anywhere and everywhere they can, because they will have no way of knowing where the threshold is.[430]

Marriage Penalized by Health Care Bill: People have discovered there is language in the bill that will make health care less expensive for single people than if you are married. Thus, married couples would actually be penalized.

The *Wall Street Journal* reports, "Some married couples would have to pay thousands of dollars more for the same health insurance coverage as unmarried people living together." (http://www.kaiserhealthnews.org/Daily-Reports/2010/January/07/ Health-Bill-Policy-Round-Up.aspx.)

Why are Obama and Other Congressmen not Willing to State that They Would Take Such a Program for Themselves and Their Own Families? On August 8, on the "ABC Obama Special on Health Care," Obama was asked, "Mr. President, will you and your family give up your current health care program and join the new 'Universal Health Care Program' that the rest of us will be on? Obama ignored the question and didn't answer it! A number of senators were asked the same question and their response was . . . we will think about it! It was also announced August 9 that the Kennedy Health Care Bill has written into it that Congress will be exempt.

Obviously, there must be something very flawed about the various health care plans if President Obama and Congressmen themselves don't want it. But it is good enough for us lowly peons, the rest of middle and lower Americans. It appears that this bill is patterned after the Mexican one that they are trying to implement by the year 2010, where 5 percent of the people, the wealthy get to have private medical care, and the rest of the nation get to have their inferior national health care system.

Former Reporter for ABC, John Stossel (on 20/20 Show) Reveals Just How Bad Obama's Health Care Plan Would Be: (*AmericasNewsToday.org*): On a 20/20 television broadcast, July 31, 2009, John Stossel showed a news clip of Obama speaking before a crowd promising that his bill would create health care for everyone and cost less than the present system, which experts stated would not be possible. Sally Pipes of the Pacific Research Institute said that the only way government can do that is to control the amount of money that is spent on health care and to ration the care. There will be much more of a demand for health care than the government is willing to pay, so there will be "long waits just like they have in Canada and Great Britain."

Stossel's broadcast showed hundreds of people in England waiting in line just to register for a dentist. He stated that for some people, the waits are so long, it is just not worth it. They do it themselves. One man reattached his tooth with super glue. Some pull their own teeth with pliers and vodka. Some patients protest because the government won't pay for the drugs they say they need.

Obama denies that his program will be a government-run health care system. But earlier he admitted that he would like a "single-payer" system, which would have to be government-run. Sally Pipes said, "He does want government-run health care; he just wants to go about it in a slow way, so people won't realize what is happening to them." Many others agree that Obama's plan will build a bridge to government-run health care where there will be long waiting lines and have loss of access to care.

Stossel Interviewed Canadian Doctor, David Gratzer, Author of *The Cure, How Capitalism Can Save American Health Care:* He stated that under the Canadian system, people have to wait six months or longer to finally be seen. "Some of them die, that's what happens." Other Canadian doctors told Stossel that their system is cracking. Even in the emergency rooms, people have to wait for 24 hours to finally be seen. There is no other hospital they could go to. They are all at capacity.

Stossel stated that 1.7 million Canadians cannot get a family doctor. One town, outside Toronto, holds a lottery. Once a month, the town clerk pulls four names out of a box of those who would like a family doctor, and then calls them on the phone informing them that they can now be on a certain doctor's list of patients. How long after that they actually get to see the doctor is another story.

There are businessmen who help Canadians get to America for treatment. They are a sort "health-care middle man" who make money on Canada's rationed health care system. One woman had a blocked artery that kept her from digesting her food. She had lost fifty pounds and was starving. She hired Rick, the health broker, to help her get to a hospital in Washington state, where she saw an American doctor, who told her she would have died in a few weeks if she had waited any longer. In Canada, her surgery was called "elective." She told Stossel, "the only thing elective about this surgery was—I elected to live."

Another woman, who was about to give birth to quadruplets, had to fly to Montana to a hospital. All the neo-natal units in Canada were too crowded. Actress Natasha Richardson fell while skiing outside Montreal and needed a high-tech trauma center, but there wasn't one within hundreds of miles and no helicopters to take her to one. Stossel gave examples of a famous Spanish tenor, a sheik from the United Arab Emirates, Italy's Prime Minister, and Arch Bishop Desman Tutu who all had government-run health care in their own countries, but they preferred coming to the USA for treatment from American doctors.

It Takes Profits to Have the Money and Incentive to Do Medical Research: "Yes, our profit-driven medical centers are expensive and sometimes wasteful," Stossel said, "but it is that pursuit of profit that gives us inventions that save lives." Dr. Gratzer added, "This is the country of medical innovation. This is the country where people come when they need treatment." "In America, we are surrounded by medical miracles. Death by cardiovascular disease has dropped by 2/3 in the last 50 years. You have to pay a price for that type of advancement," Stossel stated.

Grace Marie Turner of the Gaylon Institute says, "Breakthroughs like birth control pills and robotic limbs could not have happened without the possibility of big profit." She also added that she would like companies to come up with other cures such as for Parkinson's disease, for cancer and for Alzheimers. "Unless there is a reward for them to do that, we are not going to have those new medicines." Stossel interjected, "But government has researchers. We have the NIH (National Institute of Health)?" Turner replied that government is only responsible for 4% of the drugs on the market today.

Innovation and Fast Treatment Comes from People Having the Freedom to Pursue Profit: Stossel mentioned that in Canada, there is one medical profession that does work for profit. It offers easy access to cutting edge technology, available all the time, where patients hardly have to wait and can be seen within 24 hours or a week. Stossel adds that you have to bark or meow to get that kind of treatment. In other words, there is better care for animals than for humans, because the veterinary clinics are run for profit, just as the medical profession used to be.[431]

How the Majority of Doctors Feel About Obama's Health Care: Most doctors are not happy with either the House bill or the Baucus bill. "This is war," said Dr. George Watson, a Kansas physician and president-elect of the Association of American Physicians and Surgeons, (AAPS). "This is a bureaucratic boondoggle to grab control of health care. Everything that has been proposed in the 1,018-page bill will contribute to the ruination of medicine."

Dr. Jane Orient, executive director of the AAPS, told the Washington Examiner: *Promised coverage is not the same thing as care. All you're getting is a place in the waiting lines.*

A survey in the fall of 2009 of 270,000 primary care physicians by the Physicians Foundation found that if health care reform passes, 30% expect to see fewer patients, 13% will find something that does not involve patient care and 11% plan to retire altogether.[432]

My nephew, Dr. Jared Probst, a family physician in Salt Lake City, Utah, told me in a telephone interview, September 6, 2009, that he and other doctors have been informed that if a health care bill passes, no matter what version, all doctors will then get the same wages—and probably very low wages, compared to what doctors are able to earn under a free-enterprise system of medicine. It won't matter if they are a specialist who has spent many additional years and money studying and getting an advanced degree and has great debts in student loans to pay back. He also said that so many of his fellow doctors have said they would rather quit than be part of such a highly regulated, socialized medicine system.[433]

In a poll that was reported on March 20, 2010, on Brian Sussman's show, KSFO radio, 45% of doctors stated that if the health care bill passes, they will consider retiring early or quitting. That would be a loss of 360,000 doctors in our nation.

Why are they so opposed to Obama Care? They say that it would essentially mean the end of their autonomy, their ability to make their own medical decisions. Medical privacy will be a thing of the past. It will destroy the free market system of health care and drive up costs. There will be price controls on doctors and on hospitals. The doctors wages will be cut by 21%. They are already having a hard time paying off their student loans to get through medical school. If Obama Care passes, it will be extremely hard.

Massachusetts was used as an example of how socialized medicine causes over-crowded waiting rooms and less motivation for people to want to become doctors. Since they passed their own version when Mitt Romney was governor, there are so few doctors for the amount of patients, that they are having to resort to group visits.

The Boston Globe, November 30, 2008, showed a picture of nine patients seated together to visit one doctor. Talk about reduced quality care and loss of privacy!

It was also mentioned that the cost of health care in Massachusetts is $47 million over the cost of what it was supposed to be. No wonder the people in Massachusetts voted for Scott Brown who used his opposition to socialized medicine in his campaign slogans.

The Stealth and Deception Used in Getting Obama Care Passed: In spite of all the thousands of tea party rallies, town hall meetings and hundreds of thousands of letters and telephone calls to Congressmen against the Health Care Bill, under the leadership of Nancy Pelosi, the Speaker of the House, the House version of the Health Care Bill passed November 8, 2009, by a vote of 220 to 215. The bill ended up with 1900 pages and has an estimated cost of implementation of $1 trillion. What a cost for a bill that is named, "Affordable Health Care for all!"

The Senate version was passed Christmas Eve morning, after many coercions, bribes, and twistings of arms of various senators had taken place. The Senators were already exhausted, having been held over the previous weekend, with votes taken on both Saturday and Sunday. Many were just plain worn out and wanted to get home for Christmas. Democrat Senators, who previously had been opposed, caved in, such as Ben Nelson of Nebraska and Mary Landrieu of Louisiana. They both gave into the enormous bribes and promises granted to their states for their yes vote. Nelson got 100% of medicaid to be paid by the federal government for the state of Nebraska forever. That has been labeled the "Cornhusker Kickback." Landrieu's bribe was $300 million also for medicaid. It has been called the "Louisiana Purchase."

The vote was strictly party-line. Sixty Democrat Senators voted for it and 39 Republicans against it. The estimated cost of the Senate Health Care Bill would be $871 billion.[434]

Once Congress was back in session in January, the House and the Senate had to hammer out their different versions and combine them into one bill that

Obama was in hopes would be passed before his state of the union speech the end of January 2010.

However, because of the January special election in Massachusetts of Republican Scott Brown to the US Senate, Obama no longer had enough votes in the Senate to push the Health Care through, so, fortunately, all came to a halt until March, when another big push for its passage happened. This caused an amazing amount of new Tea Party Rallies, Town Hall Meetings, and unending calls, letters again to Congress urging them to vote against it.

As you will see, some amazingly "unorthodox" methods were used to try to get Obama Care passed again.

How "Sausage" is Made, "Deem and Pass, Slaughter, and Self Executing Rule": Most Americans have been stunned and shocked as they watched the various shenanigans that have taken place over the past year to try to get Obama Care passed. We had no idea that elected officials were capable of such skulduggery, backroom deals, political payoffs, strong-arm tactics and underhanded methods for getting their bills past, no matter what!

Otto Von Bismarck, who, in 1871, unified Germany and became the first German Chancellor, made the following statement which certainly describes what we have witnessed. He said, "Laws are like sausages. It's better not to see them being made."

When I quoted this statement to a friend, he replied with, "What Congress is doing with this health care bill is actually an insult to good sausage." I couldn't agree with him more.

What does "Deem and Pass" mean? According to Brian Sussman's radio show, March 17, since Pelosi and Reed knew that they could not get enough votes in the Senate to pass the newly revised health care bill, they would just pretend that since the Senate had voted for another version of it before in December, (before Senator Scott Brown was elected) they will just "deem" that the Senate has voted for the bill and call it "passed."

They have enough votes in the House to pass the revised bill, so they can then say that the bill has passed both the House and the Senate as is required by law.

What a sneaky, underhanded way to pass a law! Congressmen say that they do this quite often, but it is just about small things, about amendments to bills, not something so large that it will involve 1/6 of our economy as health care does.

It is interesting how "deem and pass" sounds just like "demon pass," which is a more accurate description of what the whole process is.

"Slaughter" is another term used for the same skulduggery, which definitely makes one think of the smelly "sausage" that is produced. It also is a descriptive term of what Obama, Nancy Pelosi, Harry Reed, and the liberal Democrat Congress are doing to our U.S. Constitution and the whole rule of law. They are slaughtering it and cutting it up into pieces to suite their whims and their socialist agenda.

I am in hopes that the third term used, "self-executing rule" will have some long-term effects on those most responsible for the final "sausage" that has been mangled together in the many different versions of this health care bill and what is finally squeezed out.

Constituents back home will remember how their congressmen ignored the will of the people, and, hopefully, their actions will cause a "self-executing" effect. These weasel politicians will be "executed out" of ever holding public office again.

Pelosi's Revealing Statement: On Brian Sussman's KSFO Radio Show, March 9, 2010, he played a news clip of the Speaker of the House, Nancy Pelosi, making the following statement about the health care bill. She stated: "We have to pass it, then we can find out what's in it." With such "brilliant" wisdom coming out of the mouths of our elected officials, no wonder we are in such a sad state of affairs in our nation.

The following was sent to me by my friend, Charlotte Iserbyt, October 9, 2009. We are not sure who wrote it, but it is very clever and very true about how wacky the passing of the Health Care Bill would be:

> *Let me get this straight. We're going to pass a health care plan, written by a committee whose head says he doesn't understand it, passed by a Congress who hasn't read it, but exempts themselves from it, signed by a president who also hasn't read it . . . with funding administered by a treasury chief who didn't pay his taxes . . . and financed by a country that's nearly broke. What possibly could go wrong?*

The "Smelly Sausage"—Obama Care Passed: In spite of another large rally against Obama Care, held Saturday, March 20, in front of the Congressional buildings in Washington D.C.; tens of thousands more phone calls coming into Congress from constituents from all over the nation, on Sunday evening, March 21, Obama Care passed by a vote of 219 to 212. All the Republicans voted against it, joined by 36 Democrats.

Scary Provisions to Implement the Bill: Obama is going to authorize and give jobs to 16,500 IRS agents who will be the ones to make sure Americans are compliant to the bill and get their health insurance or they will be fined. What do income tax agents have to do with health care? They have about as much to do with it as student loans does. None of this makes sense, but it was never intended to, unless you understand the Marxist mindset that the "ends justify the means." Whatever means you use to get there is perfectly acceptable to them.

Obama's Mentor, Saul Alinsky and His Rules for Radicals: If what you see going on with Obama, his Many Czars, his loyal supporters in the pro-Democrat Congress and the legislation they are passing, does not make any sense, you need to read the book *Rules for Radicals*, written in 1971 by one of Obama's radical mentors, Saul Alinsky. Or, if you prefer the Cliffnote version, read a small booklet written by former Communist, now conservative author, columnist, and speaker, David Horowitz, *Barack Obama's Rules for Revolution The Alinsky Model.*

Alinsky wrote the blueprint for what Obama and his cohorts are all about. They are following his same pattern. The Stimulus Bill, the Hate-Speech Bill, the Health Care Bill, Cap and Trade, Amnesty for Illegal Aliens, and all that Obama has attempted in his first term of office as President, has nothing to do with his "nice-sounding" desires to want to help desperate banks, the auto industry, the insurance companies, the mortgage companies, and the poor unfortunate people who have no health insurance.

The overall motive behind Obama's actions is "achieving the revolution, the total transformation of America into a socialist state." To him and his radical czars, whatever they can do to achieve that transformation is perfectly acceptable. Again, "The ends justify the means." That is why you saw Obama and his cronies arm twisting, bribing, promising all sorts of extra benefits, giving rides on Airforce One, inviting people to the White House and giving false promises about the advantages of his health care bill.

Who cares if something is legal or moral? Alinsky only cared for the practical effects on the revolution. Since he did not believe in God, he did not have any moral conscience to restrain himself. He shared the opinion of the Russian author, Dosteovsky, who wrote, "If God does not exist, then everything is permitted."

Alinsky also shared the same beliefs as Castro and used his famous quote: "With the revolution everything is possible; outside the revolution nothing is possible." As David Horowitz states, to Alinsky, "The revolution—the radical cause—is the way, the truth and the life."

Empire State Building Lit in Honor of Communist China's 60th Anniversary, September 30—Would This have Been Allowed Under Any Other President?

Could it be because of Obama's love affair with socialism/communism that this anniversary was allowed?

According to a FOX news story, the majority of people in New York City and throughout the nation were shocked and highly opposed to the decision to allow the city's highest beacon, the Empire State Building (102 stories high), the symbol of American's free enterprise system—into a shining monument honoring the 60th Anniversary of the Red Chinese communist revolution, September 30, 1949.

In the evening the Empire State Building was illuminated in red and yellow lights to celebrate the anniversary of the bloody communist takeover. The tower is lit in white most nights, but nearly every week gets splashed with color to honor holidays and heroes—red, white and blue for Independence Day, green for St. Patrick's Day, true blue to honor heroes.

The building's managers say they have honored a host of countries, including Canada, India and Australia, but as of September 30 that list now includes one of the world's largest communist regimes, with a deadly history in genocide and violation of human rights.

Red Chinese History of Genocide and Human Rights Abuse: According to researcher Chang Jung, the Communist revolution and its aftermath may have been deadlier than any world war. As many as 72 million people died as a result. During the Great Famine of 1958-1962, 36 million Chinese were starved to death as a result of Mao's "Great Leap Forward," a government policy meant to industrialize the nation. During those years, "peasants ate bark, maggots, bird droppings, human flesh—anything to survive—as government storehouses stood full with grain and other cereals," neither the first nor last in China's troubled line of violations of human rights. The article does not mention the present day abuses, of forced abortions, only allowing one child to be born per family.

Comments by Americans about the Honoring of the Chinese Revolution: About 40 protesters stood outside the Empire State Building in the morning of September 30 as China's New York consul attended a ceremony the managers of the Empire State Building said was to honor "the 1.3 billion Chinese people and the 60th anniversary of their country." Here were some of the comments made by the protestors:

Arthur Waldron, a history professor at the University of Pennsylvania: "China gets treatment that other dictatorships can only dream of—a free pass on human rights. China remains strongly oppressive—but we make a lot of money, and we have a tendency to romanticize the country, confusing her brilliant cultural heritage with the current communist regime."

"Will we light it in honor of Tibet?" He thought there would be an outcry if another brutal regime were so honored by the tower. "Would we have lit the Empire State Building for the USSR knowing what we do about the Gulag?"

Lhadon Tethong, a leader of the demonstrators from Students for a Free Tibet: "Because the Empire State Building is such a cultural icon . . . this touches a chord close to home for people," "The lights on the building are a symbol of support for the Chinese state—for a totalitarian state," which ignores the country's "abominable record on human rights, on liberty."[435]

October 9, 2009, Nobel Peace Prize Went to President Obama: Obama was awakened early in the morning that he had a telephone call from Norway and that he had been selected for the prestigious award, the Nobel Peace Prize. He said he was very surprised, very humbled by it, was not sure why he had been selected, but he said he would accept it. He also said that he would donate the $1,400,000 to charity, but he was not sure which charity. I have an idea; he could use the money to pay for the expensive flight himself over to Norway and back to get the award, instead of having tax payers pay for him. Here are the words he spoke at his press conference concerning it:

> I am both surprised and deeply humbled by the decision of the Nobel
> committee. Let me be clear; I do not view it as a recognition of my own
> accomplishments, but rather as an affirmation of American leadership
> on behalf of aspirations held by people in all nations. To be honest,
> I do not feel that I deserve to be in the company of so many of the
> transformative figures who've been honored by this prize.[436]

Shock Over Obama's Nomination for the Peace Prize: Most journalists expressed disapproval that Obama was chosen over 205 other well-qualified candidates, many of whom had risked their lives in saving or helping others, or in a cause they had been involved in for many years to better the world.

These are some of the statements made by journalists as reported on Brett Baier's Fox News Program, October 9, 2009:

- **Ana Marie Cox**, *Air America* Correspondent, *"Apparently, Nobel Prizes are being given to anyone who is not Bush."*
- **Jennifer Loven**, *Associated Press* Correspondent, *"He won, but for what?"*
- **Ezra Klein**, *Washington Post*, *"Obama also awarded Nobel Prize in Chemistry. 'He just has great chemistry.' Says Nobel Committee."*

- **Peter Beinart,** Political Writer, *The Daily Beast, "I like Barack Obama as much as the next liberal, but this is a farce."*
- **Michael Russnow**, *Huffington Post Writer*, "*Whatever happened to awarding for deeds actually done?*" He compared this to "*giving an award to a young director for films we hope that he or she will produce.*"
- **Charles Krauthammer,** *FOX News*, Contributor, "*The award is a farce. What's he done? . . . Obama got it for his general splendidness and for the kind of fuzzy internationalism in which he offers engagement and bending a knee to the United Nations.*
- **Bill Kristol,** Editor, *Weekly Standard: ". . . I think he should have said no. That would have been the real humble thing to do and the smart thing politically to do."*
- **Juan Williams**, National Public Radio: *"It is unbelievable, when you think about it. He's only been in office eight months. It does not make sense . . . This is really, I think, an anti-Bush statement coming from the Nobel Committee. . . . The odd part, of course, is we are still fighting wars in Iraq and Afghanistan. Guantanamo Bay [prison] is still open . . . maybe they want this as a forerunner of what might be yet to come."*
- **Jeff Birnbaum**, *Washington Times* and *FOX News* Contributor: *"I guess this proves that you really can become anything you want in America . . . This diminishes the value of one of the world's most important award.* [437]
- **The *Times of London*:** "Rarely has an award had such an obvious political and partisan intent. It was clearly seen by the Norwegian Nobel committee as a way of expressing European gratitude for an end to the Bush Administration. . . The prize risks looking preposterous in its claims, patronizing in its intentions and demeaning in its attempt to build up a man who has barely begun his period in office, let alone achieved any tangible outcome for peace."[438]
- **Australia's *World Today*, Former Minister Alexander Downer:** "Frankly to be nominated after he has been in office for 11 days and to win the prize after he has been in office for less than nine months, I think it discredits the whole system. . . it is clearly a completely political decision. Not a decision based on merit. It does make the whole system a bit of a farce. . . It is a pity that Mr. Obama did not refuse the award."[439]

Why Did the Nobel Committee Select Obama?: The Chairman of the Nobel Peace Prize Committee, Thorbjorn Jagland, stated at the press coverage, October 9, that the committee had chosen Obama unanimously, mainly for: his efforts to "strengthen international diplomacy and cooperation;" trying to stop the use of nuclear weapons; for his support and promotion of the United Nations and his "playing a more constructive role in meeting the great climatic challenges the world is confronting."[440]

However, at the actual event in December, I wonder if the committee also did not have regrets that they had selected Obama.

Obama Received the Nobel Peace Prize But Offended the Norwegians: Obama travelled to Oslo, Norway, to receive what used to be a "coveted" prize. On December 11, he gave his acceptance speech before an audience of 700 distinguished guests.

However, due to the fact that he had just pledged to send 30,000 more troops in a major expansion of the Afghanistan war just 9 days before accepting the prize, and the war in Iraq was still continuing, it was a most unusual speech. There was not much he could say about peace. He instead spoke about war, trying to justify the fact that America is still engaged in the two wars, and he is the commander-in-chief of those wars. He stated, "There will be times when nations—acting individually or in concert—will find the use of force not only necessary but morally justified." (Reuters News, December 11, 2009)

Maybe the judges and the Norwegian people were disappointed with Obama because the wars are still going on, but it appears that even more Norwegians were disappointed by Obama's rude behavior while he was in Norway. He refused to attend the various events that were planned in his honor: the peace center exhibit, an evening concert, a meeting with children and a press conference. The worst of all, however, was he snubbed the king. He refused the traditional invitation to a private lunch with King Harald V of Norway.

According to a poll that was taken, 44 % of the Norwegian people found Obama to be rude to the King; 53% were upset that he did not attend the traditional concert, and more than a third did not believe he deserved the peace prize.

Marie Simonsen, political editor at *Dagbladet*, one of Norway's biggest daily newspaper, stated, *"I'm very disappointed. You get the impression he is not proud of the prize."* (http://www.thedailybeast.com/blogs-and-stories/2009-12-09/obamas-oslo=snub/full/)

Obviously, Obama is not proud of it. When one receives something one does not really deserve, it has no real meaning, and one is instead rather embarrassed.

I agree with some of the previously mentioned commentators, it would have been far better if he would have done the honorable and noble thing and declined the award, admitting that he did not deserve it. People would have had far more respect for him than they do now.

Obama's Speech at the Copenhagen Climate Summit Fell Flat: As the international luster of the "brilliant" Obama star was dimmed in Norway, it continued to fade in Copenhagen. Those pushing the climate change fraud were in hopes that Obama's speech would do the trick and convince the hesitant industrialized nations to go along with the enormous financial demands being asked of them to "offset their carbon footprint" and give to less developed nation—"to save the planet from eminent destruction."

However, Obama's speech did nothing. According to the UK newspaper, *the Guardian*, it "disappointed and fueled the frustration" of the conference.

Obama began his speech by saying, "I come not to talk, but to act." But there was no real action on his part, or commitment that he gave for the USA to "embrace the bold measures" being asked of them. He said nothing of the $100 billion that Hillary Clinton said the USA would be willing to give to "help developing nations adapt to climate change." Obama also said nothing of pressing the US Senate to pass more climate change legislation.

Hugo Chavez, the communist dictator of Venezuala, who once patted Obama on the back as a good buddy, now criticized his speech and called it "ridiculous."

Other statements critical of the speech were made by Tim Jones, a spokesman for the World Development Movement, who stated, "The president said he came to act, but showed little evidence of doing so. He showed no awareness of the inequality and injustice of climate change. If America has really made its choice, it is a choice that condemns hundreds of millions of people to climate change disaster."

Other environmental groups made similar statements against Obama's speech, such as a spokesperson from Friends of the Earth, who said, "Obama has deeply disappointed not only those listening to his speech at the UN talks, he has disappointed the whole world." (http://www.guardian.co.uk/environment/2009/dec/18/obama-speech-copenhagen)

Could "Climate Gate" Have Dampened USA's Commitments to Global Warming?: Perhaps Obama had been told to go easy on any big, earth-shattering, binding "global funding" promises coming from the USA. It would have brought more attention to what has become known as "Climate Gate," that fraudulent science is behind the whole global warming scheme. The news of this fraud had just broken two weeks before the summit.

Thousands of e-mails between top, influential scientists had been uncovered, revealing to the world that these scientists had been distorting the data and "cooking the books" for many years concerning the earth's true temperature.

Although no main-stream media would write about it, millions of people across the globe had found out about "Climate Gate" via the internet. They now know that our world is not getting warmer; it is actually in a period of global cooling.

In fact, the very day that Obama was speaking, outside in Copenhagen, an extremely cold blizzard was raging. The entire, expensive, time-consuming summit was indeed a fraud!

Assessment of Obama: A Canadian journalist, Howard Galganov, made the statement in November, 2008, shortly after Obama was elected, that by six months those who had voted for him would realize what a terrible mistake they had made. He wrote an article August 20, 2009 reminding us of that fact and said: "When Obama won the Presidency with the help of the LEFTIST Media, Hollywood and Entertainment liberals, Ethnic Socialists (ACORN), Stupid Non-Business Professionals and Bush Haters, I wrote: "It won't take 6 months until the people figure this guy out and realize how horrible a mistake they've made. And when they come to that realization, the damage to the United States of America will be so great, that it will take a generation or more to repair—IF EVER!"

Galgonov Gives the Following Reasons for Obama's Terrible First Six Months:

- His low polls even within his own party, "Obama is going under for the 3rd time with polling under 50%;" [As of March 2010, he had a 43% approval rating. It continues to go down each month he is in office.]
- His unpopular Healthcare Reform Bill that he is using "Chicago Bully tactics" to try and pass.
- The Cap and Trade or (Cap & Tax) bill that Galgonov thinks has seen its end.
- The Stimulus Package (Tax and Spend) which has caused his popularity to be in "FREE-FALL."
- The TARP package that "he took and ran with from President Bush.
- His promises of the closing of Gitmo and ending the War on Terrorism that have not been kept.
- Comparing Obama with Bush at six months into his first term, "Bush was ahead in the Polls;"
- Comparing him with the 12 preceding Presidents—"Obama ranks 10th."
- On a poll asking who would you vote for today between Obama and Mitt Romney—"It's a dead heat."

- On a poll between Obama and Sarah Palin—Obama's only 8 points ahead, and Palin hasn't even begun to campaign.
- "Obama wants to be everywhere where he shouldn't be."
- He insults Israel, America 's only real Middle East ally and favors instead "Palestinian despots and murderers."
- He travels the world apologizing for America.
- He lectures others how to do it right, when the truth is, "he has no experience at doing anything other than getting elected."
- He declared to the Moslem world that America "is not a Christian nation," but heaps praises on Islam.
- He compared the "plight of the Palestinians to the Holocaust."

Golvanav Gives Some Suggestions: "Maybe, if America's first Emperor would stay home more and travel less, and work a little bit instead of being on television just about every day, or forget about his Wednesday Date Nights with his wife, or stop running to 'papered' Town Hall Meetings, perhaps he would have a little bit of time to do the work of the nation."

[However, after seeing what happened when Obama stayed home, March 18-21, 2010, postponing his trip to Indonesia so he could get his health care bill passed, maybe we all wish he would just go on traveling more. His million dollar trips will cost nothing compared to the trillion dollar socialized medicine program, that Obama will now usher into our nation.]

Golvanav Makes Another Prediction: "Obama will probably not finish his four-year term, at least not in a conventional way." Golvanav thinks that maybe the Democrats themselves will either force him to resign or figure out a way to have him thrown out. Maybe they will finally admit that he really isn't a born U.S. Citizen and that will be a good way for the Democrats to get rid of him. Or perhaps they will make Obama their own "lame duck president." The Democrats realize with Obama "their fortunes are rapidly becoming toast," and they can't go on blaming Bush for everything. "That game's already begun to wear real thin." The mantra used to be "We don't want four more years." "The new mantra will soon become: WE DON'T WANT 6 MORE MONTHS!"[441]

A Summary of Barack Obama's Ten Months in Office (October, 2009): Bonnie O'Neal, Vice President of California Eagle Forum, wrote the following assessment of Obama: "More and more people are seeing this president as grossly inexperienced, but instead of surrounding himself with experts with wisdom, he has brought in Chicago thugs and the most left-leaning people he could find. . .

Obama's record-setting poll numbers have plummeted with record-setting speed. Tuesday, September 29, the president hit his lowest approval yet during his young term in office—45 percent of voters in a daily Rasmussen Reports tracking poll said they approve of the president's performance. Fifty-three percent disapproved!

Even though more than four out of five Democrats approve of Obama's overall performance as president and the same percentage of Republicans disapprove, Obama's biggest headache is with self-described independents: Sixty-six percent disapprove.

Here is a real "kicker!" Joe Biden and Obama claim the stimulus plan is working. Nothing could be further from the truth: 15.1 million Americans are currently out of work.

The National unemployment rate was 4.9% at the start of this recession in January. Today that rate has spiked to 9.8%. In 14 states unemployment rate is more than 10%. And the liberal media keep making excuses and refuse to state Obama's Stimulus Plan is a monumental failure. AND, there is no Plan B, unless you want to consider this Administration just denying the facts and saying everything is improving. His base is desperate to believe that lie, and so they ignore the whole subject. BUT, we can't afford to do that any longer.

This is not the Administration I want being involved in my Health Care. So far they have gotten very little right. Why should we trust them with anything?"

Some People Are Questioning Who is Really Behind Obama Running the Government? A group of attorneys in Australia who have a publication called "The NoBull Newsletter," sent out an article, November 22, 2009, entitled, "Who's Really Running the Show?"

The article states that more and more people are beginning to see that Obama is really an empty suit, completely inept for the huge job he is supposed to be performing. They agree that he can give good speeches, but question who writes the speeches? Who is really behind the scenes calling the shots and making the decisions telling him what to say and what to do? The following is a quote from the article:

> The more I watch the man, the more I see a person who appears to be the "face" of some other entity or group. He seems like a "front man." And it is becoming clear that his strings are being pulled by someone else. He does not appear to be the man in command of the ship of state. At least, he is not in the driver's seat. (The website is http://www.bullson.com.au/default.htm.)

Chapter Fifteen

A One-World Religion

As has already been alluded to in previous chapters, the plans of the one-world elitists included, from the beginning, not only a one-world government, but a one-world economy, a one-world military, and a one-world religion. What kind of a religion would it be? It would definitely not be Bible - believing Christians or Jews. The founders and supporters of globalism are for the most part atheists, Satanists, or belong to pagan, Eastern or New-age religions. They are joined by Muslims. They are all united in their hatred of Christianity and orthodox Judaism. They have been trying to water them down by polluting their true Biblical beliefs or by actually destroying populations of Christians and Jews. Much of that has been going on across the globe. The Muslims also have as their ultimate goal a one-world theocracy under Islam Sharia law.

Birth of the New-Age Religion: Most people think of the New-Age religion as something that started in the 1960s, but it actually started much earlier. It really is not new at all; it is just the old paganism given a new name.

Madame Helena Petrovna Blavatsky, who lived from 1831-1891, is widely regarded as the High Priestess of the New Age movement. She started her Theosophical Society in New York City in 1875, which, essentially, has the same beliefs as the old paganism and the New Age.

She taught that we should look to Eastern religions for their esoteric wisdom, the universal brotherhood of mankind, and unity among all religions—except, of course, monotheistic religions such as Christianity, Judaism, and Islam, who believe in one God, and they could not be reconciled with "individual enlightenment."

Madam Blavatsky believed Christians had created their own gods to look like them. She said, "Esoteric philosophy. . . refuses to accept any of the gods of the so-called monotheistic religions, gods created by man in his own image and likeness, a blasphemous and sorry caricature of the ever unknowable."

Madame Blavatsky cursed the God of the Bible as "capricious and unjust." Like the "enlightened" Masons, she believed the Bible had it all backwards. "It was really Satan who was the victim of Jehovah." Satan was the gentle serpent who spoke only words of "sympathy and wisdom." She believed Satan to be "the real creator and the benefactor, the father of Spiritual mankind."

She had lived several years in India and Tibet and claimed that she had had "astral projection," and could communicate with the spirit world. She claimed to have written several books under the direction of dead "Masters of Wisdom," Tibetan holy men who communicated telepathically with her from the Himalayas, while she was in England.

After her death in 1891, the mantle of leadership went to Annie Besant, a member of the Fabian Socialist Society of England and close friends with George Bernard Shaw and H.G. Wells. She also penned many occultic writings to add to those of Blavatsky.

Besant was followed by Alice Bailey, who launched the Lucifer Publishing Company to print all the theosophical writings and a periodical called Lucifer. But since the Christian world was not quite ready for such a name, she changed the name to the Lucis Publishing Company. She also established the Lucis Trust, which serves as the umbrella organization for a variety of globalist/New Age/occult organizations and programs that are catalysts to the emerging new world religion.

Some of these New Age organizations are: the Arcane School, World Goodwill, Triangles, Lucis Publishing, Lucis Productions, Lucis Trust Libraries, and the New Group of World Servers.

The Lucis Productions have regularly weekly "globalist" broadcasts that are beamed across the world from the UN University for Peace in Costa Rica.

The Lucis Trust was the first NGO to be accepted by the United Nations. It works side by side with the UN to promote a one-world government and a one-world ecumenical, nature and earth worshiping religion without any Christ in it.[442]

Various Attempts to Unite People in an Ecumenical "One-World Religion:" (with the obvious absence of Bible-believing Christians and Orthodox Jews): In the preparation for a one-world religion, the goal is to first form ecumenical clusters of religions and to get them to all believe somewhat the same. Of course, the name of Jesus Christ must be left out. "His teachings are too judgmental and divisive." Also, the atheists and those who worship Satan do not like the name of Christ and try to avoid hearing it or ever mentioning it.

2000, August 28-31, Millennium World Peace Summit of Religious and Spiritual Leaders, United Nations Building, New York City: Religious and spiritual leaders gathered from all over the world for the first religious summit. The attendees signed on to a pledge of 8 promises. There were no real Bible-believing Christians invited and no mention of Christ. The honorary chair and CNN founder Ted Turner endeared himself to the crowd by promoting the New Age concepts that there are many ways to heaven. He said, "The thing that disturbed me was that my religion, the Christian sect, was very intolerant, not of religious freedom, but we thought we were the only ones going to heaven."[443]

September, 2002, UN Global Peace Summit for Women, Geneva, Switzerland: Hundreds of female religious leaders from every religious persuasion and from every nation were gathered under the auspices of the United Nations. Some of the groups even professed to represent Christian churches, but according to a report by Wendy Griffith of CBN News, "Ushering in the One-World Religion," "it was clear that Jesus was not invited." His name was never mentioned in the entire summit and neither was the Bible.

Ms. Griffith quotes Robert Maginnis, a former director of the Family Research Council, who said of the summit, "I can see the possibility that it's the globalization of world religion." He said it appeared that "the hidden agenda was to unite people under one religious umbrella so they would more peacefully accept the UN's radical political goals." What are those goals? "The United Nations is very anti-life, anti-faith, anti-family, they're anti-national sovereignty, but they are pro one-world government," Maginnis stated.

Griffith writes in her article, "Christian scholars say the Bible warns of a time when all the world will unite under a false global religious and political system . . . it appears the UN could be taking the first steps in that direction."

Maginnis believes the UN is "taking the Muslim community, the Christian community, the Hindus, the Confucians and all the many hundreds of religious groups, trying to identify key leaders," and trying to co-opt them into cooperating together with the UN.

True Christians do not believe that is possible; there is only one way to heaven, not hundreds of ways. Christ said, "I am the way, the truth and the life and no man comes to the Father except by me."

A supposed Christian minister, Reverend Joan Brown Campbell was the co-chair of the Global Peace Initiative. In her talk she lit a candle, a symbol of light shining in darkness, a symbol of peace. She and others spoke about peace and "harnessing their feminine energies" to bring peace to a hurting planet, but neither she nor anyone else ever mentioned the Prince of Peace, Jesus Christ.

When asked why she would not mention Christ, Rev. Brown Campbell said, "That's not a purposeful intent. This is a meeting, of course, of people of all religions . . . I mean everyone here would say there is a God; this is not a group of Atheists, this is a group of people of faith, and for everyone there is a god-person by whatever name."[444]

The belief that there are many ways to heaven was also part of the New Age gospel at the Geneva summit. Another American woman, Ms. Strong said, "I'm very close to the Buddhists, the Taoists, the native Americans and uh, peace to me is being one with the source." When asked if she was referring to God "the Creator," she said, "Well, I don't necessary call it Creator, but, it's one name."

Maginnis summary of the world religious summit—that left out Christ—was the following:

> "The name of Jesus has power and that's why Satan doesn't like it; he doesn't want to hear it in the halls of the UN, whether it be in New York City or in Geneva. So when Ms. Campbell presents herself as a representative for Christians, where does the name Christian come from? It comes from Jesus Christ, the Lord and Savior; and if you don't invoke His name in the context of world religion, then I think you've fallen far short and clearly you've done a disservice to Christianity because He is the center of our salvation."[445]

One World New-Age Religion Murals Portrayed at the Masonic Denver New World Order Airport: I had heard that the Denver airport was labeled "the New World Order Airport." I really had no idea why except it is the most unusual architecture that I have ever seen, looking like a series of white large tents all stuck together. However, once I saw the unusual art and murals that are inside, I understood why it has that name. There are also mysterious carvings in the floor and statues that depict the concept of what will have to take place to usher in the New World Order.

Why is it called the Masonic airport? What did the Masons have to do with it? It was the Denver Masonic Grand Masters who commissioned the architects and artists. There is a Masonic capstone on the south side of the airport that was placed there March 19, 1994, that shows the Masonic symbol of a compass and square and states the following: "This capstone contains messages to the people of Colorado in 2094." Dedication Capstone laid by Grandmaster W. Gray Sr." (There was the name of a second Grand Master given whose name was hard to read on the picture I saw of the capstone.) Underneath the date of 1994 are the words: "New World Airport Commission Contributors" and gives the names "Martin Marietta aeronautics, Fentress Bradburn architect and Zimmerman metals."

I had seen a slide presentation of the unusual murals by the author Dr. Len Horowitz who spoke for a group in Rohnert Park, California, in 2001. A year later, I had a two-hour stopover at the Denver airport en route to back east, so I thought I would see them for myself. This was in September of 2002. I asked a woman who worked at the information desk if she could tell me where the murals were. She pretended she did not know what I was talking about. She said they had an art museum but had never heard of any murals. I went to the art museum and asked there. The woman there also pretended she did not know what I was talking about. I finally found a janitor and asked him. He took me right to them. They were in two different remote hallways that did not seem to get much traffic. I sat and examined them and took pictures of them.

There are many different You Tube videos about the murals and about the strange architecture of the airport and tunnels underneath. With all due respect, I will give statements first from a pro-mural video clip, supposedly giving the artists interpretation. It makes disparaging remarks about anyone who thinks they have anything to do with Masons and the Illuminati and conspiracies. I will follow with my own comments and some from other sources about the real meaning of the murals.

The pro-mural You Tube video is by Jay Moody and Fekseco Productions entitled "Facts Behind the Denver Airport Conspiracy." It states that it is not uncommon to have grand masters of the Masonic order lay the capstone. It was a tradition in Europe where they laid the capstones of many great cathedrals since the masons were the builders of them. It also shows a picture of George Washington, wearing his Masonic apron laying the cornerstone for the US Capitol building in Washington D.C. in 1793. It states that other cornerstones were laid for the building of the city and of the Whitehouse.

The video gives the name of the artist who was commissioned to paint the murals, Chicano artist named Leo Tanguma, who is Mayan. He was assisted by some local students. According to this video he was free to do whatever he wanted and was not told by the Masons to portray the scary themes that he painted. His other art work also portrays "social themes" with native American and Mexican symbolism. His murals at the airport contain the same symbolism but "orientated to an international audience." He calls the murals the "Children of the World's Dream of Peace," depicting the human journey from brutality to peace.

Mural One: A man dressed in NAZI uniform with a gas mask on his face, with a machine gun in one arm and an Arab-looking curved sword in the other, is standing with dead children under his feet and a women at the left holding a dead child weeping. Behind her, are other adults, carrying dead children and a few, who are left alive, are being taken off on a dark trail, all weeping. There is a trail of gaseous fumes circling above the soldier going off to the left (obviously depicting some form of chemical or biological warfare—why the NAZI soldier needs a gas mask). His sword is piercing into the chest of a dove.

Tanguma, the artist, states this mural is to depict world-wide "incarnation of warfare, oppression and destruction," with children lying huddled under the sword of conquest, that the women represents Mother Mary weeping for her children, showing a mother's pain. He did not use the word genocide, but that is what it appears to be—massive killing of people by their own government.

In the lower right hand corner is a piece of paper lying with a poem written on it stating: "I once was a little child who longed for other worlds, but I am no longer a child for I have known fear. I have learned to hate. How tragic, then, is youth which lives with enemies, with gallows ropes. Yet I still believe that I only sleep today, that I will wake up, a child again, and start to laugh and play." At the bottom of the poem is the name of the girl who supposedly wrote it, "Hama Herchenberg, 14 years old, died December 18, 1943, Auschwitz Concentration Camp."[446]

Dr. Len Horowitz believes that the sword piercing into the dove is a symbol of the attack on Christianity, since the dove has always been a Christian symbol. Those striving for a New World Order know that Christians are their biggest stumbling blocks and will need to be wiped out. Horowitz also believes that the chemical and biological warfare sprayed above the head of the soldier could already be going on with the chem trails that we see coming out of airplanes that do not dissipate but spread out and soon cover the whole sky. Who knows what strange chemicals are in these trails and what they are doing to us.[447]

One man on another You Tube clip shows an eagle at the top of the soldier's hat and wonders if the artist is depicting an American soldier, that the American soldiers are being portrayed as so evil they will kill their own people. (One You Tube clip said that this mural has been painted over in recent years or has been removed.)

The first mural of a NAZI-looking soldier in a gas mask and depicting doom and destruction.

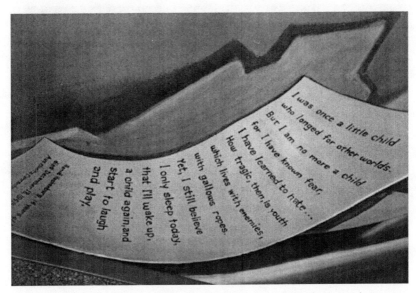

The letter (enlarged) shown at at the bottom of the first mural. It is supposedly written by a young girl who survived a concentration camp.

Mural Two: Above this mural is a rainbow instead of the gaseous fumes. The children of the world are depicted dressed in their native costumes, happily coming together with guns and swords, wrapped in their native nation's flags. The child depicting America is a boy dressed in a Cub Scout uniform. They are bringing their bundles to a German boy in the center who is hammering them with a hammer and an anvil, beating them into "plowshares and pruning hooks," instruments of peace. (Isaiah 2:4 and Micah 4:3) Below his feet under the anvil is the dead NAZI soldier with his gun lying by his side and with two doves sitting on top of it.

The pro-mural You Tube clip quotes the whole scripture that is stated in Isaiah 2:4 and asks the question, "Did the Illuminati write the Bible too?" In other words, the mural is just an innocent portrayal of the scripture in Isaiah, and we are not to think it is coming from the Illuminati or think anything sinister about it.

My answer to this is: The prophecies found in Isaiah and Micah are speaking of the time of peace after the 2nd coming of Christ, and it will be under His direction that the people will beat their swords into plowshares and spears into pruning hooks. It is not under the direction of a sinister one-world government.

The second mural showing all the children of the world bringing their armaments wrapped in their nation's flags to be hammered into plow shears.

An enlargement from the second mural showing the little boy who is representing the USA, dressed as a cub scout. The US flag is wrapped around the swords along with a flag of a girl who looks like she is Chinese.

Mural Three: According to the artists, Mural 3 and 4 are called "In Peace and Harmony with Nature." However, Mural 3 shows they are not quite there yet. It shows the children of the world lamenting the destruction of the earth and the extinction of life. Rare and exotic animals are shown inside glass boxes, as if they are now extinct and are just museum pieces. The artist states the world's native populations are dying off as a result of "colonialism." In the background, there is a forest fire raging, and a city is hardly visible encircled by dark smoke.

One of the girls is holding a Mayan tablet with the date showing December 21, 2012, which alludes to the Mayan prophecy and calendar that on that day, the earth is going to go through an ending as we know it, and a rebirth will begin. As has already been mentioned, the artist, Mr. Tanguma, is Mayan.

The artist shows three dead women lying at the bottom of the mural in caskets. One is black holding some symbols that she worshiped; one is Latino, holding an idol that she worshiped, and one is white with blond hair holding a rose, a Jewish star and a Christian Bible on her chest. She is lying on a red, white, and blue quilt. According to what is written on the You Tube video, the artist was originally going to have the coffins just filled with "people of color," but he decided that white people are also suffering as a result of "global militarism."

What is interesting to see is that the children do not seem to be sad about the dead people, just the dead animals. Some have tears in their eyes, either holding or observing the dead animals. They do not seem to be very disturbed at all by the dead people lying at their feet. Obviously, the children have been well trained to be good little environmentalists who believe animal species take priority over human life.

The third mural shows three dead women lying in coffins and children above who appear to only be concerned about the endangered species.

Mural Four—The Ushering in of a One World New-Age Pagan Religion:
Now the children are all happy, dancing together in their native costumes. There is the same bright rainbow over their heads as in the second mural. The children are facing and moving towards a boy seated in the center who looks like he is from India, with a golden halo over his head resembling a Christ or Buddha-like figure. He is holding a flowering tree. The artist says it is "a symbol of peace or rebirth." The tree has a bright light reflecting from it; it appears that the children closest to it are worshipping it.

Worshipping of a Plant—the Symbol of Mother Earth, or Paganism: All the other religions are gone, represented by the three dead women in the previous mural. However, the Masonic religion is alive and well, portrayed by a boy dressed in the costume of the Scottish Right Masonic Order, with Masonic symbols on his chest.

All the extinct animals, fish, and birds are alive again. This mural depicts a new world, like a new Garden of Eden, where all can live in order and peace, now that populations have been greatly reduced and the bad, judgmental religions are gone. What seems to be missing are any adults. Could the adults not adjust to the changes of the New World Order? In all of the last three murals there were no adults except for dead ones, just children were alive.

The fourth mural shows all the children of the world dancing happily and coming towards the center of the picture where they are obviously worshiping a plant that glows with a bright light. Behind the plant, is a sort of Christ-like or Buddha-like figure. Of course, all the endangered species are now alive and well, but no adults are pictured. At the top is a rainbow that crosses the picture.

A close up of the glowing plant and the children's faces full of adoration.

This pro-mural video ends with the words, "Native American themes are common in the Denver airport." Some Navaho words are inscribed in the floor "DZIT DIT GAII" which means "sacred white mountain." Is that what the white-tent like roof of the airport is trying to depict? Is the whole airport supposed to be a sacred white new-age mountain?

The You Tube clip then states that parts of the murals and other paintings have since been removed from the airport because too many people were complaining that they were offensive. The National Coalition of Censorship and the ACLU have been protesting the removal. So, perhaps some of them may have been restored.[448]

The Hierarchy of Masons Believe in a One-World Religion with Lucifer, "the Great Light" in Charge: The murals go along exactly with what Masonry would like us all to believe about the future of the world, that there will someday be a one-world religion. Here is the quote again from Chapter 10, that was given then by Albert Pike, one of the revered Masonic leaders:

> God's plan is dedicated to the unification of all races, religions and creeds. This plan, dedicated to the new order of things, is to make all things new—a new nation, a new race, a new civilization and a

new religion, a nonsectarian religion that has already been recognized and called a religion of "The Great Light."[449]

The Strange Statues and Other Art at the Denver Airport: There are many artifacts that correlate with a New World Order. Outside the airport one can see a large statue of a horse standing rearing up with his forefeet in the air. The horse is opaque looking, but with eyes that glow red which are rather scary looking. Some think he is representing a horse of war, or could he be the pale horse of death spoken of in the Book of Revelations? (Revelations 6:8)

Inside the airport are other strange statues and art forms that depict people looking like robots, held in separate compartments, and standing above you in the baggage department are scary looking gargoyles. On the floor, right in front of the first mural that shows the NAZI soldier with the deadly bio-chemical gas going out above him, is located an inlay that shows an old cart and inside the symbols AUAG. Some say that AUAG is related to the chemical symbols for gold and silver. Others believe it stands for a new strain of hepatitis called Australia Antigen, which is also symbolized by AUAG, which could be depicting the gas that was used to kill the many people in the genocide that the mural is depicting.

Architect of the Airport with a Swastika Layout and Deep Tunnels Underneath: The airport was built in 1995 on 53 square miles. Denver already had a functioning airport, but that was abandoned for this one. According to one You Tube video, the airport is the capstone for an underground city. Some people are calling it Area 52. (Area 51 is a secret underground airbase near Las Vegas, Nevada.) When looking down at an aerial view of the airport, the view has shocked many. The building and runways resemble a NAZI swastika.

Many passengers find it a little bit odd and even scary that they have to travel underground to get to the terminal they need to go to. There are reports that there are five large buildings that are 150 feet deep underground, with large tunnels connecting them and large holding rooms that have sprinkling systems. When asked why they were built and what they are being used for, the answer is for storage. Storage of what and why so deep down?

There are also barbed-wire fences that surround the airport and face the inside rather than outside; in other words they are there for keeping people inside.[450]

As one can see, there are many interesting questions about this mysterious airport and its art and architecture. I recommend that the reader check it out for yourself, either in person when you are at the airport or go to the various You-Tube videos that show the murals and art. (My son had a long stopover at the Denver Airport in February, 2010. He tried to find the murals, but told me that they were no where to be seen, so perhaps it is true that they have now been removed.)

The Georgia GuideStones, America's Stonehenge, Depict a One-World New Age Religion, with a New Set of Ten Commandments: On one of the highest hilltops in Elbert County, Georgia, stands a huge monument of four solid granite tablets supporting a capstone on top. Built in 1980, the monument stands 19 feet tall and weigh 119 tons. The tablets are positioned in such a way as to allow the viewing of the North Star through a hole at eye level near the center of the monument.

On the four stones, engraved in eight different languages, are 10 Guides, or "Commandments for the Age of Reason." A cement plaque in the ground by the side of the monument states, "Let These be Guide stones to an Age of Reason. Obviously this is referring to a book by Thomas Payne, called the *Age of Reason,* which was a very anti-Christian book.

The Guidestones' Origin and Purpose: The origin of the strange monument is shrouded in mystery. No one knows the true identity of the man, or men, who commissioned its construction. All that is known for certain is that in June, 1979, a well-dressed, articulate stranger visited the office of the Elberton Granite Finishing Company and announced that he wanted to build an edifice to transmit a message to mankind. He identified himself as R. C. Christian, but it soon became apparent that was not his real name. The man he spoke to was Joe H. Fendley, the now retired president of Elberton Granite. Fendley said that Mr. Christian told him that he represented a group of men "who wanted to offer direction to humanity," but wished to remain anonymous.

According to Dr. Stan Monteith, who has written about the Georgia Guidestones and even has a separate website about them, they are "an important link to the Occult Hierarchy that dominates the world in which we live." He said that he has been to Elberton and visited the public library where he found a book written by the man who called himself R.C. Christian. Therein, Mr. Christian stated that the monument he erected was in recognition of Thomas Paine and the occult philosophy he espoused. People in the surrounding areas of Elberton say that they have seen strange occult and mystic ceremonies going on during the night at the guidestones. According to Dr. Stan, only one religious leader in the area had the courage to speak out against the American Stonehenge, and he has recently relocated his ministry.

Dr. Stan also believes that "the group who that commissioned the Georgia Guidestones is one of many similar groups working together towards a New World Order, a new world economic system, and a new world spirituality." It is important to understand "the dark spiritual forces that are behind them" or we will not understand the "unfolding of world events."

The Messages Engraved on the Guidestones: They deal with four major topics: (1) Governance and the establishment of a world government, (2) Population and reproduction control, (3) The environment and man's relationship to nature, and (4) A new spirituality.

The Ten Commandments of the "Age of Reason" Written on the Stones:
1. Maintain humanity under 500,000,000 in perpetual balance with nature.
2. Guide reproduction wisely—improving fitness and diversity.
3. Unite humanity with a living new language.
4. Rule passion—faith—tradition—and all things with tempered reason.
5. Protect people and nations with fair laws and just courts.
6. Let all nations rule internally resolving external disputes in a world court.
7. Avoid petty laws and useless officials.
8. Balance personal rights with social duties.
9. Prize truth—beauty—love—seeking harmony with the infinite.
10. Be not a cancer on the earth—Leave room for nature—Leave room for nature.

Comments and Interpretation of the Meaning of these Guidestones:
1. **Population Control:** The world's population is approaching 7 billion. Limiting the population to 500 million would require the extermination of nine-tenths of the world's people! This reduction of the world's population fits perfectly into the philosophies of the Illuminati and the New World Order, who believe there are just too many people on the planet and killing the majority of the "useless eaters" would be a benefit to the world. This also gives a clue as to where Mr. Christian is coming from and who his friends are who contributed to the funding of the monument.
2. **Reproduction Must be Controlled:** How exactly is this to be accomplished? Abortion, war, genocide, disease? Apparently some sort of government intervention would be necessary.

3. **Government Would Even Control our Language:** Would it be against the law to speak any other language than what the government has decided upon?

4. **Who will be Doing the Ruling of Passion, Faith, and Tradition?** If it were left to the individual and self restraint, that would be all right. But since none of the rest of these commandments seem to be left to the individual, it is assumed this one would also be under the control of big government, which makes it very frightening. Our freedom of speech, religion, and traditions would be under the rule of government.

5. **It is Government's Responsibility to Protect all People:** Would this assume that we no longer would have the right to bear arms and protect ourselves?

6. **A World Court Would be Part of a World Government:** This foreshadows the current move to create an International Criminal Court and a world government through the United Nations.

7. **Elimination of "Petty Laws":** This would allow the New World Order to streamline the legal code, to decide what is petty and what isn't. Could the Bill of Rights be considered "petty laws?"

8. **Common Good over Individual Rights:** This insinuates that individual rights should be stripped away for the benefit of the whole.

9. **Whose Truth are We to Prize?** There is no mention of the absolute truth that comes from the Christian God. "Seeking harmony with the infinite" reflects the current effort to replace Judeo-Christian beliefs with a new-age spirituality.

10. **"Be not a Cancer":** This last commandment resonates with the same evil of the first. By insinuating that mankind has become a cancer to the earth, then it would not really be considered bad to wipe out 9/10s of the population, would it? This gives us a stronger hint that Mr. Christian and his cronies are new-age environmentalists who have little regard for the life of man.

Dr. Stan believes the message of the American Stonehenge also foreshadows the current drive for accepting the environmentalists' concept of "Sustainable Development." He warns us that whenever you hear the term "Sustainable Development," you should substitute it with "socialism" to be able to understand what is really means.

He also believes that the ideas engraved on the Georgia Guidestones are very similar to those espoused in the Earth Charter, as you will see below." Dr. Stan ends his comments about the Guidestones with this statement:

The fact that most Americans have never heard of the Georgia Guidestones or their message to humanity reflects the degree of control that exists today over what the American people think. We ignore that message at our peril.[451]

The Georgia Guidestones Promoting a New Spirituality

Another Website Asks the Question Could the Guidestones be Some Joke?
Pamela Jean of the *Digital Journal* answers with: "Would a group of individuals who wish to remain anonymous spend the massive amounts of money, the actual amount having never disclosed, to erect something of this nature as a joke?" It does not appear that anyone, after reading the ten commandments engraved in the stone, seems to think it is a joke.

In fact, Jean states various faiths have circulated petitions to have the Guidestones torn down. "Its message is ominous and does not set well; . . . a world, in which a government is put in position to determine who should live and who should die, how one may worship one's individual faith, and also be stripped of one's individuality is chilling."

The Guidestones Fit in with Bible Prophecy and the Book of Revelations:
Miss Jean states that those who have studied Bible prophecy find that the message written on the stones actually fits in "quite succinctly with the predictions given in the Book of Revelation. Satan will rise to power and rule and reign over the entire world—until his eventual demise."

Jean states that those who are informed and believe in the existence of "The Illuminati" feel that they have been planning "massive depopulation for decades, which will one day manifest itself in the form of massive plagues, a series of biological attacks, or any number of other means to eliminate most of the people inhabiting the planet."

Most of the Work of Manual Labor on Planet Earth is Finished; the Workers can be Eliminated: Pamela Jean also mentions a profound concept that most of us have probably never thought of.-

         -. lots of people are not really necessary. . The earth is in pretty good shape and "only needs minor maintenance."

> Much of the natural resources have been mined, cultivated, and stockpiled in warehouses and store shelves around the world. Since most of the 'work' is done, now the workers are simply in the Illuminati's way, and consuming resources that they want for themselves . . . and they plan to eliminate most of us in accordance with the first commandment of the Georgia Guidestones' 500 million population cap.[452]

Earth Charter and the New Age Green Religion: As we have seen from the previous information, proponents who are planning for a one-world religion definitely plan on it being a green, earth-worshiping religion, in other words, "pantheism," or just the old-fashioned "paganism."

The Earth Charter (EC) illustrates the religion part even more, by making it appear as if it is a modern day "Ten Commandments. The EC is even carried around in an "arc of hope," similar to the "arc of the covenant," that carried the Ten Commandments for the Children of Israel.

The EC was written by the "green duo," Mikhail Gorbachev and Maurice Strong. It was unofficially presented before a UNESCO meeting in Paris, France, in March of 2000, and officially launched in June, 2000 at the Peace Palace, at The Hague, in the Netherlands.

It is interesting to find out that the EC has almost the same message as the Georgia Guidestones. There is emphasis on these four elements: 1) control of reproduction 2) world governance 3) the importance of nature and the environment and 4) a new spirituality.

The Mission Statement for the EC: On their website, is stated what their purpose is: "to promote the transition to sustainable ways of living and a global

society founded on a shared ethical framework that includes respect and care
for the community of life, ecological integrity, universal human rights, respect
for diversity, economic justice, democracy, and a culture of peace."

One of the 16 principle that supports their mission statement includes the
following: "adopt at all levels sustainable development plans and regulations."
Remember the definition of sustainable development is top down, central control,
that is highly regulated, where there is almost no development and very little
that is sustainable. In other words it is socialism/communism.

The next principle in their mission statement is a global society, or global
government. That will certainly not be one bases on the "free enterprize system."
That is considered "greedy" and not "sustainable" in the green handbook.

A "shared ethical framework" and "economic justice" is just newspeak for
redistribution of wealth, to take from those who have and give to those who
have not. In other words again we're back to socialism/communism.

Universal human rights means supporting the United Nations Declaration
on Human Rights, which lists many nice sounding rights, but then, essentially,
lets us know our basic rights do not come from God; they come from the United
Nations, and "where the UN giveth, the UN can taketh away."

Respect for diversity includes acceptance of abortion, the homosexual agenda
and same-sex marriage, which the UN and the EU are trying to to push into
every country.

They want their global society to be a Democracy, not a Republic.
Democracy means majority rule, where the rights of the individual are not
important; everything is based on "the common good."

"A culture of peace" means no opposition to the UN plans. One of EC
supporting principles mentions getting rid of the military in each nation -
"demilitarize national security systems to a non-provocative level and convert
military resources to peaceful purposes."

At the end of the EC website, they recommend "in order to build a
sustainable global community, the nations of the world must renew their
commitment to the United Nations, and fulfill their obligations under existing
international agreements. . . " In other words, we are to go along nicely with all
UN policies, happily pay our UN obligations which will soon be a global tax,
as we are moved into a one-world government.

The New Spirituality: As I mentioned already, there is nothing new about
the new-age movement. It is just bringing us back to the old paganism, where
man worships the creation, rather than the Creator, exactly what we are warned
against in Romans 1:25.

As you watch a video clip on the Earth Charter website, that is celebrating their past 10 years, music is playing in the background about "redemption, and forgiveness." The video ends with a picture of a book that shows a Christian church with a cross on the steeple entitled Generating the Renewable Energy of Hope, an Earth Charter Guide to Religion and Climate Change, Nov., 2009. Obviously they are trying to win over the Christians to their way of thinking, so we can all be one big happy new-age, earth worshiping world. (http://www. earthcharterinaction.org/content/articles/432/1/Earth-Charter-Initiative-10-years-at-a-glance/Page1.html)

Islam: There is one other religion that the Illuminati have to contend with, one that also seeks to dominate and take over the world and form a theocracy—Islam. It is growing faster than any other religion. Many of them are militant and ruthless in their desire to achieve their goals. What will the Illuminati do with them? Presently, it appears they are working along with them. Communism and Islam seem to be very good companions in Africa and other nations where they are seeking for dominance and control. Who knows what the final outcome will be?

The Islam Religion Intends to be a One-World Theocracy with Any Opposition Either Converted to Islam or Wiped Out: Donna Hearne, the head of the Constitution Coalition, puts on wonderful education conferences every January or early February in St. Louis, MO. For many years she has included speakers about Islam and the threat the religion is not only to our Constitution, our Judeo/Christian heritage and religious beliefs, but to our education system and our way of life. Her organization has published a little booklet called *In Our Backyard, Is Radical Islam in the U.S. a Serious Concern?* In chapter four, "Islam—A Complete Way of Life," the booklet gives many quotes from Islam leaders who tell us they definitely believe their religion is a complete way of life and there is no room for any other religion, or any other political system. Here are some of them:

> **Anjem Choudary** (A British-born, self-styled Muslim cleric, who has been investigated by British police because of his extremist statements. He spoke the following before students at Dublin's Trinity College, as reported in the Irish Examiner, October 26, 2007): "*Followers of Islam could not accept secular authority . . . There will be strife. It could be political, it could be ideological, it could be military struggle.*"

Choudary quoted Lebanon-based Mr. Mohammad who had lost his asylum status in England after saying that the British people brought the London bombings on themselves: *'Islam was a complete way of life that could not yield to any other way. Islam is a complete system of living, the Shariah system. Islam has political beliefs—it cannot co-exist with another political belief.'*

Zaid Shakir (formerly the Muslim chaplain at Yale University): stated that Muslims cannot accept the legitimacy of the American system, which is *'against the orders and ordainments of Allah. To the contrary, the orientation of the Quran pushes us in the exact opposite direction.'*

Ahmad Nawfal (a leader of the Jordanian Muslim Brethren, who speaks often at American Muslim rallies): *"The United States has no thought, no values, and no ideals; if militant Muslims stand up, with the ideology that we possess, it will be very easy for us to preside over this world."*

Jaafar Sheikh Idris (the founder of American Open University, which supports Shariah law): He has denounced the U.S. system of democracy as *'the antithesis of Islam'* and argued that no man has the right to make laws outside Allah's laws expressed in the Quran.

Omar M. Ahmad (President of NAIF—North American Imams Federation): *"Islam isn't in America to be equal to any other faith, but to become dominant. The Quran, the Muslim book of scripture, should be the highest authority in America, and Islam the only accepted religion on Earth . . . No one can be a Muslim who makes or freely accepts or believes that anyone has the right to make or accept legislation that is contrary to that divine law."*

Keith Ellison (Islamic Congressman from Minnesota): was present at the NAIF conference when Omar said these words. Keith Ellison also spoke at to the same conference. It is pretty alarming to think that we have an elected member of Congress who shares in these beliefs against his own nation and form of government!

Siraj Wahaj (A black convert to Islam, the first Muslim to deliver the daily prayer in the U.S. House of Representatives. This comment was made a year later before a group of Muslims in New Jersey): "If we were united and strong, we'd elect our own emir (leader) and give allegiance to him . . . Take my word, if 6-8 million Muslims unite in America, the country will come to us."

Obama's Strong Islam Background: We may not only have the first black president in the White House, but we may have the first Muslim president as well. Obama had strong instruction in the Muslim religion in his childhood, which seems to still be with him. When he and his mother and little sister were living in Indonesia with his stepfather, Obama's picture was shown in his school yearbook and his religion was listed as Muslim.

There is an amazing You Tube video clip that shows all of Obama's many speeches praising the Islam religion. His only comments about Christianity is that America is no longer a Christian nation. **(http://www.youtube.com/**

Much has been written about Obama's communist influences as he was growing up. Islam and Communism are quite compatible. They seem to coexist quite well in many parts of the world. They both believe in totalitarian regimes and cruel methods in subjugating their people. Islam also teaches that the ends justify the means. In fact, the Koran tells people that it is okay to lie, steal, cheat, and kill for the sake of Allah.

How the Islam Religion is Spreading in the United States: The book *In Our Backyard*, gives several ways the Muslims are spreading their beliefs: through education, the prison system, and by accommodations—as people are giving in more and more to their demands.[453]

Education, My Personal Experience Having to Teach Islam: I had to teach a two-week unit on Islam as a substitute teacher in a 7th grade World History class at Healdsburg, CA, in 2002. I saw for myself, firsthand, the pro-Islam bias that exists in the textbook and the anti-Christian propaganda that is also clearly obvious. The textbook I was asked to teach from, called *Through the Centuries*, suggested the following things for me as the teacher to do: I was to give all the students a Muslim name; have them come dressed in Muslim attire; pretend they were making a pilgrimage to Mecca; have them make a prayer rug; have them memorize certain prayers in the Quran, and memorize the "Five Pillars of Islam."

What I Did Instead: I thought to myself, whatever happened to the rule teachers are supposed to be teaching under—separation of church and state? No way would I be allowed to ask students to do such things and promote the Christian religion; why am I now allowed to promote the Muslim religion in such a way? So, I thought, if I can now teach a religion, I think I will teach the religion of my choice.

The text started off saying that the Muslims and the Jewish people both came from the same Father Abraham, so I wrote his name on the board and wrote under it his two sons, Ishmael and Isaac. I told them   it was from

Ishmael that Mohammad had come, and it was from Isaac that many famous people in the Bible had come. I asked if anyone might know some of them. A boy raised his hand and asked, "Is that where Moses comes from?" I said, "Yes! Very good! And the Muslims do recognize Moses as a prophet, as well. Would you like me to tell you more about Moses?" They said yes, so I did. But to start off I had to first tell them the story of Joseph being sold into Egypt, and how the children of Israel ended up in Egypt. That was such a fascinating story, and the students had so many questions that it took up most of the period.

That is how each day went. I would try in every way to incorporate a little of the Bible stories in my lessons, so the students would know what the cousins of the Muslims were all about, as well. When it came to the memorizing of the Five Pillars of Islam, I went over them with them, but then I gave them each a lovely copy of the Ten Commandments to see what creed that their cousins lived by, a creed coming from God received by the hand of the Prophet Moses. I asked them to examine the two creeds, side by side, and see if any of the creeds matched up. The only one was the first one, "There is no other God but Allah," and "Thou shalt have no other gods before me," from the Ten Commandments. It was good for the students to compare the two and to read the Ten Commandments, perhaps for some their first experience doing so. They read such things as: "Thou shalt not steal, Thou shalt not kill, Thou shalt not bear false witness against your neighbor, Thou shalt not commit adultery." None of these are found in the Five Pillars. Muslims are allowed to lie, to kill, to steal, if it is done to promote Allah.

Examples of Bias toward Islam and Anti-Christian Statements: I have since had to teach from the newer textbook called *World History, Medieval and Modern Times,* published by McDougal Little, 2006. It is even more biased than the first one. Here are a few examples from the book showing how it is promoting Islam and putting down Christianity:

Islam is Referred to Over and Over Again as a "Kind, Tolerant" Religion: "Muhammad forgave the Meccans," after he conquered them. (p. 94) (The truth is he took the women and children as slaves, and he cut off the heads of the men.)

"The caliphs showed tolerance to those they conquered." (p. 98)

"The conquered people welcomed the Muslim armies as liberators." (p. 100)

"Muslims let conquered people keep their own religion if they wished to do so. (p. 101)

"Over time, many people converted to Islam. They were attracted by Islam's message of equality and hope for salvation." (p. 101)

"There was much blending of cultures under Muslim rule." (p. 101)

The Truth—Islam is not a Tolerant Religion: As the reader has already read from the beginning quotes from some of the Muslim leader in America, Islam is not tolerant of other religions and never has been. It does not believe in living side by side with other religions or governments. Its goal is to take over the whole world with a one-world theocracy. Muhammad taught his followers to cut off a person's head or worse if they would not accept Allah and Islam. Such is stated in the Quran.

"I will cast terror in the hearts of those who disbelieve. Therefore strike off their heads and strike off every fingertip of them. (Quran 8:12)

Garments of fire have been prepared for the unbelievers. Scalding water shall be poured upon their heads, melting their skins and that which is in their bellies. They shall be lashed with rods of iron. (Quran 22: 19-22)

"Christians are not Tolerant and Do not Treat Others as Equals:" The following are some of the statements and pages in the textbook that teach anti-Christian statements:

"Alfonso I became the ruler of the Kongo. He converted to Catholicism and made it the official religion of the Kongo. The class system changed. The gap widened between the nobles, who were educated Christians, and the commoners." (p. 197) [So, in other words, when people become Christians, they look down on the common people, but Muslims treat everyone equally.]

"The Portuguese (Christians) used more Africans as slaves." (p. 197) [The text never mentions the many slaves that the Muslims took when they would conquer people.]

"Another legacy of the Crusades was rising Christian hostility toward Jews . . . More and more Christians believed that non-Christians were their enemy. Muslims, however, allowed Jews and Christians to live in peace in most cases. Many Crusaders who stayed in Palestine came to respect Muslims, but Christian intolerance toward Jews continued." (p. 330)

Pro-Islam, Anti-Christian Indoctrination and Propaganda: There are two chapters devoted to promoting Islam in the textbook, the beginning of Islam and the spreading of Islam, with not a single chapter devoted to Christianity. Christianity gets one page talking about the birth of Christ in the chapter on the Roman era, and it gets a smattering of pages here and there throughout the book, most of it not very complementary, such as: what is written about the crusades; the Spanish inquisition; wars between Christian nations and the slave market. In total, the textbook has 78 pages promoting Islam and 44 that mention Christianity or Christians.

Whenever the text mentions Muhammad, his title is given, "the Prophet Muhammad," (ie. pp. 83,89, and 93) as if it is a given fact that is what he was. Children soon learn that is his name. When the text tells of the birth of Christ, it states that that Christ is believed by his followers to be the son of God, but he is never given the title "Christ, the son of God."

If a child is not growing up in a Christian home or attends a Christian church, by the end of the school year, using this textbook, he would have a very negative view of Christianity and a very positive view of Islam, exactly what the textbook is trying to achieve. Such one-sided teaching is not education; it is indoctrination. (More is written on this subject, where the funding is coming from and how Islam is able to have such influence on American schools in the book *The Incremental Chipping Away of the Once Great USA*, soon to be published.

"One Faith of God" Under the UN: Towards the end of Chapter Seventeen on the Timeline, there is a section written about a one-world government Constitution that is already prepared and ready to go under the auspices of the United Nations. It already has a website. (http://one-faith-of-god.org/covenant/one_faith_0010.htm) The website also has some very interesting statements about uniting all Christian and Jewish religions in "One Faith of God." They can't quite figure out how to do that with the Islam religion, so they leave them by themselves, with "One-Islam," but the Jews and all Christian religions are to be united and watered down into something that does not resemble either religion. Why are they doing this? According to the website as written in 2008:

> The faith has fragmented into factions, into supporters of different regional religious leaders. There is no unified and single religious leadership that all Christians and Jews can look to as their one voice. This is the purpose of One-Faith-Of-God. To give all Christians and Jews around the world an idea greater than any divided and misguided loyalties. To unite as one, to heal the world, to protect the world and to give back life to the solar system. [Kind of sounds like a New Age religion, where we will worshiping the world and the solar system.]
>
> It shall be a mission of the Union that the United Nations shall eventually pass all necessary motions and direction that the sovereign

state of One Faith be established with the constitution written. [How nice to know that our united religion will be under the auspices of the United Nations.]

An Elected "Most Holy Messiah:" All people will be united by believing in one "supreme, most holy, most worthy servant of God." [Kind of makes you think of Obama, doesn't it, especially when we see the indoctrination in our public schools, where some children are chanting his name like some kind of God. I wonder if there will be some punishment for those who cannot accept or believe in this "supreme, most holy, most worthy servant of God."]

> By article 55 of the constitution of One-Faith-Of-God, the supreme earthly representative of God and the great spirits shall be the Messiah (moshiach), who shall be elected every ten years by the faithful members of One-Faith-Of-God." The Messiah (moshiach) shall be the most holy, the most worthy servant of God, and the office of the Messiah shall stand forever as testimony to the great love and forgiveness of God in placing his trust and authority to elect his Earthly representative in the very hands of each and every member of One-Faith-Of-God. (Henry Lamb, "The New Constitution for America's Union," *WorldNetDaily.com*, April 19, 2009.)

That should certainly make all Christian and Jews happy—the long awaited promised Messiah will not be coming down from heaven, but gets to be elected by the people, for a ten-year term of office, and then we get to have a new Messiah. And, of course, he will have to be an ecumenical Messiah who is new-age and goes along with the worship of nature, mother earth, and the "solar system,"

The Christian belief is that Jesus Christ is the Messiah and will be returning. Christ is the creator of the earth and the solar system We are to worship Him, not His creations. The Jews are still awaiting their Messiah, but both orthodox Christians and Jews believe that the Messiah of these last days will destroy all false religions and evil governments—not be part of it, as this new UN constitution is proposing.

Christians believe Christ will usher in his Thousand Year Millennium and time of peace. Only then will the world have true peace. Then will we beat our swords into plowshares and know war no more (Isaiah 2:4) and (Micah 4:3), and the lamb and the lion will lie down together. It will be a theocracy with the Messiah in charge. I don't think He will relish the UN replacing him every ten years with someone else. In fact, I do not believe the evil UN will be in existence anymore, once the true Messiah has come.

However, before the 2nd Coming, there is going to be a short period of time when the New World Order does get to be in control of the entire world and there will be a one-world government, economy, and religion. We can postpone it as courageous Americans and others have been doing, standing for liberty and truth, but it is prophesied, and it is best to know about it so we can prepare for it.

When is the "One-Faith-of-God" to Be Officially Launched? When you check out the above website (2009 version) and click on the supposed "Christian History Timeline," be prepared to read the most biased, anti-Christian, fictitious history you can ever imagine. They show a timeline of events that supposedly have already happened and what is yet to happen.

The One-Faith-of-God was supposedly to have already started in 2006. Somehow, most of us missed that news. (Maybe that means the timeline is running behind schedule.) As you see below, the first elections of 144,000 and of the Messiah are to be held in 2010. There are three major events that are to then take place in 2012.

2010—First national elections of leadership of One-Faith-Of-God for every nation on Earth

2010—International democratic election by members of One-Faith-Of-God of the Messiah in the name of God

2012—Great Conclave of One-Heaven between One-Islam, One-Spirit-Tribe and One-Faith-of God; the election of the leadership of One-Heaven and the closing of the gates of Hell forever [Isn't that nice that Hell essentially will no longer exist. These people think there power is incredible.]

2012—Official recognition by the United Nations of the State of One Jerusalem

2012—Officially the "last days" and the "end of time" as end of traditional Jewish and Christian calendar and creation of new Universal Calendar

It is interesting how this timeline coincides with the pagan Mayan calendar that also ends in 2012, and a new calendar begins. It is also interesting to read what they have listed as the "religious facts of Christianity," which are full of distortions, pagan beliefs and lies, and portray Christians as the most evil, misguided society on earth.

"Christian Beliefs": Here are some of the distortions given as Christian "fundamental philosophy" on their website (http://one-faith-of-god.org/religion_christianity/facts.htm):

Theism (god)—Ancient Pagan Trinitarian Monotheism based on power, fertility, war and human sacrifices;

Ultimate reality—Heaven is a fable, there is no redemption, only power to the ancient God, Mother Goddess and their son (a Trinity of Father, Son, and Holy Spirit). Except those born of Noble (Sadducean) blood, all others are ignorant sheep who blindly follow a lie;

Human nature—Created good, but now born sinful;

Purpose of life—Know, love and serve God, but never know the real God to whom you serve (Satan, Mother Goddess)."

So, according to this website, Christians, unbeknown to us, are really worshipping an ancient pagan trinity of Father, who is really "Satan, a Mother Goddess, and their son," whom is called the Holy Spirit. The Christian religion is based on "power, fertility, war, and human sacrifices."

Could the person writing this website be describing his own pagan religion and trying to make it appear that all people are really worshipping the same god, or someday will be forced to? He is very open as to who that god is—Satan.

No Mention of Christ Anywhere: It is very interesting in the timeline and the listing of facts of Christianity on this website that, there is no mention of Christ as the person we are worshipping. Nor is he even listed as the founder of the Christian faith. It, obviously, shows that whoever is writing this information has the same aversion to using the name of Jesus Christ, as do others who worship Satan or pagan gods. Paul of Tarsus is listed as the founder, much later than when he lived, by about 200 years, and very disparaging things are written about him. Could the reason for why the name of Christ is missing is that those who worship Satan are afraid to speak or write the name of Jesus Christ? They are afraid of the power that his name holds. (http://one-faith-of-God. org/religion_christianity/facts.htm)

The timeline is much kinder to Judaism. Most of the historical facts and the statement of the Jewish beliefs are accurate. They almost have it right, except they go way off on a limb and list John the Baptist as the founder of Judaism. (http://one-faith-of-god.org/religion_judaism/facts.htm.)

Christian Bias and Forthcoming Persecution: If a child is not raised in a Christian home; does not have association with Christians who truly live their religion; is taught in the public schools, where Christianity is put down and Islam is praised, where a green, nature-worshiping religion is taught and promoted, where "diversity and multiculturalism" are also worshiped, and anyone who has a different opinion of morality is considered guilty of "hate speech;" if a child listens to President Obama give speeches saying that the US is no longer a Christian nation; and if a child looks at such twisted information about Christianity as is on the aforementioned website, then, no wonder, when that child grows up, he or she has such a distorted view and dislike for Christianity.

In this once great Christian nation, settled primarily by Christians seeking religious liberty, we can now see an anti-Christian bias rising, which could turn into persecution, as has been prophesied would happen in the last days.

The Book of Revelations Prophesizes of a Time When there will be a One-World Religion under Control of Satin (Referred to as the Beast and his Representative, the Anti-Christ): Chapter 13, verse 1, describes the beast rising up out of the sea having seven heads and ten horns and upon the horns are ten crowns. Most people interpret the beast to represent the dictator of a one-world government and one supreme ruler of that government. The heads, horns, and crowns represent the major unions of nations, with their rulers who have now been united to be part of the world government.

The Beast Will Deceive the People by Performing a Great Miracle Causing them to Worship Him and the Dragon: Verse 3 tells that one of the ten heads was wounded and died, but the beast was able to heal the wound and brought him back to life, a miracle that made all the world hold the beast in great awe and be afraid of him. Verse 4 states that in worshipping the beast, the people are really worshipping Satan, who gave power unto the beast. Verse 4 also shows how afraid the people will be—"Who is like unto the beast, who is able to make war with him." Verse 8—all people who dwell on the earth will worship him, except for the Christians who have their names written in the "book of life of the Lamb who was slain for the world."

Verse 6: The Beast Speaks Blasphemy Against God and Persecutes the Saints, the Followers of Christ: The beast is victorious and he "overcomes the saints." Verse 7—"the beast will have power over all kindreds, tongues and nations."

A Second Beast with Two Horns, (who looks like a lamb but speaks like a dragon) will Join the First. This one is referred to as the Anti-Christ. More Miracles and Wonders will Happen: Verses 11-13—The anti-Christ will cause fire to come down from heaven in the sight of men and other miracles.

He will convince more people to worship the beast. Many will be deceived and will worship the beast.

An Image of the Beast will be Made by the Anti-Christ: Verses 14-15—The image will be able to speak, as if it were alive. Those who will not worship the image of the beast will be killed.

How Long will the Beast and the Anti-Christ Rule Over the Earth? It could be from 3 ½ years to 6 ½ years. According to Revelations 13, verse 5, it will be forty-two months, which is **3 and ½ years.** The Book of Daniel in the Old Testament gives two different answers—Chapter 8 speaks of the last days and the Anti-Christ, described as a goat with horns. Verse 12 states that he will cast truth to the ground and will practice and prosper. Verse 13 asks the question how long will this "transgression of desolation" last? Verse 14 answers the question with 2,300 days which is **6 and 1/3 years.** In Chapter 12, however, the question is asked again and the answer in verse 7 is given as "a time, times and a half." Time is interpreted as one year so it is one year plus two years plus one half a year equaling—**3 and ½ years.** In verse 11 it is stated as one thousand two hundred and ninety days—which is **3.5** years and in verse 12, it is given as one thousand three hundred and thirty five days which is **3.6** years.

The Wise Shall Understand and Be Blessed for Waiting: According to Daniel 12:10, "the wicked shall do wickedly, and none of the wicked shall understand, but the wise shall understand." And Verse 12 states "blessed is he that waiteth" and cometh to the end of the 3.6 years.

The Last Days will Be Similar to the Time of Noah—With People Unconcerned and Unprepared for Any Disaster: I know this is all very hard to think of, especially when times are still somewhat all right. We have not really entered into a period of desolation or tribulation yet. In the entire chapter of Mathew 24, Jesus answers his disciples' questions about what will be the signs of the end of the world and before his second coming. He tells them (verses 6-7) of wars and rumors of wars, of famines, pestilences, and earthquakes, a terrible time (verse 15) of desolation and great tribulation, (verse 21) "such as was not since the beginning of the world," (verse 9) that the Christians will be greatly persecuted and killed, that they will have to flee unto the mountains. (Verse 24) There will be false Christs and false prophets such as the anti-christ, that shall show "great signs and wonders and shall deceive the very elect." (Verse 37-39) Christ says that the last days will be as in the days of Noah—people were eating and drinking, getting married, having a good time, totally unaware that anything bad was going to happen to them. No one was prepared but Noah and his family. Even though Noah had tried to warn them, the people would not listen, so they were all destroyed. (Verse 15) Christ says that those who read his prophecy will understand, and they will watch and be ready. (Verses 42-44)

What Can Christians Possibly Do to Watch, Prepare and Be Able to Endure These Difficult Times? As both Daniel and Christ tell us, the righteous will understand, be prepared and will be blessed for being able to endure these difficult time. Some Christians believe that they will escape all these times of tribulations, that the Lord loves them and will "rapture" them away before any of this happens. I tell them that, just in case that does not happen in the time period they think it should, it is good to have a Plan B. They should also get prepared to survive for a long time.

Like our pioneer forefathers before us, we must be self sustaining—to have our own sources of food such as gardens with non-hybrid seeds that will keep reproducing—not the hybrid seeds that are now sold on the market that will only grow one year. We will need a supply of long storing food in case we can't have a garden because of famine, drought or bad weather. We will need a large supply of water and a way to purify it. We will need a supply of wheat and to make your own bread, you will need a supply of oil, yeast, honey or sugar, powdered milk, and salt. We will need a wheat grinder that does not need electricity to grind our wheat to make our own bread.

There may be times of no electricity, either because of storms or because of wacky environmental policies, that are already brewing, such as shutting down all coal mines, which are still the major source of electrical power in the USA, or there may be some "smart meter" that will be forced upon your home, and your electricity will be under the control of your power provider. They can turn down your electricity or just turn it off. Such is already happening in countries in Europe and is starting in California.

We may need to have a generator or some way of producing our own energy, or learn how to live without it. We will need a way to produce heat in the wintertime and some way to cook and bake our food without electricity.

We will need to have our homes fully paid for, to be out of debt. We will need to have some livelihood—a product that we can produce which can be bartered or traded with others for what we need. Perhaps it is a good idea to have some gold and silver coins tucked away that can be used for bartering or buying or selling. (Of course, they may be outlawed, as gold was under FDR, especially if the one-world government wants us to be on a total cashless system.)

I know it is hard to imagine our once great, free nation ever coming to such a state of tyranny, and it would be much easier to believe that all is well, but for those of you who do see the transformation of America going around us, I hope you will take this warnings seriously.

During the short time of freedom that we still have left before the national/ international ID card with an RFID chip will be mandated for all of us; before an RFID implant will be forced upon us, before we could become a total police state, that you can begin preparing.

Think through every aspect of your daily life, from morning until night—what you would need so you and your family can survive and remain free without having to compromise your beliefs and come under total government control by taking an implanted RFID chip. Plan and prepare accordingly. If you are prepared, you will have less need to fear. You will not have to panic or give in through fear or desperation and take the mark and be forced to worship the false God that it represents.

Christians Know How the Last Chapter Ends: As frightening and unsettling as these last days are and will become, it is reassuring to know that we know how it is going to end. We know that Christ will return for his 2nd Coming, that all his enemies will be destroyed, that he will usher in the millennium, a thousand years of peace, righteousness, and happiness. This knowledge can give us hope and help us to endure some rough times ahead.

Chapter Sixteen

The NAFTA Super Highway and Maps
Public/Private Partnerships

In spite of the denials that President Bush and others have stated about any super highways being built, there is overwhelming evidence that there are plans for such, and the infrastructure is being prepared for them. These highways are all part of the NAFTA/ North American Union plan.

Sometimes you have to go to the Mexicans to get the truth, as with the following statement by Jose Natividad Gonsales, the governor of the Mexican province of Nuevo Leon. He is talking about the first roadway that was to be built, the Trans Texas Corridor:

> "The Trans Texas Corridor is not just the NAFTA Superhighway; but the Logistical Trans-Corridor of North America, uniting Mexico, the U.S. and Canada." This was said in a meeting where U.S. Secretary of Transportation, Mary Peters, was in attendance. At the same meeting, according to the Mexican press, Mexico's transportation secretary announced that President Calderon and President Bush had agreed to "an economically integrated North America."[454]

Public Private Partnership, the Funding Mechanism to Make Superhighways Possible

"Public Private Partnerships (PPPs)" Created: This was the new title for the government selling America's infrastructure to private companies. American Association of State Highway and Transportation officials even set up their own website to sell the idea of "Public-Private partnerships.[455]

So, it is not just the executive branches of all three countries and their agencies that are selling out their own sovereignty, it is also private corporations, who are a strong driving wind bringing their wealth, influence, and extensive advertising budgets. Banks and mortgage companies also join the partnerships forcing borrowers to comply as a stipulation for receiving loans.

Private companies are now systematically buying up water treatment plants in communities that are in financial straits (which include many in our nation). The PPPs have control over the water supply of the community and can jack up the prices to whatever they want. They are not your elected officials, so there is nothing you, the citizen, can do about it. Private companies are buying control of the U.S. Highway systems through PPPs with the state departments of transportation. It is a PPP that is now in control of the TTC (Trans Texas Corridor). One million Texans would lose their land if all goes according to the original plan.

2005, July 29—President Bush Signed a Bill Which Permits and Promotes the Charging of Tolls on Existing and Planned Interstate Highways, Bridges, and Tunnels: Before the passage of the bill, known as SAFETEA-LU, or "Safe, Accountable, Flexible, Efficient Transportation Equity Act: A Legacy for Users," it was generally illegal to charge tolls on roads built with Federal funds. What's more, the tolls collected would be automatic, requiring universally compatible toll transponder tags on every vehicle. SAFETEA-LU makes possible a variety of programs, all aimed at forcing Americans to pay to travel. The following is written on the Federal Highway Administration website about SAFETEA-LU:

> *Innovative finance*—SAFETEA-LU makes it easier and more attractive for the private sector to participate in highway infrastructure projects, bringing new ideas and resources to the table. Innovative changes such as eligibility for private activity bonds, additional flexibility to use **tolling** to finance infrastructure improvements, and broader TIFIA and SIB loan policies, will all stimulate needed private investment.

"Interstate System Reconstruction & Rehabilitation Pilot Program": This program allows for the tolling of existing interstate highways, bridges, and tunnels, and to fund repair of existing highways. These are some of the provisions of the program:

- "Interstate System Construction Toll Pilot Program" authorizes tolling existing facilities on the interstate system to fund new interstate highways.
- "Value Pricing Pilot (VPP) Program" allows new tolls on existing toll free facilities such as high occupancy vehicle (HOV) lanes, tolls on new lanes added to existing highways, and electronically collected variable tolls on existing and new toll facilities.

- "Express Lanes Demonstration Program" allows tolling to finance new lanes. Automatic toll collection is REQUIRED and revenue collected may be used to provide a reasonable rate of return on PRIVATE financing, operation, and maintenance costs.
- "High Occupancy Vehicle (HOV) Facilities, SAFETEA-LU Section 1121 (23 USC 166)" authorizes states to build high occupancy toll (HOT) lanes on interstate and non-interstate facilities.[456]

Cintra-Zachry, the Public/Private Partner to Build the TTC: In December of 2004, the Texas Department of Transportation "partnered" with Cintra-Zachry, a private Spanish investment firm, Cintra, and a Texas construction firm, Zachry to have them build three enormous road ways crossing Texas, called the Trans Texas Corridor (TTC). Cintra is short for *"Concesiones de Infraestrucas de Transporte, S.A."* Cintra-Zachry would invest $6 billion in the construction of the first segment of the Super Corridor. They would then turn it into toll roads, charging 15 cents a mile.

According to a fact sheet put out by a group in Texas called Corridor Watch, Cintra is one of the world's largest private sector developers of transportation infrastructure, having invested in highways in Spain, Ireland, Chile, Portugal, Toronto, Canada and they financed the building of the Chicago Skyway.

Zachry Construction Corporation was started in 1924 and is based in San Antonio, Texas. It is rated as one of the nation's top 25 construction companies.[457]

Cintra-Zachry and TXDOT Filed a Law Suit to Keep Their Plans Secret: The *Newsweek* article that tried to portray Ron Paul as a conspiracy nut because he believed the TTC was part of a NAFTA Superhighway and part of the North American Union, made the TTC sound like just a simple benign highway construction job and Cintra and Zachry as two very fine companies just doing their best to fulfill a job. If that is the case then why did Cintry-Zachry and the Texas Department of Transportation file a law suit with the Texas Attorney General to keep their plans secret from the public for where the highways would be built? Is that what reputable people do? The groups fighting this had to file a freedom of information request to find out where the highways were being planned.

Who Would Really Benefit the Most from a NAFTA Superhighway? Dr. Jerome Corsi answers that question in his article in *Human Events*, August 9, 2006, entitled, "China Wins NAFTA Superhighway Battle."

Corsi states that Red China has invested heavily in developing deep-water ports in Mexico to bring "unprecedented" volumes of containers into the USA along the emerging Super Highway. China will be the "economic winner in the North American Union free market." (And here we thought it was all about the security and prosperity of the USA, Canada, and Mexico.)

Hutchinson Ports, a wholly owned subsidiary of China's Hutchinson Whampoa Limited (HWL) is investing millions to expand two ports, Mananillo on Mexico's Pacific Coast and Punta Colonet, a Mexican bay in Baja, California. They are being expanded to become a 10 to 20 berth facility capable of processing some 6 million standard 20-foot long TEUs (industry terminology for the 20-foot equivalent unit, a single standard container).

HWL Ltd. is the holding company of billionaire Li Ka-shing, a well-known businessman, whose companies make up 15 percent of the market capitalization of the Hong Kong Stock Market." He is well connected to Communist Red China, COSCO, the China Ocean Shipping Company, and was trying to purchase "Global Crossing," but was denied the right to do so by a US Senate Committee, because of his strong ties to communism.

Global Crossing controls a significant percent of all the fiber optics currently leaving the United States.

What Would the Trans Texas Corridor Do to Texas? The TTC project originally called for a 4,000-mile network of transportation corridors, including a rail system, 1,200 feet wide, to be built across the state. The plan would have affected over a million people, taken about a half million agricultural acres out of private hands, chopped up farmland and ranches, cut through counties and school districts. The planned routes would have expanded the existing highways I-35 and I-69.

The building of the corridors would have cost an estimated $184 billion to be paid through a 50-year lease with the Spanish company, Cintra who partnered with the Texas company, Zachary. The roads would be completed in phases and turned into toll roads. The state and federal government would no longer have any control over the roads, and the tolls could continue to be raised to whatever CINTRA and Zachary wanted.

Battle in Texas to Fight the TTC: Back in 2003, the legislation was passed authorizing the building of the TTC, but it was tucked away in a huge Transportation Bill, which no one paid much attention to. However, by March, 2007, Texans had been alerted as to what was going on. A senate hearing was held about the TCC, where thousands of outraged Texans showed up to speak out against it. They have been fighting it ever since.

Texans did not like the idea of their state being chopped up by the building of such mammoth roads and the annexing of so much private land and the eminent domain taking that would be going on. They also did not like the agenda behind the NAFTA Superhighway and the North American Union and did not want their state to be the first wing of destroying American sovereignty.

After a five-year battle, the opponents finally appeared victorious in 2008, and the head of the TTC, Amadeo Saenz, admitted defeat. The plans were being stopped. However, a year later, it was found out that the elitists behind this plan, including the "supposed" conservative governor Rick Perry, had quietly changed the name of the TTC and were going forward with it, building it incrementally in small segments thinking the vigilant Texans, who had fought it so hard, had gone back to normal life or to sleep and would not notice.

So, once again, the troops had to rally and put on another battle. By October of 2009, it appeared they were once more victorious. Even the governor admitted that the TTC was dead.

Is the TTC Really Dead?: Out of curiosity, I wanted to check the old website that they once had for the TTC to see if it was still there. The link to the Trans Texas Corridor website used to show a map of where the two massive highways were planned at *http://ttc.keeptexasmoving.com/flash/interactive_map/ interactive.htm.* I checked the website and another site came up in its place. So I checked it. It was mainly talking about water in Texas—*http://www.window. state.tx.us/specialrpt/tif/southtexas/infrastructure.html.* But if you keep reading, at the very end is a section on transportation and, according to what is written, the TTC is still alive and well. Either they did not get the memo that the TTC is supposed to be dead and buried, or this is just all part of a new act of "smoke and mirrors" and political "slight of hand" going on. Here is what is written on the website as of October, 2009:

> While the implementation of NAFTA has brought more people, trade and economic development to the South Texas region, it has also brought more traffic congestion issues to the region. To alleviate traffic congestion, promote economic development and better connect the region's agricultural, trade and economic centers with markets throughout the state and nation, TxDOT is developing three "trade corridors," or special transportation routes designed to make truck traffic more efficient. These include the Ports-To-Plains Trade Corridor, the Trans-Texas Corridor 35 (TTC-35) and the I-69/ Trans-Texas Corridor.

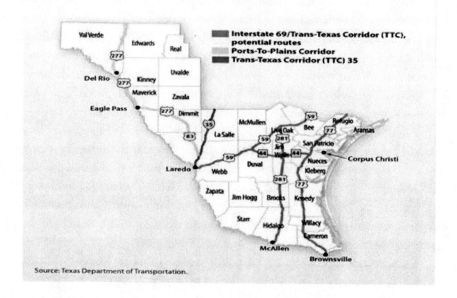

Source: Texas Department of Transportation.

Map Showing the Original Plans for Three Texas Corridors

Texas Trade Corridors:

1. **Ports-to-Plains Trade Corridor**: The website describes this roadway as a connection from the inland "Port of Laredo to Denver and on to various locations in the Great Plains." This corridor would be different from the other two going through Texas because this one would not be a toll road or require the construction of new roads. The Texas Department of Transportation, TXDOT, would just "improve and expand existing roads and rights of way."

2. **Trans-Texas Corridor 35:** This is described as a "multi-use trade corridor incorporating existing and new highways, railways and utilities, and connecting Laredo with markets in central and north Texas and throughout the nation." It will run parallel to Interstate 35, northwest from Laredo toward San Antonio and on to Oklahoma. "Plans call for TTC-35 to be built over the next 50 years" and to include: "lanes for passenger vehicles and trucks; railways; commuter railways; and infrastructure for utilities (water, oil and gas, and transmission lines for electricity)."

   How will it be built? The website says that state, federal and private (toll) dollars will be used to construct the roads. And the website does admit that "in some areas . . . significant amounts of rights of way (land) will be acquired from landowners." But it is "expected to have only limited effects on South Texas land owners, however, because there are enough existing rights of way on either side of Interstate 35 to accomplish most of the additional building proposed for TTC-35." [I'm afraid when one looks at the blown up picture of what this expansion will look like—four football fields wide, one realizes that the statement of "limited effect" is not true at all. It would have an enormous effect on any property that it is going through.]

3. **Interstate 69/Trans-Texas Corridor:** The website describes this highway as similar to TTC-35 but connecting Laredo, McAllen, and Brownsville to markets in the east and northeast Texas and on to the Chicago and on to Canada.

    It would be financed the same as TTC-35 with state, federal and private toll dollars. The website states, "At this time, the need for additional rights of way from landowners has not yet been established."[457] Of course, if it is going to be just like TTC-35, it will also be 4 football fields wide and will have an equally enormous affect on property owners in the areas it is going through.

The TTC Raises Its "Dead" Head Again: I received an article, March 21, 2010, coming from Terri Hall, the founder and leader of Texans Uniting for Reform and Freedom (TURF), one of the groups who have been fighting the Trans Texas Corridor for several years. Much of this information is also coming from a personal phone call with Terri on March 22. She told me that not only is the TTC alive once again, but so is Governor Rick Perry's support for it, as well as that of President Obama. Obama also supports NAFTA, the amnesty for illegal aliens that it is calling for, open borders between all three countries and the entire Super highway system. Terri also told me of Canada's support and what the future goals are for all of the above.

Even though the TTC was proclaimed dead in 2009 because of all of the opposition against it, just as I predicted, it is raising its head again, with the new name, "Innovative Connectivity Plan (ICP)."

Terri said that once Rick Perry had received the Republican nomination for governor, and his reelection seemed pretty sure, he began again his support for the "TTC" now named "ICP."

What is very disturbing is that Perry ran a campaign to regain the Republican nomination on his strong stand for "state's rights" against the encroaching power of the federal government. All the while, he was still very much in the pocket of the internationalists. Maybe Perry does not believe in a takeover of Texas by the federal government, but international and world government is okay? Doesn't that sound a little bit hypocritical?

The Detrimental Effects of NAFTA and Obama's Support for it: In her article, Terri Hall retraced the history of NAFTA and reminded us of the fact that the two U.S. Presidents, who were behind it and who supported it, were both members of the elite CFR and the Trilateral Commission (TC), George Bush Sr. and Bill Clinton. And NAFTA's chief architect was the U.S. Trade Representative Carla Hills, who also belonged to the TC.

Terri describes NAFTA as just the opposite of "free trade." It is instead "government managed trade," "heavily tilted in favor of foreign countries." NAFTA fails to "insist on reciprocity, and overly taxes American goods while providing tax breaks on foreign imports."

Terri emphatically states that "NAFTA has done more to hurt the U.S. manufacturing sector than any other government policy in recent history. In fact, more than one million Americans have lost jobs due to NAFTA." [Some believe it is closer to 300 million jobs lost.]

In his campaign for president, Obama said he would like to see parts of NAFTA "renegotiated," but such language is no longer mentioned. He, instead, is pushing for even more "free" trade agreements to be signed with other countries, such as: Australia, New Zealand, Singapore, Chile, Peru, Vietnam and Brunei on an Asia-Pacific regional free-trade agreement, South Korea, Panama, and Columbia.

Canada's Renewed Support for the NAFTA Superhighway: Canadian officials have shown renewed interest in a multi-modal trade corridor along I-35, so that they can facilitate bringing in cheap NAFTA goods.

Winnipeg is planning to build an inland port similar to those in San Antonio, Dallas, and Kansas City. The port in Kansas City has ceded sovereign U.S. territory to Canada and Mexico with the flags of all three countries flying over it.

From Winnipeg, Canada, there will be "a multi-modal trade corridor being built southward along I-35." Winnipeg officials have stated they intend to run a logistics and trade corridor that would include rail and high speed highways all the way to Mexico as an "Asia-Pacific gateway" connecting to Toronto and Montreal.

The Plans for the TTC (as of March, 2010): Within days of Governor Perry winning the Texas primary, March 2, as the Republican candidate, he and

TxDOT revealed their plans to continue to push the TTC "piece by piece all the way up to the Red River." TTC-69 (also given the name I-69 to make it appear more harmless), was never stopped and is still moving forward. In fact, expansion of US 77 is already underway in the valley as part of the initial leg of what will be known as TTC-69/I-69; Ports to Plains (to run from Mexico all the way to Alberta, Canada) and La Entrada de Pacifico are two other active TTC corridors, that show that nothing has changed with their construction either, except their shedding the official name of the Trans Texas Corridor.

As Terri Hall writes, this proves the TTC's "demise was mere illusion designed to put Texans back to sleep while politicians get re-elected and quietly build it, segment by segment, under the radar."

Here are other aspects of the various expansions: The SH 130 toll road will continue northward; the first leg will be TTC 35, from Georgetown around Austin, extending south to San Antonio; the expansion of US 281 south of San Antonio feeds into the I-35 corridor and will move the corridor northward; the new TTC segment from Waco to Hillsboro, fills the gaps of "free" lane I-35 expansion, and will also likely become some form of foreign-owned toll road, similar to segments 5 & 6 of SH 130, and the TTC-69 is planned to go from the Rio Grande Valley northeast to Texarkana and eventually up through Michigan.

How will they be built? A TTC-69 public private partnership(called CDA in Texas), was awarded to ACS of Spain and Zachry of San Antonio in June of 2008. In August of 2009, the Perry-appointed-Texas Transportation Commissioner, Ned Holmes, asked for the TTC-69 contract to be approved by the Texas Attorney General, Greg Abbott. Perry wanted this contract signed before the citizens of Texas could step-in to stop it.

Perry's son, Griffin, works for UBS, the financial arm of the ACS consortium who won the development rights for TTC-69. Could there be a little Perry "special interest "going on here?

Future Long-Range Goals of the NAFTA Superhighway: Terri Hall describes the following destinations for the "piece by piece" projects: Ports to Plains is to run from Mexico all the way to Alberta, Canada; La Entrada de Pacifico, will traverse through the Big Bend area. (They are planning to cede Big Bend to international interests by deeming it an "international" park, essentially to join it with Mexico's "Big Bend" on the other side of the U.S. border.); Future sea-ports will be connected with Far-East ocean shipping lanes; Federal transportation dollars will be steered into several local projects over time, and then connect the segments into a singular, identifiable system.

Ports to Plains Alliance: This is the coalition pushing the development of the Ports to Plains trade corridor. They completed a trade mission to Alberta and promoted the West Texas Trade Summit in San Angelo, held February 19, 2010, where the goal was to promote both trade and multi-national corridors in Texas and Mexico.

The Ports to Plains Alliance also hosted an "Energy Summit," April 8-9, 2010, in Colorado. The alliance is mirroring the efforts of other public private partnerships (partially tax-funded) like TTC-69's Alliance for I-69, and the big I-35 coalition, called the North America Supercorridor Coalition or NASCO.

Terri Hall ends her article with: "So don't fall for the rhetoric, Texans. As Ronald Reagan used to say, "trust but verify," and the verifiable facts point to the "Trans Texas Corridor briskly moving ahead on all fronts."

"Remain vigilant to stop the biggest land grab in Texas history and to protect our sovereignty. Your freedom depends on it!"

Make the connections. . . Read more about how privatizing government functions comes at great cost to taxpayers."(Terri Hall, "Trans Texas Corridor is Still Alive," March 22, 2010, *http://www.texasturf.org/*)

Terri does describe one section of Texas that has been able to rid themselves of the TTC by their own hard work and innovative "coordination plan." It is described in Chapter Eighteen about Hope.

Is the NAFTA Super Highway Being Built in the Rest of the Nation? Because of all the attention that has been on Texas with their battle against the TTC that has gone on since 2004, not much has been said about other areas across the nation with any highways being built. However, I have heard reports from friends who say they have seen mammoth highways being built in remote areas of the Northwest and others have said they have seen bridges being greatly widened to make it possible that a huge highway could cross. Yes, I believe the preparations are being laid and the plans are still going forward.

My good friends, Mary and Dick Wolbert, who drove across the northern states to Minnesota the summer of 2009, told me that they saw and took pictures of enormous highways being built somewhere between Wyoming and North Dakota. They saw perfectly good highways that look brand new (because they are in remote areas and hardly receive any traffic) being torn up and retrofitted with steal grid frames underneath, as if they are expecting some very heavy trucks, or artillery, or something to be travelling on them. My friends asked some of the construction crew why this was being done? They were told it was to make the highways hold up better in cold weather. If that is true, why would the perfectly good highways that obviously had held up fine in cold weather, now be deliberately torn up?

NAFTA Superhighway Maps Designed by NAFI: As you will see, there are two maps that used to be shown on websites to give a conceptualization of the "desired" routes of the super highways connecting through Mexico, the United States, and Canada. There is also a map of Texas showing the plans for the TransTexas Corridor (TTC). Who came up with these routes? They were proposed by the North American Forum on Integration (NAFI)—a group that was begun in 2002, headquartered in Montreal, Canada. NAFI consists of wealthy industrialists, academies, and politicians whose aim it is to break down barriers to the North American Union and provide a quick flow of goods, services, and people through the three countries. The main actors in NAFI are members of the Council on Foreign Relations and their related organizations based in Mexico and Canada.

NAFI's Objectives: According to their own website—(emphasis added): "NAFI aims to address the issues raised by **North American integration** as well as identify new ideas and strategies to reinforce the **North American region**." They hope to achieve these objectives by: 1) Making the academic world, the public and decision-makers aware of the challenges posed by **integration between the three NAFTA countries**; 2) Identifying the **elements of the North American agenda** which would allow the **consolidation and reinforcement of the North American region**; 3) Favoring the creation of North American networks to set the basis for a trilateral dialogue.

NAFI's Conferences and their Titles: To educate people about North American Integration, NAFI holds various conferences. These are ones that have been held in the past and their titles:

March, 2003, Montreal, Canada, "Beyond Free Trade: **Strengthening North America**"

April, 2004, Monterrey (Mexico) "**North American Energy Resources**" and the creation of a **North American energy fund**.

2005-2009, Conferences for Students called "Triumvirate": [These were already written about in greater detail in the Chapter about Robert Pastor, who is on the board of NAFI and has been very much involved in promoting a NAU among students.] A hundred students attend these mock parliament sessions from 15 different universities and participate playing various roles—either as legislators, lobbyists or journalists.

Economic and Political Integration: NAFI's first objective is to make "the public and decision makers aware of the challenges of **economic and political integration** between the three NAFTA countries."

1994—North America's SuperCorridor Coalition, Inc. (NASCO) was Formed: According to their website March, 2007, they were very proud of who they are and blatantly spoke of their international corridor connections. Now their website is totally different. They try not to mention any international connections at all. Obviously, they have been getting a lot of criticism from concerned citizens, and they were told to redo their website. This is what they had written about themselves and their purpose as of March 3, 2007. (Websites change as people find out what is going on, so it may be different today.)

> "NASCO is a non-profit organization dedicated to developing
> the world's first international, integrated and secure, multi-model
> transportation system along the international Mid-Continent
> Trade and Transportation Corridor to improve both the trade
> competitiveness and quality of life in North America . . . The
> NASCO Corridor encompasses Interstate Highways 35, 29 and 94,
> and the significant east/west connectors to those highways in the
> United States, Canada, and Mexico. The Corridor directly impacts
> the continental trade flow of North America. Membership includes
> public and private sector entities along the Corridor in Canada, the
> United States and Mexico . . . From the largest border crossing in
> North America (the Ambassador Bridge in Detroit, Michigan, and
> Windsor, Canada), to the second largest border crossing of Laredo,
> Texas and Nuevo Laredo, Mexico, extending to the deep water Ports of
> Manzanillo and Lazaro Cardenas, Mexico, and to Manitoba, Canada,
> the impressive, tri-national NASCO membership truly reflects the
> international scope of the Corridor and the regions it impacts . . .
> NASCO has received $2.25 million in Congressional funding to be
> administered by the US Department of Transportation (USDOT) for
> the development of a technology integration and tracking project."

North American Inland Port Network (NAIPN): This is a sub-committee of NASCO and is also mentioned on their website. It was given the task of developing an active inland port network along the corridor to alleviate congestion at maritime ports and our nation's borders. In other words, NAIPN is the organization that is making sure that cheaper ports are being built in Mexico that will bring in goods and unload them with cheaper costs by avoiding the more expensive ports in California where longshoremen charge more money.[458]

The following map is what used to be on the NASCO (North American Super Corridor Organization) website. They were very proud of it. It has since been taken down. It used to show arrows pointing to the flow of traffic from Mexico up through the United States to Canada. They also had written on the map, "You built it" (as if this is something we all agreed to and were proud of).

The NASCO Map Now on their Website: As of November 2009, their website has a disclaimer saying "This map is not a blueprint or a plan of any kind" . . . the highways shown exist already." (Do you think they were getting lots of opposition to their map that used to say "You built it?")

At least the NASCO map leaves the state borders in of the USA, but notice no borders for any provinces in Canada or Mexico and no borders between the three countries.

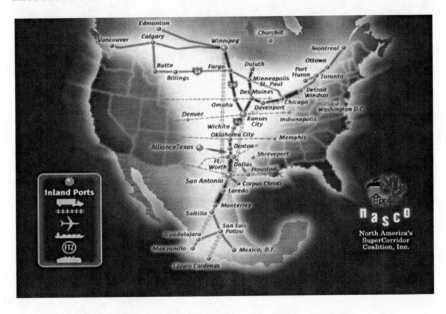

NASCO Map that no longer exists on their website

NAFI's North American Map: As you will see in the map that NAFI created, it has divided the USA into four major corridors: Pacific Corridor, Central Western Corridor, Central Eastern Corridor, and the Atlantic Corridor. Not shown are the 80 interconnecting "high priority corridors," that will be linked onto them inside the United States.[459]

The NAFI website is written in both English and French. The French translation and abbreviation for NAFI is *"FINA."* The website is *www.fina-nafi. org.*

NAU Map of NAFTA Superhighway

This map is taken from one that appeared in the New American magazine. [460] What is written on the side was hard to read so I printed it below: (To view the map and read the entire magazine articles about it go to *http://www.scribd.com/ doc/469972/North-American-Union-New-American*)

> This map is a conceptualization of the Super Highways now underway to connect the United States, Canada, and Mexico to help bring about the creation of a North American Union similar to the European Union. The map's travel corridors show the desired routes of the new Super Highways as proposed by the North American Forum on Integration (NAFI)—a group of wealthy industrialists, academies, and politicians whose aim it is to break down barriers to the North American Union. The main actors in NAFI are members of the Council on Foreign Relations or related organizations based in Mexico and Canada.
>
> NAFI, whose first objective is to make "the public and decision makers aware of the challenges of *economic and political*

integration between the three NAFTA countries," is following the country-integration plan of the European Union. (Emphasis added.) That plan used the idea of "free trade" to make steps toward integration sound appealing to the public. Though the North American Union would devastate the American middle class, the Super Highways are being touted as facilitating free trade and bringing about prosperity in the three countries.

NAFI's vision is being enacted right now. Eighty separate, but interconnected "high priority corridors," are being initiated in the United States. To find a complete list of the 80 intended Super Highway projects, go to *http://www.aaroads.com/high-priority/table. html.*[461]

FIELD OF FREEWAYS: Computer image depicts stretch of proposed NAU's borderless transit corridor.

Description—Computer Image Giving an Idea of all the Lanes and the Width: This picture shows a computer image of what the super high way would look like: 1200 feet wide, about the width of four football fields side by side, (more than a quarter mile), with 10 traffic lanes, six for cars (three going north, three going south), four lanes for trucks (two lanes going north, two lanes going south). There will be six rail lines: two for commuter rails, two for freight, and two high speed passenger rail lines. There will also be a 200-ft. wide utility corridor for water, oil, gas, communications, data and electricity.

Under Foreign Control: The Trans Texas Corridor would be under the control of a foreign corporation, which would be responsible for building the highway and then collecting the toll on it for the next half a century, 50 years. That company is Cintra, (Cintra Concesiones de Infraestrusturas) a Spanish corporation, owned by the King of Spain, which is partnering with a Texas company, Zachry Construction. The Texas Department of Transportation (TxDOT) then is partnering with Cintra-Zachry, who will invest $6 billion in the construction of the first segment of the SuperCorridor, and then give it to TxDOT, along with another $1.2 billion for the right to build and operate the TTC for the next 50 years.

Rudy Giuliani Connection: Former Mayor of New York City, Rudy Giuliani, has an embarrassing connection to the TTC. Bracewell & Giuliani, a law firm he joined as senior partner in 2005, is the exclusive legal counsel for the above mentioned Spanish firm, Cintra, that has been granted the right to operate the toll road in the TTC project. It is most interesting that none of this has ever been mentioned or questioned in all the debates or public appearances that Giuliani had in his run as a top Republican candidate for President of the United States. (Of course, none of the candidates were ever asked about the TTC or the SPP, or anything about a movement towards a North American Union. Ron Paul would periodically get a question or a joke about it, and the reporters would make fun of him for believing in it.)[462]

Mexican Ports Would Put USA Longshoremen and Truckers Out of Work: U.S. longshoremen belong to a union which has helped them get higher wages. They earn over $100,000 a year while Mexican longshoremen earn maybe $10.00 an hour. American truck drivers belong to the teamsters union which demands for them higher wages. Mexican truck drivers have no union and also come cheap. Thus, by bypassing U.S. ports and American truck drivers and using Mexican ports (specifically Manzanillo and Lazaro Cardenas) and Mexican truck drivers or rail instead, it will cost much less to bring goods into our country. All those involved can have bigger profits. The big containers, that are coming from under-market labor in China and other Asian countries, will be placed onto Mexican trucks or rail cars and sent on their way to the United States and Canada.

Why Such Mammoth Super Highways and Who Would Benefit? Lots of big corporations and stores will benefit from finding cheaper and faster ways to bring in produce and goods from foreign markets. Various U.S. government agencies, dozens of state agencies, and scores of private NGOs (non-governmental organizations) have been working behind the scenes to create the NAFTA Super Highway. Many of these groups belong to NASCO, the North American Super Corridor Coalition. They are the group that came up with the design of the superhighway. It is obvious that their design aims to connect Mexico, Canada, and the U.S. into one big transportation system, expediting and bringing together the North American Union.[463]

The NASCO design purposely had bypassed the existing highways because they wanted to provide new areas of commerce for themselves and their partners, commerce such as gas stations, restaurants, hotels that could only be accessed through their superhighway toll roads. Other competing businesses would no longer be accessible and would be forced out of business.

The Destruction of Sovereign States and Nations, Broken up By Broad Corridors: As with just about every idea that is being presented for regional and world government, the elitists have been scheming and writing about these things for many years. I discovered a quote by H.G. Wells, the famous Fabian Socialist writer who has written about socialistic, futuristic plans in several of his books. This quote is from *The Shape of Things to Come*, written back in 1936, his description of the year 2040. (I darkened the most important parts.)

> If most of the divisions and barriers of the period of the sovereign states had disappeared, if there were no longer castles, fortifications, boundaries and strategic lines to be traced, there were still many indications that the world was under control and still not quite sure of its own good behavior. The carefully planned system of aerodromes to prevent any untoward developments of the free private flying that had been tolerated after 2040 was such an indication, and so was the strategic import plainly underlying the **needlessly wide main roads that left no possible region of insurrection inaccessible**. From the air or on a map it was manifest that the world was still 'governed.' **The road system was like a net cast over a dangerous beast.**[464]

So, in summary, these giant superhighways will not only serve to expedite trade and bring cheaper goods into the three nations, but the real underlying reason for them is to break up states and national boundaries, and make it much easier to establish regional government of the states and the nations. If there is no longer a state with state boundaries, there will no longer be a state national guard to protect that state. The "needlessly wide main roads" will make no "region of insurrection" accessible. The road system will be like a "net cast over a dangerous beast."

The Port of Entry—Kansas City, Missouri: If all goes according to the NAFTA Superhighway plan, foreign trucks will not have to stop at the border coming in from Mexico to Texas. The border will just be a speed bump for them. They will proceed across Texas, Oklahoma and on to Kansas City, Missouri, which has been designated as the port of entry. And guess who gets to operate the port? None other than Mexico! Phyllis Schlafly wrote in her November 2006 Phyllis Schlafly Report: "Kansas City, Missouri, is planning to allow the Mexican government to open a Mexican customs office in conjunction with the Kansas City Smart Port. This will be the first foreign customs facility allowed to operate on U.S. soil."

> This spring [2006], city officials signed off on a 50-year lease for the Mexican facility, with an option for 50 more years . . . The council earlier this year earmarked $2.5 million in loans and $600,000 in direct aid to SmartPort, which would build and own the inland customs facility and sublet it to the Mexican government through agreements with U.S. Customs and Border Protection . . . SmartPort meanwhile is seeking a $1.5 million grant from the U.S. Economic Development Administration to purchase high-tech gamma-ray screening devices for drive-through inspections of truck cargo" The Mexican trucks will cross border in FAST lanes, checked only electronically by the new "SENTRI" system. Thus, the trucks will not have to be opened for inspection, just drive under a big scanner that will read the bar codes on the merchandise inside. What if the bar codes have been falsely marked? What if inside are really lots of guns and ammunition, but are marked with bar codes for Chinese trinkets and toys? Why have so few Americans heard anything about this? We are purposely being kept in the dark. Even the *Kansas City Star* paper admits that "Confusion and secrecy have been hallmarks of the ambitious project."[465]

Putting the U.S. in danger: Several writers and radio columnists have mentioned the danger of Mexican truck drivers, who don't have to abide by U.S. safety standards, nor do they have very safe trucks. But the biggest danger could be the kind of merchandise that will be brought in without any real inspection. Drugs, ammunition, even soldiers could be smuggled in. This is revealed in the following e-mail message:

> Put yourself in the mind of a military strategist. Cargo arriving from China and other countries will arrive at the port in Mexico. Trucks

will be loaded there and 'sealed.' The purpose of the seal is supposedly security and efficiency—so that trucks don't have to be stopped and searched at borders and trucking check points. This is what's called the 'trusted shipper' program. Trucks sealed at the port will be able to travel to their warehouse destination in the U.S. without being stopped. Between the rail lines and the 'trusted shipper' trucks delivering straight to warehouses, enough Chinese troops could be brought into our country to take it over within a few weeks. You don't need an overwhelming number of troops when the attack is a surprise and the troops are strategically located for quick strikes on the centers of power.

The 'free trade' agreements have been selling our country out from under us—selling off infrastructure, encumbering U.S. assets through credit. The NAFTA highway and a sneak attack is a way that the traitors in our government could be turning us over to the creditor nations—China in particular. Think that's far fetched? Then give one good reason for this highway when we have major ports on both seacoasts. How does the 'trusted shipper' provide security for the United States? Think about it. [466]

European Union Toll Roads All Privatized: For those skeptics who still can't believe such a thing as a NAFTA Superhighway is planned, already leased and will be operated by foreign companies such as Cintra, a company from Spain, look at what is happening in Europe, our role model for all of this. According to an article by Jerome Corsi in *Human Events,* June 30, 2006, just about all major toll roads in Europe are now privatized:

> Italy's state-owned toll authority, Autostrade SpA, was sold to private investors in the late 1990s (and will soon be merged with Spain's Abertis, creating a vast 6,7000 km (4, 200 mile) network of private toll roads throughout Western Europe). In France, the three largest toll enterprises in which the government had retained controlling interest, Autoroutes Paris-Rhin-Rhone (APRP); Soeiete du Nord et de L'Est de la France (SANEF. Operator of the Autoroute du Sud), were put up for sale in late 2005; their privatization is currently in process of being completed. By the end of the year, 8,175 km (5,109 miles) of France's toll roads will be in private hands, according to the French toll road association, AFSA. In Spain and Portugal, all major toll roads are, likewise, in private hands. [467]

Much of America's Infrasructure, Ports, Terminals and Toll Roads are Already Privatized: According to Phyllis Schlafly, American infrastructure is already being sold off, little by little. We were all alarmed at the news of 22 East and Gulf port operations being sold to Dubai Ports World, a maritime company controlled by a Middle East government. Now we find out from Homeland Security, that 80% of our 3,200 terminals nationwide are operated by foreign companies and countries. The Pocahontas Parkway, in Virginia, is already leased to an Australian company for 99 years. An Australian-Spanish partnership is now leasing the Indiana tollroad for 75 years. In 2005, Chicago sold a 99-year lease to the same firm for $1.8 billion, and the tolls are expected to double. The tolls from the U.S. side of the tunnel between Detroit and Windsor, Canada, also belong to an Australian company.

Why the big rush to sell our infrastructure? The answer is usually follow the money. Many state and local governments are in debt. It is nice to have that big amount of money coming in, so politicians can cover their runaway budget deficits. They ignore the fact that U.S. citizens must now pay tolls to foreign landlords for three or four generations. [468]

In the next chapter you will see a timeline of the major events that have taken place in the past 100 years moving us closer to regional government and to a transformation of the USA. As one can see, many years and many events have gone into preparing for this time, moving us ever closer to world government. The elitists truly plan on all the objectives of the Gomberg map and their other goals to come to fruition. All the unions, and regions will then be run by a totally centralized world government operating under UN mandates.

Chapter Seventeen

Timeline to a Transformed USA and Regional Government Merger from 1910-2010

As you have read in the proceeding chapters, much stealth, deception and secrecy has gone into transforming the USA and moving us closer to socialism and regional government. In this chapter, you will have a 100-year review of the major events that have prepared the way for the mighty socialist transformations that we have seen already happening and those which lie ahead. Our timeline begins with 1910 and ends with the year 2010.

Is the Timeline on Time? The elitists have had various dates set for when their objectives were to be fulfilled for regional and world government. FDR thought it would happen under his reign, soon after the United Nations was established. George Orwell thought it would happen by 1984; that is why he wrote his book by the same title to warn us about it. Others thought it would happen by the turn of the century of 2000. Robert Pastor and the CFR had planned that by 2010 all would be in place to form a North American Union. There is still a plan that by 2015, a strong, binding connection of the Americas to the EU will be happening, through the Transatlantic Common Market and Transatlantic Policy Network.

However, fortunately, over the years, many glitches have come into the globalist plans, and they have not been able to meet their timelines. The glitches have come because of wise, informed, patriotic Americans, who know and understand the Constitution and the principles upon which this nation was founded. They could see how far we were drifting away from them. These people have gotten involved, informed others, spoken out, kept an eagle-eye on their elected officials and have even run for office themselves. Through their efforts, the runaway ship of state has been brought back on course, time and time again.

Perhaps, it will still be possible to turn the ship this time, and the present elitist goals set for 2010 and 2015 can be delayed or even defeated. However, many are worried that this time it may be too late.

Our ship of state has never before been so heavily laden with such enormous debt. Remember the wise statement, "a nation of debtors is a nation of slaves." Perhaps, we are no longer the free people we thought we were. Maybe we no longer have the freedom or the ability to turn the ship. There are too many heavy chains of debt dragging it down.

The billowing sails of the free-enterprise system, that helped to hold our ship up right and to sail a straight course, have never been so shot full of holes. Perhaps the sails can no longer hold up against the powerful winds of evil, conspiring men and their corrupting influences.

The sturdy rope that held fast and firm our anchor, the foundation of our nation, the gospel of Jesus Christ, has never been so frayed before. It is almost chewed through by secular sharks and rats.

The chart or map—to keep us on a straight course, to keep us from getting lost or hitting the rocks—was our wonderful, inspired Constitution, which has never before been so ignored and so trampled on.

Nor have we ever had before standing at the helm, a captain who is so unqualified, unprepared and ineligible. Nor does he seem at all proud of his ship of state and speaks disparagingly of it whenever the occasion arises. Could it be, in actuality, that Captain Obama is more like an eloquent, con-artist pirate, who has captured the ship of state, manned it with his crew of 40 plus pirate/czars, and together they are fleecing the ship? They already have taken $787 billion for their pirate stash to use at their discretion? Obama and his pirate crew have also weighed down the ship of state by $3 trillion additional debt.

Has everything to protect our nation now become so weakened that all it will take is one more crisis, one more major storm, one more blast of a large financial disaster, and our ship of state will be destroyed?

Is it too late to turn the ship and bring it back on course one more time? Is it too late to keep it from sinking in enormous debt? Is it too late to keep it from falling into the hands of even more pirates—this time globalist pirates who seek to plunder every last item of any worth: our sovereignty, nationhood, our resources, our Republic, Constitution, and what is left of our free enterprise system, our rights, liberties and property?

Notice at the end of this chapter there is a reference to a new constitution that has already been written for all of the Americas, not just for North America. Will that ever come into being? Much depends on what we, citizens of the United States of America, can still do to preserve our nation, our Constitution, our freedoms and liberties with the time we still have left.

Let us learn from the lessons of these past 100 years to help determine the answers to what our future will bring.

Many of the following events have been mentioned in greater detail in previous chapters. This chapter will give just a brief synopsis of the event, the date, and who or what caused it to happen. One can see that the incremental chipping away of our foundation and freedoms and our move to socialism/communism could not have happened by chance. This has been an organized effort over many years.l

1910—A Secret Meeting on Jekyll Island in Georgia to Draw Up Plans for the Federal Reserve: Seven wealthy bankers and politicians met at the private resort owned by J.P. Morgan, Jekyll Island, off the coast of Brunswick, Georgia. These seven men represented one-fourth of the total wealth of the entire world. The purpose of the meeting was to devise a scheme to sell a "Central Bank" to the U.S Congress and start imposing a centrally-controlled monopoly over the banks, economy and currency of America as existed in European countries.[470]

1913, December 22—The Federal Reserve (A Central Bank) was Created: It was called the Glass-Owen bill and it, passed quickly just before Christmas vacation, when some Congressmen had already left to go home, and the others were tired and in no mood for debates. It was signed into law the next day by President Woodrow Wilson. The Federal Reserve is neither federal nor a reserve. Our federal government has no control over it, other than to appoint its director every 14 years. It has never been audited. It is an international cartel of wealthy bankers, who have a monopoly and absolute control over the economy of our nation. The Fed has also been responsible for taking our nation off the gold and silver standard so they can create "fiat" money without any backing, creating enormous inflation over the years and devaluation of the dollar.[471]

1913—The Graduated Income Tax was Passed, and the Sixteenth Amendment was added to the Constitution: This is something our founding fathers never wanted. Before this time, people paid sales taxes and we had tariffs, import taxes on goods coming into the U.S., and that seemed to be enough to take care of all of the money we needed. Our nation had very little debt compared to now. Our Constitution never intended for such a tax to be laid on U.S. Citizens. However, both a central bank and graduated income tax are part of the Ten Planks of the *Communist Manifesto*. They are a big part of the road to socialism and regional government that has helped to made our nation very ripe for communism.

1915, May 15—the Lusitania was Sunk by a German submarine with 128 Americans on Board: The Germans knew the Lusitania was not just a regular passenger ship but was carrying ammunition to bring to the British for war against the Germans. They placed ads in American papers warning Americans to not get on the ship, but their warning was not heeded. The elite knew and had planned for this tragedy to happen. They knew it would take the loss of American lives, to convince the American people to change their minds about being involved in World War I.[472]

1917, April—US Entered World War I: Woodrow Wilson, who campaigned on the slogan of keeping us out of war, was the one who got Congress to approve our entering the war.

1918, November 11—World War I Ended: During our short one and one-half years in the war, 116,708 American soldiers lost their lives and 228,000 were wounded. The war cost us $33 billion, leaving us in debt $25 billion. War is one of the biggest debt builders for nations, exactly what a central bank likes. The powerful bankers of the world love to foment wars and keep them going while they fund both sides of the wars. [473]

1919, Versailles Treaty, President Wilson Presented his Fourteen Points: The Points had been written by his advisor, a very left-leaning socialist, Edward Mandell House. The last point called for a general association of nations to be formed. This resulted in the League of Nations.

1920, US Senate Refused to Ratify the Versailles Treaty or Entry into the League of Nations: The Senate recognized it for what it was—entrance into a world government and an attack on our US Constitution.

1921, July 29—The Council on Foreign Relations (CFR) Was Founded in New York City: This took place under the direction of Edward Mandell House, and with the help of their sister organization, the Royal Institute of International Affairs, RIIA. The founders were wealthy bankers and people who already had a socialist one-world agenda in store for our nation. The purpose—to so infiltrate and gain control over government that the CFR members could circumvent the Constitution and not let it prevent them from achieving their world government agenda. The Rockefellers were involved from the beginning and often have assumed leadership roles. They donated the land for the headquarters in New York City. Major funding for the CFR comes from the Rockefeller and Carnegie Foundations.

Amazingly, since that time, every administration has had more and more CFR members involved. Often either the president or vice president is CFR and sometimes both. The majority of the cabinets are members. Clinton had 548 CFR members in his cabinet. George Bush Jr. had 516.[474] Who knows what the final count will be on Obama's cabinet since he keeps creating new czar positions?

1929-39—The Great Depression Hit Our Nation: This was actually caused by the Federal Reserve, something they had planned all along. It was under the deception of "stabilizing our economy," making sure there would be no more "booms or busts," or "runs on banks," that the legislation was passed to create the Federal Reserve, and yet they created the biggest bust and run on banks in history. Why would the wealthy bankers want to create a depression for our country? Under a crisis, pretending to solve it, they were able to close down more independent banks, gain more of a monopoly over the economy, usher in more federal reserve notes that replaced real, honest currency, and get us off the gold standard. It could then cause our nation to go into greater and greater debt and have to borrow more money. Why? By nations having to borrow money is how banks make their money from the interest on the loans. [475]

1932—FDR Became President: He caused our slippery slope to socialism called "The New Deal." He, along with the Federal Reserve, caused the Great Depression, and his socialist programs prolonged it. It didn't end until America entered World War II. He also created the National Resource Planning Board (NRPB), which he was planning to use to break up the states and get rid of state and local government. He was able to stack the Supreme Court with fellow Masons who shared his socialist views. As Mark Levin writes in his book, *Liberty and Tyranny*, "It was not long before the Court became little more than a rubber stamp for Roosevelt's policies."[476] FDR served three terms as president until his death in 1945.

1933—The US was taken off the Gold Standard Under President FDR: The Federal Reserve could now create more fiat money, devalue the dollar, and in the process make enormous money for themselves. Using fiat money is a way of taking more and more money from the people (like a "tax"), but since the people don't understand what is going on, they don't complain as much as they would if they were told their taxes were being raised.

1941, December 7, Japanese Attacked Pearl Harbor: Two thousand American soldiers were killed and eleven naval vessels were sunk or destroyed. FDR had plenty of warning about the Japanese attack. He could have warned Pearl Harbor and saved our soldiers and our vessels, but he needed that terrible tragedy to get the American people to be willing to enter into war again.[477]

1941, December 8, U.S. Declared War on Japan, Germany, and Italy: The U.S. was once again involved in a deadly world war.

1942—The Gomberg Map was Published: It laid out the plan for ten large regional governments, with 41 objectives written at the bottom. Some believe it was FDR who asked for the map to be drawn and wrote the objectives himself. The bottom of the map does state his "Four Freedoms Speech," leaving in the part about a world-wide reduction of armaments to such a point . . . that no nation can . . . commit an act of aggression . . . anywhere in the world.

1944, July, in Bretton Woods, New Hampshire, the International Monetary Fund and World Bank were Established: Their stated purpose was to help war-torn and undeveloped nations across the globe. Their real purpose was to set up central banks and central planning for the economies for each country, placing them under their control. It was also to terminate the use of gold as a basis for their currencies in every country so fiat money could be created out of thin air. Governments could then avoid the discipline of gold and not have to pay a penalty for having their currencies drop in value on world markets. Without gold, markets, values and currencies could be more easily manipulated. When all countries were off the gold standard, the IMF and the World Bank could inflate all fiat money at the same rate. The IMF and the World Bank were also necessary to prepare the way for establishing the United Nations.

1945, April 12, FDR Died and his Vice President Harry S. Truman Took Over: Truman was FDR's third Vice President and had only served three months, when FDR died. It was under his administration that the war ended, but the atomic bombs were dropped on Japan, and the United Nations was officially begun, Israel became a nation. Truman was elected in 1948 for a second term.

1945, May 8, Germany surrendered: The end to the war was in sight.

1945, August, Two Atomic Bombs Destroyed Nagasaki and Hiroshima, Japan: Was this terrible tragedy necessary when Germany had just surrendered, and the end of the war was approaching?

1945, September 2, Japan surrendered: World War II was officially ended leaving 60 million dead; 35 million were civilians, 25 million were soldiers. America lost 405,400 soldiers.[478]

1945, October 25,—The United Nations was Created: The UN was acclaimed as "the best hope for world peace." One hundred and forty-one wars have taken place across the globe since.

1954 The Founding of the Bilderbergers at Hotel de Bilderberg in the Netherlands: The Bilderbergers are a secretive group of powerful globalists who wield much influence over national governments and the election of world leaders. They are all striving for the same goal of world government.

1961-1963, John F. Kennedy was President: He had to face several hard decisions, Bay of Pigs, Cuban Missile Crisis, and the Vietnam War. One of his sad legacies is his "behind the scenes" support for world-wide disarmament, as you will read next.

1961—General and World-wide Disarmament Proposed: "Freedom From War"—Publication 7277 was published by the Department of State. Its subtitle was "The United States Program for General and Complete Disarmament in a Peaceful World." This is a little known attack on our 2nd amendment rights coming from the UN 16th General Assembly by way of our Department of State and signed by President John F. Kennedy.

It is asking for all nations to go through three stages of disarming the entire nation: 1) Reduction of nuclear weapons and other weapons and the eventual elimination of all nuclear weapon stockpiles, with a Commission of Experts to do the inspecting of all nations who have such weapons; be allowed to 2) Further reduction of weapons, reduction of armed forces of nations, strengthening of the UN forces and the strengthening of the Disarmament Organization; 3) States would only retain minimal forces; minimal non-nuclear armaments required for maintaining internal order and would provide agreed manpower for a U.N. Peace Force, which would be equipped with agreed armaments, all others would be destroyed.[479]

1963, November 23, Assassination of John F. Kennedy in Dallas, Texas, an Example to Future Presidents of Who is Really In Charge: Many people are suspicious that the truth of this assassination has been covered up, that there were multiple bullets that were shot at the president, not just from Lee Harvey Oswald, and that it was one from the back that actually killed him, not Oswald's that came from above.

One theory is that Kennedy was trying to get rid of the Federal Reserve, that he had even signed on June 4, 1963, a little known Executive Order 11110, that would basically strip the Federal Reserve of its power to loan money to the US government and it would soon be out of business. The Christian Law Fellowship researched this matter and say that this order has never been repealed, just ignored.[480] Whatever the truth is, Kennedy's assassination has probably served as a warning for future presidents to go along with the powerful elitists who are really giving the marching orders or else.

1963—Lyndon Baines Johnson Became President: (CFR) He was Kennedy's Vice President and took over after his assassination. He continued FDR's New Deal; he just changed the name to the "Great Society." He kept us involved and focused on the Vietnam War throughout his term, while, back home, he promoted one socialist program after another. He furthered "regional government" with "total planning and total management by unelected officials." He signed the first Gun Control Act of 1968 which brought the Law Enforcement Alliance of America (LEAA) into existence. LEAA's mission was to make massive changes so that our national military and our police departments could be placed under the United Nations for its use as a "rapid response mechanism." Johnson laid the groundwork for the World Wide Military Command and Control System that was built at the Massachusetts Institute of Technology—Research Engineering (MITRE). (The above information was taken from the large historical binder sent by Bernadine Smith, November, 2008.)

1968— Club of Rome (COR) was Established: This is the extreme environmental group that was started by Aurelio Peccei, of Italy. It is made up of many wealthy elite members, all pushing for population control by spreading scare tactics of the scarcity of the earth's resources.

1969-1974 Richard Nixon (CFR) Became President: He ended the Vietnam War. However, many bad things happened during his administration, such as: he the Environmental Protection Agency (1973); the Endangered Species Act (ESA) and Roe vs Wade were passed under his watch, all which are very anti-people. As you read in the chapter about the Bilderbergers, Nixon was opposed to the GATT treaty and went against it, even though the CFR and the Bilderbergers told him to support it. Daniel Estulin believes that is the reason Nixon was forced to resign from being the president as an example to all other presidents that you had better "march to the same drum beat" that the elite want you to or out you go. [481]

1974—Gerald Ford Became President: Nixon was forced to resign over the scandal of Watergate, and his Vice President took his place. Ford was not a member of the CFR, but the person he was advised to appoint to fill the office of Vice President was—Nelson Rockefeller, who just happened to be the older brother of the man who served many terms as the director of the CFR, David Rockefeller. (Gerald Ford became a member of the CFR after his presidency.)

1974—Fast Track Legislation was Passed: This gave the President the authority that rightfully belongs to Congress "to regulate commerce with foreign nations."[482] The president could now freely negotiate treaties and other trade agreements with foreign nations and then simply present them to Congress for a straight up and down vote, with no amendments possible, and with only 20 hours for debate allowed. There is little opportunity for public involvement. Government becomes less and less that "of the people, by the people and for the people."[483]

1973—The Trilateral Commission was Begun: It was founded by David Rockefeller and Zbigniew Brzezinksi to be the international "mother ship" above all the other secretive societies pushing for global government.

1974—Robert Pastor Prepared the Way for the Give Away of the Panama Canal: Pastor was a member of the Trilateral Commission and the Council on Foreign Relations, was the executive director of the Commission on US-Latin American Relations, aka, the Linowitz Commission, which prepared the way for the giveaway of the Panama Canal.

1976—Jimmy Carter, First Member of Trilateral Commission Elected President of the United States: He had the backing of Brzezinksi who had tutored Carter in globalist philosophy and foreign policy. Carter then selected no less than a third of his cabinet from The Trilateral Commission.

1977—Carter and the Giveaway of the Panama Canal: Carter appointed Brzezinski as his National Security Advisor, who then appointed Robert Pastor as director of the Office of Latin American and Caribbean Affairs. Pastor became the Trilateral Commission's point man to lobby for the Panama Canal giveaway with the help of Sol Linowitz, who was appointed as temporary ambassador to Panama (thus avoiding the Senate confirmation.)[484]

1978—The Foreign Intelligence Surveillance Act (FISA) Passed: It is a federal law prescribing procedures for the physical and electronic surveillance and collection of "foreign intelligence information" between "foreign powers" and "agents of foreign powers" (which may include American citizens and permanent residents engaged in espionage and violating U.S. law: §1801(b)(2)(B)) on territory under United States control. The act created a court which meets in secret, and approves or denies requests for search warrants. Only the number of warrants applied for, issued and denied, is reported. In 1980 (the first full year after its inception), it approved 322 warrants. This number has steadily grown to 2224 warrants in 2006. In the period 1979-2006 a total of 22,990 applications for warrants were made to the Court of which 22,985 were approved (sometimes with modifications; or with the splitting up, or combining together, of warrants for legal purposes), and only 5 were definitively rejected. The Act was amended by the USA PATRIOT Act of 2001, primarily to include terrorism on behalf of groups that are not specifically backed by a foreign government. An overhaul of the bill, the Protect America Act of 2007 was signed into law on August 5, 2007. It expired on February 17, 2008.[485]

1980—Ronald Reagan became the President: He was not a member of the CFR or the Trilateral Commission, but his Vice President was, George Bush Sr. During the Reagan-Bush Presidency; 257 CFR members held posts as US government officials.[486]

1984, June 14, illegal Immigration News Conference: Reagan gave dire prediction about the state of our nation because of illegal immigration: "But the simple truth is that we have lost control of our own borders, and no nation can do that and survive." Did Reagan do anything to solve this problem? No, he did just the opposite.

1986—Reagan signed the Immigration and Reform Act of 1986: This rewarded 3 million illegal aliens, mostly from Mexico, with US citizenship. This did nothing to solve the problem but only enticed more to come. The Act included employer sanctions, making it against the law for employers to hire illegal aliens, but these sanctions were never enforced. The IRCA Amnesty,

sold to the American people as a never-to-be-repeated action, encouraged
millions more of illegal aliens, flooding across our borders, hoping for a repeated
amnesty.[487]

1988—George H. W. Bush Became President: He continued to have key
appointments made to his cabinet from the CFR and T.C. membership and did
nothing to stop illegal immigration. He also gave many speeches in which he
spoke about promoting a "New World Order."[488]

1990—Bush Passed another Immigration Bill: This increased the level
of legal immigration by several hundred thousand to 675,000 annually.

1991—More Environmental Threats by the Club of Rome: Under the
leadership of New-Age leader, Aurelio Peccei, the Club of Rome published
the following statement, "Searching for a new enemy to unite us, we came up
with the idea that pollution, the threat to global warming, water shortages,
famine and the like would fit the bill . . . All these dangers are caused by human
intervention . . . The real enemy, then is humanity itself."[489]

**1992—Rio de Janeiro, the UN Biodiversity Treaty was Signed by
George Bush:** and 150 heads of state from various countries. It was based on
the pseudo-scientific theory known as the "Wildlands Project," the radical idea
of David Foreman of "Earth First," that 50% of our nation should be put back
into pre-Columbian wilderness conditions, allowing for migrating corridors for
animals, with no borders. "Eventually a wilderness network would dominate a
region and thus would itself constitute the matrix, with human habitation being
the islands." Fortunately, before our US Senate could vote on this treaty to ratify
it, sight unseen, a conservative scientist, Dr. Michael Coffman, was able to reveal
to them the truth about the radical, extreme "Wildlands Project," upon which
it was based and the treaty was withdrawn from the floor. (However, Clinton
implemented it anyway by executive order in 1996.) [490]

More on the Wildlands Project: In case you can't quite believe such a
thing as the Wildlands Project was ever taken seriously, go to their website.
They still exist and are very proud of themselves and their goals. Here is what
they state:

The goal of the Wildlands Project is to set aside approximately fifty (50)
percent of the North American continent (Turtle Island) as "wild land" for the
preservation of biological diversity.

The project seeks to do this by creating "reserve networks" across the
continent. Reserves are made up of the following:

- "Cores, created from public lands such as National Forest and Parks
- Buffers, often created from private land adjoining the cores to provide
  additional protection

- o Corridors, a mix of public and private lands usually following along rivers and wildlife migration routes
- o The primary characteristics of core areas are that they are large (100,000 to 25 million acres), and allow for little, if any, human use.
- o The primary characteristics of buffers are that they allow for limited human use so long as they are "managed with native biodiversity as a preeminent concern."
- o Moral and ethical guidelines for the Wildlands Project are based on the philosophy of Deep Ecology.
- o The eight point platform of Deep Ecology can be summarized as follows:
- o All life (human and non-human) has equal value.
- o Resource consumption above what is needed to supply "vital" human needs is immoral.
- o Human population must be reduced.
- o Western civilization must radically change present economic, technological, and ideological structures.
- o Believers have an obligation to try to implement the necessary changes."

The Wildlands Project, itself, is supported by hundreds of groups working towards its long-term implementation. Implementation may take 100 years or more. The Wildlands Project has received millions of dollars in support from wealthy private and corporate foundations such as the Turner Foundation, Patagonia, W. Alton Jones Foundation, Lyndhurst Foundation, etc.[491]

1992 (October)—NAFTA, North American Free Trade Agreement was Negotiated: Under the executive leadership of President George H.W. Bush and Carla Hills, both members of the Trilateral Commission NAFTA was created. Bush wanted to have credit for his work, so just before his term ended, he staged an "initialing" ceremony, though NAFTA had not yet been put through Congress and he did not have the authority to actually sign it into law.[492]

1992—Ross Perot Ran for President: as an Independent and Vehemently Opposed to NAFTA. He made his famous statement that if NAFTA passes, "there will be a giant sucking sound going south . . ." Some people believe that Perot was actually a pawn of the elite to mess up the conservative vote and ensure that Clinton did win, which may have been the case. Nevertheless, what he said of NAFTA proved to be true.[493]

1992—William Jefferson Clinton Became President for 8 years: Clinton had been the chairman of the T.C. and appointed 14 members of the TC to his cabinet. Clinton invited three former presidents to the White House to stand with him in praise and affirmation for NAFTA, Carter, Bush, and Gerald Ford. Only Ford was not a member of the CFR or T.C. The academic community was also enlisted to support NAFTA, with a petition drawn up by an MIT professor, Rudiger Dornbusch and signed by 12 living Lobel laureates in economics and 283 faculty members from other universities.[494]

1993—Henry Kissinger, Cyrus Vance and Other Members of the Trilateral Commission Promoted NAFTA: Millions of dollars were spent to spread lies of NAFTA's benefits to the American people. Kissinger said, "NAFTA would be the most constructive measure the United States would have undertaken in our hemisphere in this century."[495]

A few months later he said, "It will represent the most creative step towards a new world order taken by any group of countries since the end of the Cold War and the first step toward an even larger vision of a free-trade zone for the entire Western Hemisphere. NAFTA is not a conventional trade agreement, but the architecture of a new international system." Doesn't that sound a little bit similar to what the Trilateral Commission stated was their original goal—"creating a New International Economic Order."[496]

1994—NAFTA Became Law: Fast Track procedures became implemented once more and NAFTA was rushed through with the House passing it 234-200 and the Senate passing it by 61-38. Even though NAFTA is in every sense of the word a very binding treaty, because it was not called a treaty, but an agreement, it did not have to have the Senate's 2/3 vote but passed with a simple majority.[497]

"Giant Sucking Sound Going South": NAFTA promised greater exports, better jobs and better wages, but since 1994, just the opposite has occurred. It has become exactly what Ross Perot predicted—many U.S. jobs have gone south or have just closed down. According to Pat Buchanan, "The U.S. has lost some 1.5 million jobs, and real wages in both the U.S. and Mexico have fallen significantly. "NAFTA was never just a trade deal: Rather, it was an 'enabling act to enable U.S. corporations to dump their American workers and move their factories to Mexico."[498] By 2009, it was more like 3 million jobs that have been lost and rising each month.

Declining Living Standards: "The vast majority of American workers have experienced declining living standards, not just a handful of losers." Alan Tonelson, author of *Race to the Bottom.*[499] "Much praise has been heard for the few 'winners' that NAFTA has created, but little mention is made of the fact that the Mexican people are the deal's big losers. Mexicans now face greater unemployment, poverty, and inequality than before the agreement began in 1994," A Mexican economist and scholar Miguel Pickard.[500]

NAFTA—Attack on American Jobs: A columnist writes about NAFTA in her reporting about the passage of CAFTA, which barely squeaked by in the U.S. Senate.

> " . . . this vote is another sign of the widespread opposition to CAFTA, an agreement based on NAFTA, whose failed record includes the loss of a million American jobs and over 38,000 American family farms, while in Mexico over 1.5 million farmers have been pushed off their land and manufacturing wages have plummeted. The massively unpopular bill could only squeak through a traditionally pro-"free trade" Senate through last minute fake "deals" on two issues: sugar and labor. According to a recent study by Public Citizen, 89% of all such "deals" to win trade votes in the past have never been fulfilled." (*http://www.citizen.org/pressroom/release.cfm?ID=1968* [501]

1994—Post Capitalist Society was Published by Peter F. Drucker: Business writer, Drucker, has had a great deal of influence in pushing globalism among business leaders and professors in our business schools. His book contains chapter titles such as: "From Nation State to Megastate; Transnationalism, Regionalism, Tribalism; The Needed Government Turnaround." The following is a quote from his book referring to the combining of Mexico, Canada, and the United States of America. "The Economic integration of the three countries into one region is proceeding so fast that it will make little difference whether the marriage is sanctified legally or not."

1994, Miami—The First Summit of the Americas was Held: Bill Clinton signed onto it, integrating the USA into "hemispheric integration," for all of the Americas. This is one of the statements on their website, "We reiterate our firm commitment and adherence to the principles and purposes of the Charters of the United Nations and of the Organization of American States (OAS).[502]

1994—North America's SuperCorridor Coalition, Inc. was Formed (NASCO): NASCO's purpose as originally stated on their website was to develop "the world's first international, integrated, and secure, multi-model transportation system along the international Mid-Continent Trade and Transportation Corridor."

North American Inland Port Network (NAIPN): This is a sub-committee of NASCO and is also mentioned on their website. It was given the task of developing an active inland port network along the corridor to alleviate congestion at maritime ports and our nation's borders. (In other words, NAIPN is the organization that is making sure that cheaper ports are being built in Mexico that will bring in goods and unload them with cheaper costs by avoiding the more expensive ports in California where longshoremen charge more money.[503]

1995—Dallas, Texas: Anti-American, pro-Mexican Statement made by President of Mexico: Ernesto Zedillo, to an audience of U.S. citizens of Mexican descent, "You are Mexicans, Mexicans who live north of the border." i.e. you owe loyalty to Mexico, not Uncle Sam.[504]

1995—The Goal of "Progressive Regionalization" as Preparation for World Government: This was expressed in an address given by Zbigniew Brzesinski, former U.S. National Security Advisor: "We cannot leap into world government in one quick step . . . The precondition for eventual globalization—genuine globalization—is progressive regionalization."[505]

1996—Biodiversity Treaty Was Signed by Bill Clinton: A further attack on property rights and sovereignty was implemented by President Clinton, who signed into law, by executive order, the Biodiversity Treaty (Agenda 21) and created the President's Council on Sustainable Development, which details his blueprint to implement Agenda 21. Under Agenda 21, the primary purpose of government is to no longer serve or protect the people. Rather it is to protect nature from people on eco-socialist principles. Sustainable Development is based on three E's—Equity, economy, and ecology. The real meanings of these terms are: equity—take from those who have and give to those who have not; economy—redistribution of wealth with the elite in charge; ecology—plants and animals have more rights than humans. [506]

1997—Open Border Statement made by President Zedillo of Mexico: In Chicago, before a La Raza Meeting, another pro-open border statement was made by President Zedillo, essentially erasing the borders between Mexico and the U.S. "I have proudly affirmed that the Mexican nation extends beyond the territory enclosed by its borders." Of course, this brought the La Raza members wildly cheering to their feet. (La Raza is a very militant, pro-Mexican organization that is found on most college campuses. Most of their speakers are always condemning white man for being "racist," but they even label fellow Mexicans and blacks as "racist," such as talk show host Terry Anderson of Los Angeles, anyone who dares to speak out against illegal immigration. Patriot Americans who have heard La Raza members speak, view them as the most "racist" of all because they are always putting down others for their race. La Raza means "the race," in Spanish.) [507]

1998, Santiago, Chile: The Second Summit of the Americas was held, again signed by Bill Clinton, moving the member nations closer to "hemispheric integration."[508]

1998—Duel Mexican-American Citizenship Instigated: Mexico changed its constitution to restore citizenship to Mexican-Americans who have taken an oath of allegiance to the United States and renounced loyalty to their own country. What was the purpose in doing this? The Mexican Government wanted to loosen the ties of loyalty that the former Mexican citizens had to the United States and to re-knit their ties of loyalty to Mexico. They also wanted to then persuade Mexican-Americans to vote Mexico's interests in the USA, put Mexico first, even if you have taken an oath of allegiance to the United States.[509]

2000—George W. Bush Became President: He was not a member of the CFR or the TC (as was his father), but his Vice President, Dick Cheney is, as is his wife, Lynn Cheney, as were our many of his cabinet. He is a total supporter of NAFTA and all of its provisions and has tried to further involve all of the Americas with his support of CAFTA (Central America Free Trade Agreement) which was passed by 2 votes after midnight in July, 2005. Bush is also in total support of the FTAA (Free Trade Area of the Americas), which has been put on the back burner for awhile.

2000, March 15—The Earth Charter was Announced: Supposedly it was created by 100,000 people in 51 countries under the direction of Mikhail Gorachev and Maurice Strong, Chairman of the Earth Council. It was an outcome of the 1992 Agenda 21 Earth Summit and was to serve as the spiritual guide for the earth, reflecting "universal spiritual values," which are really pantheistic teachings of earth worship. The principles of the Earth Charter are incorporated into global governance as defined in the UN Commission on Global Governance's 1995 report Our Global Neighborhood and A Charter for Global Democracy.[510]

2000, July 2—Mexican President Vicente Fox Proposal: Fox proposed a 20-30-year time line for the creation of a common North American market.[511]

2001, April 22—the Declaration of Quebec City: It was signed by President Bush, in which he made a "commitment to hemispheric integration" and to the United Nations in preparation for the passing of the FTAA (Free Trade Area of the Americas). Phyllis Schlafly wrote about the hemispheric part. "After a communist dictator took over Venezuela, "hemispheric" was quietly scaled down to the Security and Prosperity Partnership of just North America.[512]

Another writer, William J. Gill, said the following about the Declaration of Quebec City and President Bush: "President George W. Bush carried Bill Clinton's model for merging the U. S. economy with all Latin America to the hemispheric conference of 34 heads-of—state and made an impassioned plea for them to help him ram the Free Trade Area of the Americas (FTAA) through our Congress.[513]

Fortunately, enough citizens became aware of the FTAA and Bush was not able to get it passed. Perhaps, that was another reason why the NAU was now on "fast track." It was to serve as a pre-curser to preparing for the FTAA. The Declaration of Quebec City was shown at the beginning of the chapter on the UN, showing where all this movement to form regional governments and unions is coming from.

2001, July 2, *Wall Street Journal* Article —"Open NAFTA Borders? Why Not?": This catchy title and article were written by the late "supposed" conservative columnist, Robert Bartley, as an editorial in the *Wall Street Journal*. (Bartley passed away a year later at age 66.) Here is a quote from his article:

"Reformist Mexican President Vicente Fox raises eyebrows with his suggestion that over a decade or two NAFTA should evolve into something like the European Union, with open borders for not only goods and investment but also people. He can rest assured that there is one voice north of the Rio Grande that supports his vision. To wit, this newspaper." [514]

The editor of the *New American*, Bill Jasper, has the following to say about Bartley's article: "Yes, Robert Bartley, the supposed paragon of conservatism, was indeed a secret one-worlder, and this was evident many years ago to alert readers of the Journal. In more recent years, Bartley began inching out of the one-world closet and showing his real globalist colors."

In this article Bartley was so bold as to essentially announce the "Journal's support for dumping U.S. sovereignty and transforming the United States into a vassal of a hemispheric superstate modeled after the European Union."

2001—Robert Pastor Published His Book Toward a North American Community: It was released just a few weeks before the 9-11 attack and received little attention. [514] In his book he supports the idea of having a currency for all three countries called an amero with a Central Bank of North America.

2001, September 11, New York City, the Terrible Tragedy of 9-11: Close to 3000 people lost their lives, including 343 firefighters, as the Twin Towers Trade Buildings came down. As was written in Chapter Eleven, there are many questions that need to be answered about this tragedy. It instigated the Patriot Act, the War on terrorism with Iraq and Afghanistan and has affected and restricted many of our basic freedoms.

2001—October 26, The USA Patriot Act Passed: Just 1 and 1/2 months after 911, Congress passed the 342 page bill, which is based on a similar one in Russia. It was passed sight unseen, five minutes after it was presented, in the middle of an anthrax scare.

2001, December, "Smart Border Declaration" Signed: U.S. Homeland Security Secretary Tom Ridge and Canadian Deputy Prime Minister John Manley signed this 30-point action plan to enhance the security of our shared border, while facilitating the legitimate flow of people and goods."[515]

2002—Madrid, Spain, Mexican President Vicente Fox Told What the Long Range Plan Is: "Eventually, our long-range objective is to establish with the United States . . . an ensemble of connections and institutions similar to those created by the European Union, with the goal of attending to future themes as important as . . . the freedom of movement of capital, goods, services and persons. The new framework we wish to construct is inspired in the example of the European Union.[516]

2002, NAFI, North American Forum on Integration, was formed: Its objectives are: making the public and decision-makers aware of the challenges of economic and political **integration** between the three NAFTA countries; identifying new ideas and strategies to reinforce the North American region; establishing a new tradition of North American multi-disciplinary meetings and alternating in the three countries; favoring the creation of North American networks to set the basis for a trilateral dialogue; identifying elements of a North American agenda to put forward integration beyond the reduction of tariffs; putting on the political agenda the idea of creating a North American Investment Fund that would stimulate Mexican economic growth and gaining the support of public opinion and decision-makers regarding the advantages of such a fund. It also promoted the model parliament sessions that were mentioned in Chapter Eleven.

2002, September 9—Smart Border Action Plan: A discussion was held by President Bush and Prime Minister Chretien. An update on the plan was produced by the White House on December 6, 2002.[517]

2002, November 1-2, Robert Pastor delivered "A Modest Proposal to the Trilateral Commission: It was at the plenary session of the TC in Ontario, Canada. His paper was drawing directly from his book Toward a North American Union. His proposal and seven recommendations were adopted by the TC.[518]

2002, December—Bi-national Agreement on Military Planning: This was signed by U.S. Secretary of State, Colin Powell and Canada.

2002—David Rockefeller Wrote his book *Memoirs:* He blatantly revealed his family's goal to create a one-world government: "Some even believe we are part of a secret cabal working against the best interest of the United States, characterizing my family and me as 'internationalists' and of conspiring with others around the world to build a more integrated global political and economic structure—one world, if you will. If that's the charge, I stand guilty, and I am proud of it."[519]

2003, January—NASPI (North American Security and Prosperity Initiative) was Launched: It was done by the Canadian Council of Chief Executives to propose a comprehensive North American strategy integrating economic and security issues.

2003—The TransTexasCorridor Became Part of the Transportation Bill in Texas: It was done very sneakily, attached at the end of the session when no one had any time to really read the many pages of the bill.

2004, February—Robert Pastor's Paper "North America's Second Decade," was Published: It was published by the Council on Foreign Relations. This paper advocates further North American integration.

2004, June—Chicago, "Extra-Territorial, Pro-Mexican-American Nation" Statement Made by Mexican President Vicente Fox: It was made before a Mexican-American community. He declared, "We are Mexicans that live in our territories, and we are Mexicans that live in other territories. In reality, there are 120 million that live together and are working together to construct a nation." Pat Buchanan adds, "In other words, the construction of his nation is taking place inside our nation. Is that not sedition?"[520]

2004, August—CAFTA, Central American Free Trade Agreement, was Passed: It was signed by the governments of Costa Rica, El Salvador, Guatemala, Honduras, Nicaragua and the Dominican Republic, a free trade agreement with the United States. The agreement still had to be passed by the congress of each country. Many of the same arguments against NAFTA pertain to CAFTA and what we can look forward to if an FTAA, Free Trade Agreement of all the Americas ever passes. These are all in preparation for an entire American Union.

2004 (October 15) An "Independent" Task Force on the Future of North America was Launched: It was done by the TC and the CFR to "examine regional integration in five spheres of policy: "deepening economic integration, reducing the development gap, harmonizing regulatory policy, enhancing security, and devising better institutions to manage conflicts that arise from integration and exploit opportunities for collaboration." Each country had 23 members serving on the task force. Each country had a representative from the Trilateral Commission: Carla Hills (U.S.), Luis Rubio (Mexico) and Wendy K. Dobson (Canada). Robert Pastor served as the U.S. Vice Chairman. [521]

2004, October—The Canada-Mexican Partnership (CMP) was Launched During the Visit of President Fox to Ottawa: The CMP was formed when President Fox of Mexico met with the Prime Minister of Canada in Ottawa, Canada.[522]

2004, November 1—The Independent Task Force on the Future of North America was Formed: It is a trilateral effort charged with developing a road map to promote "North American security and advance the well-being of citizens in all three countries." The task force is a sponsored by the CFR.

2005, March 23, Security and Prosperity Partnership (SPP) was Formed: (At Baylor University, Waco Texas) The heads-of-state of all three countries, President Bush, Vicente Fox of Mexico, and Prime Minister Martin from Canada, met for a summit.

The joint statement on the SPP described it as an initiative to: "establish a common approach to security to protect North America from external threats, prevent and respond to threats within North America, and further streamline the security and efficient movement of legitimate, low-risk traffic across our shared borders."[523]

2005, March 29, Mexico, USA, Canada Agree To Review NAFTA, Change Name (*El Financiero*, a Mexican Newspaper): The report told that in Waco, Texas, the governments of the three countries had agreed to an "in-depth revision," but not a renegotiation, of the (North American) Free Trade Agreement (NAFTA), which included a name change. Thirteen years after it was signed, the trade agreement between the three countries would now called the Security and Prosperity Partnership of North America (SPP).

The report also stated that the three leaders, George Bush, Paul Martin, and Vicente Fox, discussed the "priority" of their partnership, "the security of North America," which included protection against "terrorism, drug trafficking, organized crime, trafficking in persons, and smuggling." They also promised to "conclude the first stage" and bring in a "new era" of trade agreements that included a "common energy strategy."

However, there was nothing mentioned about what this article calls "the thorniest bilateral issues" for Mexico—"migration." [524]

2005, May 11— The Real ID Act Was Passed and Signed Into Law by President Bush: If the states were willing to go along with this law, it would have mandated all sorts of standard "biometrics" added to the card, essentially turning their state drivers' licenses into national ID Cards, at the states' expense, costing them billions. Fortunately, 24 states passed legislation against it, so it has never been implemented.

May 17, 2005—The Council on Foreign Relations Published a Major Report on the SPP: Only two months after the Security and Prosperity Partnership (SPP) was announced by President Bush, Mexico's Vicente Fox, and Canada's Paul Martin in Waco on March 23, 2005, the CFR's document was published explaining SPP's goals and methodology. It was posted on the U.S. State Department website, thereby confirming its authenticity.

It was there on the State Department website that Phyllis Schlafley saw the report, started investigating it, and wrote her first article about it in her June, 2005, Phyllis Schlafly Report. News of the SPP began to snow ball to other conservative groups and a mounting opposition began to form. The CFR report explains that the three SPP amigos at Waco "committed their governments" to "Building a North American Community" by 2010 with a common "outer security perimeter," "the extension of full labor mobility to Mexico," allowing Mexican trucks "unlimited access," "totalization" of illegal aliens into the U.S. Social Security system, and "a permanent tribunal for North American dispute resolution."

2005, May 17—Pastor's Paper Was Published Entitled "Building a North American Community": Report of the Independent Task Force on the Future of North America. This was issued by the task force after they met three different times, once in each country. Many of the recommendations they suggested in this paper were almost the same as those given by Robert Pastor in his "Modest Proposal" back in 2002. They are essentially a five-year plan for the implementation of a North American Union. (President Bush has denied any connection of these to what the SPP is doing and their documents, but according to Tom DeWeese, they have proven to be identical.)

2005, June—Kelo vs. City of New London was passed by the Supreme Court: This got rid of the pesky supreme law of the land (5th Amendment) which prohibits the taking of private land and handing it over to other private entities? How fortunate that the globalist-infested Supreme Court legislated from the bench by re-writing the takings clause of the 5th Amendment in Kelo vs. City of New London. Now the Supremes say it is okay to force people to sell their land to private developers who promise a kickback to the government, we are free to proceed with the taking of millions of acres of private land for the building of NAFTA Super Highway and the tolling of America's roads, bridges, and tunnels.[525]

2005, June 9—Senate Foreign Relations Committee Hearing: Chairman Richard Lugar featured Task Force member Robert Pastor. Pastor revealed further details of the plan for a continental perimeter, including an integrated plan for transportation and infrastructure that includes new North American highways and high-speed rail corridors.[526]

2005, June 27—SPP Meeting in Ottawa, Canada, Attended by Michael Chertoff, Head of Homeland Security: He stated, "We want to facilitate the flow of traffic across our borders." The White House issued a press release endorsing the Ottawa report and calling the meeting "an important first step in achieving the goals of the Security and Prosperity Partnership."[527]

2005, June 28—CAFTA was Passed by the House:, by 2 votes, and Signed into law in August by President Bush: This is what was said of the vote in the House by Ron Paul, Congressman from Texas, "Congress passed a multinational trade bill known as CAFTA last week, but not without a feverish late night vote marred by controversy and last-minute vote switching. Leaving aside the arguments for or against CAFTA itself, the process by which the bill ultimately passed should sicken every American who believes in representative government."[528]

2005, Extra-territorial Statement made by Carlos Gonzales Gutierrez, the Head of the Institute of Mexicans Abroad: "The basic concept is that the Mexican nation goes beyond the borders that contain Mexico. You can feel part of our nation without being on our territory. For the first time we are exporting our politics. Many Mexicans now live 'transnational' lives, with one foot in the other. This contributes to everyone's well-being." Pat Buchanan adds, "What these Mexican politicians are saying is that Mexico extends into the United States, and the first loyalty of all men and women of Mexican ancestry is, no matter where they live, to Mexico.[529]

2005, July 29—President Bush Signed a Bill Which Permits and Promotes the Charging of Tolls on Existing and Planned Interstate Highways, Bridges, and Tunnels: This is written about in the last chapter. The bill known as SAFETEA-LU, or "Safe, Accountable, Flexible, Efficient Transportation Equity Act: A Legacy for Users," made it now legal to charge tolls on roads built with Federal funds, what formerly had been illegal. The tolls collected would be automatic, requiring universally compatible toll transponder tags on every vehicle.

2006, January 31-February 1, A SPP "Public Health Threats Technical Meeting" Held in Ottawa, Canada: The official name of the meeting was, "Enhancing Preparedness Plans and Mutual Assistance for Pandemic Influenza and Other Emerging Public Health Threats in North America." This meeting did not include representatives from Mexico. The documents identify Health and Human Services personnel assigned to various SPP working groups such as: communications, legal, foreign nationals, epidemiology, and travel and border issues. Judicial Watch, who found out about this meeting through the Freedom of Information Act stated, "These documents are of particular interest given the scandal of the tuberculosis-infected American who traveled over the U.S.-Canadian border unimpeded by border authorities.[530]

2006, March 30-31, Cancun, Mexico, The Second Annual Summit Meeting for the SPP Was Held: It took place between Bush, Fox and the new Canadian Prime Minister, Stephen Harper. It was summed up by Vicente Fox in the following: "We touched upon fundamental items in that meeting. First of all, we carried out an evaluation meeting. Then we got information about the development of programs. And then we gave the necessary instructions for the works that should be carried out in the next period of work . . . We are not renegotiating what has been successful or open the Free Trade Agreement. It's going beyond the agreement, both for prosperity and security."[531]

2006, April 29—A Foreign Company, Dubai, Took over Nine US Military Facilities with Congress' Approval and Little Media Coverage: As USA military basis, ports, and other key infrastructures are sold to foreign entities, what does that do to our ability to defend ourselves against any kind of a foreign invasion? Could this all be part of the plan to destroy our American sovereignty and move us towards regional government? Here is the quote from the Associated Press news about the sell out of nine military facilities to the Dubai Co. of April 29:

> President Bush has approved the takeover by a Dubai-owned company of American plants that make parts for jets and tanks after a review that seems to have satisfied lawmakers who helped block an earlier Dubai deal. The AP report also said, "Initial reaction from Capitol Hill was favorable."

The following is the outrage expressed by Pastor Chuck Baldwin about this in his column for *News With Views*, May 5, 2006:

> Specifically, the Dubai company takes over control of at least nine factories, including military production facilities in Connecticut and Georgia. Dubai settled the deal for $1.2 billion. Therefore, Dubai will now take over operations of factories that produce engine components and turbine blades for military platforms. Clients include Boeing, General Electric, Honeywell, and Pratt and Whitney. Please understand that when we talk about a Dubai company we are talking about a foreign government! . . .a state-owned company . . .
>
> Unlike the private British companies that formerly held these contracts, the Dubai company is a state owned company. Yes,

Martha, that means that a foreign government, a government that has direct ties to terrorists, is now in charge of several U.S. military facilities! And the reaction to this foreign takeover on Capitol Hill was "favorable."

Not only was this Dubai deal received favorably in Washington, D.C., the mainstream media has virtually ignored the story. Be honest. How many of you even knew this happened? The story to which I alluded at the top of this column came from page 8C of my local newspaper. [The *Pensacola News Journal*, 4/29/06] That's right. Page 8C. No front page or even second, third, or fourth page news for this one. Does anyone smell a rat?

If the American people truly understood the depth and degree to which America's big business and political leaders are mired in international commercial activities, it would probably scare us half to death! No wonder the Bush administration and members of Congress allow and even encourage illegal immigration. No wonder virtually everything we buy anymore is made outside the United States. No wonder America's factories are almost all closed down. No wonder it doesn't matter to a tinker's dam how many letters we write or phone calls we make to our lawmakers in Washington . . . [532]

2006, June 15—A Meeting took place of the NACC (North American Competiveness Council): It consisted of government officials and corporate CEOs from the three countries. The purpose of the meeting was to "institutionalize the North American Security and Prosperity Partnership and the NACC, so that the work will continue through changes of administrations."[533]

2006, September 12-14, A North American Forum was Held in Banff, Alberta, Canada:, Present and past elected officials from all three countries met with corporate, military, academic, financial, industrial, and think tank members. U.S. participants included former Secretary of State George Shultz, Defense Secretary Donald Rumsfeld, Admiral Tim Keating, Commander of NORAD, and Robert Pastor, the "Father of the North American Union." Discussion items at the conference included "A Vision for North America," "Toward a North American Energy Strategy," and "Demographic and Social Dimensions of North American Integration."[534]

Canadian author Mel Hurtig attended the meeting in Banff, Canada. Here is what he wrote concerning it: "We're talking about such an important thing . . . we're talking about the integration of Canada into the United States. For them to hold this meeting secret and to make every effort to avoid anybody learning about it, right away you've got to be hugely concerned.[535]

"The Public Has Been Kept in the Dark"—The Toronto Star, Toronto, Canada, September 12, 2006: It revealed the secrecy behind the NAU meetings. Here is the entire quote. "The public has been kept in the dark while business elites have played a lead role in designing the blueprint for this more integrated North America."[536]

2007, April—Texas Corridor Moratorium Bill Victory: The Texas Senate passed the bill 27 to 4 and the House passed it 139 to 2. The bill put a two-year moratorium on public/private toll roads, which put a significant road block in front of the Trans-Texas Corridor (TTC). [537]

However, the bill was vetoed by Governor Perry after the legislative session ended. Texas legislators meet only every two years, so there was nothing they could do until two years later.

2007, August 19-21—Montebello, Ottawa, Canada, SPP Reunion Meeting of Bush, Prime Minister of Canada, Steven Harper, and Felipe Calderon Mexico. Topics at this conference were: integrating and harmonizing regulations between Mexico, Canada and the U.S and providing U.S. military of assistance to Mexico. It was clearly driven by the American Competitiveness Council representing the top 10 multinational corporations from each of the three nations seeking ways to open borders and integrate private business into government policy making.[538]

There was a large gathering of conservative groups there to protest, (mainly led by the American Policy Center, Eagle Forum, Howard Phillips, and Jerome Corsi), but these groups were not allowed within 25 miles of the Fairmont Le Chateau Montebello resort, where the meetings were taking place. Montebello is about 50 miles outside of Quebec.[539]

Because of the comments and concerns of many Americans, Canadians, and Mexicans, that were appearing more and more on the internet and alternative media about the SPP and the movement to form a NAU, the heads of state of all three countries had to pretend this concern was all unfounded (just as the heads of state of the major nations of Europe did with the European Union).

"Bush mocked the idea of a merger of a North American Union as a fantasy of conspiracy theorists. 'It's quite comical actually, to realize the difference between reality and what some people on TV are talking about.' Calderon laughed it off, too. 'I'd be happy with one foot in Mexicali and one in Tijuana.' **But according to Pat Buchanan, "Felipe is talking about one foot in Mexico and one in Los Angeles."**[540]

Hologram on back of licenses   Logo on the SPP Website

2007, September 6—The North American Drivers License: It was first produced in North Carolina. According to Jerome Corsi who wrote about the license on *World Net Daily*, the license has a hologram of the North American continent on the back. It looks exactly like the map of the logo that you see on the SPP website. A resident of North Carolina and president of Americans for Legal Immigration, William Gheen, was very upset about the new licenses and was going to refuse to get one. He said, "I object to the loss of sovereignty that is proceeding under the agreements being made by these unelected government bureaucrats who think we should be North American instead of the United States of America." Marge Howell, spokeswoman for the North Carolina DMV, affirmed to *WND* the state was embedding a hologram of North America on the back of its new driver's licenses. According to her, "It's a security element that eventually will be on the back of every driver's license in North America."[541]

2007, September 2—"Mexico Does Not End at the Border," shocking statement by Mexican President, Felipe Calderon, at the National Palace in Mexico in his "State of the State" address: This reveals what the Mexican government really believes about the borders. "Mexico does not end at its border. Where there is a Mexican, there is Mexico." Pat Buchanan writes about this for World Net Daily and adds, "This astonishing claim . . . brought his audience wildly cheering to their feet."

2007, September 9—"Buenas Noches, America!": An article by Pat Buchanan reveals the huge number of illegal aliens already in the United and what the number could be by 2060. He states the plans of the politicians to erase the borders and asks, "Can we stop this or have we reached the point of no return?"

Today, already, there are 45 million Hispanics in the United States, Perhaps Half from Mexico, and 37 million immigrants. Now, Steve Camarota of the Center for Immigration Studies projects—using official Census Bureau figures of 1.25 million legal and illegal immigrants entering and staying in the United States every year—a U.S. population of 468 million by 2060. We will add as many people—167 million—in the next half-century as the entire population of the United States when JFK was elected. Some 105 million of these folks will be immigrants and their children. That 105 million is equal to the entire population of Mexico, whence most of these folks will be coming. No wonder Mexican presidents are coming out of the closet about what is up. They know the gringos can't stop it, for they have the American establishment on their side. Buenas noches, America![542]

2007, September—New York City, a Meeting of the North American Public/Private Partnership and Infrastructure Finance Conference: Attendees were told that there is $100 billion and perhaps as much as $400 billion available for PPP financing of new privately operated toll roads in the U.S. with the majority of the funds coming from foreign investments. Many of the contracts between government and private corporations contain a "no-compete clause," meaning that the corporations have the power to charge whatever they want and no one will be allowed to compete with their fees. That essentially allows them to become a monopoly. I thought we had laws against monopolies in our country?

2007, October—Larry King Interview with Former Mexican President Vicente Fox about a New Currency. King asked him, "I would like to know how you feel about the possibility of having a Latin American united currency?" Fox answered essentially, yes, it would happen but it would take awhile.[543]

2007, November—Another Attack on American Sovereignty, the UN Law of the Sea Treaty, LOST, Again Voted on by the US Senate. According to Cliff Kinkaid of Accuracy in Media, who did much research into the background of this treaty, it was created back in 1982 by Sam Levering and his wife Miriam, two very left leaning globalists and members of the World Federalists, who advocate "a federalist system binding all countries under a central world government with limited powers." Levering formed the "Neptune Group" to lobby for the treaty. But it was soundly rejected. However, like most bad ideas the liberals try to force upon us, they never really die. They keep rising up again and again, and here we are facing it again.

What Would the Law of the Sea Treaty Do? One of the main priorities of the Law of the Sea Treaty would be "to provide the U.N. with sustained and independent sources of funding." A book published by WFA, *A New World Order: Can It Bring Security to the World's People?*, stated "One of the most popular concepts identified as an independent source of revenue is the ocean and sea beds." LOST would create an International Seabed Authority to grant "leasing rights to private corporations for mining concessions and operations." "Certain fees and sharing of technology are also involved." This Seabed Authority was created by the Convention on the Law and the Sea of 1994, and already created the "authority" to collect international revenue taxes to finance its activities. Hence, global taxes were born, a major step on the road to world government.[544]

Global Tribunal: LOST would also set up a tribunal to rule over the nations that sign on to the treaty. This would supposedly have jurisdiction over U.S. courts. It would be trial by magistrate, no jury of your peers, and no acquittal possible if you are found guilty.

2007—"North American Future 2025 Project" Was Published: It was published by the prestigious Center for Strategic & International Studies. It advocates "economic integration," the "free flow of people across national borders," and "policies that integrate governments." The CSIS report even calls for "harmonizing legislation" on intellectual property rights with other countries. That's a direct attack on our U.S. patent system, which is the key to U.S. leadership in inventions and innovations.

2007—The Hudson Institute published a 35-page White Paper "Negotiating North America: the Security and Prosperity Partnership:" It states that SPP is the vehicle "for economic integration" with Mexico and Canada and even "combines an agenda with a political commitment." The Hudson White Paper explains that the SPP's "design" is for the executive branch to exercise full "authority" to enforce and execute" whatever is decided by a 3-nation agreement of "civil service professionals" as though it were "law." That means evading treaty ratification and even congressional legislation and oversight.

2008, February 14—A Military Agreement Created the Groundwork for A NAU Army: The agreement was signed by Canada and the USA, allowing the armed forces of both countries to support each other in case of domestic emergencies, even one that does not involve a cross-border crisis. Combined with the Montebello pact to aid Mexican's military, this U.S. / Canadian pact essentially creates the groundwork for a North American army.[545]

April 21, 2008—North American Leader's Summit (held in New Orleans): Notice, it now has a new name. Any mention of the SPP is dropped.

According to the Phyllis Schlafly column that was sent out April 16, 2008, "North American Union, Conspiracy or Cover up?," the latest cover up for the North American Union movement is to just change the names, so people will think it has all gone away and there is nothing to worry about. **North American Leaders Summit** doesn't sound quite so innocuous, does it? No one hearing that would suspect that there is a partnership of all three countries, Mexico, Canada, and the USA to form a union.

Promoters of the TransTexas Corridor, who are getting such flack from concerned Texans, who do not want their state all divided up, are planning to change the name to "Regional loop." Mrs. Schlafly gives the name changes for several other terms that deal with illegal immigration that have aroused the attention of conservatives:

> To see what the elites are planning, you don't have to peek through keyholes or plant a spy under the table. Just read their published reports. The words most frequently used to describe their goals are "economic integration," "labor mobility," "free movement of goods, services and people across open borders," and "harmonization" of regulations. [546]

2008, March 13—"NAFTA and the SPP and the Framework for Advancing Transatlantic Economic Integration:" This was discussed by the Advisory Committee on International Economics Policy (ACIEP) at their second meeting in Washington D.C. This group was created a year earlier in April, 2007, by President Bush, German Chancellor Angela Merkel, and EU Commissioner President Jose Manuel Barraso. This framework has put the United States and the European Union on a joint path toward further transatlantic economic integration. [547]

2008 October Financial Crisis and the TARP Bill of $700 Billion Passed: This began the bailout of banks, mortgage companies, AIG, and the auto industries, that were "too big to fail." Scare tactics were used, and the blame was put on the Bush administration, with statements like "McCain would just do more of the same. It gave Obama a big boost in the polls.

November 4, 2008—Barack Obama, the First Black American Elected President: Obama campaigned on the platform of "hope and change." Many people are concerned that the "change" Obama promised is essentially the taking of the change in one's wallet from one group of people and giving it to another—in other words, redistribution of wealth. From all the socialist policies of his first year in office as President, from his Czars and other people he surrounds himself with, also from the words that have slipped out of his mouth, Obama is a true socialist who strongly believes in the socialist philosophy of redistribution of wealth. (Of course, not his own wealth, but that of others.)

Socialist Bills Passed Under Obama, Bringing the USA Closer to a Socialist State: 1) Stimulus Bill, putting our nation $787 billion in debt, which has helped the federal government to do more nationalizing of the auto industry, the banks, the mortgage companies, insurance companies; 2) Hate Crime Bill passed by attaching it sneakily to a Defense Authorization Bill. This will make the USA resemble more a socialist state by limiting our freedom of speech, especially religious expression in opposition to same-sex marriage or the teaching of homosexuality in our public schools. 3) Health Care Bill that will cost almost a trillion dollars and will force all American to have health insurance or be fined. There are many scary parts to the bill such as a national ID card that by 2013 is to become an implanatable RFID chip. It will hold all of your health records and other private information and have access to your bank account. 4) Other socialistic bills that Obama is pushing is Cap and Trade that will cost many jobs under the excuse of saving the environment and 5) an Amnesty bill for all illegals.

2010—The Target Date for Implementation of the North American Union: In achieving the goal of a new international economic and political order, nation states are to be broken up and put into regional government. The goal is to have the North American Union, the regional government planned for our hemisphere, in place by the Year 2010.

The framework has already been created by the executive branches of the governments of all three countries, Canada, Mexico and the USA, with no congressional or parliamentary oversight, without any vote, without the voice of the people.

The SPP Task Force stated, "The [SPP] Task Force proposed the **creation by 2010 of a North American community** to enhance security, prosperity, and opportunity. We propose a community based on the principle affirmed in the March 2005 Joint Statement of the three leaders that 'our security and prosperity are mutually dependent and complementary.' Its boundaries will be defined by a common external tariff and an outer security perimeter within which the movement of people, products, and capital will be legal, orderly and safe. Its goal will be to guarantee a free, secure, just, and prosperous North America."[548] (Yes, just as such a Union has done for the poor countries and people who are now part of the European Union.)

Ways to Force Amazing Change in Government: Bernadine Smith, the same lady who sent me the Gomberg Map in the early stages of writing this book, sent me a four-inch thick packet of historical records documenting the secrecy and stealth that have been going on in government for the past 100 years, bringing more power to federal and world government and bringing us closer to the globalists' plans for change. The globalists have achieved their required "changes" by using any one of the following ways or several at a time: (Bernadine Smith's website is www.libertygunrights.com.)

1. **Social Changes**—devaluation of Christian morals and ethics in the family, alteration in educational teaching standards, acceptance of dialectics and false information, no longer recognizing absolute truths, untruths taught about America's Godly Christian heritage or about Americas founding fathers and heroes. All these bring students to develop an attitude of apathy. When students are no longer proud of their nation or its history, they could care less about standing up for it or fighting for its freedoms.

2. **Economic Crisis of Major Magnitude**—This can be caused by bad trade agreements such as NAFTA; undercutting American trucking and farming industry; destroying our own industries and businesses or causing their outsourcing to foreign lands; the Fannie Mae and Freddie Mack Mortgage fiasco and the "bailout" of banks, car industries; stock market reverses; millions of Americans losing their jobs and their homes; high credit card debt; enormously high debt for cities, states, and the nation.

     This crisis could also be caused by a large state going bankrupt. That state could be California, which as of March, 2010, was $20 billion in debt. It has had a history of enormous debt for the past 10 years. Many of its cities are approaching bankruptcy. It is the nation's biggest debt issuer and is running out of credit. Californians were told that in February, 2009, we would be out of cash. To quote Governor Arnold Schwarzenegger, "The state is in terrible condition . . . We are going towards a financial Armageddon."[549]

     In a September 2, 2009, Reuter's article, the California State Controller, John Chiang, issued a report over the past fiscal year. His report "made for grim reading." Since December of 2008, "the state had to resolve a $61.7 billion budget deficit for a period of less than 1.5 fiscal years." [550] (http://blogs.reuters.com/commentaries/2009/09/02/california-debt-rush/)

3. **Catastrophes**—either man-made, such a 9/11, or natural such as earthquakes, floods, or hurricanes like Katrina that hit New Orleans with such devastations. This can cause chaos, confusion, desperation, and martial law to be declared with government take over.

4. **High Cost of Government**—resulting in huge debt, inflation, taxation and oppression of the people and eventually the collapse of government because it can no longer pay for necessary services.

5. **Corruption in Government**—Boy are we seeing that! One scandal after another: from a president lying about having sex with an intern, to congressmen lying about homosexual relationships, to a governor trying to sell a senate seat to the highest bidder. What effect do scandals by elected officials have on a nation? They result in distrust by the people. People no longer want to vote thinking there are no decent people to vote for. Corruption by government officials also help to justify immoral or dishonest actions by the people. They think if the president or governor is doing it, why shouldn't I?

6. **Collapse of Government**—resulting in chaos, anarchy and take over by a tyrant who uses the promises of bringing an end to chaos and anarchy to rise to power. People are willing to go along and obey the new leader, thankful for some form of order to end the chaos.

We can already see how some of the above motivators for change have already happened. Perhaps more will be seen in the future to help usher in the chaos needed for regional government to take place and people being willing to accept it. [551]

USA to Break Up Into Six Regions 2010? A few years ago such a prediction would have been laughed at and ridiculed, just as our financial crisis would have been laughed at. However, since then, we have several state governors and legislators who have made statements and signed 10th Amendment Resolutions that they would succeed from the union if things get much worse with the federal government trying to impose more and more regulations and controls over them. Texas is one of those.

According to pastor and columnist Chuck Baldwin, other people are starting to believe the breakup of our nation is more of a possibility now. He wrote about a report that came from Macedonian Radio and Television On-line (MRT) of an interview with Mr. Igor Panarin, Professor and Dean of the Moscow's Diplomatic Academy within the Russian Federation's Ministry of Foreign Affairs.

Panarin compared what is going on in the U.S. today with the last stages of the USSR under Gorbachev, before it collapsed. He predicted the United States will fall apart by July, 2010. He stated, "Mass immigration, economic decline, and moral degradation will trigger a civil war . . . and the collapse of the dollar." Panarin added that the USA "will disintegrate into six blocs—*and everyone will get their piece."* He added that the probability that this will happen by July of 2010 "is more than 50 percent." Why? Panarin answered:

> *The dollar is not secured by anything. The country's foreign debt has grown like an avalanche . . . By 1998, when I first made my prediction, it had exceeded $2 trillion. Now it is more than 11 trillion. This is a pyramid that can only collapse . . . It is already collapsing. Due to the financial crisis, three of the largest and oldest five banks on Wall Street have already ceased to exist, and two are barely surviving. Their losses are the biggest in history. Now what we will see is a change in the regulatory system on a global financial scale: America will no longer be the world's financial regulator.*

The *Drudge Report*, the *Wall Street Journal* and *World Net Daily* also reported on the same story. The *Wall Street Journal* stated "Prof. Panarin, 50 years old, is not a fringe figure. A former KGB analyst, he is dean of the Russian Foreign Ministry's academy for future diplomats. He is invited to Kremlin receptions, lectures students, publishes books, and appears in the media as an expert on U.S.—Russian relations."

Joseph Farah, editor of *World Net Daily*, wrote in a column regarding Panarin's predictions, "Until recently, no one took him very seriously. And then came the economic calamity that has rocked Americans and the rest of the world, too. Now, Panarin's predictions of an end of the United States, due to economic and moral collapse, is being taken seriously by many."

The Six Divisions? Panarin said the six parts would be: 1) the Pacific coast, with its growing Chinese population; 2) the South, with its Hispanics; 3) Texas, where independence movements are on the rise; 4) the Atlantic coast, with its distinct and separate mentality; 5) five of the poorer central states with their large Native American populations; 6) the northern states, where the influence from Canada is strong; Russia might even "claim Alaska."[551]

As the reader has learned in the chapter on the NAFTA Super Highway, part of the plan for the mammoth highways is to also divide our nation into six large geographical areas that will break up states and properties. People would have a hard time crossing or entering the highways except for every 40 miles.

Under Whose Control Would the Divisions Be? Panarin said, "everyone would get their piece." With no state militia or way of defending themselves, the states could be very easily taken over by any tyrant with a strong army. Panarin does not say who would be getting their "piece," but infers that the states might be taken over by other countries. [552]

Pay Up Now or Else! Brian Sussman, radio talk show host for KSFO, was filling in for Lee Rodgers' morning show, December 14-18. He asked the question of what would happen if China came calling and wanted their debt paid now? A Chinese leader would tell Obama, "We're sorry, but we can no longer hold your debt. It has become unsustainable. We demand that you pay us now."

Of course, Obama would tell China, "I'm sorry we cannot pay you back. We don't have the money." What if China then says, "All right, we will just have to take what we can take, starting with California." In a later broadcast, he added, "Maybe China would like the rich mining reserves of the Rocky Mountains and would demand them."

Sussman added that such things have happened in history before. Land has been taken by one nation from another to make up for unpaid debts.

How much Easier Would be the Move to a North American Union: When American has been transformed into a socialist state, with the federal government having nationalized our major industries (including health) and has much more centralized power; when the states are broken up into regions so state's rights no longer exist; when the state's national guard is no longer under the jurisdiction of state governors, but is called up by the regional governors, appointed by the president; when there is massive chaos, confusion and unrest; when the American dollar is worthless, how much easier it will be to move us towards a North American Union or some merger—which has been the objective all along?

Who Would Be in Charge?: In all the anarchy and confusion that would pursue, what a good time for the United Nations to come marching in like a "knight in shining armor" to save us all from anarchy and ruin. They could help create a merger of the three countries with a new currency, newly "harmonized" laws, a new constitution, a parliamentary form of government, already planned and ready to go. Maybe in the chaos and confusion, Americans, who formerly disregarded or had strong feelings against the UN, would welcome the UN, any "savior" that could bring order out of chaos and destruction.

I'm sure the European Union would be there to assist and give advice on how well they were able to form their merger, just as they are with the other unions that have been formed or are in the process. But, remember who the EU gets their marching orders from? They are also under the auspices of the UN.

What Would Regional (North American Union) Government Consist of?
If the globalists achieve their goals, the following is what we can expect. Some of these may be implemented even before the NAU is official:

- The U.S. Constitution and Bill of Rights would no longer be in effect.
- State and provincial governments would be abolished.
- All borders of the fifty states would be eliminated and the USA would have regions instead. (Canadian and Mexican provinces would also be broken up and large regions established.)
- Immigration would be unrestricted—open borders between all three countries.
- The massive NAFTA Super Highways will be built and will bring trucks and rail non stop across the borders of all three countries, making the transport of cheap Chinese-made products much easier.
- A national ID card would be required for residents of all three countries with biometrics on the card (including RFID) so people can be tracked at all times and all information on them collected in an international data center.
- All banks, businesses, industries, transportation, energy, natural resources, farms, armaments manufacturing, and all private property will be nationalized.
- Civilian law enforcement will be merged with military enforcement under the control of homeland security—in violation of Posse Comitatus. [553]
- General and complete disarmament. No government agent wants to be shot at by angry citizens who do not like having their freedoms taken away. So of course, guns and ammunition will have already been outlawed and confiscated before these changes take place.
- The American dollar will have collapsed, replaced with a common currency for all three countries.
- Most officials will be appointed, no longer elected.
- News media sources, newspapers, radio and television will all be government controlled and only give the politically correct version of the news. No more free press.

What Would World Government Consist of?

- All of the above but more of it.
- All power moved to the international level.

- International monetary controls coming from one big world central bank and one currency.
- Totally planned central society operated by un-elected managers.
- Heavy income tax and international taxes.
- No private ownership of property.
- Cradle-to-grave control of your life.
- Schools would have international controls and standards.
- Students would have their careers chosen for them according to what jobs are needed.
- Financing of the transition would at first be supplied by wealthy tax-exempt foundations, then later supplied by heavy taxation on all citizens.
- General and complete disarmament. The only one allowed to have weapons would be the police (maybe) and the world-government military.

A Constitution for All of the Americas: According to Henry Lamb, chairman of Sovereignty International and founder of the Environmental Conservation Organization (ECO), and a writer and researcher about the North American Union, one of the purposes for the SPP and its "working groups," was to integrate and harmonize American law with that of Canada and Mexico. "Of course, that would necessitate having to come up with a new constitution for all three countries. "Despite the official denials, the snickering and the ridicule, the process continues. The president, himself, may be just a pawn in a much bigger game being played by geo-political forces that also do not exist—officially."

According to Mr. Lamb, there is a coalition of individuals and organizations coming up with the proposed constitution and similar constitutions for six other regional government unions, to function under a "reformed United Nations." They do not identify who they are, but here is the link to their website *http:// americas-union.org/constitution/article_0000.htm.* They give a postal address in Sydney, Australia. (Isn't it nice to know that someone in Australia is creating a constitution for the Americas?)

When you go to their website, you will see a map of all of the Americas, North and South, and you find out that this constitution is not just for North America but for all of the Americas.

"A Perfect Covenant:" They describe their constitution as, "a perfect covenant." I always thought a covenant was a spiritual promise, between you and the Lord, such as what you take at the time of your baptism or the covenant you and your spouse take with the Lord at the time of your marriage. I wonder what kind of a covenant we will be taking with a one-world government? The only thing I can think of is a covenant of servitude, or slavery, depending how willing we are to go along with all that will be asked of us.

It is also very interesting to click on the individual parts of their proposed constitution, especially what they have written about a one-world religion and a warning for those who do not agree to go along with this religion. (This is mentioned in Chapter 15.)

The Clinton Global Initiative: When first reading the incredulous words on the website, one would tend to dismiss the whole idea as "fiction," but there are several recognizable non-government organizations identified as "dedicated to helping with the "covenant." One of those is Bill and Hillary's "Clinton Global Initiative." The Clintons have long been advocates of global government.

A Constitution Under the United Nations: You also find many references on the website to the United Nations. The U.N. Millennium Declaration of 1995 describes the goals of global governance and paves the way for the Constitution of the Americas, and the other five global "unions," which all advocate the same end goal: global governance. The North American Union is but one important step toward this goal."

The following are some of the extreme goals they have for their "one-world order:"

"A supreme council" of selected individual would advise the "secretary general" of the Americas.

Their constitution would bestow the rights that our Declaration of Independence states come from God— "life, liberty and the pursuit of happiness," but they add "the right to adequate housing, a job, food and good health."

Their constitution would abolish the concept of taxation and impose, instead, a Marxist system of "voluntary" giving determined by the wealth and productivity of each individual. Those who produce wealth would "give" more than those who do not. Those who do not produce wealth have a government-bestowed "right" to receive housing, food and living expenses provided "voluntarily" by those who do produce wealth. To ensure that the "voluntary" gifts are adequate, the constitution authorizes the government to impose fees for the services it renders, which may be applied selectively to those who "have," and not applied to those who "have not."

There would be a "supreme director" of the following: Planning; building and construction; culture and entertainment; education; employment; energy; finance; fitness and health; ecosystems; justice and more.

Each "supreme director" would be appointed by the secretary general, and would have "sole authority" over all aspects of his domain.

As Henry Lamb writes, "This proposed constitution is a wish list for the utopian one-world government pursued by some for more than a century. While officials scoff at such notions, the world continues to move closer and closer to the procedures and belief systems espoused by these advocates."

Lamb also states that even though there is no "official" connection between this proposed Constitution of the Americas and the official Security and Prosperity Partnership, many of the goals are the same." [554]

As scary as all of this sounds, it is not a done deal. In the next chapter you will see that there is much that has already happened to stop some of these programs. Americans are waking up and starting to take a stand. There is still hope.

Chapter Eighteen

What Can We Do to Stop USA Transformation?
What Has Been Done? There is Still Hope:

1. First of all, We Need to be Thoroughly Convinced and Knowledgeable About the Rightness of Our Cause. We need to be familiar with the form of government that our founding fathers established and know how to defend it. In the *Incremental Chipping Away of the Once Great USA,* much information is given on our representative form of government, how our Founding Fathers had designed it and intended for it and our freedoms to last forever, as long as the Constitution would be followed. But you will discover how devious people have been chipping away for a long time at the four elements that made up our strong civilization and nation: our form of government, economy, Judeo-Christian religious heritage and morals and our education. What is left over after all that chipping is vastly different from what our founding fathers intended for our nation.

What is the Proper Role of Government? Are we to be a big socialist state where the government does everything for the people and takes from those who have and gives it to those who have not? That is what Obama would have us think and what our children are being taught more and more in our public schools and universities. That is why anyone who is wealthy, other than the president and other elected officials, are looked down upon and called names such as "greedy." The new war that Obama has launched no longer seems to be the "war on terrorism" it is more a "war on prosperity."

Karl Marx (given the title of the "Father of Communism") and James Madison (the "Father of the U.S. Constitution") both claimed to have the answer to what the proper role of government is. Let's take a look at their opposite proposals and see what the best answer is.

Karl Marx's Proposal to Solve Poverty: Marx believed humanity's problems came from unequal distribution of wealth—when one man is poor and the other is rich there will always be conflict between the two. His solution was to take the property of both the rich and the poor and distribute it equally, leaving the ownership in the hands of the government. But what if the government likes all this property and does not want to distribute it at all? And what if the government has become so powerful that there is nothing the people can do to get their property back? Such is the case with most socialist, communist regimes, as described in the following quote by Oliver Demille:

> Marx's flaw is that in order to take property away from people the government must have power over them . . . this simply creates a new class of people—the government elite—who not only own all the property, but also hold all the power. They are much richer and more powerful than the rich man was before they took his money away in order to make everyone equal. Marxism—whether you call it communism (e.g. China), socialism (e.g. France and Britain), a social market (e.g. Germany and Japan), or monopoly capitalism (e.g. the United States)—defeats its own purpose; it sets out to eliminate classes and ends up creating the richest and most powerful class in the world. Of course, those who implemented socialism know this all along and set themselves up as the leaders of this class.

James Madison Solution: Madison and our other Founding Fathers believed that the proper role of government was not to take property away but to secure it, and to protect also man's life, liberty, his pursuit of happiness, and other "God-given rights." Government is to serve no other role than this. When government has attempted to do more than this, it creates mankind's problems, rather than alleviating them. Protection of rights creates incentive of the poor and security for the rich. This is also stated so well by Oliver Demille:

> When the poor man has adequate incentive, he soon becomes rich, while, when the rich man has security, his incentive is to be virtuous and share with the less fortunate. That is why the U.S. was so successful in its first 150 years of existence. With 6% of the world's population, it produced over 50% of the world's goods, services, and wealth. And, being secure in its wealth, it shared great amounts of money with other nations. Today, as its security decreases, there is a desire to give less . . .
>
> It is the same with individuals . . . since the . . . U.S. government began taxing people in order to redistribute wealth to the poor, the poor have lost their incentive and the wealthy have lost their security. The rich, being taxed of their rightful property, resent the intervention and insist that government is now responsible for caring for the less

fortunate. They no longer share with the poor, and the poor no longer live the American Dream that everyone can be rich. America has rejected Madison and adopted Marx. This point is especially poignant when one considers that Madison, the major architect of the U.S. Constitution, was inspired by Christ, while Marx was an avid Satan worshiper.

... In order to "help" men rather than protect them, governments attempt to tax and redistribute wealth. This system is called socialism, and it automatically steals agency and supports Satan's plan.

Demille clarifies what he believes has happened to the United States and the form of socialism that we now live under. He calls it "monopoly capitalism" and gives a good example of the Federal Reserve:

The U.S. today is controlled by monopolistic capitalists who own all the large banks and major industries, control the schools and media, and are the powers behind both the Republican and Democrat Parties and the officials in all three branches of government. Monopoly capitalism is the same as socialism, where an elite group of people control the government and the money of the nation.

The power of monopoly capitalism is illustrated by the Federal Reserve's control over U.S. money. The Federal Reserve is not part of the government, but is a private corporation which is controlled by the biggest supporters of global socialism in the world. The Federal Reserve can change the interest rate and inflation at will; it could drastically devalue our money at any given moment. With one sweep the Fed can make $100 bills worth less than a penny. The international bankers have already done so in Germany, Argentina, and other places during the past century.[555]

Our Founding Fathers Believed in the Free-Enterprise System not Capitalism and not Socialism: The free-enterprise system is vastly different than capitalism. It is run by a truly free market, by competition, not by monopolies, and without restrictive regulations, taxes, fees, etc., but alas, we have not had such a system for a long time. However, it is the "free enterprise system" that is being blamed for the present financial crisis. Former President George W. Bush, Former Head of the Federal Reserve Greenspan and President Obama have all stated as such, saying that we had put too much faith in the free-enterprise system and it failed us—therefore, we must go to a system of much more government regulations. It is not free enterprise that failed. It was the system of socialism, with all of its government controls and regulations, that caused the financial crisis, exactly as they wanted it to and exactly what Obama has planned for us, with even more restrictions, regulations and higher taxes.

Our Founding Fathers Believed that the Best Way to Govern a Person was by Teaching Them Correct Principles and then Letting Them Govern Themselves Through Self Restraints and Self Control: That is why they said often how important religion and morals were to a self-governing people. It is from the Judeo-Christian religious foundation of our nation that we received our correct principles and morals on which to base our self restraints and self controls and to govern our own lives. Ezra Taft Benson said it very well in the following:

> When government wants to solve a problem, it tries to change the outside environment in which people live. If people live in slums, the government builds new apartments and lets people move out of the slums into the new buildings. Within a year, the new buildings look like slums. The Lord works in a different way. He changes the inner man and then the men and women change their environment.[556] (paraphrased)

In other words, the way to change people's lives and their environment is by teaching them correct religious principles, which will motivate them to become better people on their own. They should then be allowed the freedom to change their own lives without government's interference. There is no motivation for change by putting people on the dole in a welfare state the rest of their lives, with government as the big nanny.

Our Founding Fathers Believed that the Best Government was that which Governed Least, Small Local Government—Closest to the People: The founders believed that the family was the basic unit of society and tried not to interfere with the authority of the parents teaching correct principles to their children; next came the authority of the church; next came city and county governments, which really did not have a lot to do if the family and the church were running smoothly. Elected officials, for the most part, were not paid. They deemed their elected positions to be ones of respect and honor, not paid professions. George Washington took no pay for the two terms that he served as President.

The founders felt that even state governments were too big to be effective and tried to limit their power. And they tried, through the Constitution, to limit the power of the federal government to only a few specified things. What was not specifically granted to the Federal government in the Constitution was to be left up to the states and to the people. Even the land that the federal government owned in Washington D.C. was to be limited to 10 square miles, no more. My, have we gone far beyond that! With the establishment of national parks, wilderness areas, protected reserves, etc., the federal government is encroaching more and more with a massive land grab of our nation. It owns 86 % of Nevada, 60% of Utah, 40% of California, and at least 1/3 of many other states.

If the goal of the Establishment were to truly solve humanity's problems, as they are professing, then they would go back to small, local, limited government. If, on the other hand, the goal is to increase the wealth and power of an elite class, a strong federal government is essential and a powerful New World Order is even better. It is obvious what the real goal is. The elite have spent the last 200 years spreading socialism, in all its many forms, governing by stealth and deception in preparation for their glorious New World Order takeover.

A Summation of the Global Framework Compared to What our Founders Established: In spite of all the chipping away and the many anti-American slogans, teachings, distortions and revisionist American history that is being taught, the structure of our American form of government and our amazing Constitution has outlived any other form on the face of the earth. It has been the best nation with a profound, history and Godly heritage, and it is still worth saving.

Floy Lilley, J.D., the chair of the Free Enterprise of the University of Texas at Austin, wrote the "forward" and the "afterward" section of the book *Reinventing Government* and gives a summary of what she feels living under a revised global system of government would be like and what she feels is essential to the preservation of our government and freedoms.

The Global Framework for Reinventing Government:

- Eliminate the individual as the basic unit of society and replace him with group organizations.
- The Socialization of will-to-accept is to precede socialization of property.
- History books will continue to be revised to even question the wisdom of the Revolutionary War.
- A small number of people will control a large number of groups beyond any accountability to voters.
- Attributes of sovereignty will be limited.

- The economic new world order will be established before the political global government is established.
- Individuals will have no voice in the new democracy.
- Americans will pay the lion's share of this global reconstruction project.
- No withdrawal from the global permanent order will be possible.

Essential Truths for Preserving Liberty

- The individual is the fountainhead of rights.
- The individual is the basic unit of government.
- Individual judgment and individual ownership of property are the basis of liberty.
- The American Revolution was a uniquely moral revolution.
- Voters need representatives who are elected and accountable to them.
- Attributes of individual sovereignty may not be limited.
- Political freedom must rest upon economic freedom.
- Individuals, not groups, participate in republics, not democracies.
- Americans are not obligated to finance any global reconstruction project.
- Withdrawal from insufferable social contracts is a basic human right.[557]
- (I have added one more) The best government is limited government, bound down by the chains of a fair, just, written Constitution, our US Constitution, the best that was ever penned by the hands of men.

2. Join With Like-Minded People and Groups. After we have become educated in the rightness of our cause, share what we know with others. There is strength in numbers. It is exciting to see how many people began joining together in 2009-2010 in the Tea Party Movement, and the 9-12 Project that you will read about shortly. But first let me tell the reader about the like-minded groups who have joined together to fight the merger of a North American Union and the NAFTA Superhighway, and the "success" that has been made.

2007 SPP Meeting in Ottawa, Canada: At the second SPP anniversary meeting, held near Ottawa, Canada, (in Montebello) August 19-21, 2007, where Bush, Calderon (from Mexico) and Harper (from Canada) met, a large number of conservatives were "there" protesting from mainly the U.S and Canada. A coalition has been formed called the "Coalition to Block the North American Union."

Members of the following groups were present: the American Policy Center, Eagle Forum, Howard Jarvis and the Conservative Caucus, Jerome Corsi, The Canadian Action Party, the John Birch Society. The SPP conference was held at Montebello, Canada, and was heavily guarded by U.S. army troops and Canadian security force. The protestors were forced to hold their rally at the Ottawa Marriot Hotel, 25 miles away (the security buffer), as close as they were allowed to assemble. However, the SPP attendees knew of the group's presence and willingness to work together to defeat this threat to our nations' sovereignties.[558]

The Canadian Action Party—the Leading Group Fighting the NAU in Canada, Formerly Led by Connie Fogel: This is what is posted on their website *www.CanadianActionParty.CA*

> The North American Union, posted on 4:10 p.m. October 26, 2006, Summary: The North American continent is being transformed from three sovereign nations (Canada, USA, Mexico) into one regional corporate power base, the North American Union. Unlike the creation of the European Union, there is no public political/academic discourse on the merits, or pros or cons of a North American Union building up to a vote within each nation as to the wish of the people to join such a union. Instead the union is being created by stealth, is already well on its way to fruition, and is being imposed on us by our own elected representatives and government with no opposition.
>
> The driving forces are corporate and military. The Chief Executive Officers of the most powerful corporations operating in the three countries want this union and have been working for some time devising their strategies and goals. Their facilitators are first, unelected officials and bureaucrats who move easily between corporations and government; second, former elected officials like John Manley, former Deputy Prime Minister of Canada; third, the heads of the three nations, Martin, Bush, and Fox; and finally, the governments and the rest of the elected members who apparently just rubber stamp what is put in front of them by the unelected officials—few questions, if any asked.
>
> The ultimate enforcement mechanism for the North American Union is a police state. The tools for the police state are "anti-terrorist" laws. Anti-terrorist laws are a ruse to strip the citizens of civil liberties in order to prevent dissent against the police state. The Orwellian justification is "security," "safety."

Because of Like-Minded Coalitions Working Together, Much Success Has Been Made in Stopping the Progress of the SPP and the NAU: It has been good to have Connie Fogel and her organization working with us.

Coming from Canada, she is a second witness to the reality of what is going on. This is not "just some pipe-dream of sensational American journalists eager to make money on a new book," as I have heard some legislators say in California when I have tried to talk to them about the SPP and the movement towards a NAU.

In spite of the secrecy and the stealth, the sneaky way that the executive branches of all three countries have been working behind the scenes promoting the North American Union, more and more Americans and Canadians were awakened to the enormity and seriousness of what was going on. We are grateful to the courageous journalists and reporters who have reported on the SPP and the movement to form a North American Union. We are also grateful to the many active citizens who have contacted their state legislators and congressmen, and we are appreciative of our elected officials who heeded our calls, investigated this on their own and have taken a stand against it. You will read about a national resolution and many State Resolutions that have been passed against the SPP, the NAU, and the NAFTA superhighway. There was also an amendment passed in the House to a transportation bill stopping the funding for the NAFTA superhighway.

As I mentioned in the chapter on Robert Pastor, he has admitted that there was just too much opposition to the SPP, and it is now dead. He would like us to think that is the case so we all will just go away. But the SPP is not dead; it just has a new name, "North American Summits," and the movement towards a NAU has expanded to include a partnership with the European Union. As you see, they are not dead, they are just buried much deeper. The elitists behind them don't want us snooping into what they are doing any more.

As you read in the last chapter, 100 years of preparation in building the framework for a North American Union and world government has been incrementally going on. They are not about to just drop it because of opposition. They are waiting for us all to become distracted in all the other issues that Obama has us busy with, which is certainly a huge number. They are also waiting for the opportune crisis to come along to usher in their union and a new currency as the solution to that crisis.

3. Learn from the European Union and Those Speaking Out and Trying to Get Out of It, Especially in the United Kingdom: We can see how the EU is usurping more and more power and taking over the government of its member nations. That is not what we want for the USA or Canada or Mexico. Maybe the few elite at the top want such a system, but the vast majority of the people do not. Our nation was established as government of the people, by the people and for the people, not government of elite, by the elite and for the elite.

We need to exert our rightful "sovereignty" and put our elected officials back in their place. They are to be our servants, not the other way around.

4. Learn from Each Other. Eagle Forum Special Training Session in November 2006: Thanks to the generosity of Eagle Forum donors, Phyllis Schlafly was able to bring many of her state presidents and other Eagle Forum leaders to Washington D.C., just before the Thanksgiving vacation for a week's training on the subject of the SPP, the NAFTA Superhighway and the movement towards a North American Union. Our trainers were none other than the best experts one could find: Dr. Jerome Corsi, himself, and Phyllis Schlafly herself, the one who first exposed all of this to the light of day in her Phyllis Schlafly Report July, 2005.

A Swarm of Eagles Met with Congressmen: After three days of extensive training from 9:00 A.M. until 5:00 P.M., and continuing on after dinner each evening, we were asked to go and share this information with our state Congressmen the last two days that we were there. When we didn't have appointments, we could continue on with the training session, which lasted through Friday. We were asked to have a cover letter and make copies of some of the most important information that we had received to give to our Congressmen. I wrote letters to fifteen California Republican Congressmen as well as a few key democrats, my own representatives and my two senators, Barbara Boxer and Dianne Feinstein. I had appointments with some of the congressman's aids. When I could not meet with anyone, I just left a packet of information for them. A week later I sent out faxes to them giving them even more information.

The only one that I got a personal return letter from was Lynn Woolsey (D), who is not my personal congresswoman, but she does represent part of Santa Rosa. She said she also had concerns and would do her utmost to investigate it. I was asking for all of the congressmen to sign on to a resolution against this, but, in her letter, she did not commit to that.

Fortunately, at a later date I was able to meet personally with Duncan Hunter in California for about 30 minutes and spoke to him about it. He did remember my letter and said he had signed on to the resolution. I was very happy to hear that.

Following is a copy of the letter that I hand delivered to various Congressmen's aids or left in their office. This one is to Duncan Hunter of California:

Sample Letter Delivered to California Congressmen

Congressman Duncan Hunter
2265 RHOB
Washington D.C. 20510

November 15, 2006

RE: Questions about the Security and Prosperity Partnership

Dear Mr. Duncan:

I am writing to you about something that I recently discovered and found to be very puzzling. I am hoping you can clarify some of the questions that I have.

I have been reading various articles and have found on a government commerce website, *www.spp.gov*, information about something that sounds very much like a treaty between the US and two other countries, Mexico and Canada. President Bush, the former President of Mexico, Vicente Fox, and Paul Martin, the former Prime Minister of Canada agreed to the Security and Prosperity Partnership in a Press Release a year ago, March 23, 2005, in Waco, Texas.

According to the Constitution, treaties between nations must be agreed to by a 2/3 vote from the Senate. NAFTA, which is really a treaty in every sense of the word, was called an agreement, so that Congress only had to pass it by a simple majority. It looks like by calling the SPP a partnership, President Bush thinks he can get around asking Congress to approve it. In fact, he is not even letting you know about it, let alone approve it. Very few have even heard of it. I am hoping, Congressman Hunter Duncan, that you might be the exception and can answer my questions about it.

The SPP organizational chart shows thirteen working groups with counterparts for all three countries. Some of those are: Manufactured goods, Energy, Food and Agriculture, Rules of origin, Health, E-Commerce, Transportation, Environment, Financial Services, Business Facilitation, External Threats to *North America*, Streamlined and Secured Shared Borders, and Prevention/Response within *North America*.

Notice all the references to "North America." So Canada, Mexico, and the United States are to be just one happy nation called North America? All this is to be done by stealth without any Congressional approval? You would think that such an important decision could be voted on at least by our elected representatives. What ever happened to our representative Republic and rule of law? Are we now a monarch and King George gets to make such decisions for us?

U.S. administrative-branch officers participating in these working groups are drawn from the U.S. departments of State, Homeland Security, Commerce, Treasury, Agriculture, Transportation, Energy, Health and Human Services, and the office of the U.S. Trade Representative.

And what are these working groups working towards? Released documents obtained through the Freedom of Information Act state that the U.S. administrative branch is working with its counterparts in Canada and Mexico to form a new trilateral group to "harmonize" or "integrate" the administrative laws of all three countries. **So we are to have our laws combined with those of two other nations without any congressional oversight or the vote of the people?**

In a SPP June 2005 "Report to Leaders" it was discovered that there is a "trusted traveler" program for North America including procedures to "enhance the use of "biometrics" in screening travelers destined to North America. **We are to be one happy nation with Mexico and Canada called "North America," with all of us labeled as "trusted travelers" able to easily go back and forth across each others borders? That will certainly eliminate the "illegal immigration" problem in our nation, won't it? No wonder President Bush has done nothing to protect our borders, with this plan in mind all along.**

I have recently also heard of the 4 football-field-wide Trans Texas Corridor (toll road) that is planned to be started in Texas, with non-stop cars and trucks crossing the Mexican Texas border at Laredo, without any inspection. The port of entry will not be until the trucks go on to Kansas City where they will then be inspected electronically. And guess what country is going to be running the port of entry—Mexico! It is called Kansas City SmartPort Inc. and is already a done deal. They seem to be quite proud of it. (Go to www.kansascity.com/mld/kansascity/business.) The toll road corridor is then to go on to Canada where again there will be no stopping and no inspection. The toll road in Texas is going to be leased to a company in Spain called Cintra, owned by the King of Spain. They will be building the massive corridor, and the toll money collected will go to Spain. **What bill in congress has authorized our city ports of entry and roads to be sold or leased to foreign countries?**

Can you imagine the enormous eminent domain taking that will be necessary of American farms, ranches, and homes to provide the area needed for those massive corridors? I assume these non-stop corridors, allowing such easy access to our nation and erasing our borders, are part of the "trusted traveler" program of the Security Prosperity Partnership? What security when we already know of so many terrorist, drug smugglers, and dangerous gangs who have already crossed our unprotected borders? Now we will be welcoming them with open arms.

This same June 2005 report mentioned "memoranda of understanding," binding contracts between the three nations, yet nowhere can one find any copy of those mou's, even with FOIA requests. **If this partnership is really good for our nation and will improve our security and prosperity, why is Bush not proud about it and why will he not tell Congress about it or seek your approval, and why is there so much secrecy and the mou's cannot be found?**

Personally, I think there is a great deal of deception going on here and I am very concerned for the future of my nation, especially when I hear how quickly they would like to have this all implemented—by the year 2010!

Congressman Hunter, I would be most appreciative if you know anything about the SPP and can answer my questions. I will be calling your office in a few days to hear your reply.

Sincerely,

E. Orlean Koehle, State President, Eagle Forum of California

5. Continue to Visit Congressmen and Legislators, Write Letters, Make Phone Calls: Other Eagle Forum leaders were writing similar letters and visiting their Congressmen from about 40 different states. So in one week's time, key Congressmen from states across our nation had been visited by a swarm of eagles and they found out about these important subjects. They could no longer say they knew nothing about it. However, some still said that it was just a figment of someone's imagination or "just pie in the sky," as was told to me by the aid of my Congressman, Democrat Mike Thompson, from Sonoma and Napa Counties in Northern California.

Thompson even wrote a letter to the editor in the *Napa Valley Register* May 27, 2007, again pooh-poohing a NAU, saying that "there is absolutely no plan for Congress to create a North American Union." (That is very true. It is not Congress who is doing it. It is the executive branches of all three governments.) I was glad that Thompson mentioned it, however. At least it gave some people, who had never heard of it before, the opportunity to read the name of a North American Union and maybe arouse their curiosity to do their own research.

Ten months later from when I first wrote to Mike Thompson and visited his office in Washington D.C., I finally got a personal letter from him, dated September 10, 2007. He sent an article entitled CRS (Congressional Research Service) Report for Congress about the SPP. He finally acknowledged that it did exist, but he said it was just an extension of NAFTA and nothing to worry about.

Gayle Resucka, State Eagle Forum President for Utah, spoke to her senator from Utah, Bob Bennett. Referring to the NAFTA Super Highway and Kansas City now becoming a port operated by Mexico, He said essentially, "That's just the way of the future. We just have to accept it." Later we found out why. As you read in Chapter Five, Bennett had not only learned to accept the whole diabolical plan to destroy the sovereignty of our nation, he was part of it on a grander scale." He had been appointed to be the Chairman over the EU and USA "Transatlantic Partnership Network, TNP."

However, I and others believe we do not have to accept globalists' "way of the future." We can and must do everything possible to try to stop it. Many of our state legislators and even some Congressmen, who have found out about it, agree. Below you will see examples of state resolutions and the Resolution #40 in Congress asking for the SPP, the NAU, and the Superhighway to be stopped. There was also an amendment passed to a transportation bill in the House sponsored by Congressman Duncan Hunter of California, which would have stopped any funding for the SPP and the NAFTA superhighway. However, it was not passed in the Senate, so it could not become law. However, it did pass by a wide margin in the House and brought more attention to this issue.

State Resolutions Against the SPP and the Movement to Form a North American Union: The following is a list of the 18 states that drew up their own resolutions, many of which have passed both houses—Idaho, Montana, Utah and Oklahoma:.

Arizona: Senate Concurrent Memorial 1002—introduced by Senator Johnson
Georgia: Senate Resolution 124—introduced by Senators Schaefer, Rogers, Douglas, Hill, and Chapman.
Idaho: House Joint Memorial 5 (HJM-5). Sponsored by Representatives Joan Wood, Cliff Bayer, Marv Hagedorn, and Senators Shirley McKague, Monte Pierce and Mel Richardson, **First state to pass in both houses!**
Illinois: House Joint Resolution 29—introduced by Representative Black
Missouri: Senate Concurrent Resolution 15—sponsored by Senator Barnitz & House Concurrent Resolution 33—sponsored by Representative Guest.
Montana: House Joint Resolution 25—introduced by Representative Rice of Montana **(passed).**
Oklahoma: Senate Concurrent Resolution 10 introduced by Oklahoma State Senator Randy Brogden.
Oregon: Senate Joint Memorial 5—sponsored by Senators George, Starr, and Whitsett and Representatives Boquist, Krieger, Nelson and Thatcher.
South Carolina: House Concurrent Resolution 3185—introduced by Representative Davenport.
South Dakota: Senate Concurrent Resolution 7—introduced by Senators Kloucek, Apa, Lintz, and Maher and Representatives Nelson, DeVries, Gassman, Jerke, Kirkeby, Noem, Betty Olson.

Tennessee: Introduced SJR-88 on February 21st, 2007.

Utah: House Joint Resolution 7—introduced by Representative Sandstrom and Senator Fife (Passed in the House by a vote of 47-24 and was finally passed in the Senate the next year).

Virginia: Senate Joint Resolution 442—introduced by Senators Lucas and Hawkins.

Washington:— Senate Joint Memorial 8004—introduced by Senators Stevens, Swecker and Benton & House Joint Memorial 4018—introduced by Representatives Roach, Dunn, McCune and Hurst.

The other states that later passed similar resolutions at least in one house were: Alabama, Colorado, Hawaii, and Texas.

Most of the State Resolutions Have Similar Language. This is the one from Idaho, " . . . urging Congress to use all efforts, energies and diligence to withdraw the United States from any further participation in the Security and Prosperity Partnership of North America or any other bilateral or multilateral activity that seeks to advance, authorize, fund or in any way promote the creation of any structure to create any form of North American Union."

Montana's Resolution: NOW, THEREFORE, BE IT RESOLVED BY THE SENATE AND THE HOUSE OF REPRESENTATIVES OF THE STATE OF MONTANA: That the Montana Legislature urge the President and the Congress of the United States to withdraw the United States from any further participation in the Security and Prosperity Partnership, any efforts to implement a trinational political, governmental entity among the United States, Canada, and Mexico, or any other efforts used to accomplish any form of a North American Union.[559]

House Congressional Resolution #40 110th CONGRESS, 1st Session, Introduced January 22, 2007, by Representative Virgil H. Goode from Virginia in the House of Representatives. It states "Expressing the sense of Congress that the United States should not engage in the construction of a North American Free Trade Agreement (NAFTA) Superhighway System or enter into a North American Union with Mexico and Canada."

Bill sponsor: Virgil H. Goode, Jr. [**VA**-5] **Co-sponsors:** Representatives: Duncan, John J., Jr. [**TN**-2]—1/22/07, Foxx, Virginia [**NC**-5]—1/22/07, Jones, Walter B., Jr. [**NC**-3]—1/22/07, Paul, Ron [**TX**-14]—1/22/07, Stearns, Cliff [**FL**-6]—1/22/07, Wamp, Zach [**TN**-3]—1/22/07, Norwood, Charles W. [**GA**-10]-1/30/07, Saxton, Jim [**NJ**-3]—2/8/07, Tiberi, Patrick

J. [**OH**-12]—2/8/07, Regula, Ralph [**OH**-16]-2/8/07, Cubin, Barbara [**WY**]-2/16/07, Tancredo, Thomas G. [**CO**-6]-2/16/07, Garrett, Scott [**NJ**-5]—2/27/07, McCotter, Thaddeus G. [**MI**-11]-2/27/07, Davis, David [**TN**-1]—3/1/07, Davis, Lincoln [**TN**-4]—3/1/07, Hunter, Duncan, [**CA**].

July 2007, The Hunter Amendment to the Transportation Bill against providing funding for the SPP and NAFTA Super Highway passed. Here is what the Press Release Stated:

> . . . Congressman Duncan Hunter (R-CA) successfully offered an amendment to H.R. 3074, the FY2008 Transportation Appropriations Act, prohibiting the use of federal funds for participation in working groups under the Security and Prosperity Partnership (SPP), including the creation of the NAFTA Super Highway. The Hunter amendment gained strong bipartisan support, passing the House by a vote of 362-63.
>
> "The proposed NAFTA Super Highway presents significant challenges to our nation's security, the safety of vehicle motorists, and will likely drive down wages for American workers," said Congressman Hunter. "Much like NAFTA, the super highway is designed to serve the interests of our trading partners and will lead to neither security nor prosperity. "This 12 lane highway, which is already under construction in Texas, will fast-track thousands of cargo containers across the U.S. without adequate security. These containers will move from Mexico, a country with a record of corruption and involvement in the drug trade, across a border that is already porous and insufficiently protected. "Unfortunately, very little is known about the NAFTA Super Highway. This amendment will provide Congress the opportunity to exercise oversight of the highway, which remains a subject of question and uncertainty, and ensure that our safety and security will not be comprised in order to promote the business interests of our neighbors."

> **NOTE:** SPP working groups were advancing a plan to build the NAFTA Super Highway—an international corridor extending between the U.S., Mexico and Canada[560]

Congressman Duncan Hunter (right) with Dr. Jerry Corsi, Phyllis Schlafly, and Orlean Koehle, at Eagle Forum Banquet.

This is an excellent piece of evidence to the nay-sayers out there, who are still bent on saying that the SPP and NAFTA Superhighway are none existent. It is also exciting to hear how the amendment passed by such a wide margin in the House. Obviously, there are many congressmen now well enough informed to know they do not want the SPP or the NAFTA Superhighway to take place. We congratulated Congressman Hunter for a job well done!

Congressman Hunter Received Eagle Forum of California's "Statesman of the Year" Award for 2008: At the annual state Education Conference, held March 29, 2008, in Rohnert Park, California, held at the Doubletree Inn, Mr. Hunter was honored with a beautiful plaque with an Eagle at the top, with the words engraved on it, "Statesman of the Year." Mr. Hunter received the award by State President, Orlean Koehle, who called him a "true statesman" for his courage to speak out about such un-politically correct issues as the SPP, the NAU, and the NAFTA Superhighway.

Congressman Hunter was one of the few candidates for president in the 2008 election who was willing to discuss the most important issues, such as: protecting our sovereignty against regional government, protecting our U.S. Constitution against harmonization and integration with two other countries, stopping the porous borders that are allowing millions of illegal aliens into our country, and stopping the NAFTA superhighways that are going to split our nation up into sections and destroy cities, school districts, and millions of peoples homes and livelihood.

So Much Progress Has Been Made that Robert Pastor Declared the SPP and The NAU Dead: As you read in the chapter about Robert Pastor, he announced that the SPP is now "supposedly" dead. Robert Pastor has left his position at American University and is off writing a book and being a part of the new-age group called "The Elders." Supposedly the TransTexas Corridor was stopped, but, it has just been given a new name as has the SPP. One cannot really believe what the elitist are telling us. Their liberal plans for world government never die; they just go underground for a while. The following tells of the amazing work of many groups in Texas to try to stop the TTC.

The Continuing Saga of the Battle in Texas Against the TTC

The ongoing saga for eight years over the Trans Texas Corridor reveals the amazing resilience of the Texas people and their willingness to once again fight a similar battle as "the Alamo."

The enemy in this modern battle is again a foreign entity—the Spanish firm called Cintra, who would be building the toll roads, and a massive conglomerate of internationalists who hope to gain much with the increased trade that would be coming up from Mexico on the wide superhighways.

The battle issue is still over property rights and sovereignty; who gets to control Texas and her highways—a large cartel of international powerbrokers or the Texas people and their locally elected representatives?

Unlike the Alamo, the foreign entity is now joined at the hip by people one would think were supposed to be protecting the Texas people and their property: the Texas governor, Rick Perry, and his cohorts; many elected representatives in the state legislature; TXDOT, the Texas Department of Transportation; and the federal government. A Texas construction company, Zachary, who would be working with Cintra, is also part of the group, as are other businesses, banks, attorneys, who hope they can cash in on some of the money somewhere. They are all part of a PPP, public/private/partnership, and they all seem determined, no matter what the Texas people say, to build the TTC, which would be the beginning of the massive NAFTA superhighway system.

It is also a story of deception, of the enormous power and money involved in the regional/international groups that have combined their forces against the Texas people.

The year 2003 is when the Texas legislators passed the plan and the design for the TTC. Maybe they did not understand then what it was really all about.

Two years later in 2005, at the end of the next legislative session, Texans began to get wind that such a thing as a big NAFTA superhighway was going to be started that would break up their counties, school districts, farms, ranches, etc. Since the Texas legislature only meets every two years, they had to wait two years to try to stop it through the legislative process.

More and more Texans began to get involved speaking out against the TTC and contacting their state legislators, who began to listen and respond. on April

19, 2007, Texas Legislators passed a two-year moratorium against any PPP from taking place. This would not have totally stopped the TTC, but it would have delayed it and put a damper on it.

However, just as the legislative session ended, Governor Perry vetoed the moratorium bill. There was no time for the legislators to reconvene to override his veto. Once more they had to wait until 2 more years to try to stop it.

Texas law says that no emergency session could be called without the governor doing the calling, and, of course, he was not about to do that. Instead he went off to the 2007 Bilderberger meeting, probably to receive lots of pats on the back for saving the TTC.

More and more people began to get involved. Thanks to talk radio, the internet and the many groups who were sending out information about the TTC, Texans began waking up and finding out just what the building of the TTC would do to their state. It would have greatly expanded I-35 and I-69 with a 4,000-mile network of corridors that would be 1,200 feet wide, would break up farmland, communities, counties, school districts, take 1/2 million agricultural acres out of private hands, and it would have cost just $184 billion.

A "maelstrom of objections" from Texan landowners began pouring in. There were 28,000 public comment letters and 47 town hall meetings held.

The Many Groups Who Worked Together to Stop the TTC: I heard representatives from three groups tell their own stories in person at a Freedom 21 Conference that took place in Dallas, Texas, July 24-25, 2008. They were: Terri Hall, of TURF, whom you read about in Chapter Sixteen. She is a young, dynamic mother of eight children. She is the one who who brought this issue on television stations in her area of San Antonio and often would be seen holding a baby in her arms. David and Linda Stall of Corridor Watch led another coalition of people fighting the TTC. Oklahoma State Senator Randy Brogden and Amanda Teagarden of OKSafe worked to pass legislation in their state that said the TTC would just have a big U-turn and go back to Texas. It was not crossing into Oklahoma!

2007—September—Texas City Mayors and School Board Superintendents Unite to Fight: Leaders in two national property rights groups, Stewards of the Range and American Land Foundation (now combined as "American Stewards of Liberty"), Dan and Margaret Byfield, Ralph Snyder of Texas, and Attorney Fred Grant of Idaho were able to meet with mayors and Superintendents of Schools in a part of Texas where the TTC would be going right through their counties. When it was explained to these elected county officials how the TTC would divide their school districts in half, wreak havoc to the farms, ranches, and businesses, they were happy to be able to sign on to a way to fight it. Attorney Fred Grant, a Constitutional Law expert, had discovered a little known law that calls for "coordination" between the plans of federal and state agencies and the plans of local governments.

East Central Texas Sub-Regional Planning (391) Commission (ECTSRPC) was formed: The commission was made up of mayors and superintendents of schools from Bartlett, Holland, Little River Academy, and Rogers. Together, they wrote a coordination plan of what their goals and objectives were, which definitely did not include a super highway going right through their territory. Then they wrote a letter explaining the law and used this wording, "Therefore, the state shall coordinate with the 391 Commission formed by the four rural municipalities and their respective school districts." They gave officials from TXDOT, the Texas Department of Transportation, a 30-day deadline in which to appear. TXDOT, at first, paid them no head, but soon found out that there was such an existing law and they were forced to obey it. They showed up on the 28th day to have a coordination meeting.

When they came, the mayors of each of the cities had television cameras and reporters present, and there was a big coverage on the evening news. TXDOT officials could do nothing but smile and say how happy they were to be able to meet with these local officials and coordinate their plans. Of course, in the meeting, the city mayors told TXDOT there was no way that their plans for their highway fit in with the municipalities plans, and they would just have to send their highway some other direction.[561]

Keeping a Continual Watch: All of the groups fighting the TTC have learned to not trust government. This is what Kenneth Dierschke said from the Texas Farm Bureau. "We must continue to hold TxDOT's feet to the fire during the next legislative session to ensure they keep their promises."[562]

Congressman Ron Paul, in his "Texas Straight Talk" column," 6/23/08, also warned the Texans to stay vigilant. He said that "constant pressure is needed to keep government in check. . . and hold politicians feet to the Constitutional fire." He also warned them that those behind the NAFTA Superhighway might try again when they think no one is looking. And, as you read in Chapter Sixteen, that is exactly what happened.

TTC Raised Its Ugly Head Again, but with a New Name: Sure enough, less than a year later, it was discovered that the new plans were to break the TTC into smaller projects but still include Highway 35 from San Antonio to Oklahoma and 1-69 from the Rio Grande Valley to Texarkana, near Arkansas, just like the original plans. The only difference, it would no longer be called the TTC. The new sneaky name is ICN "Innovative Connectivity Plan." That should fool everyone. It doesn't sound like a super corridor at all, anymore, does it? It sounds more like super glue.

In 2009, the only thing that the state legislators passed regarding transportation was renewing the Texas Department of Transportation (TXDOT), which was up for "sunset," a review process that determines whether the agency remains in existence, and if so, whether the agency is restructured. "Although the Sunset Committee proposed several changes to the governance of the department, none of the changes were enacted. Instead, the Texas Legislature extended TXDOT for two more years and made a $2 billion appropriation for the state agency."

2009 TTC More Stealth and Deception: The legislative session began with an announcement by Amadeo Saenz, the executive director of TXDOT, that the Trans-Texas Corridor was "dead." Governor Rick Perry also announced that "the days of the Trans-Texas Corridor are over." Were they telling the truth? Technically, yes, because the TTC's name has been changed. It is now being called the "Innovative Connectivity in Texas/Vision 2009" and is to be built in just small segments.

The governor later said, "We really don't care what name they attach to building infrastructure in the state of Texas. The key is we have to go forward and build it." The *Standing Ground* article states, "a significant number of road builders and businesses betting on the corridor have contributed to his campaign, so it is easy to understand why his comments indicate that the change is not much more than a public relations campaign." The governor and others were still dead set on proceeding with the TTC, just under a new name.

2009 Legislative Session Became a Stalemate for the TTC or the "Innovative Connectivity Plan": The governor and TXDOT asked for bills SB3 and HB4 to be filed, which would have reauthorized CDA's (Comprehensive Development Agreements) that would have allowed public private partnerships (foreign companies) the ability to contract with the state to build the roads. But these were never authorized. A bill to ask for a referendum to raise taxes for highway construction also did not pass.

Local Government Coordination Plan Once Again Triumphed: While the Texas legislature and the governor were at a standstill as to what to do about the TTC, it provided time for local government to use their "coordination plan" to stop once again the mammoth international highway, proof that local government can still work against big and powerful state and federal government.

The Eastern Central Texas Sub-regional Planning Commission (ECTSRPC), otherwise known as 391 Commission, contain two counties, Bell and Milam, which would have been chopped in half had the TTC been allowed to go through. They have worked tirelessly over these two years assuring TXDOT that they must obey the law and "coordinate" with them.

Since nothing was happening with road building over this time, the ECTSRPC has come up with their own transportation plan, that they called "Bartlett-to-Buckholtz, the first such plan in the state prepared "entirely from the rural perspective." They sent copies of their transportation plan to all affected state and local agencies including TXDOT. Two of the Bell County Commissioners met with the ECTSRPC and agreed to increase the miles allotted for the paving of the designated roads needed by the schools districts.

The ECTSRPC also heard back from the director of TXDOT, Armadeo Saenz, who thanked them for their transportation plan and stated, "We will use this information as we go forward with our planning efforts. We also look forward to continued coordination with your commission, along with the many partners that are involved in transportation-related issues in Williamson, Milam, and Bell counties."

Of course, at first TXDOT was not very happy at all to have to "coordinate" with these local elected county leaders, but they have found out that it is the law and they are forced to do so. What is also exciting, other such local commissions have sprung up in nine other areas of Texas, following the example of ECTSRPC.[563]

The Trans Texas Corridor Has Raised Its Dead Head Again and Again: And that is exactly what happened. On March 22, 2010, I received the sad news from Terri Hall, of TURF, that the TTC had just been "playing dead."

After Rick Perry was pretty assured that he would be reelected, he gave the go ahead for the TTC to once more proceed forward, using its new name. Each step of the project will use the original highway's name, so it will appear that they are just making repairs to old freeways as usual. They are hoping no one will suspect that they are building massive super toll roads to link together, until the project is all a done deal.

As has been mentioned before, these cocky, global elitists never give up. They just "play dead" until no one is paying attention, then they go forward again with their same plans.

However, because of the effectiveness of the American Stewards of Liberty and TURF, and "the 391 Commission" that they helped form, those parts of Texas under the jurisdiction of the commission, will remain free of the TTC. But it is planned for all the rest of Texas, just as before.

Who knows what will happen when the roads get to Oklahoma? Will they have to make a big U-turn or will a more compliant governor and legislators be in place who will be willing to allow the highway through? Or perhaps by then, the states will have been broken up into regional governments, and there will be no opposition to the NAFTA Superhighway being built no matter what former state or region it is in.

Tenth Amendment Movement

(Also Known as the State Sovereignty Movement): There are many states whose state legislators, in the early months of 2009, began passing Tenth Amendment resolutions saying that the federal government is trying to exert too much power over states rights, and they are not going to allow it to happen.

What does the Tenth Amendment state? "The powers not delegated to the United States by the Constitution, nor prohibited by it to the States, are reserved to the States respectively, or to the people." There is so much that the federal government is trying to have jurisdiction over which was never granted to them by the Constitution, yet they seem to not pay any heed to that. The Tenth Amendment movement is trying to remind the feds that there is still a Constitution and they are supposed to be following it.

The movement started with Oklahoma back in February, 2009. On February 18, its House of Representatives passed House Joint Resolution 1003 and the Senate passed the same resolution on March 4, both by a wide margin. The vote in the House was 83 to 13 and in the Senate it was 25 to 17. The resolution stated that "Oklahoma hereby claims sovereignty under the Tenth Amendment to the Constitution of the United States over all powers not otherwise enumerated and granted to the federal government by the Constitution of the United States." The resolution also stated "that this serves as Notice and Demand to the federal government, as our agent, to cease and desist, effective immediately, mandates that are beyond the scope of these constitutionally delegated powers." It directed copies of the resolution to be distributed to the president of the United States, the president of the U.S. Senate, and the speaker of the U.S. House of Representatives.

State Senator Randy Brogden, who led the legislation to stop any Trans Texas Corridor from coming into Oklahoma, also led the senate in adopting this resolution. There were several federal bills that caused the state legislation to take this action: The Real ID act, No Child Left Behind Education Bill, and now all that the federal government is imposing through their Stimulus Plan, and nationalizing so many of our industries. Senator Brogden made the following statement:

Over the last few weeks, it had become clear that the U.S. Congress was financially breaking the backs of every citizen in the country. So many of the problems our country faces would be resolved if the federal government was restricted to its constitutional powers. I have been burdened to do what is best for our nation and bring it back to its founding principles. My concern is for the future of my kids and grandkids; it's a deep-seated feeling. The state legislature is a place of interposition—we are supposed to protect the people.

Randy Brogden was asked to be one of our speakers at our 2009 state Eagle Forum conference for California that took place in May at the Calvary Chapel in Costa Mesa with 1500 people in attendance. He gave a wonderful talk, entitled "America, We Have a Problem," and was given a standing ovation.

By October, 2009, Thirty Five States Had Presented Similar States-Rights Legislation: According to a website, Small business Against Big Government (sbabg.org), 35 states have joined the Tenth Amendment movement, having at least one resolution pending. Many state legislators are now stating that if Obama's health care bill is passed (whatever version) that they will refuse to go along with it. Health care was also one of the many things not listed in the Constitution, supposed to be left up to the states, not to have a federal mandate pushing it upon the citizens.

Idaho Leads the Charge of States' Rights Against Obama Care: On March 17, 2010, St. Patrick's Day, in Boise, Idaho, Governor C.L. "Butch" Otter signed legislation requiring the state attorney to sue the federal government over any federal mandate requiring everyone in his state of Idaho to purchase health insurance.

When the governor was asked if his bill could succeed against the powerful federal government, he stated that there is similar legislation pending in 35-37 other states.

"The ivory tower folks will tell you, 'No, they're not going anywhere,'" Otter told reporters. "But I'll tell you what, you get 36 states, that's a critical mass. That's a constitutional mass." (http://www.idahostatesman.com/2010/03/17/1121021/idaho-first-to-sign-law-against.html.) [As of April, 2010, the number had risen to 39 states that were filing a law suit against the federal government.]

Let us hope that these 39 states have not taken "stimulus" money from the federal government and are not too intrenched and dependent on the federal "trough." Otherwise, it is going to be really hard to stand strong against the federal mandates, when financially you are so indebted to them. (According to another news report, even Idaho has a $200 million deficit. Of course, that is nothing compared to California's $20 billion deficit. Notice California is not one of the 39 States-Rights States. We are too far in debt and to dependent on the federal government for bailouts to still be master of our own ship.)

The Tea Party Movement

Another Sign of Hope for America: Back in February of 2009, Rick Santelli, a Chicago Stock broker was so upset with what Obama's administration was planning to do with our taxpaying dollars—to use them to bail out anyone Obama chooses, that he suggested we need a new "Boston Tea Party." The original Boston Tea Party was also about taxes: colonists protesting King George putting so many taxes on goods and services without any vote or voice of the people. It was called "taxation without representation." The final thing that was being taxed was the tea. The people in Boston, under the direction of Sam Adams, staged a large tea party, boarded the British ship that was loaded with the tea and threw it all into the Boston Harbor.

February 28, Tea Party Protests Began: People all over the nation began to pick up on Santelli's suggestion. Tea Party protests were held in Chicago, San Diego, St. Louis, Washington D.C. Greenville, South Carolina. Each weekend thereafter, other groups would get together in other cities. Through the amazing use of internet, people were able to contact each other and organize their protests. On tax day, April 15, 150 cities held such events. Some of them had thousands of people in attendance.

I was part of the Tea Party Protest that was held in Santa Rosa, CA, on April 15, and was asked to speak. I mainly spoke about the original Boston Tea Party and what we could learn from the colonists who took a stand against big government and tyranny. My self-made sign read, "A Nation of debtors is a nation of slaves." There were close to 600 people people who turned out; probably 95% of them had never done such a thing before. At the end of the speakers, we had a trumpet player play a medly of patriotic American songs, and I lead the group on a March to the state building, the federal building, and the city buildings, all within a few blocks from each other. As we were walking, we were shouting slogans, such as: "No more taxes, no more bailouts!"

Some of the signs that people had made read: "No taxation without deliberation," "Free market, not free loaders," "No more bailouts." A cute little girl was wearing a t-shirt that read, "Obama, get your hands out of my piggy bank!"

The 4th of July was another big day where more Tea Party Protests were held across the nation. A year later, there are thousands of groups that have sprung up all over the nation. In California, there are over 180.

Who are the Tea Party Members: Nancy Pelosi tries to make people think that Tea Party members are just "astro-turf," that they are paid to come out and protest. But that is not true at all.

The members are, for the most part, middle-class Americans, soccer moms, small business owners, "Mom and Pop" groups, that have just formed in the year 2009-2010. No one is paid. They are doing this spontaneously, because of their love and concern for their country.

Some are republicans, some are democrats, some are libertarians, some have no party affiliations at all. They are not at all socially conservative, but they are definitely all fiscally conservative, and they do not think that their hard-earned money is supposed to be spread around like manure to "redistribute wealth" to others. They all share a mutual concern for and oppose the rapid "transformation" and plunge to "socialism" that they see happening under Obama's administration.

Many of these people have become active in politics for the first time in their lives. They are contacting each other over the internet and announcing their events. Many are meeting at homes, at businesses, in small and large groups—many led by "soccer Moms," or small business owners. They are reading and studying the Constitution and other good patriotic books that explain the vision our Founding Father had for our nation. Some have speakers, some show videos. They are calling and writing their congressmen like never before. They are supporting good fiscally conservative candidates, many who are invited to speak at their meetings. Many, for the first time in their lives are running for office themselves.

March 13, Glenn Beck's 9/12 Project Was Launched: Radio host and FOX TV Personality, Glenn Beck started a "coming-together program" where Americans across the nation were urged to gather in groups to discuss and to share their feelings about how they feel about this nation, to strive to regain the same feelings of patriotism and love for their country that they had the day after the tragedy of 9/11 hit. That is how he came up with the name of "9/12." He also had a list of "Nine Principles and Twelve Virtues" that he wanted people to recite and to try to bring back into their lives, qualities upon which this nation was founded. They are the following:

Nine Principles: 1. America is good; 2. I believe in God and He is the center of my life; 3. I must always try to be a more honest person than I was yesterday; 4. The family is sacred. My spouse and I are the ultimate authority, not the government; 5. If you break the law you pay the penalty. Justice is blind and no one is above it; 6. I have a right to life, liberty and the pursuit of happiness, but there is no guarantee of equal rights; 7. I work hard for what I have and I will share it with whom I want to. Government cannot force me to be charitable. 8. It is not un-American for me to disagree with authority or to share my personal opinion; 9. The government works for me. I do not answer to them; they answer to me.

Twelve Values: Honesty, Reverence, Hope, Thrift, Humility, Charity, Sincerity, Moderation, Hard Work, Courage, Personal Responsibility, and Gratitude.

Glenn Beck's Suggestion for Coming Together Again on 9/12 (September 12): Boy! Did Americans heed his call and they did come together! The biggest Tea Party Express series of rallies was started in Sacramento, California, and went to major cities across the nation, finally arriving in Washington, D.C. on September 12 with an estimated crowd of 1 ½ to 2 million people, the largest group the police had ever seen assembled in front of the Capitol buildings. And what a nice group of people! There were no arrests and no trash left over. I heard that after Obama's inauguration, it took all day the next day for the trash to be picked up, but that was not the case with the Tea Party Express people. [564]

August 28, Sacramento Tea Party Express Launching Rally: I was part of this rally. It was exciting to see an estimated 8,000 people all assembled and united in our protest of what was going on in our state and nation. Many of the people and several speakers were from the Central Valley and spoke about the terrible abuse of government power depriving thousands of farmers of the use of water, causing them to lose their crops to supposedly save the "endangered delta smelt." (This was written about in greater detail in Chapter 8.) There were also 300 truckers who had come with their trucks. They had large signs on them either protesting the water being turned off, or AB 32, the wacky "green" bill that had been passed saying that they would have to retrofit their trucks to use a different kind of diesel fuel in California, costing $20,000, money most of them did not have. Many were being forced out of business.

Of course, many people were also protesting Obama's Stimulus Bill and the enormous debt that it has placed us in; others were there to speak out against, Cap and Trade, the Health Care Bill and Obama's nationalization and socialization of America. There was beautiful music sung and excellent speakers talking about all of these issues. It was exciting to see how many Californians were waking up to the truth of what has been going on around them—especially to the falsehoods behind the green movement.

Two big buses beautifully painted "Tea Party Express," were parked waiting to take the Tea Party Express members on to their next stop, Reno, Nevada. The Sacramento Rally was the beginning of a two-week series of rallies that progressed across the nation culminating in the September 12th march on Washington D.C. with an estimated 1 and ½ to 2 million people present.

If you click on the You Tube video of the Sacramento Rally, you can see some of the signs and hear the theme song playing in the background. Some of the signs were: "Congress, Read the Bill Before you Vote;" "Federal Budget for Dummies—How to avoid bankrupting the nation, first stop and read the damn thing;" "I'll keep my money and guns, you keep your change;" "Stop punishing success;" "Chains you can believe in;" "Congress, you're fired;" and "Go green, recycle Congress." Again, my sign read, "A nation of debtors is a nation of slaves."

The Theme Song for the Tea Party Express: On the You-Tube video about the rally, you could hear this music sung in the background: *We're having a tea party across the land. If you love this country come on and join our band. We're standing for freedom and liberty, because those with guts have shown us freedom ain't free. So if they call you a racist because you disagree, it's just one of their dirty tricks to silence you and me. I believe in the Constitution and all that it stands for. Anyone who tramples it should be booted out the door. To advocate in silence, that's what the peace crowd do. We're talking peaceful protest defending the red, white and blue.* "(There was one other verse I could not quite hear, and then the first two lines are sung again.)[565]

Tea Party Express in Searchlight, Nevada: On Saturday, March 27, thousands of Tea Party people rode in busses, drove cars, and flew into Las Vegas airport, again, from all over the nation. Since there was such a traffic jam for about 6 miles coming into the small town, some people just parked their cars on the side of the road and caught a ride with someone else a little farther along.

This time the Tea Party people were protesting against Harry Reid, the Senate Majority Leader, and his very liberal policies including support for the Stimulus Bill and the Health Care Bill.

Reid's home is in Searchlight, a small town of population 562. Reid is up for reelection and the Tea Party Express wanted to send a strong message to the state not to reelect him.

Sarah Palin was one of the main speakers. She told the huge crowd, "We're saying the big government, big debt, Obama-Pelosi-Reid spending spree is over, you're fired!"

One of our Eagle Forum leaders from Winchester, California was there, Shelly Milne. She was interviewed by a reporter from a newspaper in France. He asked her why the Tea Party groups are so opposed to Obama. Is it because of his black skin? Shelly answered, "I don't like the white part of him either. You know that he is half white? This has nothing to do with the color of his skin. it is the color of his politics. We are opposed to his socialist policies and how he is trying to transform America into a socialist state." The reporter seemed to really like her answer.

He did comment to Shelly that he had never seen a crowd like this. They were angry at what was going on in their country, but they were not really angry people. They were very friendly and kind to each other and seemed genuinely happy to be there. It looked like a big family gathering. Shelly agreed with him.

Shelly said that, as in all the Tea Party rallies that she had attended, when it was over and everyone had left, there was no mess to clean up. The Tea Party people are very clean and responsible.

The New York Times estimated 10,000 people had arrived for the rally. I heard Melanie Morgan, a former talk-show host for KSFO radio, interviewed on KSFO, March 29. She was the one who introduced Sarah Palin at the rally. She estimated the crowd at 35,000. She also commented on what a great group of people were there. So many people and yet so well behaved. No mess, no clean up, no crimes committed. The police also were very impressed.

The Town Hall Movement:

Along with the Tea Party movement and the 9-12 Project, during the summer of 2009 and on into 2010, concerned citizens across our nation started turning out for town hall meetings with their elected congressmen like never before. Most of these were discussing the health care bills.

I attended a town hall meeting with Congresswoman Lynn Woolsey, held in Petaluma, Sonoma County, August 31. It was held in the Veterans Memorial Building that normally holds about 500 people. People showed up two hours early. For those who showed up on time, it was impossible to find parking (I had to park seven blocks away), and it was impossible to get inside. Many were standing outside listening through the windows. There must have been 800-1000 people who turned out for it. After about an hour, the crowd began to dissipate a little, and I was able to get inside.

For the most part, the crowd was probably evenly divided over the health care issue. Maybe that is because the democrats were the ones who showed up early and stacked the decks. They sat up at the front and were the ones first up to speak. But there were also many who were outraged against the bill and against the entire concept of socialized medicine. Lynn Woolsey was asked many difficult questions and had a hard time answering them.

One of the questions that Woolsey kept trying to avoid answering was, "Would you take this kind of health care program for yourself and your family?

After being asked the question a third time, she finally admitted that all the government officials and congressmen have their own kind of health care that was really good, and she would probably stick with it. Her answer did not go over very well with the crowd.

Woolsey demonstrated the old elitist attitude from the book *Animal Farm* by George Orwell, "All animals are equal. Some are just more equal than others." These congress people truly think they are superior than the rest of us. A lowly serf kind of health care will be forced on us. They get to have the superior kind.

Town-hall meetings were going on across the nation. Most of the congressmen were absolutely shocked at the huge turnout that they were receiving at these meetings, and maybe it influenced them a little in their votes concerning it.

Disinformation and Slander Campaign Against the Tea Party Movement: The popularity and the effectiveness of the Tea Party movement, of course, has become a little worrisome and disconcerting—to say the least— to Obama, to his handlers and to the liberal agenda, so they had to figure out a way to stop this movement. Thus began a media blitz "disinformation" campaign against them.

As was mentioned in Chapter One about the "16 Ds of Deception," "disinformation" is one of the techniques used by those who seek to destroy our nation. They seek to discredit their opposition and destroy its effectiveness.

Newspaper, radio and television reports began to blacken the name of "Tea Party" groups, "9/12 Project Groups," and any groups that have the name Patriot in them, making it appear that they are radical, extreme, dangerous, and it is very "non-politically correct" to belong to them.

The reports accused some of those at the Tea Party rally that gathered March 20 (just before the final vote on the Health Care Bill, Sunday, March 21), of being "hateful, of spitting on the Democrat Congressmen, as they walked by, and of shouting out the word "nigger" to one of them who was black.

However, there is no film that picked up any such language. None of the Tea-party people heard such language, nor has any such incident ever happened before. So, instead of the news reporters covering any of the comments made about the health care bill by the Tea-party members, or what their posters said about it, all that one heard on the news was these "slanderous" remarks or "spitting" that took place. One man even offered a $10,000 reward if someone could produce one shred of evidence that such slanderous remarks actually took place. No one was ever able to produce any evidence, and the issue has been dropped from the radar screen. However, we are afraid that is just the beginning of the persecution of any conservative groups who are letting their voices be heard and speaking out against the Obama regime and their politics.

Outcome of the Health Care Bills: I'm sorry to say, the bribes, ear marks, the big-bullying tactics, keeping Congress in session either late Saturday or Sunday, not letting them go home for vacations---not even Christmas vacation, until the job was done, did the trick. In spite of their fears of not being reelected because of their outraged constituents, the majority of democrats folded and voted for the Health Care Bills.

Pelosi's House version of the Health Care Bill, was passed late Saturday night, November 8, by 5 votes. On Sunday, December 20, the final speeches were given on the Senate version, and the vote was taken at 1:00 A.M., to cut off any more debate by the half-asleep Senators. The vote was 60 to 40 Democrats to Republican. The final vote on the massive Senate Health Care bill, over 2074 pages, costing over $706.2 billion, was done the morning of Christmas Eve, 60 to 39, with all the Democrats voting for it and the Republicans against it.

The passage of these bills were done in spite of the latest polls that 61% of Americans are opposed to any form of nationalized health care. (*ABC News,* December 21, 2009)

However, thanks to the miraculous victory of Republican Scott Brown over Martha Coakley, January 19, for the U.S. Senate seat left vacant by the death of Democrat Ted Kennedy in Massachusetts, the tide shifted a little in the U.S. Senate. The democrats could no longer hold their large majority to get the final joint health care bill passed, and it had to be postponed for a while.

Finally, on March 21, as you read in Chapter Fourteen, after many bribes, coercions, twistings of arms, and back-room shenanigans, the health care bill was passed and signed into law by Obama on March 23.

How ironic that March 23 is the day in history (in 1775), that Patrick Henry gave his famous speech, "Give me liberty or give me death." How far has our nation sunk in 225 years! The liberty that has been slowly chipped away over the years now had a big hole blown through it with Obamacare.

Back in Patrick Henry's time, the colonists were angry to have British tea forced upon them with a new tax, that they had no say in. It was called "taxation without representation." We are now going to have Obama's health care forced upon us with our taxes being raised to pay for it, and we will be fined if we refuse to take it. And the voices of the people were not really heard in this issue, either. It could also be "taxation without representation." The polls were showing that Americans were opposed to Obamacare by 61 to 70%.

What Else Can We Do?

- **Continue to Learn and Stay Informed:** Thank goodness for some brave, conservative talk show hosts and television news broadcasters who keep us constantly informed and bring another viewpoint than the politically correct, liberal news of mainstream media. Thank goodness for the internet, through which people across the globe can also receive a different viewpoint (except for repressive regimes which will not allow their citizens to have free access to internet information).

  In the beginning of this book, I paid tribute to many of the talk show hosts and television news broadcasters who have kept me informed. I would like to give a special thanks to Lee Rodgers again, whom I have quoted several times in my book. Lee was the host of the KSFO morning show, from 5-9 a.m., broadcasting from San Francisco, the "belly of the beast," for probably ten years. My husband and I would wake up to him every weekday morning. He began to be like family. On February 19, 2010, he was no longer on the air. We were told he was retiring but without a word of goodbye. It was truly a great loss to all of his listening audience.

  Eagle Forum of California honored another KSFO radio host, Barbara Simpson, as our "Talk Show Host of the Year for 2007." She was selected because of the information that she was revealing that many other hosts would not touch, such as bringing Dr. Corsi on her show to talk about the SPP and the movement towards a North American Union. Barbara received Eagle Forum's Golden Microphone award.

  In 2008, the award went to Dr. Stan Monteith of Radio Liberty, who broadcasts out of Santa Cruz, another liberal hotspot. Dr. Stan broadcasts five hours a day, five days a week, and his show is picked up by many Christian stations across the nation and, of course, is also sent overseas with internet. Dr. Stan also is an author and has a vast library of conservative and historical books and tapes that he advertizes and sells on his program.

  In 2010, the Golden Microphone Award went to the following two talk show hosts: Sharon Hughes of Changing World Views on KDIA Radio 1640 AM and Brian Sussman of KSFO Radio, San Fransisco. Sharon has an afternoon program four days a week and one evening show coming out of Phoenix, Arizona. She has amazing guests who speak out on every important issue. Her website is also a great source of information, *www.changingworldviews.com.*

  Brian Sussman replaced Lee Rodgers on the KSFO morning show and is also bringing us important information. He used to be a weatherman and has just completed a book called *Climategate*, that reveals the truth about the Global Warming scare and the other untruths of the environmental movement.

- **Prayer is Essential:** We need to faithfully continue to pray for our nation and its leaders. Pray for our U.S. Constitution—that it may be restored and no longer ignored. Pray for our freedoms, that they may be here for our children and grandchildren, and pray for our sovereignty, that we may still be just one nation, one United States of America. As Congressman Tom Tancredo states, this is very urgent, **"Our culture, our language, our heritage, our sovereignty, our security, our prosperity and indeed our very survival are all at risk."** We also need to pray for discernment and wisdom that we will not be deceived, that we can recognize truth from falsehoods. And pray for protection in some very difficult times ahead.

- **But Prayer Alone Will Not Do the Job:** We are the hands the Lord needs to save this nation. We must put our belief into action. All the many hundreds of thousands of patriot Americans who have been writing letters, speaking out at hearings, calling and writing their legislators and their congressman are putting their faith into action and are making a difference.

- **We are to be Salt and Light:** To do that, we have to get out of the salt shaker and let our salt be spread around. As you know salt is a preservative. It stings a little. Sometimes we must call our legislators and congressmen to repentance if needs be. We must be willing to get out of our comfort zones, our apathy, and let our voices be heard.

- **We Are Called to Let Out Lights Shine:** Our Christian nation was to be the shining "city on the hill," a bastion of hope and freedom to all other nations. We cannot let that end. We cannot sit back and let our sovereignty, our beloved Constitution, and our way of life be taken from us.

- **Please Continue to Contact Your Elected Representatives—State Legislators and Congressmen:** Please encourage your representatives to stand by the Constitution and their oath of office to "preserve, protect, and defend" it. Ask them to read the bills before they vote on them and use the Constitution as a poof to see if these bills are worth supporting or not.

Ask them to do their own research and to find out for themselves that the movement towards regional government (either a North American Union or the transatlantic partnership with the EU) is not a hoax. This is not a conspiracy theory. It has become a conspiracy fact. The elite behind this are becoming very brazen and proud of their work as you will see in the last chapter giving their quotes supporting it. Though the mainstream media is still not saying anything about it, the plans can all be found with just a little bit of research. Encourage your legislators and representatives to sign on to resolutions already written against the Super Highway and the movement towards a North American Union, or to create their own for their state. Encourage them to be true patriots, even though it may not be the popular or politically correct thing to do at the time.

- **Continue to Prepare Yourself and Your Families for Some Rough Times Ahead:** As has been mentioned before, I strongly recommend your preparing with food storage and water stored that could last for some time, even months. Have provisions that you can use to cook and prepare your food without electricity. Get out of debt, pay off your mortgage, have some real currency—silver or gold tucked away, something that will maintain its value as the dollar continues to shrink in value.

- **Whatever You Do—Do Something!** Don't think that someone else will do it for you; this is not your battle. Read the following quote from a pastor in Germany who thought that he did not have to get involved. It did not concern him. Soon, it did concern him, but it was too late. (There were many Christians and their pastors who were also put in concentration camps. You just don't hear about them very often.)

> They came first for the Communists—but I didn't speak up because I wasn't a Communist.
> Then they came for the Jews—but I didn't speak up because I wasn't a Jew.
> Then they came for the Unionists—but I didn't speak up because I wasn't a Unionist.
> Then they came for the Catholics—but I didn't speak up because I was a Protestant.
> Then they came for me—and by that time—there was no-one left to speak up for me.
>
> —Rev. Martin Niemoller,
> Commenting on events in Germany 1933-1939

I will close this chapter with this quote that I use often as I speak about the great patriots who are mentioned throughout this book and to whom I pay tribute in my page of acknowledgments at the beginning. They are the bold ones who have been speaking out and writing about these important issues. Many of them have been scoffed at and ridiculed, but they were still willing to speak out.

In the beginning of a change, the Patriot is a scarce man—brave, hated, and scorned. When his cause succeeds, however, the

timid join him, for then it costs nothing to be a patriot." Mark
Twain.[566]

May you, dear reader, be such a patriot and may you, because or your
activism, be the "small helm" that may be able to turn the great ship of the United
State of America, save her from the rocks and get her back on course.

The next chapter gives additional quotes by many brave patriots warning
us and speaking out against the movement to regional and world government,
followed by the many elitists who are arrogantly promoting it.

Chapter Nineteen

Part 1—Quotes Warning Us Against a New World Order, Regional and World Government, and the Secret Groups Promoting Them by Patriots, Elected Officials, and Religious Leaders

Part 2—Quotes Promoting a New World Order; Regional and World Government; Socialism/Communism; a World Economy; One-World Religion; Environmental and Population Control; Quotes Against Property Rights and the Free Enterprise System—by Elitists and Globalists of America and the World

The "new world order" involves the elimination of the sovereignty and independence of nation-states, moving us to world government. This means the end of the United States of America, the U.S. Constitution, and the Bill of Rights as we now know them. The new world order proposals involve strengthening the United Nations and turning it into a true world government, complete with a world army, world parliament, world court, global taxation, and numerous other agencies to control every aspect of human life (education, nutrition, health care, population, immigration, communications, transportation, commerce, agriculture, finance, the environment, etc.). The various notions of the "new world order" differ as to details and scale, but agree on the basic principle and substance.

You will see from the many quotes that the words "new world order" have been in use for decades. They did not originate with President George Bush Sr. and his National Security Advisor, Brent Scowcroft, as they were out on a lake in a boat in 1990, as Bush said.

For those who might still be skeptical and can't quite believe there is such a movement to destroy independent nations and move us towards regional or world government, just reading the many hundreds of quotes by the elitists blatantly talking about it, should convince them otherwise. The elitists must truly believe there is no stopping them now, or they would not be quite so cocky, bold, and "in your face" in speaking openly about their plans for us, our nation, and our world.

This chapter starts with quotes by patriots, leaders, concerned citizens, authors and even some globalists who are warning us about the plans for a new world order. The rest of the chapter includes all the hundreds of quotes by the enemy proposing a new world order, regional or world governments, socialism, communism, etc. I also put in bold print anything that mentions those terms. I have the quotes divided up under various subjects.

If the quotes are not followed by their own reference number, then they came from one of four different websites: 1) *www.prisonplanet.com/articles/september2007,/250907NWOquotes*, html.
2) *http://www.amerikanexpose.com/quotes/.html*. 3) *http://www.supvril.com/nwo.html*
4) *http://www.jesus-is-savior.com/False%20Religions/Illuminati/quotes_on_the_new_world_order.html*.

The names are listed in alphabetical order and if known, they are followed by one or more of the various secretive, one-world organizations the person belongs to, abbreviated as follows: Council on Foreign Relations—**CFR**; Royal Institute for International Affairs—**RIIA;** Trilateral Commission—**TC;** Bilderbergers—**B**; Club of Rome—**COR**; Fabian Socialists—**FS**; Center for Strategic and International Studies—**CSIS**

Part 1—Quotes Exposing Regional and World Government, World Economy, Socialism, Communism, etc. and the Secret Groups Promoting Them—by Religious Leaders Authors, Patriots, Elected Officials, (both good and bad)

Army Training Manual Concerning Citizenship 1928, (Gave the true definition of democracy): *A democracy is government of the masses; Authority derived through mass meeting or any other form of 'direct' expression; Results in mobocracy [mob rule]; Attitude toward property is* **communistic**—*negating property rights; Attitude toward law is that the will of the majority shall regulate . . . without restraint or regard to consequences; Results in demagogism, license, agitation, discontent, anarchy.*

Note: Back in 1928, our schools still taught that America was a Representative Republic, based on the rule of law, and a firm and binding Constitution. We were never referred to as a democracy. The army training manual taught the truth back then. Now it is totally different. Seldom do you hear that America is a Republic. Usually, now we are referred to as a democracy by the schools and media and by even elected officials who should know better.

Bastiat, Fredric (French Economist and author of *The Law*, which reveals the terrible effects of socialism on the French people, a warning to other nations): *"The people will be crushed under the burden of taxes, loan after loan will be floated; after having drained the present, the State will devour the future."*

Benson, Ezra Taft (Former Secretary of Agriculture under Eisenhower, former President of the Church of Jesus Christ of Latter Day Saints, author of several books that stand for freedom and expose the enemy such as *An Enemy Hath Done This*, all about the United Nations):

   *"**A secret combination** that seeks to overthrow the freedom of all lands, nations, and countries is increasing its evil influence and control over America and the entire world."* (Taken from a talk given at an October, LDS Church General Conference in 1988 and written up in the Church Magazine, *the Ensign*, November, 1988, p. 87.)

Christian Science Monitor **editorial** (June 19th, 1920): *"What is important is to dwell upon the increasing evidence of the existence of a **secret conspiracy**, throughout the world, for the destruction of organized government and the letting loose of evil."*

   (September 1, 1961): *"The directors of the CFR (Council on Foreign Relations) make up a sort of Presidium for that part of the Establishment that guides our destiny as a nation."*

Churchhill, Winston, *(Former Prime Minister of England): "From the days of Spartacus-Weishaupt to those of Karl Marx, to those of Trotsky, Bela Kun, Rosa Luxembourg, and Emma Goldman, this **world wide conspiracy for the overthrow of civilization** and for the reconstitution of society on the basis of arrested development, of envious malevolence and impossible equality, has been steadily growing. It played a definitely recognizable role in the tragedy of the French Revolution. It has been the mainspring of every subversive movement during the nineteenth century, and now at last this band of extraordinary personalities from the underworld of the great cities of Europe and America have gripped the Russian people by the hair of their heads, and have become practically the undisputed masters of that enormous empire."*

Cumbey, Constance (Christian author of *Hidden Dangers of the Rainbow*): *"One of the most basic plans after the **New World Order** is established is to reduce the world's population from its present 6 billion to 2 billion."*

Dall, Curtis (FDR's son-in-law, from his book, *My Exploited Father-in-Law*): *"For a long time I felt that FDR had developed many thoughts and ideas that were his own to benefit this country, the United States. But, he didn't. Most of his thoughts, his political ammunition, as it were, were carefully manufactured for him in advance by the **Council on Foreign Relations—One World Money group**. Brilliantly, with great gusto, like a fine piece of artillery, he exploded that prepared "ammunition" in the middle of an unsuspecting target, the American people, and thus paid off and returned his internationalist political support.*

*The depression was the calculated 'shearing' of the public by the **World Money powers,** triggered by the planned sudden shortage of supply of call money in the New York money market . . . . The **One World Government** leaders and their ever close bankers have now acquired full control of the money and credit machinery of the U.S. via the creation of the privately owned Federal Reserve Bank.*

*The UN is but a long-range, international banking apparatus clearly set up for financial and economic profit by a small group of powerful **One-World revolutionaries,** hungry for profit and power."*

Demille, Oliver, and Lockhart, Keith (authors, researchers and educators. They co-authored **The New World Order**, *Choosing Between Christ and Satan in the Last Days*): *"There are many reasons why a **New World Order** is undesirable:*

*First, It is anathema to Christianity and freedom. It is based on the false and wicked philosophies of socialism and humanism . . . Promoters of the **New World Order** promise that it will eradicate the problems of war, poverty, famine, and disease. All that people must do is give up their freedom . . . This is . . . Satan's original plan . . . 'Give up your agency and I will force you all to live in peace and harmony.'*

Second, the New World Order abolishes the Constitution of the United States . . . and all the principles upon which it is based.

*Third, the New World Order model concentrates too much power in one government entity, meaning it would eventually become tyrannical. Even if it was set up with good intentions, world government would only be possible if all nations relinquished sovereignty; this would give the **New World Order** absolute power. Sooner or later someone in power would abuse it . . . A government powerful enough to rule the world would be too gigantic to stop it if it became tyrannical.*

Fourth, the New World Order is sponsored by men who are already corrupt and tyrannical. Indeed the very reason that they want a New World Order is that it will give them unlimited wealth and power over others. Their motives and plans are Satanic and evil.

Fifth, Finally, the New World Order restricts freedom; freedom of worship, freedom of speech, freedom of action, and any other freedoms that those in power might desire. Citizens of the New World Order will be slaves, property of the government, and their lives will depend on the whims of their masters." [567]

Disraeli, Benjamin (Former Prime Minister of England, from a novel he published in 1844 called *Coningsby, the New Generation):* "*The world is governed by very different personages from what is imagined by those who are not behind the scenes.*" "*The governments of the present day have to deal not merely with other governments, with emperors, kings and ministers, but also with the **secret societies** which have everywhere their unscrupulous agents, and can at the last moment upset all the governments' plans.*"

Fagan, Myron (Playwright who wrote plays to expose the conspiracy and the Illuminati. He was most responsible for exposing the many Communists that had infiltrated Hollywood): "*The idea was that those who direct the overall conspiracy could use the differences in those two so-called ideologies [marxism/ fascism/socialism v. democracy/ capitalism] to enable them [the Illuminati] to divide larger and larger portions of the human race into opposing camps so that they could be armed and then brainwashed into fighting and destroying each other.*"

Frankfurter, Felix (Supreme Court Justice, 1952): "*The real rulers in Washington are invisible and exercise power from behind the scenes.*"

Fulbright, Senator William, (Former chairman of the US Senate Foreign Relations Committee, stated at a 1963 symposium entitled: The Elite and the Electorate—Is Government by the People Possible?): "*The case for **government by elites** is irrefutable.*"

Fuller, J.F.C (Major General, British military historian, 1941): "*The government of the Western nations, whether monarchical or republican, had passed into the invisible hands of a **plutocracy**, international in power and grasp. It was, I venture to suggest, this **semi-occult power** which . . . . pushed the mass of the American people into the cauldron of World War I.*"

Goldwater, Senator Barry (Written in his book, *With No Apologies*, published in 1994): "*The Trilateral Commission is intended to be the vehicle for multinational consolidation of the commercial and banking interests by seizing control of the political government of the United States. The Trilateral Commission represents a skillful, coordinated effort to seize control and consolidate the four centers of power: political, monetary, intellectual and ecclesiastical. What the Trilateral Commission intends is to create a **worldwide economic power** superior to the political governments of the nation states involved. As managers and creators of the system, they will rule the future.*"

Golitsyn, Anatoliy (Former member of the KGB, who defected to America, author): "*The Soviet transition to a new political structure shows that the Soviet strategists are thinking, planning and acting in broad terms, way beyond the imagination of Western politicians. For this reason Western politicians cannot grasp the fact that the Soviet intention is to **win by 'democratic'** means. Through transition to a new system, the Soviets are revitalizing their own people and institutions, and they are succeeding. Contrary to Western belief, they are holding their ranks together.*"

"*The Soviet strategy of 'perestroika' must be exposed because it is deceptive, aggressive and dangerous. Gorbachev and 'glastnost' have failed to reveal that 'perestroika' is a world-wide political assault against the Western democracies . . . . It must be revealed that 'perestroika' is . . . not just Soviet domestic renewal but a strategy for 'restructuring' the whole world . . . . Gorbachev's renunciation of ideological orthodoxy is not sincere or lasting, but a tactical manoeuvre in the cause of the strategy. The Soviets are not striving for genuine, lasting accommodation with the Western democracies but for **the final world victory of Communism** . . .*" *(The Perestroika Deception, 1990)*

Harpers, July, 1958: "*The most powerful clique in these (CFR) groups have one objective in common: they want to bring about the surrender of the sovereignty and the national independence of the U.S. They want to end national boundaries and racial and ethnic loyalties supposedly to increase business and ensure world peace. What they strive for would inevitably lead to dictatorship and loss of freedoms by the people. The CFR was founded for "the purpose of promoting disarmament and submergence of U.S. sovereignty and national independence into an all-powerful **one-world government**.*"

Huxley, Aldous (author of **Brave New World,** stated in "*Brave New World Revisited,*" 1958): "*In 1931, when **Brave New World** was being written, I was* *convinced that there was still plenty of time. The completely organized society, the scientific caste system, the abolition of free will by methodical conditioning, the servitude made acceptable by regular doses of chemically induced happiness, the orthodoxies drummed in by nightly courses of sleep-teaching—these things were coming all right, but not in my time, not even in the time of my grandchildren . . . . Twenty-seven years later, . . . I feel a good deal less optimistic . . . In the West, . . . individual men and women still enjoy a large measure of freedom. But . . . this freedom and even the desire for this freedom seem to be on the wane."*

Hylan, John F. (Former New York City Mayor, 1922): *"The real menace of our republic is this **invisible government** which like a giant octopus sprawls its slimy length over city, state and nation. Like the octopus of real life, it operates under cover of a self created screen . . . . At the head of this octopus are the Rockefeller Standard Oil interests and a small group of powerful banking houses generally referred to as international bankers. The little coterie of powerful international bankers virtually run the United States government for their own selfish purposes. They practically control both political parties."*

Inouye, Senator Daniel K., (Democrat Senator from Hawaii. The following was said during the Iran-Contra scandal): *"There exists a shadowy government with its own Air Force, its own Navy, its own fundraising mechanism, and the ability to pursue its own ideas of the national interest, free from all checks and balances, and free from the law itself."*

Jefferson, Thomas (Writer of the Declaration of Independence, Third President of the United States): *"Peace, commerce, and honest friendship with all nations—**entangling alliances** with none."*[568]

Jefferson, Thomas, (1816) *"If the American people ever allow private banks to control the issue of their currency, first by inflation and then by deflation, the banks and corporations that will grow up around them will deprive the people of all property until their children wake up homeless on the continent their fathers conquered."*

Jefferson, Thomas, *"To compel a man to furnish contributions of money for the propagation of opinions which he disbelieves and abhors is sinful and tyrannical."*

Jefferson, Thomas, *"Single acts of tyranny may be ascribed to the accidental opinion of a day. But a series of oppressions, begun at a distinguished period, and pursued* *unalterably through every change of ministers (administrations), too plainly proves a deliberate systematic plan of reducing us to slavery."*

Jenner, William (Senator in a speech in 1954): *"Today the path of **total dictatorship** in the United States can be laid by strictly legal means, unseen and unheard by the Congress, the President, or the people. Outwardly we have a Constitutional government, but we have operating within our government and political system another body representing another form of government—a **bureaucratic elite, which believes our constitution is outmoded."***

Estulin, Daniel (Author of *The Bilderbergers*): *"the Council on Foreign Relations creates and delivers psycho-political operations by manipulating people's reality through a 'tactic of deception,' placing Council members on both sides of an issue. The deception is complete when the public is led to believe that its own best interests are being served while the CFR policy is being carried out."*[569]

Kennedy, Joseph, (Father of JFK, Bobby and Ted Kennedy): *"**Fifty men** have run America, and that's a high figure."* (Written in the July 26th, 1936, issue of *The New York Times*.)

McConkie, Bruce R. (Author, Leader in the Church of Jesus Christ of Latter Day Saints): *"Satan himself is the man of sin (2 Thess. 1:2-12) who rules the **secret combinations and governments of the New World Order**. The church of the devil is every false religion . . . whether parading under a Christian or a pagan banner . . . It is **secret combinations, oath-bound societies,** and the great world force of **godless Communism.**"*[570]

McDonald, Congressman Larry P. (Spoken in 1976. He was killed shortly thereafter in the Korean Airlines 747 that was shot down by the Soviets): *"The drive of the Rockefellers and their allies is to create a **one-world government combining supercapitalism and Communism** under the same tent, all under their control . . . . Do I mean **conspiracy**? Yes I do. I am convinced there is such a plot, international in scope, generations old in planning, and incredibly evil in intent."*

Mencken, H.L. (Journalist for the *Baltimore Morning Herald* and the *Baltimore Sun*, Author of *The American Language*): *"The urge to save humanity is almost always a false front for the urge to rule."*

Mencken, H.L (journalist, social critic): *"The whole aim of practical politics is to* **keep the populace alarmed**—*and hence clamorous to be led to safety—by menacing it with an endless series of hobgoblins, all of them imaginary."*

Miller, Arthur Selwyn, (Professor, Rockefeller-funded historian, spoken in 1987): *" . . . the fact is that the existence of the* **Establishment**—**the ruling class** *is not supposed to be discussed. A third secret is . . . . that there is really only one political party of any consequence in the United States . . . . The Republicans and the Democrats are in fact two branches of the same* **(secret) party.***"*

Pope John Paul I (Was Pope in 1978, only served 33 days and died perhaps of a heart attack): *"The historical experience of socialist countries has sadly demonstrated that* **collectivism** *does not do away with alienation but rather increases it, adding to it a lack of basic necessities and economic inefficiency."*

Quigley, Carroll (Former Professor at Georgetown University, mentor of Bill Clinton, author of book *Tragedy and Hope*, 1966): *"There does exist and has existed for a generation, an* **international** *. . .* **network** *which operates, to some extent, in the way the radical right believes the Communists act. In fact, this network, which we may identify as the* **Round Table Groups**, *has no aversion to cooperating with the* **Communists**, *or any other groups and frequently does so. I know of the operations of this* **network** *because I have studied it for twenty years and was permitted for two years, in the early 1960s, to examine its papers and secret records. I have no aversion to it or to most of its aims and have, for much of my life, been close to it and to many of its instruments. I have objected, both in the past and recently, to a few of its policies . . . but in general my chief difference of opinion is that it wishes to remain unknown, and I believe its role in history is significant enough to be known."*

"The powers of financial capitalism had another far reaching aim, nothing less than to create a **world system of financial control** *in private hands able to dominate the political system of each country and the economy of the world as a whole. This system was to be controlled in a feudalist fashion by the central banks of the world acting in concert, by secret agreements, arrived at in frequent private meetings and conferences. The apex of the system was the Bank for International Settlements in Basle, Switzerland, a private bank owned and controlled by the world's central banks which were themselves private corporations. The growth of financial capitalism made possible a* **centralization of world economic control** *and use of this power for the direct benefit of financiers and the indirect injury of all other economic groups."* (*Tragedy and Hope: A History of the World in Our Time* (Macmillan Company, New York, 1966.)

(Note: The Macmillan Company stopped printing the book shortly after it was published. Perhaps they were told to stop. Perhaps the book revealed too much about the secret elite who were really running the government. The elite did not have all their ducks in a row back in 1966. However, at our present day, 2009, much more can be revealed, because, as has already been mentioned, the elite think there is no stopping them now. Quigley's book is available through Radio Liberty and Dr. Stan Monteith, who was able to get the rights to print it again. Call 831-464-8295.)

Orwell, George (Author of best selling novel, *1984,* written back in 1949, as a warning to Americans of what the elitists had in store for us): *"The Party seeks entirely for its own sake. We are not interested in the good of others; we are interested solely in power. Not wealth or luxury or long life or happiness; only power, pure power . . . . Power is not a means; it is an end.* **One does not establish a dictatorship in order to safeguard a revolution; one makes the revolution in order to establish the dictatorship . . . .** *If you want a picture of the future, imagine a boot stamping on a human face—forever." (Spoken by one of the characters in the book, O'Brien to Winston.)*[571]

Reagan, Ronald (former President of the United States from 1981-1989): *"If we forget what we did, we won't know who we are. I'm warning of an eradication of the American memory that could result, ultimately, in an erosion of the American spirit.". . . "Freedom is never more than one generation away from extinction. We didn't pass it on to our children in the bloodstream. It must be fought for, protected, and handed on for them to do the same, or one day we will spend our sunset years telling our children what it was once like in the United States when men were free."* **(/Heritage/RonaldReagan.html"**Ronald Reagan**)**

Robbins, J.H. (I can find no background information about who J.H. Robbins is, but the quote is so true warning us about the environmental movement that I am including it.): *"Protecting the Environment is a ruse. The goal is the political and economic subjugation of most men by the few, under the guise of preserving nature."*

Robinson, John (Professor of Natural Philosophy at Edinburgh, Scotland, a historian, and Secretary General to the Royal Society of Edinburgh, author of a book exposing the Illuminati, ***Proofs of a Conspiracy—Against all the Religions and Governments of Europe Carried on in the Secret Meetings of Freemasons, Illuminati and Reading Societies, 1798):***

*"I have observed these doctrines gradually diffusing and mixing with all different systems of Freemasonry till, at last, an association has been formed for the express purpose of rooting out all the religious establishments, and overturning all the existing governments of Europe, the leaders would **rule the World** with uncontrollable power, while all the rest would be employed as tools of the ambition of their unknown superiors."*[572]

Roosevelt, Franklin D. (From a letter written to Colonel House, November 21st, 1933): *"The real truth of the matter is, as you and I know, that a **financial element in the larger centers has owned the Government ever since the days of Andrew Jackson.**"*

Rosenthal, A. M. (*New York Times* Editor and Columnist, written in *The New York Times*, January 1991): *"But it became clear as time went on that in Mr. Bush's mind the **New World Order** was founded on a convergence of goals and interests between the U.S. and the Soviet Union, so strong and permanent that they would work as a team through the U.N. Security Council."*

Rothbard, Murray N. (Economist and author of *The Case Against the Fed*, exposing the Federal Reserve) *"It is easy to be conspicuously compassionate if others are being forced to pay the cost."*

Rothbard, Murray N. *"Behind the honeyed but patently absurd pleas for equality is a ruthless drive for placing the **new elite at the top of a new hierarchy of power.**"*

Rummel, Dr. R.J. (Author of *Death by Government*): *"In total, during the first eighty-eight years of this century, almost 170 million men, women, and children have been shot, beaten, tortured, knifed, burned, starved, frozen, crushed, or worked to death; buried alive, drowned, hung, bombed, or killed in any other of the myriad ways **governments have inflicted death** on unarmed, helpless citizens and foreigners. The dead could conceivably be nearly 360 million people. It is as though our species has been devastated by a modern Black Plague. And indeed it has, but **a plague of Power**, not of germs."*

Schmidt, Helmut (Former Chancellor of West Germany, author of *Men and Power*): He referred to the CFR as the *"**foreign policy elite,** which prepared people for 'top-level missions in government."* *"... it had a very silent but effective way of seeing to its own succession."*

Shannon William H. (A priest of the Diocese of Rochester, a free-lance writer, founder of the International Thomas Merton Society and professor emeritus at the Nazareth College in Rochester, New York): *"In the final months of 2007 we are witnessing the stupendous success of the Big Three's [CFR, Bilderbergers and Trilateral Commission] strategy for **planetary economic hegemony** as the cacophony of their **carefully engineered global economic cataclysm** reverberates across America and around the world. It was never about buyers who didn't read the fine print when taking out liar loans. It was always about silver-tongued, ruling elite politicians and central bankers, anointed by the **shadow government**, who ultimately and skillfully stole and continue to steal governments from people and replace them with **transnational corporations**."*[573]

Shoup, Laurence H. and Minter, William (Professors who wrote a study of the CFR, "Imperial Brain Trust: The CFR and United States Foreign Policy" printed in *Monthly Review Press*, 1977): *"The planning of the UN can be traced to the **secret steering committee** established by Secretary [of State Cordell] Hull in January 1943. All of the members of this secret committee, with the exception of Hull, a Tennessee politician, were members of the Council on Foreign Relations. They saw Hull regularly to plan, select, and guide the labors of the [State] Departments Advisory Committee. It was, in effect, the coordinating agency for all the State Departments postwar planning."*

Stooksbury, Clark (Journalist, Assistant Editor of Liberty Magazine): *"They [the socialist elite] want timid, helpless people who are anxious to get in touch with their inner child, enter twelve-step programs, and run to the government with every little problem."*

Ward, Chester, (Former Admiral in the US Navy, Co-author with Phyllis Schlafly, Kissinger on the Couch, 1975, former member of the CFR, so he knew firsthand what the agenda was): *"The most **powerful cliques in these elitist groups** have one objective in common: they want to bring about the surrender of the sovereignty and national independence of the United States."*

Washington, George (General of the Revolutionary War, First President of the United States): *"It is our true policy to **steer clear of permanent alliances** with any portion of the foreign world."*

Washington, George (Spoken after Washington received a book about the Illuminati written by the Scottish Professor John Robison, *Proofs of a*

Conspiracy, exposing the **Illuminati** for the evil organization that it is.): "*It is not my intention to doubt that the doctrine of the **Illuminati** and the principles of Jacobinism had not spread in the United States. On the contrary, no one is more satisfied of this fact than I am.*" He also added "*They would shake the government to its foundations.*"[574]

Wilson, Woodrow (Former President of the United States, author of *The New Freedom*, written in 1913): "*Since I entered politics, I have chiefly had men's views confided to me privately. Some of the biggest men in the United States, in the Field of commerce and manufacture, are afraid of something. They know that there is a **power** somewhere so organized, so subtle, so watchful, so interlocked, so complete, so **pervasive**, that they better not speak above their breath when they speak in condemnation of it.*"

Wilson, Woodrow (Former President of the United States, 1919. Some historians say this statement was made shortly after Ellen, his first wife died in August of 1914. Perhaps he was feeling remorseful; his conscience was pricking him as he contemplated his own death and having to stand before his maker and give an accounting of what he had done. Most historians believe Wilson is referring in this quote to the Federal Reserve, which he signed into law in 1913. He always regretted having done so.) "*I am a most unhappy man. I have unwittingly ruined my country. A great industrial nation is controlled by its system of credit. Our system of credit is concentrated. The growth of the nation, therefore, and all our activities are in the hands of a few men. We have come to be one of the worst ruled, one of the most completely controlled and dominated governments in the civilized world. No longer a government by free opinion, no longer a government by conviction and the vote of the majority, but a government by the opinion and duress of a small group of dominant men.*"

Part 2—Statements Promoting: 1) New World Order / One-World Government; 2) Regional/Integrated Government/against Nationalism; 3) Socialism/Communism/ Leftist Democracy; 4) One-World Economic Control; 5) One-World Religion; 6) Against the Free Enterprise System; 7)World Environmental Controls Against Humans and Property Rights; 8) Population Control; 9) Gun Control; 10) Quotes Against a Free Press; 11) Mind Control

1) *New World Order / One-World Government/ Support of United Nations*

Blair, Tony (Fabian) (Former Prime Minister of Great Britain, Tuesday, October 2, 2001, Speaking about the 911 tragedy): *"This is a moment to seize. The kaleidoscope has been shaken, the pieces are in flux, soon they will settle again. Before they do, let us re-order this world around us."*

Blair, Tony (Spoken January 5, 2002): *"Other countries will not take lectures about the so-called new world order from a British prime minister who cannot deliver basic public services run by his own failing government."*

Biden, Joseph R. Jr, (CFR) (Former Senator, Vice President to President Obama): *"How I Learned to Love the New World Order"* (Article in *The Wall Street Journal*, April 1992.)

Biden, Joseph, R. Jr. (CFR) (Given in a speech in Clayton Hall, University of Delaware, October 29, 1992, during United Nations Week. His speech was entitled *"On the Threshold of the New World Order: A Rebirth for the United Nations."*) *"Thus, in setting an American agenda for a new world order, we must begin with a profound alteration in traditional thought . . . Collective security today must encompass not only the security of nations, but also mankind's security in a global environment that has proven vulnerable to debilitating changes wrought by man's own endeavors."*

Brandt, Willy, (B) (Former West German Chancellor, who resigned because one of his top personal staff members, Günther Guillaume, admitted to being a communist spy. People were suspicious that maybe Brandt was as well. Others said he resigned to avoid a looming sex scandal from being revealed.): *"The New World Order is a world that has a supernational authority to regulate world commerce and industry; an international organization that would control the production and consumption of oil; an international currency that would replace the dollar; a World Development Fund that would make funds available to free and Communist nations alike; and an international police force to enforce the edicts of the New World Order."*

Brzezinski, Zbigniew, (CFR, TC, B) (National Security Advisor to President Jimmy Carter, advisor to many presidents, including Obama): *" . . . This regionalization is in keeping with the Tri-Lateral Plan which calls for a gradual convergence of East and West, ultimately leading toward the goal of 'one world government' . . . . National sovereignty is no longer a viable concept . . ."*

Bush, George H. (CFR, TC, B, Skull and Bones), Former President of the United States: *"Out of these troubled times, our fifth objective—a **new world order**—can emerge . . . We are now in sight of a United Nations that performs as envisioned by its founders."* (September 11, 1990, Televised Address)

*"If we do not follow the dictates of our inner moral compass and stand up for human life, then this lawlessness will threaten the peace and democracy of the emerging **new world order** we now see, this long dreamed-of vision we've all worked toward for so long."* (January 1991)

*"Ultimately, our objective is to welcome the Soviet Union back into **the world order**. Perhaps the **world order** of the future will truly be a family of nations."* (Speaking at Texas A&M University, 1989)

*"We will succeed in the Gulf. And when we do, the world community will have sent an enduring warning to any dictator or despot, present or future, who contemplates outlaw aggression. The world can therefore seize this opportunity to fulfill the long-held promise of a **new world order**—where brutality will go unrewarded, and aggression will meet collective resistance."* (State of the Union Address, 1991)

*"I think that what's at stake here is **the new world order**. What's at stake here is whether we can have disputes peacefully resolved in the future by a reinvigorated United Nations."* (January 7, 1991, Interview on U.S. News and World Report)

*"And that **world order** is only going to be enhanced if this newly activated peace-keeping function of the United Nations proves to be effective. That is the only way the **new world order** will be enhanced."* (January 9, 1991, Press Conference)

*"The world can therefore seize the opportunity (the Persian Gulf crisis) to fulfill the long held promise of a **New World Order** where diverse nations are drawn together in common cause to achieve the universal aspirations of mankind."* ("State of the Union Address," January 29, 1991.)

*"For two centuries we've done the hard work of freedom. And tonight we lead the world in facing down a threat to decency and humanity. What is at stake is more than one small country, it is a big idea—**a new world order,** where diverse nations are drawn together in common cause to achieve the universal aspirations of mankind: peace and security, freedom, and the rule of law. Such is a world worthy of our struggle, and worthy of our children's future."* (*State of the Union Address,* 1991)

*"In the Gulf War, we saw the United Nations playing the role dreamed of by its founders . . . I hope history will record that the Gulf crisis was the crucible of the **new world order**."* (August, 1991, National Security Strategy of the United States, signed by George Bush) [575]

Bush, George H: "*It is the sacred principles enshrined in the **United Nations** charter to which the American people will henceforth pledge their allegiance.*" (Addressing the General Assembly of the U.N., February 1,1992).

Castro, Fidel (Communist Dictator of Cuba): "*We must establish **a new world order** based on justice, on equity, and on peace.*" (Address to the United Nations, 1979.)

Congress on World Federation: "*If totalitarianism wins this conflict, the world will be ruled by tyrants, and individuals will be slaves. If democracy wins, the nations of the earth will be united in a commonwealth of free peoples, and individuals, wherever found, will be the sovereign units of the **new world order**.*" ("The **Declaration** of the Federation of the **World**," adopted by the Legislatures of North Carolina (1941), New Jersey (1942), Pennsylvania (1943), and possibly other states.)

Falk, Richard A., (A writer and author, professor emeritus at Princeton in International Law) He wrote the following in an article entitled "**Toward a New World Order**: Modest Methods and Drastic Visions." It is also written in his book ***Toward a Just World Order*** (1975): "*The existing order is breaking down at a very rapid rate, and the main uncertainty is whether mankind can exert a positive role in shaping a new world order or is doomed to await collapse in a passive posture. We believe **a new order** will be born no later than early in the next century and that the death throes of the old and the birth pangs of the new will be a testing time for the human species.*"

Gardner, Richard N. (CFR, TTC) (Former ambassador, member of the State Department, Professor of law and international organization at Columbia, author of ***Pursuit of World Order***: US Foreign Policy and International Organization, 1965): "*If instant **world government**, Charter review, and a greatly strengthened International Court do not provide the answers, what hope for progress is there? The answer will not satisfy those who seek simple solutions to complex problems, but it comes down essentially to this: The hope for the foreseeable future lies, not in building up a few ambitious central institutions of universal membership and general jurisdiction as was envisaged at the end of the last war, but rather in the much more decentralized, disorderly and pragmatic process of inventing or adapting institutions of limited jurisdiction and selected membership to deal with specific problems on a case-by-case basis . . .*"

*In short, the **house of world order** will have to be built from the bottom up rather than from the top down. It will look like a great booming, buzzing confusion, to use William James famous description of reality, but an end run around national sovereignty, eroding it piece by piece, will accomplish much more than the old-fashioned frontal assault."* (**"The Hard Road to World Order,"** *Foreign Affairs*, April, 1974)

Gephardt, Richard, (CFR) (Democrat Congressman from Missouri): *"We can see beyond the present shadows of war in the Middle East to a **new world order** where the strong work together to deter and stop aggression. This was precisely Franklin Roosevelt's and Winston Churchill's vision for peace for the post-war period."* (*The Wall Street Journal* (September, 1990)

Gorbachev, Mikhail (COR, B) (Former President of the Soviet Union, now heads up an environmental group called "State of the World Forum." He co-authored the Earth Charter with Maurice Strong. The charter calls for **world government** and a new spirituality—one-world religion.) November 2, 1987, he addressed the Soviet Politburo and said the following:

*"In October 1917, we parted with the old world, rejecting it once and for all. We are moving toward a **new world, the world of Communism**. We shall never turn off that road! . . . Comrades, do not be concerned about all that you hear about glasnost and perestroika and democracy in the coming years. These are primarily for outward consumption. There will be no significant internal change within the Soviet Union other than for cosmetic purposes. **Our purpose is to disarm the Americans and let them fall asleep."***

*"Further global progress is now possible only through a quest for universal consensus in the movement towards a **new world order."*** (Spoken in an address at the United Nations, December, 1988, shortly after, the Berlin Wall came down and the Soviet Union was dissolved and communism "supposedly" was dead.)

Gore, Al, (CFR, B, Vice President to Clinton. The following quote was spoken by Gore in Marrakech, Morocco, April, 1994. He was there for the signing of a new world trade agreement. He arrived just a few hours after U.S. planes that were enforcing an allied no fly zone over northern Iraq accidentally shot down two U.S. helicopters, killing 15 Americans and 11 foreign officials): *"I want to extend condolences, to the families of those who died **in the service of the United Nations**."* (LA. Times, 6/12/94)

Hitler, Adolph, Supreme Fuhrer of Germany leading up to World War II: *"National Socialism will use its own revolution for establishing of a **new world order**."*

Howard, Jonathan Winston: Prime Minister of Australia, March 13, 2003, in a National Address: *"The decade of the nineteen nineties was meant to have been one in which a **new world international order**, free of the by-polar rivalry of earlier days, was to have been established."*

Humanist Manifesto II (written in 1973): *"We deplore the division of humankind on nationalistic grounds. We have reached a turning point in human history where the best option is to transcend the limits of national sovereignty and to move towards the building of a **world community** . . . We look to the development of a system of **world law and a world order** based upon transnational federal government."*(*The Humanist*, September/October, 1973.)

Humphrey, Hubert H. (Vice President with President Lyndon Johnson, presidential candidate against Richard Nixon): *"A New World Order"*—Title of his commencement address at the University of Pennsylvania, printed in the *Pennsylvania Gazette* (June, 1977)

Kissinger, Henry (CFR, TC, B) Former Secretary of State for President Richard Nixon, Advisor to many presidents, Nobel Peace Prize Winner: *"NAFTA is a major stepping stone to the **New World Order**."* (Spoken when campaigning for the passage of NAFTA.)

*"Two centuries ago our forefathers brought forth a new nation; now we must join with others to bring forth a **new world order**."* The Declaration of Interdependence, 1976

*"Our nation is uniquely endowed to play a creative and decisive role in **the new order** which is taking form around us."* (Henry Kissinger quoted in the *Seattle Post Intelligence*, 1975.)

*"My country's history, Mr. President, tells us that it is possible to fashion unity while cherishing diversity, that common action is possible despite the variety of races, interests, and beliefs we see here in this chamber. Progress and peace and justice are attainable. So we say to all peoples and governments: Let us fashion together a **new world order**."* (Henry Kissinger, in address before the General Assembly of the United Nations, October, 1975,)

Kissinger, Henry: *"Today, America would be outraged if U.N. troops entered Los Angeles to restore order. Tomorrow they will be grateful! This is especially true* *if they were told that there were an outside threat from beyond, whether real or promulgated, that threatened our very existence. It is then that all peoples of the world will plead to deliver them from this evil. The one thing every man fears is the unknown. When presented with this scenario, individual rights will be willingly relinquished for the guarantee of their well-being granted to them by the* **World Government.***"* (Bilderberger Conference, Evians, France, 1991.)

"*How to Achieve* **The New World Order,**" Title of book excerpt by Henry Kissinger, in *Time* magazine (March 1994.)

Kissinger, Henry, "*The president-elect is coming into office at a moment when there is upheaval in many parts of the world simultaneously. You have India, Pakistan; you have the jihadist movement. So he can't really say there is one problem, that it's the most important one. But he can give new impetus to American foreign policy partly because the reception of him is so extraordinary around the world. His task will be to develop an overall strategy for America in this period when, really,* **a new world order** *can be created. It's a great opportunity, it isn't just a crisis.*" (January 6, 2009, PBS Interview with Charlie Rose as reported on *World Net Daily*, by Drew Zahn)

"*Obama's task will be to develop an over-all strategy for America in this period, when really a* **'new world order'** *can be created.*" (Interview on CNBC as reported in *The New American*, April 27, 2009)

Kissinger, Henry A. "The chance for a **new world order**" (*New York Times,* January 12, 2009), (Essentially Kissinger is saying that the reason the world is facing a global financial crisis is because nation states have tried to solve their own problems on their own. It has failed. We must have a global financial system leading to a global political system)

"*An* **international order** *will emerge if a system of compatible priorities comes into being. It will fragment disastrously if the various priorities cannot be reconciled . . . The alternative to a new international order is chaos . . .*

The financial collapse exposed the mirage. It made evident the **absence of global institutions to cushion the shock and to reverse the trend.** *Inevitably, when the affected publics turned to their national political institutions, these were driven principally by domestic politics, not considerations of* **world order.***

International order *will not come about either in the political or economic field until there emerge general rules toward which countries can orient themselves . . .*

In the end, the **political and economic systems can be harmonized** *in only one of two ways: by creating an* **international political regulatory system** *with the same reach as that of the economic world; or by shrinking the economic units to* *a size manageable by existing political structures, which is likely to lead to a new mercantilism, perhaps of* **regional units.**

A new Bretton Woods-kind of global agreement is by far the preferable outcome. *America's role in this enterprise will be decisive. Paradoxically, American influence will be great in proportion to the modesty in our conduct; we need to modify the righteousness that has characterized too many American attitudes, especially since the collapse of the Soviet Union.*

McGovern, George (Former Democrat Senator from South Dakota, presidential candidate against Nixon): *"I would support a Presidential candidate who pledged to take the following steps: . . . At the end of the war in the Persian Gulf, press for a comprehensive Middle East settlement and for a* **new world order** *based not on Pax Americana but on peace through law with a stronger U.N. and World Court."* (*The New York Times*, February, 1991)

Mandela, Nelson (Former president of South Africa, Winner of Nobel Peace Prize for ending Apartheid in Africa): *"The* **new world order** *that is in the making must focus on the creation of a world of democracy, peace and prosperity for all."* (*The Philadelphia Inquirer* (October 1994)

Mubarak, Hosni, (President of Egypt): *"The renewal of the nonproliferation treaty was described as important for the welfare of the whole world and the* **new world order**." (*New York Times,* April, 1995)

Safire, William (Former speech writer for President Nixon, became a columnist for the New York Times, In this statement he is referring to the many times that President Bush used the term 'new world order' and thinks we should give him credit for coining it even though it appeared much earlier in history, even going back to Hitler and FDR): *" . . . its Bush's baby, even if he shares its popularization with Gorbachev. Forget the Hitler new order root; F.D.R. used the phrase earlier."* (*The New York Times* (February, 1991)

New York Times (Written November, 1975): *"At the old Inter-American Office in the Commerce Building here in Roosevelt's time, as Assistant Secretary of State for Latin American Affairs under President Truman, as chief whip with Adlai Stevenson and Tom Finletter at the founding of the United Nations in San Francisco, Nelson Rockefeller was in the forefront of the struggle to establish not only an American system of political and economic security but* **a new world order.**"

New York Times (April 1994): *"The Final Act of the Uruguay Round, marking the conclusion of the most ambitious trade negotiation of our century, will give birth—in Morocco—to the World Trade Organization, the third pillar of the **New World Order**, along with the United Nations and the International Monetary Fund."* (Part of full-page advertisement by the government of Morocco.)

New York Times (written October, 1940, **"New World Order Pledged to Jews,"**): *"In the first public declaration on the Jewish question since the outbreak of the war, Arthur Greenwood, member without portfolio in the British War Cabinet, assured the Jews of the United States that when victory was achieved an effort would be made to found **a new world order** based on the ideals of justice and peace."*

Nixon, Richard (CFR, B) (Former President of the United): *"He [President Nixon] spoke of the talks as a beginning, saying nothing more about the prospects for future contacts and merely reiterating the belief he brought to China that both nations share an interest in peace and building '**a new world order**."* (Excerpt from an article in *The New York Times* (February, 1972)

*"The developing coherence of Asian regional thinking is reflected in a disposition to consider problems and loyalties in regional terms, and to evolve regional approaches to development needs and to the evolution of **a new world order**."* (Richard Nixon, in *Foreign Affairs,* October, 1967)

Ohmae, Kenichi (Political reform leader in Japan): *"**New World Order:** The Rise of the Region-State"*—Title of article written by Kenichi in *The Wall Street Journal* (August 1994)

Pope John Paul II, (Karl Wojtyla): *"By the end of this decade (2000 AD) we will live under the first **One World Government** that has ever existed in the society of nations . . . a government with absolute authority to decide the basic issues of human survival. **One world government** is inevitable."* (As quoted by Malachi Martin in the book, *The Keys of This Blood.*)

Rockefeller, David, (CFR, TC, B) (Sspeaking at the Business Council for the United Nations, September 14, 1994.): *"We are on the verge of a global transformation. All we need is the right major crisis and the nations will accept the **New World Order** . . . But this present window of opportunity, during which a truly peaceful and interdependent world order might be built, will not be open for long. Already there are powerful forces at work that threaten to destroy all of our hopes and efforts to erect an enduring structure of **global interdependence**."*

Rockefeller, Nelson (CFR) (Former Governor of New York and Vice President under Gerald Ford; from a talk Rockefeller gave at Harvard, "Rockefeller Bids Free Lands Unite: Calls at Harvard for Drive to Build **New World Order**," *The New York Times*, February, 1962): *"The United Nations has not been able—nor can it be able—to shape a **new world order** which events so compellingly demand . . . The **new world order** that will answer economic, military, and political problems, urgently requires, I believe, that the United States take the leadership among all free peoples to make the underlying concepts and aspirations of national sovereignty truly meaningful through the federal approach."*

Roper, Elmo (Part of the Atlantic Union Committee that helped form NATO): *"For it becomes clear that the first step toward **world government** cannot be completed until we have advanced on the four fronts: the economic, the military, the political and the social . . . the Atlantic pact [NATO] need not be our last effort toward greater unity . . . It can be one of the most positive moves in the direction of **One World**."*[576]

Schlesinger, Arthur, Jr. (*Back to the Womb*, July/August 1993 and *Foreign Affairs*, July/August 1995): *"In defense of the **world Order**, U.S. soldiers would have to kill and die. . . . We are not going to achieve a **New World Order** without paying for it in blood, as well as in words and money."*

Scowcroft, Brent, General (CFR, CSIS) (George Bush's National Security Advisor. The following was said on the eve of the Gulf War): *"A colossal event is upon us, the birth of a **New World Order**."*

"We believe we are creating the beginning of a new world order coming out of the collapse of the U.S.-Soviet antagonisms." (August 1990), quoted in *The Washington Post* (May 1991)

The following is taken from a long commencement address that he gave at Brigham Young University, April, 1992, where he mentioned the New World Order seven times:

"... We have perhaps an unparalleled opportunity to help create **a new world order**, one more conducive to the values Americans have held dear for 200 years . . . **A new world order** will appear. The issue is not whether there will be **a new world order**, but whether the nature of **that order** will be shaped significantly by the productive involvement of the United States . . .

We are striving now to take advantage of the current world situation to shape this **new world order** and thus finally to secure peace. The dimensions of our *involvement are primarily three-fold: political, economic, and security, and suggest what the **new world order** can and should become . . .*

*In the political realm, our strategy is to support and encourage the force of **political pluralism** . . . to every culture . . . For the U.S., **interdependence** is not a policy, it is an inescapable fact of our existence . . .*

*One school of thought would be for us to keep the peace and bring about the **new world order** on our own, to be the world's policemen, to provide American solutions everywhere . . . The current forces of **nationalism** alone would bar success for any such hedgemonical design.*

*In sum, **a new world order,** congenial to U.S. interests and values, will not merge by accident. Nor will it emerge by itself. It will take constant attention, effort, and indeed some sacrifice . . . You, all of you, will be involved in this enterprise, whatever path you choose for your own lives."*

(April, 1992, Commencement Address given at Brigham Young University in Provo, Utah. Before his talk, General Scowcroft was given an honorary doctor's degree.)[577]

Talbot, Strobe (CFR) (Former Deputy Secretary of State for Clinton):—*"Within the next hundred years . . . nationhood as we know it will be obsolete; all states will recognize a **single, global authority**. **National sovereignty wasn't such a great idea after all.**"* (*Time Magazine*, July 20th, 1992.)[578]

Thomas, Dr. Augustus O. (President of the World Federation of Education Associations, August 1927, quoted in the book *International Understanding: Agencies Educating for a New World,*1931): *"If there are those who think we are to jump immediately into **a new world order,** actuated by complete understanding and brotherly love, they are doomed to disappointment. If we are ever to approach that time, it will be after patient and persistent effort of long duration. The present international situation of mistrust and fear can only be corrected by a formula of equal status, continuously applied, to every phase of international contacts, until the cobwebs of the old order are brushed out of the minds of the people of all lands."*

Warburg, James, (CFR) (Wealthy banker who helped establish the Federal Reserve; statement to the Senate Foreign Relations Committee on February 17th, l950): *"We shall have **world government** whether or not you like it, by conquest or consent."*

Wells, H.G., (FS) (Author, *The New World Order,* 1939): " *. . . when the struggle seems to be drifting definitely towards a world social democracy, there may* *still be very great delays and disappointments before it becomes an efficient and beneficent world system. Countless people will hate the **new world order** and will die protesting against it. When we attempt to evaluate its promise, we have to bear in mind the distress of a generation or so of malcontents, many of them quite gallant and graceful-looking people."*

Wells, H.G., (FS) (Author, *The Fate of Man,* 1939): *"This World Youth movement claims to represent and affect the politico-social activities of a grand total of forty million adherents—under the age of thirty . . . It may play an important and increasing role in the consolidation of a **new world order**."*

Welles, Sumner (Undersecretary of State for FDR; Article in *The Philadelphia Inquirer,* June, 1942): *"Sumner Welles tonight called for the early creation of an international organization of anti-Axis nations to **control the world** during the period between the armistice at the end of the present war and the setting up of a **new world order** on a permanent basis."*

(2) Quotes Promoting Regional Governments; Against Nationhood and Sovereignty

Brewster, Kingman Jr. (CFR) (Author, wrote in the 50th Anniversary edition of *Foreign Affairs,* 1971, an article entitled, "Reflections on Our National Purpose): *" . . . our purpose should be to do away with our nationality, to take some risks in order to invite some others to pool their sovereignty with ours."*

Bush, George H. (Speaking Before Duke University Graduates, *USA Today,* May 17, 1998): *"The United States must stay involved in the world and we must lead. Today there is a strange coalition at work in Washington and across the country consisting of people on the political right and the political left coming together to keep us from staying involved. Big labor and liberal Democrats are joining some Republicans on the right in calling for America to come home, (saying) we have done our part and that it's time for others to do the heavy lifting on international leadership. **And we must not listen to that siren's call of protection and isolation.**"*

Boutros-Ghali, Boutras, (Former UN Secretary-General, "An Agenda for Peace," 1992): *"The time for absolute and exclusive **sovereignty** . . . **has passed;** its theory was never matched by reality."*

Gaither, H. Rowan Jr, (President Ford Foundation; The following was told to Norman Dodd, who was investigating foundations for the Congressional Reese Commission in 1954): " . . . *all of us here at the policy-making level have had experience with directives . . . from the White House . . . . The substance of them is that we shall use our grant-making power so as to alter our life in the United States that **we can be comfortably merged** with the Soviet Union."*

Gorbachev, Mikhail (Former President of the Soviet Union, before it "collapsed" and communism supposedly "died;" from his book, *Perestroika—New Thinking for Our Country and the World, 1988*): *"It's my conviction that the human race has entered a stage where we are all dependent on each other. No other country or nation should be regarded in total separation from another, let alone pitted against another. That's what our communist vocabulary calls **internationalism** and it means promoting universal human values."*

Lord Lothian (British Ambassador to the United States, taken from a speech entitled "Wings Over History," as reported in the *London Observer*, Sunday, Nov. 27, 1983): *"But though few yet realize it, the old anarchy of multitudinous **national sovereignties is about to dissolve**—and quickly at that. World unity is, of course, at present entirely out of sight. But that the world is going to fall into **four or five main political and economic groups**, each in great measure self-supporting, each under the leadership of a great state equipped with modern military and air power, at any rate for a time, seems certain. Nothing that we can do can prevent it."*

Soros, George (A far-left billionaire stock broker, financier, and philanthropist who has helped found and contributed money to many extreme-left groups such as: the Center for American Progress, MoveOn.Org, Human Rights Watch, Media Matters and the Democrat Party. He also contributed greatly to Obama's campaign. In 2006, he wrote *The Age of Fallibility: Consequences of the War on Terror*, from which this quote comes, found in the Prologue, xv.): *"**Sovereignty** is an anachronistic concept; it has been inherited from an age when kings ruled over their subjects."*

Stalin, Joseph (Supreme Dictator of the Soviet Union): *"Populations will more readily abandon their national loyalties to a vague regional loyalty than they will for a world authority. Later the regionals can be brought all the way into a **single world dictatorship**."*

Toynbee, Arnold (RIIA) (British Professor; the following was spoken June, 1931, in a speech before the Institute for the Study of International Affairs in Copenhagen. It was later published in the RIIA Journal): *"I believe the **monster of sovereignty** is doomed to perish by the sword. We are at present working discreetly with all our might to wrest this mysterious force called **sovereignty** out of the clutches of the local nation states of the world. And all the time we are denying with our lips what we are doing with our hands, because to impugn the sovereignty of the local national states of the world is still a heresy for which a statesman or a publicist can be . . . ostracized or discredited."*

Wright, Quincy (Professor at the University of Chicago, from *the Daily Maroon*, the student newspaper at the University of Chicago): *"In order to establish permanent peace in the world, it is necessary to stop the clustering of all political loyalties around the same symbols. My point was that excessive loyalties to certain sacred cows, such as **sovereignty, nationality, neutrality, and domestic jurisdiction is ruining civilization,**"*[580]

(3) Statements Supporting Socialism/Communism/Democracy:

Fonda, Jane (Movie star, very liberal, known as "Hanoi Jane" for her betrayal of American soldiers during Vietnam; this is a statement from her speech at Michigan State University, 1970): *"I would think that, if you understood what **communism** was, you would hope, you would pray on your knees that we would become **communist**."*

Gorbachev, Mikhail (Former President of the Soviet Union, author): *"Those who hope that we shall move away from the socialist path will be greatly disappointed. Every part of our program of perestroika . . . is fully based on the **principle of more socialism and more democracy** . . . **More socialism means more democracy, openness and collectivism in everyday life** . . . We will proceed toward better socialism rather than away from it. We are saying this honestly, without trying to fool our own people or the world. Any hopes that we will begin to build a different, non-socialist society and go over to the other camp are unrealistic and futile. Those in the West who expect us to give up socialism will be disappointed . . . I would like to be clearly understood . . . we, the Soviet people, are for socialism . . . . **We want more socialism and, therefore, more democracy.**"* (*Perestroika—New Thinking for Our Country and the World*, 1988)

Gorbachev, Mikhail: *"I am a Communist, a convinced Communist! For some that may be a fantasy. But to me it is my main goal."* (*New York Times,* 1989.)

Hayden, Tom (U.S. Congressman): *"**Communism** is one of the options that can improve people's lives." (New York Times,* 1975.)

Manuilskii, Dmitrii Z. (Ukraine Delegate to the UN, the Lenin School on Political Warfare, 1931): *"War to the hilt between **communism** and capitalism is inevitable. Today, of course, we are not strong enough to attack. Our time will come in thirty or forty years. To win, we shall need the element of surprise. The Western world will need to be put to sleep. So we shall begin by launching the **most spectacular peace movement** on record. There shall be electrifying overtures and unheard of concessions. The capitalist countries, stupid and decadent, will rejoice to cooperate to their own destruction. They will leap at another chance to be friends. As soon as their guard is down, we shall smash them with our clenched fist."*

Hitler, Adolph (Supreme Fuhrer of Germany leading up to World War II): *"**National Socialism** will use its own revolution for establishing of a **new world order** . . ." "Our ideology is intolerant . . . and peremptorily demands . . . the **complete transformation of public life** to its ideas."*

Rockefeller, David, (CFR, TC, B) *"Whatever the price of the Chinese Revolution, it has obviously succeeded not only in producing more efficient and dedicated administration, but also in fostering high morale and community of purpose. **The social experiment in China under Chairman Maos leadership is one of the most important and successful in human history.**"* (Statement in 1973 about Mao Tse-tung: NY Times 8-10-73.)

Shaw, George Bernard, (Fabian Socialist) (Playwright and author; from his *Intelligent Woman's Guide to Socialism and Capitalism,* 1928): *"Under **Socialism** you would not be allowed to be poor. You would be forcibly fed, clothed, lodged, taught, and employed whether you liked it or not. If it were discovered that you had not the character and industry enough to be worth all this trouble, you might possibly be executed in a kindly manner . . ." [This is compassionate liberalism?]*

Shearer, Derek (Former ambassador to Finland under Clinton, now Professor of Diplomacy and World Affairs at Occidental College; the following was written in *Reason,* 1982): *"Socialism has a bad name in America, and no amount of wishful* *thinking on the part of the left is going to change that . . . . The words* **Economic Democracy** *are an adequate and effective replacement."*

Thomas, Norman (U.S. Socialist Presidential Candidate): *"The American people will never knowingly adopt* **Socialism***. But under the name of 'liberalism' they will adopt every fragment of the* **Socialist** *program, until one day America will be a* **Socialist** *nation, without knowing how it happened."*

United Nations—UNESCO Publication, *Foundations of Lifelong Education,* 1976: *"Education should aim not so much at acquisition of knowledge . . . [today] there is less need to know the content of information . . . [There should be a] transformation of life in totality . . . [a]* **profound commitment to social tasks** *. . .* **Achievement of socialist countries** *. . . have laid the foundation of a way of life which makes everyone understand its individual relevance . . ."*

Wells, H.G. (FS) (A co-founder of the Fabian Socialists, author, *The New World Order,* 1939): *"The New Deal is plainly an attempt to achieve a working socialism and avert a social collapse in America; it is* **extraordinarily parallel to the successive 'policies' and 'Plans' of the Russian experiment***. Americans shirk the word 'socialism', but what else can one call it? . . . This new and complete Revolution we contemplate can be defined in a very few words. It is (a) outright world-socialism, scientifically planned and directed, plus (b) a sustained insistence upon law, law based on a fuller, more jealously conceived restatement of the personal Rights of Man, plus (c) the completest [sic]a freedom of speech, criticism, and publication, and a sedulous expansion of the educational organization to the ever growing demands of the new order . . . . Putting it at its compactest, [sic]it is the triangle of Socialism, Law, and Knowledge which frames the Revolution that may yet save the world."*

Wells, H.G. (Written in *The Fate of Man,* 1939) *"The crisis [the Great Depression] discovered a great man in Franklin Roosevelt . . . None too soon he has carried America forward to the second stage of democratic realization. His New Deal involves such* **collective controls** *of the national business that it would be absurd to call it anything but* **socialism***, were it not for a prejudice lingering on from the old individualist days against that word . . . Both Roosevelt and Stalin were attempting to produce a huge, modern, scientifically organized,* **socialist state, the one out of a warning crisis and the other out of a chaos."***

(4) A One-World Economic Control, One Currency:

Devesa, Domenec Ruiz (World Bank economist; from the *Streit Council Journal*, Fall 2007): "... *economic integration must and will lead to political integration,* since an integrated market requires common institutions producing common rules to govern it."

Roosevelt, Franklin Delano, (CFR) (Former President of the United States, Started the Road to Socialism/Communism with his program called the New Deal): *"The real truth of the matter is, as you and I know, that a financial element in the larger centers has owned the Government ever since the days of Andrew Jackson."* (Found in a letter written by FDR to Colonel House, November 21st, 1933.)

Rothschild, Mayer Amschel (Wealthy banker who had five sons and set them up over a bank in the leading countries in Europe. Rothschild was the co-founder of the Illuminati and the main financer of it, 1828): *"Allow me to issue and control the money of a nation, and I care not who writes the laws."*

Rothschild, Mayer Nathanial (One of the sons of the Rothschild banking dynasty. Nathanial was present and helped in the planning for the Federal Reserve, America's Central Bank; Given in a speech to a gathering of world bankers, February 12, 1912. The following year, the newly incorporated Federal Reserve was started, headed by Mr. Rothschild.): *"Let me control a peoples currency and I care not who makes their laws . . ."*

Warburg, Paul (CFR) (A very wealthy banker who helped start the Federal Reserve; Spoken before the Senate Foreign Relations Committee 2/17/1950): *"We shall have world government whether or not we like it. The only question is whether world government will be achieved by conquest or consent."*[581]

Wells, H.G. (FS) (Author, *The New World Order*, 1939): *"Directly we grasp this not very obscure truth that there can be, and are, different sorts of money dependent on the economic usages or system in operation, which are not really interchangeable, then it becomes plain that a collectivist world order, whose fundamental law is such a Declaration of Rights as we have sketched, will have to carry on its main, its primary operations at least with a new world money, a specially contrived money, differing in its nature from any sort of money conventions that have hitherto served human needs. It will be issued against the total purchasable output of the community in return for the workers' services to the community."*

(5) One-World Religion (Definitely Not a Christian Religion)

American Institute of Judaism (Excerpt from article in *The New York Times*, December, 1942): *"The statement went on to say that the spiritual teachings of religion must become the foundation for the **new world order** and that national sovereignty must be subordinate to the higher moral law of God."*

Bailey, Alice (Occult leader, author of *Externalization of the Hierarchy*, written in 1946, p.573): Bailey believed that "the Great One" would reinstate the Ancient Mysteries Religion as the **New World Order Religion**. *"These Mysteries, when restored, will unify all faiths."*[582]

North American Conference on Religion and Ecology (May 18, 1990. Press conference at the National Press Club in Washington, D.C. on the occasion of the "Caring for Creation" conference): *"It is now apparent that the ecological pragmatism of the so-called pagan religions, such as that of the American Indians, the Polynesians, and the Australian Aborigines, was a great deal more realistic in terms of conservation ethics than the more intellectual monotheistic philosophies of the revealed religions."*

Spangler, David (Director of Planetary Initiative, United Nations): *"No one will enter the **New World Order** unless he or she will make a pledge to worship Lucifer. No one will enter the **New Age** unless he will take a Luciferian Initiation."*

The Newschwabenland Times: (A blog site) *"Man's evil actions historically are ascribed to his divisions into many different religions. Therefore, much emphasis is being laid on the re-uniting into **one religion**. The current Ecumenical Movement is leading the charge toward this all-important goal. In a seminar held in Boston in August, 1991, the current New England Director of the Theosophical Society stated that, at the proper moment in world history the Roman Catholic Pope would travel to Jerusalem to address a world-wide religious conference. In his speech, he would declare all the **world's religions to be united into One**."*[583]

(6) Quotes that Show How America no Longer Has a Free Press:

Callaway, Oscar (U.S. Congressman, 1917): *"In March, 1915, the J.P. Morgan interests, the steel, shipbuilding, and powder interests, and their subsidiary organizations, got together 12 men high up in the newspaper world and employed them to select the most influential newspapers in the United States and sufficient* *number of them to control generally the policy of the daily press . . . . They found it was only necessary to purchase the control of 25 of the greatest papers.*

An agreement was reached; the policy of the papers was bought, to be paid for by the month; an editor was furnished for each paper to properly supervise and edit information regarding the questions of preparedness, militarism, financial policies, and other things of national and international nature considered vital to the interests of the purchasers."

Cohen, Richard M. (CFR) (Senior Producer of CBS political news): *"We are going to impose our agenda on the coverage by dealing with issues and subjects that we choose to deal with."*

Goldberg, Bernard (author, reporter, commentator; quoted by Harry Stein in the June 13-19, 1992, TV Guide): *"We in the press like to say we're honest brokers of information and it's just not true. The press does have an agenda."*

Graham, Katherine (CFR, B) (Former Washington Post Director): *"We live in a dirty and dangerous world. There are some things the general public does not need to know and shouldn't. I believe democracy flourishes when the government can take legitimate steps to keep its secrets, and when the press can decide whether to print what it knows."*

Rockefeller, David (CFR, B, Co-founder of TC, Spoken at a Bilderberg Meeting in Baden-Baden, Germany, 1991): *"We are grateful to the Washington Post, The New York Times, Time Magazine and other great publications whose directors have attended our meetings and respected their promises of discretion for almost forty years. It would have been impossible for us to develop our plan for the world if we had been subjected to the lights of publicity during those years. But, the world is now more sophisticated and prepared to march towards a **world government**. The supranational sovereignty of an intellectual elite and world bankers is surely preferable to the national auto-determination practiced in past centuries."*

Salent, Richard (CFR) (Former President, CBS News): *"Our job is to give people not what they want, but what we decide they ought to have."*

Swinton, John (Editor of the New York Times): *"There is no such thing as an independent press in America, unless it is in the country towns. You know it and I* *know it. There is not one of you who dares to write your honest opinions, and if you did, you know beforehand that it would never appear in print.*

"I am paid $150.00 a week for keeping my honest opinion out of the paper I am connected with. Others of you are paid similar salaries for doing similar things. If I should permit honest opinions to be printed in one issue of my paper, like Othello, before twenty-four hours, my occupation would be gone.

"The business of the New York journalist is to destroy truth; to lie outright; to pervert; to vilify; to fawn at the feet of Mammon; to sell his country and his race for his daily bread. We are the tools and vessels for rich men behind the scenes. We are intellectual prostitutes."

(7) Anti-Free Enterprise/Capitalism Statements

Caldicott, Helen (Union of Concerned Scientists): *"Free Enterprise really means rich people get richer. They have the freedom to exploit and psychologically rape their fellow human beings in the process . . .* **Capitalism** *is destroying the earth."*

United Nations—UNESCO Publication, *Foundations of Lifelong Education*, 1976: *"Achievement of socialist countries . . . have laid the foundation of a way of life which makes everyone understand its individual relevance . . . [whereas* **capitalism**] *lays the foundation of rivalry and aggression and encourages exaggerated consumption, [making] man a slave of ambition and social status symbols . . . [Lifelong learning promotes] equality of end result, and not merely of opportunity . . . [and] fosters equality in terms of opinions, aspirations, motivation, and so on . . . There is a dilemma—if lifelong education were to be based on the aim of increasing the yield of business enterprises and economic growth, it would merely serve to establish a totalitarian, one-dimension society."*

Shaw, George Bernard, (FS) (author, playwright): *"It is a historic fact, recurrent enough to be called an economic law, that* **capitalism**, *which builds up great civilizations, also wrecks them if persisted in beyond a certain point. It is easy to demonstrate on paper that civilization can be saved and immensely developed by, at the right moment, discarding capitalism and changing the private property profiteering state into the common property distributive state . . . Not until the two main tenets of socialism:* **abolition of private property** *(which must not be confused with personal property), and equality of income, have taken hold of the people as religious dogmas, as to which no controversy is regarded as sane, will a stable socialist state be possible."*

(8) Statements Supporting World Environmental Controls of Resources, Global Warming, Redistribution of Wealth, Statements Against People and Against Property Rights

Benedict, Richard (State Department employee working on assignment from the Conservation Foundation): *"A global climate treaty must be implemented even if there is no scientific evidence to back the greenhouse effect."*

Berle, Peter (President of the National Audubon Society): ***"We reject the idea of private property."***

Clinton, William (Former President of the United States): *"Our overriding environmental challenge tonight is the worldwide problem of climate change, global warming, the gathering crisis that requires worldwide action."* ("State of the Union Address," 1998.)

Davis, John (Editor of *Earth First! Journal*): *"I suspect that eradicating small pox was wrong. It played an important part in balancing ecosystems."* ***"Human beings, as a species, have no more value than slugs."***

***Economist* editorial:** *"**The extinction of the human species may not only be inevitable but a good thing** ... This is not to say that the rise of human civilization is insignificant, but there is no way of showing that it will be much help to the world in the long run."*

Ehrlich, Paul (Professor of ecology at Stanford University, author of the *Population Bomb*, 1968, that predicted hundreds of millions of people would starve to death in the 1970s because of over population. It didn't happen, but he is still highly respected and his many scare tactics continue.): ***"Giving society cheap, abundant energy ... would be the equivalent of giving an idiot child a machine gun."***

Foreman, David (of Earth First!): *"We must make this an insecure and inhospitable place for capitalists and their projects ... We must reclaim the roads and plowed land, halt dam construction, tear down existing dams, free shackled rivers and **return to wilderness** millions of tens of millions of acres of presently settled land."*

Gorbachev, Mikhail, (Former President of the Soviet Union; written in an article called "From Red to Green," *Audubon Magazine*, 1994.) *"Now that we* *are rid of this syndrome of imposing the communist model on people, now that we've given them the chance to get rid of this dogma, I have to tell you Americans that you've been pushing your American way of life for decades. You thought it was perfection itself, the ultimate achievement of human thought . . . There has to be a different approach . . . Americans have to be more modest in their desires. We have to stimulate human qualities in people rather than greed . . ." "What we're talking about is creating new forms of life on the basis of new values."*

Gregg, A. (COR) (Quoted in *Mankind at the Turning Point*, 1974): ***"The world has cancer, and the cancer is man."***

Gore, Al (Former Vice President, Presidential Candidate, Senator, Author, spoken at Putting People First, 1992)) ***"The task of saving the earth's environment must and will become the central organizing principle of the post-Cold War world."***

Hayes, Dennis ("Earth Day Agenda" 1970): *"I suspect that the politicians and businessmen who are jumping on the environment bandwagon don't have the slightest idea of what they are getting into. They are talking about emission control devices on automobiles, while we are talking about **bans on automobiles**."*

Hubbard, Barbara Marx (Psychologist, member and futurist/strategist of Task Force Delta; a U.S. Army think tank): ***"One-fourth of humanity must be eliminated from the social body.*** *We are in charge of Gods selection process for planet earth. He selects, we destroy. We are the riders of the pale horse, Death."*

King, Maurice (Professor in Africa who believes the world should have a one-child policy): ***"Global Sustainability requires: 'the deliberate quest of poverty . . . reduced resource consumption . . . and set levels of mortality control."***

Lovins, Amory (Chairman and Chief Scientist of the Rocky Mountain Institute, author and co-author of many books on renewable energy and energy efficiency, Rocky Mountain Institute): *"Complex technology of any sort is an assault on human dignity. It would be little short of disastrous for us to discover the source of clean, cheap, abundant energy, because of what we might do with it."*

Marx, Karl, and Engels, Frederich (authors of the Communist Manifesto, 1888 edition): *"In this sense, the theory of the Communists may be summed up in the single sentence: Abolition of private property."*

*1. **Abolition of property** in land and application of all rents of land to public purposes.*
3. Abolition of all rights of inheritance.
7. Extension of factories and instruments of production owned by the State; the bringing into cultivation of waste-lands, and the improvement of the soil generally in accordance with a common plan.

National Wilderness Institute, "Endangered Species Blueprint," *"**Pure guesswork** has become the basis of a forecast that has been published in newspapers to be read and understood as a scientific statement."*

Neddick, Sherry (Greenpeace Leader): *"**This is a political game.** It has nothing to do with science. It has nothing to do with health and safety."*

Noss, Dr. Reed F., (Leader in The Wildlands Project): *"**The collective needs of non-human species must take precedence over the needs and desires of humans."***

Oppenheimer, Michael (Environmental Defense Fund): *"... **the only hope for the world is to make sure there is not another United States: We can't let other countries have the same number of cars, the amount of industrialization, we have in the U.S.** We have to stop these Third-World countries right where they are. And it is important to the rest of the world to make sure that they don't suffer economically by virtue of our stopping them."*

Peterson, Russell (National Audubon Society President): *"We have the opportunity to avoid choices like nuclear power which will come back to haunt us 30 years from now."*

HRH Prince Philip, Duke of Edinburg (Of the World Wildlife Fund, Reported by Deutsche Press Agentur (DPA), August, 1988): *"**In the event that I am reincarnated, I would like to return as a deadly virus, in order to contribute something to solve overpopulation."***

HRH Prince Philip, Duke of Edinburgh (In his Foreword to *If I Were an Animal*; United Kingdom, Robin Clark Ltd., 1986): *"I just wonder what it would be like to be reincarnated in an animal whose species had been so reduced in numbers that it was in danger of extinction. What would be its feelings toward the human species whose population explosion had denied it somewhere to exist? ... I* *must confess that I am tempted to ask for reincarnation as a particularly deadly virus."*

Rosenberg, Ernest (President and CEO of Occidental Petroleum Corporation): *"The move towards controlling less and less pollution at greater and greater expense—until you are spending everything to control nothing—is one of the big water quality problems we are facing in the future."*

The Neuschwabenland Times (htttp://groups.yahoo.com/group/ TheNeuschwabenlandTimes/message/15): *"Our current emphasis on man's devastating effects upon the earth and upon Global Warming and pollution are* **designed to convince people that only united, drastic action from the United Nations can save this planet from collapse.***"*

Singer, Peter (the "Father of Animal Rights"): ***"Christianity is our foe. If animal rights is to succeed, we must destroy the Judeo-Christian Religious tradition."***

Strong, Maurice (Head of the 1992 Earth Summit in Rio de Janeiro): ***"Isn't the only hope for the planet that the industrialized civilizations collapse? Isn't it our responsibility to bring that about?"***

United Nations—*Our Global Neighborhood*, 1995: *"To keep global resource use within prudent limits while the poor raise their living standards, affluent societies need to consume less . . . Population, consumption, technology, development, and the environment are linked in complex relationships that bear closely on human welfare in the global neighborhood. Their effective and equitable management calls for a systemic, long-term, global approach guided by the principle of* **sustainable development***, which has been the central lesson from the mounting ecological dangers of recent times. Its universal application is a priority among the tasks of* **global governance.***"*

Watson, Lyall (South African botanist, zoologist, biologist, anthropologist, ethnologist, and author of many new age books, among the most popular of which is the best seller *Supernature; The Financial Times*, 15 July, 1995): ***"Cannibalism is a radical but realistic solution to the problem of overpopulation."***

Watson, Paul (Director of the "Sea Shepherd Conservation Society" and a co-founder of "Greenpeace"):

"I reject the idea that humans are superior to other life forms . . . Man is just an ape with an overly developed sense of superiority."

"The secret to David McTaggart's (early officer in Greanpeace) success is the secret to Greenpeace's success: **It doesn't matter what is true . . .** *it only matters what people believe is true . . . You are what the media define you to be. [Greenpeace] became a myth, and a myth-generating machine."*

Wildavsky, Aaron (political scientist, author): *"The Environmentalists Dream is an* **Egalitarian Society** *based on: rejection of economic growth, a smaller population, eating lower on the food chain, consuming a lot less, and sharing a much lower level of resources much more equally."*

Wirth, Timothy (former Democrat Congressman from Colorado, who served as Clinton's Assistant Secretary of State. He is now serving as President of the United Nations Foundation and Better World Fund): *"We've got to ride the global warming issue.* **Even if the theory of global warming is wrong, we will be doing the right thing—in terms of economic policy and environmental policy."**

Wurster, Charles (Leader in the Environmental Defense Fund): *"People are the cause of all the problems;* **we have too many of them; we need to get rid of some of them, and this (ban of DDT) is as good a way as any."***

(9) Population Control Statements

Adolph Hitler (Former Supreme Fuhrer of Germany, author of *Mein Kampf,* 1923): **"The sacrifice of personal existence is necessary to secure the preservation of the species."**

Bailey, Alice (Author of ***The Externalization of the Hierarchy***, p. 548, states that war will be used to drastically reduce populations): *"The atomic bomb will be turned over to the* **One-World Government** *and will be used against any nation who refuses to go along with the* **New World Order."***

Cooper, Bill (Author of ***Behold A Pale Horse***, p. 49, quotes a document from the Bilderberg Secret Society): *"Since most of the general public will not exercise [economic] restraint . . . [we must] take control of the world by the use of economic silent weapons in a form of* **quiet warfare** *and reduce [the dangerous levels of consumption] of the world to a safe level by a process of benevolent slavery and genocide."*[584]

Cousteau, Dr. Jacques, (scientist, environmentalist): *"In order to stabilize world population, we must eliminate 350,000 per day."*

Human Manifesto II #14: *"Advocate that **the world community** . . . engage in cooperative planning concerning the use of rapidly depleting resources . . . **population growth must be checked.**"*

Huxley, Sir Julian (Fabian Socialist) (First Director General of UNESCO, 1946-1948): *"Even though it is quite true that any radical eugenic policy will be for many years politically and psychologically impossible, it will be important for UNESCO to see that the eugenic problem is examined with the greatest care, and that the public mind is informed of the issues at stake so **that much that now is unthinkable may at least become thinkable.**"*

HRH Prince Philip, Duke of Edinburgh (Preface to *Down to Earth* written by Prince Philip, 1988, p. 8): *"I don't claim to have any special interest in natural history, but as a boy I was made aware of the annual fluctuations in the number of game animals and the need to **adjust the 'cull' to the size of the surplus population.**"*

Sanger, Margaret (Outspoken atheist and socialist, founder of the Voluntary Parenthood League in 1914, which later became Planned Parenthood; responsible for opening the first birth control clinic in the United States in New York City): *"**The most merciful thing that the large family does to one of its infant members is to kill it.**"*

Thropy, Miss Ann (pseudonym, writer for *Earth First! Journal*): *"... **as radical environmentalists, we can see AIDS not as a problem, but as a necessary solution.**"*

Turner, Ted (wealthy billionaire and supporter of radical environmentalism, from an interview with Audubon magazine): *"**A total world population of 250-300 million people, a 95% decline from present levels, would be ideal.**"*

(10) Gun Control—Outlawing Use of Guns and Armaments and Defense/Military

Brady, Sara (Chairman, Handgun Control, spoken to Sen. Howard Metzenbaum, written in the National Educator, January, 1994, p.3): *"Our task* *of creating a socialist America can only succeed when those who would resist us have been **totally disarmed.***"

Clark, Joseph, S., (U.S. Senator, spoken on the floor of the Senate, March 1, 1962, about PL 87-297 which calls for the disbanding of all armed forces and the prohibition of their re-establishment in any form whatsoever.): " . . . ***This program [PL 87-297] is the fixed, determined and approved policy of the government of the United States.***"

Clinton, Bill (Former US President, spoken on 3-22-94, MTVs "Enough is Enough"): *"When we got organized as a country and we wrote a fairly radical Constitution with a radical Bill of Rights, giving a radical amount of individual freedom to Americans . . . and so a lot of people say there's too much personal freedom. When personal freedom is being abused, you have to move to limit it. That's what we did in the announcement I made last weekend on the public housing projects, about how we're going to have **weapon sweeps** and more things like that to try to make people safer in their communities."*

Gartner, Michael (journalist, *USA Today*, 1992): *"There is no reason for anyone in this country, anyone except a police officer or a military person, to buy, to own, to have, to use a handgun . . . . **And the only way to do that is to change the Constitution.**"*

Kennedy, John F. (Former President of the United States, author of *Future of the United Nations Organizations*, 1961): ***"To destroy arms, however, is not enough.*** *We must create even as we destroy—creating world-wide law and law enforcement as we outlaw world-wide war and weapons."*

Owens, Major (Congressman from New York (D), stated in 1992 when he introduced H. J. Res. 438): *"The second article of amendment to the Constitution of the United States is repealed."*

Wells, H.G, (FS) (Author H.G. Wells, *The New World Order*, 1939*): **"Armament should be an illegality everywhere, and some sort of international force should patrol a treaty-bound world. Partial armament is one of those absurdities dear to moderate-minded 'reasonable' men. Armament itself is making war. Making a gun, pointing a gun, and firing it are all acts of the same order. It should be illegal to construct anywhere upon earth any mechanism for the***

specific purpose of killing men. When you see a gun it is reasonable to ask: Whom is that intended to kill?”

(11) Indoctrination, Propaganda, Mind Control to Get People to Go Along with What Leaders Want; Plans for Those Who They Cannot Reprogram

Goering, Hermann (President of the Reichstag, Nazi Party, and Luftwaffe Commander in Chief): *"Naturally the common people don't want war: Neither in Russia, nor in England, nor for that matter in Germany. That is understood. But, after all, IT IS THE LEADERS of the country who determine the policy and **it is always a simple matter to drag the people along**, whether it is a democracy, or a fascist dictatorship, or a parliament, or a communist dictatorship. Voice or no voice, the people can always be brought to the bidding of the leaders. That is easy. All you have to do is tell them they are being attacked and denounce the peacemakers for lack of patriotism and exposing the country to danger. It works the same in any country."*

Golitsyn, Anatoliy (former member of the KGB, author of the *The Perestroika Deception*, 1990): *"They [the Soviets] intend . . . to induce the Americans to adopt their own 'restructuring' and convergence of the Soviet and American systems using to this end the fear of nuclear conflict . . . . Convergence will be accompanied by blood baths and political **re-education camps** in Western Europe and the United States. The Soviet strategists are counting on an economic depression in the United States and intend to introduce their **reformed model of socialism** with a human face as an alternative to the American system during the depression."*

Gonzalez, Henry (U.S. Representative, August 29, 1994): *"The truth of the matter is that you do have those standby provisions, and the statutory emergency plans are there whereby you could, in the name of stopping terrorism, apprehend, invoke the military, and **arrest Americans and hold them in detention camps.**"*

Delgado, Dr. Jose, M.R. (Director of Neuropsychiatry, Yale University Medical School, Congressional Record, No. 26, Vol. 118, February 24, 1974): *"We need a program of psychosurgery for political control of our society. The purpose is physical control of the mind. Everyone who deviates from the given norm can be surgically mutilated. The individual may think that the most important reality is his own existence, but this is only his personal point of view . . . **Man does not have the***

right to develop his own mind . . . We must electronically control the brain. Someday armies and generals will be controlled by electronic stimulation of the brain."

Heaton, K. Maureen (An expert on the New World Order and Mind Control, author of *The Impossible Dream*. This quote comes from the *National Educator*): *"One of the least understood strategies of the world revolution now moving rapidly toward its goal is the **use of mind control as a major means of obtaining the consent of the people who will be subjects of the New World Order**."*

Huxley, Aldous (Author of bestselling futuristic book, *Brave New World*, foreword to the 1946 edition): "A really efficient totalitarian state would be one in which the all-powerful executive of political bosses and their army of managers control a population of slaves who do not have to be coerced, because they love their servitude. To make them love it is the task assigned, in present-day totalitarian states, to **ministries of propaganda,** newspaper editors and schoolteachers . . . . The greatest triumphs of propaganda have been accomplished, not by doing something, but by refraining from doing. Great is truth, but still greater, from a practical point of view, is **silence about truth**."

Speer, Albert (Hitler's Minister for Armaments at his trial after World War II): *"Hitler's dictatorship differed in one fundamental point from all its predecessors in history. It was the first dictatorship in the present period of modern technical development, a dictatorship which made complete use of all technical means for the domination of its own country. Through technical devices like the radio and the loud-speaker, **eighty million people were deprived of independent thought. It was thereby possible to subject them to the will of one man . . .**"*

References

Where to go to do research: Go to whatever search engine you use and type in the words North American Union or NAU, or SPP, or NAFTA Superhighway. Many sites will come up. I recommend the following: www.worldnetdaily. com *www.eagleforum.org; www.JBS.org; www.Canadian ActionPartyCA.org; www.Freedom21.com;* Check out the many You Tube segments of Lou Dobbs broadcasts on CNN news on the above topics. Even though he is no longer with CNN news, hopefully these broadcasts are still able to be seen. Search "European Union" and see all the information about it. Would we want the USA to give up her sovereignty and liberty to some day become part of such an all-encroaching, power-hungry octopus, that is seeking to entangle the entire earth in her tentacles?

For the bigger picture, search under the words: new world order and one-world government. You will be amazed as to what pops up.

I also recommend the many books listed in the footnotes and the following articles found at wwwWND.com:

Feds threaten Texas over superhighway funds plan;
NAFTA Superhighway hits bump in road; Houston: The Wal-Mart of North
    American Union;
Commerce chief pushes for 'North American integration; *Idaho lawmakers want*
    out of SPP;
Texas Ports plan for Chinese containers; 'Don't pave our land' Farm Bureau
    pleads;
Lawmaker battles Trans-Texas Corridor; House resolution opposes North American
    Union;
U.S. parkway leased to Aussie firm; Residents of planned union to be 'North
    Americanists';
Official calls super highway 'urban legend; 10 most underreported stories of 2006;
PREMEDITATED MERGER; Congressman Battles North Americanization;

North American Union leader says merger just crisis away; Analysts: Dollar collapse would result in 'amero';

U.S. dollar facing imminent collapse?; London stock trader urges move to 'amero;'

'Bush doesn't think America should be an actual place'; Mexico ambassador: We need N. American Union in 8 years

Congressman: Superhighway about North American Union; 'North American Union' major '08 issue?;

Resolution seeks to head off union with Mexico, Canada; Documents reveal 'shadow government';

Tancredo: Halt 'Security and Prosperity Partnership'; North American Union threat gets attention of congressmen;

Top U.S. official chaired N. American confab panel; N. American students trained for 'merger';

North American confab 'undermines' democracy; Attendance list North American forum;

North American Forum agenda; North American merger topic of secret confab;

Feds finally release info on 'superstate'; Senator ditches bill tied to 'superstate';

Congressman presses on 'superstate' plan; Feds stonewalling on 'super state' plan?;

Cornyn wants U.S. taxpayers to fund Mexican development; No EU in U.S.;

Trans-Texas Corridor paved with campaign contributions?; U.S.-Mexico merger opposition intensifies;

More evidence of Mexican trucks coming to U.S.; Docs reveal plan for Mexican trucks in U.S.;

Kansas City customs port considered Mexican soil?; Tancredo confronts 'superstate' effort;

Bush sneaking North American superstate without oversight?;

End Notes

Chapter One—Koehle Family Story During World War II, Deceptive Preparations for the EU in Germany, Ten D's Strategy for a Stealth Plan, Conspiracy Theories or Conspiracy Facts?

1 Monte Kuligowski, "Obama's 'Christian Nation,' *www.americathinker.com/2009/04/ Obama_Christian_nation_/htmthel/.*

Chapter Two—The Parallel of US Integration to the European Union, Government by Stealth and Deception, The War on the Middle Class

2 James Perloff, "Unattractive Union," *The New American*, May 11, 2009.

3 Lou Dobbs, *War on the Middle Class,* How the Government, Big Business, and Special Interest Groups are Waging War on the American Dream and How to Fight Back, (Viking Penguin Group, New York City, NY, 2006), pp. 9-10.

4 Taylor Caldwell, "Saving the Middle Class," (*The New American*, June 23, 1997), p. 39.

5 William Norman Grigg, *America's Engineered Decline,* (JBS, Appleton, WI, 2004), pp. 1-2.

6 Lyndsay Jenkins, *Britain Held Hostage* and *The Last Days of Britain*, interviewed on a video called "The Real Face of the European Union," The Campaign for Truth in Europe by the UK Independent Party, *www.ukip.org*, and Defenders of the Realm, *www.campaignfortruth.com.*

7 "The Origins of 1919-1939—The History of the European Union and European Citizenship" *http://www.historiasiglo20.org/europe/anteceden.htm.*

8 *http://www.politicos.co.uk/books/24918.htm?ginPtrCode=10410&identifier=.*

9 John McManus, "The European Template," (*The New American*, April 16, 2007), pp. 39-40.

10 *http://www.inplainsite.org/html/European-Union,html.#Babel.*

Chapter Three—The Politically Correct History of the EU, The "Evils of Nationalism"

11 "The Origins of 1945-1957—The History of the European Union and European Citizenship" *(http://www.historiasiglo20.org/europe/anteceden.htm.)*

12 Ibid.

13 "Jean Monnet: 1888-1979," "The History of the European Union: The European Citizenship," *(http://www.historiasiglo20.org/europe/monnet.htm)*.

14 *http://europa.cu/abc/history/foundingfathers/churchill/index_en.htm*.

15 15 Ibid.

16 "The Origins of 1945-1957—The History of European Union and European Citizenship."

17 Ibid.

18 Booker and North, *The Great Deception: The Secret History of the European Union* (New York: Continuum Books, 2003), p. 86-87.

19 Dr. Jerome R. Corsi, PH.D, *The Late Great USA*, (World Ahead Media, Los Angeles, CA), pp. 3-4.

20 Op.cit., "The Origins of 1945-1957."

21 Op.cit., Jenkins, *Britain Held Hostage* and *The Last Days of Britain*.

22 *http://www.ena.lu/mce.cfm*.

23 *http://en.wikipedia.org/wiki/Passport*.

24 *http://www.statewatch.org/news/2005/jan/02update-visas-biometrics.htm*.

25 Michael Scheiffler, "Reversing an Act of God with a Modern Tower of Babel," *(http://www.biblelight.net/Tower-of-Babel.htm)*.

26 Corsi, Op.cit, pp. 4-5.

27 Michael Kirby, Chief Justice of the High Court of Australia, "Trans-Tasman Union—was Sir Douglas Graham Right? *http://www.lawfoundation.net.au/resources/kirby/papers/19990819_transtas.html*,5/6/01.

Chapter Four—The Truth About the EU and its Background, People and Groups in Europe Who Oppose it, the New Constitution now Called a Treaty, Latest Irish Vote

28 Edward Spalton, Letter Sent to Kitty Werthman from Derby, England, October 7, 2006.

29 "From the First Draft of a European Constitution to the Constitution of Europe," European Navigator, *http://www.ena.lu/*.

30 "French Voters Reject First EU Constitution," May 30, 2005, *http://www.chinadaily.com.cn/english/doc/2005-05/30/content_446789.htm*.

31 "Dutch Say "No" to the EU Constitution," June 2, 2005, *http://news.bbc.co.uk/2/hi/4601439.stm*.

32 Ibid.

33 Philip Day, "The Real Face of the European Union," DVD, Campaign for Truth, *http://www.global-elite.org/node257*.

34 Ann Schibler, "What We Can Learn from the EU," DVD Review of The Real Face of the European Union, (*The New American*, March 3, 2008), pp. 31-32.

35 Kitty Werthman, Telephone Interview, October 3, 2007.

36 *www.flynnfiles.com*, 4/27/07, as reported in Stop the North American Union website, *http://www.conservativeusa.org/northamericanunion.htm*.

37 "Council of Europe Pushes Abortion as Part of Cairo Conference Anniversary," Catholic Family and Human Rights Institute, Oct. 2, 2009, *www.c-fam.org*.

38 *http://www.bloomberg.com/apps/news?pid=newsarchive&sid=auf.VyeKMWks*.

39 "Obama Wants Turkey to Join the European Union," (*The New American*, April 27, 2009), p. 6.

40 "Turks are Conquering Germany," *http://www.disclose.tv/forum/topic9780.html#*.

41 "The EU, The UK and Regionalization," Interview by Wik Heerma of Edward Spalton, Philadelphia Trumpet and Crown Productions, *http://www.youtube.com/watch?v=r5TWAykw6bw*.

42 George F. Will, "The What of Nations?" (*Newsweek*, April 20, 2009).

43 *http://www.telegraph.co.uk/news/worldnews/europe/eu/6157877/Germany-passes-legislation-to-ratify-Lisbon-treaty.html*.

44 Christopher Story, "The Irish Referendum is Null and Void," *Sovereign Independent*, Oct. 5, 2009.

45 Sarah Foster, "Ireland Says 'Yes' to the New World Order," *NewsWithViews.com*, Oct. 20, 2009.

46 Christopher Booker, "Ireland's EU Referendum is the Last Stand Against the Project," *http://www.telegraph.co.uk/comment/6235273*.

47 Bojan Pancevski in Brussels, "Tony Blair, President of the EU," October 4, 2009, *http://www.timesonline.co.uk/tol/news/world/europe/article6860257*.

48 "Fifty Plus Reasons for Leaving the EU" *http://www.youtube.com/watch?v=nGe7n 9j4_3g&feature=related*.

49 "Common Purpose Exposed," *http://www.cpexposed.com/*.

50 *http://www.bbc.co.uk/blogs/dailypolitics/andrewneil/2009/07/so_just_what_is_a_quango.html*.

51 Charlotte Iserbyt, "Refuse the National ID Card," NewsWithViews.com,February 13, 2005).

Chapter Five—"Transatlantic Economic Integration," Binding the USA with the EU, Other Unions Now Forming—Other Unions and Common Currencies Now Forming

52 John F. McManus, "EU Déjà vu in the Caribbean," (*New American*, February 2, 2009), p. 27.

53 James Perloff, "Unattractive Union," (*The New American*, May 11, 2009), p. 13.

54 Dr. Jerome Corsi, PH.D, "THE NEW WORLD DISORDER, Bush OKs 'integration' with European Union. Congress never asked about new obligation," (WorldNetDaily.com., May 8, 2007).

55 W. Cleone Skousen, *The Five Thousand Year Leap, The Miracle that Changed the World*, (National Center for Constitutional Studies, Idaho, 2006), pp. 268 and 271.

56 Orlean Koehle, *A Closer Look at the Real ID Act, Giving Up A Whole Lot of Liberty for a Little Bit of False Security*, (Small Helm Press Associate, Santa Rosa, CA, 2009), p. 47.

57 *http://www.tpnonline.org/.*

58 *http://www.eurunion.org/partner/erusrelations/TEC*, htm.

59 Corsi, "Seven-Year Plan Aligns U.S with Europe, Jan. 16, 2008. *http://www.worldnetdaily.com/news/article.asp?ARTICLE_ID=59713.*

60 Perloff, Op.cit. p. 13.

61 Connie Fogal, *http://www.canadians.org/action/2008/18-Sep-08.html.*

62 "Latin America's Free Trade Agreements with the European Union—an Agenda for Domination," August, 2008, *www.grain.org.*

63 John F. McManus, "EU Déjà vu in the Caribbean," (*The New American*, February 2, 2009), pp. 27-29.

64 Ibid. p. 31.

65 Robert Pastor, *Towards A North American Community, Lessons From the Old World for the New*, (Peterson Institute for International Economics, Washington D.C., 2001), pp. 172-173.

66 Carlos Prado, "The Socialist United States of Latin America?" *http://www.revolutionradio.org/2008/05/29/the-socialist-united-states-of-latin-america/.*

67 Joshua Goodman, "South American Presidents Agree to Form Unasur Bloc" (Update 3), May 23, 08, *http://www.bloomberg.com/apps/news?pid=2067001$sid+abWOMOeJUK7Y.*

68 Ibid.

69 *http://www.africa-union.org., http://www.afrimap.org/newsarticle.php?id=1265\t_blank*

70 Ibid.

71 Felix Osike, "Region to Have Single Currency by 2012." Global Policy Forum, August 20, 2007.

72 *http://wapedia.mobi/en/Central_Asian_Union.*

73 *http://www.aseansec.org/5612.htm, "http://www.europe.org.sg/en/eu_in_asia/eu_asean.htm" www.europe.org.sg/en/eu_in_asia/eu_asean.htm*

74 *http://en.wikipedia.org/wike/Asia_Cooperartion_Dialogue.*

75 Gemma Daley, "Rudd Wants European-Style Union," Bloomberg, June 5, 2007, *http:/www.bloomberg,com/apps/news?pid+20601081&sid+alf7aj40zhFk&refer+Australia.*

76 Daryl Mason, "Australia and New Zealand Locked Out of New 'Asian Union' on Orders of China," Bloomberg, November 21, 2007, http://yournewreality.blogspot.com/2007/11/indonesia-vietnam-thailand-malaysia.html.

77 William Busse, "Does Mexico Have the Solution for U.S. Healthcare?" Aug. 20, 2009, *http://www.examiner.com/x-16231-Maricopa-County-Conservative-Examiner?showbio.*

78 http//protect-the-earth.org/, and http://heal-the-earth.org/climate_change/climate_change_pole_shift.htm.)

79 www.americas-union.org.

Chapter Six—Early Plans For Regional Government, World War I and II, the League of Nations, The Gomberg Map of 1942, the Nations of the World Already Divided into Ten Major Regions

80 George Washington, "Farewell Address," (American Daily Advertiser, Philadelphia, September 19, 1796).

81 John F. McManus, *Changing Commands, The Betrayal of America's Military,* (JBS, Appleton, Wisconsin), pp. 89-90, Quoting from Colin Simpson's *The Lusitania* (Boston: Little, Brown, 1972), p. 157.

82 James Perloff, *Shadows of Power, The Council on Foreign Relations and the American Decline,* Western Island, Appleton, Wisconsin, p. 68.

83 *http://wiki.answers.com/Q/How_many_people_died_in_World_War_2.*

84 *http://strangemaps.wordpress.com/,http://history.sandiego.edu/gen/.maps/1900s/1942world4000.jpg.*

85 Phyllis Schafly, "Pursuing the 'North American' Agenda—Is America For Sale? *The Phyllis Schlafly Report,* September, 2006, p. 4.

86 "Strange maps," Op.cit.

Chapter Seven—Regional Government Inside the United States, Maps Dividing the USA into Regions, FDR's National Resources Planning Board under the UN, Attempts to Eliminate State and Local Governments

87 Delbert Clark, "Nine Groups Instead of the 48 States," *The New York Times Magazine,* April 21, 1935.

88 Bernadine Smith, Personal Telephone Interview, September 8, 2009.

89 Clark, Op.cit.

90 "The New Deal Built the New World Order," *http://www.batr.org/gulag/081903. html.*

91 Bernadine Smith, "Franklin Delano Roosevelt, Administrator of the Transformation into Global Government," Binder of Information on Regional Governments," (Compiled and sent 10/08).

92 Bernadine Smith, "The Twilight of the States," Second Amendment Committee, PO Box 1776, Hanford, CA 93232.

93 Farewell Address Delivered by Governor Ralph L. Carr, Governor of Colorado, Before the Joint Session of the Colorado Legislature, Thirty Fourth Session, January 8, 1943, at Denver, Colorado.

94 Bernadine Smith, "Yesterday's Plans—Today's Reality," Binder of Information on Regional Governments," (Compiled and sent 10/08), p. 4.

95 Personal interview with Supervisor John Moorlach, June 19, 2009.

96 *http://quickfacts.census.gov/qfd/states/06/06073.html.*

97 Smith, Op.Cit., Series of newspaper articles on the attempt to eliminate county and city governments.

98 W. Cleone Skousen, *The Making of America,* (The National Center for Constitutional Studies, Malta, ID, 1986), pp. 48-51.

Chapter Eight—The United Nations—Its Founding and Ultimate Purpose—Regional and Global Government, The Green World Order

99 *http://www.summit-americas.org/eng-2002/quebeccity-summit.htm.*

100 Bob Hillman, *Reinventing Government, Fast Bullets and Culture Change,* 2001, (*http://www.freedom.org*), p. 41.

101 Henry Lamb, *The Rise of Global Governance,* (Sovereignty International, Inc. Hollow Rock, TN and Bango, ME, 2008), p. 27.

102 Edward J. Griffin, *The Creature From Jekyll Island,* (American Media, Westlake Village, CA, 1994) pp. 85-87.

103 Doug Bandow, "The IMF: A Record of Addition and Failure,"*Perpetuating Poverty: The World Bank, the IMF, and the Developing World* (Washington, D.C.: Cato Institute, 1994), p. 19.

104 William F. Jasper, *The United Nations Exposed,* (The John Birch Society, Appleton, Wisconsin, 2001), pp. 174-175.

105 Griffin, Op.cit., p. 89.

106 Steve Bonta, *Inside the United Nations, a critical look at the UN,* (The John Birch Society, Appleton, Wisconsin, 2003,) p. 7.

107 Dr. John Coleman, *Diplomacy by Deception,* (Joseph Publishing Co, Carson City, NV, 1993), pp. 14-15.

108 Jasper, *The United Nations Exposed*, pp. 58-59.

109 Coleman, Op.cit., p. 24.

110 Ibid., p. 16.

111 Dr. Stanley Monteith, *Brotherhood of Darkness*, (Hearthstone Publishing, Oklahoma City, Oklahoma, 2000), p. 18.

112 Jasper, Op.cit., pp. 42-43.

113 "United Nations," *World Book Encyclopedia*, (World Book Inc., Vol. 20, 1993), p. 52.

114 *http://en,wikipedia.org/wiki/list_of_wars,1945-2009.*

115 Samuel L. Blumenfeld, *NEA, The Trojan Horse in American Education*, (Paradigm Company, Boise, Idaho, 1984,) p. 194.

116 William Benton, in his address before the 1st meeting for the U.S. National Commission for UNESCO, Sept. 23, 1946, in "Review of the United Nations Charter: A Collection of Documents," U.S. Senate Document #87, a report of the Subcommittee on the UN Charter, 83rd Congress, 2nd Session, Jan. 7, 1954.

117 "In the Classroom: Toward World Understanding," UNESCO Publication, No. 356 (Paris, Georges Lang, 1949), p. 58.

118 Lamb, Op.cit., p. 31.

119 Center for Civic Education, *We the People, The Citizen and the Constitution, Teacher's Guide*, Calabasas, CA, 1994, p. 178-179.

120 Center for Civic Education, *We the People, The Citizen and the Constitution*, Calabasas, CA, 1994, p. 207.

121 Ibid, p. 208.

122 *We The People,* Teacher's Guide, pp. 136-161.

123 Allen Quist, *FedEd, The New Federal Curriculum and How It's Enforced*, Maple River Education Coalition, St. Paul, MN, 2002, p. 26.

124 Michael S. Coffman, *Saviors of the Earth*, (Chicago, Illinois, Northfield Publishing Co. 1993) pp. 221-222.

125 *http://wapedia.mobi/en/Convention_on_the_Elimination_of_All_Forms_of_Discrimination_Against_Women#5.*

126 Chris Carter, "UN Convention on the Rights of the Child Would Threaten the American Family," *http://www.familysecuritymatters.org/publications/id.2220/pub_detail.asp.*

127 Lamb, Op.cit., pp. 50-63.

128 Monteith, Op.cit., p. 43.

129 Larry Abraham and Franklin Sanders, *The Greening*, (Soundview Publications, 1993), pp. 99-102.

130 Steve Milloy, *Green Hell: How Environmentalists Plan to Control Your Life and What You Can Do to Stop Them*, (Washington D.C., Regenery, 2009).

131   James Perloff, "Exposing the Green World Order," (*The New American*, August 31, 2009) pp. 29-31.

132   "Klamath Falls Bucket Brigade Protests Water Shutoff," *http://www.heartland.org/ publications/ environment%20climate/article/10413/Klamath_Falls_bucket_brigade_ protests_water_shutoff.html.*

133   *http://www.klamathbasincrisis.org/articles06/pastsymbol031206.htm.*

134   Devvy Kidd, "Klamath Falls Farmers Destroyed by Illegal Species Listing," *http:// www.newswithviews.com/Devvy/kidd86.htm.*

135   Ibid.

136   *http://vodpod.com/watch/1943363-saving-water-in-fresno-devin-nunes.*

137   Brad Wilmouth, "Former Democrat/Actor Paul Rodriguez Begs Obama to Side With Farmers Over Endangered Fish," September 18, 2009, *http://newsbusters.org/ blogs/brad-wilmouth/2009/09/18/fmr-dem-actor-paul-rodriguez-begs-obama-side-w- farmers-endangered-fis.*

138   Kidd, Op.cit.

139   *http://www.gdrc.org/u-gov/global-neighbourhood/chap1.htm.*

140   *http://quotes.liberty-tree.ca/quotes_by/barry+goldwater.*

141   Ezra Taft Benson, *An Enemy Hath Done This,* (Parliament Publishers, Salt Lake City, UT, 1969), pp. 160-161.

142   Dr. John Coleman, *Conspirator's Hierarchy: The Story of the Committee of 300,* (American West Publishers, Carson City, NV., 4th Edition, Revised and Updated, 2006), p. 25.

143   Benson, Op.cit, pp. 207-208.

Chapter Nine—Chief Architects of the UN—the Royal Institute for International Affairs and the Council of Foreign Relations

144   Dr. Stanley Monteith, *Brotherhood of Darkness,* (Hearthstone Publishing, Oklahoma City, Oklahoma, 2000), pp. 95-96.

145   William Jasper, "Global Fusion," (*The New American*, April 27, 2009), p. 16.

146   Myron Fagen, "The Illuminati and the CFR Expose," Transcript of Tape, 1960, *http://forums.skadi.net/showthread.php?t=102669.*

147   "Council on Foreign Relations, "*http//en.wikipedia.org/wiki/council_on_foreign_ relations.*

148   Professor Arnold Toynbee, a member of the Royal Institute for International Affairs, in a June, 1931, speech before the Institute for the Study of International Affairs in Copenhagen, Denmark. Quoted by Tony Pearce, "Is There Really a New World Order?" posted on *www.saltshakers.com/midnight/nwo.html.*

149   *www.cfr.org./about/mission.html.*

150 Pat Robertson, *The New World Order*, (Word, Inc., Dallas, Texas, 1991), p. 97.

151 Dr. Carroll Quigley, *Tragedy and Hope, a History of the World in Our Time*, (New York, Macmillan, 1966), p. 32.

152 *http://www.cfr.org/publication/8102/building_a_north_american_community.html.*

153 Hillary Rodham Clinton, "Foreign Policy Address at the Council on Foreign Relations," Washington, D.C., July 15, 2009, *http://www.state.gov/secretary/rm/2009a/july/126071.htm.*

154 Daniel Estulin, *The True Story of the Bilderberg Group*, (Trine Day, Walterville, Oregon, 2007), p. 81.

155 Ibid, p. 117.

156 Allen Ide, "What the CFR Really Is," Letter to the Editor published in the Delaware State News, Dover Delaware, Feb. 27, 2007.

157 Estulin, Op.cit., p. 120.

158 John F. McManus, *The Insiders, Architects of the New World Order*, (JBS, Appleton, Wisconsin, 2004), pp. 9-125.

159 Wikipedia website, Op.cit.

160 Estulin, p. 120.

161 David Rockefeller, Bilderberg Meeting, June 1991. Baden, Germany.

162 Monteith, Op.cit., p. 31.

163 Myron C. Fagen, *Illuminati and the Council on Foreign Relations,* transcribed from a tape, date unknown, probably in the 1960s after the death of JFK, *http://www. biblebelievers.org.au/illuminati.htm.*
http://www.illuminatiarchives.org/category/council-on-foreign-relations/.

Chapter Ten—More Powerful Support for the UN, Other Secretive Organizations Supporting Regional and World Government

164 McManus, Op.cit. p. 20.

165 Griffin, *Creature from Jekyll Island*, p. 295.

166 William F. Jasper, *Global Tyranny Step by Step, The United Nations and the Emerging New World Order*, (Western Islands, Appleton, WI, 1992), pp. 244-247.

167 Estulin, p. 251.

168 Ibid, p. 21.

169 Ibid. p. 318.

170 Ibid. pp. 41-44.

171 *http://www.worldnetdaily.com/news/article.asp?ARTICLE_ID=55917.*

172 Hilaire du Berrier, HduB Reports, September, 1991, pp. 1-2 as reported by William F. Jasper, The United Nations Exposed, pp. 46-47.

173 Estulin, p. 95.

174 Ibid, pp. 80-81.

175 Brian Sussman, as reported on the Sussman Show, KSFO Radio Show, February 5-6, 2008.

176 Estulin, Op.cit. pp. 24-25.

177 Ibid., p. 153.

178 Phyllis Schlafly, *A Choice Not an Echo,* (Pere Marquette Press, Alton, Illinois, 1964), pp. 102-104.

179 Estulin, Op.cit., p. 1.

180 Ibid. pp. 10-11.

181 Ibid. p. 15.

182 Ibid, pp. 5-7.

183 Ibid. p. 59-60.

184 Ibid, p. 22.

185 Ibid, p. 187.

186 William Shannon, *http://www.catelog.americancatholic.org.*

187 Barry Goldwater, *With No Apologies,* (Berkley Books, New York, 1979), p. 293.

188 Patrick Wood, "Toward a North American Union," The August Review, Global Elite Research Center, *www.August Review.com.* 2006, p. 1.

189 Richard Gardner, *The Hard Road to World Order,* Foreign Affairs, 1974, p. 558 (Foreign Affairs is the magazine published by the Council on Foreign Relations.)

190 McManus, Op.cit. p. 22.

191 Gary Allen, *None Dare Call it Conspiracy,* (Concord Press, Rossmoor, California, 1971), pp. 122-123.

192 *http://www.lse.ac.uk/collections/pressAndInformationOffice/newsAndEvents/ archives/2006/ FabianWindow.htm.*

193 *Wikipedia, "Fabian Society," http://en.wikipedia.oprg/wiki/Fabian_Society.*

194 *www.cluboffrome.org/hist/ho7.htm.* (June, 1999).

195 Dr. Stan Monteith, *The Brotherhood of Darkness,* (Hearthstone Publishing, Ok. City, OK, 2000), p. 41.

196 *http://www.theforbiddenknowledge.com/jardtruth/clubof rome.htm.*

197 *http://www.bibliotecaplyades.net/sociopolitica/esp_sociopol_clubrome09.htm.*

198 *http://www.cluboffrome.org/organization/membership.php.*

199 Monteith, Op.cit. pp. 78-79.

200 *http://www.iamthewitness.com/Daryl*BradfordSmith_Rothschild.htm.

201 William H. McIllhany, "A Primer on the Illuminati," (*New American,* June 22, 2009), p. 33.

202 The Illuminati and the Protocols, *http://jahtruth.net/illumin.htm#Protocols%20Proof,* p. 3 of 182.

203 Jan Swafford, "The Town that Made Beethoven," *Tufts Magazine*, Medford, MA., Volume XV, Number 3, Spring 2008, pp. 40-41.

204 "Der Grosse Drahtzieher (The Big String Puller), *Focus*, 14, 1994, pp. 156-158.

205 McIllhany, Op.cit. p. 34.

206 *http://www.crystalinks.com/illuminati.html.*

207 Manly P. Hall, *Lectures on Ancient Philosophies*, (Philosophical Research Society, Inc., 1984), p. 433.

208 Albert Pike, *Morals and Dogmas*, (Supreme Council of the Thirty Third Degree of the Scottish Rite, 1871), pp. 104, 819, 321.

209 Manly P. Hall, *The Lost Keys of Freemasonry*, (Macoy Publishing, Richmond, Virginia, 1923), p. 48.

210 Monteith, Op.cit., pp. 120-128.

211 *http://www.calodges.org/no406/FAMASONS.HTM.*

212 Paul Fisher, *Behind the Lodge Door*, (Tan Books, Rockford, Illinois, 1994), p. 244, paraphrased by Stan Monteith, *Brotherhood of Darkness*, p. 129.

213 Pike, Op.cit., p. 219.

214 C. William Smith, "God's Plan in America," (*The New Age Magazine*, September 1950, Vol. LVIII, No 9), p. 531.

215 Eugene Lennhoff, *The Free Masons,* translated from the German by Einar Frame, (Addlestone, England, Lewis Masonic Books, 1934, 1994,) pp. 168-171.

216 Manly P. Hall, *The Secret Destiny of America*, (The Philosophical Research Society, Inc. Los Angeles, California, 1944), p. 72.

217 Corrine McLaughlin, & Gordon Davidson, *Spiritual Politics*, (Ballentine Books, 1994) p. 297.

218 Paul Kurtz, *Humanist Manifestos I and II*, (Prometheus Books, New York, 1973), pp. 13-23.

219 history.ucsb.edu/ . . . /33d/projects/protzion/DelaCruzProtocolsMain.htm.

220 Myron Fagen, "The Illuminati and the CFR Expose," Transcript of Tape, 1960, *http://forums.skadi.net/showthread.php?t=102669.*

221 Monteith, Op.cit. pp. 130-131.

222 Dr. John Coleman, *Conspirator's Hierarchy: The Story of the Committee of 300*, (American West Publishers, Carson City, NV., 4th Edition, Revised and Updated, 2006), pp. 326-332.

223 Ibid, pp. 13-17.

224 C. Rhodes, Documents presented in the Rhodes House, Oxford, England. In: Aydelotte F. *The Vision of Cecil Rhodes:* A Review of the First Forty Years of American Scholarships. (London: Geoffrey Cumberlege, Oxford University Press, 1946), pp. 3-5.

225 Carroll Quigley, *The Anglo-American Establishment, from Rhodes to Cliveden*, (Sisyphus Press, State College, PA, 1982), p. 11.

226 Dennis Cuddy, *President Clinton Will Continue the New World Order*, (Oklahoma City, Southwest Radio Church, 1993), p. 5.

227 Coleman, Op.Cit., p. 230.

228 Ibid, p. 320.

229 Estulin, Daniel, *The True Story of the Bilderberg Group*, (Trine Day, Walterville, OR, 2007), pp. 57-58.

230 Ibid. p. 114.

231 Ibid. p. 58.

232 *http://www.sourcewatch.org/index.php?title-Committee_of_300.*

233 "North Atlantic Treaty Organization, (NATO)" *World Book Encyclopedia*, Volume 14, (World Book Inc. Chicago, 1984), pp, 366-367.

234 Dr. Leonard G. Horowitz, *Death in the Air, Globalism, Terrorism, and Toxic Warfare*, (Tetrahedron Publishing Group, Sandpoint, ID, 2001), pp. 314, 396.

235 John McManus, *Changing Commands, The Betrayal of America's Military*, (John Birch Society, Appleton, Wisconsin, 1995), p. 20.

236 Ibid, pp. 105-107.

237 Ibid, p. 33.

238 *http://en,wikipedia.org/wiki/list_of_wars,1945-2009.*

239 Horowitz, Op.Cit, pp. 13-14 and 196-198.

240 Blog Comment by Eddie to LA Times article by Brian Doherty, "Gun Rights Fight Isn't Over," June, 27, 2008, *http://infowars.com/the-gun-right-fight-isn't-over.*

241 Coleman, Op. Cit. p. 280.

242 Ibid, p. 304.

243 John Harlow, "Billionaire Club in Bid to Curb Overpopulation," (*Sunday Times of London*, May 24, 09) *http://www.timesonline.co.uk/tol/news/world/us_and_americas/article6350303.ece.*

244 William F. Jasper, "The New Jacobin Elite," (*The New American*, July 6, 2009), p. 44.

Chapter Eleven—Chapter Eleven, NAU Stealth and Deception A Go-Go! CFR's Robert Pastor—the "Father of the NAU," Pastor's Objectives Including International ID Cards, Universities and Multi-National Corporations Promoting the NAU, the Present Stealth Campaign

245 David Horowitz, *www.DiscoverTheNetworks.org.*

246 Jerome Corsi, "Meet Robert Pastor: Father of the North American Union," *http://www.freerepublic.com/focus/news/1672386/posts.*

247 Dr. Jerome R. Corsi, *The Late Great USA, The Coming Merger with Mexico and Canada,* (World Ahead Media, Los Angeles, 2007), p. 24.

248 Ibid. p. 35.

249 Corsi, "Meet Robert Pastor" Op.cit.

250 Robert A. Pastor, *Towards a North American Community: Lessons from the Old World* (Washington, D.C.: Institute for International Economics, August, 2001).

251 Ibid pp. 100-102.

252 *North American Forum on Integration (NAFI), http://www.fina-nafi.org/eng/ triumvirat07/ default.asp? langue=eng&menu=triumvirat.*

253 *http://www.fina-nafi.org/eng/triumvirat09/default.asp.*

254 *http://www.wnd.com/news/article.asp?ARTICLE_ID=55596.*

255 Jerome Corsi, "North American Parliament under way," May 28, 2008, *http:// worldnetdaily.com/index.php?fa=PA3.GE.view&pageId=65582.*

256 "North American Leaders Unveil Security and Prosperity Partnership, International Information Programs," *www.U.S.Govt.org.*

257 *http://www.spp.gov/.*

258 *http://www.tradeobservatory.org/headlines.cfm?refID=69922.*

259 "Building a North American Community," Report of the Independent Task Force on the Future of North American, Council on Foreign Relations, 2005.

260 Tom DeWeese, "North American Union Fact Sheet," April, 2008.

261 Corsi, "Meet Robert Pastor," Op.cit.

262 *http://www.cfr.org/publication/8173/north_american_community_approach_to_ security.html.*

263 Pastor, Robert, "North America A Partial Eclipse and a Future Community," 2007, *http://www.american.edu/ia/cnas/pdfs/workingpaper5_rp_hussain.pdf.*

264 Schlafly, Phyllis, "England's Call to Repeal our Declaration of Independence," *www. EagleForum.org, April 30, 2008.*

265 *http://www.asu.edu/clas/nacts/bna/csos.html.*

266 *http://www.marc.org/NAW/speakers.html.*

267 Lou Dobbs, *War on the Middle Class,* (Viking Penguin Group, New York, NY, 2006), pp. 100,101,109.

268 William Norman Grigg, *America's Engineered Decline,* (JBS Appleton, Wisconsin, 2004) p. 41.

269 *http://online.wsj.com/public/article/SB117500805386350446-cRRynUb3zQgR2Yx n8wFOt96EOlE_20070404.html?mod=blogs.*

270 *http://asunews.asu.edu/20090210_nactsreport.*

271 Jerome Corsi, "University Reshuffles 'North American Union Architect,' January 24, 2008, *http://worldnetdaily.com/index.php?fa=PAGE.view&pageId=45702.*

272 Jennifer Loven, AP White House Correspondent, "*Obama attending first US-Canada-Mexico Summit http://news.yahoo.com/s/ap/20090809/ap_on_go_pr_wh/ obama.*

273 Phyllis Schlafly, "What Happened in Guadalajara," *The Phyllis Schlafly Report,* September, 2009, p. 4.

274 Loven, Op.cit.

275 Schlafly, Op.Cit.

276 Loven, Op.cit.

277 *http://www.cfr.org/publication/8102/building_a_north_american_community.html.*

Chapter Twelve—Big Brother is Watching Over Us: National ID Cards and Databases—Part of a Police State; The History of ID Cards in the USA; The USA Patriot Act; The Department of Homeland Security; The Real ID Act of 2005; The Western Hemisphere Travel Initiative; The Pass ID Bill; RFID Chips; Police State in Hardin, Mont

278 Kurt and Orlean Koehle, Home Video of Interview with Wagner Family in Dresden, Germany, April,1989.

279 Nelson Kelleigh, "White House Wants 'Informants' to Rat Out Critics," *radiok@ bellsouth.net*, 8/5/09.

280 Ibid.

281 *http://www.foxnews.com/politics/2009/08/28/senate-president-emergency-control-internet/.*

282 Phyllis Schlafly, "Liberty vs. Totalitarianism," *http://www.eagleforum.org/psr/july98/.html.*

283 Ibid.

284 *http://en.wikipedia.org/wiki/List_of_identity_card_policies_by_country.*

285 William Norman Grigg, *Liberty in Eclipse, The War on Terror and the Rise of the Homeland Security State,* (The Welch Foundation, New Mexico, 2007), pp, 124-128.

286 *http://industry.slashgeo.org/industry/07/08/13/48233.shtml.*

287 Rhys Blakely, "India to Issue all 1.2 Billion Citizens with Biometric ID Cards," July 15, 2009, *http://www.timesonline.co.uk/tol/news/world/asia/article6710764.ece.*

288 Ibid.

289 *http://www.guardian.co.uk/politics/2009/jun/30/identity-cards-pilots-airports.*

290 Jim Powell, "John Locke Natural Rights to Life, Liberty, and Property," Aug. 1996, Vol. 46, Issue: 8, *http://www.thefreemanonline.org/featured/john-locke-natural-rights-to-life-liberty-and-property/.*

291 Schafly, Op.cit.

292 Ibid.

293 Phyllis Schlafly, "Is the Era of Big Government Coming Back?" *http://www. eagleforum.org/psr/2002/feb02/psrfeb02.shtml.*

294 Schlafly, "Liberty vs. Totalitarianism," Op.cit.

295 Grigg, Op.cit. pp. 111-114.

296 *http://killfile.newsvine.com/_news/2008/08/25/1783040-in-1995-joe-biden-basically-wrote-the-patriot-act—.*

297 *http://en.wikipedia.org/wikiUSA_Patriot_Act.*

298 Paul, Ron, Congressman, "Privacy and Personal Liberty," *http://www.ronpaul2008. com/issues/privacy-and-personal-liberty/.*

299 Tom DeWeese, "Total Surveillance Equals Total Tyranny," (*The DeWeese Report,* American Policy Center, Virginia, September 1, 2003).

300 Jennifer Lee, "Upgraded Driver's Licenses Are Urged as National ID's," January 8, 2002, *http://www.nytimes.com/2002/01/08/national/08LICE.html.*

301 Phyllis Schlafly, *http://www.eagleforum.org/column/2002/jan02/02-01-30.shtml.*

302 Tom DeWeese, "Homeland Insecurity, Deconstructing the Constitution, (*The DeWeese Report,* American Policy Center, Virginia, Nov. 14, 2002).

303 *http://en.wikipedia.org/wiki/Real_ID_Act.*

304 Orlean Koehle, *A Closer Look at the Real ID Act—Giving Up a Whole Lot of Liberty for a Little Bit of False Security,* (Small Helm Press Associate, Santa Rosa, CA, March, 2008).

305 Robert Pastor, "A North American Community Approach to Security," testimony—Senate Foreign Relations Committee, *http://www.senate.gov/-foreign/ testimony/2005/PastorTestimony050609.pdf.*

306 Jim Harper, *http://www.cato-at-liberty.org/2009/07/07/does-the-pass-id-act-protect-privacy/*).

307 *http://www.washingtonwatch.com/bills/show/111_SN_1261.html.*

308 *http://edlabor.house.gov/documents/111/pdf/publications/.AAHCA-BillText-071409. pdf.* pp. 58-59.

309 Sharon Hughes, "Obama Administration Scrubs 'Cash for Clunkers' Government Control Wording from Website," (*ChangingWorldViews.com,* August 4, 2009).

310 Thomas Jefferson, letter to A. H. Rowan, 1798; archived at *http://etext.virginia. edu/jefferson/quotations.*

311 Alberto Gonzales, US Attorney General, statement made at a January 18 Senate Judiciary Committee Hearing, as reported by the *San Francisco Chronicle,* January 24, 2007.

312 Grigg, Op.cit. pp. 15-18.

313 Ibid, pp. 173-176.

314 Ron Paul, "Statement on H.R. 3773—FISA Amendment Act of 2008," *http://www. house.gov/paul/congrec/2008/cr031408h.htm.*

315   Grigg, Op.cit. pp. 196-198, and David Lohr, "Randy Weaver: Siege at Ruby Ridge," http://www.trutv.com/library/ crime/gangsters_outlaws/cops_others/ randy_weaver/21.html.

316   "Waco—Military Documents were Destroyed," *http://www.apfn.org/apfn/waco_mil. htm.*

317   Grigg, Op.cit. pp. 199-201

318   Ibid, pp. 152-157.

319   Chuck Baldwin, "Ravenwood Comes to America," October 9, 2009, *http://www. chuckbaldwinlive.com/hardin-mt.html.*

320   Sarah Gravlee and Nick Lough, Reporters about "Hardin, Montana American Private Police Force," KULR-8 TV Billings, Montana, Oct. 4-5, 2009, *www.kulr8. com/news/local/63488352.html?*

321   *http://newswithviews.com/BreakingNews/breaking168.htm.*

322   Joseph Farah, "Between the Lines, Barack Obama's Plan for Giant Police Force," July 15, 2008, *http://www.wnd.com/index.php?fa=PAGE.printable&pageId=69601.*

323   Chuck Baldwin, Op.cit.

324   *http://www.nytimes.com/2009/05/14/us/14explorers.html.*

325   Jane Sutton, "Recession Fueling Right Wing Extremism," April 14, 2009, *http:// uk.reuters.com/* article/idUKTRE53D5SH20090414?pageNumber=2&virtualBra ndChannel%3b=0&sp%3b=true&sp=true.

326   John Spring, (former talk show host) "Paper on the Real ID Act of 2005," KLAA Radio, 830 AM, Los Angeles, johnspring@gmail.com.

327   Charlotte Iserbyt, *NewsWithViews.Com.*, October 16, 2003.

328   Ibid.

329   Ibid.

330   "Freedom from War," The United States Program for General and Complete Disarmament in a Peaceful World, Publication 7277, US. State Department, 1961.

331   Iserbyt, Op.cit., Oct. 16, 2003.

332   Betty Freauf, "Earth Day, May Day and Watermelons," *NewsWithViews*, April 26, 2003.

333   Ibid.

334   *The New American*, "Bush's Tribute to the New European Soviet," June 17, 2002.

335   *The New American*, "Disarmament Love Fest in Moscow, June 17, 2002.

336   *EUobserver.com, 4/10/03.*

337   Charlotte Iserbyt, "Refuse the National ID Card," *NewsWithViews.com*, February13, 2005.

338   *http://dprogram.net/2009/07/12/ex-ibm-employee-reveals-tv-abandoned-analog-band-to-make-room-for-rfid-chips/.*

339   Koehle, Op.cit., pp. 52-61.

340   *http://dprogram.net/2009/07/12/ex-ibm-employee-reveals-tv-abandoned-analog-band-to-make-room-for-rfid-chips/.*

341   *http://verichipcorp.com* (2007).

342   Ibid (2009).

343   Grigg, pp. 135-137.

344   *http://www.computerweekly.com/Articles/2009/08/06/237215/uk-national-id-card-cloned-in-12-minutes.htm#.*

345   Aaron Bolinger, "Medical Microchip for People May Cause Cancer," p. 15, Associated Press, 2007, *http://www.msnbc.msn.com/id/20643620.*

346   *http://wistechnology.com/article.php?id=2044.*

347   *http://www.youtube.com/watch?v=wJBZSzIh5Fo.*

Chapter Thirteen—The Financial Crisis, America's Central Bank, How the Crisis Promotes a NAU, a World Economic Order, and a World Currency

348   Thorndike Barnhart Dictionary, (Doubleday and Company, New York, 1952), pp. 297, 181; Websters New Dictionary, (Wiley Publishing, Inc. Cleveland, Ohio, 2003), pp. 236,612,134; and The World Book Dictionary, (World Book Inc., Chicago, 1985), p. 774, 420.

349   Tom DeWeese, "Free Enterprise Did not Cause the Market Meltdown," (*The DeWeese Report*, November, 2008), p. 3.

350   Ibid, p. 4.

351   *http://nymag.com/daily/intel/2008/09/what_happened_at_lehman_in_30.html.*

352   Ellen Brown, September 7th, 2009, *http://www.webofdebt.com/articles/economic9-11.php.*

353   Daniel Henniger, "Mad Max and the Meltdown," (*Wall Street Journal*, Nov. 20, 2008).

354   The DeWeese Report, Op.cit. p. 4.

355   Richard C. Gross, "Public Lashing: Fannie, Freddie execs excoriated at House Hearing," (*Washington Times*, 12/15/08).

356   *The DeWeese Report*, Nov. 2008, p. 4.

357   G. Edward Griffin, *Creature from Jekyll Island*, p. 23 and p. 472.

358   *http://quotes.liberty-tree.ca/quote/charles_lindbergh_quote_419b, and Griffin, p. 470*

359   *www.campaignforliberty.com.*

360   *http://quotes.liberty-tree.ca/quotes_by/barry+goldwater.*

361   G. Edward Griffin, *Creature from Jekyll Island*, pp. 204-207.

362   Brian Sussman, KSFO, San Francisco, Evening Radio Talk Show, June 1, 2009.

363   Michele Bachmann, *http://thehill.com/blogs/congress-blog/education/59191-government-to-take-over-all-student-loans-rep-michele-bachmann.*

364 Lee Rodgers, KSFO San Francisco, Morning Radio Talk Show, April 4, 2009.

365 *www.politickerNJ.com/2751/torrecelli-economy-stimulus-package-cit-bank,February,20,2009.*

366 Lee Rodgers, KSFO Radio Morning Show, "Actual Unemployment: 15.8%"—*http://voices.washingtonpost.com/economy-watch/2009/05/actual_us_unemployment_158.html.*

367 Sharon Hughes Radio Program "Changing World Views," September 21, 2009.

368 Dr. Jerome R. Corsi, "The New World Disorder, Goodbye U.S. dollar, Hello Global Currency," (*The Eco-logic Powerhouse,* June, 2007,) pp. 13-14.

369 Herbert G. Grubel, "The Case for the Amero: The Economics and Politics of a North American Monetary Union," *Fraser Institute,* 1999. *http://oldfraser.lexi.net/publicanions/critical_issues/1999/amero/section_03.html.*

370 Dr. Jerome R. Corsi, *The Late Great USA, The Coming Merger with Mexico and Canada,* (a WND Book, World Ahead Media, Los Angeles, CA, 2007), pp. 42-43.

371 Robert A Pastor, "A North American Community: A Modest Proposal to the Trilateral Commission," (Delivered in Toronto, Ontario, Canada, November 1-2, 2002). *http://www.american.edu/ia/cnas/pdfs/PastorTrilateral.pdf.*

372 *http://www.foreignaffairs.org/20070501faessay86308/benn-steil/the-end-of-national-currency.html.*

373 "Premeditated Merger," World Net Daily, Op.Cit.

374 Peter B. Kenan and Ellen E. Meade, *Regional Monetary Integration,* (A CFR Book, Cambridge University Press, Nov. 2007), *http://www.cfr.org/publication/14534.*

375 Phyllis Schlafly, Op.cit.

376 Warren Mass, "From Riches to Rags, Equal Opportunity Poverty Comes to Zimbabwe," (*New American,* March 30, 2009).

377 *http://wherestheinterest.com/2009/02/05/adrian-rogers-what-one-person-receives-without-working/.*

Chapter Fourteen—Obama's Socialized America

378 Rush Limbaugh, *http://www.rushlimbaugh.com/home/daily/site_101209/content/01125108.guest.html.*

379 Susan Jones, "'Spread the Wealth Around' Comment Comes Back to Haunt Obama," October 15, 2008, *http://www.cnsnews.com/public/content/article.aspx?RsrcID=37539.*

380 Samuel J. Wurzelbacker with Thomas N. Tabback, *Joe the Plumber, Fighting for the American Dream,* (Pearl Gate Publishing, Austin, TX, 2008), p. 17 and p. 118.

381 Dr. Jerome R. Corsi, *The Obamanation, Leftist Politics and the Cult of Personality,* (Threshold Editions, Simon and Shuster, NY, 2008), p. 46.

382 Sharon Churcher, "A drunk and a bigot—what the US presidential hopeful HASN'T said about his father." *London Daily Mail*, January, 2007. (Rob Chilly, contributed to this story. He is freelance journalist who interviewed relatives and friends of Obama Sr. in Kenya.)

383 Corsi, Op.cit. p. 18.

384 Churcher, *Daily Mail*, Op.cit.

385 Corsi, Op.cit. p. 74.

386 Obama, Barack, *Dreams from My Father: A Story of Race and Inheritance*, (New York: Crown, 2004) p. 67-68.

387 Churcher, Op.cit.

388 Obama, Op.cit. p. 93.

389 Corsi, Op.cit. pp. 17-91.

390 Ibid, pp. 182-183.

391 "BORN IN THE USA? Is this really the smoking gun of Obama's Kenyan birth? Attorney files motion for authentication of alleged 1960s certificate from Africa," *WorldNetDaily.com*, August 2, 2009.

392 *http://www.wnd.com/index.php?fa=PAGE.view&pageId=100613) http://www.wnd.com/index.php?fa=PAGE.view&pageId=105764) http://www.wnd.com/index.php?fa=PAGE.view&pageId=105764) http://www.wnd.com/index.php?fa=PAGE.view&pageId=105764).*

393 Devvy Kidd, Obama's Ineligibility, How Deep Does the Corruption Go?" September 23, 2009, *http://newswithviews.com/Devvy/kidd470.htm.*

394 Drew Zahn, "Born in the USA? 49 of 50 states never saw certification of eligibility," *WorldNetDaily.* 9/27/09.

395 *http://www.wnd.com/index.php?fa=PAGE.view&pageId=103626 > and http://www.resistnet.com/profiles/blogs/us-army-reserve-major-from-Florida.*

396 Hagmann and McLeod, "Media Blackout Concerning Obama's Eligibility for President," August 4, 2009, *TheNortheastIntelligenceNetwork*.com, and *judi@canadafreepress.com.*

397 "Kenyan-Born Obama All Set for Senate Seat," *East Standard Ltd,* Nairobi-Kenya, June 27, 2004, *http://web.archive.org/web/20040627142700/eastandard.net/headlines/news26060403.htm.*

398 Wood, Patrick, "Trilateral Commission members to the most important government positions, (*August Review*, January 30, 2009)."

399 "A Presidency Fit for a King," *New American*, March, 2009.

400 *http://features.csmonitor.com/politics/2009/04/01/ho-hum-another-obama-nominee-doesnt-pay-taxes/.*

401 *http://glennbeck.blogs.foxnews.com/2009/06/09/rise-of-the-czars/.*

402   *http://video.newsmax.com/?bcpid=20972460001&bclid=22770166001&bctid=424 84643001&s=al&promo_code=8A9E-1.*

403   Chris Moody, "Exactly How Much Taxpayer Money Went to ACORN?" *http:// biggovernment.com/2009/09/18/exactly-how-much-taxpayer-money-went-to-acorn/#.*

404   *http://www.nola.com/politics/index.ssf/2009/10/acorn_embezzlement_was_5_milli. html.*

405   David A. Patten, Obama's Top Aide Gaspard Tied to ACORN, September 28, 2009, *http://www.newsmax.com/insidecover/obama_acorn_gaspard/2009/09/28/265678. html.*

406   Sharon Hughes, "Welcome to Czarist America, #3, Regulatory Czar, Cass Sustein, 9,28,09, *www.changingworld views.com.*

407   *http://en.wikipedia.org/wiki/Mattachine_Society.*

408   *http://www.missionamerica.com/oldagenda26.php.*

409   Sharon Hughes, "Welcome to Czarist America #2—The Green Czar, Van Jones," 9/21/09 *www.ChangingWorldviews.com.*

410   *http://www.edmunds.com/cash-for-clunkers/stimulus-bill.html.*

411   *http://en.wikipedia.org/wiki/Car_Allowance_Rebate_System.*

412   *http://www.washingtonauto credit.com/bad-credit-car-loans/2009/08/dealersend-cash-for-clunkers-before-government/.*

413   *w w w . G l e n B e c k c a r s . g o v p r o g r a m ,   h t t p : / / w w w . y o u t u b e . c o m / watch?v=d7mzAz5fuMI&NR=1.*

414   *http://www.cnn.com/2009/POLITICS/09/06/obama.adviser.resigns/index.htm.*

415   Hughes, Op.cit.

416   Andrea Lafferty, *How Many Czars Does One President Need? http://www. traditionalvalues.org/modules.php?sid=3708.*

417   Drew Zahn, "Do you know you're paying for Michelle Obama's 22 assistants?" WorldNetDaily, August 5, 2009, *http://obambi.wordpress.com/2009/08/05/do-you-know-youre-paying-for-michelle-obamas-22-assistants/ http://www.politicsdaily. com/2009/07/06/what-michelle-obamas-staffers-earn/.*

418   San Francisco, Dec. 18 (Reuters) and the Glen Beck Show, Feb. 17, *www.GlenBeck. com.*

419   *http://www.mirror.co.uk/news/top-stories/2009/06/01/michelle-obama-s-1m-date-in-new-york-115875-21405350/.*

420   *http://www.factcheck.org/2009/07/michelles-european-vacation/.*

421   Joseph Williams, "Obama's Trip to Paris Raises Some Eyebrows," *Globe,* June 5, 2009. *http://www.boston.com/news/nation/washington/articles/2009/06/05/ obama_family_vacation_to_paris_raises_some_eyebrows/.*

422 *http://www.washingtonexaminer.com/opinion/blogs/beltway-confidential/Michelle-Obama-Its-a-sacrifice-to-travel-to-Europe-to-pitch-for-the-Olympics—For-Oprah-and-the-president-too—But-were-doing-it-for-the-kids-62928957.html.*

423 Jim Clark, "We Won"—On to Copenhagen!" October 2, 2009, *http://www.postchronicle.com/commentary/article_212259738.shtml?ref=rss.*

424 Rush Limbaugh, Talk Radio Show, October 2, 2009.

425 *http://blog.heritage.org/2009/06/25/new-heritage-video-cap-tax-wont-save-the-earth/#.*

426 *http://www.guardian.co.uk/uk/2009/dec/01/climate-change-scientist-steps-down.*

427 *http://thecaucus.blogs.nytimes.com/2009/10/08/house-passes-expanded-hate-crimes-bill/.*

428 *http://www.cnn.com/2009/POLITICS/09/15/carter.obama/index.html.*

429 *http://www.centerforajustsociety.org/press/default.asp?nav=publications.*

430 American Family Association, *www.AFA.net*, Action Alert, September 29, 2009.

431 "ABC Health Special with John Stossel," Aug. 8, 2009.

432 *http://www.cnn.com/2009/politics/12/24/health.care/index.html.*

433 Telephone interview with Dr. Jared Probst of Salt Lake City, September 6, 2009.

434 *http://www.investors.com/NewsAndAnalysis/Article.aspx?id=508242#.*

435 *http://www.foxnews.com/story/0,2933,557823,00.html. (Story of Empire State Building Lit Up for Red China.)*

436 http://blog.taragana.com/n/text-of-obamas-remarks-on-winning-the-2009-nobel-peace-prize-191925/.

437 http://www.foxnews.com/story/0,2933,563503,00.html.

438 http://www.foxnews.com/story/0,2933,564306,00.html.

439 *http://www.abc.net.au/news/stories/2009/10/12/2711565.htm*

440 http://blog.taragana.com/n/obama-wins-nobel-peace-prize-in-vote-seen-as-encouraging-his-promise-of-diplomacy-disarmament-192150/.

441 Howard Galgano, "It Won't Take Six Months," *http://jaykeating.wordpress.com/category/congress/.*

Chapter Fifteen—A One-World Religion

442 William F. Jasper, *Global Tyranny. . . Step by Step*, Western Islands Publishers, Appleton, Wisconsin, 1992, pp. 213-216.

443 *http://www.prisonplanet.com/ushering_in_the_one_world_religion.htm.*

444 Wendy Griffith, "Ushering in the One-World Religion," *www.CBNNews.com.*

445 Ibid. *http://www.youtube.com/watch?v=rYWic-Udt4E&NR=1&feature=fvwp.*

446 Dr. Len Horowitz, *http://www.youtube.com/watch?v=rYWic-Udt4E&NR=1&feature=fvwp.*

447   Dr. Horowitz speaking at Sonoma State University about the Denver Airport murals, Rohnert Park, CA., 2001.

448   *http://www.youtube.com/watch?v=rYWic-Udt4E&NR=1&feature=fvwp.*

449   C. William Smith, "God's Plan in America," (*The New Age Magazine*, September 1950, Vol. LVIII, No 9), p. 531.

450   Zahra Malik and Chris Cheong, "The Mysteries of the Denver Airport," *http:// www.youtube.com/watch?v=JjjIy1DOOgs&NR=1.*

451   *http://www.radioliberty.com/stones.htm.*

452   Pamela Jean, "The Georgia Guidestones, Are These the New World Order 10 Commandments?" 8/23/07 *http://www.digitaljournal.com/article/218931/The_Georgia_Guidestones_Are_These_The_New_World_Order_10_Commandments_.*

453   *In Our Backyard, Is Radical Islam in the U.S. a Serious Concern?,* (The Constitution Coalition, St. Louis, Missouri, 2008), pp. 22-23.

Chapter Sixteen—The NAFTA Superhighway

454   Tom DeWeese, "NAU Fact Sheet," April 2008, p. 5.

455   *http://international.fhwa.dot.gov/pubs/pl09010/index.cfmary.htm.*

456   *http://ops.fhwa.dot.gov/tolling_pricing/index.htm*

457   *http://www.corridorwatch.org/ttc/pdf/fact%20sheet%20-%20Cintra-Zachry%20-%20 031105%20FINAL.pdf*

458   North America's Super Corridor Coalition, Inc. NASCO *http://www.nascocorridor. com/pages/about/about.htm.*

459   *http://www.window.state.tx.us/specialrpt/tif/southtexas/infrastructure.html*

460   *http://www.nascocorridor.com/pages/about/about.htm.* (March 9, 2007).

461   *The New American,* October 2, 2006, pp. 22-23.

462   *http://www.aaroads.com/high-priority/table.html.*

463   Cliff Kincaid, "Giuliani Linked to NAFTA Superhighway," Accuracy in Media, aim.org, May 14, 2007.

464   Dr. Jerome Corsi, "Bush Administration Quietly Plans NAFTA Super Highway," *Human Events,* 6/12/2006.

465   H.G. Wells, *The Shape of Things to Come*

466   Phyllis Schlafly, "Scanning the News about North American Integration," *The Phyllis Schlafly Report,* Alton Illinois, November 2006, citing the *Kansas City Star,* 7-18-06.

467   Davis, Vicky, e-mail message from *"http://us.f829.mail.yahoo.com/ym/ Compose?To=eyeswideoopen@yahoo.com"* sent July 04, 2006 5:56 AM.

468   Dr.Jerome R. Corsi, "Investors Push NAFTA Super-Highways," *Human Events,* June 30, 2006, (*http://www.humaneventsonline.com/article.php?print=yes&id=15839*).

469   Phyllis Schlafly, "Pursuing the North American Agenda, Is America for Sale?," *The Phyllis Schlafly Report,* September, 2006, p.4.

Chapter Seventeen—The Timeline to A North American Merger 1910-2010

470 Edward R. Griffin, *Creature from Jekyll Island, A Second Look at the Federal Reserve,* pp. 1-12, 460-463

471 Ibid, pp. 204-207

472 Ibid, pp. 247-248

473 Ibid, pp. 217-218

474 John F. McManus, *The Insiders, Architects of the New World Order,* (JBS, Appleton, Wisconsin, 2004), pp. 9-125.

475 Griffin, pp. 471-503

476 Mark R. Levin, *Liberty* and *Tyranny,* A Conservative Manifesto, (Threshold Editions, New York, NY, 2009, p. 7.)

477 James Perloff, *Shadows of Power,* (Western Islands, Appleton, WI, 1988), p. 68.

478 *http://wiki.answers.com/Q/How_many_people_died_in_World_War_2.*

479 "Freedom from War, The United States Program for General and Complete Disarmament in a Peaceful World," (Publication 7277, US. State Department, 1961).

480 *http://www.john-f-kennedy.net/thefederalreserve.htm.*

481 Daniel Estulin, *The True Story of the Bilderberg Group,* p. 217.

482 *US Constitution,* Article 1, Section 8.

483 "Fast Track Talking Points," Global Trade Watch, Public Citizen.

484 Patrick Wood, "Toward a North American Union," p. 8.

485 Robert A. Pastor, *The Carter Administration and Latin America: A Test of Principle,* (The Carter Center, July 1992), p. 9.

486 *http://en.wikipedia.org/wiki/Foreign_Intelligence_Surveillance_Act.*

487 John F. McManus, *The Insiders, Architects of the New World Order,* (The John Birch Society, Appleton, Wisconsin, 2004), p. 51.

488 Daniel Sheehy, *Fighting Immigration Anarchy: American Patriots Battle to Save the Nation,* (Author House, 2005), p. 24.

489 George H. Bush, "Presidential Address: Bush Announces War on Iraq as Part of the New World Order," (*Congressional Quarterly,* January 19, 1991), p. 197.

490 Michael S. Coffman, *Saviors of the Earth, The Politics and the Religion of the Environmental Movement,* (Northfield Publishing, Chicago, 1994), pp. 195-197.

491 *http://www.wildlandsprojectrevealed.org/htm/summary.htm.*

492 Patrick Wood, "Toward a North American Union," p. 3.

493 Ross Perot, "Excerpts from Presidential Debates," 1992.

494 John MacArthur, "The Selling of Free Trade," (University of California Press, 2001), p. 228.

495 *Washington Post,* op-ed, "Kissinger and Vance," May 13, 1993.

496 *Los Angeles Times*, op-ed, "Kissinger," July 18, 1993.

497 Patrick Wood, Op.Cit., p. 5.

498 Pat Buchanan, "The Fruits of NAFTA," *The Conservative Voice*, March 10. 2006.

499 Alan Tonelson, *The Race to the Bottom*, (Westview Press, 2002), p. 89.

500 Miguel Pickard, "Trinational Elites Map North American Future in 'NAFTA PLUS,'" IRC Americas Website.

501 Deborah James, "CAFTA Squeaks by Senate with Tiniest Margin Ever for Trade Bill in History," *http://www.commondreams.org/views05/0701-28.htm.*

502 *http://www.summit-americas.org/Documents%20for%20Quebec%20City%20 Summit/Quebec/ Declaration%20of%20Quebec%20City%20-%20Eng%20-%20 final.htm.*

503 *http://www.nascocorridor.com/pages/about/about.htm.* (March 9, 2007).

504 Pat Buchanan, "Buenas Noches, America," *(http://www.humanevents.com/article. php?id=22261), 9/9/07.*

505 Zbigniew Brzesinski, Speech at Mikhail Gorbachev's "State of the World Forum," October, 1995.

506 Michael Shaw, Understanding Sustainable Development Agenda 21, (Freedom 21, Santa Cruz, 2005), pp. 8-10

507 Buchanan, "Buenas Noches, America."

508 *http:/www.summit-americas.org.*

509 Buchanan, Op.Cit.

510 Coffman, Op.Cit. pp. 12-13.

511 Tom DeWeese, Op.Cit., p. 4.

512 Phyllis Schlafly, "Economic Integration on the March," *The Phyllis Schlafly Report*, Alton, Illinois, August, 2007, p. 1.

513 William J. Gill, "Bush Pledges Wide-Open 'Free' Trade for Hemisphere at Quebec City Summit," *(http://www.aaminc.org/newsletter/v7i2/v7i2p6.htm).*

514 Robert J. Bartley, "Open NAFTA Borders, Why Not?" *The Wall Street Journal*, July 2, 2001, *(http://www.opinionjournal.com/columnists/rbartley/?id=95000738.)*

515 Patrick Wood, Op.Cit., p. 5.

516 DeWeese, Op.Cit.

517 Buchanan, Op.Cit.

518 Robert A. Pastor, "A Modest Proposal to the Trilateral Commission," 2002.

519 David Rockefeller, *Memoirs*, (Random House, Inc., New York, 2002), p. 405.

520 Buchanan, "Buenas Noches, America."

521 DeWeese, Op.Cit. p. 4.

522 Ibid.

523 "North American Leaders Unveil Security and Prosperity Partnership, International Information Programs," *www.U.S.Govt.org.*

524 *http://www.tradeobservatory.org/headlines.cfm?refID=69922.*

525 Bob Dacy, "It's the law! Feds Pave the Way to Toll and Privatize the Interstate Highways as Part of American Union," *www.Infowar.com*, June 29, 2006.

526 DeWeese, Op.Cit.

527 Ibid.

528 Ron Paul, "The Poison Sausage Factory," Aug. 2, 2005, LewRockwell.com.

529 Buchanan, "Mexican Presidents, This is America."

530 "PremeditatedMerger," WorldNetDaily, June 6, 2007.

531 Concluding Press Conference at Cancun Summit, Vicente Fox, March 31, 2006.

532 Pastor Chuck Baldwin, "Dubai Co. Takes Over Nine US Military Facilities," *NewswithViews.com.* 5/5/06.

533 DeWeese, Op.Cit.

534 Ibid.

535 DeWeese, Op.Cit. p. 1.

536 Ibid.

537 *Jacksonvilleprogress.com*, 5-2-07.

538 DeWeese, Op.Cit.

539 DeWeese, "American Policy Center News Release," Aug. 20, 2007.

540 Buchanan, "Buenas Noches, America!"

541 Dr. Jerome R. Corsi, "Premeditated Merger, North American Union Driver's License Created," *(http://www.worldnetdaily.com/news/article.asp?ARTICLE_ID=57502.)*

542 Buchanan, OpCit.

543 DeWeese, Op.Cit. p. 4.

544 Kincaid, Cliff, "Sinister Secrets of the U.N. Sea Treaty," *http://www.usasurvival.org/ck11.05.07.html.*

545 DeWeese, Op.Cit. p. 8.

546 Phyllis Schlafly, "North American Union, Conspiracy or Cover up?" April 16, 2008.

547 Dr. Jerome Corsi, "Bush OK's Integration with European Union," May 8, 2007, http://www. wnd.com/news/article..asp?ARTICLE_ID=55584.

548 Bernadine Smith, Information condensed from a large packet about "change" sent by the 2nd Amendment Committee of Hanford, California, October, 2008.

549 Reuters, "California Budget Shortfall Seen Nearing 42 Billion," San Francisco, December 11, 2008, (http://www.reuters.com/article/ idUSTRE4BA73C20081212.)

550 http://blogs.reuters.com/commentaries/2009/09/02/california-debt-rush/.

551 Smith, Op.Cit.

552 *http://www.chuckbaldwinlive.com/c2009/cbarchive_20090929.html.*

553 Posse Comitatus was a law passed back in 1878 that forbids the military from being used in civilian police enforcement. However, the law does allow for some exceptions—under emergencies, natural disasters and rebellion and under the orders of the president.

554 Henry Lamb, "The New Constitution for America's Union," *Worldnetdaily.com*, April 19, 2008.

Chapter Eighteen—What Can We Do to Stop USA Transformation? What Has Been Done? There is Still Hope

555 Oliver Demille and Keith Lockhart, *The New World Order, Choosing Between Christ and Satan in the Last Days,* (Dakota Productions, Payson, Utah, 1992), pp. 71-72.

556 Ibid, p. 70.

557 Robert P. Hillman, *Reinventing Government, Fast Bullets and Culture Change,* "forward and afterward" written by Floy Lilley, J.D, (Free Enterprise, University of Texas, Austin, 2001), p. 89.

558 DeWeese, "Chronological History for the Establishment of the North American Union," p. 8.

559 *www.stopthenau.org.* "current summary of state and federal resolutions."

560 *http://www.house.gov/list/speech/ca52_hunter/Nafta_hgwy_amendment.shtml.*

561 Notes from Stewards of the Range 2007 Annual Property Rights Conference, Oct. 26-27, 2007, John Ascuaga's Nugget, Reno, Nevada.

562 *http://www.worldnetdaily.com/index.php?fa=PAGE.printable&pageId=67133.*

563 "Superhighway Standstill," *Standing Ground*, Taylor, Texas, September, 2009, pp. 6-7.

564 *http://www.the912project.com/.*

565 *http://www.youtube.com/watch?v=F3XyQVYZ_jA.*

566 *http://www.phnet.fi/public/mamaa1/twain.htm.*

Chapter Nineteen—Quotations Promoting Regional Government, World Government, the New World Order, World Economic Order, Environmental Order and World Religion

567 Oliver Demille and Keith Lockhart, *The New World Order, Choosing Between Christ and Satan in the Last Days,* (Dakota Productions, Payson, Utah, 1992), pp. 26-27 and 44.

568 W. Cleone Skousen, *The Five Thousand Year Leap, The Miracle that Changed the World*, National Center for Constitutional Studies, Idaho, 2006, pp. 268 and 271.

569 Estulin, p. 117.

570 Demille, Op.cit. p. 44.

571 George Orwell, *1984*, (Harcourt Brace Jovanovich, Inc. New York, 1949.)

572 John Robinson, *Proofs of a Conspiracy—Against All the Religions and Governments of Europe Carried on in the Secret Meetings of Freemasons, Illuminati, and Reading Societies*, 1798. (Republished by CPA Book Publishers, Boring, Oregon.) (The book can be found at Radio Liberty, 831-464-8295.)

573 William Shannon, *http://www.catelog.americancatholic.org*.

574 "The Illuminati Spreads to America," *http://21stcenturycicero.wordpress.com/nwo/ enemies-within/the-illuminati-spread-to-america/*.

575 John McManus, *Changing Commands, The Betrayal of America's Military*, (John Birch Society, Appleton, Wisconsin, 1995), p. 20.

576 Ibid, p. 33.

577 Brent Scowcroft, "Commencement Address at Brigham Young University," April, 1992, BYU Learning Resource Center, Cassette Tape AC3911.

578 Strobe Talbot, "The Birth of the Global Nation," *Time Magazine*, July 20, 1992.

579 Bob Hillman, *Reinventing Government, Fast Bullets and Culture Change*, 2001, (*http://www.freedom.org*), p. 41.

580 David Rockefeller, as quoted in the New York Times, August 10, 1973.

581 Gary H. Kah, *En Route to Global Occupation*, (Huntington House Publishers, Lafayette, Louisiana, 1991), p. 33.

582 Rabbi Marvin S. Antelman, "Part III: The Activities of Eighteenth Century Revolutionary Societies," 1974, *http://www.geocities.com/cliff_shack/ eliminateopiate1_8.html*.

583 *http://groups.yahoo.com/group/TheNeuschwabenlandTimes/message/15*.

584 Ibid.

LaVergne, TN USA
15 January 2011
212481LV00001B/1/P